Handbook of
Midlife Development

WILEY SERIES ON ADULTHOOD AND AGING
Michael Smyer, Editor

Handbook of
Midlife Development

Margie E. Lachman

John Wiley & Sons, Inc.

New York • Chichester • Weinheim • Brisbane • Singapore • Toronto

Library of Congress Cataloging-in-Publication Data:

Handbook of midlife development / [edited by] Margie E. Lachman.
     p.   cm. — (Wiley series on adulthood and aging)
   ISBN 0-471-33331-X (alk. paper)
   1. Middle age.   I. Lachman, Margie E.   II. Series.
  HQ1059.4 .H36 2001
   305.244—dc21   00-050984

Printed in the United States of America

10 9 8 7 6 5 4 3 2 1

To my husband, Ron Spiro, and my children, Julia and Neil,
for their ongoing love and support,
and to my father, Robert J. Lachman,
for setting high standards and encouraging me
to pursue my dreams.
I am honored to be part of your lives.

Contributors

Advisory Editors

Paul B. Baltes
Max Planck Institute for
   Human Development

Hazel Rose Markus
Stanford University

Contributing Authors

Hiroko Akiyama, PhD
Senior Associate Research Scientist
Institute for Social Research
Department of Psychology
The University of Michigan
Ann Arbor, Michigan

Carolyn M. Aldwin, PhD
Professor
Department of Human and
   Community Development
University of California—Davis
Davis, California

Toni C. Antonucci, PhD
Program Director
Institute for Social Research
Professor
Department of Psychology
The University of Michigan
Ann Arbor, Michigan

Vern L. Bengtson, PhD
AARP/University Professor of
   Gerontology
Professor of Sociology
Andrus Gerontology Center
University of Southern California
Los Angeles, California

Rosanna M. Bertrand, PhD
Postdoctoral Fellow and Visiting
   Lecturer
Psychology Department
Brandeis University
Waltham, Massachusetts

Susan Bluck, PhD
Assistant Professor
Institute on Aging
University of Florida
Gainesville, Florida

Cindy M. de Frias, MS
Graduate Student in Psychology
Department of Psychology
University of Victoria
Victoria, British Columbia, Canada

Roger A. Dixon, PhD
Professor of Psychology
Department of Psychology
University of Victoria
Victoria, British Columbia, Canada

Caleb E. Finch, PhD
Andrus Gerontology Center
University of Southern California
Los Angeles, California

Elena L. Grigorenko, PhD
Associate Professor
Moscow State University
Research Scientist
Yale University
New Haven, Connecticut

Beth Halpern, PhD
Research Associate
Department of Psychiatry
SUNY Health Science Center
Brooklyn, New York

Jutta Heckhausen, PhD
Professor
Department of Psychology and
    Social Behavior
University of California—Irvine
Irvine, California

Margaret Hellie Huyck, PhD
Professor
Institute of Psychology
Illinois Institute of Technology
Chicago, Illinois

Jungmeen E. Kim, PhD
Assistant Professor
Clinical and Social Sciences in
    Psychology
Mt. Hope Family Center
University of Rochester
Rochester, New York

Margie E. Lachman, PhD
Professor
Psychology Department
Brandeis University
Waltham, Massachusetts

Michael R. Levenson, PhD
Associate Research Psychologist
Department of Human and
    Community Development
University of California—Davis
Davis, California

Carol Magai, PhD
Dean of Research
Long Island University—Brooklyn
Brooklyn, New York

Scott B. Maitland, PhD
Assistant Professor
Department of Family Relations
    and Applied Nutrition
University of Guelph
Guelph, Ontario, Canada

Dan P. McAdams, PhD
Professor
Human Development and
    Psychology
Northwestern University
Evanston, Illinois

Usha Menon, PhD
Assistant Professor of
    Anthropology
Department of Psychology,
    Sociology and
    Anthropology
Drexel University
Philadelphia, Pennsylvania

Alicia Merline, MA
Graduate Student
Institute for Social Research
Department of Psychology
The University of Michigan
Ann Arbor, Michigan

Phyllis Moen, PhD
Ferris Family Professor of Life
   Course Studies and Professor of
   Human Development and of
   Sociology
Cornell University
Ithaca, New York

Stella Oh, MA
Research Assistant
Department of Psychology
Yale University
New Haven, Connecticut

Norella M. Putney, MA
Doctoral Candidate
Department of Sociology
Andrus Gerontology Center
University of Southern California
Los Angeles, California

Avron Spiro III, PhD
Research Scientist
Massachusetts Veterans
   Epidemiology Research and
   Information Center
VA Boston Healthcare System
Assistant Professor
Department of Epidemiology and
   Biostatistics
Boston University School of Public
   Health
Boston, Massachusetts

Ursula M. Staudinger, PhD
Professor of Psychology
Department of Psychology
Dresden University
Dresden, Germany

Robert J. Sternberg, PhD
IBM Professor of Psychology and
   Education
Department of Psychology
Yale University
New Haven, Connecticut

Harvey L. Sterns, PhD
Director, Institute for Life-Span
   Development & Gerontology
Professor, Department of
   Psychology
The University of Akron
Research Professor of Gerontology
Northeastern Ohio Universities
   College of Medicine
Akron, Ohio

Susan Krauss Whitbourne, PhD
Professor of Psychology
University of Massachusetts—
   Amherst
Amherst, Massachusetts

Foreword

UNTIL RECENTLY, MIDLIFE was an almost unstudied territory in human development. This unexplored part of the life span had received relatively little attention from students of human development, who tended to concentrate on childhood, adolescence, or old age. There were no major research institutes devoted to the middle years, in contrast to the other periods in the life course. As a consequence, there is much ignorance and myth about midlife.

What we think occurs in the midlife period is based on imperfect knowledge, and some of our widely shared cultural beliefs are likely to be wrong. As such, they stand as untested, unvalidated premises on which millions of persons make decisions. Probably there are as many myths about the middle years as there were about aging 25 years ago, before the new research in gerontology. These misperceptions and misinformation are transmitted from one generation to the next, constituting our cultural legacy of thought about what happens in middle age.

The time has come to rid ourselves of these obsolete ideas about middle age and replace them with new knowledge based on scientific research. We need to understand who succeeds and who fails, who does well and who does poorly, in sustaining personal health and happiness and productive social behavior. We want to know the causal factors in the lives of those who continue to increase in growth and mastery, who make full use of their powers along lines of excellence. We should understand the characteristics of those who keep going, and those who, essentially, quit trying—and we should know about those who started late, from a poor beginning, and nevertheless reach exceptional achievements across the many roles of midlife.

We have had seventy-five years and more of theories about midlife development, some of modest scope, some grand and all-encompassing. Scientific research on midlife was rare. During the past decade of the 1990s there has been a move from speculation to study, from relying on volunteer discussion groups to the use of representative samples of middle-aged persons, from reliance on individual interviews to the use of reliable and valid measurements.

The new research has been interdisciplinary from the start. The new scientific inquiries have drawn experts trained in diverse areas, and the authors contributing to this volume exemplify this diversity of interest. The references in their chapters span many fields of study—among them cognition, genetics, neurology, and economics, as well as the more traditional fields of psychology, sociology, and anthropology.

The authors of these chapters were confronted by several challenges and they have, in their work, met them successfully. First, they have integrated the pertinent research findings from three levels of inquiry—the social, psychological, and biomedical—so that we get a full picture of these topics being considered, whether it is physical aging, personality, work, families, or other aspects of midlife development.

Second, their reviews successfully bring together the two main perspectives and orientations in studies of midlife, those of life-span development and of life course analysis. The reviews cover research on the timing and ordering of status transitions and on the comparative experiences of different birth cohorts, and combine it with descriptions of the sequence of individual development through this period of life, and the connections between earlier and later developmental events.

Third, the authors clearly recognize the variability between individuals in midlife development—both within cultures and across cultures. They also understand that it is not particularly useful to ask whether or not people change during midlife; everyone changes, but some more than others, and in different ways. The right question is: What are the conditions that cause some to change in certain ways, and others to stay the same? They do not make a case against the importance of antecedent experiences in childhood and youth, but note that new antecedents of midlife development are added that did not exist before, are mixed into this stream, and create new trajectories of development.

The publication of a Handbook is a scholarly tradition in the sciences, and the publication of this first *Handbook of Midlife Development* is a signal that a new area of scientific inquiry has appeared. The editor and her advisory editors selected notable leading scholars to prepare the chapters. The editors and authors have made a major contribution to the field of midlife development. Everyone who is interested in this field is truly grateful to them.

ORVILLE GILBERT BRIM
Lifetrends

Preface

The afternoon of human life must also have a significance of its own and cannot merely be a pitiful appendage to life's morning. (Carl Jung, 1933, p. 109)

THIS IS THE FIRST handbook on the topic of midlife development. Currently there is an intense interest in the middle years of the life span due, in large part, to the confluence of major demographic shifts and research breakthroughs. The population explosion of middle-aged adults and the rapid growth in our knowledge about this age period have led to the identification of midlife as a segment of human development worthy of study in its own right. The baby boom generation is moving through midlife in record numbers. In the year 2000, there were over 80 million babyboomers in the United States between the ages of 35 and 54. This cohort represents about 30% of the U.S. population. The effort to differentiate midlife from other periods of human development also reflects a growing interest in optimization of aging. If we can identify the roots of aging earlier in adulthood, it may be possible to delay, minimize, or prevent some of the biopsychosocial changes that occur in later life. With the rapid release of new research findings about midlife, the timing is right for a handbook dedicated to this lengthy, central period of the life span.

Much of the previous research relevant to midlife has been done without a direct focus on this age period. Research on topics such as career changes, preretirement planning, menopause, cardiovascular disease, child-rearing, the empty nest, caregiving, or grandparenting, although not billed specifically as midlife research, has nevertheless been devoted to the study of middle-aged adults. One of the largest research enterprises focused directly on the middle years, conducted by The John D. and Catherine T. MacArthur Foundation Research Network on Successful Midlife Development (MIDMAC), recently completed its 10-year agenda. The findings from their large representative survey of Midlife in the United States (MIDUS) are making their way into the medical, developmental, psychological, and social journals, a summary volume is due to be published in 2001, and plans are underway to extend the survey to a second wave. The literature on midlife is likely to continue growing at a fast pace.

The chapters in this *Handbook* provide a synthesis of findings from many different arenas, bringing them together under one cover. For some topics included in this volume, the picture about midlife is still sketchy, and the authors were challenged to extrapolate from work on other age periods, usually old age. In so doing, the authors raise interesting questions about continuity and change and whether some areas of midlife can be characterized as an extension of young adulthood or a precursor of things to come in later life.

In most topic areas, research and theory on aging is much further along in its development compared to midlife. There are three separate handbooks about aging in the fields of Psychology, Social Sciences and Biology, and their fifth editions are due out shortly. Although a number of edited books on midlife have been published over the past 20 years, there are no journals dedicated to midlife. Research on midlife is usually published in the aging journals and included in textbooks on adult development and aging. Until now there has not been enough information to require a textbook dedicated to middle age. This is changing, with new courses being offered on the topic of midlife and textbooks devoted specifically to this age period on the horizon.

The authors who contributed to this volume were asked to provide state-of-the-art reviews of the literature, not necessarily all-inclusive, but reflecting their vision of directions for future theory and research on their topic. They were asked to take a biopsychosocial approach to midlife with a life-span developmental perspective. In addition, the authors were asked to be particularly sensitive to issues of gender, cohort differences, and ethnic and cultural variations in their coverage. The *Handbook* is rich with contributions on a myriad of topics from key scholars in the field. Thanks to them, for the first time we can enjoy the synthesis of years of work touching on midlife now collated and integrated into one comprehensive work. This *Handbook on Midlife* signals the coming of age of this area of inquiry in the field of human development.

I wish to thank the many people who have made this *Handbook* a reality. Michael Smyer, the Editor for the Adult Development and Aging Series at John Wiley, first identified the need for a summary volume on midlife. I am grateful to him for his vision and for inviting me to edit this *Handbook*. This volume would not have been published without the hard work of the able staff at John Wiley and Sons. I especially would like to acknowledge Jennifer Simon and all members of the editorial staff and production group for pushing me and the authors to meet the deadlines and for bringing this book to fruition. I wish to thank my advisory editors, Paul B. Baltes and Hazel Rose Markus for suggesting ways to shape the volume and identifying potential contributors. I value their wisdom and friendship. The key to a successful edited book is having the right set of chapters. I thank all the authors for their excellent contributions and hard work.

I want to express gratitude to my MIDMAC colleagues, especially Bert Brim, the chair, who inspired me and provided incredible opportunities for learning and collegiality. The 10 years I spent as a member of MIDMAC marked my entry into midlife both chronologically as well as professionally. The intellectual exchanges among eminent scholars and esteemed colleagues from many disciplines have enriched my life in many ways and contributed immensely to the quality of this volume. I also gratefully acknowledge the financial support I received to conduct my work from the John D. and Catherine T. MacArthur Foundation and from the National Institutes on Aging.

My colleagues, students, and staff at Brandeis University have been supportive and stimulating over the past 20 years. I especially wish to thank Joe Cunningham, Kimberly Prenda, Heather Walen, Mick Watson, Suzie Weaver, Art Wingfield, Judy Woodman, and Leslie Zebrowitz. They were encouraging and available for guidance while I was working on this volume, as always. I thank the members of the Life-span Lab for making sure that things ran smoothly when I was preoccupied with getting this volume completed.

My family deserves much credit for enabling me to devote extended hours to this project. My children, Julia and Neil, have become self-sufficient and reliable, using good judgment, and always willing to take on more responsibility, allowing me time to complete my work. I am proud of you. Finally, I give thanks to my husband for sharing daily responsibilities and life. No matter how frantic things are, with his sense of humor and laid-back perspective on life, Ron is always there cracking a joke, making us laugh, and putting a different spin on things. My heartfelt and sincere thanks to you all.

MARGIE E. LACHMAN

Introduction

Middle-aged life is merry, and I love to lead it,
But there comes a day when your eyes are all right
But your arm isn't long enough to hold the telephone book
where you can read it. (Ogden Nash, 1952, p. 5)

Middle-aged adults seem to be preoccupied with how well they *see* and how good they *look*. It's not surprising, considering the term *midlife* conjures up images of reading glasses, thinning or graying hair, sagging chins, fatigue, backaches, hot flashes, forgetfulness, loss of sex drive, grown children leaving home, parents becoming sick or dying, and a multitude of other changes in the physical, psychological, and social realms. Do these experiences we typically associate with midlife truly represent the central themes of the middle years of the life span, or are they just popular misconceptions promoted and exaggerated by talk shows, magazines, and birthday cards? When middle-aged adults experience new challenges or unwelcome changes, do they trigger a midlife crisis or do they create opportunities for growth and adaptation? One thing is clear—there are many views of midlife. At one extreme, the notion of midlife as a period of turmoil or crisis (Levinson et al., 1978; Sheehy, 1976) is in stark contrast to the view that midlife is the period of peak functioning and responsibility (Neugarten, 1968). Are those beyond forty "over the hill," or does "life begins at forty?" (Pitkin, 1932).

Over 25 years ago, Neugarten and Datan (1974) remarked that midlife, in contrast to old age, had received little attention from lifecycle scholars. They commented that opposing views of researchers and clinicians "led to a somewhat unbalanced view of middle age as either plateau or crisis" (p. 592). On the one hand, many researchers believed that personality is stable during adulthood and that nothing of great significance occurs until senescence. In contrast, clinicians espoused the view that there are problems and crises in mental health brought on by physical changes and social upheavals. Much has been learned over the past quarter century, yet still less is known about the middle years than the later years of the life cycle, leading Brim (1992, p. 171) to refer to the middle years as the "last uncharted territory in human development."

Some well-known conceptualizations of midlife have emerged from clinicians' accounts of their middle class, middle-aged clients' problems (see Hunter & Sundel, 1989). As a result, midlife is often portrayed as a time of crisis and unrest (Farrell & Rosenberg, 1981; Jacques, 1965; Oldham & Liebert, 1989). Subsequent research with more diverse samples has uncovered a more balanced perspective (Baruch & Brooks-Gunn, 1984; Eichorn, Clausen, Haan, Honzik, & Mussen, 1981; Giele, 1982; Lachman & James, 1997; Rossi, 1994; Ryff & Kessler, in press; Ryff & Seltzer, 1996; Willis & Reed, 1999). In contrast to the view from clinical populations, survey-based findings have characterized those in middle age as being on top of their game, "no longer driven, but now the drivers" (Neugarten, 1974, p. 98). These disparate views can be reconciled if the experiences of midlife are considered from multiple perspectives, recognizing the vast range of possibilities and variations by historical period, timing of events in the life course, gender, culture, race, ethnicity, and social class. The goal of this first edition of the *Handbook of Midlife Development* is to offer such a multidisciplinary and contextual perspective on midlife.

MIDLIFE ISSUES AND CENTRAL DOMAINS

What are the most prevalent issues that are faced by those in midlife? A national survey conducted by the American Board of Family Practice (1990) showed that changes in physical conditions, health, and mental functioning, as well as getting older, were considered the worst aspects of midlife. Respondents especially expressed concerns about increases in chronic illness and being overweight. The best things reported about midlife reflected feelings of more personal control and freedom. Being settled and having life experience were considered the best things, having financial security, and the freedom and independence that come with grown children were also frequently cited. Improving relationships with family and friends, caring for a frail parent or helping children, and saving for retirement were noted as important goals during midlife (American Board of Family Practice, 1990). Thus, it appears that the midlife experience includes both gains and losses (Baltes, 1987; Neugarten & Datan, 1974). For example, the loss of fertility at menopause is sometimes experienced as a gain in sexual freedom (Rossi, 1994). Or, the loss of the active parent role when children move out of the home is often accompanied by newfound gains in marital satisfaction and opportunities for exploring new interests, growth, and fulfillment (Ryff & Seltzer, 1996). The contents of the *Handbook,* drawing on fields such as psychology, sociology, anthropology, human development, economics, biology, epidemiology, and medicine, reflect the wide range of issues and concerns that are integral to persons in the middle years of the life span. It is a time when themes of juggling multiple roles and achieving balance in life are front and center.

During midlife, there is a tension between the changes in physical functioning and social roles and the psychological resources available to deal with them. All indications are that although middle-aged adults may be faced with multiple challenges, they also are well equipped in many ways to handle them (Aldwin & Levenson, Chapter 6; Heckhausen, Chapter 11; Lachman & James, 1997). For most people in middle age, physical (Avis, 1999; Whitbourne, Chapter 4) and cognitive changes (Dixon, deFrias, & Maitland, Chapter 8; Sternberg, Grigorenko, & Oh, Chapter 7; Willis & Schaie, 1999) occur gradually and do not lead necessarily to disability or impairment. Although some aspects of cognitive functioning may show declines, the middle-aged adult has the resources and experiences to compensate for them (Miller & Lachman, 2000). Most middle-aged adults function well psychologically (Lachman & Bertrand, Chapter 9), and are effective at regulating emotions (Magai & Halpern, Chapter 10)and coping with change (Aldwin & Levenson, Chapter 6; Heckhausen, Chapter 11).

In addition to physical changes, middle age often involves a restructuring of social roles (Bumpass & Aquilino, 1995), especially in the work (Sterns & Huyck, Chapter 13; Kim & Moen, Chapter 14) and family realms (Antonucci, Akiyama, & Merline, Chapter 15; Putney & Bengston, Chapter 15). Midlife adults have a wide range of circumstances involving their children, determined in part by their social class, children's ages, and geographical propinquity (Ryff & Seltzer, 1997). Some have young children still in the home, and others have grown children who live on their own, or perhaps return to the home after a separation or divorce. Those who had children in their twenties or early thirties will often become grandparents during the early part of their middle years. Midlife adults also must confront changes in their relationships with their own parents, especially due to declining health or death. One of the harsh realities of middle age is captured in the statistics about the number of living parents. According to the National Survey of Families and Households, as adults enter midlife, 41% have both parents alive, while 77% leave midlife with no parents alive (Bumpass & Aquilino, 1995). What these figures do not convey is the emotional anguish and turmoil associated with parental loss. The experiences of midlife adults are complicated by the mobility of our society, in which adult children are often faced with the long distance monitoring of parents with failing health and decreased ability to live independently (Putney & Bengtson, Chapter 15). Adding to the complexity of dealing with parents' illness is that the midlife adult usually has multiple responsibilities at home and in the workplace. This intergenerational, multi-role squeeze in midlife has led to the label, "sandwich generation."

WHAT IS MIDLIFE?

The U.S. Census Bureau (1990) reports there are 74 million middle-aged adults, between the ages of 40 and 60, comprising 27% of the population. This represents an increase of 6% over the past decade, and the numbers are expected to increase by 1% over the next decade. No wonder marketers, not to mention researchers and publishers, are targeting this age group.

According to the online Oxford English Dictionary (2000), the word *midlife* first appeared in Funk and Wagnalls Standard Dictionary in 1895. Midlife is defined as "the part of life between youth and old age." Yet, the boundaries for midlife are fuzzy with no clear demarcation. Subjective views of the midlife period show a wide age range (American Board of Family Practice, 1990, Lachman, Lewcowitz, Marcus, & Peng, 1994; Neugarten & Datan, 1974).

Those between the ages of 40 and 60 are typically considered to be middle-aged, but there is at least a 10-year range on either end, so that it is not uncommon for some to consider middle age to begin at 30 and end at 75. In fact, one-third of Americans in their 70s think of themselves as middle-aged (National Council on Aging, 2000). Research shows that the subjective boundaries of midlife vary positively with age (Lachman et al., 1994). The older one is, the later the reported entry and exit years for the midlife period (Lachman & Bertrand, Chapter 9). Middle-aged adults typically report feeling about 10 years younger than they are (Montepare & Lachman, 1989). Although midlife is a relatively long period, ranging from 20 to 40 years, it has not yet been divided into subperiods akin to the young-old, old-old distinction used to describe later life (Neugarten & Hagestad, 1986).

Middle age is a long period with a great deal going on in many different realms. In both the family and work domains, middle-aged adults play an important role in sharing their experience and transmitting their values to the younger generation (McAdams, Chapter 12). The middle aged are involved with taking care of the young and the old. They may be launching children, adjusting to having children return home, becoming grandparents, taking care of a widowed or sick parent, or getting used to being the oldest generation in the extended family after both parents have passed away. In the work domain, middle-aged adults may reach their peak in position and earnings. They also may be faced with multiple financial burdens from rent, mortgage, child care, college tuition, loans to family members, or bills from nursing homes. They also may decide or be forced to change jobs, face age discrimination, or begin planning or saving for retirement.

For middle-aged adults, health is generally good, and most of the physical changes do not cause disability or alter life styles, even if they do raise concerns and lamentations about the woes of getting older (Whitbourne,

Chapter 4). Some who are less fortunate are faced with chronic illnesses, disease, or health problems that place limitations on their activities (Spiro, Chapter 5). Among those in their early 40s, only 7% report having a disability (Bumpass & Aquilino, 1995). The number of men and women with some form of disability more than doubles by the early 50s (16%) and nearly triples by the early 60s (30%). Thus, for many adults, midlife is characterized by increasing health problems, and this is particularly true for those with low socioeconomic status (Bumpass & Aquilino, 1995). Although adults report an increase in poor health from early to late midlife, during the same period, there is a decrease in negative emotions and an increase in positive mood (Mroczek & Kolarz,1998). The picture is one of relatively good emotional and psychological health even in the face of stress and declines (Lachman & Bertrand, Chapter 9; Magai & Putney, Chapter 10). There is much evidence for the use of compensatory strategies, resilience, and adaptive behaviors during the middle years (Heckhausen, Chapter 11).

OVERVIEW OF THE HANDBOOK

The *Handbook* is organized in four sections, covering the theoretical, physical, psychological, and social aspects of midlife development. This reflects the multidisciplinary nature of the *Handbook,* with all chapters addressing the interplay of biomedical, psychological, and social factors during the middle years.

Staudinger and Bluck in Chapter 1 review existing theoretical perspectives, including stage models, and demonstrate the utility of the life-span view for guiding research on midlife. The dynamic nature of changes in the middle years can be represented as both gains and losses. The midlife experience is determined by both biological and cultural/environmental influences. In fact, midlife does not exist as a concept in all cultures (Shweder, 1998).

By comparing the nature of the middle years in American, Japanese, and Hindu societies, Menon, Chapter 2, demonstrates variations in the construction of middle age. To illustrate, she points out that even if midlife were defined on the basis of the midpoint of the life span, this too would vary both within and between cultures as a function of the length of life.

Biologically based changes in midlife do not appear to be as dramatic as in other periods of the life span. It is not necessarily a long period of quietude, but one marked by contrasts. Some individuals begin to show health declines during the middle years and others pass through midlife with a clean bill of health. Problems of obesity, chronic illness, cardiovascular disease, as well as changes in sensory functioning, emerge in the middle years. The incidence of illness and disease is tied to many factors such as social class, lifestyle, and heredity. One of the major shifts in the middle years occurs in the area of reproduction, especially for women. Finch, Chapter 3, discusses midlife, from a biologist's perspective, as a period of decreased fertility or fecundity. The definition of midlife varies by species and life expectancy. There is wide variability in health, and genetic influences such as ApoE are prominent in midlife. ApoE has been associated with cognitive dysfunction and ischemic heart disease, and Finch proposes that it should be considered in relation to psychosocial outcomes. Interestingly, middle age has been studied by biologists to enable the study of reproductive aging free of the confounds of disease.

 Whitbourne, Chapter 4, reviews the major physical changes that often occur in middle age. She points out that the timing and magnitude are quite variable and many of these changes are not inevitable. With a healthy diet and exercise, for example, decrements can be delayed or even avoided. Her coverage of the different body systems highlights the interdependence of hormonal cardiovascular, respiratory, and other functions. Spiro, Chapter 5, applies a multidisciplinary, life-span approach to the understanding and treatment of health in midlife. Diseases of midlife can be prevented by minimizing risk factors. Health is presented as a multifaceted construct, and is considered a primary basis for well-being. In the context of chronic illness, midlife adults need to find ways to cope or compensate for losses. Aldwin and Levenson, Chapter 6, point out the connection between stress and health and highlight the need for good coping skills in midlife. They point out there are many stresses that midlife adults encounter in multiple domains of life, such as death of parents or compromised health, and yet most middle-aged adults are able to achieve growth and wisdom in the face of these stressors.

Sternberg, Grigorenko, and Oh, Chapter 7, summarize the evidence for mixed patterns of growth and decline in intelligence. They make an important distinction between practical and academic forms of intelligence and show their differential trajectories of change during adulthood. They present interesting evidence for the development of tacit knowledge and highlight the importance of learning from experience. Midlife provides many good opportunities for making intellectual contributions, given the position of the middle-aged in the family, in the workplace, and in society. In another cognitive domain, there is a common belief that memory declines in midlife, and many people complain that they are becoming more forgetful. Dixon, DeFrias, and Maitland, Chapter 8, provide a clear and cogent review of what we do know about memory in midlife, con- cluding that there is not much evidence for widespread memory decrements in the middle years. They propose new directions for research such as looking at the influence of hormonal changes and metamemory on memory functioning.

Lachman and Bertrand, Chapter 9, examine how personality affects the midlife experience. They summarize the key theories on personality that can inform research in this area. Not all aspects of personality are stable. The self plays an important role in midlife, serving as a resource for negotiating the physical changes and social stresses that may be encountered. No one is immune to the complexities of midlife. Yet, those who feel a sense of mastery and control are better able to meet the challenges head on and find effective strategies for reducing or dealing with stress. Magai and Halpern, Chapter 10, explore the emotional aspects of development in midlife, considering both positive and negative affect. This newly emerging area of research is ripe with possibilities for understanding ways in which adults negotiate the terrain of the middle years, including death of one's parents as well as parenting one's children. The concept of emotional regulation is described and applied to the midlife experience. Heckhausen, Chapter 11, explores the psychosocial resources that are at the disposal of the midlife adult. These protective factors help in the adaptation to the losses, developmental deadlines, multiple roles, and other challenges associated with midlife. She engages in a creative analysis of processes such as social comparison and assimilation and accommodation. Although primary control plays a central role in the middle years, it becomes a less effective strategy compared to secondary control in circumstances where goals are unattainable.

McAdams, Chapter 12, presents a comprehensive and insightful coverage of the generativity construct, a central theme in the middle years. Moving leaps and bounds beyond the original Eriksonian view, he discusses the variations in generativity by race/ethnicity and history/cohort. The multifaceted and multidimensional view of generativity, in the domains of parenting and societal involvement, reflects the critical role that commitment to others plays in the development of well-being in midlife.

Sterns and Huyck, Chapter 13, convincingly make the case for the centrality of work during the middle years. They cover career development and consider the variations by gender, cohort, culture, and race. The progression of career trajectories including job mobility and reentry into the workforce in midlife are highlighted. Unemployment and layoffs may have a different impact depending on the age of the person or whether or not they occur in the context of a good job market.

Kim and Moen, Chapter 14, expand the coverage of the work cycle to the transition to retirement. They consider the context of preretirement, identifying the impact of historical variations, timing, planning, adjustment, and resources that are brought to bear on retirement decisions. This work is integrated with work on agency and the self as well as societal transitions. Variations by gender, ethnicity, and cohort are considered and emphasized.

Putney and Bengtson, Chapter 15, provide a compelling analysis of the role of families and intergenerational relationships in midlife within the context of ethnic and gender variations. They cover important midlife phenomena such as the sandwich generation, caregiver stress, grandparenting, family conflict, kinkeeping, the boomerang generation, co-residence, and the cluttered versus empty nest. Antonucci, Akiyama and Merline, Chapter 16, highlight the supportive role of social relationships in midlife. The midlife adult is a major supporter but also reaps the benefits of support from others as they negotiate the trials and tribulations of midlife. Social relations provide a major source of satisfaction and contribute to well-being and health in midlife (Walen & Lachman, 2000). The absence of support or the experience of strain can wreak havoc on middle-aged adults, leading to stress and illness. Relationships in midlife involve not only the family but also friends and coworkers, and differences by gender are important to consider.

There are many interesting questions about midlife that are addressed throughout the *Handbook* chapters. Can midlife experiences be traced to characteristics or events from earlier in life, such as personality, social relations, or education? Does midlife provide a window on aging? To what extent can we prepare for old age during midlife? What can we do in midlife to optimize the later years? The authors consider whether there is continuity from young adulthood through midlife and into old age. Resources accumulated during the middle years can serve as the basis for security during later life, whether in the economic, social, physical, or psychological realms. How much can be done to make up for omissions and losses (e.g., can we take calcium supplements to make up for poor nutrition or thinning bones? Can advanced education or a challenging job in midlife protect us from cognitive declines?).

Together, these chapters provide an account of the ways middle-aged adults can take charge of their lives. There is accumulating evidence for ways to compensate for or even postpone aging-related losses that begin during midlife. For example, weight-bearing exercise can remediate muscle loss (Whitbourne, Chapter 4). Psychological resources can come into play in adapting to the physical and social losses that occur during midlife. When desired outcomes are not attainable, it is possible to utilize secondary control or accommodative processes (Heckhausen, Chapter 11; Brandstadter & Renner, 1990; Whitbourne & Connolly, 1999) for adjustment. Selective optimization processes enable the resilient adult to draw on social and psychological resources to compensate for biological decline (Staudinger & Bluck, Chapter 1).

It is my sincere hope that this *Handbook* provides us with a clearer vision of midlife, by collating and integrating the work conducted on this age period, and suggesting directions for future investigation. If some aspects of midlife are still fuzzy, this can serve as an incentive to explore new territories to bring midlife development into clearer focus, with or without reading glasses. A better understanding of middle-aged adults can have far-reaching consequences. These can extend not only to those who are in midlife, but also to those who are younger or older in the family, in the work place, and in society as a whole. All who are touched by, influenced by, and cared for by the middle-aged are also likely to benefit.

REFERENCES

American Board of Family Practice. (1990). *Perspectives on middle age: The vintage years.* Princeton, NJ: New World Decisions.

Avis, N.E. (1999). Women's health at midlife. In S.L. Willis & J.D. Reid (Eds.), *Life in the middle: Psychological and social development in middle age* (pp. 105–147). San Diego, CA: Academic Press.

Baltes, P.B. (1987). Theoretical propositions of life-span developmental psychology: On the dynamics between growth and decline. *Developmental Psychology, 23,* 611–626.

Baruch, G., & Brooks-Gunn, J. (Eds.). (1984). *Women in midlife.* New York: Plenum Press.

Brandstadter, J., & Renner, G. (1990). Tenacious goal pursuit and flexible goal adjustment: Explication and age-related analysis of assimilative and accommodative strategies of coping. *Psychology and Aging, 5,* 58–67.

Brim, O.G. (1976). Theories of the male mid-life crisis. *Counseling Psychologist, 6,* 2–9.

Brim, O.G. (1992). *Ambition: How we manage success and failure throughout our lives.* New York: Basic Books.

Bumpass, L.L., & Aquilino, W.S. (1994). *A social map of midlife: Family and work over the middle life course.* Vero Beach, FL: John D. and Catherine T. MacArthur Foundation Research Network on Successful Midlife Development.

Eichorn, D.H., Clausen, J.A., Haan, N., Honzik, M.P., & Mussen, P.H. (Eds.). (1981). *Present and past in midlife.* New York: Academic Press.

Farrell, M.P., & Rosenberg, S.D. (1981). *Men at midlife.* Boston: Auburn House.

Giele, J.Z. (Ed.). (1982). *Women in the middle years: Current knowledge and directions for research and policy.* New York: Wiley.

Hunter, S., & Sundel, M. (Eds.). (1989). *Midlife myths: Issues, findings, and practice implications.* Newbury Park, CA: Sage.

Jacques, E. (1965). Death and the mid-life crisis. *International Journal of Psychoanalysis, 46,* 502–514.

Jung, C.G. (1933). *Modern man in search of a soul.* New York: Harcourt, Brace & World.

Lachman, M.E., & James, J.B. (1997). *Multiple paths of midlife development.* Chicago: University of Chicago Press.

Lachman, M.E., Lewkowicz, C., Marcus, A., & Peng, Y. (1994). Images of midlife development among young, middle-aged, and older adults. *Journal of Adult Development, 1,* 201–211.

Levinson, D.J., Darrow, C.N., Klein, E.B., Levinson, M.H., & McKee, B. (1978). *The seasons of a man's life.* New York: Knopf.

Miller, L.S., & Lachman, M.E. (2000). Cognitive performance and the role of health and control beliefs in midlife. *Aging, Neuropsychology, and Cognition, 7,* 69–85.

Montepare, J., & Lachman, M.E. (1989). You're only as old as you feel. Self-perceptions of age, fears of aging, and life satisfaction from adolescence to old age. *Psychology and Aging, 4,* 73–78.

Mroczek, D.K., & Kolarz, C.M. (1998). The effects of age on positive and negative affect: A developmental perspective on happiness. *Journal of Personality and Social Psychology, 75,* 1333–1349.

Nash, O. (1952). Peekaboo, I almost see you. In *The private dining room and other new verses.* Boston: Little, Brown.

National Council on the Aging. (2000, March). *Myths and realities 2000 survey results.* Washington, DC: National Council on Aging.

Neugarten, B.L. (Ed.). (1968). *Middle age and aging: A reader in social psychology.* Chicago: University of Chicago Press.

Neugarten, B.L., & Datan, N. (1974). The middle years. In S. Arieti (Ed.), *The foundations of psychiatry* (Vol. 1., pp. 592–608). New York: Basic Books.

Neugarten, B.L., & Hagestad, G. (1976). Age and the life course. In R. Binstock & E. Shanas (Ed.), *Handbook of aging and the social sciences* (pp. 35–55). New York: Van Nostrand-Reinhold.

Oldham, J.M., & Liebert, R.S. (Eds.). (1989). *The middle years: New psychoanalytic perspectives.* New Haven, CT: Yale University Press.

Oxford English Dictionary Online. (2000). Oxford, England: Oxford University Press.

Pitkin, W.B. (1932). *Life begins at forty.* New York: McGraw-Hill.

Rossi, A.S. (Ed.). (1994). *Sexuality across the life course.* Chicago: University of Chicago Press.

Ryff, C.D., & Kessler, R. (in press). *Portraits of midlife in the United States.* Chicago: University of Chicago Press.

Ryff, C.D., & Seltzer, M.G. (1996). *The parental experience in midlife.* Chicago: University of Chicago Press.

Sheehy, G. (1976). *Passages.* New York: Dutton.

Shweder, R. (Ed.). (1998). *Welcome to middle age! And other cultural fictions.* Chicago: University of Chicago Press.

U.S. Census Bureau. (2000, November). *Resident population estimates of the United States by age and sex.* Washington, DC: Author.

Walen, H.R., & Lachman, M.E. (2000). Social support and strain from partner, family, and friends: Costs and benefits for men and women in adulthood. *Journal of Social and Personal Relationships, 17,* 5–30.

Whitbourne, S.K., & Connolly, L.A. (1999). The developing self in midlife. In S.L. Willis, & J.D. Reid (Eds.), *Life in the middle.* (pp. 25–46). San Diego, CA: Academic Press.

Willis, S.L., & Reid, J.D. (1999). *Life in the middle: Psychological and social development in middle age.* San Diego, CA: Academic Press.

Contents

SECTION I

FRAMEWORKS AND CONTEXTS

CHAPTER 1

A View on Midlife Development from Life-Span Theory

URSULA M. STAUDINGER and SUSAN BLUCK

HAS DEVELOPMENTAL RESEARCH SO FAR NEGLECTED MIDLIFE?

HISTORICALLY, DEVELOPMENTAL PSYCHOLOGISTS have concentrated largely on childhood and adolescence, detailing the challenges of and progression through these life phases. That trend has changed over the past 40 to 50 years as adult development has increasingly become a topic for research. So far, however, this research has focused primarily on later life. The existence of the whole field of gerontology provides evidence of the importance that psychology and other disciplines have attached to understanding late adulthood. When one looks across the life span, the gap in research on midlife development is apparent. Several books, however, have provided a useful foundation to begin filling this gap (e.g., Lachman & James, 1997; Rossi, 1994; Ryff & Seltzer, 1996; Shweder, 1998; Willis & Reid, 1999). To start our discussion of midlife from a life-span developmental perspective, we examine the reasons for the relative scarcity of theory and research concerning midlife.

The authors acknowledge the many valuable discussions with colleagues from the Max Planck Institute for Human Development, and colleagues from the Network on Successful Midlife Development of the MacArthur Foundation (Chair: Orville G. Brim). Susan Bluck is now at the University of Florida, Gainesville.
Note: The adjective "life-span" is used for consistency with other chapters, although the authors use "lifespan" in other publications.

3

IS MIDLIFE A DISTINCT PHASE OF LIFE?

One reason for the scarcity of research on midlife may be that there is no clear demarcation of midlife, at least not as clear as the ones for childhood as the beginning and for old age as the end of life. Thus, the first intriguing question to answer is whether midlife indeed exists as a life phase, and if so, when it begins and ends.

Although age 30 is a cultural marker of adulthood, it is an ambiguous signal of the beginning of middle age. While media messages tell individuals that they are leaving youth behind at age 30, people do not really experience the largely negative, cultural press of being "over the hill" until age 40 (Brooks-Gunn & Kirsh, 1984; Whitbourne & Connolly, 1999). Several researchers have noted that chronological age is a much more useful predictor of children's abilities than it is of adults' development (e.g., Baltes, Reese, & Lipsitt, 1980; B. Neugarten & Datan, 1996; Whitbourne & Weinstock, 1979). In general, midlife is an uncharted period in which chronological age does not seem to be a salient marker. Despite this, the studies reviewed next suggest that some agreement exists in lay theories of when midlife begins and ends.

What can be learned from individuals' subjective conceptions of when midlife begins and ends? In a sample of middle-aged respondents (B. Neugarten, Moore, & Lowe, 1965), the most frequent conception of a middle-aged man or woman was of someone who was 40 to 50 years old. Interestingly, in the same sample, to be labeled "young," individuals had to be between 18 and 24, and to be "old" was reserved for those 60 to 75 years of age. Thus while people may have a central conception of who is middle-aged, it leaves gaps in the life span. Age 40 is middle-aged, but what about the period between 24 and 40 years, and that between age 50 and 60? This border area on either side of the central period of middle age leaves room to interpret one's own, and others' middle-aged status. This notion is supported by a large, life-span study of subjective age that found that individuals in the 30-to-40 age range exhibit the greatest variability in reporting their subjective age (Goldsmith & Heiens, 1992).

Similar research has identified a more differentiated profile of midlife and where it fits into the life span (Shanan & Kedar, 1980). Participants from adolescence through 78 years, were asked to divide the life span into as many periods as they saw fit. The periods describing the central part of the life span included adulthood (30–50 yrs.), and middle adulthood (50–60 yrs.). This points to the same conclusion as previously discussed, though with a somewhat different age range. Individuals may see middle age as a fairly defined period, while viewing the transition into that period as largely undefined so that the transition period might or might not also be considered part of middle age. The period that is simply called "adulthood" by these respondents may provide a wide boundary for an individual's progression into the midlife period. Another way to look at the period called "adulthood" by this group is that middle age is the part of life that needs no qualifier. One is neither young, nor old. Thus, this finding suggests that middle age may be the period in which one simply is an adult, and that means being in the middle of the two other more defined categories, early and late adulthood.

In two other studies, corresponding normative conceptions of the age at which midlife begins and ends have been identified (Cameron, 1969; Drevenstedt, 1976). These two studies suggest that middle age is the period between 40 and 55 years, thereby encompassing parts of both periods identified in the studies reviewed earlier. Generally, one might conclude that midlife begins somewhere around 40 and ends by 60 (see also MIDMAC, 1999), but that at both edges of midlife there is a flexible, vague boundary. One factor affecting how people define midlife is their own current age. Thus, in two of the reported studies, the respondents—who were themselves middle-aged—suggested a later ending for midlife (55 or 60 instead of 50 years), and also used a higher age boundary to describe when individuals enter old age (65 instead of 60 years; Cameron, 1969; Drevenstedt, 1976).

Another factor affecting how society, and individuals, define midlife is the cohort to which they belong. In fact, it is demographic changes (especially declining birth rate and increased life expectancy) that are seen as responsible for the current societal view of midlife as a discrete period (in Western cultures; Gullette, 1998). Thus, given the changes in the societal and life-course structures, a definition of midlife linked to chronological age most likely will differ between cohorts (see also Schaie & Willis, 1986). Taking a life-span perspective encourages a definition of midlife that abstracts from chronological age. It considers the multiple contexts of midlife and their related opportunities and challenges, as well as the resources available and their distribution.

Midlife may be the most central period of life, that which is referred to generally when aiming at adulthood without qualifying it as either "early" or "late." Its exact age boundaries are unclear, and while the time from age 40 to 60 seems to comprise middle age, the boundaries are open to interpretation. Interpretation may be affected by one's own current age, as well as the historical period. This lack of a precise definition and the sense that it may not be well described by reference to chronological age but instead involve subjective perceptions of multiple paths through various domains, may have restricted the development of a clear agenda for research. The limited value of chronological age with regard to defining midlife shifts our attention to the developmental tasks of midlife. Again, however, not just a single task but several challenges can be identified.

Thus, as elaborated later it may be useful to define midlife using metacharacteristics.

Does Midlife Present Life Problems Worth Psychological Study?

A second reason midlife may have been understudied is a seeming lack of societal and psychological reasons to do so. In the past 50 years, psychologists have focused on the study of areas in which individuals have problems negotiating life (Seligman & Csikszentmihalyi, 2000). Thus, one reason midlife was not studied was that it was not considered a particularly problem-stricken phase of life. From a societal perspective, by midlife investment in socialization on average should have paid off. By this point, individuals should have been socialized into roles and are usually contributing to society. Consequently, they neither need more socialization investment (as children do) nor do they normatively require external help and care due to health or frailty issues (as old and very old adults may). They provide no problems that psychologists, and more generally society, must respond to; they are, instead, one of the pillars that maintain societal functioning. In contrast, the identification of old age as a societal problem because of the growing number of older people in Western industrial nations has contributed to increased gerontological research. Further, the perception that midlife does not present particular problems to individuals may help explain why psychological research has not yet made midlife a focus of attention. When our perspective, however, focuses on understanding basic developmental processes as well as the ways to support successful development, midlife is rich in aspects to be explored.

Midlife may be better defined by a pattern of characteristics than simply by chronological age. As such, the relation of chronological age to social, psychological, and biological age may offer a way to study midlife in context. There is no consensus that any single biological or social event constitutes the lower boundary of middle age, and retirement can be seen as an upper boundary, in some cohorts, only for men (B. Neugarten & Datan, 1996). Some have suggested that middle age is the time between when the youngest child leaves home and when the spouse dies (Treas & Bengtson, 1982). Although specific events such as these play critical roles, individuals measure their age and life phase using a combination of social, psychological, and biological markers that are only sometimes tied to particular events (see also Moen & Wethington, 1999).

Although no consensus exists concerning the entry and exit points of midlife, there is more agreement concerning the sequence of developmental tasks that normatively occur in this period. By midlife, individuals are expected to have established a family, found a clear career direction in which they will peak during midlife, and have taken on responsibility with respect to their children, their own aging parents, and sometimes their community. These multiple roles influence the ecology of midlife for each individual (Reid & Willis, 1999), as well as provide individuals with the chance to customize their own experience (Moen & Wethington, 1999).

While midlife itself has been relatively understudied, research pertinent to midlife appears in the domains and events that are central to its definition. When considering the social, psychological, and biological experience of midlife, relevant research is available in several areas: the social domain (e.g., family and parenting, friendship across the life span), the psychological realm (e.g., change and continuity in self, personality, and well-being), and the biological arena (e.g., changes in sexual function and bodily functions—menopause, incidence of disease). Researchers have explored such topics as the "midlife crisis" (Jacques, 1965), menopause (Voda, Dinnerstein, & O'Donnell, 1982), the effects of caring for both children and aging parents ("the sandwiched generation"; Davis, 1981); the "empty nest" (e.g., Rubin, 1979); and the transition to retirement and leisure (Atchley, 1982).

Taking this task- or event-specific perspective, the oft-made claim that little research exists on midlife may be overstated. In fact, many research areas provide useful information for understanding the multiple challenges and problems of midlife development. However, midlife has only recently been identified as a developmental period worth studying as a whole. One of the current challenges to the field is to integrate findings from various areas to develop a view of the important events and transitions of midlife, whether these be drawn from work that is largely psychological, social, or biological. Life-span theory offers the opportunity to view these multiple contexts of aging as interrelated. From there, research designed with a focus on midlife may examine events and transitions in terms of both problems and achievements (see also Heckhausen, Chapter 11 this volume, for a discussion of midlife as a time of both vulnerability and resilience).

MIDLIFE: IS IT MORE THAN ONE PHASE?

A final reason that midlife may have received relatively little specific research attention is that it may be too heterogeneous a phase. Not only do individuals take different pathways through midlife (interindividual variability; Moen & Wethington, 1999), but it is a life phase in which one is both leaving youth and entering old age. The beginning of midlife and the latter part of midlife have similarities, but also have quite different demands (Goldhaber, 1986). Previous research on midlife has sometimes painted it as a time of crisis, sometimes as the prime of life, and some-times as a period of stability and routine (Farrell & Rosenberg, 1981), thus making it difficult to form an integrated view from which to gener-ate research.

Consideration of the possibility of a young-midlife and a late-midlife may add precision to our research endeavors. It may also make it possible to reconcile seemingly contradictory findings. The first part of midlife may involve more growth and building of resources than losses, and that relation may start turning around toward the end of midlife (Bühler, 1953). While young-midlife involves consolidating family and career, is-sues of late midlife may revolve around such things as health concerns, preparing for retirement, and becoming a grandparent. When entering midlife, one still feels young, and the sense that one is reaching the mid-point of life is something that must be weighed, considered, and ac-cepted. By the time one is leaving midlife, this transition is complete and the issue is no longer one of realization but of finding ways to lead a ful-filling life despite inevitable losses (e.g., B. Neugarten & Datan, 1996).

Although other reasons may also exist for the historical paucity of re-search interest in midlife, we have identified three major reasons: Midlife is not easily defined in terms of chronological age; from a societal and probably also individual perspective, it does not present problematic events and transitions; and it may be better conceptualized as two dis-tinct phases. As discussed later in this chapter, these barriers to the pro-ductive study of midlife are effectively eliminated when one views midlife through life-span developmental theory.

A SELECTIVE REVIEW OF THEORETICAL PERSPECTIVES ON MIDLIFE

In this section, we provide a selective review of some theorists who have either directly discussed midlife or made salient observations concerning midlife as part of a larger theoretical framework. The review is not exhaus-tive but considers the way the middle period of life has been conceptual-ized, especially the convergence between viewpoints. This convergence serves as a guideline to the critical themes that must be included to provide an overarching theoretical approach to middle age. The section is organ-ized around three of these themes: time orientation, the balance between work and relationships, and opportunities for growth and generativity.

SOCIAL, BIOLOGICAL, AND PSYCHOLOGICAL TIME: BÜHLER'S AND NEUGARTEN'S CONTRIBUTIONS

The first salient theme that has guided previous theories of midlife is the extent to which development in this period is biologically versus socially structured. As opposed to early development, in which biological unfolding plays a key role in the individual's progress, adulthood is governed more by social, cultural, and environmental constraints and opportunities (Baltes, Lindenberger, & Staudinger, 1998) though certain biological events may also be important (e.g., menopause; Parlee, 1984). While early childhood may be characterized as running on a biological clock, much of adulthood is governed more, or at least conjointly, by a social clock (B. Neugarten et al., 1965). This notion of the clock of life, whether biological or social, brings our attention to the *temporal aspect* of life-span development, and particularly what it means to be "in the middle."

Neugarten's work (for a compilation, see D. Neugarten, 1996) challenges researchers to critically examine the role of time in development by asking whether the way in which developmental psychology has studied children is also appropriate for the study of adults. While she supports research approaches that examine continuity as well as those that examine discontinuity, the most interesting contributions of her thinking about midlife come from examining discontinuities. Primarily, she argues that adults' sense of time and timing plays a role that is not seen earlier in life. One no longer measures life as time since birth, but as time left to live. For adults, the blending of past, present, and future becomes a psychological reality (e.g., Ryff, 1991). This changing view of time allows adults not only a sense of self, but a sense of self across time, that is, a sense of their own life cycle. Middle-aged individuals evaluate themselves as having shown personal growth since their younger years, and look to the future with the expectation of further personal growth (Ryff, 1991). In late midlife, one may begin to contemplate the end of the life cycle. This sense of impending endings has been linked to increased socioemotional selectivity (e.g., Carstensen & Turk-Charles, 1998).

B. Neugarten points out that awareness of one's own life cycle has consequences for the individual's goal choices and priorities, and it also allows for comparison with others. The individual compares his or her own progress through the life cycle with a view of the expected, or normative, societal timing of major events and transitions. When studying midlife, researchers are alerted to examine not only what events are important for adaptation, but also how the on-time or off-time sequencing of major life events changes how they are experienced, or what they mean to the individual. She suggests that this "normal, expectable life cycle" that individuals carry in their heads allows them to compare themselves to their peers in terms of how they are facing both occupational and family challenges in midlife. Research has shown that individuals do indeed carry stereotypes about what one should have accomplished by midlife and use them to make judgments about others (e.g., Krueger, Heckhausen, & Hundertmark, 1995).

Midlife has been seen as a plateau, as a peak, and as a crisis (e.g., menopause, men's declining sexual prowess, midlife depression, retirement, the empty nest). The importance of timing may be helpful when it comes to deciding between the three. Although a minority of individuals may react to the normative transitions of midlife with nonadaptive styles, this is true of any life stage (B. Neugarten & Datan, 1996). As such, midlife is seen by Neugarten as a potential period of crisis only to the extent that the normative events of midlife are experienced off-time, or to the extent that normative progress through this life phase is interrupted by unexpected events. In addition, while midlife events sometimes require major coping efforts, people often view them in retrospect as being meaningful turning points through which they gained new insights (Wethington, Cooper, & Holmes, 1997).

Besides the timing of major events (e.g., marriage, childbearing, widowhood), B. Neugarten also outlines such transitions as the increasing responsibility for aging parents, the awareness of the self as the bridge between generations, the need to establish relationships with adult children's marriage partners, and grandparenthood, as important for midlife development. In facing these relationship challenges, as well as the occupational challenges of midlife, the emerging theme in midlife is the view of self as the socializer, no longer the socialized. Thus, Neugarten's view of midlife emphasizes the maturity of the individual at midlife, with the capacity for taking on important roles and purposively acting to create benefits for oneself and others. In this way, she addresses generativity through her discussion of adulthood as a time when one creates not only biological but social heirs.

Through the choice and pursuit of life goals, and through the ability to selectively assess and reassess one's path through adulthood, the individual is the creator of his or her own environment in midlife. The extent to which one effectively interacts with, and changes his or her environment, or even sees the need to make his or her own choices, depends on that person's own life history, including social factors such as class and culture (Baltes et al., 1998; for a review of culture and midlife, see Shweder, 1998).

If midlife is a time of challenge and potential stress (e.g., the conflict between caregiving and career; see Marks, 1998), it is also a time of achievement. This emphasis on the creative activities and products of the middle-aged, and how they are related to time perspective, is fundamental to the view of the life course outlined by Charlotte Bühler (1968). Her humanistic view of life-course development emphasizes the pursuit of goals to establish meaning and reach fulfillment in life. Thus, she views the individual as attempting to harmonize the duality between seeking comfort and accomplishing selected goals. The extent to which one tends toward accomplishment over comfort depends, among other things, on one's temporal perspective. Bühler contends that though we live in the present, we have goals that reach into the future, and we are always affected by our past. Those who mostly focus on the present (e.g., children) seek largely comfort. The period of midlife brings the consideration of past and future into balance; the individual tries to use what has been learned in the past to promote future goal achievement and fulfillment. In this view, while midlife is a biological midpoint or a time when physical growth is complete and decline has not yet really begun, midlife also offers as yet unknown possibilities for self-fulfillment and accomplishment through balancing the past and the future. This potential is also reflected in Maslow's (1962) claim that self-actualization is not possible at least until one leaves the period of youth.

As individuals progress through the life cycle, with both the biological and social clocks ticking away, the accumulation of experience and the varying ways in which individuals have organized that experience, lead them to very different places. The experience of the diachronicity of life (i.e., extending into the past and the future) taking center stage in adolescence plays a central role in midlife (see Staudinger, 1999).

As described in the section on life-span developmental theory, the view of life as having a temporal flow in which midlife is both the result of one's previous developmental history, and a staging ground for later life, is taken up in one of the propositions of life-span psychology. While life trajectories become more varied as we move across the life span, two domains—family and career, or love and work—are important for most individuals at middle age. Several researchers have focused on the normative stages that may be expected as people attempt to achieve a balance in these two domains, and others, across midlife.

FINDING A BALANCE: JUNG'S AND LEVINSON'S THEORIES

A second theme seen in previous theorizing is the idea of midlife as a time when individuals are attempting to find balance in various ways. Part of Jung's view (1971) is that midlife is a time when a more whole and balanced gender identity begins to emerge that allows individuals greater autonomy over choices and roles than is offered by the unitary, society-driven, sex-role orientation of the young. More recent empirical work has suggested that when individuals move toward a more androgynous identity in midlife, this may be a source of pleasure, but sometimes also causes embarrassment (Huyck, 1999).

In combination with this move toward androgyny, Jung postulated that midlife is a time when one's level of extraversion and introversion also come into greater balance. He argued that young adulthood demands a largely extraverted orientation to meet the challenges of establishing work and family, and the middle years allow for a balancing in which individuals also begin to turn inward and explore their own subjective experience to a greater extent. In general, Jung viewed midlife as a turning point at which one gradually comes to realize that the values and ideals developed earlier in life are not sufficient for moving meaningfully through the second half of life. He states, "We cannot live the afternoon of life according to the program of life's morning; for what was great in the morning will be little at evening, and what in the morning was true will at evening have become a lie" (Jung, 1971, p. 17). Other theorists pick up this theme by examining the types of challenges that are specific to midlife.

Levinson's (1978) stage theory of adult male development is based on his research on the similarities in the patterns of men's lives across the adult years. Here again, we see a consideration of the extent to which interaction of biological and social influences affect the structure of midlife. A purely biological view might frame midlife as a plateau between the growth of youth and the decline of later life. While that may be the approximate biological architecture of midlife, Levinson set out to determine if there are also social patterns of development within adulthood. Thus, his theory is similar to Neugarten's, in that it is based on the idea that while biological changes may result in stages of development in childhood, social and cultural changes are just as likely to structure the life course in predictable ways in adulthood. According to Levinson, early adulthood (about age 18–45) is conceived as a time in which men establish an adult identity and take up the challenges of settling themselves in the workforce, develop an intimate partnership, and start a family. Middle adulthood (about age 45–65) is a time when men have often achieved these earlier goals, but are striving to find meaning in life more generally. He posited the midlife crisis as an attempt for men to review their lives and reorder their priorities. Here the temporal theme reviewed in the preceding section emerges again. The crisis is a result of looking at one's achievements thus far and questioning their meaningfulness in terms of the life lived and life left to live. In Levinson's sample, the resultant changes in priorities often involved more emphasis on relationships and less on career than was seen in earlier adulthood. Though the notion of a midlife crisis as normative has been debated (for a review, see Rosenberg, Rosenberg, & Farrell, 1999), this change in priorities reflects another basic tenet of much thinking about midlife, that a major task is to find an adaptive and meaningful balance between love and work, or communion and agency in one's life.

Because of the often different nature of women's roles and responsibilities in midlife, Levinson's theory does not describe women's experience particularly well. Although with women's increasing involvement in the labor force, some of his ideas surely are applicable. Frieze (1978) has described the complicated scenario that greets women in midlife (at least current midlife cohorts): Since women are usually primary caregivers to children, and sometimes also to aging parents (both their own and their husband's), their ability to balance agency and communion is further challenged. Often, women must step out of their career path, or reduce their involvement in career, to have and raise children. In such cases, women must begin to establish a career, and then reenter the workforce once their children enter school. The ways that women make choices concerning trade-offs between work and family may be affected by the extent to which they are socialized to place value on independence and affiliation (Gilligan, 1982). More generally, gender may be as important as life stage in understanding individuals' attitudes and feelings concerning marriage, parenting, and friendships (e.g., Huyck, 1999; Lowenthal, Turner, & Chiriboga, 1975).

The reviewed theories converge on the notion that midlife is an important time for finding balance. It has been suggested that underlying the balancing and reprioritizing the importance of agency and communion in midlife is a more fundamental change in individuals' gender identity. Jung (1971) introduced the idea that individuals move from sex-role stereotyped behavior in young adulthood to a more balanced gender profile across midlife. While both men and women must balance the dual challenges of work and relationships across midlife, their trajectories through midlife are affected by the value they place on these two domains and on societal gender-stereotyped expectations concerning their commitment to each domain. Life-span developmental theory puts these particular ways in which individuals strive for balance in midlife in a larger perspective. As discussed in the section on life-span theory, the ability to achieve balance may be based on a successful matching of investment of resources and life demands in midlife.

HAVIGHURST AND ERIKSON: GENERATIVITY IN MIDLIFE

While much research focuses on the challenges of midlife and the conflicting demands of work and family, or caregiving for both children and elders (not necessarily simultaneously), concepts such as "life as learning" and "generativity" put the challenges of midlife in a positive light. Havighurst (1972) viewed not only midlife but each life phase as a time for attempting and achieving various developmental tasks. Each life phase presents the individual with a new set of life conditions to be met with, and so "the human individual learns his way through life" (p. 1). The emphasis on learning and mastering tasks reflects the underpinnings of the theory: The course of adult development is prescribed to some extent by societal institutions (e.g., family, church, government, media, economy) and individual development occurs within that larger framework. Thus, the individual is challenged to contribute not only to the well-being of self and family but also to the larger community.

Havighurst also sees two of the general tasks of middle age as reaching and maintaining a satisfactory career level, and maintaining positive relationships: relating to one's spouse as a person, helping teenage children prepare for the adult world, and adjusting to and assisting aging parents. These goals mirror the concerns with agency and communion seen in other theories, but additional developmental tasks are also seen as particularly important in midlife. These include accepting the physiological changes of midlife, achieving adult social and civil responsibility, and developing satisfying leisure-time activities. As such, Havighurst's view of midlife extends beyond the psychosocial life (career and relationships) to also include both higher (societal responsibilities) and lower (biological concerns) levels of analysis. All these developmental tasks are both structured by society and chosen by the individual, and offer opportunities for the middle-aged individual to learn more about life and about the world while making a contribution to others' well-being.

Erikson's (e.g., 1980) view of development also puts midlife in a larger context by adopting a life-span perspective in which life tasks (psychosocial crises) are generally age-graded, but also cumulative across life, and open to reemergence depending on life circumstances. His stages of industry, intimacy, and generativity are respectively expressed in the challenges of career, marriage, and parenting. While all three remain important across adulthood, the challenge of generativity versus stagnation is specific to midlife. Erikson argues that it is in this period that the mature individual has the skills and resources to give to others. He defines generativity as any activity that is motivated by concern for the next generation. Thoughtful and caring parenting involves generativity, though having children in itself does not resolve this psychosocial task. Through giving, or concern for the next generation, adults not only assist others or develop society, but are able to step outside their own concerns to expand their view of life beyond themselves and their own time. Erikson claimed that this new perspective wards off feelings of self-centered stagnation and offers new insights into one's own life. Thus, midlife brings with it, at least for some segments of the population, an opportunity for assuming responsibility and authority, and a greater sense of self-direction and self-understanding (Goldhaber, 1986). The middle years are ones in which individuals act as leaders of families, organizations, and communities (Schaie & Willis, 1986). Their engagement in these multiple roles, and through it their generativity, has been linked to later well-being (e.g., Vandewater, Ostrove, & Stewart, 1997). While generativity involves giving of oneself to others, particularly the next generation, individuals may also benefit in terms of well-being by feeling that they have made a meaningful contribution to society as they enter their later years (Keyes & Ryff, 1998).

McAdams and de St. Aubin (1992) have elaborated Erikson's view of generativity in a psychosocial model (see also McAdams, Chapter 12, this volume). Inner desires and cultural demands are seen as working in tandem to influence one's concern for the next generation and belief that the human enterprise is meaningful or worthwhile. These beliefs, desires and demands lead to generative activities such as creating or maintaining things that benefit the community. One of the reasons midlife is a prime time for generative acts is that this is when the demands of work and family challenge individuals to make agentic and communal offerings of themselves to their offspring and to the larger community. These generative achievements often become part of the individual's life story or conception of self (McAdams, Hart, & Maruna, 1998) and are often remembered when older adults look back at midlife (Conway & Holmes, 1999).

Individuals may, however, enter midlife with different capacities for achieving generativity. Social structure affects individuals' health and educational opportunities and thus may indirectly affect their opportunities for generativity and well-being (Baltes et al., 1998; Ryff & Singer, 1998). What types of factors affect the extent to which people are generative in midlife? Havighurst's (1972) notion that the tasks of midlife are set by societal expectations and constraints, and Erikson's (1980) view of the individual placing him- or herself in a wider temporal and historical context through generativity, are concepts that are further elaborated in contextualistic views of development, such as Bronfenbrenner's (1979) human ecology model of development. While stage theories that describe how people normatively progress through adulthood have merit, the individual life circumstances of each adult also influence development, resulting in individual trajectories through midlife. The human ecology model delineates influences in the immediate environment (e.g., workplace, home), the interrelation of various integrated and conflicting environments (e.g., having a part-time job while raising a child), as well as the larger external environment (e.g., living in a city versus a rural home). Finally, the overarching values of one's culture and society influence life choices and development. While midlife may present all individuals with the same fundamental tasks, the exact nature of those tasks and the opportunity for mastery, and therefore for generativity, also differ somewhat from one individual to the next. Life-span theory has made such a contextualistic view of development a cornerstone (cf. Baltes et al., 1980).

A person who is in the middle years, realizing that time passed and time left to live may be equal, and facing the need to balance career and family, is also in a prime period for achievement; for giving to others; and for learning about oneself by what he or she gives to others. According to Erikson, resolution of this midlife developmental task sets the stage for the development of integrity in later life.

In this section, we have reviewed several prominent and partially contradictory theories of midlife with special focus on three themes: time perspective, balancing life demands, and generativity. Research on midlife has not always, or maybe even often, been guided by theory. While sometimes based within a theoretical framework, much research on midlife has focused on specific life events or situations that normatively occur in midlife. The life-event framework for studying adult development examines the critical events and transitions that individuals face, how they cope with those transitions, and how this results in functional and dysfunctional outcomes for different individuals (Hultsch & Plemons, 1979). Besides an analysis of specific events, the timing, sequencing, and accumulation of life events and transitions are also important to the trajectory that individuals face, and how they adapt to midlife and aging (Lerner & Hultsch, 1983). In the following section, we present the life-span perspective on midlife development. It demonstrates how life-span theory not only incorporates many important features of past theoretical work on midlife but also provides a sophisticated framework for future theory development and empirical research that may further our understanding.

A VIEW ON MIDLIFE DEVELOPMENT FROM LIFE-SPAN THEORY

What is life-span developmental theory? Why would we expect to learn something new about midlife by taking this perspective? In the following pages, we present six central propositions of life-span theory (see also Baltes et al., 1998; Staudinger, Marsiske, & Baltes, 1995), show how these relate to the central themes in extant midlife research and theory, and develop the consequences that these propositions may have for the study of midlife. Table 1.1 summarizes the propositions as well as the implications for the study of midlife development.

For many people, life after young adulthood is still connected with negative stereotypic expectations, such as the belief that middle-aged people are either crisis-stricken or bored, and that old age is largely a period of decline and despair. The life-span view presented here argues against such simplistic views of development. Conceptualizing development across the life span as multidimensional, multidirectional, and modifiable challenges models of midlife development and aging that are oriented exclusively toward decrements (Baltes, 1993; Riley & Riley, 1989; Rowe & Kahn, 1987).

Table 1.1

Summary of Life-Span Propositions and Their Implications for the Study of Midlife Development

Concept	Proposition	Implications for the Study of Midlife Development
Life-Span Development	Ontogenetic development is the lifelong change in adaptive capacity influenced by biology and culture. No age period holds supremacy in regulating the nature of development.	What are the particular characteristics of development in midlife? It isn't useful to study midlife in isolation. It is crucial to consider precursors and outcomes of midlife.
Development as Gain-Loss Dynamic	Development implies not only growth (gains) but also decrements (losses). With increasing age, losses outweigh gains. A multidimensional, multidirectional, and multifunctional conception of development results from this perspective.	Midlife is characterized by a "tie" in the relation of gains to losses. Some domains of functioning are still increasing, many maintain functioning, while others have already begun to decline.
Life-Span Changes in the Dynamic between Biology and Culture	Biological influences on development become more and more detrimental with increasing age. Cultural support of development continues and is needed more with increasing age.	Midlife and midlife are not the same. Given the changing ratio of gains and losses, there may be a need to distinguish between early and late midlife.
Life-Span Changes in the Allocation of Resources	In conjunction with the culture-biology dynamic, an age-related reduction in overall resources is assumed. Resources are used to serve three major functions: growth, maintenance and recovery, and regulation of loss. As losses increase with increasing age, maintenance, recovery, and regulation of loss become more and more prominent.	Midlife is characterized by many challenges and threats as well as resources. Thus, midlife implies a major effort in managing resources and needs. Though maintenance and recovery may be most prominent in midlife, both growth and loss management are also invested.

(continued)

17

Table 1.1 Continued

Concept	Proposition	Implications for the Study of Midlife Development
Life-Span Development Is Modifiable	Throughout life, development demonstrates plasticity. The range and limits of developmental plasticity are central to life-span research.	Even though the range of selection is reduced by midlife, there still is possibility for change. Examining the range and limits of plasticity in midlife puts an emphasis on optimization instead of repair.
Ontogenetic and Historical Contextualism	The influences of biology and culture follow three logics: age-graded, history-graded, and nonnormative.	The characteristics of midlife are cohort-specific and may depend on the cultural-historical context.

Source: Modified and extended from Baltes, Lindenberger, and Staudinger, 1998.

DEFINING LIFE-SPAN DEVELOPMENT

The first proposition of life-span theory is that ontogenetic development is the lifelong *selective change in adaptive capacity* as it is influenced by the interaction between biology and culture. No age period holds supremacy in regulating development. The central feature of the developmental process is "transactional adaptation" (e.g., Lerner, 1984, 1986) or "person-environment interaction" (e.g., Magnusson, 1990). Development is not simply the passive unfolding of prewired maturational programs, or the mechanistic reaction of organisms to environmental stimuli. Development is the outcome of a constant and active process of the individual's transaction with changing contextual influences, including age-graded changes of the genome and historical transformations of society. The individual is actively selecting developmental contexts, can change contexts, and is simultaneously changed by contexts. Such ideas have been perfectly captured by the concept of developmental tasks introduced by Erikson and Havighurst.

This notion implies that biological models that view development as being limited to the first half of life, and as being followed by aging in the second half are inadequate to describe human development from a psychological perspective. At all ages, development implies concurrent and successive gains and losses, which can be either dependent on or independent of each other (see also Uttal & Perlmutter, 1989).

The notion of lifelong development thus implies that when studying midlife, a first task is to investigate what development in midlife is like. It is no longer self-evident that midlife development is either only growth or only decline. Instead, its own unique characteristics must be identified. Second, when considering development as extending from conception until death, we are not interested in looking at one life phase by itself and in isolation. The particulars of any given life phase need some points of comparison to be identified. Thus, it does not seem useful to exclusively study middle-aged adults; young and old comparison groups should be included as well.

Young and old comparison groups are essential when determining the precursors and the consequences of midlife. Examining young and older comparison groups, however, is still rarely done as can be seen when reviewing the literature on midlife development (for an exception, see, e.g., Lachman & Weaver, 1998). Most studies that focus on midlife in terms of their theoretical interest also focus exclusively on midlife in terms of samples (e.g., Klohnen, Vandewater, & Young, 1996). When comparison age groups are included, most often younger ages leading up to midlife are studied, and rarely old age following midlife (e.g., Helson & Klohnen, 1998; Vandewater et al., 1997). Including young, middle-aged, and old adults in a study without having a theoretical focus on midlife, however, does not make it a sufficient study. A life-span approach to the study of midlife development calls for both a theoretical framework that focuses on midlife as well as the inclusion of young and old comparison samples.

The notion of development as transactional adaptation further implies that it is not only psychological functioning that changes with age but also the contexts (and their associated risks and resources), and the functional consequences (evaluative criteria) of development. Considering the example of language and cognitive development, it is not only proficiency that changes or develops with age, but also the contexts of acquisition and application in everyday life. Furthermore, the criteria according to which language and cognitive proficiency are evaluated undergo age-related change. Whenever development is considered from a life-span perspective, these three interlocking parameters of development (level of functioning, sources or contexts, functional consequences) are the focus of analysis.

In relation to midlife, this implies that from a life-span perspective, researchers should not stop at investigating the level of intellectual functioning in middle-aged adults but also ask what the contexts are for intellectual functioning in midlife and how these contexts influence intellectual functioning. Further, life-span researchers also ask how intellectual performance is evaluated: What is expected of middle-aged adults, what are the functional consequences of intellectual development in midlife? Willis and Schaie (1999) interpret their findings of midlife peak performance in reasoning as well as verbal abilities by describing how midlife offers contexts of career development and familial responsibilities (e.g., financial management) that may support such increases. A further interpretation is that in contrast to old age when society starts to excuse poor intellectual performance, adults in midlife are expected to be highly efficient and knowledgeable.

Life-span development can be a continuous (cumulative) or discontinuous (innovative) process. Continuity is provided by the intimate relationship, family, and friendship context and for males most likely by the work context as well. But as we develop or age, we are also constantly confronted with new internal and external developmental contexts that may give raise to discontinuity. This phenomenon is captured, by the theoretical concept of "developmental tasks" (both in the practical and intrapsychic sense) that change over the life course (e.g., Erikson, Erikson, & Kivnick, 1986; Havighurst, 1972; Levinson, 1978). When middle-aged women reenter the workforce after their children have grown up, they are confronted with new developmental contexts. These contextual challenges are reflected in marked increases (more strongly for women than for men) in some intellectual domains (e.g., Willis & Schaie, 1999). Early retirement (e.g., Atchley, 1982), unemployment (Moen & Wethington, 1999), or widowhood (e.g.,

Wortman & Silver, 1990) in midlife are other life-span contexts where issues of discontinuity take center stage. Furthermore, health and functional changes that arise as a consequence of biological aging, such as decreases in sensory functioning, can serve as sources for developmental innovation and/or disruption in midlife (Merrill & Verbrugge, 1999). As such, midlife can be characterized as both continuous and discontinuous depending on the domain of functioning being considered and the particular life events faced by individuals.

DEVELOPMENT AS A GAIN-LOSS DYNAMIC

Development not only implies growth (gains) but also implies decrements (losses). Life-span development includes the full range of directional possibilities: gain, stability, and loss. The process of development should not solely be described as a continued progression to higher levels of functioning, nor as a constant decline.

Contrary to widely held beliefs about childhood as a period of universal progression, losses occur even early in life. Piaget (1965), for example, described some visual illusions that increase with age and others that decrease with age. He ascribed this loss in visual accuracy to advancement in cognitive stage, in this case the development of conceptual schemata. Similarly, in contrast to equally widely held beliefs about the pervasiveness of decline with aging, there continue to be gains in later life. In language development, individuals may continue to modify and expand their verbal knowledge through middle adulthood and even into old age (e.g., Horn & Hofer, 1992). In a similar vein, there is evidence that middle-aged adults demonstrate peak or high performances (compared with young and old adults) in such areas as everyday problem solving, life-problem solving, and work-related expertise (e.g., Denney, 1989; Ericsson & Smith, 1991; Staudinger & Baltes, 1994). Even in the field of memory, which is notorious for its age-related declines, there are facets such as implicit memory (i.e., unintentional memory; Graf, 1990; Howard, 1991) or autobiographical memory (e.g., Bluck, Levine, & Laultere, 1999; Cohen, 1998), which evince stability and some increase across the life span. In terms of self- and emotion-regulation, research has demonstrated that midlife seems to bring advances (e.g., Labouvie-Vief, DeVoe, & Bulka, 1989; Labouvie-Vief, Hakim-Larson, & Hobart, 1987). Certainly, to define what constitutes a loss and what constitutes a gain is highly complex and dependent on age-graded, history-graded, and idiosyncratic influences (for a more extended discussion of this topic, see Baltes et al., 1998).

The life-span perspective conceives development as a system of changes that encompasses positive and negative directions and consequences (Baltes, 1987; Weinert, 1994). When considering the overall balance between gains and losses across domains, a generally positive or negative picture may emerge, but with increasing age, the balance between gains and losses becomes increasingly negative.

When reviewing research on midlife development, it seems that midlife is characterized by a tie in the relation of gains and losses. Some domains still show progress or stability, while others have already begun to show decline. In some respects, "midlifers" look like young adults and in other respects they look like older adults. This tie between gains and losses can

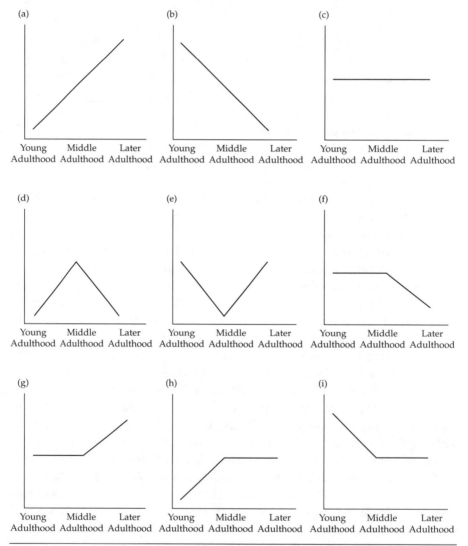

Figure 1.1 Theoretically derived schematic developmental life-span trajectories. Each of the nine trajectories depicts a certain characteristic of midlife. The trajectories apply equally to subjective experience and developmental processes.

be related to some quite different life-span trajectories. Figure 1.1 shows theoretically derived developmental trajectories illustrating the many different ways that midlife can be situated in the middle of the life span.

Middle age can be indistinguishable from youth and old age (trajectory c). Middle age can also be unique—either better or worse than both youth and old age (trajectories d and e). The "true" middle position is illustrated by trajectories (a) and (b). Middle age can be better than youth and worse than old age (trajectory a). Or the other way around, middle age can be worse than youth but still better than old age (trajectory b). Middle-aged adults may be found to be like young adults (trajectories f and g), but they may also be found to be like old adults (trajectories h and i) depending on the domain under study.

Given these multiple trajectories, a useful contribution to the literature would be completion of a meta-analytic study that systematically reviews available evidence on midlife development by sorting results into these categories to gain a better understanding of overall midlife development. Empirical examples can be found for all these trajectories. However, the relative frequency of each trajectory across available studies still is unclear. Knowing the frequency distribution of these trajectories may help researchers to form a picture of what it feels like from the inside to be in the middle. Do individuals in midlife primarily experience themselves as operating at lower levels than before, including the prospect of stability for the years to come (trajectory i)? Or do they more commonly experience increased levels of functioning and an expected continuation of this increase in the future (trajectory a)? These trajectories are not only interesting in terms of subjective experiences of midlife development, but also important in understanding the developmental processes of midlife such as stability, growth, and decline.

Based on a cross-sectional comparison, it was found that growth aspects of personality (e.g., self-acceptance, environmental mastery) follow as many as five different trajectories (b, c, f, h, g; Figure 1.1; Ryff & Singer, 1998). In the case of internal control beliefs in central life domains, such as marriage, work, finances, or health, four trajectories were identified (a), (c), (g), and (i) (Lachman & Weaver, 1998). So far, the curvilinear trajectories (d) and (e) seem to be underrepresented, though some evidence is also available for them in a study on the life-span development of attitude change. In this study, it was demonstrated that susceptibility to attitude change is lowest in midlife (trajectory e) fitting very well with Neugarten's characterization of midlife as moving from being socialized to being a socializer. The finding of attitude stability is complemented by evidence showing that at the same time attitude importance and certainty are at their highest in midlife (trajectory d; Visser & Krosnick, 1998). When moving to the domain of cognitive development, the Seattle longitudinal study provides evidence for almost all the depicted trajectories. Perceptual speed follows trajectory (b), development of verbal ability and verbal memory reflects trajectory (h), logical and spatial reasoning follow trajectory (d), and finally the development of numerical reasoning follows trajectory (f).

Within the same individual, at the same moment in time, some functions may be increasing while others are decreasing or remaining stable. Normal development in adolescence, for example, includes increases in physical competence that are concurrent with decreases in the ability to acquire additional languages. Normal midlife development includes normative biological losses (e.g., Finch, 1990), and some losses in some areas of intellectual functioning, while other domains of intellectual functioning and personality functioning may show stability and even increase (e.g., Baltes, Staudinger, & Lindenberger, 1999).

According to the life-span perspective, development across midlife (as development in other life phases) is characterized by the simultaneous as well as successive occurrence of increases (gains), decreases (losses), and maintenance (stability) in transactional-adaptive capacity. Thus development is multidirectional, it encompasses the increase, maintenance, and decrease of functioning across different domains. This implies that development is multidimensional rather than unidimensional (e.g., intellectual functioning involves distinct categories such as fluid versus crystallized intelligence; or personality is composed of five different dimensions). Thus, when midlife development is approached from a life-span perspective, it is important to distinguish between the overall balance of developmental gains and losses across domains as well as the domain-specific trajectories for particular functions. Such a point of view is consistent with a multilevel or systemic approach to development (Ford, 1987).

Development unfolds in many different domains of functioning. There is no unitary developmental process that affects all dimensions of an individual in the same way. Although changes in some domains of functioning in an individual will tend to be correlated, it is possible for individuals to experience changes in some areas that are independent of changes in others. In the psychological sphere, personality functioning in adulthood seems to develop rather independently of physical functioning (e.g., Baltes, 1993; Smith & Baltes, 1993). When studying development, then, it may often be more meaningful to speak of domain-specific trajectories for particular functions (e.g., Karmiloff-Smith, 1992). The "overall development" of a person would represent some complex admixture of development along specific dimensions. From a life-span perspective, therefore, midlife is neither synonymous with stability, nor with growth, nor with decline. With increasing age, however, the overall balance of gains to losses in level of functioning and available reserves across the different domains of development becomes less positive. Midlife may mark the break-even point in the overall relation of gains to losses.

Life-Span Changes in the Dynamic between Biology and Culture

What may be underlying this change in the gain-loss ratio as individuals move through life? Baltes (e.g., 1997) has argued that it is both age-related decline in levels of biological functioning, and age-related increase in the need for a complex infrastructure of cultural support. Culture here refers to the entirety of psychological, social, material, and symbolic (knowledge-based) resources that humans have developed over millennia and that are transmitted across generations (e.g., Cole, 1991; Shweder, 1991). After biological maturity, the expressions and mechanisms of the genome decline in functional quality with age. Our body is biologically well equipped until the end of the reproductive and parenting phase. Thereafter, evolution has not had much of a chance to optimize our biology (yet) because evolutionary selection primarily works through the mechanisms of reproduction and parenting (for a more extended discussion of these issues, see Baltes et al., 1999). At the same time, humankind has successfully developed culture in such a way that it is more and more capable of compensating for biological decline, at least to a certain degree. Without doubt, humans are in need of culture from the very start of their existence, but with increasing age the complexity and sophistication of cultural structures supporting human development increases.

The two main influences on human development, biology and culture, follow a certain life-span path. For midlife development, this implies that the tie between gains and losses could be grounded in a biological decline that is only at its beginning and a cultural "infrastructure" that challenges as well as supports development during midlife. Pursuing this line of argument a bit further, however, may make it necessary—as mentioned—to distinguish two phases of midlife: early (40–50 yrs.) and late (51–60 yrs.) midlife. Some of the theories of midlife development described earlier, such as Levinson's, also suggest that such a subdivision should be meaningful.

Early midlife (on average) may still be dominated by the assets culture provides. We reap the harvest from our efforts in education, career, relationship, parenthood, and biology is predominantly still on our side. Whereas toward the later phase of midlife, it may (on average) be the case that the biological declines and the societal challenges start to outweigh assets. Examples of social-cultural challenges are the empty-nest situation (when children leave home); in the career realm, the first indicators of approaching retirement may become noticeable; and intimate relationships may be tested for their endurance. With regard to biological declines, the literature supports the view that after age 50 biological declines become more prominent. Biological losses are described that only come to the foreground around age 50 (e.g., decrease in muscle strength, decreases in sensory functioning, increase in cardiovascular diseases). Such bodily changes reach a noticeable level around age 50 (Merrill & Verbrugge, 1999).

According to our knowledge of the literature on midlife development, studies including such a differentiation between early and late midlife are not yet broadly available (e.g., Hooker & Kaus, 1994; Lachman & Weaver, 1998). Some studies do exclusively focus on the early phases of midlife, between age 40 and 50 (e.g., Bromberger & Matthews, 1996; Helson & Klohnen, 1998; Vandewater et al., 1997). Should such a cut-point find empirical support after further investigations of the multiple domains of midlife development, it would seem useful to subdivide samples into groups of early midlifers ranging from 40 to 50 years and late midlifers ranging from 51 to 60 years of age.

LIFE-SPAN CHANGES IN THE ALLOCATION OF RESOURCES

Related to the notion of the gain/loss ratio, and the forces underlying the changes in this ratio is the observation that organisms have limited resources and that these resources change in their range and fixedness across the life span (Baltes & Baltes, 1990). The gain/loss argument goes beyond the simple observation of multidirectionality in one or more developmental domains. Developmental domains are not independent of each other. A dynamic interplay ensues between gains and losses. Thus, a first limitation on resources results from investment into a specific path of development. No individual can do all things; there must be a selection of courses of action from the broader universe of possible plans. This idea has a long history in developmental science, and is similar to Waddington's idea of canalization (Edelman, 1987; Waddington, 1975). Under the assumption of limited adaptive resources, every selection of a developmental path necessarily implies that other possibilities have not been chosen; the selection of one developmental alternative (even if it has been "preselected"; e.g., by the genome) necessarily implies the loss of potential to engage in many other developmental courses. In this sense, all development, including alternatives we would traditionally classify as exemplifying progressive growth, are complemented by an element of loss. One example is the negative side effects of professional specialization. With increasing proficiency in a particular career during midlife, one loses some potential to invest in proficiency in other careers. Similarly, by choosing a mate, one gains security and attachment, but at the same time loses the freedom and variation related to changing partners.

A second limitation on resources and their development ensues from age-related changes in the overall level and variability of resources. Across the life span, the totality of resources available for development decreases. Midlife stage presents the individual with many competing developmental task domains such as those involving career, children, and aging parents.

Although an individual in midlife usually has a high level of internal and external resources, the sheer number of demands can present a risk situation by exceeding those available resources (e.g., Brim, 1992). This suggests that the gain-loss dynamic shows configurations specific to age and life period. These should be considered when evaluating life-span scenarios for developmental optimization, protection against losses (maintenance of functioning), and recovery from dysfunction in midlife.

Three adaptive tasks differ in prevalence across the life span and require differing resource allocations: growth, maintenance and/or recovery (resilience), and regulation of loss. The adaptive task of growth refers to behaviors that aim at reaching higher levels of functioning or adaptive capacity. Under the heading of maintenance and/or recovery are behaviors that refer to the stability of functioning in the face of challenge or the return to previous levels after a loss. The task of regulation of loss indexes behaviors that organize adequate functioning at lower levels when maintenance or recovery is no longer possible.

In previous work, we have suggested that there is a systematic pattern to these life-span changes in the relative allocation of resources (Staudinger et al., 1995). In childhood, and up until young adulthood, the primary allocation of resources is oriented toward growth, and in old age resources are increasingly needed to regulate losses. Figure 1.2 illustrates that midlife, according to this logic, should be characterized by a predominance of maintenance and recovery. Yet, considerable resources are still allocated to growth (especially in early midlife), while some resources are already needed for investment in the regulation of loss (more so in late midlife).

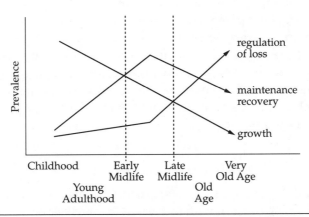

Figure 1.2 The allocation of reserve capacity to the three functions, growth, maintenance/recovery, regulation of loss, follows a life-span script. In midlife, resources are primarily invested in maintenance and recovery, but also growth (especially in early midlife) and regulation of loss (especially in late midlife) play a role. The management of resource investment emerges as an important developmental task.

When it comes to the allocation of resources, midlifers again take a middle position between the young and the old. In some domains of life, they are using their resources for growth as do young adults and in others they invest in maintenance, repair, and also probably some management of loss. This is reflected in findings such as that women in midlife begin investment in a career after having raised children: They invest in their professional growth (e.g., Moen & Wethington, 1999). It is also reported, however, that a number of challenges to normal functioning arise during midlife, such as change in the intimate relationship, changes in bodily functions and body image that require resources to achieve maintenance, and sometimes also recovery, of normal functioning (e.g., Klohnen et al., 1996).

One of the resource issues of midlife often cited in the recent literature is the notion of the sandwiched generation (e.g., Davis, 1981). This term refers to middle-aged persons who have to care for aging parents as well as for their adolescent children. The empirical "truth," however, is that the sandwich position is not very prevalent among 40- to 60-year-olds. It certainly is not a mass phenomenon in midlife. Once the aging parents become in need of care, the (average) midlifer's children are already out of the house and leading independent lives. However, the sandwich position is not a myth when it comes to managing the responsibilities at work, at home, and toward aged parents (e.g., Halpern, 1994; Marks, 1998). This sandwich position primarily concerns women, who still are most commonly the primary caretakers of old parents. Data concerning this management of conflicting responsibilities also demonstrate how one domain of life, such as work, can provide for the replenishing of resources as well as its exhaustion. Social interactions at work or even the need to think about other things than the family can be a resource for dealing with the caregiving task toward aging parents (e.g., Halpern, 1994; Marks, 1998).

The changing pattern of resource investment across midlife offers a metalevel for viewing developmental tasks in this phase. The extent to which resources are expended on growth, maintenance/recovery, and loss may change even from early to late midlife. At a general level, being able to match resources and life demands may be predictive of developmental success in midlife.

LIFE-SPAN DEVELOPMENT IS MODIFIABLE

Another central feature of life-span theory, related to the notion of resources, is a strong concern with the plasticity of development. Plasticity of development refers to the fact that any given developmental outcome is but one of numerous possible outcomes. The search for the range and limits of human plasticity, including its age-related changes, is fundamental and unique to the study of life-span development (cf. Baltes et al., 1998;

Lerner, 1984; Magnusson, 1996). Plasticity denotes the range of latent reserves of functioning. It encompasses both the reserves currently available and those that may become available in the future. Not only will an individual differ in developmental status across different domains, but the same individual may also differ within one domain at different assessments across a day, a week, or a month (Nesselroade, 1991). For example, a one-time assessment of intellectual functioning ignores that an individual's scores on intelligence tests can change depending on factors such as anxiety, fatigue, perceived relevance of the test, and level of baseline performance (Cornelius, 1986; G.V. Labouvie, Hoyer, Baltes, & Baltes, 1974). Individuals can also improve their performance substantially as a simple function of practice ("warming up")—the degree to which currently available reserve capacity is activated. This applies across adulthood; in old age, however, the range of reserve capacity is increasingly limited (e.g., Baltes et al., 1999).

Assuming that development is characterized by plasticity provides an interactive and dynamic view of the gene-environment interaction. The focus on plasticity brings to the foreground that "humans have a capacity for change across the life span from birth to death . . . (and that) the consequences of the events of early childhood are continually transformed by later experiences, making the course of human development more open than many have believed" (Brim & Kagan, 1980, p. 1). The notion of plasticity also opens vistas on intervention-oriented research that explores the possibilities of optimizing midlife development.

The implication of the notion of plasticity for the understanding and study of midlife development is that any finding so far reported about what midlife is like does not have the character of a natural law but is open to modification given the provision of appropriate circumstances. Bodily changes can be influenced to a certain degree by lifestyle features and health behavior (Merrill & Verbrugge, 1999). Levels of intellectual functioning are open to improvement given the right training intervention. So far, however, midlife has not been the focus of such intervention efforts as cognitive decline during midlife is limited (Willis, 1990). Range and limits of plasticity in midlife are still open to systematic investigation. The sandwich position (work, care of older parents) that many women are facing in midlife would be an ideal circumstance for exploring the plasticity of functioning in midlife. Questions such as "When, and for which individuals, does this situation result in stress?" or "How is this stress experienced and how can it be reduced?" could guide such explorations. Thus, the life-span developmental view of plasticity in behaviors and trajectories through midlife directs our focus not only to develop interventions for those who have problems in midlife, but also to take a salutogenic approach, with a focus on optimizing the midlife experience (Staudinger et al., 1995).

Ontogenetic and Historical Contextualism Characterizes Life-Span Development

When development is described as the outcome of ongoing processes of transactional adaptation in selected domains, analytic attention must shift to the question: What intra- and extrapersonal conditions are transacting to produce a developmental outcome? Ontogenetic and historical contextualism (Baltes et al., 1980; Lerner & Kauffman, 1985; Riegel, 1976) posits—in contrast to organismic and mechanistic views of development (e.g., Overton & Reese, 1973)—that development is always the simultaneous and complex outcome of forces of nature and nurture, of genes and environment, of intra- and extrapersonal influences. To better understand the fabric of developmental contexts, three logics organizing environmental and biological influences as well as their interaction must be considered: the normative age-graded, the normative history-graded, and the nonnormative logic (Baltes et al., 1980). This three-pronged system of biological and contextual influence serves important functions in understanding interpersonal and intercultural similarities as well as differences in developmental trajectories (e.g., Baltes & Nesselroade, 1984; Dannefer, 1984). Age-graded, history-graded, and nonnormative influences combine to produce similarities and differences in developmental challenges and opportunities. The age-graded logic refers to developmental conditions of a biological or societal nature that are normative linked to chronological age, such as menopause or retirement. The nonnormative logic refers to developmental circumstances that are closely linked to the life circumstances of a particular individual. In the following, however, we pay particular attention to the role of historical influences on development.

Cultural and historical influences represent, in effect, one area or one level of the broader set of contextual influences that affect development (e.g., Lerner & von Eye, 1992). In the development of life-span theory and research, they have always obtained special attention. Historical periods and cultural changes condition and shape the opportunity structures to which individuals have access. Social structures are constantly evolving, and vary across cultures and socioeconomic groups. Major historical events (e.g., war, economic depression, migrations) and historical changes in technology (e.g., introduction of antibiotics, increasing availability of food, the growing role of the computer in society) affect the level and direction of psychological development (e.g., Baltes, 1968; Caspi, 1987; Elder, 1998; Riegel, 1972; Riley, 1986; Schaie, 1965). Elder showed that the Great Depression had long-term effects on the psychosocial adjustment of American men. That effect, however, was moderated by age during the Depression, and prior family socialization practices. It was found that during times of economic hardship people marry earlier, try to enter the workforce earlier, and deemphasize higher education. These events that occur in early adulthood certainly carry their influence into midlife. Such individuals then may find themselves in a marriage that they would have not chosen at a later age or locked into a profession because they did not invest in higher education.

One major demonstration of the important role of history has been suggested by life-span developmental research on cohort differences (e.g., Baltes, Cornelius, & Nesselroade, 1979; E.W. Labouvie & Nesselroade, 1985; Schaie, 1965). Using longitudinal and cross-sectional sequential research methodologies, multiple birth cohorts of individuals (i.e., individuals born at the same period in historical time) can be followed over time. Such designs permit the examination of whether individuals born in different sociocultural conditions evince differences in developmental trajectories. That is, when comparing the developmental trajectories from different birth cohorts (here, taken as an *index* of the broad body of contextual differences in such variables as education, medicine, economic conditions), are there differences in level, direction, and dispersion of functioning?

In the intellectual domain and for adulthood, cohort differences in intellectual functioning can be sizable: Over historical time, comparing adults in the range from early adulthood to old age born from 1889 until 1966, some intellectual abilities studied have shown increase (e.g., verbal, spatial, and reasoning ability), while others have shown stability (numerical ability) or even decrease (word fluency) over generational birth cohorts (e.g., Willis & Schaie, 1999). Moreover, the identification of historical effects may not require a very broad sampling of birth cohorts. Even when birth cohorts separated by an average of 15 years are studied over only a 3-year longitudinal interval, a substantial influence of birth cohort on cognitive functioning has been detected (Hultsch, Hertzog, Small, McDonald-Miszczak, & Dixon, 1992). If we define midlife as extending from age 40 to age 60, a period of 20 years, early and late midlifers may show cohort differences in their cognitive development.

In a similar way, a study of psychosocial development in adulthood, also employing a cohort-sequential design, identified cohort effects (Whitbourne, Zuschlag, Elliot, & Waterman, 1992). Researchers using an inventory based on Erik Erikson's model of psychosocial development, and comparing young and middle-aged adults, found that the late-life developmental task of reaching integrity versus falling into despair was less favorably resolved by the later-born cohorts. The authors suggested that this may be due to a historical erosion in philosophical values in the society (Whitbourne et al., 1992). Or, it was reported that some personality changes observed in currently middle-aged women, such as feelings of liberation and even elation (Stewart & Ostrove, 1998), may reflect—at least to a certain degree—that these women did not have many life choices in young adulthood because of gender stereotypes and socioeconomic conditions at that time. Consequently, it will be interesting to see whether coming generations of women who indeed have had more freedom to make life choices as young adults will feel the same amount of elation when they reach midlife.

The very notion of midlife as a life phase has been claimed to be subject to historical relativity (e.g., Moen & Wethington, 1999). We would not go as far as arguing that midlife is only an invention of modern times, but it makes intuitive sense that prolonged life expectancy as well as advances in medical treatment, nutrition, and lifestyle, have set the delimiters of midlife at higher ages. In earlier times, a 30-year-old may have been thought of as middle-aged and a 50-year-old as being old. Nowadays, we observe a prolongation of younger adulthood as well as of middle adulthood. What was called old age, is more and more likely to be counted as middle age now. It is open to discussion whether the age inflationary trend (due at least partly to negative aging stereotypes—people do not want to be considered old) should be mirrored in the scientific study of midlife and old age as well. Regardless of how we label them, it may be more fruitful to link life phases, particularly midlife, to a certain constellation of developmental resources and challenges rather than to chronological age per se.

In closing, the propositions of life-span development offer a useful set of lenses through which to view midlife development. The six propositions lead to insights that encompass past theoretical work and help to guide future research. First, seeing midlife as part of the ongoing flow of life-span development suggests that midlife development is best studied by including both a young and an old comparison group. Next, midlife may best be defined as the period in life where the overall ratio of gains and losses is at a break-even point, where challenges and resources are still in balance. Here, we are also signaled to look beyond overall gains and losses to consider how these gains and losses play out in particular life domains. Further, given the changing ratio of gains and losses, there may be a need to distinguish between early and later midlife as these may be characterized by different events and different resource investment profiles. The view of midlife as characterized by plasticity also highlights the potentials of midlife that are still waiting to be systematically discovered. Finally, as time passes, researchers will need to pay attention to the historical and societal changes that may affect midlife in the years to come.

REFERENCES

Atchley, R.C. (1982). Retirement as a social institution. *Annual Review of Sociology, 8*, 263–287.

Baltes, P.B. (1968). Longitudinal and cross-sectional sequences in the study of age and generation effects. *Human Development, 11,* 145–171.

Baltes, P.B. (1987). Theoretical propositions of life-span developmental psychology: On the dynamics between growth and decline. *Developmental Psychology, 23,* 611–626.

Baltes, P.B. (1993). The aging mind: Potential and limits. *Gerontologist, 33,* 580–594.

Baltes, P.B. (1997). On the incomplete architecture of human ontogeny: Selection, optimization, and compensation as foundation of developmental theory. *American Psychologist, 52,* 366–380.

Baltes, P.B., & Baltes, M.M. (1990). Psychological perspectives on successful aging: The model of selective optimization with compensation. In P.B. Baltes & M.M. Baltes (Eds.), *Successful aging: Perspectives from the behavioral sciences* (pp. 1–34). New York: Cambridge University Press.

Baltes, P.B., Cornelius, S.W., & Nesselroade, J.R. (1979). Cohort effects in developmental psychology. In J.R. Nesselroade & P.B. Baltes (Eds.), *Longitudinal research in the study of behavior and development* (pp. 61–87). New York: Academic Press.

Baltes, P.B., Lindenberger, U., & Staudinger, U.M. (1998). Life-span theory in developmental psychology. In R.M. Lerner (Ed.), *Handbook of child psychology* (5th ed., pp. 1029–1143). New York: Wiley.

Baltes, P.B., & Nesselroade, J.R. (1984). Paradigm lost and paradigm regained: Critique of Dannefer's portrayal of life-span developmental psychology. *American Sociological Review, 49,* 841–846.

Baltes, P.B., Reese, H.W., & Lipsitt, L.P. (1980). Life-span developmental psychology. *Annual Review of Psychology, 31,* 65–110.

Baltes, P.B., Staudinger, U.M., & Lindenberger, U. (1999). Lifespan psychology: Theory and application to intellectual functioning. *Annual Review of Psychology, 50,* 471–507.

Bluck, S., Levine, L.J., & Laultere, T.M. (1999). Autobiographical remembering and hypermnesia: A comparison of older and younger adults. *Psychology and Aging, 14,* 671–682.

Brim, O.G., Jr. (1992). *Ambition: How we manage success and failure throughout our lives.* New York: Basic Books.

Brim, O.G., Jr., & Kagan, J. (1980). Constancy and change: A view of the issues. In O.G. Brim & J. Kagan (Eds.), *Constancy and change in human development* (pp. 1–25). Cambridge, MA: Harvard University Press.

Bromberger, J.T., & Matthews, K.A. (1996). A longitudinal study of the effects of pessimism, trait anxiety, and life stress on depressive symptoms in middle-aged women. *Psychology and Aging, 11*(2), 207–213.

Bronfenbrenner, U. (1979). *The ecology of human development.* Cambridge, MA: Harvard University Press.

Brooks-Gunn, J., & Kirsh, B. (1984). Life events and the boundaries of midlife for women. In G. Baruch & J. Brooks-Gunn (Eds.), *Women in midlife* (pp. 11–30). New York: Plenum Press.

Bühler, C. (1953). The curve of life as studied in biographies. *Journal of Applied Psychology, 19,* 405–409.

Bühler, C. (1968). The general structure of the human life cycle. In C. Bühler & F. Massarik (Eds.), *The course of human life: A study of goals in the humanistic perspective* (pp. 12–26). New York: Springer.

Cameron, P. (1969). Age parameters of young adult, middle-aged, old and aged. *Journal of Gerontology, 24,* 201–202.

Carstensen, L.L., & Turk-Charles, S. (1998). Emotion in the second half of life. *Current Directions in Psychological Science, 7,* 144–149.

Caspi, A. (1987). Personality in the life course. *Journal of Personality and Social Psychology, 53,* 1203–1213.

Cohen, G. (1998). Aging and autobiographical memory. In C.P. Thompson, D.J. Herrmann, D. Bruce, J.D. Read, D.G. Payne, & M.P. Toglia (Eds.), *Autobiographical memory: Theoretical and applied perspectives* (pp. 105–123). Mahwah, NJ: Erlbaum.

Cole, M. (1991). A cultural theory of development: What does it imply about the application of scientific research. *Learning and Instruction, 1,* 187–200.

Conway, M.A., & Holmes, A. (1999). *Psychosocial stages and the availability of autobiographical memories.* Manuscript submitted for publication.

Cornelius, S.W. (1986). Classic pattern of intellectual aging: Test familiarity, difficulty and performance. *Journal of Gerontology, 39,* 201–206.

Dannefer, D. (1984). Adult development and social theory: A paradigmatic reappraisal. *American Sociological Review, 49,* 100–116.

Davis, R.H. (1981). The middle years. In R.H. Davis (Ed.), *Aging: Prospects and issues* (3rd ed., pp. 201–233). Los Angeles: Andrus Gerontology Center.

Denney, N.W. (1989). Everyday problem solving: Methodological issues, research findings, and a model. In L.W. Poon, D.C. Rubin, & B.A. Wilson (Eds.), *Everyday cognition in adulthood and late life* (pp. 330–351). New York: Cambridge University Press.

Drevenstedt, J. (1976). Perceptions of onsets of young adulthood, middle age, and old age. *Journal of Gerontology, 31,* 53–57.

Edelman, G.M. (1987). *Neural Darwinism: The theory of neuronal group selection.* New York: Basic Books.

Elder, G.H., Jr. (1998). The life course and human development. In R.M. Lerner (Ed.), *Handbook of child psychology. Volume 1: Theoretical models of human development* (5th ed., pp. 939–991). New York: Wiley.

Ericsson, K.A., & Smith, J. (Eds.). (1991). *Toward a general theory of expertise: Prospects and limits.* Cambridge, MA: Cambridge University Press.

Erikson, E. (1980). *Identity and the life cycle.* New York: Norton.

Erikson, E.H., Erikson, J.M., & Kivnick, H. (1986). *Vital involvement in old age: The experience of old age in our time.* London: Norton.

Farrell, M.P., & Rosenberg, S.D. (1981). *Men at midlife.* Dover, MA: Auburn House.

Finch, C.E. (1990). *Longevity, senescence, and the genome.* Chicago: University of Chicago Press.

Ford, D.H. (1987). *Humans as self-constructing living systems: A developmental perspective on behavior and personality.* Hillsdale, NJ: Erlbaum.

Frieze, I. (1978). *Women and sex roles.* New York: Norton.

Gilligan, C. (1982). *In a different voice.* Cambridge, MA: Harvard University Press.

Goldhaber, D. (1986). *Life-span human development.* New York: Harcourt Brace Jovanovich.

Goldsmith, R.E., & Heiens, R.A. (1992). Subjective age: A test of five hypotheses. *Gerontologist, 32,* 312–317.

Graf, P. (1990). Life-span change in implicit and explicit memory. *Bulletin of the Psychonomic Society, 28,* 353–358.

Gullette, M.M. (1998). Midlife discourses in the twentieth-century United States: An essay on the sexuality, ideology, and politics of middle-ageism. In R.A. Shweder (Ed.), *Welcome to middle age (and other cultural fictions)* (pp. 3–44). Chicago: University of Chicago Press.

Halpern, J. (1994). The sandwich generation: Conflicts between adult children and their aging parents. In D.D. Cahn (Ed.), *Conflict in personal relationships* (pp. 143–160). Hillsdale, NJ: Erlbaum.

Havighurst, R.J. (1972). *Developmental tasks and education.* New York: David McKay.

Helson, R., & Klohnen, E.C. (1998). Affective coloring of personality from young adulthood to midlife. *Personality and Social Psychology Bulletin, 24*(3), 241–252.

Hooker, K., & Kaus, C.R. (1994). Health-related possible selves in young and middle adulthood. *Psychology and Aging, 9*(1), 126–133.

Horn, J.L., & Hofer, S.M. (1992). Major abilities and development in the adult period. In R.J. Sternberg & C.A. Berg (Eds.), *Intellectual development* (pp. 44–49). New York: Cambridge University Press.

Howard, D.V. (1991). Implicit memory: An expanding picture of cognitive aging. *Annual Review of Gerontology and Geriatrics, 11,* 1–22.

Hultsch, D.F., Hertzog, C., Small, B.J., McDonald-Miszczak, L., & Dixon, R.A. (1992). Short-term longitudinal change in cognitive performance in later life. *Psychology and Aging, 7,* 571–584.

Hultsch, D.F., & Plemons, (1979). Life events and life-span development. In P.B. Baltes & O.G. Brim (Eds.), *Life-span development and behavior* (Vol. 2). New York: Academic Press.

Huyck, M.H. (1999). Gender roles and gender identity in midlife. In S.L. Willis & J.D. Reid (Eds.), *Life in the middle: Psychological and social issues in middle age* (pp. 209–232). San Diego, CA: Academic Press.

Jacques, E. (1965). Death and the midlife crisis. *International Journal of Psychoanalysis, 46,* 502–514.

Jung, C.G. (1971). *The portable Jung.* New York: Viking Press.

Karmiloff-Smith, A. (1992). *Beyond modularity: A developmental perspective on cognitive science.* Cambridge, MA: MIT Press.

Keyes, C.L.M., & Ryff, C.D. (1998). Generativity in adult lives: Social structural contours and quality of life consequences. In D.P. McAdams & E. de St. Aubin (Eds.), *Generativity and adult development: How and why we care for the next generation* (pp. 227–264). Washington, DC: American Psychological Association.

Klohnen, E.C., Vandewater, E.A., & Young, A. (1996). Negotiating the middle years: Ego-resiliency and successful midlife adjustment in women. *Psychology and Aging, 11*(3), 431–442.

Krueger, J., Heckhausen, J., & Hundertmark, J. (1995). Perceiving middle-aged adults: Effects of stereotype-congruent and incongruent information. *Journals of Gerontology 50B*, 82–93.

Labouvie, E.W., & Nesselroade, J.R. (1985). Age, period, and cohort analysis and study of individual development and social change. In J.R. Nesselroade & A.V. Eye (Eds.), *Developmental and social change: Explanatory analysis* (pp. 189–212). New York: Academic Press.

Labouvie, G.V., Hoyer, W.F., Baltes, M.M., & Baltes, P.B. (1974). An operant analysis of intelligence in old age. *Human Development, 17*, 259–272.

Labouvie-Vief, G., DeVoe, M., & Bulka, D. (1989). Speaking about feelings: Conceptions of emotion across the life span. *Psychology and Aging, 4*, 425–437.

Labouvie-Vief, G., Hakim-Larson, J., & Hobart, C.J. (1987). Age, ego level, and the life-span development of coping and defense processes. *Psychology and Aging, 2*, 286–293.

Lachman, M.E., & James, J.B. (Eds.). (1997). *Multiple paths of midlife development.* Chicago: University of Chicago Press.

Lachman, M.E., & Weaver, L. (1998). Sociodemographic variations in the sense of control by domain: Findings from the MacArthur Studies of Midlife. *Psychology and Aging, 13*(4), 553–562.

Lerner, R.M. (1984). *On the nature of human plasticity.* New York: Cambridge University Press.

Lerner, R.M. (1986). *Concepts and theories of human development* (2nd ed.). New York: Random House.

Lerner, R.M., & Hultsch, D.F. (1983). *Human development: A life-span perspective.* New York: McGraw-Hill.

Lerner, R.M., & Kauffman, M.B. (1985). The concept of development in contextualism. *Developmental Review, 5*, 309–333.

Lerner, R.M., & von Eye, A. (1992). Sociobiology and human development: Arguments and evidence. *Human Development, 35*, 12–33.

Levinson, D.J. (1978). *The seasons of a man's life.* New York: Knopf.

Lowenthal, M.F., Turner, M., & Chiriboga, D. (1975). *Four stages of life.* San Francisco: Jossey-Bass.

Magnusson, D. (1990). Personality development from an interactional perspective. In L.A. Pervin (Ed.), *Handbook of personality: Theory and research* (pp. 193–222). New York: Guilford Press.

Magnusson, D. (Ed.). (1996). *The life-span development of individuals: Behavioural, neurobiological and psychosocial perspectives.* Cambridge, England: Cambridge University Press.

Marks, N.F. (1998). Does it hurt to care? Caregiving, work-family conflict, and midlife well-being. *Journal of Marriage and the Family, 60*, 951–966.

Maslow, A. (1962). *Toward a psychology of being.* Princeton, NJ: Van Nostrand Reinhold.

McAdams, D.P., & de St. Aubin, E. (1992). A theory of generativity and its assessment through self-reports, behavioral acts, and narrative themes in autobiography. *Journal of Personality and Social Psychology, 62*, 1003–1015.

McAdams, D.P., Hart, H.M., & Maruna, S. (1998). The anatomy of generativity. In D.P. McAdams & E. de St. Aubin (Eds.), *Generativity and adult development: How and why we care for the next generation* (pp. 7–43). Washington, DC: American Psychological Association.

Merrill, S.S., & Verbrugge, L.M. (1999). Health and disease in midlife. In S.L. Willis & J.D. Reid (Eds.), *Life in the middle* (pp. 78–104). San Diego, CA: Academic Press.

MIDMAC. (1999). *What is midlife?* Vero Beach, FL: Life Trends. Available: http://midmac.med.harvard.edu

Moen, P., & Wethington, E. (1999). Midlife development in a life course context. In S.L. Willis & J.D. Reid (Eds.), *Life in the middle* (pp. 3–24). San Diego, CA: Academic Press.

Nesselroade, J.R. (1991). Interindividual differences in intraindividual change. In L.M. Collins & J.L. Horn (Eds.), *Best methods for the analysis of change* (pp. 92–105). Washington, DC: American Psychological Association.

Neugarten, B.L. (1996). Continuities and discontinuities of psychological issues into adult life. In D.A. Neugarten (Ed.), *The meanings of age: Selected papers of Bernice L. Neugarten* (pp. 88–95). Chicago: University of Chicago Press.

Neugarten, B.L., & Datan, N. (1996). The middle years. In D.A. Neugarten (Ed.), *The meanings of age: Selected papers of Bernice L. Neugarten* (pp. 135–159). Chicago: University of Chicago Press.

Neugarten, B.L., Moore, J.W., & Lowe, J.C. (1965). Age norms, age constraints, and adult socialization. *American Journal of Sociology, 70,* 229–236.

Neugarten, D. (1996). *The meanings of age: Selected papers of Bernice L. Neugarten.* Chicago: University of Chicago Press.

Overton, W.F., & Reese, H.W. (1973). Models of development: Methodological implications. In J.R. Nesselroade & H.W. Reese (Eds.), *Life-span developmental psychology: Methodological issues* (pp. 65–86). New York: Academic Press.

Parlee, M.B. (1984). Reproductive issues, including menopause. In G. Baruch & J. Brooks-Gunn (Eds.), *Women in midlife* (pp. 303–313). New York: Plenum Press.

Piaget, J. (1965). *The moral judgment of the child.* New York: Free Press.

Reid, J.D., & Willis, S.L. (1999). Middle age: New thoughts, new directions. In S.L. Willis & J.D. Reid (Eds.), *Life in the middle* (pp. 276–280). San Diego, CA: Academic Press.

Riegel, K.F. (1972). Time and change in the development of the individual and society. In H.W. Reese (Ed.), *Advances in child development and behavior* (Vol. 7, pp. 81–113). New York: Academic Press.

Riegel, K.F. (1976). The dialectics of human development. *American Psychologist, 31,* 689–700.

Riley, M.W. (1986). The dynamics of life stages: Roles, people, and age. *Human Development, 29,* 150–156.

Riley, M.W., & Riley, J.W.J. (1989). *The quality of aging: Strategies for interventions* (Vol. 503). Newbury Park, CA: Sage.

Rosenberg, S.D., Rosenberg, H.J., & Farrell, M.P. (1999). The midlife crisis revisited. In S.L. Willis & J.D. Reid (Eds.), *Life in the middle: Psychological and social issues in middle age* (pp. 47–70). San Diego, CA: Academic Press.

Rossi, A.S. (Ed.). (1994). *Sexuality across the life course.* Chicago: University of Chicago Press.

Rowe, J.W., & Kahn, R.L. (1987). Human aging: Usual and successful. *Science, 237,* 143–149.

Rubin, L.B. (1979). *Women of a certain age: The midlife search for self.* New York: Harper & Row.

Ryff, C.D. (1991). Possible selves: A tale of shifting horizons. *Psychology and Aging, 6,* 286–295.

Ryff, C.D., & Seltzer, M.M. (Eds.). (1996). *The parental experience in midlife.* Chicago: University of Chicago Press.

Ryff, C.D., & Singer, B. (1998). Middle age and well-being. In H.S. Friedman (Ed.), *Encyclopedia of mental health* (Vol. 2, pp. 707–719). San Diego, CA: Academic Press.

Schaie, K.W. (1965). A general model for the study of developmental problems. *Psychological Bulletin, 64,* 92–107.

Schaie, K.W., & Willis, S.L. (1986). *Adult development and aging* (2nd ed.). Boston: Little, Brown.

Seligman, M., & Csikszentmihalyi, M. (Eds.). (2000). Positive psychology [Special issue]. *American Psychologist, 55.*

Shanan, J., & Kedar, H.S. (1980). Phenomenological structuring of the adult lifespan as a function of age and sex. *International Journal of Aging and Human Development, 10,* 343–357.

Shweder, R.A. (1991). *Thinking through cultures.* Cambridge, MA: Harvard University Press.

Shweder, R.A. (Ed.). (1998). *Welcome to middle age (and other cultural fictions).* Chicago: University of Chicago Press.

Smith, J., & Baltes, P.B. (1993). Differential psychological aging: Profiles of the old and very old. *Ageing and Society, 13,* 551–587.

Staudinger, U.M. (1999). Social cognition and a psychological approach to an art of life. In F. Blanchard-Fields & T. Hess (Eds.), *Social cognition, adult development and aging* (pp. 343–375). New York: Academic Press.

Staudinger, U.M., & Baltes, P.B. (1994). Psychology of wisdom. In R.J. Sternberg (Ed.), *Encyclopedia of human intelligence* (Vol. 2, pp. 1143–1152). New York: Macmillan.

Staudinger, U.M., Marsiske, M., & Baltes, P.B. (1995). Resilience and reserve capacity in later adulthood: Potentials and limits of development across the life span. In D. Cicchetti & D. Cohen (Eds.), *Developmental psychopathology* (Vol. 2, pp. 801–847). New York: Wiley.

Stewart, A.J., & Ostrove, J.M. (1998). Women's personality in middle age: Gender, history, and midcourse corrections. *American Psychologist, 53*(11), 1185–1194.

Treas, J., & Bengtson, V.L. (1982). The demography of mid- and late-life transitions. *Annals of the American Academy of Political and Social Science, 464,* 11–22.

Uttal, D.H., & Perlmutter, M. (1989). Toward a broader conceptualization of development: The role of gains and losses across the life span. *Developmental Review, 9,* 101–132.

Vandewater, E.A., Ostrove, J.M., & Stewart, A.J. (1997). Predicting women's well-being in midlife: The importance of personality development and social role involvements. *Journal of Personality and Social Psychology, 72,* 1147–1160.

Visser, P.S., & Krosnick, J.A. (1998). Development of attitude strength over the life cycle: Surge and decline. *Journal of Personality and Social Psychology, 75*(6), 1389–1410.

Voda, A., Dinnerstein, M., & O'Donnell, S. (Eds.). (1982). *Changing perspective on menopause.* Austin: University of Texas Press.

Waddington, C.H. (1975). *The evolution of an evolutionist.* Edinburgh, Scotland: Edinburgh University Press.

Weinert, F.E. (1994). Altern in psychologischer Perspektive. In P.B. Baltes, J. Mittelstrass, & U.M. Staudinger (Eds.), *Alter und Altern: Ein interdisziplinärer Studientext zur Gerontologie* (pp. 180–203). Berlin, Germany: de Gruyter.

Wethington, E., Cooper, H., & Holmes, C.S. (1997). Turning points in midlife. In I.H. Gotlib & B. Wethington (Eds.), *Stress and adversity over the life course: Trajectories and turning points* (pp. 215–231). Cambridge, MA: Cambridge University Press.

Whitbourne, S.K., & Connolly, L.A. (1999). The developing self in midlife. In S.L. Willis & J.D. Reid (Eds.), *Life in the middle: The psychological and social developments of middle age* (pp. 25–45). San Diego, CA: Academic Press.

Whitbourne, S.K., & Weinstock, C.S. (1979). *Adult development: The differentiation of experience.* New York: Holt, Rhinehart and Winston.

Whitbourne, S.K., Zuschlag, M.K., Elliot, L.B., & Waterman, A.S. (1992). Psychosocial development in adulthood: A 22-year sequential study. *Journal of Personality and Social Psychology, 63,* 260–271.

Willis, S.L. (1990). Contributions of cognitive training research to understanding late life potential. In M. Perlmutter (Ed.), *Late-life potential* (pp. 25–42). Washington, DC: Gerontological Society of America.

Willis, S.L., & Reid, J.D. (Eds.). (1999). *Life in the middle.* San Diego, CA: Academic Press.

Willis, S.L., & Schaie, K.W. (1999). Intellectual functioning in midlife. In S.L. Willis & J.D. Reid (Eds.), *Life in the middle* (pp. 234–250). San Diego, CA: Academic Press.

Wortman, C.B., & Silver, R.C. (1990). Successful mastery of bereavement and widowhood: A life-course perspective. In P.B. Baltes & M.M. Baltes (Eds.), *Successful aging: Perspectives from the behavioral sciences* (pp. 225–264). New York: Cambridge University Press.

CHAPTER 2

Middle Adulthood in Cultural Perspective: The Imagined and the Experienced in Three Cultures

USHA MENON

MIDDLE AGE: What images does that phrase most readily conjure up? For much of the twentieth century, the images that prevailed in middle-class Anglo-American culture revolved around the meaning implicit yet central to the idea of middle age—that of the "declining years." Failing eyesight, graying hair, creaking joints, aching muscles, sagging chins, fading memory, a "midlife crisis," or other variations on these themes of decline and loss predominated in the popular imagination. As early intimations of mortality, they were believed to announce, unambiguously and insistently, that life's peak experiences were over. So, do these images continue to predominate in the Anglo-American cultural world? Or, is an alternate, competing set of images emerging? And what about indigenous conceptions of this life phase in other contemporaneous cultural worlds, among, say, the Japanese or Hindus?

In this chapter, I explore the cultural fictions of middle age, or "middle-hood"—to use Plath's (1975) less culturally loaded term—as they have been imagined, taken shape, and lived in three very different cultural settings: middle-class Anglo-America, middle-class Japan, and upper-caste Hindu society in rural India. The meanings surrounding this phase of life are not necessarily uniform, neither in the subculture where the connotations previously described have been the most salient—middle-class Anglo-America—nor in other cultural traditions. The very term *middle age* is problematic because it is so heavily saturated with meanings, that have evolved in a particular sociohistorical and cultural context, stressing

40

decline, both physical and mental, as this life phase's distinctive experiential flavor. Middle age is a "cultural fiction" (Shweder, 1998) that gathers "realness" only in one particular cultural world. Not surprisingly, other cultural worlds have produced their own, equally real cultural fictions to imagine and describe this phase—the Oriya Hindu *prauda*, for example, or the Japanese *ichinin-mae*—each the product of cultural assumptions about the life course and the meaning and purpose of life.

As Bradd Shore (1998) has noted, such "simple cross-cultural comparisons are difficult" (p. 103) because "perceptions of age are always mediated by cultural models of a life course" (p. 103). Therefore, while attempting a comparative study of the middle phase of life in three cultural contexts, I also describe their models of the life course. In the process, I tease out and elaborate on the assumptions, sometimes implicit, that prevail in each of these cultural contexts about personhood, human nature, and the relationships between the passing of time, membership in society, and appropriate conduct.

Before discussing these three cultural models and the middle phase of life, I need to make explicit a central assumption in this chapter. I am aware that every human being everywhere actively interprets, shapes, and alters his or her reality, and I recognize the variability and personal significance of individual experience. Every person's experience of adult development, irrespective of cultural context, has its own unique "trajectory" (Vatuk, 1987, p. 25). Nevertheless, each culture has its own particular way of representing the life course, such representations are part and parcel of the worldview of its members, and they, therefore, reflect meanings both salient and significant within these different cultural traditions.

LATE ADULTHOOD: HINDU[1] IMAGES AND EXPERIENCES

Plath (1975) suggests that middle age is an aspect of life in modern, industrialized societies: The longer life expectancies that often follow modernization have resulted in societies that must define and understand the extended period of active life between youthfulness and senility. But, he may not be entirely correct in this inference. Traditional Hindu thinking,[2] premodern in its origins and formulations, has also wrestled with the

---

[1] Hindu beliefs and practices vary greatly according to region and caste affiliation, to name but two of the more significant differences between people who claim to be Hindu today: It is almost impossible, therefore, to generalize and represent all Hindus. In this chapter, therefore, the various conceptions of adulthood presented are specifically linked to particular Hindu communities.

[2] Much of traditional Hindu thinking can be traced back to the various Dharmasastras, medieval texts that contain Hindu thought on law, morality and society.

problem of demarcating the human life course in appropriate and meaningful ways. Focusing exclusively on the experiences of men, ancient Hindus conceptualized the human life course as being divided into four stages: the student/apprentice (*brahmacharya*), householder (*grhasthya*), forest dweller (*vanaprastha*), and renouncer (*sanyasa*).

Although neither the term *middle age* nor any rough equivalent of it is ever used, it is possible to interpret this four-stage sequence in a more modern idiom and identify middle age as coinciding with the third stage of life (Kakar, 1998), that of the forest dweller. Chronologically speaking, the Dharmasastras define this life stage as beginning at 50 years and ending at 75—rather too old for the modern understanding of middle age perhaps, but then these texts were working with human life spans that lasted a hundred years. During this stage, between the bustling activity of the householder's life and the probable senility of the renouncer, a man begins the process of disengagement in preparation for the final, radical break, the last stage of life, when he is required to renounce the world and all its entanglements.

Renunciation, as many observers of Hindu India have noted (Dumont, 1970; Heesterman, 1985), is one of the more enduring cultural ideals in Hindu society. Renouncers continue to be a part of Hindu India's social landscape although the vast majority of Hindus today do not consider a radical renunciation of the world and its ways to be a viable or practical option. Instead, they aspire to achieve the less extreme ideal of nonattachment, of not being bound to the fruits of one's labor in this world. As Madan observes, nonattachment is what emerges when renunciation is "translated into the householder's idiom" (1987, p. 3).

In the Hindu moral code, renunciation or its more this-worldly version, nonattachment, are the paths to achieving the ultimate goal of every human life,[3] *moksa*, the final release from *samsara*, the perpetual cycle of rebirths and redeaths. Renunciation or nonattachment is thought to guarantee final release to those who practice it because it enables people to refine themselves, cleanse themselves of all desires, unsated desire being at the root of rebirth. Practically every aspect of Hindu social life manifests the value attached to self-refinement (*samskriti*). Thus, the moral significance attached to the correct and sincere performance of one's duties, however unpleasant one may find them, emerges from the cultural understanding that doing one's duties uncritically and unquestioningly will, in and of itself, lead to self-refinement.

To understand this cultural emphasis on self-refinement, it is necessary to appreciate certain distinctive features of the Hindu worldview. In

---

[3] For Hindus, life—fleeting, lacking constancy, characterized by loss—is defined as suffering and, therefore, not necessarily an experience that people seek to repeat endlessly.

Hindu thought, the manifest world is in flux, and this includes both the social and the natural, a distinction that Hindus rarely make. Hindus further assume that everything in this universe is material[4] because even apparently nonmaterial things like thought, gaze, space, and time have relational properties. Within this world, varied entities are constantly engaged in transacting, exchanging, and transforming.

From the Hindu perspective, transactions affect the transactors profoundly, transforming them, because "what goes on *between* actors are the same connected processes of mixing and separation that go on *within* actors" (Marriott, 1976, p. 109, emphasis in original). Therefore, it is impossible to separate actors from their actions: Actors act as they do because of their particular natures (*svabhava*) and because of the particular codes of conduct (*svadharma*) that are inherent in them, but such action alters not merely the person at whom it is directed but also the actor who originates the action. Similarly, Hindus tend not to distinguish between mind and body, between spirit or consciousness and matter, and between the "moral" and the "natural." Those who give and receive as well as what and how they give and receive are, indissolubly and simultaneously, both substance and code. Furthermore, substance-and-code are seen as residing in "particles" that can be exchanged, ingested, reproduced, exuded, excreted, and that are in constant circulation.

This transactional thinking, together with the belief in the materiality of all phenomena and the constant circulation of substance-and-codes, leads to a particular definition of the body and a particular understanding of personhood. Hindus conceive their bodies as relatively unbounded and porous containers that are shared, exchanged, and transformed all across life, through events like birth and marriage, and acts like sharing food and space (see Daniel, 1984; Inden & Nicholas, 1977; Lamb, 1993; Trawick, 1990). All human bodies are permeable, but those of women are far more so because women menstruate and reproduce, implying both women's need to be more circumspect as well as their greater potential for being remade and transformed.

As exchanges between people are thought to be inherent and inevitable, Hindus use this theory of the relative permeability of the human body to deliberately refine their physical substances. Throughout the life course, therefore, through daily practices (*nityakarma*) and explicit rituals of refinement (*samskaras*), Hindus regulate, manipulate, and

---

[4] Matter can and is distinguished and ranked in terms of its "grossness" (*sthulata*) and its "subtlety" (*sukshmata*), the former including all that is less refined, less generative, and therefore, less imbued with power (*sakti*) and value (*mulyam*) while "subtle" refers to all that is more refined, and more generative. Thus, knowledge is more subtle and more transformative than wealth, wealth more subtle than land, land more subtle than food, which itself is more subtle and transformative than garbage (Marriott, 1976).

transform themselves. Because of the continual exchanging that people are engaged in, the consequence of merely living and being in this world, people are always mixed, and Hindus recognize the sheer impossibility of making radical separations or perfect purifications. Impurities are thought to be part of everyday life and all humans oscillate between relative purity (*suddhata*) and relative impurity (*asuddhata*). Men's physical substance assure them greater purity when compared with women but their greater involvement in the public domain means that, as they go through life, they become progressively more unrefined and coarse.

Hindus do not believe that human beings exist prior to, or outside, society. Neither do they believe that society comes into being because humans enter into a voluntary contract to maximize their self-interest. Far from subscribing to any idea of "ontological individualism" (Bellah, Madsen, Sullivan, Swidler, & Tipton, 1996, p. 143), social arrangements are seen as part of nature and as more enduring and fundamental than the people who participate in them. Furthermore, Hindus believe that the primary goal of any social group is to reproduce itself. Only by doing so can human societies transcend the ravages of time. And for them, the family, established through the sacrament of marriage, represents the most appropriate site for such social reproduction.

Marriage, therefore, is the most significant ritual of refinement that men and women experience. For a man, marriage launches him on the path toward maturity, and promotes him to becoming the reproductive head of the household and the performer of household rituals. For a woman, it is a transformative ritual (Manu, 2, p. 67): She is remade into the substances of her husband and his family and, among upper-caste Hindus, marriage is the ritual through which a woman attains the ritual purity of the twice-born (*dvija*). A potent auspiciousness—a predominantly female attribute—is thought to suffuse a married woman. The auspiciousness that all married women embody is marked by particular signs of auspiciousness that every upper-caste married Hindu woman wears on her person. Through wearing these signs, a married woman creates a magical aura of protection that is believed to maintain her husband's health and long life.

Purity and auspiciousness, correlates of self-refinement, are important concerns for most Hindus and they order much of Hindu society. Given their understandings of personhood and the nature of social relations, Hindus conceive purity as having at least "three intersecting meanings" (Mines, 1990, p. 113). The first of these refers to that which is less mixed, in the sense of being less exposed to external influences—thus, those who have withdrawn from sexual activity, who are reclusive, who are no longer involved in the physical care of the very young and the very old would have this kind of purity. The second meaning of purity refers to that possessed by those who control the exchanges they engage in. Given that all social interactions are thought to be hierarchically structured, the exchange of substance-and-code is asymmetrical: The more dominant give more than they receive, and therefore, absorb less of the qualities of the subordinate. Thus, those who are senior, older, or superior are also purer. The third meaning has to do with order and coherence: thus, a postmenopausal woman is considered pure because she can maintain bodily coherence, she is no longer subject to childbirth and menstruation, natural events and processes that are thought to destroy such coherence (Marriott, 1990).

The Hindu understanding of auspiciousness has to do with fecundity, generativity, and prosperity. While women's ability to reproduce is celebrated and worshiped as auspicious, it necessarily requires participating in the natural processes of menstruation and childbirth, as well as being involved in the nursing of infants and the care of small children, with all their accompanying impurities. These processes and activities, auspicious and generative though they certainly are, keep women alternating between conditions of relative purity and impurity for most of their lives. Purity and auspiciousness, therefore, are two orderings that do not necessarily work in the same direction. For some women during the middle years of their lives, when their reproductive and caregiving duties are over and their husbands are still alive, purity and auspiciousness do work in the same direction, reinforcing each other. They make the older, postmenopausal, sexually inactive, no-longer-caregiving, but still-married mother the purest and most auspicious of women.

In this cultural world, dominated by the ideal of renunciation or nonattachment; by a concern for self-refinement, purity, and auspiciousness; and by a vision of the human life course that is divided into age-appropriate activities, how do people conceive adulthood? The Indian psychoanalyst Sudhir Kakar asserts (1998) that for most Hindus in rural north India middle age, in the Anglo-American sense, is a phenomenon that has escaped them. Only the Westernized elite, exposed over many years to a steady influx of Western ideas and concepts, can claim any familiarity with the dominant images of decline and loss associated with the Anglo-American notion of middle age. For the rest, according to the responses volunteered by Kakar's subjects in rural north India, there are only three phases: childhood, youth, and old age. According to this indigenous perspective, one moves from youth to old age without transiting through an intermediate phase. Only when Kakar pushed his Hindi-speaking subjects did they recall *adher-awastha,* the middle condition, the phase of life that lies between youth and old age. And while the Hindi term *adher-awastha* does include the idea of declining years, it also connotes the mature intelligence and wisdom that comes from experience, from simply having lived in the world for many years.

In trying to explain this apparent lack of cultural salience that middle age seems to be suffering from, Kakar suggests that this life phase may not be recognized in contemporary India as an independent, clearly identifiable period. Instead, it may be conceived as the beginning of old age, an introductory phase that heralds the onset of the last phase of life. And the precipitating event that announces the arrival of middle age and the impending arrival of old age, Kakar says, relying on his clinical experience, "is the marriage of the first child—whether son or daughter—and the confrontation with the procreative activity of one's offspring" (1998, p. 78). Middle age for men and women, then, is marked by changing roles within the family—from father to father of a married (and therefore, sexually active) son or daughter and from mother to mother of a married son or daughter. Kakar speculates that this "psychological transition of men and women into middle age" would occur at about 45 for men and around 40 for women living in urban areas while the equivalent ages for men and women living in rural areas would be a couple of years younger.

There are, however, other conceptions of adulthood within the Hindu cultural world. Thus, in the temple town of Bhubaneswar, in eastern India, where I have done fieldwork for several years (for more on this community, see Mahapatra, 1981; Seymour, 1999; Shweder, 1991), Oriya Hindus say that one enters the middle phase of life when one occupies certain family roles, performs well-defined kinds of duties and shoulders particular kinds of responsibilities (Menon & Shweder, 1998). Thus, Oriya Hindu women enter mature adulthood—the middle phase of life— when they occupy one of two particular family roles: that of senior wife (*purna bou*) or still-married mother of married sons (*sasu*).[5] Oriya Hindu men regard themselves as mature adults[6] when they are the fathers of

---

[5] In an extended family, senior wives (*purna bous*) are mature women, mothers of adolescent children, who are senior to other, younger mothers. *Purna* is an interesting word because, while in this context it connotes seniority, it more commonly denotes *fullness* or *completeness*. With age, the birth of children, the entry of other younger sons' wives, a woman progresses to become a *complete* son's wife—*purna bou.*

The English term *mother-in-law* (*sasu*) does not quite capture the meanings embedded in *sasu*. A Hindu marriage is not a contract and Hindu marriage rituals are believed to transform the physical substance of a woman into that of her husband's and the family she is marrying into (Inden & Nicholas, 1977). Thus with the passage of time, as a woman assimilates into her conjugal family, there is less and less that distinguishes her from her husband's mother (*sasu*) in terms of her physical substance.

[6] Folk wisdom in the temple town, and elsewhere in the Hindu world, has it that Hindu men become mature adults only after the death of their fathers; till that happens they are just sons, frozen in immaturity, always overshadowed by the presence of their fathers.

adolescent and adult children (*bapa*) and fathers of married sons (*sasur*). The distinctive difference between female and male family roles associated with mature adulthood is that the critical, defining characteristic of the former is the condition of being married, while with the latter, it is the idea of fatherhood. As described later in this chapter, a widower with children can be a mature adult, but a widow cannot.

As a mature adult, an Oriya Hindu woman has a substantial degree of control over her own body and her actions, but more importantly, she has considerable control over the activities of others within the family. In addition, she feels central to the order and material prosperity of the family and others acknowledge this centrality. Furthermore, she now approaches divinity without restriction. Not surprisingly, this ability to maintain regular, uninterrupted connections with divinity characterizes the still-married mother of married sons more than the senior wife because, as discussed, purity and auspiciousness converge in her person.

Oriya Hindu men become mature adults when, as fathers themselves, they replace their fathers both in the process of decision making within the family and in the family's interface with the rest of the community. At this point in time, they are at the pinnacle of mature adulthood, but like Kakar's north Indian subjects, the actual marriage of an adult child— and for Oriya Hindus, unlike Kakar's subjects, the child must be a son— signals the beginning of the end of this phase of mature adulthood. Given the patrilineal, patrilocal cast of extended families in the temple town, even after men marry and are generally thought to have become young adults, their family role continues to be that of a son: Marriage does not instantaneously transform their family role as it does women's. There is no family role labeled "new" husband that is the equivalent of new wife. Rather, within four or five years of marriage and fatherhood, a young husband and new father is invited by his father to share in the duties and responsibilities of managing an extended family, most of which relate to the family's relationships with the outside world. This involvement usually marks the beginning of the gradual, almost imperceptible shift for a man from being a young adult to becoming a mature adult.

And this brings me back to the distinctive difference between the male and female experience of mature adulthood. No natural event or experience can stop a man's gradual progress from young adulthood through mature adulthood to old age. A man's entry and experience of mature adulthood depends on his being a father. People in the temple town recognize the possibility that, for a variety of reasons, a couple may not be able to procreate. But this is not a major problem because culture has devised a way of trumping biology—adoption. Adopting children belonging to one's close relatives, perhaps a sister's or brother's child, happens frequently in this neighborhood, and just as marriage rituals are thought to change the physical substance of the woman into that of the family she is marrying into, rituals are performed that alter the child's substance permanently into that of his or her adoptive parents.

For women, however, it is an entirely different story: Everyone recognizes that particular events and experiences can obstruct the sequence of life phases. Thus, early widowhood or a woman's decision to leave her husband jeopardizes the process of adult female development as Hindus conceive it. A young widow or a married daughter who chooses to return to her father's home permanently will never experience mature adulthood.

The reason is fairly obvious. As mentioned, being married is integral to becoming a mature adult woman. In that sense, a young widow or a married daughter who has permanently returned to her father's home is an anomaly that goes against order and coherence. From a practical point of view, there are no particular family roles that she can occupy and therefore, no well-understood, defined duties and responsibilities that she can fulfill. But there is more to her anomalousness than just that.

In the Hindu worldview, marriage rituals are thought to begin the transformation of the physical substance of a woman in real and substantial ways into that of her husband and his family. Within a few years of living and sharing with the conjugal family and being sexually active with her husband, this process of transformation is completed and a woman and her husband are thought to become one, in the sense that he has incorporated her into his body—not, and this is important to remember, that they have both merged to form a single body or that she has incorporated him. Therefore, in the Hindu cultural world, a widow should not *be*—in the natural order of things, she should have died with her husband. Her very survival is a moral outrage, an indication of the decay and corruption that characterize the modern world. The reverse, however, does not hold true—a man could easily survive his wife's death. In explaining the difference, Oriya Hindus of the temple town often use the following analogy: losing one's wife is like losing a limb or an organ, extraordinarily painful, almost impossible to bear, but not against the natural order of things.

Similarly, when a married woman chooses to return permanently to her father's home, she too is trying to undo the transformations that marriage and the subsequent years of married life have wrought in her. Both young widows and separated women are stigmatized as inauspicious because they are thought to go against the natural progression of life; they add to the disorder and confusion that already characterize the world today.[7] They can, therefore, never partake in the experience of mature

---

[7] According to Hindu thought, there are four epochs or world-times and we live today in the most corrupt and degenerate of these, the *Kaliyuga*. But this epoch, it is thought, will end in the total disintegration of the world, and the first and most moral of these epochs, *Satyayuga* or the Age of Truth, will be reborn.

adulthood and all that it means—autonomy, dominance, productivity, and coherence. In fact, Oriya Hindu women are fully aware that this phase of life is hardly guaranteed to all women, and this in their opinion, confers a special meaning to its experience. When a woman achieves and experiences a long mature adulthood, she considers herself to be singularly blessed, interpreting the experience as a sign that divine grace has touched her life.

When Oriya Hindus are asked to characterize mature adulthood, they describe this phase as one of complete immersion in the affairs of this world. They regard this as the decisive phase in a person's life, in the sense that it sets the tone for the rest of life: An accomplished and successful mature adulthood portends a relatively satisfying and content old age. As a mature adult, a person begins to savor autonomy and dominance over others; but these privileges come together with a heavy set of responsibilities: maintaining and increasing the material prosperity and spiritual well-being of the family.

The Freudian paradigm tends to assume that successful adulthood is achieved only when a person detaches him- or herself from the family, thus becoming independent and autonomous (Freud, 1960), two attributes thought to be typical of adulthood. Oriya Hindus would disagree with this conception of adulthood on both counts. For them, becoming a mature adult requires continued and substantial involvement with the family, while retaining a distinct sense of self. They describe it, not as some kind of egocentric inner process that requires detaching oneself from others, but rather, as one that entails expanding oneself more comprehensively to include others. Furthermore, as any observer of the dynamics of Oriya Hindu families would agree, this increased involvement in the family does not come at the cost of dependency and loss of autonomy. To infer that it did would be to assume that behavior compliant with cultural norms and social roles reflects an unquestioning conformity to them. Instead, among Oriya Hindus, mature adults not only possess a deep familiarity with norms and roles but they have, more importantly, developed the ability to use them strategically, to mold them to suit their own needs and to further their own ends vis-à-vis others in the family or others in the community. As the Rudolphs have remarked while discussing adulthood among the Rajputs of north India, "the interdependence characteristic of the extended family often calls for initiative, individuality, and autonomy" (1978, p. 167) on the part of mature adults.

No single psychological theme predominates during mature adulthood—at least not in the way it is experienced by Oriya Hindus in the temple town of Bhubaneswar. Here, both men and women—but many more women than men—consider mature adulthood to be the most satisfying period in a person's life. They assert that mature adulthood provides them with opportunities for achieving well-being that previously were and subsequently will become unavailable to them. However, the latter part of this life phase is tinged with anxiety and fearfulness: Two anxieties, in particular, reduce women's feelings of well-being. First is the prospect of widowhood and all the connotations that Oriya Hindus attach to that condition; and second is the process of growing old, of losing the ability to care for oneself physically and of becoming dependent on others (see Vatuk, 1990).

Men share this anxiety about a future of helplessness and dependence. But for them, the well-being and contentment of mature adulthood is already somewhat diluted by the marriages of their children, in particular, those of their sons, because these events are harbingers of what lies ahead: an old age that should, according to cultural ideals, be characterized by renunciation. As Kakar has observed for north Indians, among Oriya Hindus of the temple town, too, a couple withdraws from sexual activity once their eldest son marries and brings his new wife into the family. Any breach of this custom, if it were to become known in the neighborhood,[8] brings great shame to the entire family. Kakar, therefore, suggests that the midlife crisis that plagues all Hindu men has less to do with their agonizing about having reached the peak of life, with nothing left to look forward to, and more to do with their having to resolve the conflict between cultural demands that they renounce sex once their own children marry and become sexually active and their own personal desire to continue to be sexually active.

As far as Oriya Hindu women of the temple town are concerned, however, most display little regret at the cessation of sexual activity. In their view, sexual activity and the exchange of substances during intercourse is inherently polluting, though unavoidable in terms of the need to perpetuate the family. However, with the marriage of a son, the responsibility of reproduction is passed on to the younger couple. This is also the time when a woman goes through menopause. Women in this neighborhood, both young and old, keenly feel the impurity of menstruation.[9] They refer to menstruation as "the curse of the seasons" (*rtu sapo*) and they look forward with almost palpable relief to menopause, when the "curse of the seasons ends" (*rtu sapo bandha heigola*). Withdrawing from sexual activity, together with menopause, enables these women to maintain bodily purity more easily, and therefore, enjoy unrestricted access to divinity—one of the signal privileges of mature adulthood.

---

[8] As when a married mother becomes pregnant at the same time as her son's wife does—and such events do occur in this neighborhood.
[9] Observing menstrual taboos involves having to stay out of the kitchen, out of contact with other members of the family, especially one's children, having to eat out of leaf plates, not being able to bathe or oil one's hair—all these barriers to life-as-usual serve to make these women feel out of sorts.

Women, however, are not exempt from experiencing a midlife crisis of their own, and theirs, too, has as its theme renunciation—renouncing the control and supervision of household activities. As Vatuk (1983, p. 71) has observed for a group of north Indian Hindus, men give up being involved in the household and its activities quite readily, perhaps because they have always been peripheral. In contrast, most women resist household authority being wrested from them. From the moment they stepped over the threshold as new wives, these women have been heavily invested in the household and its affairs, but only as mature adults have they actually exercised power and influence, and been central to its activities. Not surprisingly, they find it to hard to hand over family responsibilities to the next generation and they often resist doing so, despite such behavior being culturally valued and rewarded.

THE MEANINGS OF MATURITY: THE JAPANESE CONCEPTION OF ADULTHOOD

One of the more enduring elements in Western folklore (Rohlen, 1978, p. 129) about Japan centers on the idea that, in this cultural world, aging is viewed positively: The old are respected, even indulged, and they enjoy great freedom. As Ruth Benedict observed more than a half century ago, "the arc of life" in Japan is shaped like "a great shallow U-curve with maximum freedom allowed to babies and to the old" (1946, p. 253). Of course, old age is not adulthood: It is the last not the middle phase of life and together with the first phase of life—infancy—enjoys special privileges. And in contemporary Japan, as Plath (1972) has demonstrated, there is ample evidence that such attitudes toward aging and the old, part of Japan's Confucian tradition, are hardly all-pervasive. Nevertheless, most observers who study the Japanese cultural world would agree (Lock, 1993, 1998; Plath, 1980; Rohlen, 1978) that the Japanese have a unique perspective on the process of aging and age has particular salience in Japanese society.

In trying to describe and explain this perspective in a comprehensive and detailed manner, I run the risk of homogenizing all Japanese, of blurring the individual differences that exist and presenting an entire people as a monolithic entity. And I certainly do not wish to do so. At the same time, perhaps the Japanese articulate a degree of cultural self-consciousness that encourages those who observe and comment on their culture and society to assume such homogeneity. Margaret Lock, for example, talks of the "remarkable uniformity in the creation of family life" and ascribes it to "a national sensitivity about movement through the life course since at least the beginning of this century" (1998, p. 56).

Despite this caveat about the danger of making unwarranted generalizations, one can still say that, in Japan today, age continues to order social rank and the exercise of authority. To even a casual observer, it is readily obvious that Japan's leaders, whether in business, academics, or politics, are generally older than most of their counterparts in other parts of the world. Even in the world of entertainment, where a huge premium is usually placed on youthful beauty, Lock (1998) reports that older women are appreciated and valued not merely for their artistic talents but even for their beauty. In the Japanese cultural world, therefore, age, is associated positively with both power and creativity.

But this, while accurate, is a superficial representation of Japanese understandings about aging. A closer examination reveals a highly elaborated national discourse on aging: a complex narrative that weaves together several disparate elements from Japan's various traditions—themes of loss, regret, and fear that are elaborated on in classical literary texts (Formanek, 1992, cited in Lock, 1998), dating back to the period between the fourteenth and seventeenth centuries, as well as the more positive orientations to aging that can be traced to Japan's Confucian and Zen Buddhist traditions. In trying to identify what is distinctive about Japanese understandings of aging, at least two related aspects need to be mentioned: first, the Japanese conception of aging as a process of social maturation; and second, the Japanese view that the different phases of life offer endless opportunities for continual personal improvement.

According to the first, a person moves through life as a member of a particular age-grade: He or she matures as a social being and learns about age-appropriate behavior through participating, with fellow members, in community and family rituals.[10] Lock reports that, even today, birthdays are infrequently celebrated as markers of individual maturation and aging; biological transformations evidently take second place to "social maturation" as a member of a family and the community. Rohlen suggests that this underemphasis of biology reflects the Japanese view that socialization is an all-important process that lasts a lifetime, the clearly understood purpose of which is to create a human being. The Japanese, therefore, see all of life as "a time of becoming, not being" (1978, p. 132) for all humans. As Caudill and Weinstein have observed in their comparative study of child care in Japan and the United States, the Japanese see a newborn as "a separate biological organism" that has to be incorporated into society through "increasingly interdependent relations with others" (1969, p. 12). Becoming human is not guaranteed simply through the passage of time; nor is it restricted to a particular period of life. The moral connotations attached to becoming human require that people work at this process throughout their lives.

---

[10] Although, according to Lock, modernization has led to the former becoming more rare—except in some rural areas—and the latter more important in contemporary Japan.

And as for the second noteworthy aspect of Japanese understandings of aging, the Japanese recognize and experience aging as a natural process, in the sense that it involves "submitting" oneself to nature and thereby having access to what is truly real, to a "nature-given reality" (Rohlen, 1978, p. 130). He describes this unique understanding of the relationship between humans, nature, and the passing of time in the following way:

> The Japanese have an acute awareness of aging viewed as a subtle change in one's relationship with the world. They live in a society ordered around differences in age. They speak a language that to be spoken properly requires a precise knowledge of the relative ages of the parties concerned. Women especially dress according to a rather minutely worked out aesthetic that relates patterns and color to fine gradations in age. And the Japanese inhabit a cultural world profoundly concerned with the turn of seasons, of years, and of whole lives. (p. 130)

Given this cultural desire to become one with nature and experience bodily changes as natural changes, the Japanese seek to mirror in their personal lives the changes that occur so smoothly and so predictably in the seasons. Every season is appreciated for having its own distinctive qualities, its own special beauties. Similarly, every phase of life represents a distinct set of experiences and opportunities, and is thus valued for its own unique potentiality. At one level, the Japanese attitude to the passing of time can be characterized as "fatalistic" (Rohlen, 1978): All phenomena in the manifest world, it is thought, must inevitably submit to time, and human beings are no exception. To resist in any kind of way, to try and combat the ravages of time is an exercise in futility—a sign of immaturity or folly or both. But, and this is an important qualification, an integral element of this submission to time is to simultaneously explore the potential available for self-cultivation and human perfectibility in every phase of life. Rohlen identifies this aspect of the Japanese attitude toward aging as what is particularly "fascinating" (p. 130). The fatalism that the Japanese display toward aging, therefore, comes with a particularly striking twist: While accepting, without resistance, the effects of aging, the Japanese are extraordinarily concerned with the challenges and potential for human perfection that the process brings in its wake.

Plath identifies this aspect of aging as part of Japan's Confucian-inspired "heritage of possibilism" (1980, p. 5)—the idea that age is no bar to continual personal improvement. Thus, the traditional Japanese understanding of aging is "much more profound and challenging" (Rohlen, 1978, p. 130) than just the notion that age, in and of itself, must be respected and the aged valued because they embody the experience and wisdom of years. While acknowledging that the passing of time cannot be resisted and will always result in change, the Japanese strive to achieve in their lives "valued, meaningful change" (p. 132) that "centers on personal growth, demands considerable effort and application, looks to a release from the 'self' rather than to its satisfaction, and stands as the most important yardstick of personal achievement and the life well led" (p. 130).

The Japanese define and understand personal growth in a particular kind of way, as revolving around the idea of "pure action." In Japanese thought, "pure action" is said to result when the motivation for it is totally pure. And motivation becomes unquestionably pure when one's sense of self is completely obliterated. Successful obliteration of the self implies becoming part of nature, blending seamlessly with the patterns and rhythms of nature, no longer even aware of the action one performs. As Plath (1980) says, "You are not 'communing' with nature, but *are* nature, moving with it in bursts of spontaneity that express the greatest truth of human nature (p. 47, emphasis in original). By their very nature, these moments of "truth, beauty, and purity" occur suddenly, without warning, and are usually short-lived. However, one can, and indeed should, always "cultivate a readiness, even a passionate readiness" (p. 47) for their occurrence.

While this may sound too esoteric and abstract for most people, both Japanese and non-Japanese, it has practical implications for the way ordinary Japanese live their lives. It explains the voluntary and rigorous practice of total, unquestioning obedience to the demands of the moment, till one achieves "expertness" in whatever one is doing. It also explains the strong commitment that the Japanese display—men to work and women to mothering. According to this logic, commitment leads to expertness, which readies a person for those moments of pure action when in the midst of the humdrum activities of the workaday world, truth and beauty converge.

The association between men and work and women and mothering is hardly random. It represents the gender-differentiated paths toward personal growth that Japanese culture has traditionally considered appropriate. For women, the path to personal growth and the opportunity to experience pure action is through striving for private rather than public goals, through becoming "good wives and wise mothers." For men, the proper sphere of activity is, and always has been, the public domain: They achieve personal growth and possibly moments of pure action through sincere and diligent work.

This adherence to traditional understandings is perhaps surprising, given the radical and tumultuous changes that Japan experienced in the past century. World War II and its aftermath have extracted a psychic cost from the Japanese people. And this, together with the rapid economic growth that characterized much of the second half of the twentieth century, has had inevitable social consequences. Modern patterns of employment have reshaped the careers of many in the workforce, and the two-generational nuclear family has become the national norm, transforming forever the "social context and institutional meaning" (Rohlen, 1978, p. 144) of working and parenting for the Japanese. Nevertheless, the rather "intense Japanese commitment to work (and mothering)" (p. 144) has not altered to any substantial degree.

An even greater surprise is that, despite modernization, the pulse of life for men and women remains so strikingly different. For most of the twentieth century, women constituted a high proportion of the Japanese workforce, but these were generally unmarried, younger women. On getting married, women are expected to give up working and devote their entire energies to being good wives and wise mothers. Thus, gender differentiates and defines differently the male and female life cycles. Perhaps this is what Plath means when he writes "women's tempo remains bound up with the home and the rhythm of the generations to a degree approached by only the most homebodyish of men" (1980, pp. 138–139). And while biology does play a greater role in shaping the female life cycle than it does the male, even a clearly physiological change in female biology such as menopause (*kônenki*) is seen as part and parcel of the general process of aging. The particular symptoms of *kônenki*—stiff shoulders, headaches, dizziness, dry mouth, for example—are thought to belong to the broader, more general set of signs associated with aging and are not isolated and identified as a disease or even as indicating a gradual and permanent decline in physical health.

Ideally, the Japanese believe that a married woman's vocation, her calling, should be that of "specialist homemaker" or "professional wife" (Plath, 1980, p. 139), tapping into those qualities of nurturance and caring that nature, it is supposed, has bestowed on all women (Lock, 1998). This may not always be possible: A woman may have no alternative but to work, and work hard, helping run the farm or family business, while caring for home and family. Nevertheless, Lock claims that the experience of marriage and motherhood is identical for all Japanese women, irrespective of class or educational levels: Women marry in the mid to late 20s and by their mid-30s, their families consisting of the requisite two children are complete. She explains this unusual similarity in women's life experiences as a result of the national discourse on aging[11] that focuses and elaborates on the various phases of life and appropriate life cycle development.

From the Japanese perspective, the transformation on marriage from an often thoughtless, spoiled daughter into a caring, expert wife can only be achieved through self-discipline and obediently performing one's

---

[11] Lock (1998, p. 56) says that in Japan since the turn of the twentieth century, a "genre of writing" known as "people's life span" discussed and elaborated in great detail the ideal life course for people in diverse life circumstances.

duty. And in discussing this transformation in retrospect, Plath's female interviewees tend to remember and emphasize the painfulness of the process: In the interviews, there is a constant refrain of remarks like "I worried myself thin in the early years," "I killed my sense of self the day I married" (1980, p. 139).

In these narratives, the transition from young to mature adulthood is told in terms of acquiring "expertness" in managing the household's affairs, and in supervising the activities of other family members while supporting them through the various exigencies of their lives. In an important sense, however, this transformation, because it is only one half of a reciprocal relationship, can never occur in isolation. A junior wife cannot become an "expert" senior wife as long as the latter continues to live: As Plath says, "The senior wife by her very presence continues to define the junior's juniority" (1980, p. 162). A junior wife may control the domestic activities of the household, but she will never have access to that peak position in the classic path to maturity until the older woman dies. Thus, 42-year-old Mrs. Furuya, acknowledged by her peers as capable and socially adept, does not feel fully mature because her husband's mother—the senior wife—is still alive: she has been a junior wife for 18 years and though her husband, since his father's death two years ago, has shouldered the entire responsibility of the family business, his mother has yet to surrender the reins of the household to his wife (Plath, 1975, p. 55).

The meanings of female maturity, however, are changing in contemporary Japan: paradoxically enough, marriage and child rearing are becoming more important today than ever before. A Japanese woman is thought to "flower" when she gives birth to children: Childbearing has always been recognized as the highest achievement that a woman can aspire to in terms of "social responsibility, sacrifice, and the expenditure of creative energy" (Rohlen, 1978, p. 145). And in contemporary Japan, where most men are salaried workers, their wives are unlikely to be junior wives waiting to be promoted to senior wives in "stem-family households" (Plath, 1980, p. 163). Instead, these women are more likely to be living in the relative isolation of nuclear families.[12] And, not surprisingly, in this social context, they derive meaning and purpose in their lives, not, as in the past, from the smooth and efficient organization and management of a large household, but primarily from marriage and child rearing.

For men, as I have already mentioned, the avenue to pure action lies in the sphere of work. The average Japanese man today is a salaried worker, employed by either the government or a company. Men, therefore, should

---

[12] The emergence of the two-generation, nuclear family as the national norm portends the disruption that will occur in most of these women's lives and the loneliness that they are likely to experience when their children finally leave home (Rohlen, 1978).

achieve their moments of pure action by adhering diligently and sincerely to a bureaucratic career path. In the companies and government offices where most Japanese men work, educational qualifications and personal abilities are undoubtedly necessary for career advancement but the critical variable that decides "rank, responsibility, status, and monetary reward" is seniority and its corollary, experience (Rohlen, 1978, p. 144). In describing the world of Japanese workers, Rohlen says,

> The hierarchy of bureaucratic authority in factories as well as in offices is age graded. A man is judged relative to his age-mates, all working their way up in competition with one another. The obvious failures are those who are not promoted at various crucial age-determined stages. The bureaucratic framework, in sum, creates an ideal career arc that progresses slowly from subordination to supervisory position, from dependence and inexperience to a capacity to lead and assist others, from the necessity of humility to the necessity of self-confidence. (p. 144)

Rohlen (1978) suggests that this structure of bureaucratic authority with its heavy emphasis on seniority and experience is inspired by the attitudes and ideals of traditional family businesses. Sons learned the tools of their fathers' trades as their fathers' apprentices. With time and systematic application, they became experienced in all aspects of the business and slowly they began to replace their old fathers in the day-to-day operations of the business. But the latter never became totally irrelevant: Their opinions were regularly sought and their advice always valued. In some sense, the senior generation never retired. In Rohlen's words, this model "tied authority to both seniority and to experience, and it visualized personal growth as the product of discipline and experience" (p. 144).

Modern organizations in Japan, whether in the corporate or public sector, try to recreate these idealized and traditional family relationships, but fail because of the structure and scale of their organizations. It is simply impossible to promote all employees at beginning and subordinate levels to positions that carry the same authority and respect that fathers in traditional families were entitled to and customarily enjoyed. The idea that companies and government offices are analogous to "big families" and that all employees are "family members" is harped on unceasingly but, for most employees, it does not ring true—the gap between the ideal and the real is too great to sustain such a myth. Promotion at particular "age-determined stages," as Rohlen (1978) has commented, works to winnow out all those who have not made the grade: only a small handful of men in their late 40s and early 50s are fortunate enough to rise to senior management positions. As modern equivalents of fathers in traditional families, only they "assume the satisfying role of respected seniors" (p. 144). But the vast majority of older employees, despite being "family members," do not ascend to higher management positions and inevitably retire and go home. And the worst of it is that, very often, economic necessity compels these retirees to look for another job in another company at a subordinate level. As Plath says, older Japanese men do not look forward to "retirement" from work; instead, they look to "rehirement" (see Plath, 1980, pp. 89–90).

For many Japanese men, therefore, the realities of work in a postindustrial society are tending to seriously undermine the intensity of their commitment. Traditionally, work has not only been the fulcrum, the entire point, of existence for Japanese men, it has also been the medium through which they could realize pure action. A disciplined, single-minded commitment to work enabled a man to cultivate and develop his inner resources, prepare himself for those sudden "bursts of spontaneity" when "truth, beauty, and purity" converge to make for a human life's peak experiences. But work in contemporary Japan is tending not to provide those opportunities any longer. And thus, Rohlen suggests that while "the conception of male adulthood as 'flowering' in the toil of work will undoubtedly remain the major theme," "new and different species of human fulfillment" (1978, p. 145) are likely to emerge, redefining the central experiences of male maturity.

When one compares the meanings of female maturity to male maturity in contemporary Japan, Japanese women enjoy a clear advantage over their menfolk: motherhood, "the pinnacle of socially recognized productive maturity" (Rohlen, 1978, p. 145), remains an option open to all women. For men, the possibility of achieving such "socially recognized productive maturity" is strictly limited by the organizational parameters and the circumstances of their work in a postindustrial society. Many, therefore, may never accomplish anything approaching "socially recognized productive maturity."

Apart from persevering as salaried workers or as mothers, Japanese men and women also seek to achieve personal growth by pursuing secular forms of "spiritual education" (Plath, 1980, p. 49). Thus, corporations and government agencies organize training sessions for all employees, both new and old: While skeptics decry these sessions as attempts to create and maintain a submissive labor force, most employees derive meaning from participating in them because they believe that they can achieve personal growth through cultivating "expertness" (Rohlen, 1973). Even more remarkable is that many ordinary Japanese, during the middle period of their lives, deliberately engage in avocations that cultivate and develop their inner resources: fully half of Plath's interviewees in his study of adulthood in Japan were enrolled in classes to learn the traditional arts of calligraphy, the Tea-ceremony, flower arrangement, or the reciting of No-drama texts. Their goal, they told him, was not merely to develop their skills but, more importantly, their "discipline and self-composure" (1980, p. 49).

The highly elaborated national discourse on the life cycle in Japan had traditionally identified the middle years of life as that "relatively undifferentiated part of the life cycle that commenced with marriage and lasted until ritual entry, at age 60, into old age" (Lock, 1998, p. 56). Modern Japanese, however, appear to have a more nuanced view of the middle years: Plath's subjects bracket this phase of life as beginning in the 40s and ending around age 60. Two years, designated as the "danger years" (*yakudoshi*), fall during this period of middle life: age 33 for a woman and age 42 for a man. And while there is little cultural consensus as to their origins and functions, Plath says that they continue to be observed by most people. During a danger year and sometimes during the year preceding and succeeding, one is supposed to lead a circumspect life in quiet meditation, buying amulets and visiting shrines in search of peace, before returning to the normal business of living. While there has been some effort on the part of the Japanese media to link these danger years with imported, primarily Western notions of midlife crisis, most ordinary Japanese reject such attempts to find cross-cultural similarities.

The traditional term for the middle period of life has been *sōnen*, its chief meaning being the "prime of life." Plath, however, suggests that there is more than just this one Japanese term for the Anglo-American term "middle age." The word currently used is *chūnen* and in Plath's opinion it is the most literal translation of middle age, though dictionaries do not elaborate on its etymological roots. There is also the premodern term *shōrō*, or "beginning old age," which Plath thinks is a better gloss for middle age because it includes meanings of loss and decline, but its infrequent usage, now and in the past, makes it a poor equivalent for the Anglo-American term.

While those of Plath's subjects who were over 40 did not resist the term *chūnen* being used to describe them, they often suggested other terms—unconnected with aging or age per se—that they feel sound better because they connote fullness, activity, or weight in the sense of wielding authority (see Plath, 1975). In common with most other cultures, there are, in Japan, no ceremonies or public recognition of a person's transition into middle age. The end of middle age, however, which coincides with the beginning of old age, is marked by a traditional ceremony held in the sixtieth year of life that is observed by some but not all Japanese. And while no one today is likely to consider 60 as old, it marks the threshold soon after which Japanese become eligible for Medicare and Social Security benefits.

The most distinctive feature about traditional Japanese understandings of aging is that time is not seen as a factor that erodes life's prospects;

rather, the passage of time and aging is thought to allow people to appre-
hend the deeper, more essential truths of life. The Japanese most certainly
recognize the physical facts of maturation and aging, but they do not grant
these physical changes any great or overwhelming significance. Japanese
culture and society favor the mature and the old over the young, not only
because the former have the accumulated experience of a lifetime, but also
because they are supposed to have spent that time cultivating themselves
as human beings, being self-disciplined and persevering, developing and
maintaining personal integrity and social responsibility. A great deal is
demanded of a mature adult in Japanese society, but maturity also holds
out the promise of freedom, ease, and relaxation. Plath's respondents used
the term *atsukmashisa*, glossed as "boldness" or "nerve," to describe the
ways in which they had changed with age: With age and experience, the
Japanese feel, one can afford to relax and take liberties even with time-
honored customs and practices (1980). And many of the women who participated in Lock's study are eagerly awaiting old age because they can
then give up displaying "feminine reserve" (Lock, 1998, p. 59), they can be
as forward as they please without incurring social censure. The Japanese
view middle age as an opportunity for each person to come into his or her
own, to experience and display his or her individuality and uniqueness.

MIDDLE AGE: THE PREDOMINANT ANGLO-AMERICAN CONCEPTION OF THE TWENTIETH-CENTURY

Middle-class Anglo-America possesses the uniquely twentieth-century
advantage of "mass longevity" (Plath, 1980, p. 1),[13] an advantage that is
likely to change forever the way people perceive the life course and its
various stages. The traditional sequence of life stages seems hardly adequate; it needs to be expanded to accommodate the two or three extra
decades that people are living today when compared with those who
lived just a couple of generations ago. Thus, in an interesting, insightful
piece, entitled "What Do You Call People Who Used to Be Old," that appeared in the editorial columns of the *New York Times* (July 2, 2000),
Dudley Clendinen refers to a Harris Poll conducted by the National
Council on Aging that found that nearly half the people between the ages
of 65 and 69 consider themselves to be "middle-aged," as do one-third of

---

[13] The countries of northern and western Europe and Japan share in this phenomenon of
"mass longevity." And as Plath (1980) points out, Japan's experience of this demographic
transition is particularly noteworthy because it has occurred the most rapidly—within
the lifetime of those born in the second half of the twentieth century.

those in their 70s. Marveling at what he terms the "advancing vitality of age," he tells the following, fascinating anecdote:

> On a plane to Florida this year, I sat with a woman of 60, on her way to her winter home. Her latest boyfriend, a businessman of almost 70, had acquired a certain cachet in his peer group when sued by a young woman for sexual harassment. That did not bother my planemate so much because she believed him when he said the woman came after him, and so did the jury at the trial. But it troubled her mother, who is 85, and who found out about it when her fifth husband, who is 91, saw notice of it in a business journal he gets at his office.

As Clendinen remarks, the vocabulary needed to talk about these extended lives has not yet been developed: Even the clinical psychologist Elliott Jaques, himself now 83 years old, who coined the highly evocative and enduring phrase "midlife crisis" more than 35 years ago is at a loss; comparatively speaking, his suggestion of the phrase "the third stage of adulthood" to describe the period between 62 and 85 years sounds less than catchy.

Inevitably, these expanded lifetimes will challenge current popular conceptualizations of the life course, as well as the particular life stage known as middle age—but how? Will the fact that the 70s and 80s are becoming commonly experienced as a physically and mentally vigorous period of a person's life make a difference in the ways that youth and middle age have customarily been understood and defined? Is it conceivable that understandings about aging and old age will change so radically that a person of 60 will be thought of as continuing to grow, rather than as growing old? Will the prevailing cult of youth (Gullette, 1998; Rohlen, 1978) finally be undermined?

Since the mid-1960s, several empirical studies have examined how men and women negotiate middle age but no consensus has emerged from their findings. Instead, generally speaking, their findings diverge into two contradictory understandings about the process of aging: Some have emphasized the positive aspects of middle age, focusing on the accumulated resources that middle age brings, both internal and external, enabling a person to confront the challenges of life with equanimity; while others highlight the negative aspects, the crises that supposedly characterize this period, the growing recognition that life is finite and the reluctant, painful resignation to the reality of time passing.

Neugarten's study of 100 successful middle-aged men and women (1968) exemplifies the first kind of representation. It presents its middle-aged subjects as people in comfortable control of their life circumstances and no longer expected to follow social roles: They alter and redefine social rules; because of the status and knowledge that they have accrued over the years, they confidently manipulate their social environments; and finally, sheer experience interacting with others allows them to adapt their feelings and impulses more reflexively and more appropriately. Other studies (Estes & Wilensky, 1978; Levinson, 1978; Lowenthal & Chiriboga, 1972) have, more or less, replicated the generally optimistic tenor of Neugarten's findings.

However, some psychoanalysts and psychiatrists working with clinical data have come to rather different conclusions: They tend to see crisis in middle age as a universal, developmental certainty—the "midlife crisis" (Jaques, 1965). While clinical data can quite justifiably be faulted for focusing on a sample that is not representative of the general population, the inference drawn from these studies about increased stress and dissatisfaction during middle age has been supported by some surveys and epidemiological studies (see Leighton, 1959; Pineo, 1968; Rollins & Feldman, 1970; Srole, Langner, Michael, Opler, & Rennie, 1962).

Farrell and Rosenberg (1981) in their investigation of middle-aged men emphasize the importance of social class and access to wealth and education in refracting the experience of middle age: Only upper middle class, wealthy, and well-educated men have the psychological resources to cope with the demands of adult life. At middle age, most men find that the maturity they assume they have developed is a thin resource, insufficient to prevent them from "falling into the traps of material failure, lost self-esteem, or extreme self-estrangement" (p. 217). Farrell and Rosenberg claim that American society "establishes expectations and criteria for success that most men will never attain" (p. 216), and men, having internalized these expectations, judge themselves to be failures with only themselves to blame. Even researchers, who represent middle age as a relatively good period of life to be in, are somewhat skeptical about the high level of satisfaction reported by their middle-aged respondents (Lowenthal & Chiriboga, 1972). They are especially suspicious of the discrepancy between husbands and wives' reports of marital satisfaction during middle age, wives reporting greater dissatisfaction than their husbands.

Even a less than thorough overview of the body of work done on middle age reveals that the more optimistic representations of midlife experiences have come primarily from studies done with predominantly upper-middle-class subjects with access to higher education and wealth and/or survey research using questionnaires—not a methodology that encourages candor from respondents—rather than from clinical interviews or health surveys. Apart from this, Farrell and Rosenberg (1981), in their review of work done on adult male development, suggest that research findings on middle age are often contradictory for the following three reasons: The period of middle age is defined differently by different researchers; there may be methodological problems with respect to the choice of sample and other techniques of data collection; and finally, adult male development may not conform to a single model—it may occur along multiple paths defined variably in terms of ethnicity, social class, and access to economic and psychological resources.

Generally speaking, researchers tend to agree that middle age begins at 40 and ends at 60 years of age. However, even this aspect of middle age is not accepted unquestioningly by all. Some researchers identify the late 30s as part of this life phase while others do the same for the late 60s, contriving to make middle age a period of time that is nearly as long as half a normal life span (Farrell & Rosenberg, 1981). Part of the reason for this lack of agreement could be that they appear to be working on different parts of this extended length of time yet continue to describe their research as focusing on middle age. Thus, some examine the "empty nest" phase when children have left home; others look at a more generalized time period, not associated with any particularly significant events; and still others zoom in on the experience of a predefined developmental crisis that is supposed to hit home during a precise chronological period.

But perhaps, there is no need to be too concerned about this dissensus in academia regarding middle age: According to Gullette (1998), when ordinary middle-class Anglo-Americans reflect on the meanings of age, they rarely look to scholarly studies for the truth about aging. Instead, she says that they rely on the popular press, films, novels, and television shows to tell them that "truth." But even in the world of popular culture, the meanings of aging and middle age abound in confusion. There are primarily two truths that vie for people's attention: the one that claims that everyone "dreads" (p. 5) aging, that middle age is the time when one slips into it, and that the dominant theme in the story of middle age is "decline" (p. 10); and the other, more optimistic counter discourse, some of it emerging from academia, that seeks to persuade people that middle age is a good time to be in. Gullette, however, contends that the counter discourse, despite its sunny message, falls on deaf ears because it lacks the emotional intensity and immediacy that "the bad news about midlife aging" (p. 7) possesses so abundantly. Thus, in all the din of conflicting meanings, the one that is heard the most often, the most insistently, and the most insidiously, is that of aging as "an unavoidable decline, like a curse" (p. 5). And, significantly enough, despite the inevitability of aging, the timing of this decline is vague and unclear: Gullette suggests that part of the power of "middle ageism" derives from this uncertainty about its onset—what she terms its "perverse undecidability" (p. 27). And she goes further to argue:

> Adolescence has now come to be the *psychological* threshold of socialization into midlife aging. This is currently the age when the young (presumably, girls first) absorb the cult of youth for the first time, pick up the technologies

of youthfulness, learn to notice "aging" in others and be disgusted by it, and thus lay the groundwork for fearing decline and watching for it not much later on in their own life course. p. 12, emphasis in original)

Generally speaking, then, middle-class Anglo-Americans can be said to conceive the human life course as an individual's journey from birth to death, an irreversible sequence of stages, in which chronological years or biological events mark significant milestones. In this conception, middle age is thought to mark the beginning of the end of life; it exemplifies the decline and loss of potency, physical beauty, and mental acuity that is seen as characteristic of carefree youth; and frequently, it is perceived as a time of crises. Even when there is an attempt to extol the attractions of aging or middle age, it takes the form of identifying those elements that embody some typically youthful quality. For most middle-class Anglo-Americans, then, "It is youth that epitomizes the American sense of well-being, and we pay homage to its gods time and again throughout an adulthood that inevitably leads us away from many of its perquisites" (Rohlen, 1978, p. 130).

Leaving aside for the moment the cult of youth that dominates popular culture, a distinctive feature of this Anglo-American conceptualization of the life course is its emphasis on the individual. Maturation and aging are not social experiences that a person goes through as a member of a family and community; rather, they are solitary "engagements" (Plath, 1980) that an individual undertakes as an independent entity. This is hardly surprising given the prevailing ethos of individualism. The institution of privacy, the cultural salience and significance of autonomy, child-rearing practices designed to nurture and develop independence, all symbolize the value and worth a human being is thought to embody "simply because as an individual he is of consequence" (Trilling, 1972, p. 24).

And what effect does this highly developed sense of individualism have on the way people understand and experience aging? The most obvious is that changes in individual biology eclipse the social experience of aging. More importantly, because of enormous significance granted to human biology, advances in science and medical technology have medicalized the entire process of aging; growing old is now redefined and diagnosed as a set of medical problems that are in need of treatment. And, while Gullette quite rightly exhorts us to "look at the nineties boom in menopause discourse, the prostate scare, the heart-disease news for women, the reemergence of the word 'testosterone' in contexts of male sexual decline" (1980, p. 6), medicalization has been less than even-handed in its treatment of women.

As Lock points out, for much of the twentieth century, in North America, men negotiating middle age were thought to be exempt from biological aging and attention was paid only to their work life, but women's midlife experiences were examined as being entirely determined by their biology: "The pathological Menopausal Woman takes center stage and, in recent years, has virtually obliterated any other way of understanding female middle age" (Lock, 1998, p. 46). Pathologizing menopause, as Kaufert and Lock suggests, implies assuming that the sole purpose of a woman's existence is to reproduce and once that natural ability ends (signaled by menopause), a woman has outlived her utility and, therefore, by definition, her postmenopausal life cannot but be one devoid of all meaning (Kaufert & Lock, 1991). The overwhelming significance given to female biology in determining a woman's life course seems excessive. However, according to Lock, not only does it represent quite accurately the thinking of the medical establishment for most of the past century, but it also explains satisfactorily the formulation of the "normative crisis model," by the same establishment, to describe female middle age—despite contradictory empirical evidence that suggests that most women do not greet menopause with despair and depression (see Avis & McKinlay, 1991). As Alice Rossi explains, women were supposed to be traumatized psychologically because it meant the end of their "true function, namely that they couldn't conceive anymore" (quoted in the *Chicago Tribune,* February 16, 1999). Because birth control pills have granted women control over their reproductive capacity for the past several decades, this pathologizing of menopause is curious; perhaps it reflects the perspective of a predominantly male medical establishment[14] that is only recently beginning to lose credibility.

Significantly enough, the end of the twentieth century also saw the end of this "double standard of aging" (Sontag, 1972), a target of feminist ire way back in the 1970s. Referring to over a hundred years of social history in the United States, Gullette (1998) marshals impressive evidence to support her claim that most men, today, are as vulnerable to the invidious influences of the "decline ideology" as women. Life in a postindustrial society, characterized by uncertainty and insecurity in jobs and wages, and the ubiquitous fiction of midlife male menopause contrive to create age anxiety in all but the most privileged of men. Disagreeing vehemently with those who hold that "the only honest narrative about the life course is a decline" (p. 27) and assuming that "little in midlife aging is bodily and that nothing considered 'bodily' is unaffected by culture" (p. 4), she suggests that middle age has no specific beginning in Anglo-American conceptions because people have been "getting older younger" (p. 17). A self-avowed radical social constructionist, she declares:

---

[14] It needs to be mentioned that several prominent women, including intellectuals like Simone de Beauvoir (1953) and Susan Sontag (1979), shared this view.

In the United States in the twentieth century, aging no longer means a geriatric physical process, and it can begin long before marked events like retirement or the last of the children leaving home. Although widely shared, its core is a private emotion: fear of being not-young. In other words, it is a culturally cultivated chronic disease with an adolescent exposure and a no-later-than-midlife onset. (p. 17)

Lately, a counternarrative about the middle years of life has emerged. With the findings of the enormously comprehensive 10-year study of almost 8,000 adults by the MacArthur Foundation Research Network on Successful Midlife Development being made public in early 1999, an alternative, more optimistic characterization of this life phase has become available. Its upbeat message is implicit in its use of the term "midlife development" when talking of aging into the middle years: there appears to be an attempt to get away from the negative connotations of "decline" attached to the more commonly used phrase, middle age. This alternative characterization takes on two of the more persistent myths that dominate the Anglo-American conceptualization of middle age—the midlife crisis and the psychological and physical costs of menopause—and produces solid empirical evidence to refute them. Thus, midlife crises seemingly afflict only 1 in 10 persons of those surveyed; half the post-menopausal women interviewed claim not to have experienced hot flushes—"the sine non qua of menopause" in the West (Lock, 1998, p. 63)—and most greet the end of menstruation with "only relief" rather than suffer the depression and distress that psychoanalysts and gynecologists claim to have observed.

Apart from enjoying good physical health, most midlifers assert that they have very satisfying relationships with children, other family members, and friends. "The midlife years appear to be a time of psychic equanimity, good health, productive activity and community involvement" (*New York Times,* February 16, 1999), and one can only agree with Gilbert Brim, the director of the research network, when he is quoted in the same article as saying, "On balance, the sense we all have is that midlife is the best place to be."

But, does this alternative, slightly different story about aging and middle age that has recently emerged qualify as a counternarrative? Does it belong to the genre of counternarratives that actively elaborate on what Gullette rather dismissively describes as the "politics of optimism and recuperation" (1998, p. 5)? Does it make the substantial claim that life gets progressively better with age, that each successive phase of life provides a fresh opportunity to cultivate oneself and perhaps gain a deeper understanding of the essential truths of life—that adulthood and even old age give humans "stature, movement, optimism" (Rohlen, 1978, p. 145)?

Well, no. The MacArthur study makes far more modest claims. Basically, it contends that middle age, contrary to most popular thinking in middle-class Anglo-America, is a good period in a person's life, perhaps even the best. And it also highlights the future risks of old age. Thus, the complaints of losses in "personal growth and purpose in life" by older midlifers are interpreted as portending the decline and losses that are likely to characterize the next phase of life, that of old age. As Carol Ryff, a psychologist and one of the researchers associated with the project, is reported as having said: "The message for people in midlife is to be mindful of what's ahead" (*New York Times,* February 16, 1999). This study has not abandoned the decline ideology that is said to characterize Anglo-American conceptualizations of the life course; however, it suggests a radically different timing—instead of occurring in the fourth decade of life, decline and losses are now thought to occur in the sixth or seventh decade. And this marks an important shift in cultural understandings about aging: Middle age is being redefined as the prime of life for middle-class Anglo-Americans. While this redefinition can be ascribed, in part, to today's stupendous advances in medical science and technology, much of it reflects ordinary people's recognition of the advantages of middle age: having a greater sense of control over themselves and their environment and more satisfying relationships with spouses, children, other family members, and friends.

CONTRASTS AND COMPARISONS

Each of the three conceptions of middle age presented in this chapter emerges as a unique cultural fiction, each the product of cultural assumptions about the life course and the meaning and purpose of life. For middle-class Anglo-Americans, the purpose of life is to be free, mobile, active, able to pursue one's interests without hindrance or undue influence; for the Japanese, traditionally speaking, a valued, meaningful life centers on personal growth, the cultivation of one's talents and abilities through considerable effort and application; and for the Hindu, the ultimate though often unspoken goal of life is renunciation, achieved not necessarily through a radical disengagement from this world but by detaching oneself through self-refinement from selfish action and from the fruits of all action.

Speaking as an Anglo-American about the relationship between an individual and society, Plath says:

> We enter society out of concession to animal weakness and practical need. But social participation can only diminish us; our highest self is realized in peak experiences that take us out of the ruck of society. Our cultural

nightmare is that the individual throb of growth will be sucked dry in slavish social conformity. All life long, our central struggle is to defend the individual from the collective. (1980, p. 216)

The Japanese and Hindus, in contrast, participate in social relations because they believe that that is the only way available to fully experience one's humanity: One realizes who one is and where one is going through interrelationships and interdependencies. For both Hindus and Japanese, one is never born a human being; one becomes a human being through living in society, through participating in life-cycle rituals and through following customary practice. And exclusion from the group, for both the Japanese and Hindus, is the worst kind of punishment. "Exclusion is depersonalization. . . . For without a circle of intimates to attend to it, one's human integrity is in peril, here and beyond" (p. 217): Plath is speaking of the Japanese, but he could as well be speaking of Hindus (see Kakar, 1982).

Not surprisingly, then, the most striking feature of the Anglo-American conception of adult development and aging, and one that distinguishes it from both the Japanese and the Hindu, is its emphasis on the individual as people mature and age rather than on the changing dynamics of social and familial relationships. Given this emphasis on the individual, it is perhaps to be expected that the passing of life is marked in terms of chronological years and biological events, terms rarely used by Hindus or Japanese when describing the various life phases. Despite this emphasis on chronological change, the boundaries of Anglo-American middle age appear somewhat fuzzy, and lately, the entire life phase is being extended to include chronological years that were previously categorized as old.[15] Anglo-American middle age, therefore, appears more a state of mind when life's problems, role transitions, and physiological changes accumulate till finally an individual experiences him- or herself as having become middle-aged.

In contrast to middle-class Anglo-Americans, the Japanese and Hindus conceive aging as a social process rather than the individual experience of biological transformations. Notwithstanding this similarity, the Japanese notion of possibilism is unique, nothing even remotely similar being found in Hindu understandings of maturation and aging. In that respect, Hindus tend to resemble the Anglo-American midlifers who participated in the MacArthur study: Both groups identify the middle years as the

---

[15] Another finding of the study is that middle age is apparently occurring later, chronologically speaking, than before: Thus, instead of middle age beginning at 40 and ending at 60 years of age, respondents push back the onset of middle age to 44 years of age and its end to 62 years. This postponement of the onset of middle age may reflect a muted recognition of the twentieth-century phenomenon of "mass longevity."

prime of life but with old age comes the inevitable decline and loss in physical ability and mental acuity.

In middle-class Anglo-America, the cult of youth remains preeminent. Aging is tolerated only to the extent that it allows people to retain "something of the carefree, mobile, active state typical of youth" (Rohlen, 1978, p. 130). And, in the past several decades, advances in medical science and technology have helped people postpone the inevitability of aging. By comparison, Hindu and Japanese conceptions appear more fatalistic in the sense that nature is thought to have her way irrespective of human wishes. But again, there are differences in the Japanese view of biographical time and the Hindu. The Japanese submit to the depredations of time but simultaneously see within this submission a challenge and a potential for perfecting the human self: A mature adult, someone who is completing this process of becoming human, is characterized by wisdom, self-control, and cultivated abilities. For Hindus, the passing of the years provides opportunities to refine oneself: When one submits unresistingly to the ravages of time, one is withdrawing, gradually but surely, from the desires and entanglements of this world.

Again, the emotional tone of the middle period of life reflects and corresponds to the cultural understanding about aging. Thus, mature Japanese adults, imbued by the idea of Confucian possibilism, talk of boldness (*atsukamashisa*) when describing the changes that age has wrought on them. The dominant motif of middle age among the Japanese is not decline; instead, they view middle age as an opportunity for each person to come into his or her own, a chance to experience and display his or her individuality and uniqueness. Comfortably familiar with their social roles, they can now afford to take liberties with cultural rules, they can be playful, even a little self-indulgent.

For Oriya Hindus, mature adulthood is a complicated time, emotionally speaking. As mature adults,[16] self-assured and confident of their accomplishments, they enjoy a heightened sense of well-being. However, two anxieties cloud this contentment. The first is anxiety about an uncertain future in which old age and the inevitable decline associated with it figure prominently; for Oriya Hindus, old age is a culturally devalued life phase known as a "second childhood" or "childishness," marked by complete dependence on others. And the second is about having to live up to a cultural ideal that exhorts mature adults, both men and women, to renounce the pleasures of the world, beginning with sexual activities—the precipitating event usually being the marriage of an adult child. As Kakar suggests, perhaps this is the midlife

---

[16] Interestingly enough, the Oriya term for mature adulthood, *prauda*, includes the meanings "audacity" and "boldness."

crisis that most Hindus face: "renunciation versus involvement" (1998, p. 81), requiring them, if they are to resolve this challenge positively, to develop equanimity.

For middle-class Anglo-Americans, the emotional texture of this phase of life would depend on whether they have bought into the theme of middle-age decline uncritically or not. If they did, their predominant emotion would be the acute fear of growing old; while for those who are more like the midlifers of the MacArthur Foundation's study and believe that decline occurs, but in old rather than middle age, this would be a time of considerable satisfaction and well-being, though tinged with some anxiety about the future and all that it foreshadows: Old age and the losses and decline that accompany it.

Each cultural conception of the middle years of life is, as would be expected, saturated with cultural meanings. Even elements that are commonly acknowledged as a feature of aging in all three cultural contexts—the experience of menopause, for example—acquire an entirely different emphasis and salience, once they go through the process of cultural construction. Thus, middle-class Anglo-American women today react to menopause with little more than mild relief; for Japanese women, menopause characterizes female aging but because of the underemphasis of biology within the culture, it takes its place as just another element in the larger process of human aging; and for Oriya Hindu women, menopause signals a momentous transformation in a woman's ability to maintain bodily coherence and has the immediate impact of allowing her unrestricted access to divinity, a privilege that contributes enormously to her sense of well-being.

Notwithstanding these cultural differences in the experience of middle age, there are two aspects—perhaps universal—about this life phase that all three cultural conceptions share, to a greater or lesser degree. The first is what Neugarten, when describing the conduct of a mature adult, refers to as "conscious self-utilization rather than the self-consciousness of youth" (1970, p. 78). This is a particularly apt way of describing the ways in which all the people discussed in this chapter—Japanese, Oriya Hindus, and middle-class Anglo-American participants of the MacArthur Foundation's study—experience themselves as mature adults. All, as mature adults, are confident of their abilities to judge and manage people, situations, and relationships so as to obtain the results they seek; furthermore, while continuing to be concerned about social approbation, they are no longer driven by it.

The second is the idea that the "transitions and meanings of mature adulthood are linked to transitions in the sexuality, schooling, and family formation of one's adolescent children" (Shweder, 1998, p. xvi). This theoretical insight, articulated first by Weisner and Bernheimer in their study of the midlife experiences of Anglo-Americans who had, in their youth, participated in the countercultural movement of the 1960s, suggests that for these parents "midlife actually is marked by its being yoked with the adolescent developmental transition" (1998, p. 217). And far from having only local meanings that do not travel well, this particular insight can be readily applied to the Oriya Hindu and the Japanese context. Thus, a 53-year-old Japanese employee told Plath that he would regard himself an old man only after his daughters were married and a grandchild was born: "Only after I've graduated from those events" (1975, p. 54). And similarly, for an Oriya Hindu married mother, the marriage of her son and the entry of his new wife into the family promote the mother to the very pinnacle of mature adulthood.

One could perhaps extend this metaphor of the middle and younger generation being yoked to include the older generation as well. The universal meaning attached to mature adulthood, then, would derive primarily from the centrality of its location in the life course. Being in the middle, mature adulthood takes shape and is defined in terms of linkages and connections with the generations that precede and succeed it: One is thrust into mature adulthood when the person further along in life's journey accedes to old age; and, the prestige and privilege of mature adulthood is further endorsed when the person following in one's path is being socially processed.

REFERENCES

Avis, N.E., & McKinlay, S.M. (1991). A longitudinal analysis of women's attitudes toward menopause: Results from the Massachusetts Women's Health Study. *Maturitas, 13,* 65–79.

Beauvoir, S., de. (1953). *The second sex* [H.M. Parshley,Trans.]. New York: Knopf.

Bellah, R.N., Madsen, R., Sullivan, W.N., Swidler, A., & Tipton, S.M. (1996). *Habits of the heart.* Berkeley: University of Southern California Press.

Benedict, R. (1946). *The chrysanthemum and the sword: Patterns of Japanese culture.* Boston: Houghton Mifflin.

Caudill, W., & Weinstein, H. (1969). Maternal care and infant behavior in Japan and America. *Psychiatry, 32,* 12–43.

Daniel, E.V. (1984). *Fluid signs: Being a person the Tamil way.* Berkeley: University of Southern California Press.

Dumont, L. (1970). *Homo hierarchicus: The caste system and its implications.* Chicago: University of Chicago Press.

Estes, R.J., & Wilensky, H.L. (1978, February). Life cycle squeeze and the morale curve. *Social Problems, 25*(3), 277–292.

Farrell, M.P., & Rosenberg, S.D. (1981). *Men at midlife.* Boston: Auburn House.

Formanek, S. (1992). Normative perceptions of old age in Japanese history: A study based on literary sources of the Nara and Heian periods. In S. Formanek & S. Linhart (Eds.), *Japanese biographies: Life histories, life cycles, life stages* (pp. 241–269). Vienna, Austria: Verlag der Österreichischen Akademie der Wissenschaften.

Freud, S. (1960). *General introduction to psychoanalysis.* New York: Washington Square Press.

Gullette, M.M. (1998). Midlife discourses in the twentieth-century United States: An essay on the sexuality, ideology and politics of middle-ageism. In R.A. Shweder (Ed.), *Welcome to middle age! (and other cultural fictions)* (pp. 3–44). Chicago: University of Chicago Press.

Heesterman, J.C. (1985). *The inner conflict of tradition: Essays in Indian ritual, kingship and society.* Chicago: University of Chicago Press.

Inden, R.B., & Nicholas, R.W. (1977). *Kinship in Bengali culture.* Chicago: University of Chicago Press.

Jaques, E. (1965). Death and the mid-life crisis. *International Journal of Psychoanalysis, 46,* 502–514.

Kakar, S. (1982). *Shamans, mystics and doctors.* New York: Knopf.

Kakar, S. (1998). The search for middle age in India. In R.A. Shweder (Ed.), *Welcome to middle age! (and other cultural fictions)* (pp. 75–98). Chicago: University of Chicago Press.

Kaufert, P., & Lock, M. (1991). What are women for? Cultural constructions of menopausal women in Japan and Canada. In J.K. Brown and V. Kerns (Eds.), *In her prime* (pp. 201–219). Urbana: University of Illinois Press.

Lamb, S. (1993). *Growing in the net of Maya.* Unpublished doctoral dissertation, University of Chicago.

Leighton, A.H. (1959). *My name is legion.* New York: Basic Books.

Levinson, D.J. (with Darrow, C.N., Klein, E.B., Levinson, M.H., & McKee, B.). (1978). *The seasons of a man's life.* New York: Ballantine Books.

Lock, M. (1993). *Encounters with aging: Mythologies of menopause in Japan and North America.* Berkeley: University of Southern California Press.

Lock, M. (1998). Deconstructing the change: Female maturation in Japan and North America. In R.A. Shweder (Ed.), *Welcome to middle age! (and other cultural fictions)* (pp. 45–74). Chicago: University of Chicago Press.

Lowenthal, M.F., & Chiriboga, D. (1972). Transition to the empty nest. *Archives of General Psychiatry, 26,* 8–14.

Madan, T.N. (1987). *Non-renunciation.* Delhi, India: Oxford University Press.

Mahapatra, M. (1981). *Traditional structure and change in an Orissa temple.* Calcutta, India: Punthi Pustak.

Manu. (1991). *The laws of Manu* (W. Doniger & B.K. Smith, Trans.). London: Penguin Classics.

Marriott, M. (1976). Hindu transactions: Diversity without dualism. In B. Kapferer (Ed.), *Transaction and meaning: Directions in the anthropology of exchange and symbolic behavior* (pp. 109–142). Philadelphia: Institute for the Study of Human Issues.

Marriott, M. (1990). *India through Hindu categories.* New Delhi, India: Sage.

Menon, U., & Shweder, R.A. (1998). The return of the White man's burden: The moral discourse of anthropology and the domestic life of Hindu women. In R.A. Shweder (Ed.), *Welcome to middle age! (and other cultural fictions)* (pp. 139–188). Chicago: University of Chicago Press.

Mines, D.P. (1990). Hindu periods of death impurity. In M. Marriott (Ed.), *India through Hindu categories* (pp. 103–130). New Delhi, India: Sage.

Neugarten, B.L. (1968). *Middle age and aging.* Chicago: University of Chicago Press.

Neugarten, B.L. (1970). Dynamics of transition from middle age to old age: Adaptation and the life cycle. *Journal of Geriatric Psychiatry, 4,* 71–81.

Pineo, P. (1968). Disenchantment in the later years of marriage. In B.L. Neugarten (Ed.), *Middle age and aging* (pp. 258–262). Chicago: University of Chicago Press.

Plath, D.W. (1972). The after years. In D. Cowgill & L. Holmes (Eds.), *Aging and modernization* (pp. 133–150). New York: Meredith.

Plath, D.W. (1975). The last Confucian sandwich: Becoming middle-aged. *Journal of Asian and African Studies, X(1/2),* 51–63.

Plath, D.W. (1980). *Long engagements.* Stanford, CA: Stanford University Press.

Rohlen, T. (1973). *For harmony and strength: Japanese white-collar organization in anthropological perspective.* Berkeley: University of Southern California Press.

Rohlen, T. (1978). The promise of adulthood in Japanese spiritualism. In E.H. Erikson (Ed.), *Adulthood* (pp. 129–147). New York: Norton.

Rollins, B.C., & Feldman, H. (1970). Marital satisfaction over the family life cycle. *Journal of Marriage and the Family, 32(1),* 20–28.

Rudolph, S.H., & Rudolph, L.I. (1978). Rajput adulthood: Reflections on the Amar Singh diary. In E.H. Erikson (Ed.), *Adulthood* (pp. 149–171). New York: Norton.

Seymour, S. (1999). *Women, family, and child care in India.* Cambridge, England: Cambridge University Press.

Shore, B. (1998). Status reversal: The coming of aging in Samoa. In R.A. Shweder (Ed.), *Welcome to middle age! (and other cultural fictions)* (pp. 101–137). Chicago: University of Chicago Press.

Shweder, R.A. (1991). *Thinking through cultures.* Cambridge, MA: Harvard University Press.

Shweder, R.A. (1998). Introduction: Welcome to middle age! In R.A. Shweder (Ed.), *Welcome to middle age! (and other cultural fictions)* (pp. ix-xvii). Chicago: University of Chicago Press.

Sontag, S. (1972). The double standard of aging. *Saturday Review, 55,* 29–38.

Srole, L., Langner, T., Michael, S., Opler, M., & Rennie, T. (1962). *Mental health in the metropolis.* New York: McGraw-Hill.

Trawick, M. (1990). *Notes on love in a Tamil family.* Berkeley: University of Southern California Press.

Trilling, L. (1972). *Sincerity and authenticity.* Cambridge, MA: Harvard University Press.

Vatuk, S. (1983). The family life of older people in a changing society: India. In J. Sokolovsky (Ed.), *Aging and the aged in the third world: Regional and ethnographic perspectives* (Pt. 2, p. 71). Williamsburg, VA: College of William and Mary, Department of Anthropology.

Vatuk, S. (1987). Power, authority and autonomy across the life course. In P. Hocking (Ed.), *Dimensions of social life: Essays in honor of D.G. Mandelbaum* (pp. 23–44). Berlin, Germany: Mouton de Gruyter.

Vatuk, S. (1990). To be a burden on others: Dependency anxiety among the elderly in India. In O.M. Lynch (Ed.), *Divine passions: The social construction of emotions in India* (pp. 64–88). Berkeley: University of Southern California Press.

Weisner, T.S., & Bernheimer, L.P. (1998). Children of the 1960s at midlife: Generational identity and the family adaptive project. In R.A. Shweder (Ed.), *Welcome to middle age! (and other cultural fictions)* (pp. 211–257). Chicago: University of Chicago Press.

SECTION II
BIOMEDICAL ASPECTS

CHAPTER 3

Toward a Biology of Middle Age

CALEB E. FINCH

THIS CHAPTER EXPLORES issues in defining the midlife or middle-age phases of the human life course from evolutionary and comparative perspectives. Particular emphasis is given to the reproductive system and brain, and a common human gene variant for a blood lipoprotein apolipoprotein E, the apoE4 isoform, that increases the risk of impaired cardiovascular health and cognition during middle age. Although there is extensive work on the menopause, middle age has received little attention among biomedical gerontologists (Finch, 1991). For example, middle age is not identified in the index or chapter subheadings of two widely used textbooks of biological gerontology (Arking, 1998; Digiovanna, 2000). Nonetheless, the domain of middle age is necessarily included in the many longitudinal studies of human and animal aging. Moreover, at least one journal, *Neurobiology of Aging,* has a general policy that animal studies should include intermediate age groups, as well as the extreme ages of "young" and "old." Many of our studies on reproduction and on the brain have emphasized the middle-age domain, because we wished to study aging phenomena in the absence of diseases of aging.

As a biologist who studies the neurobiology of aging and life history evolution, I have been stimulated by the widely divergent views of middle

I am grateful for critical comments by Nilay Patel (USC). Many of these ideas were germinated during discussions at meetings of the MacArthur Foundation Networks on Successful Aging and Middle-age. The experimental work from my lab was supported by grants from the NIA, Alzheimer Association, the American Federation of Aging Research, and the John Douglas French Foundation for Alzheimer's Disease.

age among social scientists, who to varying degrees are concerned with cultural agism and rigid concepts of human psychosocial developmental stages. The MacArthur Foundation's program, Studies of Successful Midlife Development is a new platform for research on middle age. Some of the present volume's authors, who are members of this program have considered the diversity of adult human outcomes at midlife including cultural norms (Lachman & James, 1997; Shweder, 1998), parenting (Ryff & Seltzer, 1996), sexuality (Rossi, 1994), sense of control (Lachman & Weaver, 1998), and other measures of self-esteem and happiness (Mroczek & Kolarz, 1998). These discussions go far beyond traditional models; for example, Erikson's psychoanalytic-based stages do not name an explicit midlife stage in the transitions between "young adulthood, adulthood, and old age" (Erikson, 1984). While remaining aware of these often politicized psychosocial and psychoanalytical contexts, I am focusing here on the biological substrates of middle age. As general references on the biology of aging and on the evolution of life span, I suggest four books that were written for a general audience: Finch (1990), Rose (1991), Stearns (1999), and Wachter and Finch (1997); the latter two edited volumes contain detailed discussion of many topics treated in this chapter; the articles referred to are indicated by an asterisk (*), as well as by cited authors.

DEFINITIONS OF MIDDLE AGE

The human biology of aging and its evolution may be understood in the terms of population biology, which gives insights into the forces of natural selection that influence the human gene pool and therefore the outcomes of aging that are under genetic control (*Rose, 1991; Charlesworth, 1994; *Stearns, 1999). I first examine the feasibility of a demographic definition of middle age. As a starting point, one might consider midlife as *the midpoint of life expectancy* (50% survivorship), which in developed countries would mean a midlife point of about 40 years. This demographic criterion leads to an absurdity, albeit one that is instructive.

Figure 3.1A contrasts the survivorship in the human population of a contemporary poor country and a rich country. In both populations, the maximum life span is over 100 years, as observed throughout the world (*Wachter & Finch, 1997; Vaupel et al., 1998). The upper limits of life span are subject not only to the average yearly mortality and the population size (Finch & Pike, 1996), but also to the leveling off of the acceleration of mortality rates. Given the enormous diversity of human environments and disease profiles at different ages, it is surprising how uniform mortality rate accelerations are after puberty in human populations, such that mortality rates double about every 8 years during the adult years in the majority of populations (Finch, 1990; Finch et al., 1990). The mortality rate reaches a

(A)

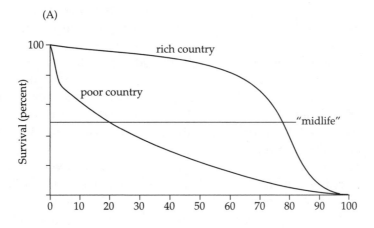

(B)

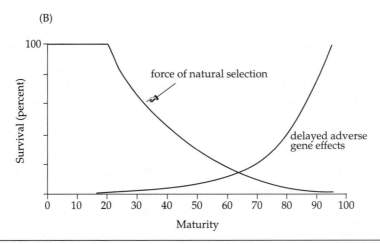

Maturity

Figure 3.1 Survival curves and the force of natural selection. (A) Illustrative survival curves of human populations, representing a rich country with low infant mortality and life expectancy at 20 years (maximum female fecundity) of about 60 years versus a poor country with high overall mortality rates and life expectancy at 20 years of about 30 years. (B) Representation of the declining force of natural selection after maturity in a natural population due to the loss of adults from natural hazards as in the poor country in Panel A. The evolutionary theory predicts that the declining force of natural selection would be permissive for the accumulation of genes in the population that have delayed adverse consequences, such as cancer, vascular disease, and Alzheimer's disease. The theory, however, does not predict which diseases will arise or their schedule of risk by age group.

maximum of about 50% mortality per year after 100 years (Vaupel et al., 1998). More generally, the typical survival curve in natural populations looks like a downhill slope of the poor country in Figure 3.1A, in which only a small subpopulation survives into middle age. The converse has become true for survival curves of industrial countries, which are increasingly "rectangularized" with a strong proportion of senescent mortality (Figure 3.1A). Nonetheless, as noted, annual mortality rates accelerate more or less smoothly during adult life until very advanced ages, when they approach a maximum.

In populations with high infant mortality and low life expectancy from birth onward, the time of middle age, when calculated at 50% of life expectancy, would occur soon after the onset of reproduction. Using 1990 examples from United Nations data that approximate Figure 3.1A, life expectancy at birth varied from Sweden (77.6 yr) to Malawi (48.8 yr) (Kinsella & Taueber, 1992), which spans a range of about 30 years. Hunter-gatherer groups such as the Aché of eastern Paraguay, have similarly high overall mortality and low life expectancy in the 40–50 year range (*Kaplan, 1997). Thus, the demographic point of middle age would occur at 40 years in Sweden (reasonable), but at 20–25 years for Malawi and hunter-gatherers (absurd). Moreover, the onset of midlife would differ markedly between men and women because of gender differences in life expectancy at birth that vary about 10 years between the highest and lowest national populations (Kinsella & Taueber, 1992). Even greater differences might be found among the lowest demographic strata of some national populations afflicted with HIV, which shortens life expectancy by 20 or more years. Thus, calculations based on 50% of the life expectancy at birth do not give a general index of middle age for all populations.

A better approach to defining middle age may be to consider it in relation to the life expectancy of those who survive to produce their first child, which is typically at least several years after puberty. For example, Aché women who reach the typical age of first reproduction, about 19–20 years, have a life expectancy of about 65 years (*Kaplan, 1997), which allows for a postreproductive phase of about 15–20 years. Moreover, calibrating middle age to the onset of reproduction takes account of demographic differences in the onset age of puberty, which can vary up to 5 years, depending on growth rates, which are affected by nutrition and infectious disease. Relatively few viable births occur within the first 3–5 years of menarche, even in cultures favoring early marriage, because of the high initial incidence of spontaneous miscarriage. This phase of "adolescent sterility" is followed by nubility, or reproductive maturity (Ashley-Montague, 1957; Hassan, 1980). (Even in laboratory rodents with puberty at 2 months, full reproductive maturity does not develop for another 2–4 months, with markedly more viable pups in the second litter than the first.) In typical populations of developed countries, more than 90% of children are born to women aged 20–40 years; the typical ages of paternity are slightly shifted to about 3 years later (e.g., Lancaster, 1994).

As a working criterion for demarcating the beginning of middle age in human populations, I suggest the age of 40 years. At this age, most women show sharp decreases in fecundity, about 5 years before menopause, even in the absence of birth control (Gosden, 1985; vom Saal, Finch, & Nelson, 1994). In developed countries, the age of 40 is typified by general good health, according to formal indicators of physical and mental competence, and self-reported well-being (Siegler, 1997; Thomas, 1997). This working definition is also applicable to men. Despite the absence of a sharp decline in reproduction that corresponds to the menopause, most births are fathered by men younger than 60 years. One record age of paternity is 94 years (Seymour, Duffy, & Koerner, 1935), which is 35 years later than the oldest documented maternal age at birth (Fergusson, Taylor, & Watson, 1982). The range of these individual variations is represented in Figure 3.2. In general, the range of individual variations increases with each successive stage: gestation < puberty < middle age. The duration of health during middle age appears to be one of the most variable.

Defining middle age in relation to the major adult reproductive phase is also consistent with the strong demographic shift to later parental ages, which means that both sexes are pressing the barriers of biological upper age limits to reproduction (Easterlin & Crimmins, 1985). Assisted reproduction at later ages may become common in personal life history strategy

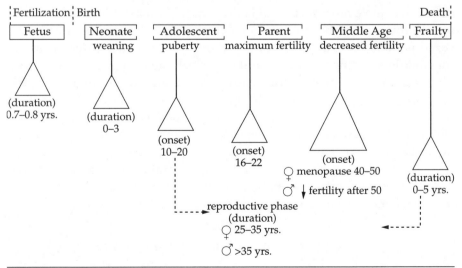

Figure 3.2 Variable stages in human life history. Original figure of author, redrawn from Finch (1997a).

(e.g., cyropreservation of eggs for decades, against future contingencies; Djerassi, 1999), and may become more generally available than to just an economic elite. Such a trend would, of course, further press the definition of middle age. Moreover, most populations are showing rapid increases in the oldest old (*Vaupel, 1997). The greatest documented life span is that of Jean Calment, who lived to 122 (Allard, Lèbre, & Robine, 1998). Assuming her menopause at 50, Mme. Calment had a postmenopausal phase of 70 years, which was twice the duration of her postpubertal phase. She lived independently and in good health for more than 50 postmenopausal years, for which she may be accorded a second record, the longest middle-age phase. When tested cognitively at 118 years for verbal memory and language fluency, she was ". . . comparable to persons with the same level of education in their eighties and nineties," and performed even better when retested 6 months later (Ritchie, 1995). Based on data from France, Ritchie (1998) calculated that the life expectancy without dementia occupies 67% of remaining life expectancy at age 97.

A growing subpopulation of humans now maintain mental acuity and a considerable degree of physical competence into the 9th or 10th decades, or beyond, which greatly extends the domain of middle age. This is a revolutionary change from the traditional view that senility begins at 60, as epitomized in Sir William Osler's infamous bad joke in his "Fixed Period" speech of 1905 "that old men should be chloroformed at sixty" (Beach, 1987).

Lastly in this discussion on definitions of middle age, I return to the differences between populations. Subgroups within most national populations may be found that have life expectancies at birth or puberty which closely resemble more fortunate national populations; in particular, these may be found in higher socioeconomic strata (SES). In general, the less favored populations have higher early mortality from attributed causes in the middle-age range that are similar to older age groups in favored populations: In both cases, most deaths are attributed to circulatory and heart diseases (e.g., World Health Statistics Annual, 1988). Nonetheless, further inquiry about causes of morbidity at middle age might reveal etiologies of particular diseases due to gene-environment interactions that differ between subgroups, which may not be apparent in national averages. An open question is whether major cultural differences in expectations for the outcomes of aging (e.g., articles in Shweder, 1998) could include gene-environment interactions in particular subgroups.

CANONICAL PATTERNS OF AGING

In contrast to the major demographic differences in human survivorship and life expectancy, some biological changes in humans seem to be widely shared across the present world populations (Table 3.1). I select

Table 3.1
Canonical Age Changes in Mammals

	Ovarian Oocyte Loss/Infertility[a]	Bone Loss	Tumors & Cancers; Genetic Influences on Target Cells	Atherosclerosis	Brain Glial Activation[b]	Dopamine Receptor, Decrease in Number (density)[b]	Amyloid Deposits in Brain (Aβ)[c]
Lab rodent	Complete mid-life loss of oocytes and fertility	M&F	M&F	+	+	+	0
Dog	?/ Fertility maintained		M&F	+	?	?	+
Rhesus monkey	Complete midlife loss of oocytes and fertility	M&F	M&F	+	+	+	+
Human	Complete midlife loss of oocytes and fertility	M&F	M&F	+	+	+	+

Notes: Certain aging changes are shared by placental mammalian species across a 30-fold range of life spans, from mouse to human. The shared subset of canonical aging changes can be found in short- and long-lived species that descended from common ancestors 70 to 100 million years ago. For detailed references, see Finch (1990), Finch (1993), and Finch and Kirkwood (2000).

[a] The mammalian ovary is generally characterized by its irreversible loss of irreplaceable oocytes from birth onward. Reproduction must cease when oocytes are depleted.

[b] Brain glia (microglia and astrocytes) show activated phenotypes during normal aging of laboratory rodents, rhesus, and humans. Although glial activation is often associated with neurodegenerative diseases, its occurrence in healthy middle-aged rodents (T.E. Morgan et al., 1999) suggests that this marker is of aging, rather than age-related disease. The attenuation of glial activation by diet restriction in aging rats (T.E. Morgan et al., 1999) indicates that local oxidative damage (a chance event) may be a factor: Food restriction decreases the load of oxidized proteins and lipids, which can activate glia.

[c] Amyloid β-peptide (Aβ) deposits in the brain are found by the mean life span in all mammals so far examined which live more than 10 years (Finch & Sapolsky, 1999; Funato et al., 1998). The amyloid deposits accumulated with "normal aging" are more diffuse than those found in Alzheimer's disease, where there is also much greater neuron death than in normal aging. Laboratory rodents do not accumulate brain Aβ amyloid deposits, unless made transgenic with human Alzheimer's mutations.

two examples from a large list of changes that have been recognized to occur during middle age, changes in reproduction and changes in brain dopamine neurotransmission. I also discuss how blood elevations of IL-6 may be a marker for the end of middle age. Chapter 4, by Susan Whitbourne, provides a broader survey of physiological changes during middle age.

Menopause occurs at a median age of about 50 years, over a range of 45–55 years (90% of women) (Gosden, 1985; Gosden & Faddy, 1998). The differences reported between samples of different countries and SES strata (1–5 years) could be confounded by malnutrition and disease which can impair regular fertility cycles, and by cultural biases on self-reported age at menopause. There is no reason to presume that the age at menopause has changed much in human history during the past 10,000 years when human populations have grown explosively and enjoyed increasing protection from predators and disease. Although menopause is the definitive time of fertility cessation, fertility declines sharply during the preceding several years, as the remaining stock of ovarian egg cells (oocytes) becomes depleted (Figure 3.3) (Gosden, 1985; vom Saal et al., 1994). The sharp decline in live births is associated with major increases of defective embryos, which are either resorbed or spontaneously aborted. Even so, the incidence of birth defects accelerates remarkably, such that nearly 10% of births by 50-year-old mothers have chromosomal abnormalities, chiefly Down syndrome (trisomy 21). Concurrently with depletion of the oocyte stock, the numbers of growing follicles, which produce estrogens, also become fewer, so that there is an overall trend for gradual diminution of blood estrogens, even before menopause.

The main basis for menopause is ultimately the exhaustion of the ovaries' stock of irreplaceable oocytes and primary follicles, which are formed in the fetus before birth. No new oocytes are added and the existing stock is lost irreversibly, with an exponential decline approximately like a radioactive decay curve (Figure 3.3A, B). More than 50% of the oocytes present at birth are lost by the time of puberty (Gosden, 1985; vom Saal et al., 1994) (Figure 3.3). During 30 years of regular cycles, a woman may ovulate up to 400 of the original 2 million potential eggs by the time of menopause. However, in preagrarian cultures with extended nursing, a women might ovulate less than 50 eggs during her lifetime. The minimum number of oocytes and follicles required to maintain regular fertility cycles is about 1,100 (Gosden & Faddy, 1998). The major decrease of sex steroids after menopause includes >90% decrease of estradiol and progesterone.

Individuals vary widely in the precise degree of estrogen deficits after menopause, because a significant amount of estrogens can be made by fat cells and because some estrogens (phytoestrogens) may be ingested through the diet. Estrogen deficits after menopause can have major influences on

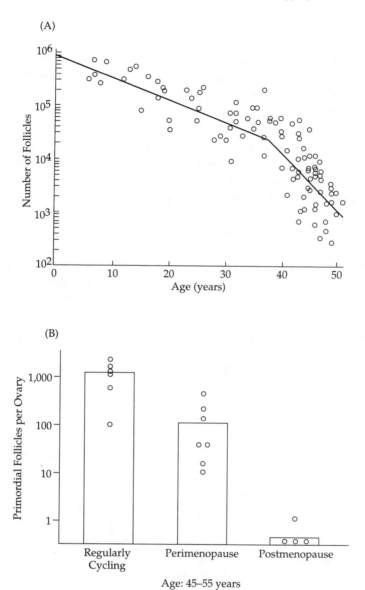

Figure 3.3   Menopause associated with the exhaustion of ovarian egg cells. The rate of ovarian aging is measured by the loss of primary follicles, each of which contains a single oocyte. (A) The probability of oocyte loss is independent of the total number remaining. These kinetics resemble the decay of radioactivity and fit a linear regression of *log (number total follicles or oocytes) versus age* in humans, representing data for neonates from Block (1952, 1953) and Richardson et al. (1988). Note the accelerating loss of oocytes by 40 years, when > 99% of oocytes are lost. From vom Saal et al. (1994). (B) Premenopausal women (45–50) years vary > 1000-fold in the numbers of remaining oocytes and follicles. Redrawn from Richardson et al. (1987).

health. In women, accelerated bone loss (osteopenia) is linked to the loss of estrogens at menopause during midlife. In turn, the thinning of bone increases the risk of osteoporotic fractures at later ages, which is associated with high risks of morbidity and mortality. Thus, one factor in the risk of bone fractures can be traced to the limited numbers of ovarian follicles that are formed before birth.

Shorter-lived mammals also show similar reproductive changes during middle age, which can be considered as one of a set of canonical changes of aging in mammals in general (Table 3.1). Reproductive changes are obvious in females from species that have been so far examined from about half of the 17 orders of placental mammals. Fixed (i.e., irreplaceable) stocks of ovarian oocytes are found in placental mammals, which last shared a common ancestor more than 50 million years ago (Finch, 1994) (Figure 3.4). Thus, menopause due to loss of oocytes and follicles appears to be an ancient phenomenon of aging in placental mammals, which would be considered as a *primitive trait* by evolutionary biologists. The absence of a definitive equivalent to menopause in some primates (Finch & Sapolsky, 1999) and birds (Nisbet et al., 1999; Ottinger, Nisbet, & Finch, 1995) could represent genetically determined species variations in rate of oocyte loss. The finite stock of ovarian oocytes gives a basis for an extensive postreproductive phase of life history in animals besides humans, to be described.

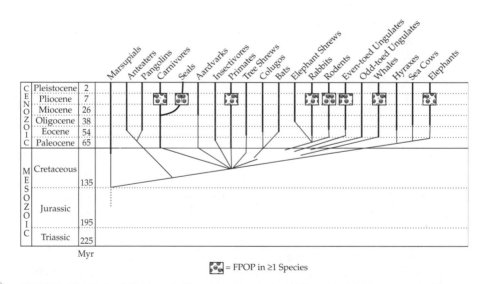

Figure 3.4   Distribution of fixed populations of primary oocytes (FPOP) in different phylogentic orders of mammals. Data are available for about 50% of the mammalian orders. The thick vertical lines approximate the depth of the fossil record. From Finch (1994).

Male mammals, in contrast to females, in general do not have marked declines in gonadal function at midlife and maintain some degree of spermatogenesis into the later years (Finch, 1990; vom Saal et al., 1994). Blood levels of testosterone tend to decline after 60 years, with wide individual differences, such that a few men retain youthful levels at later years. Testosterone is produced by the Leydig cells of the testis, which appear to decrease progressively during aging, but at a much slower rate of decline than ovarian follicles. Individual men vary widely in sexual activity during middle age (*Rossi, 1994). Contrary to some popular beliefs, there is no strong relationship between blood testosterone, libido, and sexual performance, at least above a minimum level of testosterone (e.g., Fahmy, Mitra, Blacklock, & Desai, 1999; vom Saal et al., 1994). Thus, testicular functions are not as strong determinants of activities during middle age as ovarian functions are in women. Among the causes of individual differences that are widely discussed are cultural attitudes and social opportunities, but also emotional and physical health. Risk factors for reduced sexual activity include obesity and diabetes, tobacco use, and drugs used to treat depression and hypertension. Maturity-onset diabetes (type II diabetes) in particular, is associated in men with higher risk of increased erectile impotence due to vascular damage (e.g., Metro & Broderick, 1999), whereas diabetic women have higher risk of reduced sexual responses (e.g., Watts, 1994).

The inconsistent association of libido with testosterone levels during aging in men, as noted, implies complex changes in neural systems that influence sexual activities. In fact, much data from aging male and female rodents shows slow, progressive changes in neurotransmission during aging. These changes begin soon after maturity and do not have any association with diseases as currently recognized by neuropathologists (Clark, 1994; Knoll, 1997). Age changes are found in many neural pathways which utilize monoamine neurotransmitters (dopamine, norepinephrine, serotonin). Gradual age changes in various receptors for monoamines in brain systems are found during the midlife period. For example, the density of dopamine receptors per nerve cell decreases during midlife in healthy inbred male mice (Figure 3.5A) and in healthy men and women (Figure 3.5B) (reviewed in D. G. Morgan, May, & Finch, 1987; Roth, 1997). The brain region shown here is the striatum (caudate-putamen), which modulates a wide range of brain functions, directly or indirectly, including muscle tone during voluntary movement, sexual behaviors, motivation and reward, and cognition. The striatum has major input and output pathways connecting it with the frontal cortex and the limbic system, as well as to the motor systems of the brain for which it was early recognized as part of the extrapyramidal system. Humans show about 1% per year loss of striatal (caudate) D2 receptors after the age of 18 years (Wong, Young, Wilson, Meltzer, & Giedde, 1997).

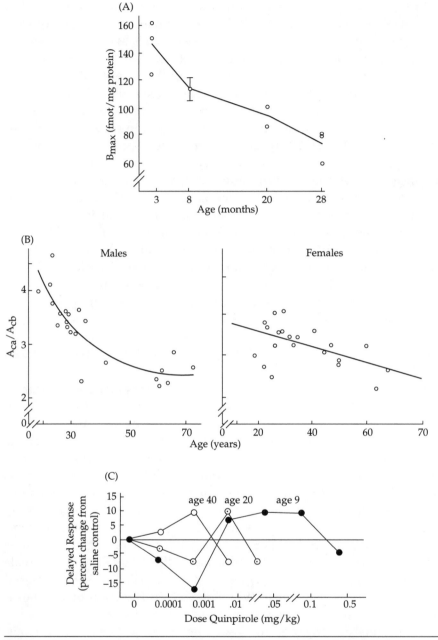

Figure 3.5 Brain dopamine receptor (D2) concentrations during normal aging. (A) Mice (C57BL/6J, male), postmortem binding data (Bmax). Redrawn from Severson and Finch (1980). (B) Humans, PET imaging. Redrawn from Wong et al. (1984). (C) Response to quinpirole, a dopamine D2 agonist, which has a biphasic dose response on delayed recall performance, a dopamine-dependent function of the prefrontal cortex. Redrawn from Arnsten et al. (1995).

Although there is no conclusive proof of the relationship between the degree of change in monoamines during aging and particular sexual functions in any species, nonetheless it is of interest that certain drugs that increase monoamine levels also enhanced sexual activity in aging rodents (e.g., deprenyl: Clark, 1994; Knoll, 1997).

Dopamine neurotransmission in the striatum has a major influence on muscle control, as illustrated by two diseases with strong trends for incidence during middle age. In Huntington's disease, caused by a rare dominant gene, abnormal jerky movements (chorea) begin typically between 20 and 50 years, and are associated with a relative excess of striatal dopamine D2 activities, due to the loss of the counterbalancing cholinergic neurons. A converse set of symptoms arise in Parkinson's disease, which is more common after 50. The muscle rigidity and tremor of Parkinson's is associated with relative deficits of striatal dopamine from loss of the nigro-striatal neurons. It is possible that the usual middle-age changes in dopamine neurotransmission contribute to age changes in reflex speed and in complex movements which are factors in the decline of athletic performance during middle age.

Monoamines are also strongly implicated in age changes of higher cognitive functions, as illustrated by an outstanding study of the delayed recall response in rhesus monkeys (Arnsten, Cai, Steere, & Goldman-Rakic, 1995). This memory function is modulated by dopamine D2 receptors in the prefrontal cortex, which interacts through defined pathways with striatum and other subcortical brain regions. In the prefrontal cortex, dopaminergic systems show marked progressive changes during aging, whereas the motor cortex and some other nearby regions are less impaired. A test of dopaminergic functions in the prefrontal cortex is the effect of a drug quinpirole that acts preferentially on dopamine D2 receptors. Quinpirole has a biphasic dose response in young adults, with low doses impairing delayed recall, but higher doses improving performance. Aging shifts the dose response curves, such that middle-aged rhesus monkeys at 20 years and old monkeys at 40 years (close to the life span) showed the memory-enhancing effects of quinpirole at progressively lower doses, but a loss of the impairment at lowest doses (Figure 3.5C). These findings suggest that dopamine deficits may contribute to some memory impairments at middle age in humans.

The mechanisms of dopamine receptor loss are not specified, but are more likely to result from neuron cell body atrophy and loss of synaptic specializations than from neuron cell death (Finch, 1993). In contrast to the general atrophic trend of neurons observed in short-lived and long-lived mammals (Finch, 1993), the glial cells in the striatum and many other brain regions become increasingly active during middle age (Table 3.1; T. E. Morgan et al., 1999). These changes are probably distinct from those associated with the amyloid β-peptide (Aβ) deposits of Alzheimer's disease, which, in cognitively normal humans are rare before the age of 70 years (Finch & Sapolsky, 1999; Funato et al., 1998).

The examples shown in Figure 3.5 can be extended to many other receptor systems that begin to show gradual changes during middle age when laboratory animals and humans are generally in excellent health. A major task ahead is to understand how these subtle changes in neurotransmission are related to individual age changes in cognitive and motor performance. Among performance trends detected during middle age are decreased speed of responses, from simple reflexes to complex processes, and increased vulnerability to disruption by conflicting stimuli that require central processing by multisynaptic circuits (The huge literature on cognitive and psychomotor aging is well covered in many handbooks and monographs).

Lastly, recent data suggest a possible blood marker for declining health that could be used as an indicator of the end of the healthy phase of middle

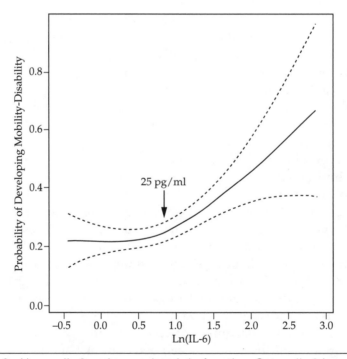

Figure 3.6 Human IL-6 and age-related dysfunction. Serum IL-6 is a predictor of frailty, a marker for the end of middle age. In the Iowa site of EPESE (the Established Populations for Epidemiologic Studies of the Elderly), a subgroup aged 71 years or older initially had no disabilities in selected activities of daily living (ADL). When interviewed 4 years later, those in the highest tertile of IL-6 had a nearly 2-fold higher risk of acquiring ADL disabilities (Ferrucci et al., 1999).

age, blood levels of interleukin-6. IL-6 is a protein made by the liver, which is a component of the "acute phase" responses during inflammation. In several community-based studies of the elderly, elevations of IL-6 are associated with an increased risk of subsequent functional loss (Figure 3.6) (Cohen et al., 1997; Ferrucci et al., 1999). The measure of functional loss is the ADL (activities of daily living scale), which include abilities for ordinary movements (sitting and standing, climbing stairs). Chronic elevations of IL-6 indicate a sustained acute phase stress response, which may arise from many causes that are harmful to health, including chronic infections and maturity onset diabetes (Pickup, Battock, Chusney, & Burt, 1997). Many chronic diseases of aging are associated with inflammatory cell activities (e.g., atherosclerosis, bone and joint conditions, and Alzheimer's disease; Finch & Longo, 2000; Finch & Marchalonis, 1996). We do not know how generally the progress of these varied conditions is reflected in blood IL-6 or other markers.

EVOLUTION OF THE HUMAN LIFE SPAN AND AGING

Middle age is clearly a highly variable phase of the life span. Moreover, during evolution, life spans can decrease or increase according to the selection pressures on reproduction. A major hypothesis on the evolution of life span and aging is that natural selection acts primarily through reproductive success, that is the efficacy of a parent to produce viable offspring. In most natural populations, the bulk of reproduction is observed to be accomplished by young adults, for the simple reason that natural hazards allow relatively few to survive to advanced ages. Typical mortality rates for even large animals like lions and elephants are in the range of 1% to 10% per year, which exceeds that of most human populations (*Austad, 1997). As a consequence, genes with adverse effects that do not emerge until later years are not selected against (Figure 3.1B). The dwindling force of natural selection gives a good explanation of why human populations have multiple genes that increase the risk of Alzheimer's disease (AD), ischemic heart disease (ISH), or other diseases that rapidly increase after middle age in most populations. The apoE gene has a common variant, apoE4, which increases the risk of *both* AD and ISH, to be described.

Population biologists describe reproductive schedules on an "r-k" continuum of life histories, in which "r"-selection enhances early onset of reproduction with larger numbers of offspring early in life (Charlesworth, 1994; Rose, 1991; Stearns, 1992, *1999). R-selection is illustrated by the Pacific salmon which breed but once and die after first spawning. K-selection represents later maturation, less intense reproduction spread over longer times and greater adult life expectancy, as illustrated by species of Atlantic salmon, which spawn at least six successive seasons (Finch, 1990). In effect, the reproductive effort can be spread out or compressed in response to natural selection.

If natural selection delays the onset of reproduction, then the evolutionary hypothesis predicts that the statistical life span will also be increased. This has been modeled in the laboratory by selecting for younger and older age of reproduction in fruit flies. Rose, Arking, and others have shown that, within 10 to 15 generations, the life spans of flies can be shortened or lengthened about 35%, with corresponding changes in the acceleration rate of mortality (Rose, 1991, *1997). The early reproducing flies produced larger numbers of eggs per clutch than the later reproducing flies. These changes are heritable and were enabled by the preexisting genetic variations in the outbred population of flies being studied. That is, the changes did not require new mutations.

A counterpart of these artificial selection experiments was described for the Virginia opossum, using populations that differed in the predators (Austad, 1993). An island population with few predators may be compared to the laboratory flies that were allowed to reproduce at later ages, whereas a mainland population with heavy predators on adults is like the young fruit flies being selected for rapid reproduction. The opossums on an island had smaller litters and lived longer with slower aging changes (collagen aging; slower acceleration of mortality), than a mainland population. Austad hypothesized that the island population was derived from the mainland, and had a lower mortality due to lower predation, as is typical of island populations.

Many human populations are showing apparently similar demographic transitions, from early and frequent reproduction in association with high mortality rates, and within one or two generations, to fewer offspring at later maternal ages, lower mortality, and longer life spans (Easterlin & Crimmins, 1985; *Gosden et al., 1999; Kinsella & Taueber, 1992). This demographic transition has a major influence on middle age, because it shifts maternal functions farther into the physiological domain of middle age, as more women become menopausal while raising their small families. It is widely assumed that, cultural, rather than genetic factors, are at work in these human transitions. Nonetheless, there could be some role of genetics. For example, the greater geographic individual mobility that is often associated with increasing economic advantage might reduce consanguineous marriages and increase outbreeding. Outbreeding is often associated with hybrid vigor and increased fecundity, which could lessen the individual drive for large numbers of offspring. Conversely, increased geographic mobility can bring increased exposure to different infectious organisms to which individuals were not genetically adapted. An approach to these complex questions might be to examine the coefficients of inbreeding in human populations that are undergoing, or have recently made the demographic transition to latter onset of reproduction and smaller families.

The hypothesis that natural selection acts mainly on the young adults who accomplish the bulk of reproduction, does not, however, preclude a role of older individuals in reproductive success. The extent of multigenerational caregiving and contributions to reproductive success is a new topic of increasing interest to evolutionary biologists and anthropologists. Multigenerational participation in child rearing is a major feature of most human societies, which involves vital roles of middle-aged or older caregivers. In some hunter-gatherers, grandmothers appear to supply as many calories to the family unit as do hunting males (Hawkes, O'Connell, Jones, Alvarez, & Charnov, 1998). However, the limited studies conducted with feral populations of animals have not shown corresponding roles of the older generation. For example, in olive baboons and lions, the presence of a grandmother did not influence infant survival (Packer et al., 1998; Sherman, 1998).

Nonetheless, there are indications of allo-parenting and other social roles for middle-aged and older individuals in diverse mammalian species. In some populations of the short-finned pilot whale, 25% of adult females may be postmenopausal (Kasuya & Marsh, 1984; discussed in *Carey & Gruenfelder, 1997; Finch, 1990, pp. 165–166). Moreover, 15% of the postreproductives were still lactating, implying that they were being suckled (lactation, once initiated, does not depend on the presence of the ovarian steroids). Kasuya and Marsh (1984) proposed that continued lactation was the result of mother-calf bonds and the particularly prolonged maternal care characteristic of pilot whales. In general, toothed whales (odontocetes), which are hunters, have complex, multigenerational social structures with extended nursing of up to 15 years, whereas baleen whales (mystecetes), which are filter feeders, have little social structure and short-duration individual relationships with early weaning at 7–11 months. There are intriguing anecdotal sightings in odontocetes that indicate allo-parenting by surrogates who are other group members (*Austad, 1997; *Carey & Gruenfelder, 1997). Further examples of postreproductive roles are discussed for Hawaiian spinner dolphins by Carey and Gruenfelder. In elephants and several other primates, older adults are active participants in their complex, multigenerational societies. With the exception of the analysis of olive baboons and lions (Packer et al., 1998) which showed no effect, none of these other examples have been analyzed for survivorship of the younger related and unrelated individuals (this is difficult to do in natural populations).

In any case, it is reasonably clear that humans are not the only mammals to survive long enough to become postreproductive with sufficiently good health to survive for extended times in their natural environments

(Austad, 1997; Carey & Gruenfelder, 1997; Finch, 1990; Finch & Sapolsky, 1999). Thus, by the present criteria, middle age as a life history stage has existed long before humans evolved, and may have appeared and disappeared according to natural selection on many occasions.

THE EVOLUTION OF APOLIPOPROTEIN E ALLELES AND MIDDLE AGE

The evolution of human multigenerational caregiving and increasing specific roles for middle-aged individuals may have been associated with the further extension of maturation and increased brain size during the past 3 million years (Finch & Sapolsky, 1999; Hawkes et al., 1998). An important genetic change that also occurred during this time was the evolution of the genetic variants of apolipoprotein E, the uniquely human apoE alleles, which, I will argue, also had an impact on the evolution of middle-age.

Human populations have three common apoE alleles of human populations (designated by geneticists as *apoE* ε2, -ε3, -ε4, which code for isoforms of the cholesterol transport protein, called for convenience apoE2, apoE3, and apoE4. ApoE4 is associated with a high risk of heart disease and Alzheimer's disease, whereas apoE2 is associated with centenarians (Beffert et al., 1998; Finch & Sapolsky, 1999; Kardia, Stengard, & Templeton, 1999; Laskowitz, Horsburgh, & Roses, 1997). The risks of these conditions in E4/E4 carriers at age 40 are about 3-fold higher than in E3/E3 carriers in most human populations. Remarkably, the great apes and other primates examined have only apoE4 (Finch & Sapolsky, 1999).

The apoE4 allele is unique among disease risk genes by its association with both familial and sporadic forms of these two major diseases. In most populations, apoE3 is the most common, followed by apoE4 and apoE2. E4 varies between extremes of >2 and <50%; northern hemisphere countries have about 80% E3 and 15% apoE4 (e.g., Mahley, 1988; Mastana, Calderon, Pena, Reddy, & Papiha, 1998; Poirier, Minnich, & Davignon, 1995). Blood cholesterol scales with the number of apoE4 alleles, which account for about 15% of blood cholesterol variance. Most other disease risk genes are associated with much smaller populations and are much rarer in the general population (e.g., early onset familial forms of heart disease and Alzheimer's disease); these early killers are caused by diverse rare and dominant genes. The term *risk factor* does not imply that all carriers, even those with two copies of an allele, will develop the disease. A small percentage of ApoE4/E4 carriers, for example, survive to 100 years in reasonable health without clinical Alzheimer's disease. These individual differences are not understood and could represent effects of yet other gene variations or of the environment, or both.

How apoE4 increases risk of *both* heart disease and Alzheimer's disease is not well understood and may reflect different biological activities of the apoE molecule in different tissues. As a blood protein, apoE is a cholesterol carrier, and the ApoE4 is associated with elevated blood cholesterol; this activity of apoE is easily understood in relation to ischemic heart disease from coronary atherosclerosis (Mahley, 1988; Poirier et al., 1995). ApoE is also found in brain cells, particularly astrocytes, where it is thought to have an important role in transporting lipids to neurons for the formation of new synapses (Arendt et al., 1997). Studies in human brains show that E4 gene carriers have less compensatory synapse formation during Alzheimer's disease. Moreover, in experiments with cultured rodent neurons, the outgrowth and sprouting of neurons was promoted when apoE3 lipoprotein was added to the cultured cells, whereas adding apoE4 lipoproteins inhibited neuron outgrowth (reviewed in Finch & Sapolsky, 1999; Poirier et al., 1995; Roses, 1997). These different effects of E3 versus E4 parallel the differences in sprouting observed in Alzheimer brains.

As noted, the evolution of apoE3 from E4 is hypothesized to have occurred first by a point mutation in the coding region of the gene. This genetic change could occur by the most common type of DNA base mutation, a single base pair transition (Mahley, 1988; Finch & Sapolsky, 1999). The less common apoE2 gene can be further derived from apoE3 by repeating this mutation at another location in the apoE gene. Finch and Sapolsky (1999) hypothesized that the establishment of the apoE3 allele in the emerging populations was favored by two activities of the apoE3 protein molecule. The first activity could enhance brain development because outgrowth and sprouting of neuron processes is promoted more by apoE3. This activity of apoE3 could have been a factor in the major enlargement of the cerebral cortex, which evolved during the past 3 million years. This major brain change is associated with an increased complexity and density of neuron processes (more neuropil), whereas the numbers of neurons is less modified, as deduced from comparisons of human and great ape cerebral cortex (Buxhoeveden, Buxhoeveden, Lefkowitz, Loats, & Armstrong, 1996). The second activity favoring the spread of E3 could have been improved health at middle age, due to reduced risk of heart disease and Alzheimer's disease, which would have favored grandparental and other intergenerational caregiving in humans carrying apoE3.

APOE AS A POSSIBLE EXAMPLE OF GENETIC INFLUENCES ON MIDDLE AGE

ApoE4 carriers at middle age have a higher incidence of modest brain and heart dysfunctions that might not qualify for clinical disease. For example, apoE4 is associated in middle age with lower scores on a test of recent memory (Figure 3.7), which is a measure of hippocampal functions. The hippocampus is a seat of declarative memory and is a major target of Alzheimer's disease. The scores on this test were also correlated with the size of the hippocampus, accounting for 16% of the variance (Figure 3.7) (Reiman et al., 1998). Similar effects of apoE4 are indicated in longitudinal studies of male twins (Figure 3.7C; WWII veterans; 27th year of follow-up), the apoE4 carriers had significant cognitive declines across ages 48–63, which was greater in a subgroups with hyperglycemia and hyper-tension (Carmelli et al., 1998; Carmelli, Swan, Reed, Schellenberg, & Christian, 1999). The remaining extensive variance in brain volume must represent other factors besides apoE alleles. The other factors are not well defined, but could include individual variations of neuron numbers that

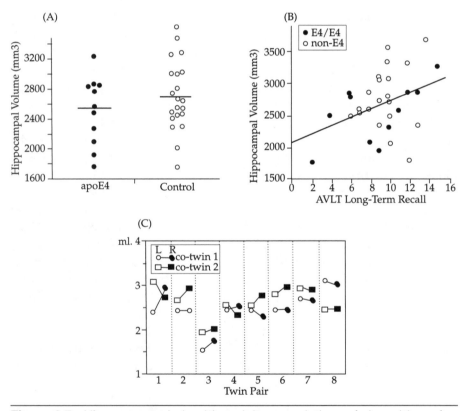

Figure 3.7 Hippocampus in healthy adults: correlations of size with perfor-mance. (A) Hippocampal volume and apoE4 allele. Redrawn from Reiman et al. (1998). (B) Hippocampal volume and memory (AVLT recall). Redrawn from Reiman et al. (1998). (C) Hippocampal volume varies between twin pairs and within (left vs. right brain). Data of Plassman et al. (1997). From Finch and Kirkwood (2000).

arise during development (Finch & Kirkwood, 2000). Ongoing studies may show if the apoE4 deficits existed before middle age, possibly as a mild developmental defect.

Heart functions at middle age also show clinically silent effects of apoE4. In two studies, exercise-induced angina pains characteristic of "silent ischemia" occurred at a two-fold higher rate in apoE4 carriers. These individuals had no symptoms of heart disease at rest (Katzel, Fleg, Paidi, Ragoobarsingh, & Goldberg, 1993; Nakata et al., 1996). The latter study found more silent ischemia in E4/E4 carriers aged 64 years mean than at 57 years, which indicates progressive atherosclerosis.

Returning to the evolutionary discussion, it is reasonable to infer that the greater average physical and mental capacity of middle-aged individuals carrying apoE3 would have also favored a greater role in multigenerational caregiving and could have allowed the emergence of human grandmothering effects in postreproductive (i.e., middle-aged caregivers). In effect, the evolution of apoE3 could have expanded the domain of middle age in human populations.

On the basis of these clinical studies, I propose evaluating the apoE genotype in relation to different psychosocial outcomes of middle age. For example, the presence of mild relative deficits in memory at middle age might discourage some individuals from pursuing further education or new social contacts. The silent ischemia associated with apoE4 would also tend to inhibit participation in physically demanding professions and recreation, including sex. It would be interesting to look for interactions between apoE4 and blood levels of sex steroids (androgens and estrogens) in both men and women to identify subgroups of reproductive activities that are presently recognized by physical health status (Edwards & Booth, 1994; McKinlay & Feldman, 1994; Schiavi, 1994).

NONGENETIC VARIATIONS IN MENOPAUSE: A ROLE OF DEVELOPMENTAL VARIATIONS IN CELL NUMBERS

Many psychosocial analyses of middle age have emphasized the extraordinary range of individual variations. I suggest that one source could arise during development, through random variations in cell numbers (this topic is treated at length in Finch & Kirkwood, 2000). A glimpse of these complex and surprising processes comes from studies of identical twins. Identical twins do not go through menopause at the same year. Typically, cotwins differ by several years and can differ up to 11 years (Snieder, MacGregor, & Spector, 1998) (Figure 3.8). Dizygous (DZ) twins of the same sex differ even more. Elsewhere I have argued that these variations in reproductive

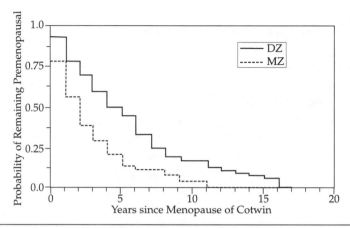

Figure 3.8 Differences between cotwins (MZ, monozygous; DZ, dizygous) in the age at menopause. Redrawn from Sneider et al. (1998).

aging are derived from variations in the initial stock of oocytes (potential egg cells) at birth (Finch 1997; Finch & Kirkwood, 2000).

While there are no data on ovaries of monozygous (MZ) cotwins, data from inbred mice shows a remarkable 3-fold range of differences between individuals in the numbers of ovarian oocytes found at birth (Jones & Krohn, 1961). Because the same variations of oocyte numbers are found in unrelated human neonates (Block, 1953) (Figure 3.9), it is plausible that these variations in humans are not entirely due to genetic variations, which would be consistent with the different ages of menopause in identical twins.

Experimental studies show in mice that surgically removing part of the ovarian tissue accelerates the onset of reproductive senescence according to predictions from the equation on the rate of oocyte loss (Nelson & Felicio, 1986). A human counterpart of this experiment may be found in Turner's syndrome, which causes gonadal dysgenesis and oocyte deficiencies with premature menopause (Finch & Kirkwood, 2000; Gosden, 1985).

How could genetically identical individual mice begin life with such huge individual numbers of oocytes? These variations are already found in the developing ovary (Tam & Snow, 1981). Moreover, the primordial germ cells that give rise to oocytes have been shown to divide a random number of times when cultured from mouse embryos (Ohkubo, Shirayoshi, & Nakatsuji, 1996). Many types of cells show a great deal of random variation in cell division potential, which can be observed when daughter cells are separately cloned (Figure 3.10). All of this plays out later in life as a nonheritable variation in the onset of the postreproductive phase that defines middle age.

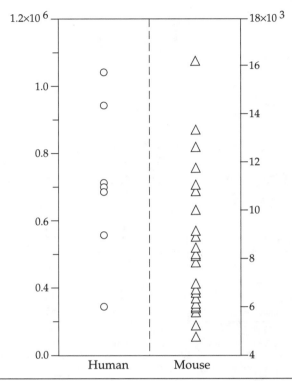

Figure 3.9 Variations in numbers of ovarian oocytes in neonates. From Finch and Kirkwood (2000). Left, human infants (Swedish, consanguinity unknown) who died at birth, mostly from asphyxia during labor. In the author's words: "The number of primordial follicles seems to vary greatly in newborn infants." Drawn from tabular data of Block (1953). Right, mouse (RIII strain); redrawn from graphed data of Jones and Krohn (1961a).

As noted, the consequences of menopause are loss of fertility with the exhaustion of the egg cells, but also loss of sex steroid production. Post-menopausal estrogen deficits are of particular importance, because they are now widely recognized as major risk factors for heart attacks and for bone fractures that may be ameliorated significantly by estrogen replacement (Beale & Collins, 1996; Nasr & Breckwoldt, 1998). Correspondingly, the mortality from heart disease in women is about 85% less than that in men, aged 35–44 years (Uemura & Pisa, 1985). Women who have premature menopause (before 43 years) have accelerated risk of bone fractures (Ohta et al., 1996). Thus, chance individual variation in the numbers of oocytes formed before birth can have major influences on the condition of health during middle age.

Moreover, as shown in Figure 3.7, even identical twins have different sizes of their hippocampus. Elsewhere, it is argued that these individual

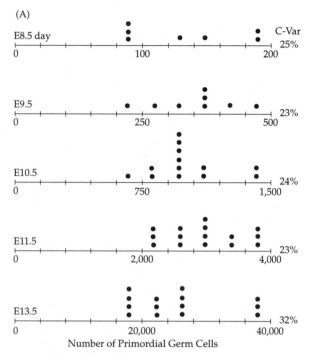

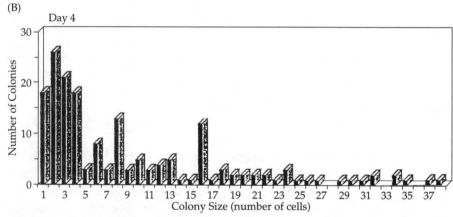

Figure 3.10   Primordial germ cell (PGC) numbers in the early mouse embryo. From Finch and Kirkwood (2000). During gestation, PGCs arise in the extraembryonic mesoderm at day 7. The PGCs migrate in columns through the wall of the hindgut (day 8.5); then within the dorsal mesentery (day 9.5), and finally to the genital ridges, where they collect at the site of the future ovary (day 10.5–11.5). (A) The distribution of PGC numbers per embryo. Redrawn from Tam and Snow (1981). (B) Clonal studies of PGC proliferation during primary culture. Single PGCs were plated and colony size (numbers of PGCs) counted during the following 5 days, which corresponds to the end of PGC proliferation and ovary formation *in vivo*. The 50-fold range of colony size shows clonal variations in proliferation and in cell death. Redrawn from Ohkubo et al. (1996).

variations represent different numbers of neurons that arise during brain development, possibly through the same types of stochastic variation in cell proliferation as found in the developing ovary (Finch & Kirkwood, 2000).

CONCLUSION

This chapter considered middle age as a phase within the wide range of individual variations in timing of internally and externally perceived events and changes across the life history. The younger bound of middle age could be taken as the age group that has just completed the last birth required for population stability. However, the multiplicity of trajectories in the life course resists a hard definition of middle age in the human life course, because of the individual variations and exceptions. The age of these bounds must shift with varying mortality rates from environmental dangers and disease patterns, which may be influenced by effects of apolipoprotein E gene variants. A higher incidence of ischemic heart disease and mild cognitive dysfunctions is associated with apoE ε4 in some middle-aged samples. Another source of variations in performance at middle age may be random variations in cell numbers in the ovary and hippocampus that arise during development. In conclusion, myriad developmental, heritable, and environmental factors are at work in determining activities during middle age.

REFERENCES

Allard, M., Lèbre, V., & Robine, J-M. (1998). *Jeanne Calment: From van Gogh's time to ours, 122 Extraordinary years.* New York: Freeman Press.

Arendt, T., Schindler, C., Bruckner, M.K., Escherich, K., Bigl, V., Zedlick, D., & Marcova, L. (1997). Plastic neuronal remodelling is impaired in patients with Alzheimer's disease carrying apolipoprotein, ε4 allele. *Journal of Neuroscience, 17,* 516–529.

Arking, R. (1998). *Biology of aging* (2nd ed.). Sunderland, MA: Sinauer.

Arnsten, A.F., Cai, J.X., Steere, J.C., Goldman-Rakic, P.S. (1995). Dopamine D2 receptor mechanisms contribute to age-related cognitive decline: The effects of quinpirole on memory and motor performance in monkeys. *Journal of Neuroscience, 15,* 3429–3439.

Ashley-Montague, M.F. (1957). *The reproductive development of the female with special reference to the period of adolescent sterility.* New York: Julian Press.

Austad, S.N. (1993). Retarded senescence in an insular population of Virginia opossums (Didelphus virginiana). *Journal of Zool, 229,* 695–708.

Austad, S.N. (1997). Postreproductive survival. In K. Wachter & C.E. Finch (Eds.), *Between Zeus and the salmon: The biodemography of longevity* (pp. 161–174). Washington, DC: National Academy Press.

Beach, T.G. (1987). The history of Alzheimer disease: Three debates. *Journal of History Medicine and Allied Sciences, 42,* 327–349.

Beale, C.M., & Collins, P. (1996). The menopause and the cardiovascular system. *Bailliere's Clinical Obst. Gynaecol, 10,* 483–513.

Beffert, U., Danik, M., Krzywkowski, P., Ramassamy, C., Berrada, F., & Poirier, J. (1998). The neurobiology of apolipoproteins and their receptors in the CNS and Alzheimer's disease. *Brain Res Brain Res Rev, 27,* 119–142.

Block, E. (1953). Quantitative morphological investigation of the follicular system in newborn female infants. *Acta Anat, 16,* 201–206.

Buxhoeveden, D., Lefkowitz, W., Loats, P., & Armstrong, E. (1996). The linear organization of cell columns in human and nonhuman anthropoid TpT cortex. *Anat. Embryol, 194,* 23–36.

Carey, J.R., & Gruenfelder, C. (1997). Population biology of the elderly. In K. Wachter & C.E. Finch (Eds.), *Between Zeus and the salmon: The biodemography of longevity* (pp. 127–60). Washington, DC: National Academy Press.

Carmelli, D., Swan, G.E., Reed, T., Miller, B., Wolf, P.A., Jarvik, G.P., & Schellenberg, G.D. (1998). Midlife cardiovascular risk factors, ApoE, and cognitive decline in elderly male twins. *Neurology, 50,* 1580–1585.

Carmelli, D., Swan, G.E., Reed, T., Schellenberg, G.D., & Christian, J.C. (1999). The effect of apolipoprotein E epsilon 4 in the relationships of smoking and drinking to cognitive function. *Neuroepidemiology, 18,* 125–133.

Charlesworth, B. (1994). *Evolution in age-structured populations* (2nd ed.). Cambridge, New York: Cambridge University Press.

Clark, J.T. (1994). Sexual function in altered physiological states: Comparison of effects of hypertension, diabetes, hyperprolactinemia, and others to normal aging in male rats. *Neuroscience Biobehaviour Review, 19,* 279–302.

Cohen, H.J., Pieper, C.F., Harris, T., Rao, K.M., & Currie, M.S. (1997). The association of plasma IL-6 levels with functional disability in community-dwelling elderly. *Journals of Gerontology: Series A, Biological Sciences and Medical Sciences, 52,* M201–M208.

Digiovanna, A.G. (2000). *Human aging: Biological perspective* (2nd ed.). New York: McGraw-Hill.

Djerassi, C. (1999). Sex in an age of mechanical reproduction. *Science, 285,* 53–54.

Easterlin, R.A., & Crimmins, E. (1985). *The fertility revolution.* Chicago: University of Chicago Press.

Edwards, J.N., & Booth, A. (1994). Sexuality, marriage, and well-being: The middle years. In A.S. Rossi (Ed.), *Sexuality across the life course* (pp. 233–260). Chicago: University of Chicago Press.

Erikson, E.H. (1984). Reflections on the last stage–and the first. *Psychoanalytic Study of the Child, 39,* 155–165.

Fahmy, A.K., Mitra, S., Blacklock, A.R., & Desai, K.M. (1999). Is the measurement of serum testosterone routinely indicated in men with erectile dysfunction? *British Journal Urology International, 84,* 482–484.

Ferrucci, L., Harris, T.B., Guralnik, J.M., Tracy, R.P., Corti, M.C., Cohen, H.J., Penninx, B., Pahor, M., Wallace, R., & Havlik, R.J. (1999). Serum IL-6 level and the development of disability in older persons. *Journal of American Geriatric Society, 47,* 639–646.

Finch, C.E. (1990). *Longevity, senescence, and the genome.* Chicago: University of Chicago Press.

Finch, C.E. (1991). Middle-age: An evolving frontier in gerontology [Editorial]. *Neurobiological Aging, 12,* 1–2.

Finch, C.E. (1993). Neuron atrophy during aging: Programmed or sporadic? *Trends in Neuroscience, 16,* 104–110.

Finch, C.E. (1994). The evolution of ovarian oocyte decline with aging and possible relationships to Down syndrome and Alzheimer disease. *Exp Gerontol, 29,* 299–304.

Finch, C.E. (1996). Biological bases for plasticity during aging of individual life histories. In D. Magnusson (Ed.), *The lifespan development of individuals: A synthesis of biological and psychosocial perspectives* (pp. 488–501). Cambridge, England: Cambridge University Press.

Finch, C.E. (1997). Comparative perspective on plasticity in human aging and life spans. In K. Wachter & C.E. Finch (Eds.), *Between Zeus and the salmon: The biodemography of longevity* (pp. 245–267). Washington, DC: National Academy Press.

Finch, C.E. (1998). Variations in senescence and longevity include the possibility of negligible senescence. *Journal Gerontol, 53A,* B235–B239.

Finch, C.E., & Kirkwood, T.B.L. (2000). *Chance, development, and aging.* Oxford, England: Oxford University Press.

Finch, C.E., & Longo, V. (2000). The gero-inflammatory manifold. In J. Rogers (Ed.), *Neuroinflammatory mechanisms in Alzheimer's disease: Basic and Clinical Research.* Basel, Switzerland: Birkhäuser Verlag.

Finch, C.E., & Marchalonis, J. (1996). An evolutionary perspective on amyloid and inflammatory features of Alzheimer disease. *Neurobiological Aging, 17,* 809–815.

Finch, C.E., & Pike, M.C. (1996). Maximum lifespan predictions from the Gompertz mortality model. *Journal of Gerontol, 51,* B183–B194.

Finch, C.E., & Ricklefs, R.E. (1991). Age structure of populations [Letter]. *Science, 254,* 799.

Finch, C.E., & Rose, M.R. (1995). Hormones and the physiological architecture of life history evolution. *Q Rev Biol, 70,* 1–52.

Finch, C.E., & Sapolsky, R.M. (in press). The reproductive schedule, ApoE, and the evolution of Alzheimer disease. *Neurobiol Aging.*

Fergusson, I.L.C., Taylor, R.W., & Watson, J.M. (1982). *Records and curiosities in obstetrics and gynecology.* London: Balliere.

Funato, H., Yoshimura, M., Kusui, K., Tamaoka, A., Ishikawa, K., Ohkoshi, N., Namekata, K., Okeda, R., & Ihara, Y. (1998). Quantitation of amyloid beta-protein (A beta) in the cortex during aging and in Alzheimer's disease. *American Journal Pathol, 152,* 1633–1640.

Gosden, R.G. (1985). *The biology of menopause: The causes and consequences of ovarian aging.* San Diego, CA: Academic Press.

Gosden, R.G., Dunbar, R.M., & Haig, D. (1999). Evolutionary interpretations of the diversity of reproductive health and disease. In S.C. Stearns (Ed.), *Evolution in health and disease* (pp. 108–120). Oxford, England: Oxford University Press.

Gosden, R.G., & Faddy, M.J. (1998). Biological bases of premature ovarian failure. *Reprod Fertil Development, 10,* 73–78.

Hassan, F.A. (1980). The growth and regulation of human population in prehistoric times. In M.N. Cohen, R.L. Malpass, & H.G. Klein (Eds.), *Biosocial mechanisms of population regulation* (pp. 305–311). New Haven, CT: Yale University Press.

Hawkes, K., O'Connell, J.F., Jones, N.G.B., Alvarez, H., & Charnov, E.L. (1998). Grandmothering, menopause, and the evolution of human life histories. *Proceedings of the National Academic of Science, USA, 95,* 1336–1339.

Hoffman, G.E., & Finch, C.E. (1986). LHRH neurons in the female C57BL/6J mouse brain during reproductive aging: No loss up to middle-age. *Neurobiology of Aging, 7,* 45–48.

Jones, E.C., & Krohn, P.L. (1961). The relationships between age, numbers of oocytes, and fertility in virgin and multiparous mice. *Journal Endocrinol, 21,* 469–496.

Kaplan, H. (1997). Evolution of the human life course. In K. Wachter & C.E. Finch (Eds.), *Between Zeus and the salmon: The biodemography of longevity* (pp. 175–211). Washington, DC: National Academy Press.

Kardia, S.L., Stengard, R., & Templeton, A. (1999). An evolutionary perspective on the genetic architecture of susceptibility to cardiovascular disease. In S.C. Stearns (Ed.), *Evolution in health and disease* (pp. 231–245). Oxford, England: Oxford University Press.

Kasuya, T., & Marsh, H. (1984). Life-history and reproductive biology of the short-finned pilot whale [Globicephala macrorhynchus] off the Pacific coast of Japan. In W.F. Perris, R.L. Brownell, & D.P. DeMastan (Eds.), *Rep International Whale Commission* [Special issue 6].

Katzel, L.I., Fleg, J.L., Paidi, M., Ragoobarsingh, N., & Goldberg, A.P. (1993). ApoE4 polymorphism increases the risk for exercise-induced silent myocardial ischemia in older men. *Arteriosclerosis Thromb, 13,* 1495–1500.

Kinsella, K., & Taueber, C.M. (1992). *An aging World II* (Reports, P25, 92–3). Washington, DC: U.S. Bureau of the Census.

Knoll, J. (1997). Sexual performance and longevity. *Experimental Gerontology, 32,* 539–552.

Lachman, M.E., & James, J.B. (Eds.). (1997). *Multiple patterns of midlife development.* Chicago: University of Chicago Press.

Lachman, M.E., & Weaver, S.L. (1998). Sociodemographic variations in the sense of control by domain: Findings from the MacArthur studies of midlife. *Psychology and Aging, 13,* 553–562.

Lancaster, J.B. (1994). Human sexuality, life histories, and evolutionary ecology. In A.S. Rossi (Ed.), *Sexuality across the life course* (pp. 39–62). Chicago: University of Chicago Press.

Laskowitz, D.T., Horsburgh, K., & Roses, A.D. (1997). Apolipoprotein E, a gene with complex biological interactions in the aging brain. *Neurobiology of Disease, 4,* 170–185.

Mahley, R.W. (1988). Apolipoprotein E: Cholesterol transport protein with expanding role in cell biology. *Science, 240,* 622–630.

Marcusson, J.O., Morgan, D.G., Winblad, B., & Finch, C.E. (1984). Serotonin-2 binding sites in human frontal cortex and hippocampus: Selective loss of S-2A sites with age. *Brain Res, 311,* 51–56.

Mastana, S.S., Calderon, R., Pena, J., Reddy, P.H., & Papiha, S.S. (1998). Anthropology of the apolipoprotein E (ApoE) gene: Low frequency of ApoE4 allele in Basques and in tribal (Baiga) populations of India. *Ann Human Biol, 25,* 137–143.

McKinlay, & Feldman, H.A. (1994). Age-related variation in sexual activity and interest in normal men: Results from the Massachusetts male aging study. In A.S. Rossi (Ed.), *Sexuality across the life course* (pp. 261–286). Chicago: University of Chicago Press.

Metro, M.J., & Broderick, G.A. (1999). Diabetes and vascular impotence: Does insulin dependence increase the relative severity? *International Journal Impotence Research, 11,* 87–89.

Morgan, D.G., May, P.C., & Finch, C.E. (1987). Dopamine and serotonin systems in human and rodent brain: Effects of age and degenerative disease. *Journal of American Geriatrics Society, 35,* 334–345.

Morgan, T.E., Xie, Z., Goldsmith, S., Yoshida, T., Lanzrein, A-S., Stone, D., Rozovsky, I., Perry, G., Smith, M.A., & Finch, C.E. (1999). The mosaic of brain glial hyperactivity during normal aging and its attenuation by food restriction. *Neuroscience, 89,* 687–699.

Mroczek, D.K., & Kolarz, C.M. (1998). The effect of age on positive and negative affect: A developmental perspective on happiness. *Pers Soc Psychol, 75,* 1333–1349.

Nakata, Y., Katsuya, T., Rakugi, H., Takami, S., Ohishi, M., Kamino, K., Higaki, J., Tabuchi, Y., Kumahara, Y., Miki, T., & Ogihara, T. (1996). Polymorphism of the apolipoprotein E and angiotensin-converting enzyme genes in Japanese subjects with silent myocardial ischemia. *Hypertension, 27,* 1205–1209.

Nasr, A., & Breckwoldt, M. (1998). Estrogen replacement therapy and cardiovascular protection: Lipid mechanisms are the tip of an iceberg [Review]. *Gynecology Endocrinology, 12,* 43–59.

Nelson, J.F., & Felicio, L.S. (1986). Radical ovarian resection advances the onset of persistent vaginal cornification, but only transiently disrupts hypothalamic-pituitary regulation of cyclicity in C57BL/6J mice. *Biol Reprod, 35,* 957–964.

Nisbet, I.C., Finch, C.E., Thompson, N., Russek-Cohen, E., Proudman, J.A., & Ottinger, M.A. (1999). Endocrine patterns during aging in the common tern (Sterna hirundo). *General Comparative Endocrinology, 114,* 279–286.

Ohkubo, Y., Shirayoshi, Y., & Nakatsuji, N. (1996). Autonomous regulation of proliferation and growth arrest in mouse primordial germ cells studied by mixed and clonal cultures. *Experimental Cell Research, 222,* 291–297.

Ohta, H., Sugimoto, I., Masuda, A., Komukai, S., Suda, Y., Makita, K., Takamatsu, K., Horiguchi, F., & Nozawa, S. (1996). Decreased bone mineral density associated with early menopause progresses for at least ten years:

Cross-sectional comparisons between early and normal menopausal women. *Bone, 18,* 227–231.

Ottinger, M.A., Nisbet, I.C., & Finch, C.E. (1995). Aging and reproduction: Comparative endocrinology of the common tern and Japanese quail. *American Zoologist, 35,* 299–305.

Packer, C., Tatar, M., & Collins, A. (1998). Reproductive cessation in female mammals. *Nature, 392,* 807–811.

Paolisso, G., Rizzo, M.R., Mazziotti, G., Tagliamonte, M.R., Gambardella, A., Rotondi, M., Carella, C., Giugliano, D., Varricchio, M., & D'Onofrio, F. (1998). Advancing age and insulin resistance: Role of plasma tumor necrosis factor-α. *American Journal Physiol, 275,* E294–E299.

Pickup, J.C., Battock, M.B., Chusney, G.D., & Burt, D. (1997). NIDDM as a disease of the innate immune system: Association of acute-phase reactants and interleukin-6 with metabolic syndrome X. *Diabetologia, 40,* 1286–1292.

Plassman, B.L., Welsh-Bohmer, K.A., Bigler, E.D., Johnson, S.C., Anderson, C.V., Helms, M.J., Saunders, A.M., & Breitner, J.C. (1997). Apolipoprotein E epsilon 4 allele and hippocampal volume in twins with normal cognition. *Neurology, 48,* 985–989.

Poirier, J., Minnich, A, & Davignon, J. (1995). Apolipoprotein E: Synaptic plasticity and Alzheimer's disease. *Annals of Medicine, 27,* 663–670.

Reiman, E.M., Uecker, A., Caselli, R.J., Lewis, S., Bandy, D., de Leon, M.J., De Santi, S., Convit, A., Osborne, D., Weaver, A., & Thibodeau, S.N. (1998). Hippocampal volumes in cognitively normal persons at genetic risk for Alzheimer's disease. *Annals of Neurology, 44,* 288–291.

Ritchie, K. (1995). Mental status examination of an exceptional case of longevity: J.C. aged 118 years. *British Journal of Psychiatry, 166,* 229–235.

Ritchie, K. (1998). Establishing the limits of normal cerebral aging and senile dementias. *British Journal of Psychiatry, 173,* 97–101.

Rose, M.R. (1991). *The evolutionary biology of aging.* New York: Oxford University Press.

Rose, M.R. (1997). Toward an evolutionary demography. In K. Wachter & C.E. Finch (Eds.), *Between Zeus and the salmon: The biodemography of longevity* (pp. 96–107). Washington, DC: National Academy Press.

Roses, A.D. (1997). Apolipoprotein E, a gene with complex biological interactions in the aging brain. *Neurobiology Disease, 4,* 170–185.

Roses, A.D., & Saunders, A.M. (1997). ApoE, Alzheimer's disease, and recovery from brain stress. *Annals of the New York Academy of Sciences, 826,* 200–212.

Rossi, A.S. (Ed.). (1994). *Sexuality across the life course.* Chicago: University of Chicago Press.

Roth, G.S. (1997). Age changes in signal transduction and gene expression. *Mechanisms of Ageing Development, 98,* 231–238.

Ryff, C.D., & Seltzer, M. (Eds.). (1996). *The parental experience in midlife.* Chicago: University of Chicago Press.

Schiavi, R.C. (1994). Effect of chronic disease and medication on sexual functioning. In A.S. Rossi (Ed.), *Sexuality across the life course* (pp. 313–340). Chicago: University of Chicago Press.

Severson, J.A., & Finch, C.E. (1980). Reduced dopaminergic binding during aging in the rodent striatum. *Brain Research, 192,* 147–162.

Severson, J.A., Marcusson, J., Winbald, B., & Finch, C.E. (1982). Age-correlated loss of dopaminergic binding sites in human basal ganglia. *Journal of Neurochem, 39,* 1623–1631.

Seymour, F.I., Duffy, C., & Koerner, A. (1935). A case of authenticated fertility in a man of 94. *Journal of the American Medical Association, 105,* 1423–1424.

Sherman, P.W. (1998). The evolution of menopause. *Nature, 392,* 759–761.

Shweder, R.A. (1998). *Welcome to middle age (and other cultural myths).* Chicago: University of Chicago Press.

Siegler, I.C. (1997). Promoting health and minimizing stress in midlife. In M.E. Lachman & J.B. James (Eds.), *Multiple patterns of midlife development* (pp. 243–255). Chicago: University of Chicago Press.

Snieder, H., MacGregor, A.J., & Spector, T.D. (1998). Genes control the cessation of a woman's reproductive life: A twin study of hysterectomy and age at menopause. *Journal of Clinical Endocrinol Metabolism, 83,* 1875–1880.

Stearns, S.C. (1992). *The evolution of life histories.* New York: Oxford University Press.

Stearns, S.C. (1999). Introducing evolutionary thinking. In E.C. Stearns (Ed.), *Evolution in health and disease* (pp. 3–15). New York: Oxford University Press.

Tam, P.P.L., & Snow, M.H.L. (1981). Proliferation and migration of primordial germ cells during compensatory growth in mouse embryos. *Journal of Embryology Experimental Morphology, 64,* 133–147.

Thomas, S.P. (1997). Psychosocial correlates of women's self-rated physical health in middle adulthood. In M.E. Lachman & J.B. James (Eds.), *Multiple patterns of midlife development* (pp. 257–291). Chicago: University of Chicago Press.

Uemura, K., & Pisa, Z. (1985). Recent trends in cardiovascular mortality in industrialised countries. *World Health Stat. Quarterly, 38,* 142–162.

Vaupel, J.W. (1997). Trajectories of mortality at advanced ages. In K. Wachter & C.E. Finch (Eds.), *Between Zeus and the salmon: The biodemography of longevity* (pp. 17–37). Washington, DC: National Academy Press.

Vaupel, J.W., Carey, J.R., Christensen, K., Johnson, T.E., Yashin, A.I., Holm, N.V., Iachine, I.A., Kannisto, V., Khazaeli, A.A., Liedo, P., Longo, V.D., Zeng, Y., Manton, K.G., & Curtsinger, J.W. (1998). Biodemographic trajectories of longevity. *Science, 280,* 855–860.

vom Saal, F.S., Finch, C.E., & Nelson, J.F. (1994). The natural history of reproductive aging in humans, laboratory rodents, and selected other vertebrates. In E. Knobil (Ed.), *Physiology of reproduction* (2nd ed., Vol. 2, pp. 1213–1314). New York: Raven Press.

Wachter, K., & Finch, C.E. (1997). *Biodemography of aging.* Washington, DC: National Academy of Sciences.

Watts, R.J. (1994). Sexual function of diabetic and nondiabetic African American women: A pilot study. *Journal of National Black Nurses Association, 7,* 50–59.

Wong, D.F., Wagner, H.N., Jr., Dannals, R.F., Links, J.M., Frost, J.J., Ravert, H.T., Wilson, A.A., Rosenbaum, A.E., Gjedde, A., Douglass, K.H., Petronis, J.D.,

Folstein, M.F., Touhg, J.K.T., Burns, H.D., & Kuhar, M.J. (1984). Effects of age on dopamine and serotonin receptors measured by positron tomography in the living human brain. *Science, 226,* 1393–1396.

Wong, D.F., Young, D., Wilson, P.D., Meltzer, C.C., & Gjedde, A. (1997). Quantification of neuroreceptors in the living human brain: III. D2-like dopamine receptors: Theory, validation, and changes during normal aging. *Journal of Cereb Blood Flow Metab, 17,* 316–330.

World Health Organization. (1988). *World Health Statistics Annual.* Geneva, Switzerland: Author.

CHAPTER 4

The Physical Aging Process in Midlife: Interactions with Psychological and Sociocultural Factors

SUSAN KRAUSS WHITBOURNE

THE PHYSICAL AGING PROCESS technically begins when an individual is conceived, as the passage of time is associated with changes in each cell of the body. However, for practical purposes, aging is not considered a relevant phenomenon in an individual's life until some point in adulthood. The onset of aging in adulthood does not occur at one specific point, however. Age-related changes in the body accumulate gradually and at different rates in the various bodily systems. Furthermore, although aging is essentially a biological process, the rate and timing of age-related changes interact in significant ways with psychological and sociocultural factors. There are several underlying assumptions on which this chapter is based. The first is that, as already stated, aging in middle adulthood and beyond is essentially but not entirely a biological process. Psychologists have tended to ignore the role of physical aging when discussing changes in personality and social functioning throughout adulthood. However, it is crucial to be aware of the normal age-related changes that adults can and do experience. The goal of this chapter is to provide such an orientation.

The second assumption of this chapter is that some physical changes are not inevitable. Individuals play an active role in affecting the rate of aging throughout adulthood. Although it may be an exaggeration to state that adults can "control" the rate of their own aging, adults can either accelerate or decelerate the effects of aging on their bodies in many ways. The extent to which adults engage in these processes is theorized to be a function, in part, of the individual's use of the processes of identity assimilation and accommodation (Whitbourne & Collins, 1998). According to identity process theory (Whitbourne, 1996), identity assimilation is the process adults use to maintain a consistent sense of the self over time. Through identity assimilation, changes with regard to aging are interpreted in terms of the individual's existing identity. When these changes can no longer be assimilated, the individual's identity accommodates to incorporate the new information about the self. Optimal physical aging occurs when individuals achieve a balance by maintaining their positive view of the self over time while adapting their behaviors to compensate for or prevent age-related losses. For the most part, optimization of the aging process occurs in individuals who adopt a "use it or lose it" approach by maintaining a certain level of physical activity. At the same time, individuals who age optimally recognize the need to avoid the "bad habits" that can accelerate the aging process.

The third assumption of this chapter is that aging is a multidimensional and multidirectional process. The interaction of physical, psychological, and social factors must at all points be examined and considered. Although it is tempting to regard all age-related changes in adulthood as involving loss or decline, social and cultural definitions of aging affect the way that these changes are interpreted. What is seen as a loss in some cultures is seen as a gain by people in other cultures.

Images of aging in Western society are in fact more negative than positive, and this presents a challenge both to psychologists and to individuals who are attempting to adapt to the aging process in adulthood. For middle-aged adults in particular, the challenges to identity presented by the recognition of the physical aging process make it more difficult to engage in optimal levels of preventive or compensatory activity. Although by later in adulthood, many individuals manage to avoid becoming depressed by or preoccupied with their own aging, the challenge for middle-aged adults is to incorporate these changes into their identities without being overwhelmed or demoralized.

The impact of attitudes toward aging on the adaptation of individuals to the aging process represents one way in which sociocultural factors play a role in the physical aging process. Sociocultural factors also play a direct role in affecting the opportunities available to individuals to take advantage of the strategies known to affect the rate of aging. Education and income in particular affect the extent to which individuals can learn about ways to maximize their physical functioning as well as the extent to which they can take advantage of such measures. In many cases, the effects of education and income are related to race and the differential opportunities available through the social structure to people of different races. Gender is another major sociocultural factor that affects both the opportunities that people have for engaging in age-regulatory behaviors as well as the way in which age-related changes are interpreted by the individual and others.

In this chapter, the emphasis is on explaining the most important biological changes associated with aging in the middle adult years and beyond. Due to the fact that gerontological research focuses on aging in many areas covered in this chapter, findings specific to the middle years (40–65) are not necessarily available. Researchers are increasingly including samples within this age group, or continuous samples from ages 20 or 25 and older in studies on adult age differences. In certain areas, however, it will be difficult to give specific information on the middle years. Preventive and compensatory measures will be presented where the data permit such implications to be drawn, with a focus on the activities that middle-aged and older adults can engage in to maximize their functioning in a given area. Finally, social and cultural factors will be considered where available including gender, education, income, and race (see Whitbourne, 2001, for further discussion of age-related changes in later adulthood).

THEORETICAL PERSPECTIVES

The ultimate limit to the life span is determined by biological processes, which set the pace and direction of the aging process. Biological theories attempt to explain the underlying logic to these processes. However, even those gerontologists working within the biological perspective recognize that these theories will never entirely account for the aging process as it unfolds in humans and that interactions with experiential and environmental factors must also be considered.

BIOLOGICAL THEORIES

Biological theories of aging fall into two categories: programmed aging and random error (Hayflick, 1994). Programmed aging theories are based on the assumption that aging is a genetically determined process. One argument that has long been used in support of this approach is that species vary in life span, suggesting that life span is part of our genetic makeup. For example, the life span of a butterfly is 12 weeks and the life span of a giant tortoise is 180 years (humans are in between those points with a life span of 120 years). More recently, biologists have been able to manipulate genetically the longevity of fruit flies; other researchers have identified single genes that regulate life span in laboratory worms (Jazwinski, 1996). In humans, there is evidence from large population studies in Sweden that longevity has a heritability index of .26 in men and .23 in women (Herskind, McGue, Holm, et al., 1996; Herskind, McGue, Iachine, et al., 1996).

The telomere theory proposes that defects develop in gene expression within cells that cause them to lose their ability to reproduce. As more and more cells lose the ability to reproduce (a process called replicative senescence), and become dysfunctional, organs and systems become compromised in their ability to carry out their required activities (Hayflick & Moorhead, 1961). A telomere is made up of DNA, but unlike the rest of the chromosome, which contains genes, there is no genetic information on the telomere itself. Instead, telomeres serve a protective function, keeping the ends of chromosomes from being degraded and fusing with other chromosome ends. The telomere theory of aging is based on the fact that every time a cell replicates, it loses a sequence of the DNA on the telomeres. The older the cell (the more times it has divided), the shorter the length of the telomeres. According to the theory, cells stop dividing when the short telomere length is sensed as damage to the DNA.

The random error theories propose that aging changes are the result of deleterious processes that become more frequent in later life but do not reflect the unfolding of a genetic program. The "wear and tear" theory served as a popular metaphor of aging at one time, but fell into disfavor because it was regarded as overly simplistic. More sophisticated variants of the theory have recently emerged, proposing that fatal damage to the body's cells occurs through destruction and abnormalities of DNA in the mitochrondria (Yang, Lee, & Wei, 1995). The main problem with the theory, and even the mitochondrial version of the theory, is that it is not known whether such damage is the cause or the result of aging.

The waste product accumulation theory suffers a similar problem in that the processes it describes may be a cause or an effect of aging. According to this theory, waste products build up in the body's cells and interfere with their functioning. Lipofuscin, a mixture of lipoproteins and waste products, is one of these substances. A yellowish-brown pigment that accumulates in neurons and in the muscle cells of the heart, lipofuscin is also found in aging skin cells (von Zglinicki, Nilsson, Docke, & Brunk, 1995). Although the process described by this theory is correct, and lipofuscin does show up in large amounts throughout these cells, there is no evidence that this material actually does any damage.

The cross-linking theory proposes that collagen, a ladder-shaped molecule that makes up about one-third of all bodily proteins, undergoes abnormal alterations that cause widespread changes throughout the body.

Starting at some point in middle adulthood, the rungs of one ladder start to connect to the rungs of another ladder, forming cross-links. These changes, when they occur within the skin, cause it to become increasingly rigid and to shrink in size. It is also proposed that cross-links form within the DNA, leading to deleterious changes in the genes. In evaluating this theory, it seems likely that the process it describes may have importance in affecting structures that contain cross-linked molecules, but it is unlikely that the process is a primary cause of aging.

The free radical theory, also known as the oxidative stress theory (Sohal & Weindruch, 1996), proposes that changes occur within cells as the result of the production of free radicals, highly reactive elements formed by certain molecules in the presence of oxygen. Free radicals bind to other molecules, causing them to lose their functioning. Some of the havoc that can be wreaked by free radicals includes the formation of age pigments and cross-links described earlier, as well as possible damage to the nervous system. There is some experimental support for the free radical theory. Some of this comes from research involving antioxidants, which are chemicals that prevent the formation of free radicals. A well-known antioxidant that is being widely advertised as an antiaging substance is vitamin E; another antioxidant vitamin that is receiving increasing attention is vitamin C. Free radicals can also be destroyed by superoxide dismutase (SOD), which is being sold as an anti-aging drug. Unfortunately, for those who believe that consuming large amounts of SOD can slow the aging process, it breaks down when ingested and does nothing to combat the formation of free radicals in the body (Hayflick, 1994). Nevertheless, there is evidence that longer-living species have higher levels of SOD, and it has also been shown that feeding antioxidants such as those used in food preservatives can extend the lives of laboratory animals.

One implication of the free radical theory relates to caloric restriction, in which individuals reduce their daily caloric intake. Caloric restriction has been shown in experimental animals to extend the life span. Proponents of the free radical theory propose that the effects of caloric restriction may be attributed to a reduction in the process of free radical formation. It is thought that this evidence, along with support from other lines of experimental research, will ultimately support the proposition that aging is the result of oxidative stress (Sohal & Weindruch, 1996).

Having reviewed the biological theories, it is apparent that no one approach has emerged as the ultimate explanation of the changes in physical functioning that accrue in the middle years. Furthermore, the role of psychological and sociocultural factors is recognized even within the biological perspective. Although biology may set much of the groundwork for physical aging processes, these processes occur within the context of the total individual whose actions influence the experiences that affect biological processes. The individual is also part of a larger social milieu that further influences the outcome of biological changes within the body's cells.

INTERACTIONIST MODELS

According to interactionist perspectives of aging and development, genetics and environments interact in complex ways throughout the life span. Interactions, or "transactions" (Lerner, 1995) in the immediate environment, as these occur over time, are regarded as having the greatest impact on the individual's life (Bronfenbrenner, 1995). Another important aspect of this model is the proposition that there are multiple paths in development, so that it is not possible to describe development according to a series of linear stages. Finally, the model is based on the assumption that there is "plasticity" in development, meaning that the course of development may be altered depending on the specific interactions taken by the individual in relation to the environment.

Applying the interactionist perspective to the aging process, the individual's activities are seen as affecting and being affected by genetically or biologically controlled changes in the body. The result is large individual differences in the nature and timing of age-related changes in physical and cognitive functioning. Take as an example aerobic exercise, which is an instance of an individual's direct interaction within the environment. Individuals who participate in aerobic exercise throughout the middle and later years of life are taking actions that are virtually guaranteed to delay if not offset the normal effects of aging on the cardiovascular system. The path of development for these individuals will be different from the path of the development in later life of sedentary people. This illustrates the concepts of multidimensionality (cardiovascular functioning will be affected but probably not the graying of the hair), multidirectionality (cardiovascular functioning may remain stable or even improve), and plasticity (by engaging in exercise the individual is altering the rate of the aging process). There is still an underlying biological process in existence, because aging normally takes its toll on this system, but the individual's actions in the immediate environment are altering this process.

As we explore the processes of development in middle adulthood throughout this chapter, the usefulness of the concepts of multidimensionality, multidirectionality, and plasticity will become apparent. Along with the notion of multidimensionality goes the idea that development can proceed in multiple dimensions across life. The concept of plasticity fits very well with the notion of compensation and modifiability of the aging process through actions taken by the individual. The interactionist model, then, provides an excellent basis for viewing the processes of development in the middle years.

APPEARANCE AND MOBILITY

With this background of biological theories, changes in individual systems will now be examined. In terms of personal identity, age changes in appearance and mobility are an important place to start in this review of physical changes in the middle years. These are the first changes that many adults notice, and because the outside appearance of the individual is used by others as a social cue to age, people in this society are sensitive to even small age-related changes. Changes in bodily systems that contribute to appearance may also have more significance in terms of general health and susceptibility to illness. Increases in body fat in the middle years are a prime example of such outward changes that have ramifications for health and disease. Alterations in the structures that contribute to mobility may also lead to more general problems for the individual, such as the weakening of bones that may contribute to a heightened risk of falling or development of postural changes. Although these are external changes, their implications may carry more importance for the adult's overall level of health and functioning.

The effect of social context on the individual's aging during the years of middle adulthood is particularly salient in the discussion of appearance. Individuals in Western society face social rejection and discrimination when their appearance starts to change in middle age. In a society where age rather than youth is considered beautiful, people would aspire to looking older than their years. They would not consider dyeing their hair, unless it were to bleach it pure white and they would try to accentuate rather than cover up the bags and sags that develop around their face. In Western society, people (especially women) find the aging of appearance represents a significant threat to their positive feelings about themselves as well as potentially their opportunities for employment. In this respect, then, sociocultural influences interact with identity and with biological changes taking place within the individual under the control of genetic factors.

APPEARANCE

Skin

The wrinkling and sagging of the skin take on significance early in adulthood, although they are hardly evident to most people until the 40s. Throughout the middle years of adulthood, as skin wrinkles increase in number and depth, the skin starts to lose its firmness and elasticity, leading to sagging areas such as the infamous "double chin." Other changes in the skin involve the development of discolored areas, called *lentigo senilus*. These areas of brown pigmentation (on fair-skinned people) are more likely to develop in the exposed areas of skin, on the face, hands, and arms.

Visual changes in the skin occur in part because with increasing age, the cells of the epidermis take on an irregular arrangement (Kligman, Grove, & Balin, 1985). The majority of changes occur in the dermal layer of the skin. Collagen molecules undergo the deleterious changes involved in cross-linking that make them more rigid. At the same time, elastin fibers become more brittle. The result of the changes in collagen and elastin is a loss of the skin's flexibility and ability to conform to the changing shape of the skin as the limbs move. The skin is more likely to sag because it cannot return to its original state of tension after it has been stretched out through movement.

Two other components of the skin's dermal layer show age-related changes that ultimately affect function and appearance. The sweat glands become less active, diminishing the ability to tolerate heat. The sebaceous glands, which normally secrete oils, also become less active. Consequently, the skin surface becomes drier and more vulnerable to damage from being rubbed or chafed.

Changes also occur with increasing age in adulthood in the layer of subcutaneous fat, which becomes thinner. Subcutaneous fat gives the skin its opacity and smoothes the curves of the arms, legs, and face. When it begins to thin in middle adulthood, the skin is more likely to sag and become more translucent. The fat does not disappear, though, but shifts as it begins to collect as fatty deposits around the torso.

Other changes in the coloring of the skin occur due to the development of pigmented outgrowths and angiomas, which are elevations of small blood vessels on the skin surface. Capillaries and arteries in the skin become dilated and in general are more visible due to the loss of subcutaneous fat. Large irregularities in the blood vessels known as varicose veins may develop and appear on the skin of the legs. The nails also start to show signs of aging in middle adulthood. Their growth rate slows and they become yellowish in color.

Facial appearance is affected by changes that start to accumulate in middle adulthood in the teeth, which discolor due to loss of their enamel surface and staining from coffee, tea, food, and tobacco. Current generations of middle-aged adults may suffer less from problems related to tooth loss compared to older cohorts, due to improvements in dental hygiene in the past several decades, particularly flossing. In middle adulthood, changes in the eyes also begin to affect the face's appearance. Many middle-aged adults must wear eyeglasses for reading, if not distance; in addition, the areas around the eyes become "baggy," due to accumulation of fat, fluid, and dark pigmentation.

Many of the changes in the skin are due to photoaging, age changes caused by exposure to the sun's harmful radiation. Parts of the body that are more exposed to the sun, such as the face and arms, are more likely to show the microscopic changes described here than are parts of the body that are not exposed (Takema, Yorimoto, Ohsu, Osanai, & Kawai, 1997). Sunscreen that effectively blocks the rays of the sun (at least level 15 SPF) is the most effective prevention (Farmer & Naylor, 1996). Cigarette smoking is also harmful to the skin. In addition to these preventive measures, adults can compensate for age-related changes in the skin in the years of middle adulthood. Facial massages (Iida & Noro, 1995), skin emollients, and the application of vitamin E can help offset some age-related changes (Nachbar & Korting, 1995).

Hair

Changes in the color of the hair are a universal age-related process beginning in the middle adult years and sometimes earlier. Hair color changes are not caused by the "accumulation" of gray, but by the loss of pigmentation in the hairs that remain on the head as melanin production ceases. The actual shade of gray that develops is the result of the mixture of the white (unpigmented) hairs with the remaining pigmented hairs. Eventually, for most people, all the hairs are unpigmented and the overall hair color is white. Less universal, but also frequent in occurrence is a thinning of the hair on the head. The thinning of the hair, although more obvious in men, actually occurs in both sexes. Hair loss in general results from the destruction of the germination centers that produce the hair. In the form of hair loss that is specific to males and is genetically determined, called male pattern baldness, the hair follicles continue to produce hair, but it is not visible. Although hair stops growing or becomes less visible where it is desired, it may appear in larger amounts in places where it is not welcome, such as the chin on women, the ears, and in thicker clumps around the eyebrows.

Age changes in the hair are, according to current knowledge, not preventable. For men, hair loss can have a negative effect on identity, as men are judged less attractive when they are bald unless they are highly attractive in other ways (Muscarella & Cunningham, 1996). Furthermore, the hair dyes "just for men" may have opposite effects than are intended, because people tend to look more negatively on men who use these cosmetics (Harris, 1994).

Body Build

Beginning in middle adulthood, individuals show a pronounced loss of standing height. The decline, which continues well into the 70s and 80s, is consistently demonstrated both in cross-sectional and longitudinal studies and occurs to a greater degree in women (de Groot, Perdigao, & Deurenberg, 1996; Suominen, 1997). Changes in height occur due to loss of bone material in the vertebrae, which collapse and thereby shorten the length of the spine.

There are also consistent patterns of weight changes over the years of adulthood starting as early as the 20s. Total body weight increases from early adulthood until the mid-50s, and then declines after that. Most of the weight gain that occurs through the years of middle adulthood is due to an accumulation of body fat in the torso. Weight loss that occurs after the 50s is due to loss of lean body mass; that is, muscle and bone (Baumgartner, Heymsfield, & Roche, 1995).

The accumulation of body fat is quite possibly one of the most dreaded outcomes of the aging process, becoming a source of preoccupation for adults by the 40s (Whitbourne & Collins, 1998). However, in this area there are significant preventive and compensatory measures that individuals can take to offset the aging of body build. Involvement in aerobic exercise leads to improved muscle tone and reductions in fat. Resistance training can help to offset age losses in bone content that contribute to the loss of height. Some of the most dramatic evidence for the effects of exercise on body composition comes from studies of elite athletes (Horber, Kohler, Lippuner, & Jaeger, 1996; Pollock et al., 1997). However, even the average middle-aged and older adult can see positive results within 2 to 3 months by engaging in vigorous walking, jogging, or cycling for 30 to 60 minutes a day, for 3 to 4 days a week (Vitiello et al., 1997).

MOBILITY

The structures that support movement are the bones, joints, tendons, and ligaments that connect the muscles to the bones, and the muscles that control flexion and extension. In the average person, these structures all undergo age-related changes that compromise their ability to function effectively. Beginning in the 40s, or earlier in the case of injury, each component of mobility undergoes significant age-related losses. Consequently, there is a gradual reduction of the speed of walking (Bohannon, 1997) and the development of joint pain leading to restriction of movement in daily activities (Grimby & Wiklund, 1994).

Muscles

The adult years are characterized by a progressive loss of muscle mass, a process known as sarcopenia. The number and size of muscle fibers is reduced, especially the fast-twitch fibers responsible for muscle strength (Hakkinen et al., 1996). As muscle mass decreases, it is replaced at first by connective tissue and then ultimately by fat. Accompanying sarcopenia is a loss of strength beginning in the 40s to 50s, with a decline thereafter of 12% to 15% per decade (Hurley, 1995). By contrast, isometric strength is generally maintained (Bemben, Massey, Bemben, Misner, & Boileau, 1996). These findings are consistent with the known patterns of atrophy of the fast-twitch and slow-twitch fibers. However, researchers in the area seem to agree that there is not a direct one-to-one connection between loss of muscle mass and reductions in strength (Jubrias, Odderson, Esselman, & Conley, 1997; Meltzer, 1996). There may be additional effects of changes in central nervous system function that disrupt the signals to contract received by the muscle cells (Hakkinen et al., 1996). Another factor contributing to muscle strength loss is a reduction in sensitivity in the sensory receptors in the skin of the hand (Kinoshita & Francis, 1996).

Strength training is the chief method for preventing and compensating for sarcopenia (McCartney, Hicks, Martin, & Webber, 1995, 1996). Using either progressive or high-intensity resistance training, adults can more than double their maximum muscle strength. Effective training typically involves 8 to 12 weeks, 3 to 4 times per week at 70% to 90% of the one repetition maximum. Even if an individual takes a break from an exercise program, the lost strength can quickly be regained once exercise is resumed (Taaffe & Marcus, 1997).

Bones

Bone consists of living tissue that is constantly reconstructing itself through a process of bone remodeling in which old cells are destroyed and replaced by new cells. The remodeling process is partly controlled by hormones and partly controlled by the amount of mechanical pressure placed on the bone. The greater the amount of stress placed on the bone, the more the growth of new bone cells is stimulated. The general pattern of bone development in adulthood involves an increase in the rate of bone destruction compared to renewal and greater porosity of the calcium matrix leading to loss of bone mineral content.

Estimates of the decrease in bone mineral content over adulthood are 5% to 12% per decade from the 20s through the 90s (McCalden, McGeough,

Barker, & Court-Brown, 1993) with an accompanying decrease in strength of 8.5% per decade (McCalden, McGeough, & Court-Brown, 1997). Adding to this process, microcracks develop in response to stress placed on the bones that further contribute to the likelihood of fracture (Courtney, Hayes, & Gibson, 1996). Part of the increased susceptibility to fracture of older bone can be accounted for by a loss of elasticity, meaning that it breaks rather than bends when pressure is put on it (Zioupos & Currey, 1998).

Variations exist in the rate of bone loss according to other physical factors. First of all, the rate of bone loss is greater in women, particularly those who are past reproductive age and are no longer producing the hormone estrogen in monthly cycles (Garnero, Sornay Rendu, Chapuy, & Delmas, 1996). Heavier people in general have higher bone mineral content, and so they lose less in adulthood, particularly in the weight-bearing limbs involved in mobility (Edelstein & Barrett-Connor, 1993). Genetic factors are estimated to account for about half the variability in peak bone mineral content in adulthood (Dargent & Breart, 1993). Among women, Black women have higher bone mineral content than Whites (Perry et al., 1996); and among Whites, bone loss is greater in those with fair skin (H. May, Murphy, & Khaw, 1995). Still, bone loss is generally higher in women of all races studied (Krall et al., 1997), including Whites, Blacks (Perry et al., 1996), and Chinese (Xu, Huang, & Ren, 1997). Hispanic women show similar patterns of bone loss as non-Hispanic Whites even though the risk of hip fracture among Hispanic women is lower (Villa, Marcus, Ramirez Delay, & Kelsey, 1995).

Although bone loss is not a significant problem until at least the 50s or 60s, actions taken prior to this age can have important preventive consequences. These actions are particularly important for women. Smoking, alcohol use, and poor diet exacerbate bone loss in later adulthood while bone loss can be slowed by aerobic activity, resistance training with weights, increased calcium intake prior to menopause, and use of Vitamin D (Dawson-Hughes et al., 1995; S. Murphy, Khaw, May, & Compston, 1994; Sinaki, 1996; Welten, Kemper, Post, & van Staveren, 1995).

Joints

Although most adults do not notice changes in joint functioning until their 40s, deleterious processes are at work even before the age of skeletal maturity, continuing steadily throughout the adult years (Tuite, Renstrom, & O'Brien, 1997). Structural changes occur with age in virtually every component of the joint. By the 20s and 30s, the arterial cartilage that protects the joints begins to degenerate and as it does so, the bone underneath begins to wear away. At the same time, outgrowths of cartilage begin to develop that further interfere with the smooth movement of the bones against each other within the joint capsule. In addition, fibers in the joint capsule become less pliable, reducing flexibility (Ralphs & Benjamin, 1994).

Unlike muscles, joints do not benefit from constant use. On the contrary, these deterioration processes are directly related to the amount of stress placed on the joints. Exercise cannot compensate for or prevent age-related changes. However, precautions in early adulthood can reduce the chance of losses in middle age. Most important is proper footwear, particularly during exercise. People who engage in occupational activities that involve repetitive motions of the wrist should attempt to minimize damage by the use of ergonomically designed accessories. Middle-aged individuals already experiencing joint damage can benefit from flexibility exercises that expand a stiff joint's range of motion. Exercise that strengthens the muscles supporting the joint also helps to improve its functioning (Blanpied & Smidt, 1993). Both kinds of exercise have the additional benefit of stimulating circulation to the joints, thereby enhancing the blood supply that promotes repair processes in the tendons, ligaments, and surfaces of the exercising areas.

VITAL BODILY FUNCTIONS

Age-related changes in the bodily systems that support life ultimately determine the individual's survival. Along with the nervous system, the functioning of these vital organs determines the length and the quality of life.

CARDIOVASCULAR SYSTEM

Aging of the cardiovascular system involves changes that begin in middle age in both the heart itself and the arteries that circulate blood throughout the body. The component of the heart that has the most relevance to aging is the left ventricle, which loses muscle mass and strength and increases in fat and connective tissue. The wall of the left ventricle becomes thicker and less compliant during each contraction leading the left ventricle to lose its effectiveness as a pumping mechanism. Therefore, less blood is ejected into the aorta with each contraction of the heart. The arteries become less able to accommodate the flow of blood that spews from the left ventricle. This loss of flexibility in the arteries is referred to as vasculopathology of aging (Bilato & Crow, 1996). Adding to these changes is the continuing deposit of plaque along the arterial walls of fatty substances, consisting of cholesterol, cellular waste products, calcium, and fibrin (a clotting material in the blood). Although theoretically distinct from atherosclerosis, there is a resemblance between some of the normal structural changes that begin in middle age and those associated with this arterial disease.

The primary indicators of cardiovascular efficiency are aerobic capacity, the maximum amount of oxygen that can be delivered through the blood, and cardiac output, the amount of blood that the heart pumps per minute. Both indexes decline consistently at a rate of about 10% per decade from age 25 and up so that the average 65-year-old has 40% lower cardiovascular efficiency compared to the average young adult.

Many studies show that declines in aerobic capacity occur even in highly trained athletes but that their loss of cardiovascular functioning is about half of that in sedentary individuals (Pollock et al., 1997; Trappe, Costill, Vukovich, Jones, & Melham, 1996). One major exception was an analysis of all of the available literature on exercise and aerobic capacity in women. Included in the data for this analysis were the findings on nearly 5,000 females aged 18–89 years. The declines in aerobic capacity shown by these women were *greater* for active than for sedentary women. Apparently, the active women were at a much higher level when they were young, and by the time they reached their later years their loss was greater on a percentage basis. However, although the active women may have lost an estimated 10% of their aerobic power per decade, they still were functioning at higher levels than the sedentary women, who started at a lower level early in life. Nevertheless, these findings indicate the need for replicating the results of research on male samples, which constitute the majority of studies on exercise and aging, with comparable groups of women.

Short-term training studies provide more consistent findings about the value of exercise for middle-aged and older adults (Whitbourne, 1996). To be maximally effective, exercise must stimulate the heart rate to rise to 60% to 75% of maximum capacity and this training must take place 3 to 4 times a week. The specific effects of exercise on heart muscle, however, also show gender variations. For men, exercise strengthens the myocardial muscle causing it to be more effective in exerting pressure on the left ventricle to contract and leading ultimately to more blood reaching the body's cells. For women, however, exercise does not have the same effects on ventricular dynamics (Spina, Miller, Bogenhagen, Schechtma, & Ehsani, 1996). More data are needed to understand these apparent gender differences in the relationship between exercise and cardiovascular functioning.

Apart from its effects on the heart muscle, exercise contributes to improved metabolism of dietary fat, which in turn helps reduce atherosclerotic deposits in the arteries. However, exercise must be combined with a diet that is low in saturated fats. Most of the adult population must carefully monitor cholesterol levels, particularly from middle age and upward. Although total cholesterol level decreases during this period, this decline includes a lowering of the HDL cholesterol (Ferrara, Barrett-Connor, & Shan, 1997; Wilson, Anderson, Harris, Kannel, & Castelli, 1994), that lowers the individual's risk of heart disease (Stampfer et al., 1996).

The consequences of age-related changes in the arteries include an increasing risk from middle adulthood and on in the risk of hypertension, or elevated blood pressure. Although normal aging is not associated with increased blood pressure, hypertension rates rise in older populations. For males, the risk increases from 22% to 32% of the population between the ages of 45 and 64, and 64 and over; the rates for females are 23% and 40% (Statistics, 1997). A lowering of both saturated fat and salt are known to prevent or reduce hypertension. Exercise further contributes to the effects of diet on hypertension. In addition to its physiological effects, exercise can also provide an avenue of stress reduction that can contribute to lower blood pressure in middle-aged persons.

RESPIRATORY SYSTEM

Respiration includes the mechanical process of breathing, the exchange of gases in the innermost reaches of tiny airways in the lungs, and the transport of gases to and from the body's cells that occur in these airways. Aging affects this process in part through a reduction in the strength of the respiratory muscles, and an increase in rigidity of the connective tissue in the chest wall to be expanded during inspiration and contracted during expiration. These changes have the effect of reducing the amount of air that can be pumped in and out of the lungs (Teramoto, Fukuchi, Nagase, Matsuse, & Orimo, 1995). Aging is also associated with a "failing lung" (Rossi, Ganassini, Tantucci, & Grassi, 1996) that causes the lung tissue itself to lose expandability. Consequently, all measures of lung functioning in adulthood show age-related losses from about age 40 and on (Rossi et al., 1996).

Exercise can strengthen the chest wall and thereby compensate for some loss of pumping capacity of the respiratory muscles. However, there is no measure available to offset changes that occur in the lung tissue itself. The best that can be hoped for is to minimize the effects of aging on the lungs, and this is done by not smoking cigarettes (Rossi et al., 1996). The cessation of smoking is clearly associated with improvements in lung functioning in adults over 50. In a large-scale study of almost 1,400 adults from ages 51 to 95 years, lung functioning was significantly lower in smokers than nonsmokers (Frette, Barrett-Connor, & Clausen, 1996).

URINARY SYSTEM

The urinary system is composed of the kidneys, bladder, ureters, and urethra. The kidneys filter out the harmful waste products of metabolism,
which pass through the ureters and into the bladder. In the bladder, the
waste products are combined with excess water from the blood and are
eliminated as urine through the urethra. Studies dating back to the late
1940s conducted as part of the initial phases of the Baltimore Longitudinal
Study on Aging showed that nephron loss occurs consistently throughout
adulthood at a rate of 6% per decade and that virtually all measures of
renal efficiency show a steady and consistent drop-off over time. (Davies
& Shock, 1950). This view has been challenged by more refined studies indicating that normal aging is not associated with impaired kidney functioning (Epstein, 1996; Fliser et al., 1997). However, when the kidney is
placed under stress, such as caused by illness, extreme exertion, or during
a heat wave, declines in functioning become evident. Because of the risk
of lower excretion rates, medication levels must be carefully monitored in
middle-aged and older adults who are at risk of such conditions (Montgomery, 1990).

Changes with aging may also occur in the elastic tissue of the bladder
such that it cannot as efficiently retain or expel urine. Older adults also
experience some changes in the perception that they need to urinate. Besides the intrinsic changes in the bladder that lower the rate of urinary
flow in men (Kitagawa, Ichikawa, Akimoto, & Shimazaki, 1994), many
men experience hypertrophy (overgrowth) of the prostate, a gland that
sits on top of the bladder. This puts pressure on the bladder and can lead
men to feel frequent urges to urinate, particularly at night. Despite these
changes, the majority of older adults do not experience significant problems in the area of bladder functioning, as only 2% of men and 5% of
women report bladder problems as a chronic condition (National Center
for Health Statistics, 1997). Estimates of the prevalence of urinary incontinence among the over-65 population range from a low of 6% to 8% of
those living in the community to a high of 20% to 30% or more of those
living in institutions (Iqbal & Castleden, 1997). Stress incontinence (loss
of urine during a sudden physical action) is more likely to occur in
women due to the effects of childbirth or age-related decreases in the estrogen. Urge incontinence, which involves loss of control over urinary
sphincters, is associated with prostate disease in men. Behavioral controls are often successful in treating incontinence (Burgio & Engel, 1990;
Burns et al., 1993), and Kegel exercises (contraction of the sphincters) can
help prevent stress incontinence in women. Regrettably, adult diaper ads
convey an impression that incontinence can only be corrected through
purchase of these products, and also portray middle-aged women as
prime sufferers of this condition.

DIGESTIVE SYSTEM

Physiological changes in middle and later adulthood in the digestive system appear to be relatively minor. The functioning appears to be maintained of the salivary glands (Ship, Nolan, & Puckett, 1995), esophagus (Nishimura et al., 1996), and (for people in good health), the remaining organs consisting of the stomach and lower digestive tract (Hurwitz et al., 1997).

Some cautions, however, should be thrown into this generally favorable picture. Although the normal aging process may in and of itself contribute little to changes in the gastrointestinal system, problems may occur, such as abnormal feelings of fullness (Clarkston et al., 1997). Health conditions can also interfere with absorption of nutrients (Lovat, 1996).

Many lifestyle factors that can change in middle and later adulthood contribute to the quality of digestive functioning in middle and later adulthood. These factors include family composition, financial resources, and age-related mobility and cognitive problems. Other factors reflect the exposure that individuals have through the media about the need to use dietary supplements, digestive aids, and laxatives after the age of 40 or 50. Despite the image portrayed by the media, problems such as fecal incontinence affect only a small fraction of even the over-65 population (3% of men and 7% of women) (National Center for Health Statistics, 1997).

BODILY CONTROL SYSTEMS

The regulation of bodily functions of metabolism, reproduction, and control against infection is accomplished through intricate networks of organ systems and tissues controlled by the endocrine and immune system. Changes in these systems with aging interact with those that control appearance, mobility, and the vital life functions just discussed.

ENDOCRINE SYSTEM

The endocrine system incorporates the set of glands that regulate the actions of the body's other organ systems by producing and releasing hormones into the bloodstream. The major hormonal system involves the hypothalamus and anterior (front) section of the pituitary gland. Hypothalamus-releasing factors (HRFs) act on specific cell types within the anterior pituitary gland to regulate the secretion of one or more anterior pituitary hormones that operate according to the principle of negative feedback. Pituitary hormones may also be triggered via negative feedback from a target organ signaling that it is time to produce more of the necessary substance. HRFs may also be stimulated by information sent from other parts of the nervous system. The posterior pituitary gland produces other hormones, such as antidiuretic hormone that regulates the urine-concentrating mechanism in the kidneys.

Six hormones are produced by the anterior pituitary: thyroid-stimulating hormone (TSH), adrenocorticotropic hormone (ACTH), follicle-stimulating hormone (FSH), luteinizing hormone (LH), growth hormone (GH, also called somatotropin), and prolactin. Each hormone acts on specific target cells within the body, and some (such as TSH) stimulate the production of other hormones.

For centuries, scientists have been fascinated with the prospect that the cause of aging is linked to the functions of the endocrine system. Within recent years, additional interest in this system was fostered by recognition of the importance of hormones in determining the amount and proportions of muscle, bone, and fat in the body. The potential relevance of sex hormones to this important area of functioning, and possibly to other physical and psychological functions as well, also creates heightened interest in the endocrine system in general.

Growth Hormone

There is a consistently documented decline estimated at 14% per decade over adulthood in the secretion of growth hormone (Kern, Dodt, Born, & Fehm, 1996; Toogood, O'Neill, & Shalet, 1996). A related hormone produced by the liver, IGF-1 (insulin-like growth factor-1), also shows an age-related decrease across adulthood. IGF-1 stimulates muscle cells to increase in size and number, perhaps by stimulating their genes to increase the production of muscle-specific proteins. The decline in what is called the somatotrophic axis (GH and IGF-1) is called "somatopause." Because GH production affects the metabolism of proteins, lipids, and carbohydrates, the somatopause is thought to account for several age-related changes in body composition across adulthood, including loss of bone mineral content (Boonen et al., 1996), increases in fat, and a decrease in muscle mass (Bjorntorp, 1996). Normally, GH production shows regularly timed peaks during nighttime sleep; in older adults, this peak is smaller (Prinz et al., 1995). GH also rises during heavy resistance exercise, and in adults over 70 this response is attenuated (Hakkinen & Pakarinen, 1995).

The recent media attention given to hormones and aging includes claims that GH replacement therapy is the magic potion that can stop the aging process (Taaffe et al., 1994). In addition to being extremely expensive, however, there is evidence that the side effects of this treatment outweigh any of its possible advantages (Riedel, Brabant, Rieger, & von zur Muhlen, 1994). Growth hormone is linked to joint pain, enlargement of the heart, enlargement of the bones, diabetes, and pooling of fluid in the skin and other tissues, which can lead to high blood pressure and heart failure. A safer and cheaper alternative is exercise, which can accomplish some of the positive effects of growth hormone replacement therapy, including favorable effects on growth hormone secretion and bodily composition (Brown, Birge, & Kohrt, 1997; Silverman & Mazzeo, 1996).

ACTH and Cortisol

The production of ACTH by the anterior pituitary gland stimulates the adrenal gland to produce cortisol, a glucocorticoid hormone that provides energy to the muscles during times of stress. Cortisol production is regulated by a negative feedback loop intended to protect the body from damage from the effects of unchecked rises, which include damage to the thymus gland, depression of immune responses in general, tissue damage, breakdown of proteins, and formation of fat deposits (Seaton, 1995). Increases in circulating cortisol in the blood may also be linked to damage to cells in the hippocampus (Van Cauter, Leproult, & Kupfer, 1996).

There are many advocates of the so-called glucocorticoid cascade hypothesis, which proposes that aging negatively affects glucocorticoid feedback mechanisms, resulting in dangerous increases in cortisol levels which in turn affects immune response, fat deposits, and cognition (O'Brien, Schweitzer, Ames, Tuckwell, & Mastwyk, 1994; Wilkinson, Peskind, & Raskind, 1997). In support of this hypothesis, researchers have estimated that cortisol levels rise 20 to 50% between the years 20 and 80 at a rate of 5% to 7% per decade. Based on these data, cortisol, which is also called the "stress hormone," would merit the role of a number one player in promoting the body's wear and tear in response to accumulation of life stresses (Van Cauter et al., 1996). Adding weight to this hypothesis is evidence of heightened cortisol response of older people, particularly women, to stress or physiological stimulation (Gotthardt et al., 1995; Kelly, Hayslip, & Servaty, 1996; Peskind et al., 1995; Seeman, Singer, & Charpentier, 1995).

However, not all the data point to a general collapse of the hypothalamus-pituitary axis (Gotthardt et al., 1995; Nicolson, Storms, Ponds, & Sulon, 1997). More significantly, when the data are collected longitudinally rather than cross-sectionally (which is true for all the preceding studies), there appear to be varying patterns of age changes. The available longitudinal data, which represent yearly testing of healthy older adults over a 3- to 6-year period, show that some older individuals increase, some decrease, and some remain stable in cortisol levels (Lupien et al., 1996). Interestingly, positive associations were found in this study between an anxiety scale and levels of cortisol, suggesting that variations over time in cortisol level may relate to individual differences in personality. Another factor that may play a role in cross-sectional studies is obesity. Among middle-aged men, obesity is positively related to cortisol levels (Field, Colditz, Willett, Longcope, & McKinlay, 1994). Although it is not known whether obesity causes higher cortisol levels or vice versa, the existence of such data calls into question a general hypothesis about cortisol and aging.

Thyroid Hormone and TSH

The hypothalamus-pituitary-thyroid axis consists of the hypothalamic releasing factor (TRH), thyroid-stimulating hormone (TSH), and the thyroid hormones triiodothyronine (T3) and thyroxine (T4). Thyroid hormones regulate the body's basal metabolic rate (the BMR), which begins to slow in middle age and is responsible for weight gains occurring even when caloric intake remains stable.

Despite the presumed importance in this process of the thyroid hormones and their regulators in the pituitary gland and hypothalamus, little data exist on changes in adulthood, and the published findings are not in agreement. Some researchers suggest that there are deficits in the pituitary gland (Erfurth & Hagmar, 1995), and others maintain that the problem originates in the hypothalamus (Monzani et al., 1996). Another argument is that the problem is in the level of the thyroid hormones themselves, particularly the absorption of T4 by the tissues so that more remains in the blood (Hays & Nielsen, 1994). This last finding is in agreement with some arguments that regard changes in thyroid functioning as occurring due to loss of muscle mass and a lower demand for the thyroid hormones.

Melatonin

The hormone melatonin, manufactured by the pineal gland, is involved in synchronization of circadian rhythm, the regulation of other hormones, and possibly the protection of cells against free radical damage. The production of melatonin declines with increasing age, and circulating melatonin levels are affected by certain environmental conditions, such as food restriction, which increases melatonin levels and prevents its age-related decline.

It is thought that melatonin may have beneficial effects on certain aspects of aging and age-associated diseases, especially in the brain and immune system. However, the weight of the evidence does not favor melatonin supplements. There are insufficient data on humans, the side effects have still not been completely identified, and the purity of the available supplements on the market has not been assured (Huether, 1996). Melatonin supplements can also interfere with sleep cycles if taken at the wrong time. Other side effects include confusion, drowsiness, headaches, and constriction of blood vessels, which would be dangerous in people who have high blood pressure. Finally, the dosages usually sold in over-the-counter medications may be as high as 40 times the amount normally found in the body, and the effect of such large doses taken over a long term has not been determined.

Dehydroepiandrosterone (DHEA)

One adrenal hormone outside the control of the hypothalamus-anterior pituitary axis that has been the target of considerable attention with regard to aging is dehydroepiandrosterone (DHEA). This hormone is a weak male steroid (androgen) produced by the adrenal glands. It is a precursor to the sex hormones testosterone and estrogen and is believed to have a variety of functions in the body. Some of these functions include increasing production of other sex steroids and availability of IGF-1, and positively influencing some functions in the central nervous system.

DHEA, which is higher in males than females, shows a pronounced decrease over the adult years, reducing by 80% to 90% between the years of 20 and 80. This phenomenon, termed "andrenopause" (Lamberts, van den Beld, & van der Lely, 1997), is greater in men, although men continue to have higher levels than women because they start at a higher baseline. There is some evidence that loss of DHEA is related to functional declines in various measures of physical and mental health, particularly for women (Berr, Lafont, Debuire, Dartigues, & Baulieu, 1996). Extremely low levels of DHEA have been linked to cardiovascular disease in men, some forms of cancer, trauma, and stress. Institutionalized older adults in poor health also have very low levels of DHEA. In animal studies, DHEA replacement has led to impressive increases in the strength and vigor of older animals. It is not clear how DHEA has these effects. It circulates through the blood in an inactive form, called DHEA sulfate, and becomes active when it comes in contact with a specific cell or tissue that "needs" it. When this happens, the sulfate is removed. Researchers have attempted to determine whether changes in DHEA are related to the reductions with age in insulin sensitivity (Denti et al., 1997) and immune system functioning (James et al., 1997). The relationship of DHEA decrease and testosterone levels in men is also being explored (Morley et al., 1997).

Although there are no definitive answers other than that the decline in DHEA is probably a reliable one, DHEA replacement therapy is rivaling GH and melatonin in the antiaging industry. There are some proponents in the scientific community for the use of DHEA supplements (Yen, Morales, & Khorram, 1995), but other researchers cast doubt on its utility (Barrou, Charru, & Lidy, 1997; R. Miller, 1996). Like GH therapy, there may also be some attendant risks, notably liver problems and an increase in risk of prostate and breast cancer.

Estrogen and the Menopause

The technical meaning of menopause is that it is the point in a woman's life when menstruation stops permanently, signifying the end of her reproductive potential. However, as used in common speech, menopause has come to mean the phase in middle adulthood associated with hormonal changes and loss of reproductive ability. The actual term for this process is the climacteric, a term that applies to men as well. The menopause is the last stage of a gradual biological process in which the ovaries slow in the production of female sex hormones. This process takes place over a 3- to 5-year span called the perimenopause, ending in the menopause when the women has not had her menstrual period for one year. The average age of menopause is 50 years, but the timing varies among individuals. Menopause occurs earlier in women who are thin, malnourished or who smoke.

Throughout the period preceding menopause, the production of estrogen by the ovarian follicles diminishes. Since progesterone production occurs in response to ovulation, progesterone levels also decline during this time. Reflecting the negative feedback cycle between the ovaries and the anterior pituitary gland, the production of FSH and LH also rises dramatically. In turn, the hypothalamus produces less gonadotropin-releasing factor (GnRH). It is not clear which part of the system is responsible for triggering the start of menopause: a reduction in ovarian follicles or changes in the central nervous system that cause the hypothalamus to reduce its production of GnRh (Wise, Krajnak, & Kashon, 1996). The process of estrogen decline begins about 10 to 15 years before menopause, at some point in the mid-30s. By the mid-40s, the ovaries have begun to function less effectively and produce fewer hormones. Eventually by the early to mid-50s, menstrual cycles have ended altogether. There is still some production of estrogen, however, as the ovaries continue to produce small amounts and the adrenal glands stimulate the production of estrogen in fat tissue.

Although women vary considerably in their progression through the menopause (as is true during puberty), there are certain characteristic and fairly typical symptoms. One of the most prominent is the occurrence of "hot flashes," which are sudden sensations of intense heat and sweating that can last from a few moments to half an hour. Over half of women experience hot flashes over the course of a 2-year period. These changes in perceived body temperature are the result of decreases in estrogen levels, which cause the endocrine system to release higher amounts of other hormones that affect the temperature control centers in the brain. Fatigue, headaches, night sweats, and insomnia are other physiological symptoms thought to be the result of fluctuating estrogen levels. Psychological symptoms are also reported, such as irritability, mood swings, depression, memory loss, and difficulty concentrating, but the evidence regarding the connection between these symptoms and the physiological changes involved in menopause is far from conclusive.

Along with these hormonal changes are alterations in the reproductive tract. The tissues throughout the system become thinner, less elastic, and altered in position and shape. Due to lower estrogen levels, there is a reduction in the supply of blood to the vagina and surrounding nerves and glands. The tissues become thinner, drier, and less able to produce secretions to lubricate before and during intercourse. The result is the possibility of discomfort during intercourse and greater susceptibility to infection, which is more prevalent among women over 50 (Laumann, Paik, & Rosen, 1999). In addition, the woman may become more susceptible to urinary problems such as stress incontinence (discussed earlier).

More widespread throughout the body are other effects of menopause associated with the impact of decreasing estrogen levels on other bodily systems. Loss of bone strength in women becomes much more pronounced after menopause. Atherosclerosis and high blood pressure, as well as other cardiovascular diseases, also become more prevalent among postmenopausal women. It appears that estrogen provides a protection against these diseases during the reproductive years that is lost at menopause. There are also changes in cholesterol levels in the blood associated with menopause causing postmenopausal women to be at higher risk of atherosclerosis and associated conditions. Estrogen is also thought to be a protective factor against Alzheimer's disease, and its diminution takes away this protection.

Estrogen-replacement therapy (ERT) was introduced in the 1940s to counteract the negative effects of estrogen loss on postmenopausal women. However, this proved not to be an advisable strategy. The administration of estrogen can lead to an overgrowth of the uterine lining which increases the risk of cancer and blood clots. Currently, women receiving estrogen are given lower doses along with progestin (called Hormone Replacement Therapy, or HRT) to reduce the cancer risk. Progestin causes the uterine lining to shed, triggering a few days of menstrual-like bleeding each month. Even this treatment, when taken over a long course, can increase a woman's risk of developing breast cancer. HRT can also trigger asthma and gallstones, and cause blood sugar levels to change, posing a danger to women with diabetes. Some women also suffer side effects such as tenderness of the breasts and headaches from estrogen, or bloating and depression from progestin. Another alternative is Selective Estrogen

Replacement Modulaters (SERMs) such as raloxifene. This form of hormone replacement therapy has a more targeted effect on bone loss. Other recommended approaches to use in addition to HRT to counteract the effect of hormonal changes include engaging in exercise, giving up smoking, lowering cholesterol intake, and having one alcoholic drink a day.

Hormone replacement therapy is also emerging as a preventive measure for Alzheimer's disease. Investigators in the Baltimore Longitudinal Study on Aging found this out inadvertently while collecting medical information on women being tested on measures of health and cognitive functioning. Women who were taking estrogen had higher memory scores than women who were not. In addition, participants who began ERT between their regular visits maintained stable performance on the memory tests over time. In contrast, women who never took ERT showed age-associated losses in memory over the 6-year period between testings (Kawas et al., 1997). A number of explanations of the possible role of estrogen in preventing Alzheimer's disease have emerged, including the possibility that estrogen facilitates verbal functioning throughout life (Sherwin, 1996), perhaps by maintaining serotonergic and cholinergic pathways (McEwen, Alves, Bulloch, & Weiland, 1997). Another possibility is that estrogen improves blood flow in regions of the brain affected by Alzheimer's disease (Birge, 1997).

Testosterone

The term "andropause" was coined to refer to age-related declines in the male sex hormone testosterone corresponding, theoretically, to declines in estrogen for women. Supposedly related to the andropause is a loss of sexual potency, although it is now recognized that changes in erectile functioning are more related to the circulatory than the endocrine system as well as to social factors and stress (Laumann et al., 1999). However, debate continues regarding the extent to which a drop in testosterone applies to normal aging. According to conventional wisdom and cross-sectional studies, there is a decrease in free testosterone across progressively older age groups of men starting at the age of 40 and continuing at a rate of 1% per year after that (de Lignieres, 1993). However, not all studies show this pattern, and researchers recognize that potentially confounding methodological factors exist that might account for the disparities across investigations (Maas, Jochen, & Lalande, 1997). In one rare longitudinal study, changes in testosterone levels were found to be correlated with cholesterol levels, percentage of body fat, cigarette smoking, and behavioral tendencies that predispose an individual to developing cardiovascular disease. Nevertheless, taking all these factors into account, a slight testosterone decrease was noted over the 13-year period of the study in men between the ages of 41 and 61 years (Zmuda et al., 1997).

It appears from this evidence that, unlike the clear diminution of estrogen production that occurs in women, the changes in testosterone in healthy aging men are only slight although detectable. Testosterone therapy is considered appropriate for men who have a clear hormonal deficiency, but it is not advisable for otherwise healthy middle-aged and older men to take externally administered testosterone. There is an increased risk associated with its use for developing cancer as well as other deleterious changes, such as an enlarged prostate gland, higher cholesterol, infertility, and acne. These problems outweigh any advantages that may exist for muscle strength, sexual potency, and the prevention of frailty.

IMMUNE SYSTEM

Psychologists have only relatively recently become interested in the immune system, which is now beginning to be understood as intimately connected to the nervous system, and ultimately to behaviors, thoughts, and emotions. The effect of aging on the immune system has intrigued biological researchers for years, particularly because of the existence of certain autoimmune diseases that increase in prevalence in the middle and later years, such as forms of arthritis. Advances in laboratory techniques available for studying immune system functioning have contributed to the interest in this system, and new data on aging are increasingly becoming available.

The immune system function of greatest interest to researchers in the field of aging is acquired immunity, acquired as the result of prior contact with an antigen. The mechanisms involved in acquired immunity are lymphocytes, specialized white blood cells that can develop the ability to destroy or neutralize specific antigens. Acquired immunity increases in strength and effectiveness due to the ability to acquire memory for each antigen. Normally, the body's defenses do not attack tissues that carry a marker indicating that they are "self." Instead, immune cells reside peaceably with other body cells in a state known as self-tolerance.

Two types of lymphocytes are involved in the immune response: T lymphocytes (also called T cells) and B lymphocytes (also called B cells). The two types of lymphocytes participate in different forms of the immune response. One form of T cell, known as cytotoxic T cell, is primarily responsible for cell-mediated immunity in which invading antigens that have infected a bodily cell are identified and killed. B cells are involved in humoral immunity, in which they produce antibodies that bind to and neutralize the antigen. Certain T cells also participate in humoral immunity by either activating or suppressing the B cells. Macrophages are also involved in acquired immunity by processing substances to the T cells in a form suitable for initiating the immune response. Another group of cells are called natural killer (NK) cells, which have the ability to destroy a variety of infected or tumor cells. As the name implies, the NK cells do not require prior exposure to a substance to destroy it. Both T cells and NK cells contain granules filled with potent chemicals, and both types kill on contact. The chief weapons of the T cells are cytokines, diverse and potent chemical messengers secreted by the cells of the immune system. Cytokines encourage cell growth, promote cell activation, direct cellular traffic, and destroy target cells—including cancer cells. Because they serve as a messenger between white cells, or leukocytes, many cytokines are also known as interleukins. Whenever T cells and B cells are activated, some become memory cells. The next time that an individual encounters that same antigen, the immune system is primed to destroy it quickly. The memory cells produced after the primary response may survive for decades, giving lifetime immunity to certain diseases.

Declines in immune system functioning have been suspected for many years based on observations of age-related increases in autoimmune diseases and the clinical observations that older adults are more vulnerable to influenza and many forms of cancer. However, many questions remain to be resolved, such as whether observed immune deficiencies in older adults are the result of normal aging or disease processes. In addition to the immune system being incredibly complicated, there is much disagreement in the published literature. Nevertheless, researchers feel confident enough that the observed age effects are reliable to have coined the term "immune senescence" to describe the features of the aging immune system (R. Miller, 1996).

The primary feature of immune senescence is the decline of T cell functioning, including a lowered proliferation of T cells during cell-mediated immunity, and a lowering of helper T cells in humoral immunity. There are more memory T cells and fewer naïve T cells, and as a result, the system is less able to respond to newly encountered antigens (R. Miller, 1996). The ability to produce antibodies by B cells is also compromised by the aging process, but it is not clear whether this is due to a decline in the B cells themselves or to less effective action of helper T cells. There is also some evidence for changes in certain interleukins, the substances produced by T cells. One of these, interleukin-6, increases with age, which suggests the possibility that it somehow interferes with the immune response. In contrast, interleukin-2 diminishes with age, a fact that may account for decreases in T-cell proliferation. The functioning of NK cells in the bloodstream is maintained in later life, but these cells may be less effective in the spleen and lymph node tissues, which is where they are most needed. There also may be important links between the immune and endocrine systems. For example, interleukin-2 is depressed when estrogen levels decrease.

The cause of immune senescence is commonly thought to be the involution of the thymus, which loses most of its functioning by early adulthood. Thus, the T cells that circulate in the secondary lymphoid organs are mature T cells that were produced early in the individual's life during exposure to new antigens. Countering this fact is the suggestion that the system may have more dynamic properties than would be true if anatomy were the sole determinant of immune functioning. Thus, the fact that new T cells are stimulated by existing T cells could mean that, everything else being equal, the numbers of T cells may actually remain more stable than the demise of the thymus would indicate (R. Miller, 1996). Furthermore, if the remaining T cells retain or improve their responsiveness, this would compensate for their sheer loss of numbers (Born et al., 1995). Established wisdom nevertheless regards the immune system as target of the aging process and, further, as a prime suspect in regulating length of life.

This being said, there are many interactions between immune system functioning and other physical and psychological processes. It has come to light that diet and exercise can either enhance or detract from various immune system indicators. For example, additives such as zinc and vitamin E can improve immune responsiveness (Lesourd, 1997; Sone, 1995). Conversely, older people who eat low protein diets show deficient immune functioning in addition to other serious losses in body composition (Castaneda, Charnley, Evans, & Crim, 1995). As is true for diet, the amount of exercise the individual engages in can be a factor that influences immune responsiveness. Habitual physical activity can have a positive effect on various indexes of immune functioning (Shinkai, Konishi, & Shephard, 1997; Venjatraman & Fernandes, 1997).

Given this knowledge, it will be necessary to reevaluate the existing data on aging and the immune system, in which exercise and diet were not controlled. Previous findings may have presented an overly negative picture of the effects of aging. Until more data become available on the sensitivity of the immune system to these regulatory behaviors, it is best to be aware of the potentially negative effect that aging may have in people who do not maintain ideal levels of diet and exercise. A malfunctioning immune system, as in the case of cancer, is a major contributor to mortality in middle and later adulthood.

NERVOUS SYSTEM

The nervous system exerts control over all bodily systems and behaviors. Within the central nervous system, events in the environment are monitored and responded to, thoughts are conceived and enacted, and connections are maintained with other bodily systems. The autonomic nervous system controls involuntary behaviors, response to stress, and actions of other organ systems that sustain life. The areas of greatest interest in nervous system functioning and aging include changes in neural structures and bodily control systems regulated by the autonomic system.

CENTRAL NERVOUS SYSTEM

Early research on the effects of the aging process on the nervous system was based on the hypothesis that, because neurons do not reproduce, there is a progressive loss of brain tissue across the adult years that is noticeable by the age of 30. The model of aging based on this hypothesis was called by some the "neuronal fallout model." In the years intervening since that early research, however, it is becoming clear that in the absence of disease, the aging brain maintains much of its structure and function. Research by an innovative team of neuroanatomists in the late 1970s and 1980s provided the first evidence that, when given proper amounts of stimulation in the form of mental activity, aging organisms can compensate for loss of neurons by increasing the number of synapses formed by the remaining neurons (Coleman & Flood, 1987). Improvements in methods due to the availability of brain scans as well as experimental studies involving synaptic proliferation and neuron regeneration are further responsible for the current climate of greater optimism regarding age and the nervous system. Furthermore, with refinements in the definition and diagnosis of Alzheimer's disease, researchers are increasingly able to sep- arate the effects of normal aging from the severe losses that occur in this disease and related conditions.

Another key principle that emerges from more recent studies using brain imaging techniques is that there is considerable interindividual variability in patterns of brain changes across adulthood. In one large MRI study of adults, percentages of atrophy ranging from 6% to 8% per year were reported. However, the researchers noted wide individual variation both in patterns of cortical atrophy and in ventricular enlargement (Coffey et al., 1992). Some of this variability may very well be accounted for by health status of the individual because those in good health are spared some of the effects of aging, such as reductions in temporal lobe volume (DeCarli et al., 1994). There also may be significant gender variations in the effects of aging on the brain in adulthood. There are larger increases for men than women in the ventricular spaces in the brain (Matsumae et al., 1996). Men show greater reductions than women in the frontal and temporal lobes (Cowell et al., 1994) as well as in the parieto-occipital area (Coffey et al., 1998). Conversely, men may be relatively spared compared with women in the case of the hippocampus and parietal lobes (D. Murphy et al., 1996).

In studies of the frontal lobes using both MRI and positron-emission tomography (PET) scans, age reductions appear to be more conclusively demonstrated than in studies of other cortical areas (Raz et al., 1997) with estimates ranging from a low of 1% per decade (De Santi et al., 1995) to a high of around 10% (Eisen, Entezari-Taher, & Stewart, 1996). There is also evidence for reductions in the volume of the hippocampus with increasing age in adulthood (de Leon et al., 1997; Raz, Gunning-Dixon, Head, Dupuis, & Acker, 1998). These patterns of findings are interpreted as providing a neurological basis for the behavioral observations of memory changes in later adulthood (Golomb et al., 1996; Nielsen Bohlman & Knight, 1995).

However, there are compensating factors indicating that if older adults suffer brain deficits in one area they make up for these by increasing the activation of other brain regions. In one carefully conducted PET scan study, the regional cerebral blood flow was compared in men in their 70s and men in their 20s and 30s while they were performing memory tests that differed in the types of cognitive processes involved (Cabeza et al., 1997). The younger men were more likely to use regions of the brain better designed to meet the cognitive demands of the task in contrast to the older men, who showed more diffuse but higher levels of brain activation in other areas. For example, the younger men used the left half of their frontal lobes while they were learning new material and the right half when they were trying to recall the material. The older men showed very little activity of the frontal lobe while they were learning the material but then used both the right and left frontal lobes during recall. The authors concluded from this study that older adults are capable of mustering their resources when the situation demands it, even if those resources are less efficiently organized. Other studies using PET scans have also shown that older adults to be less able to increase the blood flow to specific parts of the brain in response to tasks that demand the use of those brain regions (Ross et al., 1997). However, they may also compensate by using other brain circuits to make up for decreases in the frontal lobes (Chao & Knight, 1997).

The view that there are changes with aging in adulthood in the frontal lobes and the circuits between the limbic system and cortex is consistent with data on cognitive changes in adulthood. Nevertheless, it is important to keep in mind both the plasticity of the brain throughout adulthood and the repeated demonstrations that older people find ways around some of their neural circuitry problems. Even though their efficiency might be reduced, they have not by any means lost the ability to put their brains to work.

SLEEP

The literature on sleep in adulthood clearly refutes a common myth about aging, namely that as people grow older they need less sleep. Everyone, regardless of age, requires seven to nine hours of sleep a night (Ancoli-Israel,

1997). However, there are changes in aspects of sleep-related behavior throughout the years of adulthood that can have a significant effect on the mental and physical well-being of the middle-aged and older adult. These changes relate in part to the individual's lifestyle as well as to whatever physiological factors must be taken into account. Middle-aged individuals who are experiencing high degrees of job-related stress face different challenges in their sleep patterns than do those who lead a more relaxed daily life. Furthermore, hormonal changes, such as those associated with the menopause and growth hormone levels, further affect the individual's sleep patterns throughout the adult years.

Changes in sleeping patterns emerge gradually in later adulthood, in part as a result of biological factors, and in part in connection with psychological and social factors. It is a well-established finding that older adults spend more time in bed relative to time spent asleep. They take longer to fall asleep, awaken more often during the night, and their sleep is shallower and fragmented, meaning that it is less efficient. Older adults also spend more time lying awake before they get out of bed in the morning (Bliwise, 1992). EEG sleep patterns show some corresponding age alterations, including a rise in Stage 1 sleep and a large decrease in both Stage 4 and REM sleep. These changes occur even for people who are in excellent health. Alterations in growth hormone and particularly melatonin production and timing with age contribute to breakdowns in circadian rhythms, possibly causing an advance of the timing of sleep stages relative to clock time (Haimov & Lavie, 1997). There is some evidence that sleep disturbances become evident by the age of 50, and are more prevalent in women than men (Middelkoop, Smilde-van den Doel, Neven, Kamphuisen, & Springer, 1996).

Perhaps related to the changes in circadian rhythms at night is that at some point in middle to later adulthood, individuals shift from a preference to working in the later hours of the day and night to a preference for the morning. Several investigators have established that the large majority of older (over 65-year-old) adults are "morning" people and the large majority of younger adults are "evening" people (Hoch et al., 1992; Intons-Peterson, Rocchi, West, McLellan, & Hackney, 1998; C. May, Hasher, & Stoltzfus, 1993). The biological basis for this shift in preferences presumably occurs gradually throughout adulthood along with changes in hormonal contributors to sleep and arousal patterns. However, because after college graduation most young adults must shift from evening to morning schedules of preferred work hours, the social contributors to daytime arousal patterns would seem to have their effect earlier in the adult years. An intriguing implication of the fact that older adults prefer the morning is that studies of cognitive functioning, to the extent that they take place in the afternoon, perhaps have been systematically biased against the over-60 participants (Intons-Peterson et al., 1998).

Changes in middle and later adulthood in sleep patterns that have become problematic for the individual may be prevented or corrected by one or more alterations in sleep-related behaviors. Physical inactivity, or a sedentary lifestyle, is a major contributor to sleep problems at night. To counteract the contribution of this factor to poor sleep, the individual needs to become involved in a regular pattern of exercise (which, as already seen, has many other benefits). Using the bed or bedroom as a workplace is another behavior that can interfere with sleep. The bed and related areas become associated with work-related activities, some of which may be arousing and possibly stressful as well. The behavioral method used to counteract this contributor to sleep problems is referred to as "stimulus control." Other contributors to sleep problems are excessive intake of alcohol, an irregular sleep schedule, exercising too close to bedtime, and having coffee or smoking before going to bed. People in jobs that involve shift work or require frequent shifts in time zone are particularly likely to suffer from sleep disturbances.

Psychological disorders and medical conditions can also interfere with the sleep of the middle-aged and older adults. Psychological disorders that have a negative influence on sleep patterns include depression, anxiety, and distress over the loss of a loved one. The medical conditions that can interfere with sleep include pain due to arthritis, chronic muscle pain, osteoporosis, and cancer. Difficulty breathing is associated with chronic lung disease (COPD) and congestive heart failure. Gastroesophageal reflex (GER), although not a serious medical condition, is a digestive problem that causes heartburn and regurgitation of food. This is another contributor to sleep problems when it occurs on a chronic basis. People with Parkinson's disease or Alzheimer's disease also suffer serious sleep problems. Finally, the normal age-related changes that occur in the bladder lead to a more frequent urge to urinate during the night and thereby cause sleep interruptions. Obviously, such problems are worse for men with prostate disease or for people who suffer from incontinence. During menopause, the hot flashes that come at night due to hormonal changes can cause breathing difficulties and lead to frequent awakenings. Periodic leg movements during sleep (also called nocturnal myoclonus) can awaken the individual. All of these conditions, when they interrupt sleep, can lead to daytime sleepiness and fatigue. A vicious cycle begins when the individual starts to establish a pattern of daytime napping, which increases the chances of sleep interruptions occurring at night.

One physical condition in particular that interferes with sleep at any age but is more prevalent in middle-aged and older adults is sleep apnea, also called sleep-related breathing disturbance. People with this condition experience a particular kind of snoring in which a partial obstruction in the back of the throat restricts airflow during inhalation. A loud snore is followed by a choking silence when breathing actually stops. When the airway closes, the lack of oxygen is registered by the respiratory control centers in the brain, and the sleeper awakens. There may be 100 such episodes a night, and to make up for the lack of oxygen that occurs during each one, the heart is forced to pump harder to circulate more blood. As a result there are large spikes in blood pressure during the night as well as elevated blood pressure during the day. Over time, the person is at increased risk of heart attack and stroke. In addition, the individual experiences numerous periods of daytime sleepiness that interfere with everyday activities.

Sleep apnea is more common in older adults, perhaps affecting 8% to 10% of the over-65 population, although one comprehensive study of people monitored while asleep indicated a surprisingly high incidence of 27% (Philip, Dealberto, Dartigues, Guilleminault, & Bioulac, 1997). The causes of sleep apnea include allergies and colds that swell throat tissue, obesity, the use of alcohol, tranquilizers, and sedatives (which relax the throat muscles), and anatomical abnormalities, such as large soft palates or nasal malformations that restrict airflow. In addition to interference with sleep and possible risks of more serious medical conditions, sleep apnea seems related to poorer cognitive performance among people over 60 when it is accompanied by daytime drowsiness (Dealberto, Pajot, Courbon, & Alperovitch, 1996).

Although changes in sleep patterns occur as a normal feature of the aging process, severe sleep disturbances do not. Treatment is available from sleep specialists who can provide innovative approaches such as light therapy (which "resets" an out-of-phase circadian rhythm) and improvements in sleep habits. Exercise can also be helpful in resetting disturbed circadian rhythms (Van Someren, Lijzenga, Mirmiran, & Swaab, 1997). Much less helpful is self-medication with over-the-counter supplements of melatonin, which has no proven value and may even be harmful. Furthermore, individuals must be careful to avoid the temptation of solving sleep problems with sedative-hypnotic drugs to which tolerance quickly develops and which can also interfere with daytime alertness. These drugs may set up a cycle on top of a cycle and lead to an exacerbation of problems due to age-related changes in circadian rhythms (Vitiello, 1997).

TEMPERATURE CONTROL

It is standard news fare in the summer and winter of each year to hear that with each heat wave or cold snap older adults are at risk of dying from hyper- or hypothermia, conditions known together as dysthermia. Heat exposure was the cause of 6,615 deaths in the United States between the years 1979 to 1995. Of the over 2,700 people whose deaths were known to be linked to weather conditions, 62% occurred in people over the age of 55 years and the percentages rose sharply with each age decade (Centers for Disease Control, 1998).

These statistics are impressive, but there is reason to question the extent to which dysthermia is a function of the normal aging process. Researchers are beginning to shed doubt on the common wisdom that age alone increases the risk of hyperthermia and hypothermia. Some of the factors known to contribute to dysthermia are amount of body fat (Inoue, Nakao, Araki, & Ueda, 1992), gender (Young, 1991), and physical fitness (Young & Lee, 1997). With regard to physical fitness, for example, it is known that older adults have an impaired ability to secrete sweat in conditions of extreme heat (Inoue, 1996). The lack of body cooling mechanisms can lead to heat exhaustion and heat stroke in extreme heat conditions. However, men in their late 50s to early 70s who have greater aerobic power are known to have superior sweat gland functioning and blood flow to the skin, processes that improve body heat adaptation (Tankersley, Smolander, Kenney, & Fortney, 1991). More and more researchers seem to be concurring that in the absence of disease and in the presence of a well-trained body, middle-aged and older adults may have some impairment in thermal regulation, but not to the extent that was once believed.

Adding support to this proposition is that a variety of chronic medical conditions, many of which are more prevalent in the older population, are related to hyper- and hypothermia. Hypothermia is more likely to occur in people who have experienced hypothyroidism or other disorders of the body's hormone system, stroke, severe arthritis, or other diseases that limit mobility, and peripheral vascular disease, which limits blood flow throughout the limbs. Cognitive disorders, such as Alzheimer's disease, also increase a person's risk of hypothermia because people who are disoriented fail to take preventive action against the cold. Heat stroke and heat exhaustion are more likely to occur among people who are overweight, drink alcohol to excess, and suffer from diabetes or cardiovascular or respiratory illnesses. The disorientation, confusion, and memory problems that characterize people with dementia also make them more vulnerable to hyperthermia, because they fail to recognize that they are becoming overheated. Certain medications used in the treatment of some of these diseases that are more prevalent among older adults also increase the risk of developing a heat-related disorder.

BIOPSYCHOSOCIAL PERSPECTIVES

With this review of the body's systems as they change in the middle years and beyond, it is clear that when discussing the psychology of the middle-aged individual, physical changes and health are critical factors. By the same token, it is essential to consider psychological and sociocultural factors that affect the physical functioning of the middle-aged adult (Whitbourne, 2001). Throughout this discussion, it has been evident that individuals can ameliorate or exacerbate many normal age-related changes through the actions that they take to alter their own aging. So far, however, there is only scanty evidence regarding why people may either actively try to slow down or inadvertently manage to accelerate changes in their bodily systems (Whitbourne & Collins, 1998). Furthermore, individuals may engage in the same behaviors such as exercise or dietary control for entirely different reasons. Thus, it is difficult to determine whether individuals consciously take such actions as a response to internal awareness of the aging process (Skultety, Whitbourne, & Collins, 1999).

An overarching influence on the behavior of individuals, however, is the social context, which directly or indirectly leads adults to take actions that accelerate or retard the aging of their bodies. There is a well-established relationship between social status and mortality (Adler et al., 1994; Antonovsky, 1967). Income, education, occupation, race, gender, and ethnicity may be seen as contributing to the health and well-being of the individual in part through direct influences on the quality of life and opportunities to take advantage of age-related compensatory or preventive measures. In part, however, the social class effects are indirect, through influences on attitudes toward the aging process, which in turn influence how individuals feel about the effects of physical aging on themselves.

Evidence is emerging to support the role of social status in affecting the rate of normal aging through actions such as exercise and smoking, two behaviors that are known to affect many if not all the systems covered in this chapter (Bjorntorp, 1995; Wister, 1996). These behaviors, technically within the individual's personal control, may reflect pervasive attitudes, opportunities, and normative behaviors of people in varying occupational and educational groups. In North America and Europe, people with higher socioeconomic levels place a higher value on maintaining a healthy diet and regular pattern of exercise. In the cultures of some developing nations, where people are more concerned about not starving than about staying thin voluntarily, people hold the opposite set of social values about weight.

To investigate the role of social values on obesity, a team of international researchers attempted to determine whether there would be higher rates of obesity among the more highly educated middle-aged men in countries which equated greater weight with greater social standing. Groups of 200 middle-aged men from the rural and urban regions of each of four Asian countries were compared with 200 urban men from each of three Latin American nations. Overall, the urban Latin American men had the highest body mass indexes (BMIs) (25.3kg/m^2), followed in turn by the urban (22.2kg/m^2) and then the rural Asian men (21.4kg/m^2). There was no relationship between BMI and either income or socioeconomic status among the Latin American men although there was a tendency similar to that seen in North America for the more highly educated to have lower BMIs. Among Asian men, however, particularly in the rural areas, the manual laborers had lower BMIs than those of the managerial class (INCLEN, Group, 1996). These findings are intriguing particularly given the low rates of heart disease and death from heart disease among Asian Americans.

However, there may be independent contributors of social status to health beyond specific behaviors such as exercise and smoking. An 8-year follow-up of over 3,600 adults painted a stark picture of the heightened mortality risk for people in lower income brackets of American society (Lantz et al., 1998). People from the low and moderate income levels had a higher rate of mortality than those from the more affluent sectors of society even when controlling for differences among the income groups in health risk behaviors (smoking, alcohol intake, activity levels, and body weight) as well as age, sex, race, urbanicity, and education.

In addition to the pragmatic constraints placed on their lives, however, there may be harmful psychological effects associated with higher daily levels of stress of people in lower socioeconomic levels. People who are victims of discrimination on the basis of race, gender, age, and poverty status face constant frustration over their lack of access to resources that are readily available to others. At every point along the social class gradient, those who are in higher positions have greater abilities to influence the outcomes of their lives. Both the possession of this power and awareness of it may play important mediating roles in affecting health (Adler et al., 1994).

Furthermore, lack of control over the pace and direction of what happens during the workday, as is true in an assembly line or migrant farming job, can be equally if not more stressful. This possibility was highlighted in a 25-year follow-up study of over 12,500 male workers (aged 25 to 74) whose risk of dying from cardiovascular disease was studied in relation to the amount of control they had over their work activities (Johnson, Stewart, Hall, Fredlund, & Theorell, 1996). Even 5 years of assembly line work increased the risk of dying from heart disease. Those workers who participated in this type of work for the full period of the study had an 83% higher risk.

Personality variables must also be added to the equation in a biopsychosocial model, based on several lines of evidence that relate particular traits to higher risk of morbidity and mortality. The Type A behavior pattern is positively related to several cardiovascular disease risk factors, such as high serum cholesterol (the low-density lipoproteins) and the experience of angina pain (Edwards & Baglioni, 1991). In addition, high levels of hostility, part of the Type A pattern, are thought to be independent predictors of mortality (T. Miller, Smith, Turner, Guijarro, & Hallet, 1996). Type A personality traits may also be part of a larger constellation of cardiovascular risk factors including smoking, body weight, leisure activities, and hormonal levels (Zmuda et al., 1997).

In a study of members of the Terman sample whose mental health was assessed at midlife, the chance of dying over the following 40 years was higher for those who had shown the poorest adjustment at the time of their midlife testing (Martin et al., 1995). However, the relationship between psychological adjustment and health may go even farther back than middle adulthood. Using the data obtained from the Terman sample at childhood, it was possible to determine that those children who were high in the personality trait of conscientiousness had lower death rates than those with low childhood conscientiousness. It was not simply that the conscientious individuals avoided high-risk activities and therefore accidental death, or that they had better health habits. Instead, these highly conscientious individuals seemed better equipped to cope with life stress, build stable relationships with others, and to have high "ego strength" or a "self-healing personality" (Friedman et al., 1995). Similarly, among women studied longitudinally from college to midlife, a personality trait labeled "Intellectual Efficiency," was positively related to changes in health throughout midlife. Conversely, in these same studies, personality trait measures of hostility and anxiety were negatively related to health (Adams, Cartwright, Ostrove, Stewart, & Wink, 1998).

Further research driven by an integrative model incorporating biological, psychological, and sociocultural factors will enhance the study of physical functioning, health, social status, and identity processes. Throughout this chapter, many tantalizing possibilities have emerged regarding how and whether adults can alter the rate of aging. Ultimately, these possibilities will continue to be explored as researchers find ways to suggest how the actions of individuals and the contribution of society can influence not only the length of life but also its quality throughout the middle years and beyond.

REFERENCES

Adams, S.H., Cartwright, L.K., Ostrove, J.M., Stewart, A.J., & Wink, P. (1998). Psychological predictors of good health in three longitudinal samples of educated midlife women. *Health Psychology, 17,* 412–420.

Adler, N.E., Boyce, T., Chesney, M.A., Cohen, S., Folkman, S., Kahn, R.L., & Syme, S.L. (1994). Socioeconomic status and health: The challenge of the gradient. *American Psychologist, 49,* 15–24.

Ancoli-Israel, S. (1997). Sleep problems in older adults: Putting myths to bed. *Geriatrics, 52,* 20–30.

Antonovsky, A. (1967). Social class, life expectancy and overall mortality. *Milbank Memorial Fund Quarterly, 45,* 31–73.

Barrou, Z., Charru, P., & Lidy, C. (1997). Dehydroepiandrosterone (DHEA) and aging. *Archives of Gerontology and Geriatrics, 24,* 233–241.

Baumgartner, R.N., Heymsfield, S.B., & Roche, A.F. (1995). Human body composition and the epidemiology of chronic disease. *Obesity Research, 3,* 73–95.

Bemben, M.G., Massey, B.H., Bemben, D.A., Misner, J.E., & Boileau, R.A. (1996). Isometric intermittent endurance of four muscle groups in men aged 20–74 yr. *Medicine and Science in Sports and Exercise, 28,* 145–154.

Berr, C., Lafont, S., Debuire, B., Dartigues, J.F., & Baulieu, E.E. (1996). Relationships of dehydroepiandrosterone sulfate in the elderly with functional, psychological, and mental status, and short-term mortality: A French community-based study. *Proceedings of the National Academy of Sciences, USA, 93,* 13410–13415.

Bilato, C., & Crow, M.T. (1996). Atherosclerosis and the vascular biology of aging. *Aging, 8,* 221–234.

Birge, S.J. (1997). The role of estrogen in the treatment of Alzheimer's disease. *Neurology, 48*(Suppl. 7), S36–S41.

Bjorntorp, P. (1995). Neuroendocrine ageing. *Journal of Internal Medicine, 238,* 401–404.

Bjorntorp, P. (1996). The regulation of adipose tissue distribution in humans. *International Journal of Obesity and Related Metabolic Disorders, 20,* 291–302.

Blanpied, P., & Smidt, G.L. (1993). The difference in stiffness of the active plantarflexors between young and elderly human females. *Journal of Gerontology: Medical Sciences, 48,* M58–M63.

Bliwise, N.G. (1992). Factors related to sleep quality in healthy elderly women. *Psychology and Aging, 7,* 83–88.

Bohannon, R.W. (1997). Comfortable and maximum walking speed of adults aged 20–79 years: Reference values and determinants. *Age and Ageing, 26,* 15–19.

Boonen, S., Lesaffre, E., Dequeker, J., Aerssens, J., Nijs, J., Pelemans, W., & Bouillon, R. (1996). Relationship between baseline insulin-like growth factor-I (IGF-1) and femoral bone density in women aged over 70 years: Potential implications for the prevention of age-related bone loss. *Journal of the American Geriatrics Society, 44,* 1301–1306.

Born, J., Uthgenannt, D., Dodt, C., Nunninghoff, D., Ringvolt, E., Wagner, T., & Fehm, H.L. (1995). Cytokine production and lymphocyte subpopulations in aged humans: An assessment during nocturnal sleep. *Mechanisms of Ageing and Development, 84,* 113–126.

Bronfenbrenner, U. (1995). Developmental ecology through space and time: A future perspective. In P. Moen, G.H.J. Elder, & K. Luscher (Eds.), *Examining lives in context: Perspectives on the ecology of human development* (pp. 619–647). Washington, DC: American Psychological Association.

Brown, M., Birge, S.J., & Kohrt, W.M. (1997). Hormone replacement therapy does not augment gains in muscle strength or fat-free mass in response to weight-bearing exercise. *Journals of Gerontology: Series A, Biological Sciences and Medical Sciences, 52,* B166–B170.

Burgio, K.L., & Engel, B.T. (1990). Biofeedback-assisted behavioral training for elderly men and women. *Journal of the American Geriatrics Society, 38,* 338–340.

Burns, P.A., Pranikoff, K., Nochajski, T.H., Hadley, E.C., Levy, K.J., & Ory, M.G. (1993). A comparison of effectiveness of biofeedback and pelvic muscle exercise treatment of stress incontinence in older community-dwelling women. *Journal of Gerontology: Medical Sciences, 38,* M167–M174.

Cabeza, R., Grady, C.L., Nyberg, L., McIntosh, A.R., Tulving, E., Kapur, S., Jennings, J.M., Houle, S., & Craik, F.I. (1997). Age-related differences in neural activity during memory encoding and retrieval: A positron emission tomography study. *Journal of Neuroscience, 17,* 391–400.

Castaneda, C., Charnley, J.M., Evans, W.J., & Crim, M.C. (1995). Elderly women accommodate to a low-protein diet with losses of body cell mass, muscle function, and immune response. *American Journal of Clinical Nutrition, 62,* 30–39.

Centers for Disease Control. (1998). Heat related mortality: United States 1997. *Morbidity and Mortality Weekly Report, 47*(23), 473–475.

Chao, L.L., & Knight, R.T. (1997). Age-related prefrontal alterations during auditory memory. *Neurobiology of Aging, 18,* 87–95.

Clarkston, W.K., Pantano, M.M., Morley, J.E., Horowitz, M., Littlefield, J.M., & Burton, F.R. (1997). Evidence for the anorexia of aging: Gastrointestinal transit and hunger in healthy elderly vs. young adults. *American Journal of Physiology, 272,* R243–R248.

Coffey, C.E., Lucke, J.F., Saxton, J.A., Ratcliff, G., Unitas, L.J., Billig, B., & Bryan, R.N. (1998). Sex differences in brain aging: A quantitative magnetic resonance imaging study. *Archives of Neurology, 55,* 169–179.

Coffey, C.E., Wilkinson, W.E., Parashos, I.A., Soady, S.A., Sullivan, R.J., Patterson, L.J., Figiel, G.S., Webb, M.C., Spritzer, C.E., & Djang, W.T. (1992). Quantitative cerebral anatomy of the aging human brain: A cross-sectional study using magnetic resonance imaging. *Neurology, 42,* 527–536.

Coleman, P.D., & Flood, D.G. (1987). Neuron numbers and dendritic extent in normal aging and Alzheimer's disease. *Neurobiology of Aging, 8,* 521–545.

Courtney, A.C., Hayes, W.C., & Gibson, L.J. (1996). Age-related differences in post-yield damage in human cortical bone: Experiment and model. *Journal of Biomechanics, 29,* 1463–1471.

Cowell, P.E., Turetsky, B.I., Gur, R.C., Grossman, R.I., Shtasel, D.L., & Gur, R.E. (1994). Sex differences in aging of the human frontal and temporal lobes. *Journal of Neuroscience, 14,* 4748–4755.

Dargent, P., & Breart, G. (1993). Epidemiology and risk factors of osteoporosis. *Current Opinions in Rheumatology, 5,* 339–345.

Davies, D.F., & Shock, N.W. (1950). Age changes in glomerular filtration rate, effective renal plasma flow, and tubular excretory capacity in adult males. *Journal of Clinical Investigation, 29,* 496–507.

Dawson-Hughes, B., Harris, S.S., Krall, E.A., Dallal, G.E., Falconer, G., & Green, C.L. (1995). Rates of bone loss in postmenopausal women randomly assigned to one of two dosages of vitamin D. *American Journal of Clinical Nutrition, 61,* 1140–1145.

Dealberto, M.J., Pajot, N., Courbon, D., & Alperovitch, A. (1996). Breathing disorders during sleep and cognitive performance in an older community sample: The EVA Study. *Journal of the American Geriatric Society,* 1287–1294.

DeCarli, C., Murphy, D.G., Gillette, J.A., Haxby, J.V., Teichberg, D., Schapiro, M.B., & Horwitz, B. (1994). Lack of age-related differences in temporal lobe volume of very healthy adults. *American Journal of Neuroradiology, 15,* 689–696.

de Groot, C.P., Perdigao, A.L., & Deurenberg, P. (1996). Longitudinal changes in anthropometric characteristics of elderly Europeans: SENECA Investigators. *European Journal of Clinical Nutrition, 50,* 2954–3007.

de Leon, M.J., George, A.E., Golomb, J., Tarshish, C., Convit, A., Kluger, A., De Santi, S., McRae, T., Ferris, S.H., Reisberg, B., Ince, C., Rusinek, H., Bobinski, M., Quinn, B., Miller, D.C., & Wisniewski, H.M. (1997). Frequency of hippocampal formation atrophy in normal aging and Alzheimer's disease. *Neurobiology of Aging, 18,* 1–11.

de Lignieres, B. (1993). Transdermal dihydrotestosterone treatment of andropause. *Annals of Medicine, 25,* 235–241.

Denti, L., Pasolini, G., Sanfelici, L., Ablondi, F., Freddi, M., Benedetti, R., & Valenti, G. (1997). Effects of aging on dehydroepiandrosterone sulfate in relation to fasting insulin levels and body composition assessed by bioimpedance analysis. *Metabolism: Clinical and Experimental, 46,* 826–832.

De Santi, S., de Leon, M.J., Convit, A., Tarshish, C., Rusinek, H., Tsui, W.H., Sinaiko, E., Wang, G.J., Bartlet, E., & Volkow, N. (1995). Age-related changes in brain: II. Positron emission tomography of frontal and temporal lobe glucose metabolism in normal subjects. *Psychiatric Quarterly, 66,* 357–370.

Edelstein, S.L., & Barrett-Connor, E. (1993). Relation between body size and bone mineral density in elderly men and women. *American Journal of Epidemiology, 138,* 160–169.

Edwards, J.R., & Baglioni, A.J. (1991). Relationship between Type A behavior pattern and mental and physical symptoms: A comparison of global and component measures. *Journal of Applied Psychology, 76,* 276–290.

Eisen, A., Entezari-Taher, M., & Stewart, H. (1996). Cortical projections to spinal motoneurons: Changes with aging and amyotrophic lateral sclerosis. *Neurology, 46,* 1396–1404.

Epstein, M. (1996). Aging and the kidney. *Journal of the American Society of Nephrology, 7,* 1106–1122.

Erfurth, E.M., & Hagmar, L.E. (1995). Decreased serum testosterone and free triiodothyronine levels in healthy middle-aged men indicate an age effect at the pituitary level. *European Journal of Endocrinology, 132,* 663–667.

Farmer, K.C., & Naylor, M.F. (1996). Sun exposure, sunscreens, and skin cancer prevention: A year-round concern. *Annals of Pharmacotherapy, 30,* 662–673.

Ferrara, A., Barrett-Connor, E., & Shan, J. (1997). Total, LDL, and HDL cholesterol decrease with age in older men and women: The Rancho Bernardo Study 1984–1994. *Circulation, 96,* 37–43.

Field, A.E., Colditz, G.A., Willett, W.C., Longcope, C., & McKinlay, J.B. (1994). The relation of smoking, age, relative weight, and dietary intake to serum adrenal steroids, sex hormones, and sex hormone-binding globulin in middle-aged men. *Journal of Clinical Endocrinology and Metabolism, 79,* 1310–1316.

Fliser, D., Franek, E., Joest, M., Block, S., Mutschler, E., & Ritz, E. (1997). Renal function in the elderly: Impact of hypertension and cardiac function. *Kidney International, 51,* 1196–1204.

Frette, C., Barrett-Connor, E., & Clausen, J.L. (1996). Effect of active and passive smoking on ventilatory function in elderly men and women. *American Journal of Epidemiology, 143,* 757–765.

Friedman, H.S., Tucker, J.S., Schwartz, J.E., Martin, L.R., Tomlinson-Keasey, C., Wingard, D.L., & Criqui, M.H. (1995). Childhood conscientiousness and longevity: Health behaviors and cause of death. *Journal of Personality and Social Psychology, 68,* 696–703.

Garnero, P., Sornay Rendu, E., Chapuy, M.C., & Delmas, P.D. (1996). Increased bone turnover in late postmenopausal women is a major determinant of osteoporosis. *Journal of Bone and Mineral Research, 11,* 337–349.

Golomb, J., Kluger, A., de Leon, M.J., Ferris, S.H., Mittelman, M., Cohen, J., & George, A.E. (1996). Hippocampal formation size predicts declining memory performance in normal aging. *Neurology, 47,* 810–813.

Gotthardt, U., Schweiger, U., Fahrenberg, J., Lauer, C.J., Holsboer, F., & Heuser, I. (1995). Cortisol, ACTH, and cardiovascular response to a cognitive challenge paradigm in aging and depression. *American Journal of Physiology, 268,* R865–R873.

Grimby, A., & Wiklund, I. (1994). Health-related quality of life in old age: A study among 76-year-old Swedish urban citizens. *Scandinavian Journal of Social Medicine, 22,* 7–14.

Haimov, I., & Lavie, P. (1997). Circadian characteristics of sleep propensity function in healthy elderly: A comparison with young adults. *Sleep, 20,* 294–300.

Hakkinen, K., Kraemer, W.J., Kallinen, M., Linnamo, V., Pastinen, U.M., & Newton, R.U. (1996). Bilateral and unilateral neuromuscular function and muscle cross-sectional area in middle-aged and elderly men and women. *Journals of Gerontology: Series A, Biological Sciences and Medical Sciences, 51,* B21–B29.

Hakkinen, K., & Pakarinen, A. (1995). Acute hormonal responses to heavy resistance exercise in men and women at different ages. *International Journal of Sports Medicine, 16,* 507–513.

Harris, M.B. (1994). Growing old gracefully: Age concealment and gender. *Journal of Gerontology: Psychological Sciences, 49,* P149–P158.

Hayflick, L. (1994). *How and why we age.* New York: Ballantine Books.

Hayflick, L., & Moorhead, P.S. (1961). The serial cultivation of human diploid cell strains. *Experimental Cell Research, 25,* 585–621.

Hays, M.T., & Nielsen, K.R. (1994). Human thyroxine absorption: Age effects and methodological analyses. *Thyroid, 4,* 55–64.

Herskind, A.M., McGue, M., Holm, N.V., Sorensen, T.I., Harvald, B., & Vaupel, J.W. (1996). The heritability of human longevity: A population-based study of 2,872 Danish twin pairs born 1870–1900. *Human Genetics, 97,* 319–323.

Herskind, A.M., McGue, M., Iachine, I.A., Holm, N.V., Sorensen, T.I., Harvald, B., & Vaupel, J.W. (1996). Untangling genetic influences on smoking, body mass index, and longevity: A multivariate study of 2,464 Danish twins followed for 28 years. *Human Genetics, 98,* 467–475.

Hoch, C.C., Reynolds, C.F., Jennings, J.R., Monk, T.H., Buysse, D.J., Machen, M.A., & Kupler, D.J. (1992). Daytime sleepiness and performance among healthy 80 and 20 year olds. *Neurobiology of Aging, 13,* 353–356.

Horber, F.F., Kohler, S.A., Lippuner, K., & Jaeger, P. (1996). Effect of regular physical training on age-associated alteration of body composition in men. *European Journal of Clinical Investigation, 26,* 279–285.

Huether, G. (1996). Melatonin as an antiaging drug: Between facts and fantasy. *Gerontology, 42,* 87–96.

Hurley, B.F. (1995). Age, gender, and muscular strength. *Journals of Gerontology: Series A, Biological Sciences and Medical Sciences, 50A,* 41–44.

Hurwitz, A., Brady, D.A., Schaal, S.E., Samloff, I.M., Dedon, J., & Ruhl, C.E. (1997). Gastric acidity in older adults. *Journal of the American Medical Association, 278,* 659–662.

Iida, I., & Noro, K. (1995). An analysis of the reduction of elasticity on the ageing of human skin and the recovering effect of a facial massage. *Ergonomics, 38,* 1921–1931.

INCLEN Multicentre Collaborative Group (1996). Body mass index and cardiovascular disease risk factors in seven Asian and five Latin American centres: Data from the International Clinical Epidemiology Network. *Obesity Research, 4,* 221–228.

Inoue, Y. (1996). Longitudinal effects of age on heat-activated sweat gland density and output in healthy active older men. *European Journal of Applied Physiology and Occupational Physiology, 74,* 72–77.

Inoue, Y., Nakao, M., Araki, T., & Ueda, H. (1992). Thermoregulatory responses of young and older men to cold exposure. *European Journal of Applied Physiology, 65,* 492–498.

Intons-Peterson, M.J., Rocchi, P., West, T., McLellan, K., & Hackney, A. (1998). Aging, optimal testing times, and negative priming. *Journal of Experimental Psychology: Learning, Memory, and Cognition, 24,* 362–376.

Iqbal, P., & Castleden, C.M. (1997). Management of urinary incontinence in the elderly. *Gerontology, 43,* 151–157.

James, K., Premchand, N., Skibinska, A., Skibinski, G., Nicol, M., & Mason, J.I. (1997). IL-6, DHEA and the ageing process. *Mechanisms of Ageing and Development, 93,* 15–24.

Jazwinski, S.M. (1996). Longevity, genes, and aging. *Science, 273,* 54–59.

Johnson, J., Stewart, W., Hall, E., Fredlund, P., & Theorell, T. (1996). Long-term psychosocial work environment and cardiovascular mortality among Swedish men. *American Journal of Public Health, 86,* 324–331.

Jubrias, S.A., Odderson, I.R., Esselman, P.C., & Conley, K.E. (1997). Decline in isokinetic force with age: Muscle cross-sectional area and specific force. *Pflugers Archiv European Journal of Physiology, 434,* 246–253.

Kawas, C., Resnick, S., Morrison, A., Brookmeyer, R., Corrada, M., Zonderman, A., Bacal, C., Lingle, D.D., & Metter, E. (1997). A prospective study of estrogen replacement therapy and the risk of developing Alzheimer's disease: The Baltimore Longitudinal Study of Aging. *Neurology, 48,* 1517–1521.

Kelly, K.S., Hayslip, B., Jr., & Servaty, H.L. (1996). Psychoneuroendocrinological indicators of stress and intellectual performance among older adults: An exploratory study. *Experimental Aging Research, 22,* 393–401.

Kern, W., Dodt, C., Born, J., & Fehm, H.L. (1996). Changes in cortisol and growth hormone secretion during nocturnal sleep in the course of aging. *Journal of Gerontology: Medical Sciences, 51A,* M3–M9.

Kinoshita, H., & Francis, P.R. (1996). A comparison of prehension force control in young and elderly individuals. *European Journal of Applied Physiology and Occupational Physiology, 74,* 450–460.

Kitagawa, N., Ichikawa, T., Akimoto, S., & Shimazaki, J. (1994). Natural course of human benign prostatic hyperplasia with relation to urinary disturbance. *Prostate, 24,* 279–284.

Kligman, A.M., Grove, G.L., & Balin, A.K. (1985). Aging of human skin. In C.E. Finch & E.L. Schneider (Eds.), *Handbook of the biology of aging* (2nd ed.). New York: Van Nostrand-Reinhold.

Krall, E.A., Dawson-Hughes, B., Hirst, K., Gallagher, J.C., Sherman, S.S., & Dalsky, G. (1997). Bone mineral density and biochemical markers of bone turnover in healthy elderly men and women. *Journals of Gerontology: Series A, Biological Sciences and Medical Sciences, 52,* M61–M67.

Lamberts, S.W.J., van den Beld, A.W., & van der Lely, A.-J. (1997). The endocrinology of aging. *Science, 278,* 419–424.

Lantz, P.M., House, J.S., Lepkowski, J.M., Williams, D.R., Mero, R.P., & Chen, J. (1998). Socioeconomic factors, health behaviors, and mortality: Results from a nationally representative prospective study of U.S. adults. *Journal of the American Medical Association, 279,* 1703–1708.

Laumann, E.O., Paik, A., & Rosen, R.C. (1999). Sexual dysfunction in the United States: Prevalence and predictors. *Journal of the American Medical Association, 281,* 537–544.

Lerner, R.M. (1995). Developing individuals within changing contexts: Implications of developmental contextualism for human development, research, policy, and programs. In T.J. Kindermann & J. Valsiner (Eds.), *Development of person-context relations* (pp. 13–37). Hillsdale, NJ: Erlbaum.

Lesourd, B.M. (1997). Nutrition and immunity in the elderly: Modification of immune responses with nutritional treatments. *American Journal of Clinical Nutrition, 66,* 478S–484S.

Lovat, L.B. (1996). Age related changes in gut physiology and nutritional status. *Gut, 38,* 306–309.

Lupien, S., Lecours, A.R., Schwartz, G., Sharma, S., Hauger, R.L., Meaney, M.J., & Nair, N.P. (1996). Longitudinal study of basal cortisol levels in healthy elderly subjects: Evidence for subgroups. *Neurobiology of Aging, 17,* 95–105.

Maas, D., Jochen, A., & Lalande, B. (1997). Age-related changes in male gonadal function: Implications for therapy. *Drugs and Aging, 11,* 45–60.

Martin, L.R., Friedman, H.S., Tucker, J.S., Schwartz, J.E., Criqui, M.H., Wingard, D.L., & Tomlinson-Keasey, C. (1995). An archival prospective study of mental health and longevity. *Health Psychology, 5,* 381–387.

Matsumae, M., Kikinis, R., Morocz, I.A., Lorenzo, A.V., Sandor, T., Albert, M.S., Black, P.M., & Jolesz, F.A. (1996). Age-related changes in intracranial compartment volumes in normal adults assessed by magnetic resonance imaging. *Journal of Neurosurgery, 84,* 982–991.

May, C.P., Hasher, L., & Stoltzfus, E.R. (1993). Optimal time of day and the magnitude of age differences in memory. *Psychological Sciences, 4,* 326–330.

May, H., Murphy, S., & Khaw, K.T. (1995). Bone mineral density and its relationship to skin colour in Caucasian females. *European Journal of Clinical Investigation, 25,* 85–89.

McCalden, R.W., McGeough, J.A., Barker, M.B., & Court-Brown, C.M. (1993). Age-related changes in the tensile properties of cortical bone: The relative importance of changes in porosity, mineralization, and microstructure. *Journal of Bone and Joint Surgery, 75,* 1193–1205.

McCalden, R.W., McGeough, J.A., & Court-Brown, C.M. (1997). Age-related changes in the compressive strength of cancellous bone: The relative importance of changes in density and trabecular architecture. *Journal of Bone and Joint Surgery American, 79,* 421–427.

McCartney, N., Hicks, A.L., Martin, J., & Webber, C.E. (1995). Long-term resistance training in the elderly: Effects on dynamic strength, exercise capacity, muscle, and bone. *Journals of Gerontology: Series A, Biological Sciences and Medical Sciences, 50,* B97–B104.

McCartney, N., Hicks, A.L., Martin, J., & Webber, C.E. (1996). A longitudinal trial of weight training in the elderly: Continued improvements in year 2. *Journals of Gerontology: Series A, Biological Sciences and Medical Sciences, 51,* B425–B433.

McEwen, B.S., Alves, S.E., Bulloch, K., & Weiland, N.G. (1997). Ovarian steroids and the brain: Implications for cognition and aging. *Neurology, 48,* S8–S15.

Meltzer, D.E. (1996). Body-mass dependence of age-related deterioration in human muscular function. *Journal of Applied Physiology, 80,* 1149–1155.

Middelkoop, H.A., Smilde-van den Doel, D.A., Neven, A.K., Kamphuisen, H.A., & Springer, C.P. (1996). Subjective sleep characteristics of 1,485 males and females aged 50–93: Effects of sex and age, and factors related to self-evaluated quality of sleep. *Journals of Gerontology: Series A, Biological Sciences and Medical Sciences, 51,* M108–M115.

Miller, R.A. (1996). The aging immune system: Primer and prospectus. *Science, 273,* 70–74.

Miller, T.Q., Smith, T.W., Turner, C.W., Guijarro, M.L., & Hallet, A.J. (1996). Meta-analytic review of research on hostility and physical health. *Psychological Bulletin, 119,* 322–348.

Montgomery, S.A. (1990). Depression in the elderly: Pharmacokinetics of antidepressants and death from overdose. *International Clinical Psychopharmacology, 5,* 67–76.

Monzani, F., Del Guerra, P., Caraccio, N., Del Corso, L., Casolaro, A., Mariotti, S., & Pentimone, F. (1996). Age-related modifications in the regulation of the hypothalamic-pituitary-thyroid axis. *Hormone Research, 46,* 107–112.

Morley, J.E., Kaiser, F., Raum, W.J., Perry, H.M., III, Flood, J.F., Jensen, J., Silver, A.J., & Roberts, E. (1997). Potentially predictive and manipulable blood serum correlates of aging in the healthy human male: Progressive decreases in bioavailable testosterone, dehydroepiandrosterone sulfate, and the ratio of insulin-like growth factor 1 to growth hormone. *Proceedings of the National Academy of Sciences, USA, 94,* 7537–7542.

Murphy, D.G., DeCarli, C., McIntosh, A.R., Daly, E., Mentis, M.J., Pietrini, P., Szczepanik, J., Schapiro, M.B., Grady, C.L., Horwitz, B., & Rappoport, S.I. (1996). Sex differences in human brain morphometry and metabolism: An in vivo quantitative magnetic resonance imaging and positron emission tomography study on the effect of aging. *Archives of General Psychiatry, 53,* 585–594.

Murphy, S., Khaw, K.T., May, H., & Compston, J.E. (1994). Milk consumption and bone mineral density in middle aged and elderly women. *British Medical Journal, 308,* 939–941.

Muscarella, F., & Cunningham, M.R. (1996). The evolutionary significance and social perception of male pattern baldness and facial hair. *Ethology and Sociobiology, 17,* 99–117.

Nachbar, F., & Korting, H.C. (1995). The role of vitamin E in normal and damaged skin. *Journal of Molecular Medicine, 73,* 7–17.

National Center for Health Statistics. (1997). *Health, United States, 1996–97 and Injury Chartbook (76–641496).* Washington, DC: U.S. Government Printing Office.

Nicolson, N., Storms, C., Ponds, R., & Sulon, J. (1997). Salivary cortisol levels and stress reactivity in human aging. *Journals of Gerontology: Series A, Biological Sciences and Medical Sciences, 52,* M68–M75.

Nielsen Bohlman, L., & Knight, R.T. (1995). Prefrontal alterations during memory processing in aging. *Cerebral Cortex, 5,* 541–549.

Nishimura, N., Hongo, M., Yamada, M., Kawakami, H., Ueno, M., Okuno, Y., & Toyota, T. (1996). Effect of aging on the esophageal motor functions. *Journal of Smooth Muscle Research, 32,* 43–50.

O'Brien, J.T., Schweitzer, I., Ames, D., Tuckwell, V., & Mastwyk, M. (1994). Cortisol suppression by dexamethasone in the healthy elderly: Effects of age, dexamethasone levels, and cognitive function. *Biological Psychiatry, 36,* 389–394.

Perry, H.M., III, Horowitz, M., Morley, J.E., Fleming, S., Jensen, J., Caccione, P., Miller, D.K., Kaiser, F.E., & Sundarum, M. (1996). Aging and bone metabolism in African American and Caucasian women. *Journal of Clinical Endocrinology and Metabolism, 81,* 1108–1117.

Peskind, E.R., Raskind, M.A., Wingerson, D., Pascualy, M., Thal, L.J., Dobie, D.J., Veith, R.C., Dorsa, D.M., Murray, S., Sikkema, C., Galt, S.A., & Wilkinson, C.W. (1995). Enhanced hypothalamic-pituitary-adrenocortical axis responses to physostigmine in normal aging. *Journals of Gerontology: Series A, Biological Sciences and Medical Sciences, 50,* M114–M120.

Philip, P., Dealberto, M.J., Dartigues, J.F., Guilleminault, C., & Bioulac, B. (1997). Prevalence and correlates of nocturnal desaturations in a sample of elderly people. *Journal of Sleep Research, 6,* 264–271.

Pollock, M.L., Mengelkoch, L.J., Graves, J.E., Lowenthal, D.T., Limacher, M.C., Foster, C., & Wilmore, J.H. (1997). Twenty-year follow-up of aerobic power and body composition of older track athletes. *Journal of Applied Physiology, 82,* 1508–1516.

Prinz, P.N., Moe, K.E., Dulberg, E.M., Larsen, L.H., Vitiello, M.V., Toivola, B., & Merriam, G.R. (1995). Higher plasma IGF-1 levels are associated with increased delta sleep in healthy older men. *Journals of Gerontology: Series A, Biological Sciences and Medical Sciences, 50,* M222–M226.

Ralphs, J.R., & Benjamin, M. (1994). The joint capsule: Structure, composition, ageing, and disease. *Journal of Anatomy, 184,* 503–509.

Raz, N., Gunning, F.M., Head, D., Dupuis, J.H., McQuain, J., Briggs, S.D., Loken, W.J., Thornton, A.E., & Acker, J.D. (1997). Selective aging of the human cerebral cortex observed in vivo: Differential vulnerability of the prefrontal gray matter. *Cerebral Cortex, 7,* 268–282.

Raz, N., Gunning-Dixon, F.M., Head, D., Dupuis, J.H., & Acker, J.D. (1998). Neuroanatomical correlates of cognitive aging: Evidence from structural magnetic resonance imaging. *Neuropsychology, 12,* 95–114.

Riedel, M., Brabant, G., Rieger, K., & von zur Muhlen, A. (1994). Growth hormone therapy in adults: Rationales, results, and perspectives. *Experimental and Clinical Endocrinology, 102,* 273–283.

Ross, M.H., Yurgelun-Todd, D.A., Renshaw, P.F., Maas, L.C., Mendelson, J.H., Mello, N.K., Cohen, B.M., & Levin, J.M. (1997). Age-related reduction in functional MRI response to photic stimulation. *Neurology, 48,* 173–176.

Rossi, A., Ganassini, A., Tantucci, C., & Grassi, V. (1996). Aging and the respiratory system. *Aging, 8,* 143–161.

Seaton, K. (1995). Cortisol: The aging hormone, the stupid hormone. *Journal of the National Medical Association, 87,* 667–683.

Seeman, T.E., Singer, B., & Charpentier, P. (1995). Gender differences in patterns of HPA axis response to challenge: MacArthur studies of successful aging. *Psychoneuroendocrinology, 20,* 711–725.

Sherwin, B. (1996). Estrogen, the brain, and memory. *Menopause, 3,* 97–105.

Shinkai, S., Konishi, M., & Shephard, R.J. (1997). Aging, exercise, training, and the immune system. *Exercise Immunology Review, 3,* 68–95.

Ship, J.A., Nolan, N.E., & Puckett, S.A. (1995). Longitudinal analysis of parotid and submandibular salivary flow rates in healthy, different-aged adults. *Journal of Gerontology: Series A, Biological Sciences and Medical Sciences, 50A,* M285–M289.

Silverman, H.G., & Mazzeo, R.S. (1996). Hormonal responses to maximal and submaximal exercise in trained and untrained men of various ages. *Journals of Gerontology: Series A, Biological Sciences and Medical Sciences, 51A,* B30–B37.

Sinaki, M. (1996). Effect of physical activity on bone mass. *Current Opinions in Rheumatology, 8,* 376–383.

Skultety, K., Whitbourne, S.K., & Collins, K.L. (1999). *Identity processes and exercise patterns in adult men and women.* Paper presented at the 107th annual meeting of the American Psychological Association, Boston.

Sohal, R.S., & Weindruch, R. (1996). Oxidative stress, caloric restriction, and aging. *Science, 273,* 59–63.

Sone, Y. (1995). Age-associated problems in nutrition. *Applied Human Science, 14,* 201–210.

Spina, R.J., Miller, T.R., Bogenhagen, W.H., Schechtman, K.B., & Ehsani, A.A. (1996). Gender-related differences in left ventricular filling dynamics in older subjects after endurance exercise training. *Journals of Gerontology: Series A, Biological Sciences and Medical Sciences, 51,* B232–B237.

Stampfer, M.J., Krauss, R.M., Ma, J., Blanche, P.J., Holl, L.G., Sacks, F.M., & Hennekens, C.H. (1996). A prospective study of triglyceride level, low-density lipoprotein particle diameter, and risk of myocardial infarction. *Journal of the American Medical Association, 276,* 882–888.

Suominen, H. (1997). Changes in physical characteristics and body composition during 5-year follow-up in 75- and 80-year-old men and women. *Scandinavian Journal of Social Medicine*(Suppl. 53), 19–24.

Taaffe, D.R., & Marcus, R. (1997). Dynamic muscle strength alterations to detraining and retraining in elderly men. *Clinical Physiology, 17,* 311–324.

Taaffe, D.R., Pruitt, L., Reim, J., Hintz, R.L., Butterfield, G., Hoffman, A.R., & Marcus, R. (1994). Effect of recombinant human growth hormone on the muscle strength response to resistance exercise in elderly men. *Journal of Clinical Endocrinology and Metabolism, 79,* 1361–1366.

Takema, Y., Yorimoto, Y., Ohsu, H., Osanai, O., & Kawai, M. (1997). Age-related discontinuous changes in the in vivo fluorescence of human facial skin. *Journal of Dermatological Science, 15,* 55–58.

Tankersley, C.G., Smolander, J., Kenney, W.L., & Fortney, S.M. (1991). Sweating and skin blood flow during exercise: Effects of age and maximal oxygen uptake. *Journal of Applied Physiology, 71,* 236–242.

Teramoto, S., Fukuchi, Y., Nagase, T., Matsuse, T., & Orimo, H. (1995). A comparison of ventilation components in young and elderly men during exercise. *Journal of Gerontology: Biological Sciences, 50A,* B34–B39.

Toogood, A.A., O'Neill, P., & Shalet, S.M. (1996). Beyond the somatopause: Growth hormone deficiency in adults over the age of 60 years. *Journal of Clinical Endocrinology and Metabolism, 81,* 460–465.

Trappe, S.W., Costill, D.L., Vukovich, M.D., Jones, J., & Melham, T. (1996). Aging among elite distance runners: A 22-yr longitudinal study. *Journal of Applied Physiology, 80,* 285–290.

Tuite, D.J., Renstrom, P.A., & O'Brien, M. (1997). The aging tendon. *Scandinavian Journal of Medicine and Science in Sports, 7,* 72–77.

Van Cauter, E., Leproult, R., & Kupfer, D.J. (1996). Effects of gender and age on the levels and circadian rhythmicity of plasma cortisol. *Journal of Clinical Endocrinology and Metabolism, 81,* 2468–2473.

Van Someren, E.J., Lijzenga, C., Mirmiran, M., & Swaab, D.F. (1997). Long-term fitness training improves the circadian rest-activity rhythm in healthy elderly males. *Journal of Biological Rhythms, 12,* 146–156.

Venjatraman, J.T., & Fernandes, G. (1997). Exercise, immunity, and aging. *Aging, 9,* 42–56.

Villa, M.L., Marcus, R., Ramirez Delay, R., & Kelsey, J.L. (1995). Factors contributing to skeletal health of postmenopausal Mexican-American women. *Journal of Bone and Mineral Research, 10,* 1233–1242.

Vitiello, M.V. (1997). Sleep disorders and aging: Understanding the causes. *Journals of Gerontology: Series A, Biological Sciences and Medical Sciences, 52,* M189–M191.

Vitiello, M.V., Wilkinson, C.W., Merriam, G.R., Moe, K.E., Prinz, P.N., Ralph, D.D., Colasurdo, E.A., & Schwartz, R.S. (1997). Successful 6-month endurance training does not alter insulin-like growth factor-I in healthy older men and women. *Journals of Gerontology: Series A, Biological Sciences and Medical Sciences, 52,* M149–M154.

von Zglinicki, T., Nilsson, E., Docke, W.D., & Brunk, U.T. (1995). Lipofuscin accumulation and ageing of fibroblasts. *Gerontology, 2,* 95–108.

Welten, D.C., Kemper, H.C., Post, G.B., & van Staveren, W.A. (1995). A meta-analysis of the effect of calcium intake on bone mass in young and middle aged females and males. *Journal of Nutrition, 125,* 2802–2813.

Whitbourne, S.K. (1996). *The aging individual: Physical and psychological perspectives.* New York: Springer.

Whitbourne, S.K. (2001). *Adult development and aging: Biopsychosocial perspectives.* New York: Wiley.

Whitbourne, S.K., & Collins, K.C. (1998). Identity and physical changes in later adulthood: Theoretical and clinical implications. *Psychotherapy, 35,* 519–530.

Wilkinson, C.W., Peskind, E.R., & Raskind, M.A. (1997). Decreased hypothalamic-pituitary-adrenal axis sensitivity to cortisol feedback inhibition in human aging. *Neuroendocrinology, 65,* 79–90.

Wilson, P.W., Anderson, K.M., Harris, T., Kannel, W.B., & Castelli, W.P. (1994). Determinants of change in total cholesterol and HDL-C with age: The Framingham Study. *Journal of Gerontology, 49,* M252–M257.

Wise, P.M., Krajnak, K.M., & Kashon, M.L. (1996). Menopause: The aging of multiple pacemakers. *Science, 273,* 67–74.

Wister, A.V. (1996). The effects of socioeconomic status on exercise and smoking: Age-related differences. *Journal of Aging and Health, 8,* 467–488.

Xu, S.Z., Huang, W.M., & Ren, J.Y. (1997). The new model of age-dependent changes in bone mineral density. *Growth, Development, and Aging, 61,* 19–26.

Yang, J.H., Lee, H.C., & Wei, Y.H. (1995). Photoageing-associated mitochondrial DNA length mutations in human skin. *Archives of Dermatological Research, 287,* 641–648.

Yen, S.S., Morales, A.J., & Khorram, O. (1995). Replacement of DHEA in aging men and women: Potential remedial effects. *Annals of the New York Academy of Sciences, 774,* 128–142.

Young, A.J. (1991). Effects of aging on human cold tolerance. *Experimental Aging Research, 17,* 205–213.

Young, A.J., & Lee, D.T. (1997). Aging and human cold tolerance. *Experimental Aging Research, 23,* 45–67.

Zioupos, P., & Currey, J.D. (1998). Changes in the stiffness, strength, and toughness of human cortical bone with age. *Bone, 22,* 57–66.

Zmuda, J.M., Cauley, J.A., Kriska, A., Glynn, N.W., Gutai, J.P., & Kuller, L.H. (1997). Longitudinal relation between endogenous testosterone and cardiovascular disease risk factors in middle-aged men: A 13-year follow-up of former Multiple Risk Factor Intervention Trial participants. *American Journal of Epidemiology, 146,* 609–617.

CHAPTER 5

Health in Midlife:
Toward a Life-Span View

AVRON SPIRO III

> The only time you really live fully is from thirty to sixty. The young are slaves to dreams; the old servants of regrets. Only the middle-aged have all their five senses in the keeping of their wits.
> —Hervey Allen

THE GOALS of this chapter are to:

- Provide information on health and disease in midlife in the United States at the turn of the millennium.
- Propose a life-span developmental perspective as a framework for interpreting these and other findings on health and disease.
- Consider some recent findings in the context of this perspective, with the aim of suggesting some models and methods worthy of future study for advancing our understanding of health.

My reasons for taking this approach are rooted in the belief that models offer valuable contributions (e.g., Taylor, 1990). They provide a context for viewing and interpreting disparate data; they suggest new approaches and avenues for study; they provide a theoretical context in which to distinguish among antecedents, correlates, and consequences; and they can lead us to consider relations heretofore unexamined. A vast amount of data are currently available in the social science and biomedical literatures; my challenge is to begin to integrate these findings. Thus in this chapter, I hope to present a particular (i.e., life-span) perspective from which to understand some of the evidence, and to argue that such a perspective offers a unique vantage from which to study health during the new millennium. For other perspectives on health in midlife, see Merrill and Verbrugge (1999), or Whitman, Merluzzi, and White (1999); for alternative perspectives on health psychology, see recent chapters in the *Annual Review of Psychology* (e.g., Adler & Matthews, 1994; Baum & Posluszny, 1999; Taylor, Repetti, & Seeman, 1997) or Smith and Gallo (2001).

PRELIMINARIES

Several preliminaries must be considered prior to addressing these goals. These include addressing our understanding of the words "midlife," "life span," and "health."

THE AGES OF MIDLIFE

Midlife, perhaps the last portion of the life span to be called into study as a specific phase, may be best defined by what has not been claimed by other age-related specialties. The first portion of the life span, long divided into infancy, childhood, and adolescence, subsumes the years from birth until 18; young adulthood includes the years from 18 until perhaps 35. Old age is generally recognized to begin at 65. Concurrent with the increase in life span during the twentieth century, this last phase has been subdivided into young-old (65–74), old-old (75–84), oldest-old (85–99), and centenarians (≥100). This seems to leave the years from 35 to 64 as the province of midlife, a somewhat arbitrary conclusion, which is nevertheless shared by others (e.g., Lachman & James, 1997).

A LIFE-SPAN PERSPECTIVE

We first broach the general question, What is a life-span perspective? Later, we will turn to a consideration of how this perspective might apply to the study of health. The life-span perspective is not a specific theory per se, but rather a perspective on development (e.g., Baltes, 1987; Baltes, Lindenberger, & Staudinger, 1998). Several metatheoretical propositions characterize this perspective:

- Development is a lifelong process.
- Development is characterized by multidimensionality.
- There are always gains and losses.
- Development occurs in and is constrained by its sociohistorical context.
- The study of development is inherently multidisciplinary.

In the following sections, we consider these principles in the context of health, and use them to frame our considerations regarding health in midlife.

WHAT IS HEALTH?

The most difficult question, What is health? allows many answers, depending on one's disciplinary background, theoretical perspective, and measurement preferences. In a sense, health (like other latent variables) resembles the elephant, and we are the blind men, seeking to comprehend its entirety, but limited in our experience of it by our perspective. Where we stand and how we perceive largely determine what we will see.

Most physicians evaluate health through a focus on organ systems (e.g., heart, lungs, endocrine system) and the extent of damage therein. Psychiatrists, for whom the relevant organ system (the mind) is more difficult to study directly, have focused on the interpretation of the signs, symptoms, and self-reports of their patients. Social scientists, such as psychologists and sociologists, have also concentrated on patient self-reports of health. In contrast to these person-focused approaches, others consider health at the population level (e.g., Field & Gold, 1988; Wallace, 1994). Demographers study life expectancy, as well as birth and death rates. Economists and health services researchers consider measures of healthcare use, such as access to health care, rates of hospitalization, and physician visits. In short, clinicians study diseases; psychologists study persons; and economists study systems.

In this chapter, the focus is primarily on person-level aspects of health. However, we first consider some demographics of health and disease at the population level, to provide a sociohistorical context for the study of health in midlife.

MIDLIFE HEALTH IN CONTEXT

Earlier, we proposed an arbitrary definition of midlife as ages 35 to 64. From a life-span perspective, it is important to consider the sociohistorical context of midlife. As the new millennium begins, it seems appropriate to look back over the past 100 years in the United States, and consider some of the many relevant changes.

HISTORICAL CONTEXT

In 1900, the U.S. population was nearly 76 million persons, and the median age was 23 (U.S. Census Bureau, 1999). By 1950, the population had doubled to 151 million, and the median age was 30.2. In 1998, the population had increased 70%, to 271 million, and the median age was 35.2. In 1900, 60% of the population lived in rural areas; in 1990, only 25% did.

Life expectancy also increased, from 47.3 years in 1900 to 68.2 in 1950, to 76.5 in 1997. At the beginning of the past century, the average man lived 46.3 years; the average woman 48.3. By 1997, men lived an average of 73.6 years, and women 79.2. Over the past 100 years, life expectancy increased 60%. With this increase in life expectancy, the latter part of the life span has differentiated into varied phases of study.

In addition to changes in life expectancy, there have been many changes in aspects of health (National Center for Health Statistics [NCHS], 1998). Considering age-adjusted death rates, the overall death rate has decreased from 1950 to 1996 (see Table 5.1). The most common causes of death maintained their rank order over the past 50 years. Heart disease continues to be the leading cause of death in men; for women, cancer has surpassed heart disease as the leading killer (due to an increase in lung cancer mortality, Greenlee, Murray, Bolden, & Wingo, 2000). For both men and women, mortality due to stroke, pneumonia and influenza, and unintentional injury, decreased. Mortality from chronic obstructive pulmonary disease (COPD) increased in both men and women.

Table 5.1 presents leading causes of death in 1950 and 1996, separately for men and women (NCHS, 1998). Age-adjusted death rates are shown per 100,000 persons. Note that the overall death rate from all causes declined for both men and women from 1950 to 1996, primarily due to a decrease in the death rates for heart disease, cerebrovascular disease, pneumonia and

Table 5.1
Age-Adjusted Death Rates (per 100,000 persons)

	Men		Women	
	1950	1996	1950	1996
All Causes	1001.6	623.7	688.4	381.0
Diseases				
Heart disease	383.8	178.8	233.9	98.2
Cerebrovascular disease	91.9	28.5	86.0	24.6
Malignant neoplasms	130.8	153.8	120.8	108.8
Chronic obstructive pulmonary disease	6.0	25.9	2.9	17.6
Pneumonia/influenza	30.6	16.2	22.0	10.4
Chronic liver disease and cirrhosis	11.4	10.7	5.8	4.5
Diabetes	11.4	14.9	17.1	12.5
External causes				
Unintentional injury	83.7	43.3	31.7	17.9
Suicide	17.3	18.0	4.9	4.0

influenza, and cancer (for women only). However, death rates for cancer (in men), as well as COPD, and diabetes (men only) increased.

The types of disease that are most likely to affect health have changed over the past century (U.S. Census Bureau, 1999; U.S. Department of Health and Human Services [USDHHS], 2000). In the early years of the 1900s, infectious diseases and epidemics (such as the 1918 influenza epidemic) were common and accounted for a large proportion of deaths (Armstrong, Conn, & Pinner, 1999). There were no motor vehicle accidents; acquired immune deficiency syndrome (AIDS) did not exist. Today, chronic diseases account for about 70% of all deaths, and 60% of medical care expenditures (Centers for Disease Control and Prevention, 1999). The leading causes of death in the United States in 1900 were pneumonia (accounting for 11.8% of all deaths), tuberculosis (11.3%), and diarrhea/enteritis (8.3%). Perhaps because the average age at death was in the mid-40s, heart disease was only the fourth leading cause, accounting for 6.2% of all deaths. In 1997, however, heart disease was the leading cause, accounting for 31.4% of deaths, followed by cancer (23.3%), stroke (6.9%), and chronic obstructive pulmonary disease (6.9%); pneumonia and influenza were in sixth place, accounting for 3.7% of deaths (USDHHS, 2000). With the increase in life expectancy, there has been an increase in the role of chronic disease in mortality; in the early part of the century, most people did not live long enough for such diseases to demonstrate their lethal effects.

Consider the changes over the past 100 years in specified reportable diseases, most of them infectious. In 1950, tuberculosis affected 80.4 per 100,000 persons; in 1997, the rate was 7.4 per 100,000. Measles had a prevalence of 210.1 per 100,000 in 1950; in 1996, the rate was 0.1; the rate of acute poliomyelitis declined from 22.1 to less than .05. On the other hand, AIDS was not recognized in 1950; in 1996 the rate was 21.9 per 100,000 persons (U.S. Census Bureau, 1999).

DEMOGRAPHIC CONTEXT

In addition to situating health during midlife in a sociohistorical context, it is also of interest to consider various aspects of health across demographic groups defined for example by age or gender. Table 5.2 reports mortality rates (per 100,000 persons) from 1998 (National Vital Statistics System [NVSS], 2000), for 10-year age groups from 35 to 64. For comparative purposes, data for older adults aged 65 to 74 are also shown. Note that mortality due to all chronic diseases increases, as does mortality due to pneumonia and influenza; however, mortality due to accidents and to suicide remains relatively stable across age groups. Among the middle-aged, note that mortality due to heart disease, cancer, and diabetes

Table 5.2
Death Rate (per 100,000 persons), 1998

	Age Group			
	35–44	45–54	55–64	65–74
All	199.6	423.5	1030.7	2495.1
Heart disease	30.5	101.4	286.9	735.3
Cancer	38.2	132.3	383.8	841.3
Stroke	6.0	16.5	42.6	130.0
COPD	2.0	8.2	44.8	169.1
Accidents	34.0	31.6	32.4	48.3
Pneumonia/influenza	3.1	6.3	17.0	59.8
Diabetes	4.2	12.7	38.4	89.6
Suicide	15.4	14.8	13.1	14.1

approximately doubles each decade, but that the increase after age 55 is even larger. Age is indeed a major risk factor for mortality due to chronic disease, but whether it plays a causal role, or is simply a marker for other physiological and disease processes is a matter of some debate (G. A. Kaplan, Haan, & Wallace, 1999).

Data on mortality show strong gender and racial differences (NVSS, 2000). Men generally have higher age-adjusted mortality than do women for all 15 leading causes of death except Alzheimer's disease. Blacks have higher age-adjusted mortality than do Whites, especially for homicide and hypertension.

Table 5.3 presents data on lifetime risk of developing selected diseases. The data for cancer are from the National Cancer Institute's Surveillance,

Table 5.3
Lifetime Risk (percent) of Selected Diseases

	40–59		60–79	
	Men	Women	Men	Women
All cancer[a]	8.17	9.23	33.65	22.27
Breast	—	4.06	—	6.88
Prostate	1.90	—	13.69	—
Lung	1.29	0.94	6.35	3.98

	40		50		60		70	
	Men	Women	Men	Women	Men	Women	Men	Women
Heart disease[b]	42.4	24.9	40.8	24.6	37.9	32.7	32.4	21.1

[a] Greenlee, Murray, Bolden, and Wingo, 2000.

[b] Lloyd-Jones, Larson, Beiser, and Levy, 1999.

Epidemiology, and End Result (SEER) program (Greenlee et al., 2000); those for heart disease are from the Framingham Heart Study (Lloyd-Jones, Larson, Beiser, & Levy, 1999). Data are shown separately for men and women, and by selected age groups at time of disease onset. For men, the lifetime risk of developing cancer at age 40 to 59 is 8.17%, or approximately 1 in 12; for women, about 1 in 11. The chance of an older person developing cancer during their remaining lifetime is much higher; about 1 in 3 for men, and 1 in 4 for women.

The likelihood of developing coronary heart disease is substantially higher than that of cancer at all ages, ranging from slightly over 1 in 2 for men aged 40 to 59, to 1 in 5 for women age 70 and over. Based on data from Framingham, the American Heart Association has published risk-factor equations for predicting the likelihood of heart disease (e.g., Grundy et al., 1999); similar equations also exist for predicting the likelihood of stroke (Wolf, D'Agostino, Belanger, & Kannel, 1991).

Despite their much higher risk of developing heart disease, most women are uninformed about this risk, and report that breast cancer is their greatest disease risk (Mosca et al., 2000).

Administrative data such as those in Tables 5.1 and 5.2 are collected by the federal government via the decennial census or death records, and are obtained for the entire U.S. population. Other data on health, however, are not part of such administrative reporting systems, but are obtained from representative samples of the population, such as the National Health Interview Survey (NHIS; NCHS, 1999) or National Health and Nutrition Examination Survey (NHANES; NCHS, 1994). Table 5.4 reports data on the prevalence of chronic diseases from the 1996 NHIS.

As these data demonstrate, there are some notable differences in the prevalence of chronic conditions within midlife by gender. For example,

Table 5.4

Prevalence of Chronic Conditions (per 1,000 persons)

	45–64		65+	
	Men	Women	Men	Women
Arthritis	193.0	284.0	411.2	534.5
Diabetes	56.9	59.4	121.8	84.3
Heart disease	133.5	100.3	311.3	238.0
Hypertension	214.8	213.3	298.0	410.8
Cerebrovascular disease	16.3	9.6	93.8	44.4
Chronic bronchitis	41.0	76.1	48.8	74.1
Asthma	30.4	65.5	37.5	51.3
Visual impairment	61.0	36.4	103.8	70.0
Hearing impairment	183.4	82.9	386.8	243.2

Table 5.5

Physician Contacts (number per person per year)

	45–64		65+	
	Men	Women	Men	Women
Phone	0.6	1.1	0.9	1.2
Office	1.1	4.7	5.6	5.8
Hospital	1.0	1.0	1.3	1.1
Other	1.2	1.5	3.2	3.9
ALL	6.0	8.4	11.0	12.2

women have higher rates than do men of arthritis, chronic bronchitis, and asthma, but lower rates of heart disease and visual and hearing impairment. Rates are similar between men and women for diabetes and hypertension.

Another measure of health is presented in Table 5.5, from the 1996 NHIS (NCHS, 1999), the number of physician contacts by place for men and women in midlife and in old age. Note that women have more contacts than men at both ages; also note that physician contacts are higher for the older persons, especially for office visits and other contacts.

Table 5.6 presents information on yet another measure of health, risk behaviors (NCHS, 1998). In 1965, over half of middle-aged men were current smokers, as were 30% to 40% of women. Older adults were much less likely to be current smokers. In 1995, smoking was reduced by about 40% in middle-aged men, and by 20% to 40% among middle-aged women.

Table 5.6

Health Behaviors, United States, 1998

Current Smokers (%)				
	1965		1995	
	Men	Women	Men	Women
35–44	58.2	43.7	31.5	27.1
45–64	51.9	32.0	27.1	24.0
65+	28.5	9.6	14.9	11.5

Current Drinkers (%)				
	1985		1990	
	Men	Women	Men	Women
45–64	72.2	53.0	68.4	47.6
65+	58.2	34.7	55.6	31.3

Data on current drinking were obtained in 1985 and 1990, and show that women were less likely to be current drinkers than were men. These data also indicate slight declines in the percentage of the population who were current drinkers, but given the growing evidence that moderate (1–2 drinks per day for men, .5 to 1 for women) drinking has salutary effects for heart disease (Camargo et al., 1997; Doll, 1997; Svardsudd, 1998; Thun et al., 1998), this is not surprising.

Table 5.7 presents data on two risk factors, obtained from the first National Health Examination Survey in 1960–1962 and the NHANES III in 1988–1994 (NCHS, 1998). The prevalence of high serum cholesterol (defined as 240 mg/dl or higher) is much lower in the 1990s than in the 1960s, although it remains relatively high among older women (55 and older). Obesity is defined separately for men and for women, using body mass index (BMI), computed as weight (in kg) over height (in m) squared. In contrast to the decline in serum cholesterol, obesity is markedly higher in the 1990s than in the 1960s, posing a significant health hazard due to its association with leading causes of morbidity and mortality such as hypertension, diabetes, coronary heart disease, stroke, osteoarthritis, respiratory problems, and certain kinds of cancer (National Institutes of Health [NIH], 1998).

Table 5.8 presents data on self-rated health (i.e., responses to the single question, How would you rate your health?) from the 1996 NHIS (NCHS,

Table 5.7

Health Risk Factors

| | Percentage with High Serum Cholesterol (≥ 240 mg/dl) | | | |
| | Men | | Women | |
	1960–1962	1988–1994	1960–1962	1988–1994
35–44	33.9	19.4	23.1	12.3
45–54	39.2	26.6	46.9	26.7
55–64	41.6	28.0	70.1	40.9
65–74	38.0	21.9	65.5	41.3

| | Percentage Overweight (BMI ≥ 27.8 for men, ≥ 27.3 for women) | | | |
| | Men | | Women | |
	1960–1962	1988–1994	1960–1962	1988–1994
35–44	22.8	34.9	24.1	36.8
45–54	28.1	37.7	30.7	45.4
55–64	26.9	43.7	43.2	48.2
65–74	21.8	42.9	42.9	42.3

Table 5.8
Self-Rated Health

	25–44		45–64		65+	
	Men	Women	Men	Women	Men	Women
Excellent	41.0	35.0	30.2	25.5	16.4	16.2
Very good	32.2	33.0	28.5	28.2	22.8	23.3
Good	20.5	23.6	34.2	29.5	34.2	33.1
Fair	5.0	6.7	10.7	11.8	18.7	19.9
Poor	1.2	1.7	5.2	5.0	7.8	7.5

1999). Note that self-rated health is somewhat better in men than women during midlife, but in old age, the differences are less pronounced.

As a final indicator of health in the United States, consider Table 5.9, which presents data on a multidimensional self-report measure of health, the SF-36 (Ware, 1993). These data were obtained from 1,810 respondents aged 35 to 94 from the National Survey of Functional Health Status, conducted in 1990 to provide national norms for the SF-36 (McHorney, Kosinski, & Ware, 1994; Ware, 1990).

The SF-36 is a widely used measure, assessing 8 domains including physical, social, and mental functioning (McHorney, 1997; Spiro & Bossé, 2000; Ware, 1995). Physical functioning (*PF*, 10 items) refers to limitations in performing physical activities; role limitations due to physical health problems (*RP*, 4) refers to problems with work or other activities as a result of physical health; bodily pain (*BP*, 2) refers to the extent and severity of pain; general health perceptions (*GH*, 5) assesses beliefs about personal health now and in the future; vitality (*VT*, 4) assesses feelings of pep and

Table 5.9
National Survey of Functional Health Status, 1990

	Men				Women			
	35–44	45–54	55–64	65+	35–44	45–54	55–64	65+
PF	91	87	80	66	88	83	73	62
RP	90	86	76	60	84	80	72	56
BP	79	74	68	69	75	72	67	63
GH	78	73	67	59	74	70	63	62
VT	65	63	63	58	59	61	58	55
SF	89	86	84	80	83	83	79	77
RE	86	85	81	77	80	82	80	73
MH	77	76	77	77	73	74	73	75

Note: Values weighted for nonresponse.

energy; social functioning (*SF,* 2) measures the extent to which physical or emotional problems affect performance of normal social activities; role limitations due to emotional problems (*RE,* 3) measures problems with work or other activities as a result of emotional problems; and mental health (*MH,* 5) assesses general mental health. A single item inquires about health change during the past year, but is not part of any scale. Scale scores are transformed to range from 0 to 100, with 100 indicating best health.

These data reveal that physical functioning (assessed by the first 4 scales) was higher in men than in women, and that it was somewhat lower in successively older age groups. On the 4 scales that assess primarily mental functioning, both age and gender differences were smaller; for the 5-item scale assessing mental health per se, there were no age differences.

The SF-36 has been widely used since it was introduced in the Medical Outcomes Study (Stewart & Ware, 1992). As other multidimensional measures of self-rated health (e.g., Sickness Impact Profile [Bergner, Bobbitt, Carter, & Gilson, 1981]; WHOQOL [Bonomi, Patrick, Bushnell, & Martin, 2000]), it assesses multiple domains (e.g., physical, social, mental) as suggested by the WHO (1947) definition of health. For more information on these and other measures, see the recent reviews by McHorney (1999) or Ware (1995), or visit the following Internet sites: Researcher's Guide to the Choice of Instruments for Quality of Life Assessment in Medicine (http://www.qlmed.org), Medical Outcomes Trust (http://www.outcomes-trust.org), or the SF-36 home page (http://www.sf-36.com).

THE MANY FACES OF HEALTH: TOWARD A LIFE-SPAN PERSPECTIVE

In my initial attempt to answer the question, What is health? I demurred. I distinguished between health at the person level and at the population level, and proceeded to present some statistics on aspects of health, largely at the population level. Now it is time to begin redeeming the promissory note with respect to characterizing health at the individual level.

There seem to be nearly as many perspectives on health as there are disciplines involved in its study. Some have attempted to characterize these various views into classes, such as the biomedical model versus the biopsychosocial model (e.g., Engel, 1977). The former is reductionist, adopting molecular biology as a foundational discipline. Diseases have a pathophysiological basis, although we may not yet be able to identify the relevant cause given current knowledge. As McKinlay and Marceau (1999, p. 295) observed, "medicine . . . can count up to two but not beyond," nicely stating the dualistic, either-or categorical logic of this approach in which one is either sick or well, normal or diseased. In contrast, the biopsychosocial approach recognizes the cultural and psychosocial context of health and disease, and emphasizes the study of the person rather than of the disease. Not all diseases necessarily have a pathophysiological basis. Most mental disorders, for example, do not have an identifiable pathophysiology. Thus, within the biopsychosocial view, it is reasonable for a person to feel quite healthy despite a clinical finding of disease, and for another to feel quite sick without such a finding. As examples, consider that both hypertension and diabetes mellitus can be asymptomatic, being defined by categorical thresholds applied to the continuous variables of blood pressure (Joint National Committee [JNC], 1997) and glucose (American Diabetes Association [ADA], 1999), respectively. As many as 27% of persons with hypertension don't know that they have it (JNC, 1997), and about 50% of persons with diabetes have not been diagnosed (Harris et al., 1998). This is not to ignore the serious consequences of these conditions, but merely to indicate that many persons with these conditions are not yet diagnosed, and are likely to experience few if any symptoms in the early stages. However, a person with lower back pain can be quite indisposed, yet have no clinical finding as a basis for diagnosis. In the biomedical perspective, illness (as experienced by a patient) and disease (as recognized by a clinician) are the same; in the biopsychosocial perspective, illness and disease are overlapping but not identical constructs (Evans & Stoddart, 1990).

I agree with Engel (1977) and others (e.g., R. M. Kaplan, 1990; Wilson & Cleary, 1995) who argue that a biopsychosocial perspective on health is preferable. As a developmental psychologist who has been working in epidemiology, behavioral medicine, and health services over the past 20 years, I'd like to extend such an approach by pursuing it within a life-span perspective. This will, I hope, provide a useful organizing framework, and perhaps motivate others to consider in their own work both the conceptual and methodological implications of viewing health and disease as developmental processes.

HEALTH IS LIFELONG

The first life-span tenet mentioned, that health undergoes lifelong development and change, should cause no debate. Health is a phenomenon that develops from birth (or even before, in the intrauterine environment, Barker, 1995) and continues to change throughout life. A growing area of study takes this approach quite seriously, examining the "Barker hypothesis" of fetal programming, which postulates that much of adult disease has its origins during fetal development (Joseph & Kramer, 1996; Kuh & Ben-Shlomo, 1997; Lucas, Fewtrell, & Cole, 1999; Susser, Brown, & Matte,

1999). At least for some, health is an ideal human behavior to be considered "from womb to tomb."

From a life-span perspective, it is important to recognize that any behavior has both antecedents and consequences, and that these may be distal as well as proximal. We often give primary consideration to the proximal (in both a temporal and a spatial sense) causes of health, and ignore the more distal ones (McMichael, 1999), such as antecedents in early life (e.g., Barker, 1995), or a pervasive social context such as poverty or lack of access to health care (Lynch, Kaplan, & Shema, 1997). We would benefit greatly from models that consider health as an event that extends over both space (in the sense of social and cultural context) and time (both historical and individual [Samet, 2000; Shahar, 2000]), and from the recognition that causes and explanations must be sought at multiple levels of analysis (Anderson & Scott, 1999; Cacioppo, Berntson, Sheridan, & McClintock, 2000; Schwartz & Carpenter, 1999).

Several recent studies have illustrated the effects of mid-life behavior on subsequent health. Among several large cohorts followed prospectively, persons with a profile of low cardiovascular risk (defined on the basis of low cholesterol, low normal blood pressure, no current smoking, normal electrocardiogram, and no history of diabetes or myocardial infarction) had a 70% to 90% lower risk of coronary heart disease and cardiovascular disease, 50% to 75% lower risk of stroke, 40% to 60% lower risk of cancer, and 40% to 60% lower risk of all cause mortality, over the next 16 to 22 years (Stamler et al., 1999). Those who practiced better health habits during midlife also have longer survival, and disability became compressed (Fries, 1980) into fewer years at the end of life (Vita, Terry, Hubert, & Fries, 1998). A low-risk profile in midlife also translated into lower healthcare costs both in the short term (within 18 months; Pronk, Goodman, O'Connor, & Martinson, 1999) and in the long term (23 years; Daviglus et al., 1998).

HEALTH IS MULTIDIMENSIONAL

The second tenet, that health is multidimensional, has become increasingly clear to most social scientists over the past 20 years. Health is widely recognized as a construct with many facets, many levels, and many dimensions. Despite this, however, some behavioral scientists seem insensitive to this richness and complexity. Else why would so many attempt to measure "health" as the response to a question such as "How would you rate your current health?" (Certainly no psychologist would attempt to measure personality or cognition with a single item!) It is not that I am unequivocally opposed to using such single-item self-reports, but such a measure tells only a part of the story, and there may well be certain biases in the story that is told (Costa & McCrae, 1987; Siegler, 1997; Watson & Pennebaker, 1989). Such items are better than nothing because persons who respond that their health is fair or poor have been found in numerous studies to be at higher risk of mortality (e.g., Idler & Benyamini, 1997). But single-item measures are far from sufficient or representative of health. Many multidimensional self-report measures of health are available, and these measures are increasingly utilized in the evaluation of health status in clinical trials, healthcare systems, and national surveys (Lawton & Lawrence, 1994; McHorney, 1999; Ware, 1995).

It is a matter of some debate whether the association of negative affectivity or other personality traits with measures of self-reported health status implies that the latter are inadequate measures because of their "contamination" by aspects of personality. An alternative position, which we and others espouse, is based on the recognition that personality clearly is related to health (Friedman & Booth-Kewley, 1987). However, the magnitude of this association between personality and health varies depending on the nature of the measures and on the interval over which the association is studied. Probably the most common, but perhaps least informative, evidence relates to cross-sectional associations of personality and health, both measured by self-report. The strongest evidence would result from prospective studies of objective measures of both personality and health, but these are much less common. In our work, we have found that the personality trait of negative affectivity (Watson & Pennebaker, 1989) is associated more strongly with psychological than with physical aspects of health status (Aldwin, Spiro, Levenson, & Cupertino, 2000; Kressin, Spiro, & Skinner, 2000; Spiro, Aldwin, Levenson, & Bossé, 1990; Spiro & Bossé, 2000).

It is likely that self-report measures of personality and of health will correlate more highly because of shared sources of variance, especially if both are based on a person's self-report at a given occasion. When objective measures are used prospectively (e.g., when observer ratings of personality are correlated with physician diagnoses of subsequent disease; e.g., Peterson, Seligman, & Vaillant, 1988), the correlations are lower, because shared variance is less likely to be present, but can nonetheless be significant and indicate that various aspects of personality are associated with disease incidence. For example, there is a good deal of evidence that certain personality traits (even measured by self-report) are associated prospectively with the incidence of heart disease (Hemingway & Marmot, 1999; Kubzansky & Kawachi, 2000; Rozanski, Blumental, & Kaplan, 1999); the role of personality in cancer incidence is less clear (Contrada, Leventhal, & O'Leary, 1990; Eysenck, 1991; McGee, Williams, & Elwood, 1994).

One multidimensional characterization of health that I am particularly fond of was offered by Elinson (1988). Based on this, as well as the work of others (e.g., R. M. Kaplan, 1990; Patrick & Erickson, 1993; Stewart & Ware, 1992; Wallace, 1994; Wilson & Cleary, 1995), I propose the model of health shown in Table 5.10.

This hierarchical model illustrates the many levels, or dimensions, of health, from the physiological, the clinical, and the personal vantage points as well as the system. The model captures the distinction between "disease" (Levels 1–3), "illness" (Levels 4–6), and functional status (Level 7), with the first based on definitions made by clinicians and the latter on characterizations by the patient. The model also permits the distinction between the objective, diagnostic evaluation of the clinician and the subjective, symptomatic experience of the patient, and between the biomedical and the biopsychosocial perspectives (e.g., Engel, 1977; Evans & Stoddart, 1990; Wilson & Cleary, 1995).

A patient's experience of illness is largely based on symptoms. However, a clinician's diagnosis of disease can be based on symptoms and other patient reports, as well as on signs, physical examination, and laboratory or radiological tests. Although some diseases are symptomatic, and thus observable to both patients and clinicians (such as chronic obstructive pulmonary disease), others are asymptomatic and may not be detectable by patients. Hypertension and the early stage of diabetes are two such examples of the latter; patients with these conditions may experience no symptoms and the condition can be detected only by physiological assessment. Among symptomatic diseases, some, such as angina, have

Table 5.10

Hierarchical Model of Domains of Health

1. Tissue alterations judged by pathologists to be causes of disease or death (e.g., atherosclerosis).
2. Records produced by physiological measuring equipment and their interpretation.
3. Judgments rendered by clinicians as diagnoses (e.g., coronary heart disease).
4. Reports of people that they have a given disease (e.g., "I have a bad heart," or "my doctor told me I have angina").
5. Self-reports of observable symptoms (e.g., rash).
6. Self-reports of sensations, feelings, or thoughts not observable by others (e.g., headache).
7. Health status (reported by the person) either as a single item or by use of a multidimensional measure. (Measures of health status often assess the impact of health on physical, social, and psychological functioning.)

concomitant pathophysiological changes and can be diagnosed by health-care providers. Other symptomatic diseases have little or no such patho-physiological changes and their diagnosis relies solely on patient report (e.g., depression, back pain).

As an hierarchical framework (Anderson & Scott, 1999; Cacioppo et al., 2000), the various levels are not reducible to one another; all are required to give a complete picture of health. Each of the levels has its own valid-ity; no one level is necessarily more important or definitive than another. There is no universal "gold standard" measure of health; thus the notion of validating one measure against another is not in general a good one. Rather, it seems preferable to view the situation as one of corroboration, and to examine the extent of agreement among different measures of health. Patient reports will always be colored to some extent by other fac-tors in their lives; thus their reports of health status, disease presence or severity, or of healthcare use will not necessarily agree with more objec-tive measures such as laboratory tests, physician diagnoses, or adminis-trative records (R.M. Kaplan, 1990). Rather than assume that patients are unreliable and that their reports are subjective, we should consider first that they have motives and reasons for making one report rather than an-other, and second, that the other measures of health are neither perfectly reliable nor objective.

In some circumstances, certain levels simply are not relevant for the study of a given condition. For example, in the current state of the diagno-sis of mental disorders, there are few disorders that have an unequivocal physiological marker or that can be recorded by instruments. Instead, most clinicians rely on their evaluation of patient's reports and behaviors to make a diagnosis. But it is not only mental disorders that have little or no physiological indicators. Back pain is a common, debilitating, and costly condition, yet there is little in the way of diagnostic information available for clinicians outside of patient reports and behaviors. Medical and psy-chological conditions that are symptomatic, but that have few if any meas-urable abnormalities, generally will have low levels of agreement between patient self-reports and medical record entries (Bush, Miller, Golden, & Hale, 1989; Harlow & Linet, 1989; Heliovaara et al., 1993; Kehoe, Wu, Leske, & Chylack, 1994). However, Brown and Adams (1992) found patients to be relatively reliable in their reports of 10 healthcare events (e.g., BP measure-ment, ECG, X-ray, stool kit).

The inclusion of Level 7, functional status, allows us to incorporate the World Health Organization's (1947) explicit recognition of health as "a state of complete physical, mental, and social well-being and not only the absence of disease and infirmity." This definition makes clear the need to consider multiple dimensions, as well as multiple levels, of health.

Two important aspects of health are omitted from Table 5.10, disability and healthcare use. Disability is a condition that can result from limitations in a number of aspects of functional status (e.g., Pope & Tarlov, 1991; Verbrugge & Jette, 1994). However, because disability applies only to those whose functional limitations prevent them from meeting environmental demands, it is not necessarily a level of health relevant for all individuals. Likewise, health care was omitted for the same reason, because not all adults use health care.

One other omission from Table 5.10 should be noted, the temporal dimension. Health in its various levels and other manifestations unfolds over time, both historical and personal (Samet, 2000; Shahar, 2000). Diseases evolve (Cochrane, Ewald, & Cochrane, 2000; Nesse & Williams, 1996); symptoms and risk factors change with age (G.A. Kaplan, Haan, & Wallace, 1994; R.M. Kaplan, 1990). A life-span perspective emphasizes the importance of studying change over time. Indeed, the most important implication of adopting a life-span approach may well be viewing health as a dynamic process rather than as a stable state (e.g., Wallace, 1994).

HEALTH INVOLVES GAINS AND LOSSES

The life-span approach is also characterized by multidirectionality, and suggests a focus on positive as well as negative outcomes. We should study not only the development of disease, but also the maintenance and improvement of health. Too often, studies of health have focused on disease, illness, or disability, and ignored the positive aspects (e.g., resilience, recovery, immunity). This has changed recently, spurred by those who call for a focus on the positive aspects of health and aging (e.g., Baltes & Baltes, 1990; Rowe & Kahn, 1987, 1997), but relatively few studies have focused on maintenance or improvement of health as an outcome (but cf. Benfante, Reed, & Brody, 1985; Guralnick & Kaplan, 1989; Reed et al., 1995; Ryff, Singer, Love, & Essex, 1998; Roos & Havens, 1991). We need, from a life-span perspective, to conduct more studies to answer such questions as, What predicts who will age well? Are there behavioral factors associated with increased longevity and greater resistance to disease? Can we identify persons who are more likely to resist disease, to succeed in their treatment, or to recover from rather than succumb to illness?

Much of the behavioral science research on disease seems concerned with understanding the role of behavior in the incidence of disease; there is much less study of the role of behavior in progression, treatment, or remission of disease (e.g., DiMatteo, Lepper, & Crogham, 2000; Glasgow et al., 1999; Linden, 2000; Rozanski, Blumenthal, & Kaplan, 1999). As some examples, however, consider the work of Andersen and colleagues (Andersen, Kiecolt-Glaser, & Glaser, 1994), who proposed a biobehavioral model of adaptation to cancer, or of Denollet and colleagues (1996), who considered the role of "Type D" personality (tendency to repress emotional distress) on mortality among patients in recovery from heart attack. Such a focus on the positive aspects of health, as opposed to the negative aspects of disease, is one more reason to adopt a biopsychosocial over a biomedical approach.

THE IMPORTANCE OF CONTEXT

In the first section of this chapter, we considered some of the historical and demographic context of health, examining change in various aspects of health over the twentieth century. For some conditions, we also considered the context of gender, demonstrating that health and disease differ between men and women. A good deal of evidence suggests that socioeconomic status (as well as its components, including income and education) is another important context of health and disease (e.g., Adler et al., 1994; NCHS, 1998).

But there is more than this to adopting the tenet of contextualism in the study of health. As psychologists we seldom consider the effects of sociohistorical context on human development, despite the growing recognition that all human behavior is (at least in part) a function of such contextual factors (e.g., Link & Phelan, 1995). We are not alone; psychiatrists have been accused of "social amnesia" (Cohen, 2000), while epidemiologists have been called "prisoners of the proximate" (McMichael, 1999).

Too often, we look for individual causes of change and development, and ignore the larger context in which individuals live. As one example, consider changes in cigarette smoking over the latter half of the twentieth century (Office of Smoking and Health [OSH], 1999; Pierce & Gilpin, 1995). Initiation of cigarette use increased during several periods as a result of major advertising campaigns by manufacturers; World War II was also responsible for a large increase in the number of men who began smoking. One of the major public health interventions of the past 40 years began with the Surgeon General's 1964 report on smoking. If we attempt to account for such changes in tobacco consumption by studying individual risk factors for smoking initiation, we commit a Type III error, which is providing the right answer to the wrong question (Schwartz & Carpenter, 1999). Such errors are common when individual level analyses are undertaken to address population level questions. Schwartz and Carpenter (1999) consider homelessness, obesity, and racial differences in infant mortality to illustrate that historic changes at the social level (e.g., the rise in homelessness) cannot be explained by studying predictors of homelessness. The social context in which persons exist accounts in important ways for their health; if there is restricted access to health care in some locales, then studying barriers to access at the individual level simply reveals who is more likely to use health care, but it does little or nothing to explain why the availability of health care is limited.

Or consider the results of simulations conducted by Hunink et al. (1997), who determined that the decline in CHD mortality from 1980 to 1990 resulted primarily from improvements in treatment for patients with CHD. Primary prevention to reduce risk factors in the population at large accounted for only about 25% of the decline. Similar findings have been reported in the World Health Organization's MONICA (Monitoring Trends in Cardiovascular Disease) Project, a study of 38 populations in 21 countries. The results of this massive 10-year study, involving nearly 7 million men and women aged 35 to 64, indicated that declines in risk factors (e.g., blood pressure, smoking) were generally associated with a decline in risk of CHD (Kuulasmaa et al., 2000), but advances in medical treatment had a greater impact on reduction in coronary events and mortality (Tunstall-Pedoe et al., 2000). As in the earlier example, changes at a higher level (i.e., the healthcare system) are more responsible than individual risk factor changes for the reduction in heart disease mortality over the past 10 to 20 years. The role of the sociocultural context can be ignored only at our own peril.

The importance of socioeconomic status (SES) as a context for health has been widely recognized in recent years (e.g., Adler et al., 1994; Williams, 1990). Whether measured by education or by income, those with lower SES have lower life expectancy, higher mortality rates, greater limitations on activities due to chronic limitations, worse health behaviors (e.g., greater prevalence of smoking, heavy drinking, obesity), worse well-being, and more restricted access to health care (House et al., 1994; Lachman & Weaver, 1998; Marmot et al., 1998; NCHS, 1998). From 1960 to 1986, the SES gap in the United States widened, despite a decline in death rates (Pappas, Queen, Hadden, & Fisher, 1993). That is, although death rates declined for all SES levels, they declined more for upper than for lower levels.

In general, it seems quite clear that lower SES has significant deleterious effects on health. Lantz et al. (1998) investigated whether worse health behaviors (e.g., tobacco and alcohol use, obesity, sedentary lifestyle) in lower SES groups could reduce or eliminate the SES gradient. Their findings suggest that these behaviors accounted for only a small portion of the effect, approximately 10% to 15%. However, using multiple datasets and including psychological variables as well, both Marmot et al. (1998) and Lachman and Weaver (1998) found that the SES gradient was reduced when health behaviors and these variables were taken into consideration. Much more remains to be understood about the effects of socioeconomic status on health; both societal and individual levels must be considered.

Multidisciplinary Studies

Psychologists interested in the study of health have much to learn from other social sciences (e.g., sociology), as well as from the medical sciences (e.g., medicine, epidemiology, public health). And increasingly, clinicians are interested in collaborating with and learning from social scientists. The study of health is, and likely will remain, multidisciplinary. Despite the many difficulties of multidisciplinary research, the need is great and the rewards are many (Pellmar & Eisenberg, 2000).

LOOKING AHEAD

In concluding this chapter, I offer some suggestions for next steps in the study of health during midlife. These steps build on the life-span perspective, and suggest how to use this perspective to integrate existing data and methods toward a more systematic view of health.

Methods for Studying Health

From a life-span perspective, the importance of longitudinal data cannot be overestimated. Although cross-sectional studies have much to offer, they can easily mislead (Kraemer, Yesavage, Taylor, & Kpufer, 2000). The key questions concerning health from a developmental perspective require data collected over time. Adoption of a life-span approach suggests that certain questions be addressed, for example:

- What are the trajectories of risk factors (e.g., tobacco and alcohol use, physical activity, obesity) and is their impact on health constant across the lifespan?
- Can we identify factors that promote resilience or good health, despite declines in other aspects of health? For example, does good mental health offset some of the impact of declining physical health?
- Is the role of chronological age in health causal? Or does chronological age simply mark the increasing likelihood of decline in organ systems?
- Do personality traits such as conscientiousness modulate the effects of risky health behaviors on disease incidence?
- Can we develop causal models that integrate distal (e.g., socioeconomic access, childhood events) and proximal (e.g., smoking, obesity) effects on health and disease?

There are two types of relevant longitudinal studies for addressing such questions (Tager, 1998), one that can be labeled as prospective, and the other as repeated measures. In a prospective study, a set of variables (e.g., risk factors) is measured, perhaps only once, and a sample is followed for some time until an event (first heart attack, death, remission of cancer) occurs. Although the risk factors can be measured repeatedly, this is not necessary, and does not detract from the characterization of such a study as prospective, because the outcome is an event that occurs after the risk factors are first measured. In contrast, in a repeated measures study, the same variables are measured repeatedly over time, and are the outcome of interest. Willett, Singer, and Martin (1998) provide a useful discussion of survival analysis for prospective studies, and growth models for repeated measures studies.

In a prospective study, Spiro and colleagues (Spiro, Aldwin, Ward, & Mroczek, 1995) used men in the VA Normative Aging Study (Bossé, Ekerdt, & Silbert, 1984; Spiro & Bossé, in press) to consider the impact of personality traits measured in 1965 on the incidence of hypertension. Other prospective studies relevant to health in midlife have been conducted, such as the study by Martin et al. (1995), using data over 40 years from the Terman study to show the impact of childhood personality of midlife mental health, and then on later mortality. Everson et al. (1997) and Siegler, Peterson, Barefoot, and Williams (1992) found that the personality trait hostility was associated with subsequent coronary disease, in part through its effects on health behaviors such as alcohol and tobacco use and obesity.

In several repeated measures studies, also from the Normative Aging Study, we examined trajectories of self-reported physical and psychological symptoms over 30 years. Aldwin, Spiro, Levenson, and Bossé (1989) demonstrated that the rate of change in physical and psychological trajectories varied with age; Spiro, Aldwin, Levenson, and Bossé (1990) found that self-reported personality in 1965 was associated with the level of both physical and psychological symptoms, but only weakly with rate of change. Aldwin, Spiro, Levenson, and Cupertino (2000) identified discrete patterns of physical and mental health trajectories, and found that these patterns varied with demographic characteristics, personality traits, and health behaviors, and that different patterns were also associated with differences in extent and cause of mortality. Clipp, Pavalko, and Elder (1992) and Verbrugge, Reoma, and Gruber-Baldini (1994) have also studied health trajectories, using a combination of visual and statistical approaches. In these and other similar studies, it is likely that the effects of personality on health are underestimated, for reasons elucidated by Clarke et al. (1999).

A second issue in the design and analysis of studies from a life-span perspective recognizes the need to consider the contexts of health. In recent years, multilevel models have gained increasing use in a variety of disciplines, and offer an ideal method for examining the influence on health of contextual factors such as family, neighborhood, or healthcare provider (Duncan, Jones, & Moon, 1996). These methods are also useful for examination of spatial or geographic distribution of health and disease (Blakely & Woodward, 2000; Duncan, Jones, & Moon, 1998; Langford, Leyland, Rasbash, & Goldstein, 1999). In health psychology, these methods have been used for the analysis of daily data collected via diary or experience sampling methods (Affleck, Zautra, Tennen, & Armeli, 1999; Almeida, Neiss, & Mroczek, 1999).

Some years ago, Siegel (1985) offered several criteria for the design of studies in personality and health, but their value remains and includes more generally studies of other potential risk factors or predictors of health. First, it is necessary to adequately assess the dependent variable (i.e., health). From a life-span perspective, one should thus take into account the multidimensional nature of health. As our model of health (Table 5.10) illustrates, many levels of health can be considered; as the WHO definition of health emphasizes, there are also many dimensions (e.g., physical, mental, social).

Second, measures of independent variables should be reliable, valid, and where possible, standardized. Use of standardized measures would permit the accumulation of findings across studies. Third, when appropriate, representative samples should be obtained. High-risk or self-selected samples have limitations with respect to generalizability, but depending on the question of interest, may be the most appropriate. Finally, the study design should be longitudinal (either prospective or repeated measures); analyses should be multivariate. When possible, it is a good idea to measure potential risk factors well in advance of possible occult disease, or when this is not possible, it might be a good idea to exclude cases who develop the condition within a few years of the baseline assessment.

The issue of multivariate analysis raises a concern that is seldom addressed. In the context of a study, one is often interested in a particular risk factor and its impact on a given condition (e.g., hostility on coronary heart disease; CHD). However, to convincingly demonstrate that hostility is responsible for CHD, it is necessary to somehow adjust for the role of known CHD risk factors such as smoking, cholesterol, and hypertension. But consider that several studies have shown hostility is associated with each of these risk factors (Everson et al., 1997; Siegler et al., 1992). Covarying out their effects on CHD attenuates the effect of hostility, by removing the portion explained by the indirect effects of hostility on CHD through these risk factors. Too often we view other risk factors as confounders rather than as mediators of the relationship (Adler & Matthews, 1994). Path analysis is one way to deal with this situation, and it should be more widely used in the study of health (e.g., Niaura et al., 2000; Schnurr & Spiro, 1999).

A second consideration in the context of multivariate analysis is the issue of interaction. Far too few studies have examined the role of interactions among potential risk factors and their effects on health (e.g., Holroyd & Coyne, 1987). For example, the interactions among CHD risk factors are of great significance. Smokers with elevated cholesterol had an elevated risk of CHD (Perkins, 1989). Howard, Cunningham, and Rechnitzer (1985) identified a personality dimension similar to hardiness that moderated the effect of smoking on CHD risk factors. In addition to interactions among CHD risk factors, some have suggested that interactions among personality variables are responsible for excess risk of CHD and cancer (Denollet et al., 1996; Eysenck, 1991). As a final example of interactions in the study of health, Christensen (2000) reviews work on the "patient-by-treatment" interaction in studies of adherence.

CONCLUSION

A life-span perspective provides one framework for considering health, and offers advantages that have been discussed. It matters less, in the long run, which perspective we adopt than it does whether the perspective is generative in the sense of leading to new research and new understanding. Models are tools, and are not generally built for life. To the extent that a life-span perspective on health is used by others, it will be a valuable model. To the extent that it spurs debate and discussion, it will have also served a purpose. The seeds of health are sown in adolescence (or earlier); they are often harvested in midlife, and their effects can last until old age. A life-span perspective offers powerful conceptual and methodological tools for the study of health, and will enable us to better understand the complex trajectories of health with age.

REFERENCES

Adler, N.E., Boyce, T., Chesney, M.A., Cohen, S., Folkman, S., Kahn, R.L., & Syme, S.L. (1994). Socioeconomic status and health: The challenge of the gradient. *American Psychologist, 49,* 15–24.

Adler, N.E. & Matthews, K. (1994). Health psychology: Why do some people get sick and some stay well? *Annual Review of Psychology, 45,* 229–259.

Affleck, G., Zautra, A., Tennen, H., & Armeli, S. (1999). Multilevel daily process designs for consulting and clinical psychology: A preface for the perplexed. *Journal of Consulting and Clinical Psychology, 67,* 746–754.

Aldwin, C.M., Spiro, A., III, Levenson, M.R., & Bossé, R. (1989). Longitudinal findings from the Normative Aging Study: I. Does mental health change with age? *Psychology and Aging, 4,* 295–306.

Aldwin, C.M., Spiro, A., III, Levenson, M.R., & Cupertino, A.P. (2000). *Longitudinal findings from the Normative Aging Study: III. Personality, individual health trajectories, and mortality.* Unpublished manuscript, University of California at Davis, Department of Human and Community Development.

Almeida, D.M., Neiss, M., & Mroczek, D.K. (1999). *Age differences in daily, monthly, and weekly estimates of negative affect.* Unpublished Manuscript, University of Arizona, Department of Family Studies and Human Development.

American Diabetes Association. (1999). Screening for Type 2 Diabetes, Position Statement. *Diabetes Care, 22*(Suppl. 1), S20–S23.

Andersen, B.L., Kiecolt-Glaser, J.K., & Glaser, R. (1994). A biobehavioral model of cancer stress and disease course. *American Psychologist, 49,* 389–404.

Anderson, N.B., & Scott, P.A. (1999). Making the case for psychophysiology during the era of molecular biology. *Psychophysiology, 36,* 1–13.

Armstrong, G.L., Conn, L.A., & Pinner, R.W. (1999). Trends in infectious disease mortality in the United States during the 20th century. *Journal of the American Medical Association, 281,* 61–66.

Baltes, P.B. (1987). Theoretical propositions of life-span developmental psychology: On the dynamics between growth and decline. *Developmental Psychology, 23,* 611–626.

Baltes, P.B., & Baltes, M.M. (Eds.). (1990). *Successful aging: Perspectives from the behavioral sciences.* Cambridge, England: Cambridge University Press.

Baltes, P.B., Lindenberger, U., & Staudinger, U.M. (1998). Life span theory in developmental psychology. In R.M. Lerner (Ed.), *Handbook of child psychology, Vol. 1: Theoretical models of human development* (5th ed., pp. 1029–1143). New York: Wiley.

Barker, D.J.P. (1995). Fetal origins of coronary heart disease. *British Medical Journal, 311,* 171–174.

Baum, A., & Posluszny, D.M. (1999). Health psychology: Mapping biobehavioral contributions to health and disease. *Annual Review of Psychology, 50,* 137–163.

Benfante, R., Reed, D., & Brody, J. (1985). Biological and social predictors of health in an aging cohort. *Journal of Chronic Diseases, 38,* 385–395.

Bergner, M., Bobbitt, R.A., Carter, W.B., & Gilson, B.S. (1981). The Sickness Impact Profile: Development and final revision of a health status measure. *Medical Care, 19,* 787–805.

Blakely, T.A., & Woodward, A.J. (2000). Ecological effects in multi-level studies. *Journal of Epidemiology and Community Health, 54,* 367–374.

Bonomi, A.E., Patrick, D.L., Bushnell, D.M., & Martin, M. (2000). Validation of the United States' version of the World Health Organization Quality of Life (WHOQOL) instrument. *Journal of Clinical Epidemiology, 53,* 1–12.

Bossé, R., Ekerdt, D., & Silbert, J. (1984). The Veterans Administration Normative Aging Study. In S.A. Mednick, M. Harway, & K.M. Finello (Eds.), *Handbook of longitudinal research: Teenage and adult cohorts* (Vol. 2, pp. 273–289). New York: Praeger.

Brown, J.B., & Adams, M.E. (1992). Patients as reliable reports of medical care process: Recall of ambulatory encounter events. *Medical Care, 30,* 400–411.

Bush, T.L., Miller, S.R., Golden, A.L., & Hale, W.E. (1989). Self-report and medical record report agreement of selected medical conditions in the elderly. *American Journal of Public Health, 79,* 1554–1556.

Cacioppo, J.T., Berntson, G.G., Sheridan, J.F., & McClintock, M.K. (2000). Multilevel integrative analyses of human behavior: Complementing nature of social and biological approaches. *Psychological Bulletin, 126,* 829–843.

Camargo, C.A., Hennekens, C.H., Gaziano, M., Glynn, R.J., Manson, J.E., & Stampfer, M. (1997). Prospective study of moderate alcohol consumption and mortality in U.S. male physicians. *Archives of Internal Medicine, 157,* 79–85.

Centers for Disease Control and Prevention. (1999). *Chronic diseases and their risk factors: The Nation's leading causes of death.* Atlanta, GA: Author.

Christensen, A.J. (2000). Patient-by-treatment context interaction in chronic disease: A conceptual framework for the study of patient adherence. *Psychosomatic Medicine, 62,* 435–443.

Clarke, R., Shipley, M., Lewington, S., Youngman, L., Collins, R., Marmot, M., & Peto, R. (1999). Underestimation of risk associations due to risk dilution in long-term follow-up of prospective studies. *American Journal of Epidemiology, 150,* 341–353.

Clipp, E.C., Pavalko, E.K., & Elder, G.H., Jr. (1992). Trajectories of health: In concept and empirical pattern. *Behavior, Health, and Aging, 2,* 159–179.

Cochrane, G.M., Ewald, P.W., & Cochrane, K.D. (2000). Infectious causation of disease: An evolutionary perspective. *Perspectives in Biology and Medicine, 43,* 406–448.

Cohen, C.I. (2000). Overcoming social amnesia: The role for a social perspective in psychiatric research and practice. *Psychiatric Services, 51,* 72–78.

Contrada, R.J., Leventhal, H., & O'Leary, A. (1990). Personality and health. In L. Pervin (Ed.), *Handbook of personality* (pp. 638–669). New York: Guilford Press.

Costa, P.T., & McCrae, R.R. (1987). Neuroticism, somatic complaints, and disease: Is the bark worse than the bite? *Journal of Personality, 55,* 299–316.

Daviglus, M., Liu, K., Greenland, P., Dyer, A., Garside, D., Mannheim, L., Lowe, L., Rodin, M., Lubitz, J., & Stamler, J. (1998). Benefit of a favorable cardiovascular risk factor profile in middle age with respect to Medicare costs. *New England Journal of Medicine, 339,* 1122–1129.

Denollet, J., Sys, S., Stroobant, N., Rombouts, H., Gillebert, T.C., & Brutsaert, D.L. (1996). Personality as independent predictor of long-term mortality in patients with coronary heart disease. *Lancet, 347,* 417–421.

DiMatteo, M.R., Lepper, H.S., & Croghan, T.W. (2000). Depression is a risk factor for noncompliance with medical treatment: Meta-analysis of the effects of anxiety and depression on patient adherence. *Archives of Internal Medicine, 160,* 2101–2107.

Doll, R. (1997). One for the heart. *British Medical Journal, 315,* 1644–1668.

Duncan, C., Jones, K., & Moon, G. (1996). Health-related behavior in context: A multilevel modeling approach. *Social Science and Medicine, 42,* 817–830.

Duncan, C., Jones, K., & Moon, G. (1998). Context, composition, and heterogeneity: Using multilevel models in health research. *Social Science and Medicine, 46,* 97–117.

Elinson, J. (1988). Defining and measuring health and illness. In K.W. Schaie, R.T. Campbell, W. Meredith, & S.C. Rawlings (Eds.), *Methodological issues in aging research* (pp. 231–248). New York: Springer.

Engel, G.L. (1977). The need for a new medical model: A challenge for biomedicine. *Science, 196,* 129–136.

Evans, R.G., & Stoddart, G.L. (1990). Producing health, consuming health care. *Social Science and Medicine, 31,* 1347–1363.

Everson, S., Kauhanen, J., Kaplan, G., Goldberg, D.E., Julkunen, J., Toumilehto, J., & Salonen, J.T. (1997). Hostility and increased risk of mortality and acute myocardial infarction: The mediating role of behavioral risk factors. *American Journal of Epidemiology, 146,* 142–152.

Eysenck, H.J. (1991). *Smoking, personality and stress: Psychosocial factors in the prevention of cancer and coronary heart disease.* New York: Springer Verlag.

Field, M.J., & Gold, M.R. (Eds.). (1998). *Summarizing population health: Directions for the development and application of population metrics.* Washington, DC: National Academy Press.

Friedman, H.S., & Booth-Kewley, S. (1987). The disease-prone personality: A meta-analytic view of the construct. *American Psychologist, 42,* 539–555.

Fries, J.F. (1980). Aging, natural death, and the compression of morbidity. *New England Journal of Medicine, 303,* 130–135.

Glasgow, R.E., Fisher, E.B., Anderson, B.J., LaGreca, A., Marrero, D., Johnson, S.B., Rubin, R.R., & Cox, D.J. (1999). Behavioral science in diabetes: Contributions and opportunities. *Diabetes Care, 22,* 832–843.

Greenlee, R.T., Murray, T., Bolden, S., & Wingo, P.A. (2000). Cancer statistics, 2000: CA. *A Cancer Journal for Clinicians, 50*(1), 7–33.

Grundy, S., Pasternak, R., Greenland, P., Smith, S. & Fuster, V. (1999). Assessment of cardiovascular risk by use of multiple risk factor assessment equations. *Circulation, 100,* 1481–1492.

Guralnick, J.M., & Kaplan, G.A. (1989). Predictors of healthy aging: Prospective evidence from the Alameda County Study. *American Journal of Public Health, 79,* 703–708.

Harlow, S., & Linet, M.S. (1989). Agreement between questionnaire data and medical records: The evidence for accuracy of recall. *American Journal of Epidemiology, 129,* 233–248.

Harris, M.I., Flegal, K.M., Cowie, C., Eberhardt, M.S., Goldstein, D.E., Little, R.R., Widemeyer, H., & Byrd-Holt, D.D. (1998). Prevalence of diabetes, impaired fasting glucose, and impaired glucose tolerance in U.S. adults: The Third National Health and Nutrition Examination Survey, 1988–1994. *Diabetes Care, 21,* 518–524.

Heliovaara, M., Aromaa, A., Klaukka, T., Knekt, P., Joukamaa, M., & Impivaara, O. (1993). Reliability and validity of interview data on chronic diseases: The mini-Finland health survey. *Journal of Clinical Epidemiology, 46,* 181–191.

Hemingway, H., & Marmot, M. (1999). Psychosocial factors in the aetiology and prognosis of coronary heart disease: Systematic review of prospective cohort studies. *British Medical Journal, 318,* 1460–1467.

Holyroyd, K.A., & Coyne, J. (1987). Personality and health in the 1980s: Psychosomatic medicine revisited? *Journal of Personality, 55,* 359–375.

House, J.S., Lepkowski, J.M., Kinney, A.M., Mero, R., Kessler, R.C., & Herzog, R. (1994). The social stratification of aging and health. *Journal of Health and Social Behavior, 35,* 213–234.

Howard, J.H., Cunningham, D.A., & Rechnitzer, P.A. (1985). Personality as a moderator of the effects of cigarette smoking on coronary risk. *Preventive Medicine, 14,* 24–33.

Hunink, M.G., Goldman, L., Tosteson, A., Mittelman, M., Goldman, P., Williams, L., Tserat, J., & Weinstein, M. (1997). The recent decline in mortality from coronary heart disease, 1980–1990: The effect of secular trends in risk factors and treatment. *Journal of the American Medical Association, 277,* 535–542.

Idler, E., & Benyamini, Y. (1997). Self-rated health and mortality: A review of 27 community studies. *Journal of Health and Social Behavior, 38,* 21–37.

Joint National Committee. (1997). *The sixth report of the Joint National Committee on Prevention, Detection, Evaluation, and Treatment of High Blood Pressure.* Washington, DC: National Institutes of Health.

Joseph, K.S., & Kramer, M.S. (1996). Review of the evidence on fetal and early childhood antecedents of adult chronic disease. *Epidemiologic Reviews, 18,* 158–174.

Kaplan, G.A., Haan, M.N., & Wallace, R.B. (1999). Understanding changing risk factor associations with increasing age in adults. *Annual Review of Public Health, 20,* 89–108.

Kaplan, R.M. (1990). Behavior as the central outcome in health care. *American Psychologist, 45,* 1211–1220.

Kehoe, R., Wu, S., Leske, M.C., & Chylack, L. (1994). Comparing self-reported and physician-reported medical history. *American Journal of Epidemiology, 139,* 813–818.

Kraemer, H.C., Yesavage, J.A., Taylor, J.L., & Kpufer, D. (2000). How can we learn about developmental progress from cross-sectional studies, or can we? *American Journal of Psychiatry, 157,* 163–171.

Kressin, N.R., Spiro, A. III, & Skinner, K. (2000). Effects of personality on health-related quality of life. *Medical Care, 38,* 858–867.

Kubzansky, L., & Kawachi, I. (2000). Going to the heart of the matter: Do negative emotions cause heart disease? *Journal of Psychosomatic Research, 48,* 323–337.

Kuh, D., & Ben-Shlomo, Y. (Eds.). (1997). *A life course approach to chronic disease epidemiology.* Oxford, England: Oxford University Press.

Kuulasmaa, K., Tunstall-Pedoe, H., Dobson, A., Fortman, S., Sans, S., Tolonen, H., Evans, A., Ferrario, M., Toumilehto, J. (2000). Estimation of contribution of changes in classic risk factors to trends in coronary-event rates across the WHO MONICA Project populations. *Lancet, 355,* 675–685.

Lachman, M.E., & James, J.B. (1997). Charting the course of midlife development: An overview. In M. Lachman & J.B. James (Eds.), *Multiple paths of midlife development* (pp. 1–17). Chicago: University of Chicago Press.

Lachman, M.E., & Weaver, S.L. (1998). The sense of control as a moderator of social class differences in health and well-being. *Journal of Social and Personality Psychology, 74,* 763–773.

Langford, I.H., Leyland, A.H., Rasbash, J., & Goldstein, H. (1999). Multilevel modeling of the geographical distributions of disease. *Applied Statistics, 48,* 253–268.

Lantz, P.M., House, J.S., Lepkowski, J.M., Williamson, D.R., Mero, R.P., & Chen, J. (1998). Socioeconomic factors, health behaviors, and mortality: Results from a nationally representative prospective study of U.S. adults. *Journal of the American Medical Association, 279,* 1703–1708.

Lawton, M.P., & Lawrence, R.H. (1994). Assessing health. *Annual Review of Gerontology and Geriatrics, 14,* 23–56.

Linden, W. (2000). Psychological treatment in cardiac rehabilitation: Review of rationales and outcomes. *Journal of Psychosomatic Research, 48,* 443–454.

Link, B.G., & Phelan, J. (1995). Social conditions as fundamental causes of disease [Special issue]. *Journal of Health and Social Behavior,* 80–94.

Lloyd-Jones, D.M., Larson, M.G., Beiser, A., & Levy, D. (1999). Lifetime risk of developing coronary heart disease. *Lancet, 353,* 89–92.

Lucas, A., Fewtrell, M.S., & Cole, T.J. (1999). Fetal origins of adult disease—The hypothesis revisited. *British Medical Journal, 319,* 245–250.

Lynch, J.W., Kaplan, G.A., & Shema, S.J. (1997). Cumulative impact of sustained economic hardship on physical, cognitive, psychological, and social functioning. *New England Journal of Medicine, 337,* 1889–1895.

Marmot, M.G., Fuhrer, R., Ettner, S.L., Marks, N., Bumpass, L.L., & Ryff, C.D. (1998). Contribution of psychosocial factors to socioeconomic differences in health. *Milbank Quarterly, 76,* 403–448.

Martin, L.R., Friedman, H.J.S., Tucker, J.S., Schwartz, J.E., Criqui, M.H., Wingard, D., & Tomlinson-Keasey, C.T. (1995). An archival prospective study of mental health and longevity. *Health Psychology, 14,* 381–387.

McGee, R., Williams, S., & Elwood, M. (1994). Depression and the development of cancer: A meta-analysis. *Social Science and Medicine, 38,* 187–192.

McHorney, C.A. (1999). Health status assessment methods for adults: Past accomplishments and future challenges. *Annual Review of Public Health, 20,* 309–335.

McHorney, C.A., Kosinski, M., & Ware, J.E. (1994). Comparisons of the costs and quality of norms for the SF-36 health survey collected by mail versus telephone interview: Results from a national survey. *Medical Care, 32,* 551–567.

McKinlay, J.B., & Marceau, L.D. (1999). A tale of 3 tails [Editorial]. *American Journal of Public Health, 89,* 295–298.

McMichael, A.J. (1999). Prisoners of the proximate: Loosening the constraints on epidemiology in an age of change. *American Journal of Epidemiology, 149,* 887–897.

Merrill, S.S., & Verbrugge, L.M. (1999). Health and disease in midlife. In S. Willis & J. Reid (Eds.), *Life in the middle* (pp. 77–103). Orlando, FL: Academic Press.

Mosca, L., Jones, W.K., King, K.B., Ougang, P., Redbert, R.F., & Hill, M.N. (2000). Awareness, perception, and knowledge of heart disease risk and prevention among women in the United States. *Archives of Family Medicine, 9,* 506–515.

National Center for Health Statistics. (1994). *Plan and operation of the third National Health and Nutrition Examination Survey, 1988–94* (Vital and Health Statistics, Series 1, No. 32). Washington, DC: Author.

National Center for Health Statistics. (1998). *Health: United States, 1998 with socioeconomic status and health chartbook.* Washington, DC: U.S. Government Printing Office.

National Center for Health Statistics. (1999). *Current estimates from the National Health Interview Survey, 1996* (Vital and Health Statistics, Series 10, No. 200). Atlanta, GA: Centers for Disease Control and Prevention.

National Institutes of Health. (1998). *Clinical guidelines on the identification, evaluation, and treatment of overweight and obesity in adults: The evidence report.* Washington, DC: National Institutes of Health.

National Vital Statistics System. (2000). *Deaths: Final data for 1998.* Atlanta, GA: Centers for Disease Control and Prevention.

Nesse, R.M., & Williams, G.C. (1996). *Why we get sick: The new science of Darwinian medicine.* New York: Vintage Books.

Niaura, R., Banks, S.M., Ward, K., Stoney, C.M., Spiro, A., III, Aldwin, C.M., Landsberg, L., & Weiss, S.T. (2000). Hostility and the metabolic syndrome in older males: The Normative Aging Study. *Psychosomatic Medicine, 62,* 7–16.

Office of Smoking and Health. (1999). Tobacco use—United States, 1900–1999. *Morbidity and Mortality Weekly Report, 48*(43), 986–993.

Pappas, G., Queen, S., Hadden, W., & Fisher, G. (1993). The increasing disparity in mortality between socioeconomic groups in the United States, 1960 and 1986. *New England Journal of Medicine, 329,* 103–109.

Patrick, D.L., & Erickson, P. (1993). *Health status and health policy: Quality of life in health care evaluation and resource allocation.* New York: Oxford University Press.

Pellmar, T.C., & Eisenberg, L. (Eds.). (2000). *Bridging disciplines in the brain, behavioral, and clinical sciences.* Washington, DC: National Academy Press.

Perkins, K.A. (1989). Interactions among coronary heart disease risk factors. *Annals of Behavioral Medicine, 11,* 3–11.

Peterson, C., Seligman, M.E.P., & Vaillant, G.E. (1988). Pessimistic explanatory style is a risk factor for physical illness: A thirty-five year longitudinal study. *Journal of Personality and Social Psychology, 55,* 23–27.

Pierce, J.P., & Gilpin, E.A. (1995). A historical analysis of tobacco smoking and the uptake of smoking by youth in the United States: 1890–1977. *Health Psychology, 14,* 500–508.

Pope, A.M., & Tarlov, A.R. (1991). *Disability in America: Toward a national agenda for prevention.* Washington, DC: National Academy Press.

Pronk, N.P., Goodman, M.J., O'Connor, P.J., & Martinson, B.C. (1999). Relationship between modifiable health risks and short-term health care charges. *Journal of the American Medical Association, 282,* 2235–2239.

Reed, D., Satariano, W.A., Gildengorin, G., McMahon, K., Fleshman, R., & Schneider, E. (1995). Health and functioning among the elderly of Marin County, California: A glimpse of the future. *Journal of Gerontology: Medical Sciences, 50A,* M61–M69.

Roos, N.P., & Havens, B. (1991). Predictors of successful aging: A twelve-year study of Manitoba elderly. *American Journal of Public Health, 81,* 63–68.

Rowe, J.W., & Kahn, R.L. (1987). Human aging: Usual and successful. *Science, 237,* 143–149.

Rowe, J.W., & Kahn, R.L. (1997). Successful aging. *Gerontologist, 37,* 433–440.

Rozanski, A., Blumenthal, J.A., & Kaplan, J. (1999). Impact of psychological factors on the pathogenesis of carviovascular disease and implications for therapy. *Circulation, 99,* 2192–2217.

Ryff, C.D., Singer, B., Love, G.D., & Essex, M.J. (1998). Resilience in adulthood and later life: Defining features and dynamic processes. In J. Lomranz (Ed.), *Handbook of aging and mental health* (pp. 69–96). New York: Plenum Press.

Samet, J.M. (2000). Concepts of time in clinical research. *Annals of Internal Medicine, 132,* 37–44.

Schnurr, P.P., & Spiro, A., III. (1999). Combat exposure, PTSD symptoms, and health behaviors as predictors of physical health in older veterans. *Journal of Nervous and Mental Disease, 187,* 353–359.

Schwartz, S., & Carpenter, K.M. (1999). The right answer for the wrong question: Consequences of type III error for public health research. *American Journal of Public Health, 89,* 1175–1180.

Shahar, Y. (2000). Dimension of time in illness: An objective view. *Annals of Internal Medicine, 132,* 42–53.

Siegel, J.M. (1985). Personality and cardiovascular disease: Prior research and future directions. In A. Ostfeld & E. Eaker (Eds.), *Measuring psychosocial variables in epidemiologic studies of cardiovascular disease* (DHHS Publication No. 85–2270). Washington, DC: U.S. Government Printing Office.

Siegler, I.C. (1997). Promoting health and minimizing stress in midlife. In M.E. Lachman & J.B. James (Eds.), *Multiple paths of midlife development* (pp. 243–255). Chicago: University of Chicago Press.

Siegler, I.C., Peterson, B.L., Barefoot, J.C., & Williams, R.B. (1992). Hostility during late adolescence predicts coronary risk factors at mid-life. *American Journal of Epidemiology, 136,* 146–154.

Smith, T.W., & Gallo, L.C. (2001). Personality traits as risk factors for physical illness. In A. Baum, T. Revenson, & J. Singer (Eds.), *Handbook of health psychology* (pp. 139–173). Hillsdale, NJ: Erlbaum.

Spiro, A., III, Aldwin, C.M., Levenson, M.R., & Bossé, R. (1990). Longitudinal findings from the Normative Aging Study: II. Do emotionality and extraversion predict change in symptoms? *Journal of Gerontology: Psychological Sciences, 45,* P136–P144.

Spiro, A., III, Aldwin, C.M., Ward, K., & Mroczek, D.K. (1995). Personality and the incidence of hypertension in later life: Longitudinal findings from the Normative Aging Study. *Health Psychology, 14,* 563–569.

Spiro, A., III, & Bossé, R. (2000). Relations between health-related quality of life and well-being: The gerontologist's new clothes? *International Journal of Aging and Human Development, 50,* 297–318.

Spiro, A., III, & Bossé, R. (in press). The Normative Aging Study. In G. Maddox (Ed.), *Encyclopedia of aging* (3rd ed.). New York: Springer Press.

Stamler, J., Stamler, R., Neaton, J.D., Wentworth, D., Daviglus, M.L., Garside, D., Dyer, A.R., Lin, K., & Greenland, P. (1999). Low risk-factor profile and long-term cardiovascular and noncardiovascular mortality and life expectancy: Findings for 5 large cohorts of young adult and middle-aged men and women. *Journal of the American Medical Association, 282,* 2012–2018.

Stewart, A.L., & Ware, J.E., Jr. (Eds.). (1992). *Measuring functioning and well-being: The Medical Outcomes Study approach.* Durham, NC: Duke University Press.

Susser, E.B., Brown, A., & Matte, T.D. (1999). Prenatal factors and adult mental and physical health. *Canadian Journal of Psychiatry, 44,* 326–334.

Svardsudd, K. (1998). Moderate alcohol consumption and cardiovascular disease: Is there evidence for a preventive effect? *Alcoholism: Clinical and Experimental Research, 22,* 307S–314S.

Tager, I.B. (1998). Outcomes in cohort studies. *Epidemiologic Reviews, 20*(1), 15–28.

Taylor, S.E. (1990). Health psychology: The science and the field. *American Psychologist, 45,* 40–50.

Taylor, S.E., Repetti, R.L., & Seeman, T.E. (1997). Health psychology: What is an unhealthy environment and how does it get under the skin? *Annual Review of Psychology, 48,* 411–447.

Thun, M.J., Peto, R., Lopez, A.D., Monaco, J.H., Henley, J., Health, C.W., & Doll, R. (1997). Alcohol consumption and mortality among middle-aged and elderly U.S. adults. *New England Journal of Medicine, 337,* 1705–1714.

Tunstall-Pedoe, H., Vanuzzo, D., Hobbs, M., Mahonen, M., Cepaitis, Z., Kuulasmaa, K., Keil, U. (2000). Estimation of contribution of changes in coronary care to improving survival, event rates, and coronary heart disease mortality across the WHO MONICA Project populations. *Lancet, 355,* 688–700.

United States Census Bureau. (1999). *Statistical abstract of the United States.* Washington, DC: U.S. Government Printing Office.

United States Department of Health and Human Services. (2000). *Healthy people 2010: Understanding and improving health.* Washington, DC: U.S. Government Printing Office.

Verbrugge, L.M., & Jette, A.M. (1994). The disablement process. *Social Science and Medicine, 38,* 1–14.

Verbrugge, L.M., Reoma, J.M., & Gruber-Baldini, A.L. (1994). Short-term dynamics of disability and well-being. *Journal of Health and Social Behavior, 35,* 97–117.

Vita, A.J., Terry, R.B., Hubert, H.B., & Fries, J.F. (1998). Aging, health risks, and cumulative disability. *New England Journal of Medicine, 338,* 1035–1041.

Wallace, R.B. (1994). Assessing the health of individuals and populations in surveys of the elderly: Some concepts and approaches. *Gerontologist, 34,* 449–453.

Ware, J.E., Jr. (1990). *National survey of functional health status* [Computer file]. Boston: John E. Ware, Jr., New England Medical Center [Producer], 1991. Ann Arbor, MI: Inter-university Consortium for Political and Social Research [Distributor], 1995.

Ware, J.E. (1993). *SF-36 Health Survey Manual and Interpretation Guide.* Boston: New England Medical Center, Health Institute.

Ware, J.E. (1995). The status of health assessment 1994. *Annual Review of Public Health, 16,* 327–354.

Watson, D., & Pennebaker, J.W. (1989). Health complaints, stress, and distress: Exploring the central role of negative affectivity. *Psychological Bulletin, 96,* 234–254.

Whitman, T.L., Merluzzi, T.V., & White, R.D. (Eds.). (1999). *Life-span perspectives on health and illness.* Mahwah, NJ: Erlbaum.

Willett, J.B., Singer, J.D., & Martin, N.C. (1998). The design and analysis of longitudinal studies of development and psychopathology in context: Statistical models and methodological recommendations. *Development and Psychopathology, 10,* 395–426.

Williams, D.R. (1990). Socioeconomic differentials in health: A review and redirection. *Social Psychology Quarterly, 53,* 81–99.

Wilson, I.B., & Cleary, P.D. (1995). Linking clinical variables with health-related quality of life: A conceptual model of patient outcomes. *Journal of the American Medical Association, 273,* 59–65.

Wolf, P.A., D'Agostino, R.B., Belanger, A.J., & Kannel, W.B. (1991). Probability of stroke: A risk profile from the Framingham study. *Stroke, 22,* 312–318.

World Health Organization. (1947). The constitution of the World Health Organization. *World Health Organization Chronicle, 1,* 21.

CHAPTER 6

Stress, Coping, and Health at Midlife: A Developmental Perspective

CAROLYN M. ALDWIN and MICHAEL R. LEVENSON

MIDLIFE IS A TIME of contradictions. On the one hand, various developmental theories have depicted midlife, like adolescence, as a time of *Sturm und Drang*. Men have been thought to experience a midlife crisis, deriving from the recognition of their own mortality (Jacques, 1965). Theoretically, this leads them to make radical changes in their lifestyles, much like the character played by Kevin Spacey in the film, *American Beauty*. For women, midlife has been hypothesized to be either a time of emptiness and depression, stemming from the empty nest syndrome (Borland, 1982) or from menopause (Sheehy, 1992), or alternatively, a time of frantic overload as members of the so-called sandwich generation juggle the multiple roles of parent and caretaker for elderly parents (Brody, 1990). In contrast to these perspectives on the putative crisis of middle age, surveys routinely find individuals in midlife to have fewer psychological symptoms (Aldwin, Spiro, Levenson, & Bosse', 1989; Kessler, Foster, Webster, & House, 1992), higher levels of marital satisfaction, better life satisfaction and mastery (Keyes & Ryff, 1999)

Preparation of this chapter was supported by a grant from the National Institute on Aging (AG13006) and by Hatch Funds from the University of California at Davis. We would like to thank Ana Paula Cupertino for her helpful comments on a prior version of this chapter.

than younger individuals and, in general, to be in fairly good health (Merrill & Verbrugge, 1999).

Resolving these seemingly contradictory findings is crucial to understanding adaptational processes in midlife. Either the studies characterizing midlife as a time of high stress are wrong, or people in midlife have become expert copers, able to field much of what life tosses at them at this stage. An alternative hypothesis is that the much vaunted increase in individual variability in late life may actually begin to manifest in midlife. For some individuals, midlife is a time of struggle because they are forced to cope with problems such as job loss or failure to achieve critical goals; health problems, both of one's self and also those of parents, spouses, and siblings; problems with troubled adolescents or infertility; or divorce, widowhood, and parental bereavement. For others, midlife may be a time of achievement and relative comfort. Examining the predictors of stressors and developmental changes in coping is critical for understanding adaptation in midlife.

As Siegler (1997) pointed out, however, there is a dearth of really good information on stress and coping processes in midlife. The purpose of this chapter is to review the information that does exist on life events, daily stressors, and coping processes, and their relationships to health outcomes. We will argue that midlife is not necessarily a time of crisis for most people, but it does normatively involve serious challenges that evoke changes in adaptive strategies. Surprisingly little data exists comparing the relationship between stress and coping to health outcomes in midlife versus early adulthood or late life. While most individuals in midlife are quite healthy, it is in midlife that some individuals see the onset of chronic illness such as heart disease and diabetes. The role of stress in the onset of chronic illnesses is, at this point, not well documented. Therefore, we propose three hypotheses in this chapter. First, that some of the much vaunted individual variability in chronic illness in late life begins to manifest in midlife, and that stress and coping processes play a role in the development of serious illness in midlife.

Second, the increased risk of serious acute and chronic illnesses in midlife necessitates a different attitude toward coping with stress. In particular, individuals may place more emphasis on anticipatory coping strategies that seek to prevent the occurrence of stressors and/or minimize their damage before they occur. Finally, loss-related events may constitute new and serious challenges at midlife. The process of coping with these losses may force individuals to seriously examine themselves, their assumption systems, and their lives in general, and may form a context for the development of wisdom. Certainly, this process sets the stage for the developmental tasks of late life.

' STRESS AT MIDLIFE

In this section we briefly review evidence for and against the existence of the various crises which have been thought to be specific to midlife, such as the midlife crisis for men and menopause for women. We then examine the stressors that are likely to become more frequent in midlife, and/or have a greater impact in midlife than in early adulthood. Finally, we examine whether midlife is a more or less stressful stage than early adulthood or late life, by reviewing the few studies that exist on age differences in stressful life events and daily stressors, as well as changes in those stressors over time.

Do Men Experience Midlife Crises?

In 1965, Elliot Jacques published an extraordinarily influential paper putting forth the proposition that there is a midlife crisis. A psychoanalyst, Jacques based his hypothesis on a study of 310 artists, primarily in their 30s, who had recently had reason to confront their own mortality. This may have been occasioned either by the death of a parent, a friend, or a sibling. Facing the possibility of their own mortality led these artists to reevaluate their own lives, and sometimes created a preoccupation with death, artistic impotence, and despair, although it sometimes led to a deeper awareness and self-realization. The recognition that time is limited leads one to ask whether it is being spent wisely and, not surprisingly, can result in changing unsatisfactory careers or relationships. Levinson (1978), in an in-depth, qualitative study of about 100 men, also concluded that there was a midlife crisis. From these studies arose the "common knowledge" that men routinely experience a crisis in midlife and make radical changes in their lifestyles.

There quickly arose challenges to this point of view. Costa and McCrae (1980) found little evidence for an increase in neuroticism in midlife (which presumably should accompany any crisis). While they did find that some people were likely to experience such crises, they suggested that these individuals were likely to experience crises in their 20s and 30s, and that crises were not unique to midlife. Whitbourne (1986), in a review of this literature, characterized the midlife crisis as a "pure figment"—presumably of white males' imaginations.

Farrell and Rosenberg (1981) extensively interviewed 350 middle-aged men and 150 younger men in their 20s and 30s. They concluded that there was a variety of paths through midlife, and that there was little evidence for a midlife crisis per se. However, recently, Robinson, Rosenberg, and Farrell (1999) reinterviewed these men. Looking back over their midlife period, it became evident that while not necessarily entailing crises, it was certainly a time for reevaluation. In particular, there appeared to be a shift in their personal narrative in late middle age (i.e., the 50s), in which many men reported a turning point, which may or may not have been "heroically" resolved but may have occasioned a long, slow decline. Interestingly, the younger men, now middle-aged Baby Boomers, quite freely used the term "midlife crisis" to describe nearly any setback, either in their career or family life.

In part, much of this argument about whether a midlife crisis exists stems from a fundamental misunderstanding of Jung's (1933) original work on development at midlife. Jung argued that an individual develops a *persona* in adolescence and early adulthood that provides a means of relating to the adult world of work and family. While the self consists of both male qualities (*animus*) and female qualities (*anima*), part of the self needs to be suppressed in order to develop an adequate *persona*. In the gender-segregated time at which he was writing, a man was thought to develop his animus, focusing on competitiveness and career development, while a woman was thought to develop her anima, with a focus on nurturing children. Regardless of which qualities were suppressed, Jung argued that they reemerged at midlife. The degree to which this occasioned a crisis reflected the degree to which the characteristic of the self had been suppressed. Thus, a person who had strongly repressed an essential part of his or her nature might well experience a midlife crisis as that part attempted to reassert itself, but an individual who retained a fairly integrated balance between the anima and the animus would be spared such a crisis. Parker and Aldwin (1997) found partial support for this hypothesis in their cohort-sequential study of changes in masculinity and femininity. Individuals who were most likely to change from early adulthood to midlife were those whose personality was most imbalanced in their twenties.

Thus, rather than debating whether there is a midlife crisis, it might be useful to ask, "Who has a difficult passage in midlife, and why?" Given the bulk of the data, it is likely that, for most men, midlife is a time of achievement and satisfaction. For a certain proportion of men, however, the passage is not at all smooth. Some individuals may develop significant problems and drop out of the labor force. Bossé, Aldwin, Levenson, and Ekerdt (1987) found that these early retirees were more likely to have mental health problems. Given that the unemployment statistics do not count the long-term unemployed or the "discouraged workers," it is unclear how many men experience employment problems in late midlife, and are just "holding on" until they can draw Social Security. Similarly, Chiriboga (1989) found that men who were divorced in their 50s tended not to bounce back from this setback, and experienced serious long-term effects. As Robinson, Rosenberg, and Farrell (1999) documented, there are different pathways through midlife, and studies are needed that increase our understanding of the predictors of crises or of "long, slow declines," as well as positive adaptation.

DO WOMEN EXPERIENCE MIDLIFE CRISES?

A similar pattern of contradictory research has been seen for the view that menopause constitutes a midlife crisis for women. It has long been thought that menopause sparked clinical depression and other forms of psychosis, and some popular psychologists still subscribe to that point of view (Sheehy, 1992). Yet, population surveys show, that, for most women, menopause does not result in serious depression (Matthews, 1992; J. McKinlay, McKinlay, & Brambilla, 1987). However, the 10% of women who experience sudden drops in estrogen due to hysterectomies, chemotherapy, or late-life children may experience higher levels of depressive symptoms. There are individual differences in the difficulties with which women go through the menopausal transition. Indeed, some women even speak of "postmenopausal zest."

Interestingly, there are cross-cultural differences in ease or difficulty through which women go through menopause (Avis, 1999). In general, in those cultures in which women view menopause more positively, it tends to be relatively less problematic (see Beyene, 1986), perhaps because in some cultures, a woman's status rises postmenopause. The only universal symptom appears to be hot flashes, caused by sudden changes in hormones which result in vasodilation. Even these appear to be mitigated by diet. For example, Japanese women appear to be less likely to suffer from hot flashes, perhaps because their diet contains fairly large amounts of tofu, which is high in phytoestrogens (Payer, 1991).

Another characteristic of midlife that was thought to be highly stressful is the "empty nest" phase. In prior centuries, women often died a few years after the birth of their last child, but now only about a third of the adult life span is spent raising children. Thus, there is a considerable stretch of time in which women are free to pursue other interests. Early research suggested that this was a potential crisis for women, but Borland (1982) showed that the empty nest was simply not problematic for most women. African American women, for example, were likely to have been employed during their child-rearing years, and continued this pattern after their children left the nest. While Mexican American women were less likely to have been in the workforce, they continued their traditional caretaking roles, either for unmarried children and/or grandchildren. The only group for whom this was potentially troublesome was upper-middle-class women who had no history of working outside the home and whose children were likely to delay child rearing, thus delaying grandparenthood.

The majority of women of child-bearing age now work outside the home, and presumably will continue to do so after their children are launched. For those women who have opted out of the workforce to raise their children, there is increased acceptance of "off-time" education, with more women than ever returning to school to increase their job market potential. Moen and Wethington (1999) note that divorce may either precede or follow a return to school. The empty nest phase does not appear to constitute a generalized crisis, but it may evoke a reevaluation of life goals in women.

Finally, the crisis that women in midlife are currently thought to face is role overload from being members of the sandwich generation. This pertains to the idea that midlife is a time of great stress because individuals (mainly women) are facing simultaneous demands of caring for both adolescents and frail parents, often while juggling the demands of a career. Depending on the study, a quarter to a third of middle-aged women have the demographic potential to fit this profile, that is, have at least one living parent, an adolescent living at home, and paid employment outside the home (Bengston, Rosenthal, & Burton, 1996). However, most elders are relatively healthy up until their late 70s, by which time their grandchildren have usually reached adulthood. Consequently, only 7% of adults find themselves simultaneously caring for both elders and adolescents (Rosenthal, Matthews, & Marshall, 1991, 1996). It is surprising that more individuals in midlife (slightly over a quarter) identify themselves as caregivers for older relatives than do those in later life, of whom only 15% say they are caregiving for an elderly relative or friend. Papalia, Camp, and Feldman (1996) believe that the AARP survey on which these data are based underestimated spousal care. In dealing with older dyads, it is often difficult to determine who is the primary caregiver, and one could characterize older couples as having mutually interdependent relationships.

Still, over half of the women with a surviving parent will spend at least some time in a caregiving role (Himes, 1994). Typical caregiving tasks, averaging about 4 hours a day, include helping with shopping and transportation, household maintenance, personal care, handling finances, and supervising medications. While daughters typically take on much of the care, especially for personal assistance, sons also provide a significant amount of care, often for transportation and financial tasks (Stone, Cafferata, & Sangl, 1987). While caregiving can be an arduous, stressful task leading to burnout (Zarit, Todd, & Zarit, 1986), there are often perceived benefits of caring for a loved one. Schulz, O'Brien, Bookwala, and Fleissner (1995) report that half of spousal caregivers do not report caregiving to be a stressful experience. To our knowledge, comparable data do not exist for midlife caregivers of parents, but Bengston et al. (1996) point out that adult child-parent helping relationships are typically characterized by reciprocity, except when an elder is very frail.

In summary, it is incorrect to identify midlife as a time of crisis. While there are normative changes, most individuals appear to take these pretty much in stride. However, challenges can occur at midlife that may cause individuals to make significant changes in their lives. Perhaps Clausen's (1990) observation may be most accurate. He suggested that midlife is a psychological turning point, which may include new insights into one's self, a loved one, or a life situation that can lead to significant changes or redirections in life. Wethington reviewed a series of papers she and her colleagues conducted on turning points at midlife (Moen & Wethington, 1999). Interestingly, they found that women were more likely than men to report turning points at midlife, primarily in association with negative life events. Further, they found that severe events which were successfully resolved were most likely to be associated with psychological growth. Thus, it may be worthwhile to examine life events that are common to midlife.

Common Life Events

Parental Bereavement

Perhaps the most normative stressful life event of midlife is the death of a parent. Given that two-thirds of deaths now occur after the age of 65 (Merrill & Verbrugge, 1999), it is becoming increasingly common for adults to experience the death of their parents starting in midlife. Indeed, in the MacArthur Study of midlife, Larry Bumpass observed that individuals usually begin midlife with both parents alive and exit midlife with one or both parents dead (Lachman, 1998, personal communication). Data from Canada appear to bear out this observation. Nearly all (85%) of men and women in their early 40s have at least one living parent; this number drops to only a fifth for individuals in their 60s (Marshall, Matthews, & Rosenthal, 1993). In the United States, half of all adults have lost both parents by their mid-50s, and 75% by their early 60s (Winsborough, Bumpass, & Aquilino, 1991; cited in Papalia et al., 1996).

While relatively few studies exist of bereavement at midlife, the few that do exist suggest that this event is less stressful than other types of bereavement, especially for men (Moss & Moss, 1989). In part, this may be because it is considered to be normative. Grandparents die, and then parents. Women, especially those who were involved in caregiving, may be more likely to experience grief. Individuals who are most likely to be grief stricken are those who still lived with their parents; presumably the parents' death will result in greater disruption to their lives (Parkes, 1972).

Still, death of a parent is undoubtedly a major turning point for most people. As mentioned earlier, it may force individuals to confront their own mortality, leading to a reevaluation of their own lives. With the death of one parent may come greater responsibility, not only for their own lives, but for the remaining parent. The widowed parent is generally in need of greater support, and may desire more frequent contact with children and grandchildren. While most ill elders prefer to rely on their spouses for caretaking, the absence of the partner may result in greater demands on their adult children.

The death of a second parent may be even harder, as the adult child now becomes an "orphan." While relatively little hard data exist, it is likely that losing the buffer of the parent generation leads to a shift in identity and perhaps in values and behaviors. Moss and Moss (1989) quoted some interesting remarks by a few of their respondents from their study of midlife parental loss.

> I'm suddenly the replacement for her generation. It's like going from the middle level to the senior level in the matter of a moment. Without doubt, I feel a greater sense of finality in life. When she was here I felt that there was a cushion between me and the end of life. (p. 108)
>
> There are things that are important for my professional life since she got very sick. I made major changes in my work to increase my own professional security. Perhaps the prospect of losing her had to do with that. (p. 104)

Some studies do report serious emotional distress following death of a parent (Scharlach, 1991), with nearly half reporting physical declines (Scharlach & Fredriksen, 1993). Interestingly, though, the latter study found that many individuals also reported psychological growth from the death of their parents. In many ways, it forces one to finally "become an adult," and individuals often reported that people increased in self-confidence and maturity, and learned to value personal relationships more.

Death of a Spouse

We tend to think of widowhood as something that occurs in late life. For women, however, widowhood is fairly common in midlife. An early study by Troll (1973) pointed out that half of all widows are under 60 years of age, and most of these are in their 50s. Currently, one third of all women are widowed by the age of 65. The statistics are very different for men. It is not until the age of 75 that a third of the men become widowed (Atchley, 1997).

Spousal bereavement often causes considerable emotional distress. Widows and widowers have higher rates of depression than do married people. Many people, especially women, experience considerable economic hardship (Lopata, 1979). There is much debate over whether widowhood is more difficult for men or for women, with some studies showing higher rates of distress among women, and others among men. Lieberman (1996) believed that, while women may more openly express grief, men may also feel a profound sense of loss, as if they have "lost their anchor." The course of widowhood is very different for men and women. While men are at higher risk for coronary events a year after widowhood, they are also much more likely to remarry than are women (Parkes & Weiss, 1983). The majority of men are likely to marry within a year, while only about one third of women remarry over the next few years.

However, as Lieberman (1996) pointed out, widowhood can also be a time for growth. Women who had subordinated their lives to their families may now find themselves free of such obligations, and can rediscover aspects of themselves, long-dormant abilities that were abandoned in their 20s. About a third of the widows Lieberman studied exhibited such patterns of growth, returning to school, finding new jobs, and in general making positive adaptational changes. As one woman said: "I've grown so much . . . I see myself now as a much more effective person. I'm also more serene, more generous, and calmer. I've learned to accept things much more gracefully, and I've taken on disputes and won them" (p. 142). Far fewer of the men felt that they had grown from being widowed, although surprisingly, more men than women reported having suppressed part of their personalities for their marriage.

Lieberman identified seven factors that lead to postbereavement growth. Women who expressed a sense of dissatisfaction with their previous life often became *introspective* in their attempts to make sense of their lives. This was often spurred by *a sense of their own mortality* and the realization that there was a limited time left to their lives. Thus, many women embarked upon a *life review and reevaluation,* and actively sought out neglected aspects of themselves. Women who reported postbereavement growth also *searched for personal meaning,* had *more realistic evaluations of their marriage,* and were less likely to idealize their spouse. They also perceived the *loss as an opportunity for growth.* Interestingly, they were also *more depressed* and expressed more emotional distress, suggesting that their distress may have been a catalyst for change.

Lieberman (1996) is quick to point out that growth is not necessarily related to good adjustment, and women who did not go on an identity search did not necessarily experience worse (or better) outcomes than those who did. "Good adjustment and growth are separate and independent paths" (p. 151). As one woman remarked, "I've learned more about my strengths and I've realized that I can take care of myself. I've even started going to classes and learning about business affairs. In spite of my grieving, I can feel myself growing. I have been enriched by my despair in ways I never dreamed possible" (p. 154).

Divorce

In contrast, divorce in midlife is relatively rare. Only 13% of divorces occur over the age of 40 (Chiriboga, 1989). While there is some evidence that men and women in midlife are more dysphoric in the earlier stages of divorce than younger adults, most eventually rebound after 3 to 4 years, and women actually may have slightly higher morale (Chiriboga, 1989). However, upper-middle-class women who experience significant financial declines may be particularly bitter and depressed, even several years after the divorce (Wallerstein, 1986). Men in their 40s may rebound from divorce fairly quickly, but men in their 50s are likely to have a much harder time (Chiriboga, 1979), as do women of a similar age (Botwinnick, 1973).

Nonetheless, there is some evidence for stress-related growth after marital separation and divorce. Helson and Roberts (1994) examined correlates of ego development during midlife in their sample of the Mills College women. There was no general age-related increase in ego development. However, women who had used accommodative styles to cope with serious problems such as divorce tended to have higher levels of ego development.

Thus, the most common types of serious life events in midlife appear to be death of a parent and widowhood. While divorce is relatively rare, it may have more devastating effects, especially for individuals in late midlife. These loss events may occasion maturation and psychological growth, a theme to which we return in a later section. What is not clear from the examination of specific types of crises and life events is whether midlife is a more or less stressful life stage than either early adulthood or late life.

GENERAL LIFE EVENTS

Relatively few studies have explicitly compared whether the number and type of stressful life events change with age. Early correlational studies suggested that the number of life events decrease with age (Aldwin, 1990, 1991). However, standard life events inventories are weighted toward events that are more likely to happen to younger individuals, such as graduations, marriages, divorces, beginning new jobs, having children, and the like. Aldwin (1990) developed an inventory specifically designed to tap the types of life events that are more likely to occur to middle-aged and older people, such as death of a parent, divorce of a child, institution-alization of a spouse, and the like. She found that there was no significant correlation with age in a sample ranging from midlife through late life, al-though health-related life events did tend to show increased frequency in late life (Aldwin, 1991).

Using data from the San Francisco Transitions Study, Chiriboga (1997) also found that there were no differences in the number of life events be-tween individuals in midlife and late life, but did find that young adults reported more life events. Because young people are initiating major new roles in life, it is not surprising that their lives are more unsettled. Inter-estingly, young adults also reported more positive events.

Chiriboga (1997) also presented longitudinal change in stressful life events over a 12-year period. However, the longitudinal data did not sug-gest a strict linear decrease with age. Rather, the differences between the cohorts were maintained, and the number of events fluctuated over time, suggesting both cohort and period effects on the occurrence of stressful life events. In a 6-year longitudinal study, Yancura, Aldwin, and Spiro (1999) found that there was a nonlinear change over time, with the number of self-reported life events increasing until about age 65, and then decreas-ing into later life.

From these few studies, it would be difficult to argue that one stage of life is more stressful than another—at least in terms of major life events. The type of life events may reflect developmental stage, with younger in-dividuals reporting more gains in social roles, and older individuals re-porting more losses. However, it is not at all clear that the number of life events varies. In part, younger adults may be more comfortable with the construct of stress, and thus be more willing to report stressful life events, which may be one explanation for Chiriboga's (1997) failure to find de-creases in stressful life events with age, and the maintenance of cohort differences. More work is needed to further examine age, cohort, and pe-riod effects in the experience of stressful life events.

DAILY HASSLES

In contrast, daily hassles or microstressors show clearer developmental patterns with age (and life stage). Aldwin, Sutton, Chiara, and Spiro (1996) found that both the frequency and type of hassles changed with age. Overall, older men reported fewer hassles than middle-aged men. Not sur-prisingly, older men were less likely to report problems with work or with children, and although they were more likely to report health-related has-sles, the increase of these hassles did not fully offset the decrease in the work and parenting domains. Chiriboga (1997) also found that older adults reported more health-related hassles, but that other types clearly decreased with age, such as problems with parents, children, spouses, work, relatives, and money. Despite the increased responsibilities of midlife, the middle-aged group in Chiriboga's sample was never higher in the number of hassles reported than either younger or older groups.

SUMMARY

Despite a fairly long history of trying to characterize midlife as a time of crisis and heightened stress, there is little support for this in the literature. Putative crises turn out to be less frequent and/or less severe than initially thought, and there is little indication from the general stress literature of any increase in either stressful life events or hassles. This does not mean that midlife is not a time of change. As noted earlier, bereavement becomes more frequent, with most individuals in midlife losing one or both parents, and a large proportion of women becoming widowed. While divorce is relatively infrequent, there are some indications that divorce may be more problematic for men and women in their 50s, as is job loss. Thus, midlife, while not necessarily a time of crisis, can be a time of change. Further, there are also suggestions in the literature that this change, although painful, can engender significant periods of growth, and perhaps set the stage for the development of wisdom in late life, depending, in part, on how individuals cope with these problems.

COPING AT MIDLIFE

There are three basic views in the literature on developmental changes in coping in adulthood. Theories emphasizing decrements suggest that coping worsens with age; those emphasizing increments suggest improvements in coping ability with age; finally, those emphasizing stability suggest little or no intrinsic change with age.

Gutmann (1974) was an early proponent of the decrement theory. Based on a cross-cultural study using Thematic Apperception Tests (TATs), he proposed that coping in young adulthood is characterized by active mastery, coping in midlife by passive mastery, and coping in late life by "magical" mastery. Young adults tended to relate stories about the pictures in the TATs that were full of optimistic action, while middle-aged adults were more cautious and limited. The old adults often told stories that were not directly related to the picture at hand or in which problems seemed to resolve themselves, hence magical mastery.

In contrast, Vaillant (1977), using qualitative analysis of interviews on college-educated men, argued that there was an incremental or positive developmental shift, with young adults using "neurotic" or "immature" defense mechanisms such as denial and projection, and middle-aged individuals "mature" defense mechanisms such as sublimation. He replicated this in a sample of lower class men (Vaillant, Bond, & Vaillant, 1986), but did not find similar developmental trends in a sample of Terman women who were administered a standardized questionnaire on defense mechanisms (Bond, Gardner, & Siegel, 1987). Costa, Zonderman, and McCrae (1991) found that the more problematic defense mechanisms were negatively correlated with age in three samples of men and women, while repression/denial mechanisms were positively correlated with age. Finally, Diehl, Coyle, and Labouvie-Vief (1996), in their study of age and gender differences in defense mechanisms, found that older adults displayed more impulse control than did younger adults, who displayed more aggression.

In contrast to defense mechanisms, studies using standardized coping checklists find weaker relations with age. Using this type of quantitative methodology, McCrae (1982) argued that there was little or no age-related change in coping in adulthood that could not be attributed to differences in the types of problems faced. While older adults may use less problem-focused coping, this may reflect that they are more likely to be coping with problems such as bereavement and chronic illness, for which problem-focused coping may be less useful. Other studies have also found that older adults may report less problem-focused coping, resulting in the perception that they are more "passive." However, they also may use fewer escapist strategies, such as alcohol or drug use (for a review, see Aldwin, Sutton, Chiara, & Spiro, 1996).

Thus, depending on the measures and the sample used, older adults could be considered either better or worse copers than young adults, or perhaps coping simply does not show developmental change in adulthood. Aldwin, Sutton, Chiara, et al. (1996) set out to address this conundrum using both quantitative and qualitative methodology in over 1,000 interviews with middle-aged and older men. Middle-aged men reported more coping strategies on the coping checklists, especially problem-focused coping, than did older men; however, few age differences were seen with the qualitative, content analysis of the coping interviews. Further, there were no age differences in the perceived efficacy of their coping strategies. Aldwin et al. examined the interviews to reconcile these differences and discovered that the coping of older adults could be described in terms of energy conservation. For example, when faced with a flood in the basement, a middle-aged man might seek to analyze the problem, go to the hardware store to obtain the necessary equipment, and attempt to fix the problem himself. An 80-year-old man, in contrast, is unlikely to venture into a flooded basement. However, he may very well call a son or a plumber to come and fix the problem. On a coping inventory, the middle-aged man would have checked off three strategies, while the 80-year-old would have only checked one. In the content analysis of the interviews, however, both men would have simply been coded as using problem-focused strategies. Both strategies were equally effective, in that both resulted in fixing the plumbing problem. However, the middle-aged man expended more physical energy.

Thus, these disparate findings in the literature on coping in adulthood can be integrated through an "energy conservation" model of changes in coping strategies with age. In young adulthood, individuals have a tremendous amount of energy but relatively little experience. Thus, younger adults may use more active strategies—but not necessarily more efficacious ones. Further, young adults may be more unrealistic in their beliefs in their ability to affect the situation.

With age, people may become more effective in their coping efforts. Many problems are self-limiting, and sometimes taking a wait-and-see attitude is most effective. By middle age, adults may be more realistic about their ability to change situations. A good example of this is a song, popular in the 1960s among young baby boomers, in which the singer croons, "I'm gonna make you love me." By midlife, Bonnie Raitt bemoans that "I can't make you love me, if you don't." While this may be interpreted as Gutmann's (1974) shift from active to passive mastery, it actually may simply reflect increased realism in understanding the limits of one's own actions. This does not necessarily mean that middle-aged adults are worse copers—indeed, they may be more efficacious in choosing strategies that work, in avoiding ineffective strategies, and in being more judicious in the expenditure of their efforts.

The current coping strategies checklists tend not to tap developmental trends in coping very well. Given that such coping strategies tend to reflect environmental contingencies more than personality (Rott & Thomae, 1991), it is also possible the biggest developmental change is in a greater reliance on management strategies rather than coping processes per se. *Management strategies* refers to the ability either to avoid or to minimize the occurrence of problems (see Aldwin & Brustrom, 1997), which has also been called anticipatory or proactive coping (Aspinwall & Taylor, 1998). Rather than having to cope with a problem, it makes more sense, from an energy conservation viewpoint, to prevent the occurrence of a problem and/or minimize its effects. For example, it is more efficacious to ensure that a gas tank is full before starting a trip than to have to cope with running out of gas in the middle of the journey. This idea would help explain the curious finding mentioned earlier that hassles decrease with age, although midlife is a time of great responsibility. We hypothesize that individuals in midlife have developed better management or anticipatory coping strategies to decrease the probability of experiencing daily stressors that can be avoided with a little forethought. At this point there are no studies to support this hypothesis, but we believe it is a plausible one.

THE RELATIONSHIP BETWEEN STRESS, COPING, AND HEALTH AT MIDLIFE

General issues in health at midlife have been reviewed in this volume by Spiro (Chapter 5). Thus, we focus on the relationship between stress, coping, and health at midlife.

Stress issues are highly salient to health in midlife. Kennedy and Comko (1991) found that middle-aged women ranked stress as their number one health concern. Of the various psychosocial correlates of self-rated health, Thomas (1997) found that stress was most strongly correlated with health in a sample of middle-aged women. Compared with the healthiest quartile, the least healthy quartile reported more problems with their marriage, financial strain, and worries about their children. They were also less likely to report perceived rewards from their relationships with their husbands and the children. These studies supported earlier studies on the salience of relationship stress for midlife women by Costello (1991) and S. McKinlay, Triant, McKinlay, Brambilla, and Ferdock (1990).

None of these studies compared whether relationship stress was more important for health at midlife than for early or later life. To our knowledge, there are no studies specifically examining whether individuals in midlife are more or less vulnerable to the effects of stress, or whether coping is more or less protective at this stage of life. Based on indirect evidence, however, we argue that stress may be linked to the development of chronic illness in midlife.

We do know that individuals in late life are more vulnerable to the physiological effects of stress. Older individuals are more vulnerable to heat stress, take longer to heal from injuries, and in general have a harder time returning to homeostasis after physical insults. Also, the chronic diseases of old age, such as diabetes and cardiovascular disease, start manifesting in some individuals in midlife, especially those in their 50s and 60s (for reviews, see Spiro, this volume; Merrill & Verbrugge, 1999). Further, some risk factors appear to have stronger effects in midlife than they do in late life, in part because of survivor effects (Kaplan, Haan, & Wallace, 1999). For example, individuals who are more vulnerable to the effects of smoking, for whatever genetic or environmental reasons, are likely to succumb to smoking-related illnesses in midlife.

It is also true that, due to immune system maturation, older adults may be *less* vulnerable to many kinds of infections than are younger adults (Miller, 1996). The longer one has lived, the more infections one has been exposed to, and thus the greater the number of memory and mature T cells that encode information for fighting off specific illnesses. Very old adults are nonetheless more susceptible to some types of infections such as pneumonia. In general, though, infectious illnesses are more frequent in early adulthood, and chronic illnesses are more prevalent in mid- and late-life.

Thus, it would be interesting to determine if there is a three-way inter-action between age, stress, and type of illness. For example, we know that there is a relationship between stress and cardiovascular disease (for re-views and interesting possible physiological mechanisms, see Allen & Patterson, 1995; Benjamin & McMillan, 1998). However, rarely does a 20-year-old suffer a stress-related myocardial infarction, although it is likely that risk factors such as cholesterol levels and blood pressure may tem-porarily increase. By midlife, the cumulative insults of these risk factors may render an individual susceptible to a myocardial infarction, espe-cially for physical stressors; it is not unusual for a middle-aged man to suffer his first heart attack while engaged in unaccustomed exertion, such as shoveling snow. Psychosocial factors such as job stress may also play a role (e.g., Karasek & Theorell, 1990). By late life, vulnerability to so many different types of illnesses has increased so much that stress may result in a plethora of conditions. For example, while stress has been seen as a risk factor for stroke (Bjorntorp, 1995), it is probable that this association is stronger in late life than in mid- or early life.

Some of the inconsistencies in the stress-illness literature may be due to age differences in the effects of stress. In terms of chronic illness, it is possible that an individual's "reserve capacity" for coping with physical stressors may decrease, although the same is not necessarily true for psy-chological stressors. The shift from coping strategies to management strategies hypothesized earlier might well be in response to the recogni-tion that exposure and/or overreaction to stressors is hard on the body. Some of the men in the Aldwin, Sutton, Chiara, et al. (1996) study specif-ically mentioned learning not to get angry or too worried once they had developed problems such as hypertension. Studies are needed specifi-cally addressing these issues in order to understand what effects stress may have in midlife, and whether it is involved in the development of chronic illnesses at midlife.

STRESS, COPING, AND WISDOM AT MIDLIFE

While stress undoubtedly has adverse effects, it would be a mistake to think that all of the effects of stress are negative. As mentioned, many loss events at midlife, although painful, were accompanied by a sense of maturation and personal growth.

There is a growing literature on the positive aspects of stress, sometimes called "posttraumatic growth" (Tedeschi, Park, & Calhoun, 1998) or "the perceived benefits of stress" (Aldwin & Sutton, 1998). While coping may moderate the effects of stress, being able to perceive (and act upon) a "sil-ver lining" may result in long-term positive effects. These positive changes may include material gain; changes in perspective; stronger social bonds; increased coping skills, mastery, and self-esteem (Aldwin & Stokols, 1988); increased self-knowledge (Beardslee, 1989); ego development (Helson & Roberts, 1994); and perhaps wisdom as well (Aldwin, 1994). Whether one calls it "learning from one's mistakes," the "school of hard knocks," or "sadder but wiser," it has long been recognized that, even though certain experiences can be extraordinarily painful, they may nonetheless have maturing effects.

Aldwin and Stokols (1988) proposed a deviation-amplification model, based on Maruyama's (1963) dynamic modification to von Bertalanffy's (1969) systems theory. Most standard systems theories and stress theories posit a homeostatic model; that is, stress results in a perturbation in a baseline state, and coping serves to return the organism to that baseline. However, Maruyama argued that there were both deviation-countering mechanisms (which returned organisms to baseline), and deviation amplification mechanisms, which resulted in long-term change. Aldwin and Stokols argued that whether these long-term effects were positive or negative depended on individual and contextual factors, including chance.

Other researchers have been working along parallel lines, and the results have been remarkably similar across studies (for reviews, see Aldwin & Sutton, 1998; Park, 1998; Tedeschi et al., 1998). An early study by Affleck, Tennen, Croog, and Levine (1987) found that men who perceived benefits from having a myocardial infarction had better survival at a 5-year follow-up. Presumably these men had made improvements in their diet and health behavior habits, which may have aided in their survival. Stein, Folkman, Trabasso, and Richards (1997) showed that caregivers of AIDS patients who expressed positive appraisals of their experience were less likely to be depressed and showed more positive outcomes 12 months after bereavement. Interestingly, perceiving benefits from stressful situations can be differentiated from "making meaning." Davis, Nolen-Hoeksema, and Larson (1998), in a study of individuals coping with the loss of a family member, found that making meaning was associated with better short-term outcomes, but perceiving benefits was associated with greater long-term outcomes.

This phenomenon may be more widespread that formerly thought. Aldwin, Sutton, and Lachman (1996), in a series of studies, found that the majority of individuals could perceive long-term positive outcomes even for major low points in their lives, although most individuals acknowledged that often the effects were mixed. While some might consider this to be a form of denial, the long-term effects individuals reported often made a great deal of sense. For example, one man's low point was the burning down of his apartment building one snowy winter night. The positive outcome from this experience was that it spurred him into action to find a new and much better home for himself and his family. This would be considered a material gain. One woman spoke of the coping skills derived from having to nurse her alcoholic ex-husband through his stroke—skills that were useful when her son suffered head trauma in an auto accident. Others spoke of an increased sense of mastery, almost disbelief at what they could accomplish under extremely trying conditions. Changing values and perspectives, such as rediscovering the value of health and family, is fairly common after a brush with death.

The notion that development exists in adulthood is still a matter of some debate, in part because it is difficult to show a universal developmental progression, and there are individual differences in the life course (cf. Ford & Lerner, 1992). Langer et al. (1990) have suggested that development in adulthood follows a nonsequential pattern.

Following this, Aldwin (1994) argued that stress provides a context for development in adulthood. The rationale is fairly simple. As mentioned earlier, stress can be a challenge that encourages the development of certain coping resources. More fundamentally, stress creates uncertainty, and according to Acredolo and O'Connor (1991), uncertainty is the sine qua non for development to occur. The development of more complex schemata in the Piagetian tradition relies on uncertainty—if one does not question the truth or rightness of one's current cognitive schema, then there is no need to change it. It is only when discrepancies occur that one is forced to reexamine these schemata.

Epstein (1991) has argued that trauma can create a fundamental change in an individual's identity. He referred to trauma as the "atom smasher" of psychological research, in that it often destroys individuals' cognitive schemata about not only how the world works, but also their place in it, their own sense of identity. Traumatized individuals often speak of "picking up the pieces," of having to recreate themselves. This entails fundamental self-reflection—a difficult and often painful task. It can be argued, though, that self-reflection is the basis for the development of wisdom.

The past 10 years has seen a rebirth of interest in the construct of wisdom (for reviews, see Birren & Fisher, 1990; McKee & Barber, 1999). Psychologists have tended to define wisdom in terms of practical knowledge (Baltes & Smith, 1990), and cognitive and emotional complexity (Labouvie-Vief, 1990), although recently Baltes and Staudinger (2000) have acknowledged the importance of social judgment or justice to the central construct of wisdom as well. However, McKee and Barber (1999) have cogently argued that wisdom involves seeing through illusions. Certainly, self-delusion is a major source of unwise action, and it would stand to reason that the ability to see through illusions—whether generated by oneself, one's friends (or enemies), or the culture as a whole—is the basis of wise decisions.

Stress often forces us to examine our assumptions and the validity of our perceptions. While stress may engender more delusional thinking or actions, these will undoubtedly make a situation worse in the long run. We learn through hard experience that what we thought was truth was illusion. In the Aldwin, Sutton, and Lachman (1996) study, one woman's low point was her divorce. In her 20s, she firmly believed that if she was the perfect wife and mother, she would never be divorced. What she believed was perfection, however, was not what her husband apparently wanted, and they divorced. This woman learned that her belief system, or cognitive schema, about how marriages "worked" was an illusion—but she remained embittered and disillusioned. She could not "pick up the pieces" and construct a more realistic but positive image of herself and the world.

Baltes (1987) has long argued that development in adulthood consists of a balance of gains and losses. However, the underlying assumption has been that development consists of gains that may or may not compensate for losses, with the corollary assumption that loss is bad. However, as reviewed in this chapter, it is a mistake to think that all loss is necessarily bad, or that even painful losses do not entail some benefit. Thus, if stress challenges our assumptions and forces us to abandon unrealistic or even damaging assumptions about the world, then the loss of those assumptions is a good thing. Even losing loved ones through divorce or bereavement, as painful as this might be, still avails us the opportunity to engage in compassionate behavior such as caregiving for a dying loved one, or restraining angry remarks about one's ex-spouse for the sake of the children.

Taken further, one could even argue that loss is perhaps a necessary (but not sufficient) condition for development. Neurophysiological development in childhood requires pruning competing neurological pathways; gaining childhood roles necessitates abandoning infant roles, and so forth. It is true that in early adulthood there are many more role gains than losses. Nonetheless, the act of choosing a particular career or mate necessarily entails the loss of other opportunities. Indeed, the recognition of those losses may underlie the role of reevaluation in midlife. Reappraising those losses in terms of commitment may be one component of maturity.

One of the most difficult things to understand about Erikson's (1950) construct of ego integrity is that it involves the understanding and acceptance that one has led the only possible life that one can lead. For those of us who have not as yet reached this stage, this is difficult to comprehend. We regret our mistakes, we wonder what would have happened if we had married someone else or went into a different line of work. However, the choices and experiences that one has had constitute one's self; therefore, to accept oneself, one must understand the process through which one became what one is.

Levenson and Crumpler (1996) reviewed ontogenetic and sociogenetic approaches to adult development, and argued for a third way, which they termed a "liberative" model of adult development. Essentially, this advances the idea that adult development is constituted by progressive freedom from biosocial conditioning. The self is the primary product of biosocial conditioning. However, rather than the "self," we might better characterize this as what Jung would call the "persona," or false self. The persona can be thought of as a series of accretions—one gains social roles, material possessions, social position, habits, and assumptions about the world. Extending McKee and Barber's (1999) theory of wisdom, these accretions can be seen as the basis of illusion, and, according to Buddhist philosophy, illusion (and attachment) are the origin of suffering.

For example, people who abuse alcohol or methamphetamine often have illusions about their ability to withstand the harmful effects of those substances. These illusions blind them to the very real problems generated by their behaviors. Only when the problems become so bad that they are impossible to ignore—usually because they entail horrendous suffering—are such people finally forced to confront their illusions. According to McKee and Barber (1999), "We learn to see through illusions only by suffering through them" (pp. 154–155). While this is an extreme example, this principle can be extended to most areas of life.

Theories of wisdom also generally specify things that are gained. Birren and Fisher (1990, p. 326) define wisdom as the integration of the affective, conative, and cognitive aspects of human abilities in response to life's tasks and problems. Wisdom is a balance between the opposing valences of intense emotion and detachment, action and inaction, and knowledge and doubts.

The cognitive component can be loosely defined as perspicacity or insightfulness, which is based on both a knowledge base and higher order cognitive processes, such as the ability to comprehend complex constructs and to use dialectical and relativistic modes of thinking (Labouvie-Vief, 1990). As McKee and Barber (1999) point out, perspicacity is based on seeing through illusions, which involves abandoning assumption systems and aspects of one's persona that are destructive and unnecessary. Thus, practical experience is useful to the extent that one has gained competence but also has learned to avoid error.

The affective component not only includes emotional complexity (Labouvie-Vief, 1990), but also includes emotional balance, which is based on self-knowledge. Emotional balance refers to the capacity to examine the sources of emotions, which in turn means than one tends to become less upset when negative things occur, or not to become overwhelmed by positive experiences. We tend to think of neuroticism in terms of negative affect, but Eysenck (1987) explicitly defined neuroticism as strong, easily aroused emotions—without regard to their valence. And neuroticism is one of the better personality predictors of poor mental and physical health in adulthood (Friedman & Booth-Kewley, 1987).

Conation refers to "volition and desire," or motivation. For some, wisdom entails of necessity a moral and ethical aspect (Sternberg, 1998). In addition to higher level moral reasoning (Kohlberg & Ryncarz, 1990), wisdom entails integrity, compassion, and generosity, which is referred to as "character" in some cultures. According to Langer (1989), most of our prejudices derive from unexamined assumptions and premature cognitive commitments, which are, after all, the basis of illusion. Langer talks about "decreasing prejudice through increasing discrimination," learning not to see people through stereotypes. To the extent that one learns to see through one's illusions, one is better able to see other people simply as other humans with whom one shares a common humanity. Further, the persona, with its layers of accretions, can also be considered to consist of desires—for status, for material goods, for attention from others—which can get in the way of compassionate behavior. A young child can become overly attached to a toy and refuse to share it, whereas from the perspective of an adult, a toy is simply a toy and should be shared. The "undeveloped" adult can become overly attached to, say, status at work and refuse to share credit for a project. From the perspective of a developed adult, a project is simply a project, and credit should be shared.

Thus, wisdom entails not only the development of capacity, but also loss of the false self, with its illusions and pointless desires. Indeed, wisdom is not possible unless this false self is lost. In other words, there is no development without loss. Stressful life events form the context through which this dialectic between development and loss occurs. Coping can entail the development of self-knowledge, the loss of destructive behaviors and cognition, and an increase in compassion and empathy, or it can entail just the opposite. In midlife losses become more common: One loses parents and sometimes spouses, children grow up, and careers may pall. The stress from these losses may have devastating effects and result in the development of chronic illnesses. Yet, it is also through these losses that one may start to develop wisdom.

CONCLUSION

With reference to the French Revolution, Dickens once wrote, "It was the best of times, it was the worst of times." To a degree, this is also applicable to midlife. When we first began writing this chapter, most of our initial "take" on midlife was positive. In midlife, one has suffered through one's illusions and finally learned to avoid some of the worst mistakes of youth. One also enjoys increasing responsibilities, especially the generative ones involved in mentoring the next generation and in providing a bridge between generations. While everyday demands are great, so too are the rewards. However, then the stressors of midlife "hit." Parents died, siblings became gravely ill, job demands increased seemingly exponentially, and midlife became "the worst of times." It was thus personally interesting to find so many examples in the literature of stress-related growth at midlife, even when those stressors constituted losses. McKee and Barber's (1999) theory of loss of illusions as development of wisdom formed an interesting bridge between the loss-related stressors and personal development.

While much of this chapter is admittedly speculative, we have attempted to synthesize what is known about stress, coping, and health in midlife, and outline important areas for future work. In particular, we need to determine what role stress plays in the development of chronic illness at midlife, and whether there is a shift toward better management strategies to avoid the ill effects of stress. Finally, we are beginning to approach a consensus that wisdom is a multifaceted construct entailing cognition, conation, and emotion. The developmental processes through which wisdom develops still need to be investigated, and we have suggested some possible avenues for future research.

REFERENCES

Acredolo, C., & O'Connor, J. (1991). On the difficulty of detecting cognitive uncertain: Cognitive uncertainty and cognitive development [Special issue]. *Human Development, 34,* 204–223.

Affleck, G., Tennen, H., Croog, S., & Levine, S. (1987). Causal attribution, perceived benefits, and morbidity after a heart attack: An 8-year study. *Journal of Consulting and Clinical Psychology, 55,* 29–35.

Aldwin, C. (1990). The Elders Life Stress Inventory (ELSI): Egocentric and nonegocentric stress. In M.A.P. Stephens, S.E. Hobfoll, J.H. Crowther, & D.L. Tennenbaum (Eds.), *Stress and coping in late life families* (pp. 49–69). New York: Hemisphere.

Aldwin, C. (1991). Does age affect the stress and coping process? The implications of age differences in perceived locus of control. *Journal of Gerontology: Psychological Sciences, 46,* P174–P180.

Aldwin, C. (1994). *Stress, coping, and development: An integrative approach.* New York: Guilford Press.

Aldwin, C.M., & Brustrom, J. (1997). Theories of coping with chronic stress: Illustrations from the health psychology and aging literatures. In B. Gottlieb (Ed.), *Coping with chronic stress* (pp. 75–103). New York: Plenum Press.

Aldwin, C.M., Spiro, A., III, Levenson, M.R., & Bossé, R. (1989). Longitudinal findings from the Normative Aging Study: I. Does mental health change with age? *Psychology and Aging, 4,* 295–306.

Aldwin, C.M., & Stokols, D. (1988). The effects of environmental change on individuals and groups: Some neglected issues in stress research. *Journal of Environmental Psychology, 8,* 57–75.

Aldwin, C.M., & Sutton, K.J. (1998). A developmental perspective on post-traumatic growth. In R.G. Tedeschi, C.L. Park, & L.G. Calhoun (Eds.), *Posttraumatic growth: Positive change in the aftermath of crisis* (pp. 43–63). Mahwah, NJ: Erlbaum.

Aldwin, C.M., Sutton, K.J., Chiara, G., & Spiro, A., III. (1996). Age differences in stress, coping, and appraisal: Findings from the Normative Aging Study. *Journal of Gerontology: Psychological Sciences, 51B,* P178–P188.

Aldwin, C.M., Sutton, K.J., & Lachman, M. (1996). The development of coping resources in adulthood. *Journal of Personality, 64,* 91–113.

Allen, M.T., & Patterson, S.M. (1995). Hemoconcentration and stress: A review of physiological mechanisms and relevance for cardiovascular disease risk. *Biological Psychology, 41,* 1–27.

Aspinwall, L., & Taylor, S. (1998). A stitch in time: Self-regulation and proactive coping. *Psychological Bulletin, 121,* 417–436.

Atchley, R.C. (1997). *Social forces and aging: An introduction to social gerontology* (8th ed.). Belmont, CA: Wadsworth.

Avis, N. (1999). Women's health at midlife. In S.L. Willis & J.D. Reid (Eds.), *Life in the middle: Psychological and social development in middle age* (pp. 105–147). San Diego, CA: Academic Press.

Baltes, P.B. (1987). Theoretical propositions of life-span developmental psychology: On the dynamics between growth and decline. *Developmental Psychology, 24,* 611–626.

Baltes, P.B., & Smith, J. (1990). Toward a psychology of wisdom and its ontogenesis. In R. Sternberg (Ed.), *Wisdom: Its nature, origin, and development* (pp. 317–332). Cambridge, MA: Cambridge University Press.

Baltes, P.B., & Staudinger, U.M. (2000). Wisdom: A metaheuristic (pragmatic) to orchestrate mind and virtue toward excellence. *American Psychologist, 55,* 122–136.

Beardslee, W.R. (1989). The role of self-understanding in resilient individuals: The development of a perspective. *American Journal of Orthopsychiatry, 59,* 266–278.

Bengston, V., Rosenthal, C., & Burton, L. (1996). Paradoxes of families and aging. In R.H. Binstock & L.K. George (Eds.), *Handbook of aging and the social sciences* (4th ed., pp. 253–282). San Diego, CA: Academic Press.

Benjamin, I.J., & McMillan, D.R. (1998). Stress (heat shock) proteins: Molecular chaperones in cardiovascular biology and disease. *Circulation Research, 83,* 117–132.

Beyene, Y. (1986). Cultural significance and physiological manifestations of menopause: A biocultural analysis. *Culture, Medicine, and Psychiatry, 10,* 47–71.

Birren, J.E., & Fisher, L.E. (1990). The elements of wisdom: Overview and integration. In R.J. Sternberg (Ed.), *Wisdom: Its nature, origin, and development* (pp. 317–332). Cambridge, MA: Cambridge University Press.

Bjorntorp, P. (1995). Neuroendocrine ageing. *Journal of Internal Medicine, 238,* 401–404.

Bond, M., Gardiner, S.T., & Sigel, J.J. (1983). An empirical examination of defense mechanisms. *Archives of General Psychiatry, 40,* 333–338.

Borland, D.C. (1982). A cohort analysis approach to the empty-nest syndrome among three ethnic groups of women: A theoretical position. *Journal of Marriage and the Family, 44,* 117–129.

Bossé, R., Aldwin, C., Levenson, M.R., & Ekerdt, D. (1987). Differences in mental health among retirees and workers: Findings from the Normative Aging Study. *Psychology and Aging, 2,* 383–389.

Botwinnick, J. (1973). *Aging and behaviour.* New York: Springer.

Brody, E.M. (1990). *Women in the middle: Their parent-care years.* New York: Springer.

Chiriboga, D.A. (1979). Marital separation and stress: A life course perspective. *Alternative Lifestyles, 2,* 461–470.

Chiriboga, D.A. (1989). Divorce at midlife. In R.A. Kalish (Ed.), *Midlife loss: Coping strategies* (pp. 42–88). Newbury Park, CA: Sage.

Chiriboga, D.A. (1997). Crisis, challenge, and stability in the middle years. In M.E. Lachman & J.B. James (Eds.), *Multiple paths of midlife development* (pp. 293–343). Chicago: University of Chicago Press.

Clausen, J. (1990). *Turning point as a life course concept.* Paper presented at the annual meetings of the American Sociological Association, Washington, DC.

Costa, P.T., & McCrae, R.R. (1980). Influence of extraversion and neuroticism on subjective well-being: Happy and unhappy people. *Journal of Personality and Social Psychology, 38,* 668–678.

Costa, P.T., Zonderman, A.B., & McCrae, R.R. (1991). Personality, defense, coping, and adaptation in older adulthood. In E.M. Cummings, A.L. Greene, & K.H. Karraker (Eds.), *Life-span developmental psychology: Perspectives of stress and coping.* Hillsdale, NJ: Erlbaum.

Costello, E. (1991). Married with children: Predictors of mental and physical health in middle-aged women. *Psychiatry, 54,* 292–305.

Davis, C.G., Nolen-Hoeksema, S., & Larson, J. (1998). Making sense of loss and benefitting from the experience: Two construals of meaning. *Journal of Personality and Social Psychology, 75,* 561–574.

Diehl, M., Coyle, N., & Labouvie-Vief, G. (1996). Age and sex differences in strategies of coping and defense across the lifespan. *Psychology and Aging, 11,* 127–139.

Epstein, S. (1991). The self-concept, the traumatic neurosis, and the structure of personality. In D. Ozer, J.H. Healy, & A.J. Stewart (Eds.), *Perspectives in Personality, 3,* 63–98.

Erikson, E.H. (1950). *Childhood and society.* New York: Norton.

Eysenck, H. (1987). *The biological basis of personality.* Springfield, IL: Thomas.

Farrell, M., & Rosenberg, S. (1981). *Men at midlife.* Dover, MA: Auburn House.

Ford, D.H., & Lerner, R.M. (1992). *Developmental systems theory: An integrative approach.* Newbury Park, CA: Sage.

Friedman, H.S., & Booth-Kewley, S. (1987). The disease-prone personality: A meta-analytic view of the construct. *American Psychologist, 42,* 539–555.

Gutmann, D.L. (1974). Alternatives to disengagement: The old men of the Highland Druze. In R.A. LeVine (Ed.), *Culture and personality: Contemporary readings* (pp. 232–245). Chicago: Aldine.

Helson, R., & Roberts, B.W. (1994). Ego development and personality change in adulthood. *Journal of Personality and Social Psychology, 66,* 911–920.

Himes, C.L. (1994). Parental caregiving by adult women: A demographic perspective. *Research on Aging, 16,* 191–221.

Jacques, E. (1965). Death and the mid-life crisis. *International Journal of Psychoanalysis, 46,* 502–514.

Jung, C.G. (1933). *Modern man in search of a soul.* New York: Harcourt Press & World.

Kaplan, G.A., Haan, M.N., & Wallace, R.B. (1999). Understanding changing risk factor associations with increasing age in adults. *Annual Review of Public Health, 20,* 89–108.

Karasek, R., & Theorell, T. (1990). *Healthy work: Stress, productivity, and the reconstruction of working life.* New York: Basic Books.

Kennedy, J., & Comko, R. (1991). Health needs of midlife women. *Nursing Management, 22,* 62–66.

Kessler, R.C., Foster, C., Webster, P.S., & House, J.S. (1992). The relationship between age and depressive symptoms in two national surveys. *Psychology and Aging, 7,* 119–126.

Keyes, C.L.M., & Ryff, C.D. (1999). Psychological well-being in midlife. In S.L. Willis & J.D. Reid (Eds.), *Life in the middle: Psychological and social development in middle age* (pp. 161–178). San Diego, CA: Academic Press.

Kohlberg, L., & Ryncarz, R.A. (1990). Beyond justice reasoning: Moral development and consideration of a seventh stage. In C.N. Alexander & E.J. Langer (Eds.), *Higher stages of human development* (pp. 191–207). Oxford, England: Oxford University Press.

Labouvie-Vief, G. (1990). Wisdom as integrated thought: Historical and developmental perspectives. In R.J. Sternberg (Ed.), *Wisdom: Its nature, origins, and development* (pp. 52–86). Cambridge, England: Cambridge University Press.

Langer, E. (1989). *Mindfulness.* Reading, MA: Addison-Wesley.

Langer, E., Chanowitz, B., Palmerino, M., Jacobs, S., Rhodes, M., & Thayer, P. (1990). Nonsequential development and aging. In C.N. Alexander & E.J. Langer (Eds.), *Higher stages of human development* (pp. 114–138). Oxford, England: Oxford University Press.

Levenson, M.R., & Crumpler, C.A. (1996). Three models of adult development. *Human Development, 39,* 135–149.

Levinson, D.J., Darrow, C.N., Klein, E.B., Levinson, M.H., & McKee, B. (1978). *The seasons of a man's life.* New York: Knopf.

Lieberman, M. (1996). *Doors close, doors open: Widows, grieving and growing.* New York: Putnam.

Lopata, H. (1979). *Women as widows.* New York: Elsevier.

Marshall, V.W., Matthews, S.H., & Rosenthal, C.J. (1993). Elusiveness of family life. In G. Maddox & M.P. Lawton (Eds.), *A challenge for the sociology of aging: Focus on kinship, aging, and social change* (pp. 39–72). New York: Springer.

Maruyama, M. (1963). The second cybernetics: Deviation-amplifying mutual causal processes. *American Scientist, 51,* 164–179.

Matthews, K. (1992). Myths and realities of the menopause. *Psychosomatic Medicine, 54,* 1–9.

McCrae, R.R. (1982). Age differences in the use of coping mechanisms. *Journal of Gerontology, 37,* 454–460.

McKee, P., & Barber, C. (1999). On defining wisdom. *International Journal of Aging and Human Development, 249,* 149–164.

McKinlay, J.B., McKinlay, S.M., & Brambilla, D.J. (1987). The relative contributions of endocrine changes and social circumstances to depression in mid-aged women. *Journal of Health and Social Behavior, 28,* 345–363.

McKinlay, S., Triant, R., McKinlay, J., Brambilla, D., & Ferdock, M. (1990). Multiple roles for middle-aged women and their impact on health. In M. Ory & H. Warner (Eds.), *Gender, health, and longevity* (pp. 119–136). New York: Springer.

Merrill, S.S., & Verbrugge, L.M. (1999). Health and disease in midlife. In S.L. Willis & J.D. Reid (Eds.), *Life in the middle: Psychological and social development in middle age* (pp. 78–104). San Diego, CA: Academic Press.

Miller, R. (1996). The aging immune system: Primer and prospectus. *Science, 273,* 70–74.

Moen, P., & Wethington, E. (1999). Midlife development in a life course context. In S.L. Willis & J.D. Reid (Eds.), *Life in the middle: Psychological and social development in middle age* (pp. 3–24). San Diego, CA: Academic Press.

Moss, M.S., & Moss, S.Z. (1989). The death of a parent. In R.A. Kalish (Ed.), *Midlife loss: Coping strategies* (pp. 89–114). Newbury Park, CA: Sage.

Papalia, D.E., Camp, C.J., & Feldman, R.D. (1996). *Adult development and aging.* New York: McGraw-Hill.

Park, C.L. (1998). Stress-related growth and thriving through coping: The roles of personality and cognitive processes. *Journal of Social Issues, 54,* 267–278.

Parker, R., & Aldwin, C.M. (1997). Do aspects of gender identity change from early to middle adulthood? Disentangling age, cohort, and period effects. In M.E. Lachman & J.B. James (Eds.), *Multiple paths of mid-life development* (pp. 67–107). Chicago: University of Chicago Press.

Parkes, C.M. (1972). *Bereavement: Studies of grief in adult life.* New York: International Universities Press.

Parkes, C.M., & Weiss, R.S. (1983). *Recovery from bereavement.* New York: Basic Books.

Payer, L. (1991). The menopause in various cultures. In H. Burger & M. Boulet (Eds.), *A portrait of the menopause* (3–22). Park Ridge, NJ: Parthenon.

Robinson, S.D., Rosenberg, H.J., & Farrell, M.P. (1999). The midlife crisis revisited. In S.L. Willis & J.D. Reid (Eds.), *Life in the middle: Psychological and social development in middle age* (pp. 47–77). San Diego, CA: Academic Press.

Rosenthal, C.J., Martin-Matthews, A., & Matthews, S.H. (1996). Caught in the middle? Occupancy in multiple roles and help to parents in a national probability sample of Canadian adults. *Journals of Gerontology: Series B, Psychological Sciences and Social Sciences, 51,* S274–S283.

Rosenthal, C.J., Matthews, S.H., & Marshall, V.W. (1991). Is parent care normative? The experience of a sample of middle-aged women. In B.B. Hess & E.W. Markson (Eds.), *Growing old in America* (4th ed., pp. 427–440). New Brunswick, NJ: Transaction.

Rott, C., & Thomae, H. (1991). Coping in longitudinal perspective: Findings from the Bonn Longitudinal Study on Aging. *Journal of Cross-Cultural Gerontology, 6,* 23–40.

Scharlach, A.E. (1991). Factors associated with filial grief following the death of an elderly parent. *American Journal of Orthopsychiatry, 61,* 307–313.

Scharlach, A.E., & Fredriksen, K.I. (1993). Reactions to the death of a parent during midlife. *Omega, 27,* 307–319.

Schulz, R., O'Brien, A.T., Bookwala, J., & Fleissner, K. (1995). Psychiatric and physical morbidity effects of dementia caregiving: Prevalence, correlates, and causes. *Gerontologist, 35,* 771–791.

Sheehy, G. (1992). *The silent passage: Menopause.* New York: Random House.

Siegler, I.C. (1997). Promoting health and minimizing stress in midlife. In M.E. Lachman & J.B. James (Eds.), *Multiple paths of mid-life development* (pp. 241–256). Chicago: University of Chicago Press.

Spiro, A., III. (in press). Health at midlife. In M.E. Lachman (Ed.), *Handbook of midlife development.* New York: Wiley.

Stein, N., Folkman, S., Trabasso, T., & Richards, T.A. (1997). Appraisal and goal processes as predictors of psychological well-being in bereaved caregivers. *Journal of Personality and Social Psychology, 72,* 872–884.

Sternberg, R.J. (1998). A balance theory of wisdom. *Review of General Psychology, 2,* 347–365.

Stone, R., Cafferata, G.L., & Sangl, J. (1987). Caregivers of the frail elderly: A national profile. *Gerontologist, 27,* 616–626.

Tedeschi, R.G., Park, C.L., & Calhoun, L.C. (1998). Posttraumatic growth: Conceptual issues. *Posttraumatic growth: Positive change in the aftermath of crisis* (pp. 1–22). Mahwah, NJ: Erlbaum.

Thomas, S.P. (1997). Psychosocial correlates of women's self-rated physical health in middle adulthood. In M.E. Lachman & J.B. James (Eds.), *Multiple paths of mid-life development* (pp. 257–292). Chicago: University of Chicago Press.

Troll, L. (1973). *Early and middle adulthood.* Monterey, CA: Brooks/Cole.

Vaillant, G.E. (1977). *Adaptation to life: How the best and the brightest came of age.* Boston: Little, Brown.

Vaillant, G.E., Bond, M., & Vaillant, C.O. (1986). An empirically validated hierarchy of defense mechanisms. *Archives of General Psychiatry, 43,* 786–794.

von Bertalanffy, L. (1969). *General systems theory: Foundations, development, applications.* New York: Braziller.

Wallerstein, J.S. (1986). Women after divorce: Preliminary findings from a ten year follow-up. *American Journal of Orthopsychiatry, 56,* 65–77.

Whitbourne, S.K. (1986). Openness to experience, identity flexibility, and life change in adults. *Journal of Personality and Social Psychology, 50,* 163–168.

Winsborough, H.H., Bumpass, L.L., & Aquilino, W.S. (1991). *The death of parents and the transition to old age.* Paper presented at the annual meeting of the Population Association of America, Washington, DC.

Yancura, L.A., Aldwin, C.M., & Spiro, A., III. (1999). Does stress decrease with age? A longitudinal examination of stress in the Normative Aging Study. *Gerontologist, 39,* 212.

Zarit, S.H., Todd, P.A., & Zarit, J.M. (1986). Subjective burden of husbands and wives as caregivers: A longitudinal study. *Gerontologist, 26,* 260–266.

Section III

PSYCHOLOGICAL PROCESSES

CHAPTER 7

The Development of Intelligence at Midlife

ROBERT J. STERNBERG, ELENA L. GRIGORENKO, and STELLA OH

IN THIS CHAPTER, we review the development of intelligence and creativity at midlife. Both intelligence and creativity at this stage of life show mixed patterns of growth and decline. Studies of intelligence and its development during childhood have tended to focus on intelligence as it is traditionally defined (see Ferrari & Sternberg, 1998; Sternberg & Powell, 1983). Perhaps because traditionally defined intelligence does not seem to show major developmental trends during midlife (Sternberg & Berg, 1992), studies of intelligence and its development during midlife have tended to focus on the practical aspects of intelligence (Sternberg, 1999). In this chapter, we review this literature; we argue, as have others (e.g., Baltes, 1997; Berg, 2000), that the development of conventional "academic" intelligence and of practical intelligence show distinct trajectories at midlife.

DEVELOPMENTAL TRAJECTORIES

Many intellectual functions (mostly those contributing to the so-called general or g factor of intelligence (for reviews, see Berg, 2000; Sternberg & Berg, 1992) have been found to be associated with age across the life span. Many of these associations are complex and curvilinear, reflecting rapid

Preparation of this chapter was supported under the Javits Act Program (Grant No. R206R000001) as administered by the Office of Educational Research and Improvement, U.S. Department of Education. Grantees undertaking such projects are encouraged to express freely their professional judgment. This chapter, therefore, does not necessarily represent the position or policies of the Office of Educational Research and Improvement or the U.S. Department of Education, and no official endorsement should be inferred.

growth during the years of formal schooling and slow decline thereafter (Salthouse, 1998). However, the results of research also suggest somewhat different developmental functions for changes in performance on various *kinds* of intellectual tasks across the adult life span. In particular, data show that older adults commonly report growth in practical abilities over the years, even though their academic abilities decline (Williams, Denney, & Schadler, 1983).

Intelligence during adulthood is characterized, on one hand, by losses in the speed of mental processes, abstract reasoning, and specific characteristics of memory performance (see Salthouse, 1991, for a review) and, on the other hand, by gains in the metacognitive ability to integrate cognitive, interpersonal, and emotional thinking in a synthetic understanding of the world, self, and others (see Labouvie-Vief, 1992, for a review).

The most commonly used theoretical framework for the interpretation of findings on age-related changes in intellectual performance is that of fluid and crystallized abilities (Horn, 1994; Horn & Cattell, 1966). *Fluid* abilities are those more associated with the creative and flexible thinking required to deal with novelty, such as in the immediate testing situation (e.g., discovering the pattern in a figure sequence). *Crystallized* abilities are represented by accumulated knowledge (e.g., finding a synonym of a low-frequency word). Using this distinction, various researchers have demonstrated that fluid abilities are relatively susceptible to age-related decline, whereas crystallized abilities are relatively resistant to aging (Dixon & Baltes, 1986; Horn, 1982; Labouvie-Vief, 1982; Schaie, 1977/1978), except near the end of one's life.

The majority of these findings, however, were obtained in the framework of cross-sectional methodologies, by comparing different groups of individuals of various ages. When the same individuals are followed across time in the framework of longitudinal design, the findings show that, with respect to fluid intelligence, decline does not generally begin until the 60s and loss of crystallized intelligence occurs almost a decade later, in the 70s (Schaie, 1996).

In addition, even when there are age-based group differences in intellectual performance, there is extensive interindividual variability for specific cognitive abilities within age groups. Schaie (1996), although consistently reporting mean cross-sectional differences in overall intellectual performance, pointed out impressive variability within age groups. To quantify this variability, Schaie (1988) investigated the overlap in distributions of intellectual performance among young adults and the elderly. Even in the group of individuals of 80 years and older, the overlap was about 53%. In other words, slightly more than half of the individuals in the later age groups perform comparably to a group of young adults on measures of both crystallized and fluid intelligence.

The idea that practical and academic-analytical abilities might have different developmental trajectories has been supported in several studies (see Berg & Klaczynski, 1996, for a review). Denney and Palmer (1981) were among the first research teams to demonstrate this discrepancy. They compared the performance of adults (aged 20 through 79) on traditional analytical reasoning problems (e.g., a "twenty questions" task) and a problem-solving task involving real-life situations (e.g., "If you were traveling by car and got stranded out on an interstate highway during a blizzard, what would you do?"). One of the many interesting results obtained in this study was a difference in the shape of the developmental function for performance on the two types of problems. Performance on the *traditional* problem-solving task or cognitive measure declined almost linearly from age 20, onward. Performance on the *practical* problem-solving task increased to a peak in the 40- and 50-year-old groups, declining thereafter. Expanding on this line of research, Smith, Staudinger, and Baltes (1994) compared responses to life-planning dilemmas in a group of younger (mean age 32) and older (mean age 70) adults. Unlike the results of studies of aging and academic abilities, which demonstrated the superior performance of younger adults over the elderly, in this study, young and older adults did not differ. In addition, each age-cohort group received the highest ratings when responding to a dilemma matched to their own life phase.

Similar results were obtained in a study by Cornelius and Caspi (1987). They studied adults between the ages of 20 and 78. These researchers examined relationships between performance on tasks measuring fluid intelligence (letter series), crystallized intelligence (verbal meanings), and everyday problem solving (e.g., dealing with a landlord who won't make repairs, filling out a complicated form, responding to criticism from a parent or child). Performance on the measure of fluid ability increased from ages 20 to 30, remained stable from ages 30 to 50, and then declined. Performance on the everyday problem-solving task and the measures of crystallized ability increased through age 70.

Likewise, the neofunctionalist position, advanced by Baltes and his associates (Baltes, 1987; Baltes, Dittmann-Kohli, & Dixon, 1984; Baltes, Smith, & Staudinger, 1992; Dittmann-Kohli & Baltes, 1990), suggests that although some aspects of intellectual functioning estimated via traditional tests may decline with age, stability and growth also exist, if to a lesser extent. The approach of Baltes and his colleagues also utilizes the constructs of fluid and crystallized intelligence, although a different emphasis is placed on the relative roles and meanings of these two kinds of intelligence. Here, both aspects of intelligence are considered as coequals in defining the developmental course of intelligence. In general, Baltes argues that crystallized intelligence has been too narrowly defined and that its importance increases as one moves into adulthood and old age. In this sense, it may be inappropriate to associate a decrease in fluid intelligence with an average decline in intellectual competence.

Baltes and his associates see adult cognitive competence in terms of a dual-process model. The first process, called the *mechanics* of intelligence, is concerned with developmental change in basic information processing that is genetically driven and assumed to be knowledge-free. With aging, there is a biologically based reduction in reserve capacity (Baltes, 1987; Baltes et al., 1992). The second process, *pragmatic* intelligence, relates the basic cognitive skills and resources of the first process to everyday cognitive performance and adaptation. Measures of pragmatic intelligence within select domains are viewed as tapping abilities more characteristic of adult intellectual life than are traditional psychometric measures of cognitive abilities. Similar to empirical findings on the distinction between fluid and crystallized intelligence, the research by Baltes, Sowarka, and Kliegl (1989) showed that the mechanics of intelligence tend to decline with age almost linearly, whereas the pragmatics of intelligence tend to maintain relative stability throughout adulthood. For example, whereas linear declines were found in the speed of comparing information in short-term memory (i.e., aspects of intellectual mechanics), no age differences were registered for measures of reasoning about life planning (i.e., aspects of intellectual pragmatics).

Cognitive abilities are assumed to operate on content domains involving factual and procedural knowledge; they are regulated by higher-level, trans-situational, procedural skills and by higher-order reflective thinking (metacognition), all of which define the "action space" in which problem solving occurs within a given individual. According to this approach, successful aging entails limiting one's tasks and avoiding excessive demands. Baltes and Baltes (1990) used the concept of selection to refer to a self-imposed restriction in one's life to fewer domains of functioning as a means to adapt to age-related losses. It is assumed that by concentrating on high-priority domains and devising new operational strategies, individuals can optimize their general reserves (Baltes, 1993). By relating adult intelligence to successful cognitive performance in one's environment, this position acknowledges that not all tasks are equally relevant for measuring intelligence at different ages (Baltes et al., 1984, 1992).

Specific manifestations of pragmatic intelligence are said to differ from person to person as people proceed through selection, optimization, or compensation (Dittmann-Kohli & Baltes, 1990). Selection refers simply to diminishing the scope of one's activities to things that one is still able to accomplish well, despite a diminution in reserve capacity. Optimization refers to the fact that older people can maintain high levels of performance in some domains by practice, greater effort, and the development of new bodies of knowledge. Compensation comes into play when one requires a level of capacity beyond remaining performance potential. Salthouse (1984) was able to show that older typists, although slower on several simple speeded reaction-time tasks, were able to compensate for this deficit and maintain their speed by reading further ahead in the text and planning ahead. According to Salthouse and Somberg (1982), age-related decrements at the "molecular" level (e.g., in speed of execution of the elementary components of typing skill) produce no observable effects at the "molar" level (i.e., the speed and accuracy with which work is completed).

Charness (1981) showed similar effects with older chess players, who exhibited poorer recall in general, but were better able to plan ahead than younger, less experienced players. In related studies, older adults have been found to compensate for declines in memory by relying more on external memory aids than do younger adults (Loewen, Shaw, & Craik, 1990). Older adults must often transfer the emphasis of a particular task to abilities that have not declined to compensate for those that have (see Bäckman & Dixon, 1992, for a review of these issues). When a task depends heavily on knowledge, and speed of processing is not a significant constraint, peak performance may not be constrained in early-to-middle adulthood (Charness & Bieman-Coplan, 1994). As an example, consider chess competitions by correspondence. In these "chess-by-mail" competitions, players are permitted 3 days to deliberate each move. The mean age of the first-time winners of one postal world championship is 46. In contrast, the peak age for tournament chess, where deliberation averages 3 minutes per move, is about 30 (Charness & Bosman, 1995). A series of studies on the relationship between aging and cognitive efficiency in skilled performers has attested to the compensatory and stabilizing role of practical intelligence (Baltes & Smith, 1990; Charness & Bosman, 1990; Colonia-Willner, 1998; Hartley, 1989; Willis, 1989).

The developmental trajectory of everyday intelligence has been examined by many researchers (see Berg, 2000; Berg & Klaczynski, 1996, for reviews). The summary of the field today is that the pattern of age differences in practical intelligence differs dramatically depending on how problems are defined and what criteria are used for optimal problem solving. Berg, Klaczynski, Calderone, and Strough (1994), studying participants' own ratings of how effective they were in solving their own everyday problems, did not find any age differences. Denny and her colleagues (Denney & Palmer, 1981; Denney & Pearce, 1989) used the number of "safe and effective solutions" as the criterion of optimal problem solving and found that the highest number of such solutions was generated by middle-aged adults, with both younger and older adults offering fewer solutions. Cornelius and Caspi (1987), using the closeness between participants' ratings of strategy effectiveness and "prototype" of the optimal everyday problem solver as the criterion, found an increase in everyday problem-solving ability with adult age.

Studies have examined everyday problem solving with a neo-Piagetian approach to intellectual development in adulthood (Labouvie-Vief, 1992). According to this paradigm, in middle and late adulthood, the formal-operational reasoning of late adolescents and young adults, with its focus on logic, is replaced by more sophisticated mental structures distinguished by relativistic reasoning based on synthesizing the irrational, emotive, and personal factors. Blanchard-Fields (1986, 1994; Blanchard-Fields & Norris, 1994) stated that, when dealing with social dilemmas, older adults are superior to younger adults in their integrative attributional reasoning (i.e., reasoning based on the integration of dispositional and situational components).

Studies also have examined everyday problem solving with a neo-Piagetian approach to intellectual development in adulthood (Labouvie-Vief, 1992). According to this paradigm, in middle and late adulthood, the formal operational reasoning of late adolescents and young adults, with its focus on logic, is replaced by more sophisticated mental structures distinguished by relativistic reasoning based on synthesizing the irrational, emotive, and personal. Specifically, Blanchard-Fields (1986, 1994; Blanchard-Fields & Norris, 1994) stated that, when dealing with social dilemmas, older adults are superior to younger adults in their integrative attributional reasoning (i.e., reasoning based on the integration of dispositional and situational components).

To conclude, there is reason to believe that the developmental trajectories of abilities utilized to solve strictly academic problems do not coincide with the trajectories of abilities used to solve problems of a practical nature.

WHAT DEVELOPS?

The evidence supporting the supposition that practical intelligence has a different developmental trajectory than academic-analytical intelligence supports the relative independence of practical and academic abilities but is only one of many research advances revealing the developmental mechanisms of practical intelligence. Developmental research on practical abilities is still in its early stages. However, data available at this point shed some light on what Sinnott (1989) called the *chaotically complex* reality of practical problem solving; evidence supports the existence of different developmental trajectories (maintenance, improvement, and decline) across the life span without a pronounced preference for any single one.

There is no formal theory of the stages of the development of practical intelligence (Berg et al., 1994), unlike for academic intelligence (Piaget, 1972). Some results, however, suggest that differences in performance on practical versus analytical tasks are observed rather early (e.g., Freeman, Lewis, & Doherty, 1991).

RESEARCH ON PRACTICAL INTELLIGENCE IN ADULTHOOD

Research on practical ability is becoming more and more central to mainstream psychology (see Berg & Klaczynski, 1996, for a review). Initially, the examination of practical intelligence issued from a concern that the intelligence of adults functioning largely outside the academic environment from the moment they obtained their academic degrees and virtually for the rest of their lives was evaluated primarily by traditional tests of intelligence constructed to predict academic, not practical success.

Various aspects of the meaning of the concept of practical intelligence are expressed in diverse constructs. Some researchers define everyday intelligence as a specific expression of conventional abilities that permit adaptive behavior within a distinct class of everyday life situations (e.g., Willis & Schaie, 1986), whereas others stress the unique nature of practical abilities (e.g., Neisser, 1976; Wagner, 1987). Most psychological studies of practical abilities focus on solving problems that are ill-structured in their goals and solutions and are frequently encountered in daily life (at home, work, and in dealing with people) (e.g., Cornelius & Caspi, 1987; Denney, 1989).

Some studies have addressed the relation between practical and academic-analytical intelligence. These studies have been carried out in a wide range of settings, using a variety of tasks, and with diverse populations. We review some examples of research on problem solving and reasoning. For other reviews see Ceci and Roazzi (1994), Rogoff and Lave (1984), Scribner and Cole (1981), Sternberg and Wagner (1986, 1994), Voss, Perkins, and Segal (1991), and Wagner (2000). Taken together, these studies show that ability measured in one setting (e.g., school) does not necessarily transfer to another setting (e.g., real-world task).

EMPIRICAL INVESTIGATIONS—PRACTICAL PROBLEM SOLVING

Several studies have compared performance on mathematical problems across different contexts. Scribner (1984, 1986) studied the strategies used by milk processing plant workers to fill orders. Workers who assemble orders for cases of various quantities (e.g., gallons, quarts, or pints) and products (e.g., whole milk, 2% milk, or buttermilk) are called assemblers.

Rather than employing typical mathematical algorithms learned in the classroom, Scribner found that experienced assemblers used complex strategies for combining partially filled cases in a manner that minimized the number of moves required to complete an order. Although the assemblers were the least educated workers in the plant, they were able to calculate in their heads quantities expressed in different base number systems, and they routinely outperformed the more highly educated white-collar workers who substituted when assemblers were absent. Scribner found that the order-filling performance of the assemblers was unrelated to measures of school performance, including intelligence test scores, arithmetic test scores, and grades.

Another series of studies of everyday mathematics involved shoppers in California grocery stores who sought to buy at the cheapest cost when the same products were available in different-sized containers (Lave, Murtaugh, & de la Roche, 1984; Murtaugh, 1985). (These studies were performed before cost per unit quantity information was routinely posted). For example, oatmeal may come in two sizes, 10 ounces for $0.98 or 24 ounces for $2.29. One might adopt the strategy of always buying the largest size, assuming that the larger size is always the most economical. However, the researchers (and savvy shoppers) learned that the larger size did not represent the least cost per unit quantity for about a third of the items purchased. The findings of these studies were that effective shoppers used mental shortcuts to get an easily obtained answer, accurate enough to determine which size to buy. A common strategy was mentally to change the size and price of an item to make it more comparable with the other size available. One might mentally double the smaller size, thereby comparing 20 ounces at $1.96 versus 24 ounces at $2.29. The difference of 4 ounces for about 35 cents, or about 9 cents per ounce, seems to favor the 24-ounce size, given that the smaller size of 10 ounces for $0.98 is about 10 cents per ounce. These mathematical shortcuts yield approximations that are as useful as the actual values of 9.80 and 9.33 cents per ounce for the smaller and larger sizes, respectively, and are much more easily computed in the absence of a calculator. When the shoppers were given a mental-arithmetic test, no relation was found between test performance and accuracy in picking the best values (Lave et al., 1984; Murtaugh, 1985).

Ceci and colleagues (Ceci & Liker, 1986, 1988; see also Ceci & Ruiz, 1991) studied expert racetrack handicappers. Ceci and Liker (1986) found that expert handicappers used a highly complex algorithm for predicting post time odds that involved interactions among seven kinds of information. By applying the algorithm, handicappers adjusted times posted for each quarter mile on a previous outing by factors such as whether the horse was attempting to pass other horses, and if so, the speed of the other horses passed and where the attempted passes took place. By adjusting posted times for these factors, a better measure of a horse's speed is obtained. It could be argued that the use of complex interactions to predict a horse's speed would require considerable cognitive ability (at least as it is traditionally measured). However, Ceci and Liker reported that the successful use of these interactions by handicappers was unrelated to their IQ.

A subsequent study attempted to relate performance at the racetrack to making stock-market predictions that involved the same algorithm. Ceci and Ruiz (1991) asked racetrack handicappers to solve a stock-market-prediction task that was structured similarly to the racetrack problem. After 611 trials on the stock-market task, the handicappers performed no better than chance, and there was no difference in performance as a function of IQ. Ceci and Roazzi (1994) attribute this lack of transfer to the low correlation between performance on problems and their isomorphs. "Problem isomorphs" refer to two or more problems that involve the same cognitive processes but that use different terminology or take place in different contexts.

Additional research has shown that the use of complex reasoning strategies does not necessarily correlate with IQ. Dörner and colleagues (Dörner & Kreuzig, 1983; Dörner, Kreuzig, Reither, & Staudel, 1983) studied adults who were asked to play the role of city managers for the computer-simulated city of Lohhausen. A variety of problems were presented to these individuals, such as how best to raise revenue to build roads. The simulation involved more than 1,000 variables. Performance was quantified in terms of a hierarchy of strategies, ranging from the simplest (trial and error) to the most complex (hypothesis testing with multiple feedback loops). No relation was found between IQ and complexity of strategies used. A second problem was created to cross-validate these results. This problem, called the Sahara problem, required participants to determine the number of camels that could be kept alive by a small oasis. Once again, no relation was found between IQ and complexity of strategies employed.

The preceding studies indicate that demonstrated abilities do not necessarily correspond between everyday tasks (e.g., price-comparison shopping) and traditional academic tasks (e.g., math achievement tests). Some people are able to solve concrete, ill-defined problems better than well-defined, abstract problems that have little relevance to their personal lives, and vice versa. Few of these researchers would claim, however, that IQ is totally irrelevant to performance in these various contexts. There is evidence that conventional tests of intelligence predict both school performance and job performance (Barrett & Depinet, 1991; Schmidt & Hunter, 1998; Wigdor & Garner, 1982). What these studies do suggest is that other aspects of intelligence may be independent of IQ and are important to performance, but largely have been neglected in the measurement of intelligence. We also observe this incongruity between conventional notions of ability and real-world abilities in research on age-related changes in intellectual ability.

Developmental research on practical intelligence is moving in several directions, each of which might help us to detect the internal mechanisms of its development. Most of the work is centered on specific characteristics of practical tasks. The assumption is that if we understand the differences in the ways these tasks are formulated and solved at different stages of development, we will be closer to understanding the developmental dynamics of practical intelligence. Drawing on the distinction made earlier between academic and practical tasks suggests five main directions of research: (1) studies of developmentally variable contexts of practical problem solving; (2) studies of developmental changes in the content of practical problems encountered at different stages of development; (3) studies of the developmental diversity of the goals of practical problem solving; (4) studies of differential strategies used in practical problem solving at different periods of development; and (5) studies on developmental variation in problem interpretation and definition.

CONTEXT OF PRACTICAL PROBLEM SOLVING

There is virtually unanimous agreement on the centrality of context for understanding practical problem solving. This view, which holds that practical problem solving cannot be separated from the context in which it unfolds, is referred to as the contextual perspective (e.g., Dixon, 1994; Wertsch & Kanner, 1994). In general, the metaphor used to describe the contextual approach is that of trying to follow forever changing events (i.e., the life course is represented as being a series of changing events, activities, and contexts). When applied to studies of practical problem solving, this perspective assumes that (1) the demands posed by these contexts vary across development; (2) strategies accomplishing adaptation differ across contexts; (3) these strategies also differ across individuals, and finally; (4) the effectiveness of everyday problem solving is determined by the interaction of individual and context (Berg & Calderone, 1994).

One of the most interesting developments in studies on context and practical problem solving concerns the effect of compensation: the phenomenon in which gains in (mostly) practical intelligence balance out age-related decrements in others. Researchers argue that compensation—considered in terms of the dynamic relationship between the individual's changing cognitive skills and expectations of performance, on the one hand, and shifting contextual demands, on the other hand—should be viewed as central to cognitive aging (e.g., Dixon, 1994). One example of practical intelligence compensating for declines in *g*-based intellectual performance is older adults' effective use of external aids. One common source of external cognitive aid is other people. For example, Dixon and his colleagues (Dixon, 1994) explored the extent to which older and younger adults use same-age collaborators in solving memory problems and found that older adults use previously unknown collaborators to boost their performance levels to a much greater extent than do younger adults.

Two other important characteristics of the context in which practical problem solving occurs, which might explain some aspects of the observed development variability in practical intelligence, are the complexity and familiarity of the context.

As for the complexity of the environment in which practical intelligence unfolds, one variable that has been pointed out as extremely important for shaping the development of practical abilities in adulthood is that of the immediate conditions and demands of work (see Schooler, in press, for a review). For example, Kohn and Schooler (1983), examining a group of men between the ages of 24 to 64, longitudinally studied the link between the extent to which one's work-related activities involve independent thought and judgment and workers' creative flexibility in dealing with complex intellectual demands. They found that the more the substantive complexity of one's job, the greater the incremental gains in intellectual performance over a 10-year period. Even more astounding, a similar relationship between job complexity and intellectual performance was revealed for women doing complex housework (Schooler, 1984). Moreover, Miller and Kohn (1983) found that individuals with higher flexibility in dealing with complex intellectual activities tended to engage in more stimulating and demanding intellectual activities (e.g., reading books vs. watching television).

The major criticism of this nonexperimental evidence of the intellectual effects of doing complex work (whether in the workplace or the household) is that these designs are unable conclusively to rule out the possibility that individuals who maintain their intellectual functioning are more capable of following and staying in challenging work environments. Yet, even though the causal path is difficult to infer among individuals, the evidence that more intellectually complex work leads to enriched intellectual functioning deserves attention and more thorough investigation.

Regarding familiarity or experience with the domain in which practical problem solving is carried out, studies have demonstrated that intellectual performance is greater for both younger and older adults when individuals are given either familiar materials (Smith & Baltes, 1990) or a chance to practice prior to assessment (Berg, Hertzog, & Hunt, 1982). Yet, results are ambiguous as to whether differential familiarity can help to explain age differences in practical problem solving (Denney & Pearce, 1989).

Researchers reported, for example, that older adults perceived traditional intelligence tests as less familiar than did young adults (Cornelius, 1984). Therefore, when younger and older adults are compared on conventional intelligence tests, older adults might look worse because these tests are less familiar to them and they may have forgotten how to evoke specific strategies relevant to situations of intellectual assessment.

To explore the importance of the familiarity factor, several studies have been carried out in which younger and older adults were asked to solve problems that were constructed to be more familiar or more normative for one age group or the other. Denney and colleagues (Denney, Pearce, & Palmer, 1982) showed that, in adults, the more normative for their age group everyday problems are, the better their performance is. Similarly, Smith and Baltes (1990) found that adults perform best when the problems are more normative for their age group. As Berg (in press) pointed out, memory research utilizing tasks with familiar materials (e.g., remembering words that were in frequent use during their adulthood years versus contemporary equivalents) is consistent in showing that older adults tend to perform better with materials more familiar to them (Barrett & Watkins, 1986; Worden & Sherman-Brown, 1983).

CONTENT OF PRACTICAL PROBLEM SOLVING

The main hypothesis underlying this line of research is that the content of practical problem solving differs at different stages of development. The literature published to verify this hypothesis contains heterogeneous evidence; some is supportive (e.g., Aldwin, Sutton, Chiara, & Spiro, 1996) and some is not supportive (e.g., Folkman, Lazarus, Pimley, & Novacek, 1987) of the assertion that individuals of different ages experience different everyday problems.

Berg and colleagues (Berg & Calderone, 1994; Sansone & Berg, 1993) asked preschoolers, teenagers, college students, and adults to describe a recent problem (hassle, conflict, challenge, and so on) that they had experienced and to describe the problem in as much detail as possible. The intent was to investigate whether the types of domains of problems remain constant across development or whether different types of problems would appear for different age groups. The researchers found significant variation in the content of everyday problems across development. The everyday problem-solving content for 5- to 6-year-olds consisted predominantly of problems dealing with family (e.g., disagreements with family members) and assigned responsibilities (e.g., home chores). For 11- to 12-year-olds, everyday life problems centered on school and after-school activities and environments. No single content area dominated the everyday life of college students, and their salient problems had to do with free time, work, friends, family, and romantic relationships. Finally, the everyday problem solving of the older adults centered on the family context and health.

Barker (1978) suggested that the content of practical problem solving is determined by the ecological characteristics of a given developmental period. It has been shown that (1) college students' tasks are primarily aimed at succeeding academically, forming social networks, developing an identity, and separating from family (Cantor, Norem, Neidenthal, Langston, & Brower, 1987); (2) adults focus on a variety of tasks, ranging from starting a family and a career in young adulthood, through the pragmatic tasks of middle adulthood, to adapting to impairments of health and adjusting to retirement during old and advanced old age (Baltes et al., 1984; Havighurst, 1972; Neugarten, Moore, & Lowe, 1968).

GOALS OF PRACTICAL PROBLEM SOLVING

The goal-directedness (e.g., Goodnow, 1986; Scribner, 1986; Wertsch, 1985) of practical problem solving is one of the most often cited characteristics of practical intelligence in application. Therefore, the second line of research concerns the developmental trajectories of goals of practical problem solving.

Strough, Berg, and Sansone (1996) showed that there is developmental variation in the types of goals underlying everyday problem solving. The profile of this developmental variation reflects developmental life tasks (Cantor, 1990). Preadolescents reported more goals for task improvement, and a large portion of their problems involved the school context. Interpersonal goals appeared to be more salient to middle-aged adults than to preadolescents. Preadolescents, however, reported more other-focused assistance-recruiting goals than did adults. Older and middle-aged adults reported more physical goals than did younger individuals, and the adult group as a whole reported more affective goals than did preadolescents.

Belief in the plasticity and fluidity of human developmental goals throughout the life span also is reflected by the notion that there is no single outcome or endpoint to intellectual development in general, or to the development of practical intelligence in particular (e.g., Rogoff, 1982). The implication of this line of reasoning is that the individual and his or her context form a complex systemic unit; changes in the unit shape the content, dynamics, and adaptability of the individual's intellectual functioning in specific contexts. Thus, there is no "ideal" trajectory of intellectual development, and there is no optimal instrument assessing intellectual functioning equally well at all periods of the life span.

PRACTICAL PROBLEM-SOLVING STRATEGIES

One of the main research trajectories in the field of practical intelligence focuses on strategies used in problem solving. Among the central characteristics of strategies discussed in the research literature of the past 20 years (Belmont & Butterfield, 1969; Berg, 1989; Brown, 1975; Flavell, 1970; Naus & Ornstein, 1983; Pressley, Forrest-Pressley, Elliot-Faust, & Miller, 1985) are selectivity, goal-directedness, and intentionality. Many developmental researchers have been especially interested in strategy selection both as an individual indicator and as a developmental indicator of everyday problem-solving performance (e.g., Frederiksen, 1986; Frederiksen, Jensen, & Beaton, 1972; Lazarus & Folkman, 1984).

Most of the early developmental work on everyday problem solving has been carried out under the assumption that individuals' chosen strategies can be compared irrespective of the developmental variation in the goals motivating these strategies (Band & Weisz, 1988; Berg, 1989; Cornelius & Caspi, 1987; Folkman et al., 1987). The major theoretical hypothesis dominating the field is that greater experience with everyday problems leads to better problem solving (Baltes et al., 1984; Denney, 1982). This claim assumes that a particular type of strategy, such as primary control reflected in independent coping and problem-focused action, is a more effective way of dealing with various problems than is some other strategy, such as secondary control reflected in reliance on others and emotion-focused action (Denney, 1989; Folkman et al., 1987). Self-action was the strategy most frequently mentioned across all ages in a study of reported everyday problems (Berg, Calderone, Sansone, Strough, & Weir, 1998). Problem-focused action was most frequently mentioned for hypothetical problems (Blanchard-Fields, Jahnke, & Camp, 1995). Developmental differences have been encountered, suggesting that secondary control strategies, emotion-focused strategies, and dependence on others increase across early childhood (Band & Weisz, 1988), with further elevation in later adulthood (Brandtstaedter & Greve, 1994; Denney & Palmer, 1981; Folkman et al., 1987; Heckhausen & Schulz, 1995).

The empirical literature, however, does not uniformly support the claim that "more experience equals better problem solving" (Baltes, 1997; Berg, 1989; Cornelius & Caspi, 1987). Research suggests that strategies are differentially effective depending on the context of the everyday problem (Berg, 1989; Ceci & Bronfenbrenner, 1985; Cornelius & Caspi, 1987; Scribner, 1986). Thus, Cornelius and Caspi showed that different types of strategy (problem-focused action, cognitive problem analysis, passive-dependent behavior, and avoidant thinking and denial) were viewed as differentially effective in different contexts.

Findings regarding the localization of age differences are also somewhat contradictory. The often-cited trend in the literature is that older adults tend to use more secondary control (e.g., Heckhausen & Schulz, 1995) and less problem-focused action or primary control (Folkman et al., 1987) when compared with younger adults. Blanchard-Fields et al. (1995) found minimal age differences in problem-focused action. Furthermore, Berg et al. (1998) reported age differences for older adults only, with older people using relatively less cognitive regulation and more self-action than either college students or middle-aged adults. The situation has become even less transparent, with Aldwin et al. (1996) showing that, for the most part, age differences existed among adults only when individuals' strategies were assessed through a checklist; these distinctions were greatly reduced when individuals' strategies were elicited through open-ended interviews.

One of the possible explanations for the heterogeneity of these findings is that what develops over time is sensitivity to specific contexts. The repertoire of dealing with everyday problems is rather broad, and different modules of problem solving are used in different situations; in many ways, consistency across situations may be maladaptive (Mischel, 1984). Some researchers argue that successful everyday problem solving will involve carefully fitting strategies to the specific demands of a problem and modifying these strategies in response to changes in it (Berg & Sternberg, 1985; Rogoff, Gauvain, & Gardner, 1987; Scribner, 1986). And sensitivity to the contextual features of a problem is characteristic of a developmental factor (Mischel, 1984; Rogoff et al., 1987). Others, on the contrary, suggest that these strategies become less context-dependent with age (e.g., Kreitler & Kreitler, 1987).

Yet another, although not contradictory possibility, is that the lesson derived from experience with everyday problems is how to avoid getting into everyday problems (Berg, 1989). Thus, it is plausible that no simple relation between kind of experience and everyday problem-solving ability is likely to exist. Moreover, researchers have presented evidence demonstrating that so-called effective-across-all-context (e.g., primary) strategies fail in situations in which so-called ineffective strategies (e.g., relinquishing) work (Berg, Calderone, & Gunderson, 1990, as cited in Berg & Calderone, 1994). Certain kinds of experience may be differentially related to success at solving particular kinds of everyday problems, and development might better be construed as individuals becoming increasingly capable of modifying their strategies or avoiding potentially problematic situations (Berg, 1989; Rogoff et al., 1987).

Another line of research focuses on studying individual differences that appear to lead to more optimal problem-solving performance (e.g., Ceci & Liker, 1986; Denney, 1989; Willis & Schaie, 1986). Many factors (e.g., conventional intellectual abilities, personality traits, social skills, achievement motivation) have been shown to impact the utilization of strategies in everyday problem solving (e.g., Ceci & Liker, 1986; Charness, 1981; Kuhn, Pennington, & Leadbeater, 1983), but no specific constellations of these factors were found to be better predictors of effective problem solving.

PROBLEM INTERPRETATION (DEFINITION)

To systematize the literature on the development of everyday problem solving, Berg and colleagues have introduced the concept of "problem interpretation" (Berg & Calderone, 1994; Sansone & Berg, 1993) or "problem definition" (Berg et al., 1998). Problem interpretation arises at the intersection of the context and the individual and, in essence, is the transaction of the individual with his or her context. Problem interpretation derives from features of both the individual and the context, but it might selectively engage all or only some features. Berg and her colleagues argue that such individual and contextual features may have different weights and may be differentially combined at different stages of development; thus, the search for developmental variation in everyday problem solving should focus on the development of problem interpretation (Berg & Calderone, 1994).

As it is interactive in nature, problem definition reflects those aspects of the self and context that are activated with respect to a specific problem unfolding at a specific moment in time. Problem definition is a complex, psychological, subjective reality that, according to Berg et al. (1998), reflects the individual's goals and expectations (Bandura, 1986), determines the strategies to be used to meet these expectations and accomplish subjective goals (Vallacher & Wegner, 1987), affects the outcome attribution and meaning interpretation (Dodge, Pettit, McClaskey, & Brown, 1986), and induces the affective representation of the problem (Fleeson & Cantor, 1995).

Studies provide supportive evidence for the transactional approach to everyday problem solving. Sinnott (1989) showed that older adults' interpretations of Piagetian logical-combination problems, especially those experienced in real life (e.g., assigning relatives to sleeping locations), vary to a greater degree than do the interpretations of younger adults. Older adults tend to be more sensitive to social and interpersonal facets of the problem when compared with younger adults, who concentrate on the problem's logical aspects. Similarly, Laipple (1992) showed that older adults were less likely to interpret the situation of solving logical problems with the meaning intended by the experimenter; older adults tended to leave the logical confines of the problem and inject into the experimental situation more personal experience than did the younger adults. Chi and Ceci (1987) suggested that many types of problem solving appear to be directly influenced by the mental context the child brings to the task.

In their own work, Berg and colleagues (Berg & Calderone, 1994) registered developmental characteristics of problem definition. First, they showed that, with age, there was a decrease in the frequency of task-oriented interpretations of problems and an increase in interpersonal, self, and mixed (e.g., task and self) interpretations. In their interpretation, researchers suggest that these findings correspond to the literature on the development of the self system, according to which changes of the self system involve movement away from a concrete and specific system to one that incorporates more abstract and interrelated psychological constructs (Harter, 1983). Second, Berg et al. (1998) studied the link between the problem definition and the selection of strategies for problem solving. In general, problem definition appears to be a more precise predictor of strategy use than does problem context. Individuals who defined a problem in terms of interpersonal concerns alone were more likely to report using strategies involving regulating or including others. In contrast, individuals who defined a problem solely in terms of competence concerns were more likely to utilize strategies including independent action and less likely to engage others. Finally, the links between problem definition and strategy selection were not found to vary as a function of age.

Problem definition is very important to practical intelligence. For example, a key difference between the results of Berg et al. (1998) and those of previous research is the importance that individuals placed on the social aspects of practical problem solving. Berg and colleagues found that the majority of individual problem definitions in any age group (preadolescents, college students, and adults) involved interpersonal concerns. These problem definitions, in turn, determined the selection of strategies that involved regulating or including others. This interpretation differs significantly from the argument used in previous research. Earlier work typically assumed that reliance on others reflected ineffective problem solving because individuals exhibited dependence on others (e.g., Cornelius & Caspi, 1987; Denney & Palmer, 1981; Folkman et al., 1987). However, the reinterpretation of the role of social-dependent strategies suggests that using others to deal with everyday problems is a strategy rather well suited to particular problems (Baltes, 1997; Meacham & Emont, 1989).

DEVELOPMENT OF TACIT KNOWLEDGE

Our own program of research has been based on the notion that there is more to successfully predicting performance than just measuring the so-called general factor from conventional psychometric tests of intelligence (see Sternberg & Wagner, 1993; Sternberg, Wagner, Williams, & Horvath, 1995; Sternberg et al., 2000). We propose that tacit knowledge, as an aspect of practical intelligence, is a key ingredient of success in any domain. Tacit knowledge is the procedural knowledge one needs to function effectively in everyday environments that is not explicitly taught and that often is not even verbalized. There are those who disagree with our position (see Jensen, 1993; Ree & Earles, 1993; Schmidt & Hunter, 1993, 1998), believing that individual differences in performance are explained primarily by general cognitive ability. Some proponents of using general cognitive ability tests argue further that these tests are applicable for all jobs, have lowest cost to develop and administer, and have the highest validity (e.g., Schmidt & Hunter, 1998). But even Schmidt and Hunter acknowledge that alternative measures such as work sample tests and job knowledge tests have comparable and perhaps even higher validities than do general ability tests, and provide incremental prediction above such tests.

A program of research by Sternberg and his colleagues has examined tacit knowledge research with business managers, college professors, elementary-school teachers, salespeople, college students, and general populations. This important aspect of practical intelligence, in study after study, has been found generally to be uncorrelated with academic intelligence as measured by conventional tests, in a variety of populations, occupations, and at a variety of age levels (Sternberg, Forsythe, et al., in press; Sternberg, Wagner, & Okagaki, 1993; Sternberg et al., 1995; Wagner, 1987; Wagner & Sternberg, 1985). A major task of this tacit-knowledge research has been to identify the content of tacit knowledge and develop ways to measure the possession of tacit knowledge. Tacit-knowledge tests present a set of problem situations and ask respondents to rate the quality or appropriateness of possible responses to those situations.

Consider four main issues: (1) the relationship of tacit knowledge to experience; (2) the relationship of tacit knowledge to general intelligence; (3) tacit knowledge as a general construct; and (4) the relationship of tacit knowledge to performance.

TACIT KNOWLEDGE AND EXPERIENCE

In most of our studies, tacit knowledge was found to relate to experience, indicated either by group membership (expert versus novice) or the number of years in one's current position.

In several studies, Sternberg and his colleagues showed that individuals with less experience in a given domain tend to exhibit lower tacit-knowledge scores (Sternberg et al., 1993; Wagner, 1987; Wagner & Sternberg, 1985). Wagner and Sternberg, for example, found group differences among business managers, business graduate students, and undergraduates on 39 of the response-item ratings on a tacit-knowledge test for managers, with a binomial test of the probability of finding this many significant differences by chance yielding $p < .001$. Comparable results were obtained with Yale undergraduates, psychology graduate students, and psychology faculty on a tacit-knowledge test for academic psychologists.

In addition, Wagner (1987) found that business managers obtained the highest tacit-knowledge scores, followed by business graduate students and undergraduates, with comparable results obtained in a study of psychology professors, psychology graduate students, and undergraduates. Wagner, Rashotte, and Sternberger (1994) also found that scores on a tacit-knowledge test for salespeople correlated significantly with number of years of sales experience.

Williams and Sternberg (cited in Sternberg et al., 1995) did not find significant correlations between several experience-based measures, including age, years of management experience, and years in current position, and tacit-knowledge scores. But they did find that the importance of specific pieces of tacit knowledge varied across organizational level. Their findings suggest that it may not simply be the amount of experience but what a manager learns from experience that matters to success.

TACIT KNOWLEDGE AND GENERAL INTELLIGENCE

In proposing a new approach to measuring intelligence, it is important to show that one has not accidentally reinvented the concept of g, or so-called general ability, as measured by traditional intelligence tests. We do not dispute the relevance of general cognitive ability to performance. Schmidt and Hunter (1998) have shown that g predicts performance in a number of domains. Our aim is to show that tacit-knowledge tests measure something in addition to g. In all the cited studies in which participants were given a traditional measure of cognitive ability, tacit-knowledge test scores correlated insignificantly with g.

The most consistently used measure of g in the studies was the Verbal Reasoning subtest of the DAT. The absolute values of the correlations between tacit knowledge and verbal reasoning ranged from .04 and .16 with undergraduate samples (Wagner, 1987; Wagner & Sternberg, 1985) and .14 with a sample of business executives (Wagner & Sternberg, 1990).

One potential limitation of these findings is that they were obtained with restricted samples (e.g., Yale undergraduates, business managers). However, similar support for the relationship between tacit knowledge and g was found in a more general sample of Air Force recruits studied by Eddy (1988). The correlations between scores on the TKIM and ASVAB scales were modest, and none of the four ASVAB factors correlated significantly with the tacit-knowledge score.

Tacit-knowledge tests may also be a better predictor of managerial success than are measures of personality, cognitive style, and interpersonal orientation as suggested by the findings from the Center for Creative Leadership study (Wagner & Sternberg, 1990). Sternberg, Grigorenko, and Gil (1999) recently developed a test of common sense for the workplace (e.g., how to handle oneself in a job interview) that predicts self-ratings of common sense but not self-ratings of various kinds of academic abilities. The test also predicts supervisory ratings at a correlational level of about .4.

TACIT KNOWLEDGE AS A GENERAL CONSTRUCT

Although the kinds of informal procedural knowledge measured by tacit-knowledge tests do not correlate with traditional psychometric intelligence, tacit-knowledge test scores do correlate across domains. Furthermore, the structure of tacit knowledge appears to be represented best by a single, general factor.

Wagner (1987) examined the structure of a tacit knowledge inventory for managers. He performed two kinds of factor analyses on the tacit-knowledge scores of these business managers in his study. First, a principal-components analysis yielded a first principal component that accounted for 44% of the total variance, and 76% of total variance after the correlations among scores were disattenuated for unreliability. The 40% variance accounted for by the first principal component is typical of analyses carried out on traditional cognitive-ability subtests. Second, results of a confirmatory factor analysis suggested that a model consisting of a single general factor provided the best fit to the data. The results of both factor analyses suggested a general factor of tacit knowledge.

Similar analyses were performed on a measure of tacit knowledge for academic psychologists. Consistent with the managers' study, the factor-analytic results suggested a single factor of tacit knowledge within the domain of academic psychology. Wagner (1987) also examined the generalizability of tacit-knowledge across domains by administering both tacit-knowledge measures (for business managers and academic psychologists) to undergraduates in his study. He obtained a significant correlation of .58 between the two scores, suggesting that in addition to the existence of a general factor of tacit knowledge within a domain, individual differences in tacit knowledge generalize across domains. These findings lend support for a common factor underlying tacit knowledge; a factor that is considered to be an aspect of practical intelligence.

TACIT KNOWLEDGE AND PERFORMANCE

Finally, we have shown that tacit-knowledge measures are predictive of performance in several domains, correlating between .2 and .5 with measures such as rated prestige of business or institution, salary, simulation performance, and number of publications. These correlations, uncorrected for attenuation or restriction of range, compare favorably with those obtained for IQ within the range of abilities we have tested.

In studies with business managers, tacit-knowledge scores correlated in the range of .2 to .4 with criteria such as salary, years of management experience, and whether the manager worked for a company at the top of the Fortune 500 list (Wagner, 1987; Wagner & Sternberg, 1985). Wagner and Sternberg (1990) obtained a correlation of .61 between tacit knowledge and performance on a managerial simulation; they found that tacit-knowledge scores explained additional variance beyond IQ and other personality and ability measures. In a study with bank branch managers, Wagner and Sternberg (1985) obtained significant correlations between tacit-knowledge scores and average percentage of merit-based salary increase ($r = .48, p < .05$) and average performance rating for the category of generating new business for the bank ($r = .56, p < .05$).

Williams and Sternberg (cited in Sternberg et al., 1995) also found that tacit knowledge was related to several indicators of managerial success, including compensation, age-controlled compensation, level of position, and job satisfaction, with correlations ranging from .23 to .39.

Although much of the tacit-knowledge research has involved business managers, there is evidence that tacit knowledge explains performance in other domains. In the field of academic psychology, correlations in the .4 to .5 range were found between tacit-knowledge scores and criterion measures such as citation rate, number of publications, and quality of department (Wagner, 1987; Wagner & Sternberg, 1985). In studies with salespeople, Wagner et al. (1994) found correlations in the .3 to .4 range between tacit knowledge and criteria such as sales volume and sales awards received. Finally, tacit knowledge for college students was found to correlate with indexes of academic performance and adjustment to college (Williams & Sternberg, cited in Sternberg et al., 1993).

The program of tacit-knowledge research, as reviewed here, shows that generally tacit knowledge increases with experience, but is not simply a proxy for experience; that tacit-knowledge tests measure a distinct construct from that measured by traditional, abstract intelligence tests; that scores on tacit-knowledge tests represent a general factor, which appears to correlate across domains; and finally, that tacit-knowledge tests are predictive of performance in several domains and compare favorably with those obtained for IQ within the range of abilities we have tested.

CONCLUSION AND MAJOR QUESTIONS FOR FUTURE RESEARCH

What are some of the questions for future research about intelligence in midlife development? Although there may be many, we believe that three questions especially need to be addressed.

First, our research and that of others shows that both the more academic and the more practical sides of intelligence make a difference to performance on the job and in other aspects of life in midadulthood. Given the large literature on the importance of academic intelligence and especially of the general factor in it (see, e.g., Jensen, 1998), it is important to move beyond this literature and learn the extent to which each of the two aspects of intelligence can compensate for each other. Clearly the so-called "*g* factor" is important to various kinds of success. But so is practical intelligence. How much can people get by when they are strong in one of these aspects but not so strong in the other? Can they compensate (as in an additive model), or do they need a certain threshold of each to succeed in their jobs and in their lives?

A second important questions, we believe, pertains to the trajectory of various aspects of intelligence over the life span. Academic intelligence increases in childhood and then shows a mixed pattern in adulthood, with fluid intelligence showing some decline in later life and crystallized intelligence usually increasing until the last few years of life. How about practical intelligence? What is its typical trajectory? It is especially important to know the answer to this question in terms of job placements. Many firms these days prefer to promote younger workers into positions of authority. In doing so, are they losing out on the greater practical intelligence of older workers, or are these older workers actually losing the practical intelligence they once had?

Finally, we need better to understand the kinds of activities and interventions that can maintain intelligence of any kind in midlife. If Kohn and Schooler (1983) are correct, then having a complex job can help on maintain and even increase intelligence. Are there specific activities in which adults can engage in midlife that will help them maintain or increase their intelligence? If so, what are these activities?

Intelligence shows mixed patterns of growth and decline at midlife. In many ways, midlife is an optimal period. Crystallized and practical intelligence generally are increasing, and fluid intelligence has not yet begun to decline in most adults, or if there is a decline, it is still minor in extent. Thus, midlife is a period in which adults have the chance to make their greatest intellectual contributions, both to their own lives and to the lives of others, and many adults utilize this period of their lives to do just that.

REFERENCES

Aldwin, C.M., Sutton, K.J., Chiara, G., & Spiro, A. (1996). Age differences in stress, coping, and appraisal: Findings from the Normative Aging Study. *Journal of Gerontology: Psychological Sciences, 51B*, 178–188.

Bäckman, L., & Dixon, R.A. (1992). Psychological compensation: A theoretical framework. *Psychological Bulletin, 112*, 259–283.

Baltes, P.B. (1987). Theoretical propositions of life-span developmental psychology: On the dynamics between growth and decline. *Developmental Psychology, 23*, 611–626.

Baltes, P.B. (1993). The aging mind: Potentials and limits. *Gerontologist, 33*, 580–594.

Baltes, P.B. (1997). On the incomplete architecture of human ontogeny: Selection, optimization, and compensation as foundation of developmental theory. *American Psychologist, 52*(4), 366–380.

Baltes, P.B., & Baltes, M.M. (1990). Psychological perspectives on successful aging: A model of selective optimization with compensation. In P.B. Baltes & M.M. Baltes (Eds.), *Successful aging: Perspectives from the behavioral sciences.* New York: Cambridge University Press.

Baltes, P.B., Dittmann-Kohli, F., & Dixon, R.A. (1984). New perspectives on the development of intelligence in adulthood: Toward a dual-process conception and a model of selective optimization with compensation. In P.B. Baltes & O.G. Brim (Eds.), *Life-span development and behavior* (Vol. 6, pp. 33–76). New York: Academic Press.

Baltes, P.B., & Smith, J. (1990). Toward a psychology of wisdom and its ontogenesis. In R.J. Sternberg (Ed.), *Wisdom: Its nature, origins, and development* (pp. 87–120). New York: Cambridge University Press.

Baltes, P.B., Smith, J., & Staudinger, U. (1992). Wisdom and successful aging. In T.B. Sonderegger (Ed.), *Psychology and aging* (pp. 123–167). Lincoln: University of Nebraska Press.

Baltes, P.B., Sowarka, D., & Kliegl, R. (1989). Cognitive training research on fluid intelligence in old age: What can older adults achieve by themselves? *Psychology and Aging, 4*, 217–221.

Band, E.B., & Weisz, J.R. (1988). How to feel better when it feels bad: Children's perspective on coping with everyday stress. *Developmental Psychology, 24*, 247–253.

Bandura, A. (1986). *Social foundations of thought and action.* Englewood Cliffs, NJ: Prentice Hall.

Barker, R.G. (Ed.). (1978). *Habitats, environments, and human behavior.* San Francisco: Jossey-Bass.

Barrett, G.V., & Depinet, R.L. (1991). A reconsideration of testing for competence rather than for intelligence. *American Psychologist, 46,* 1012–1024.

Barrett, G.V., & Watkins, S.K. (1986). Word familiarity and cardiovascular health as determinants of age-related recall differences. *Journal of Gerontology, 41,* 222–224.

Belmont, J.N., & Butterfield, E.C. (1969). The relations of short-term memory to development and intelligence. In L. Lipsitt & H. Reese (Eds.), *Advances in child development and behavior* (Vol. 4, pp. 30–83). New York: Academic Press.

Berg, C.A. (1989). Knowledge of strategies for dealing with everyday problems from childhood through adolescence. *Developmental Psychology, 25,* 607–618.

Berg, C.A. (2000). Intellectual development in adulthood. In R.J. Sternberg (Ed.), *Handbook of intelligence* (pp. 117–137). New York: Cambridge University Press.

Berg, C.A., & Calderone, K. (1994). The role of problem interpretations in understanding the development of everyday problem solving. In R.J. Sternberg & R.K. Wagner (Eds.), *Mind in context: Interactionist perspectives on human intelligence* (pp. 105–132). New York: Cambridge University Press.

Berg, C.A., Calderone, K., & Gunderson, M. (1990, November). *Strategies young and old adults use to solve their own everyday problems.* Paper presented at the meeting of the Gerontological Society, Boston.

Berg, C.A., Calderone, K., Sansone, C., Strough, J., & Weir, C. (1998). The role of problem definitions in understanding age and context effects on strategies for solving everyday problems. *Psychology and Aging, 13,* 29–44.

Berg, C.A., Hertzog, C., & Hunt, E. (1982). Age differences in the speed of mental rotation. *Developmental Psychology, 18,* 95–107.

Berg, C.A., & Klaczynski, P. (1996). Practical intelligence and problem solving: Searching for perspective. In F. Blanchard-Fields & T.M. Hess (Eds.), *Perspectives on cognition in adulthood and aging* (pp. 323–357). New York: McGraw-Hill.

Berg, C.A., Klaczynski, P., Calderone, K.S., & Strough, J. (1994). Adult age differences in cognitive strategies: Adaptive or deficient. In J. Sinnott (Ed.), *Interdisciplinary handbook of adult lifespan learning* (pp. 371–388). Westport, CT: Greenwood Press.

Berg, C.A., & Sternberg, R.J. (1985). A triarchic theory of intellectual development during adulthood. *Developmental Review, 5,* 334–370.

Blanchard-Fields, F. (1986). Reasoning and social dilemmas varying in emotional saliency: An adult developmental perspective. *Psychology and Aging, 1,* 325–333.

Blanchard-Fields, F. (1994). Age differences in causal attributions from an adult developmental perspective. *Journal of Gerontology: Psychological Sciences, 49,* 43–51.

Blanchard-Fields, F., Jahnke, H.C., & Camp, C. (1995). Age differences in problem-solving style: The role of emotional salience. *Psychology and Aging, 10,* 173–180.

Blanchard-Fields, F., & Norris, L. (1994). Causal attributions from adolescence through adulthood: Age differences, ego level, and generalized response style. *Aging Neuropsychology and Cognition, 1,* 67–86.

Brandtstaedter, J., & Greve, W. (1994). The aging self: Stabilizing and protective processes. *Developmental Review, 14*, 52–80.

Brown, A.L. (1975). The development of memory: Knowing, knowing about knowing, and knowing how to know. In H.W. Reese (Ed.), *Advances in child development and behavior* (Vol. 10, pp. 103–152). New York: Academic Press.

Cantor, N. (1990). From thought to behavior: "Having" and "doing" in the study of personality and cognition. *American Psychologist, 45*, 735–750.

Cantor, N., Norem, J.K., Niedenthal, P.M., Langston, C.A., & Brower, A.M. (1987). Life tasks, self-concept ideals, and cognitive strategies in a life transition. *Journal of Personality and Social Psychology, 53*, 1178–1191.

Ceci, S.J., & Bronfenbrenner, U. (1985). Don't forget to take the cupcakes out of the oven: Strategic time-monitoring, prospective memory and context. *Child Development, 56*, 175–190.

Ceci, S.J., & Liker, J. (1986). Academic and nonacademic intelligence: An experimental separation. In R.J. Sternberg & R.K. Wagner (Eds.), *Practical intelligence: Nature and origins of competence in the everyday world* (pp. 119–142). New York: Cambridge University Press.

Ceci, S.J., & Liker, J. (1988). Stalking the IQ-expertise relationship: When the critics go fishing. *Journal of Experimental Psychology: General, 117*, 96–100.

Ceci, S.J., & Roazzi, A. (1994). The effects of context on cognition: Postcards from Brazil. In R.J. Sternberg & R.K. Wagner (Eds.), *Mind in context: Interactionist perspectives on human intelligence* (pp. 74–101). New York: Cambridge University Press.

Ceci, S.J., & Ruiz, A. (1991). The role of general ability in cognitive complexity: A case study of expertise. In R. Hoffman (Ed.), *The psychology of expertise* (pp. 218–230). New York: Springer-Verlag.

Charness, N. (1981). Search in chess: Age and skill differences. *Journal of Experimental Psychology: Human Perception and Performance, 7*, 467–476.

Charness, N., & Bieman-Coplan, S. (1994). The learning prospective: Adulthood. In R.J. Sternberg & C.A. Berg (Eds.), *Intellectual development* (pp. 301–327). New York: Cambridge University Press.

Charness, N., & Bosman, E.A. (1990). Expertise and aging: Life in the lab. In T.M. Hess (Ed.), *Aging and cognition: Knowledge organization and utilization* (pp. 343–385). Amsterdam: Elsevier.

Charness, N., & Bosman, E.A. (1995). Compensation through environmental modification. In R.A. Dixon & L. Baeckman (Eds.), *Compensating for psychological deficits and declines: Managing losses and promoting gains* (pp. 147–168). Mahwah, NJ: Erlbaum.

Chi, M.T.H., & Ceci, S.J. (1987). Content knowledge: Its role, representation, and restructuring in memory development. In H.W. Reese (Ed.), *Advances in child development and behavior* (Vol. 20, pp. 91–142). Orlando, FL: Academic Press.

Colonia-Willner, R. (1998). Practical intelligence at work: Relationship between aging and cognitive efficiency among managers in a bank environment. *Psychology and Aging, 13*, 45–57.

Cornelius, S.W. (1984). Classic pattern of intellectual aging: Test familiarity, difficulty, and performance. *Journal of Gerontology, 39*, 201–206.

Cornelius, S.W., & Caspi, A. (1987). Everyday problem solving in adulthood and old age. *Psychology and Aging, 2,* 144–153.

Denney, N.W. (1982). Aging and cognitive changes. In B.B. Wolman (Ed.), *Handbook of developmental psychology* (pp. 807–827). Englewood Cliffs, NJ: Prentice-Hall.

Denney, N.W. (1989). Everyday problem solving: Methodological issues, research findings, and a model. In I.W. Poon, D.C. Rubin, & B.A. Wilson (Eds.), *Everyday cognition in adulthood and late life* (pp. 330–351). New York: Cambridge University Press.

Denney, N.W., & Palmer, A.M. (1981). Adult age differences on traditional and practical problem-solving measures. *Journal of Gerontology, 36,* 323–328.

Denney, N.W., & Pearce, K.A. (1989). A developmental study of practical problem solving in adults. *Psychology and Aging, 4,* 438–442.

Denney, N.W., Pearce, K.A., & Palmer, A.M. (1982). A developmental study of adults' performance on traditional and practical problem-solving tasks. *Experimental Aging Research, 8,* 115–118.

Dittmann-Kohli, F., & Baltes, P.B.(1990). Towards a neofunctionalist conception of adult intellectual development: Wisdom as a prototypical case of intellectual growth. In C.N. Alexander & E.J. Langer (Eds.), *Higher stages of human development: Perspectives on adult growth* (pp. 54–78). New York: Oxford University Press.

Dixon, R.A. (1994). Contextual approaches to adult intellectual development. In R.J. Sternberg & C.A. Berg (Eds.), *Intellectual development* (pp. 350–380). New York: Cambridge University Press.

Dixon, R.A., & Baltes, P.B. (1986). Toward life-span research on the functions and pragmatics of intelligence. In R.J. Sternberg & R.K. Wagner (Eds.), *Practical intelligence: Nature and origins of competence in the everyday world* (pp. 203–235). New York: Cambridge University Press.

Dodge, K.A., Pettit, G.S., McClaskey, C.L., & Brown, M.M. (1986). Social competence in children. *Monographs of the Society for Research in Child Development, 51,* 1–85.

Dörner, D., & Kreuzig, H. (1983). Problemlosefahigkeit und intelligenz. *Psychologische Rundschaus, 34,* 185–192.

Dörner, D., Kreuzig, H., Reither, F., & Staudel, T. (1983). *Lohhausen: Vom Umgang mit Unbestimmtheir und Komplexitat.* Bern, Germany: Huber.

Eddy, A.S. (1988). *The relationship between the Tacit Knowledge Inventory for Mangers and the Armed Services Vocational Aptitude Battery.* Unpublished master's thesis, St. Mary's University, San Antonio, TX.

Ferrari, M., & Sternberg, R.J. (Eds.). (1998). *Self-awareness: Its nature and development.* New York: Guilford Press.

Flavell, J.H. (1970). Developmental studies of mediated memory. In H.W. Reese & L.P. Lipsitt (Eds.), *Advances in child development and child behavior* (Vol. 5, pp. 181–211). New York: Academic Press.

Fleeson, W., & Cantor, N. (1995). Goal relevance and the affective experience of daily life: Ruling out situation explanation. *Motivation and Emotion, 19,* 25–57.

Folkman, S., Lazarus, R.S., Pimley, S., & Novacek, J. (1987). Age differences in stress and coping processes. *Psychology and Aging, 2,* 171–184.

Frederiksen, N. (1986). Toward a broader conception of human intelligence. *American Psychology, 41,* 445–452.

Frederiksen, N., Jensen, O., & Beaton, A.E. (1972). *Prediction of organizational behavior.* New York: Pergamon Press.

Freeman, N.H., Lewis, C., & Doherty, M.J. (1991). Preschoolers' grasp of a desire for knowledge in false-belief prediction: Practical intelligence and verbal report. *British Journal of Developmental Psychology, 9,* 139–157.

Goodnow, J.J. (1986). Some lifelong everyday forms of intelligence behavior: Organizing and reorganizing. In R.J. Sternberg & R.K. Wagner (Eds.), *Practical intelligence: Nature and origins of competence in the everyday world* (pp. 31–50). New York: Cambridge University Press.

Harter, S. (1983). Developmental prospectives on the self-system. In P.H. Mussen (Ed.), *Handbook of child psychology* (Vol. 4). New York: Wiley.

Hartley, A.A. (1989). The cognitive etiology of problem solving. In L.W. Poon, D.C. Rubin, & B.A. Wilson (Eds.), *Everyday cognition in adulthood and late life* (pp. 300–329). New York: Cambridge University Press.

Havighurst, R. (1972). *Developmental tasks and education.* New York: Van Nostrand.

Heckhausen, J., & Schulz, R. (1995). A life-span theory of control. *Psychological Review, 102,* 284–304.

Horn, J.L. (1982). The theory of fluid and crystallized intelligence in relation to concepts of cognitive psychology and aging in adulthood. In F.I.M. Craik & A. Trehum (Eds.), *Aging and cognitive processes* (pp. 237–278). New York: Plenum Press.

Horn, J.L. (1994). Theory of fluid and crystallized intelligence. In R.J. Sternberg (Ed.), *The encyclopedia of human intelligence* (Vol. 1, pp. 443–451). New York: Macmillan.

Horn, J.L., & Cattell, R.B. (1966). Refinement and test of the theory of fluid and crystallized intelligence. *Journal of Educational Psychology, 57,* 253–270.

Jensen, A.R. (1993). Test validity: g versus "tacit knowledge," *Current Directions in Psychological Science, 1,* 9–10.

Kohn, M.L., & Schooler, C. (Eds.). (1983). *Work and personality.* Norwood, NJ: Ablex.

Kreitler, S., & Kreitler, H. (1987). Conceptions and processes of planning: The developmental perspective. In S.L. Friedman & E.K. Scholnick (Eds.), *Blueprints for thinking: The role of planning in cognitive development* (pp. 205–272). Cambridge, England: Cambridge University Press.

Kuhn, D., Pennington, N., & Leadbeater, B. (1983). Adult thinking in developmental perspective. In P.B. Baltes & O.G. Brim (Eds.), *Life-span development and behavior* (Vol. 5). New York: Academic Press.

Labouvie-Vief, G. (1982). Dynamic development and mature autonomy. *Human Development, 25,* 161–191.

Labouvie-Vief, G. (1992). A neo-Piagetian perspective on adult cognitive development. In R.J. Sternberg & C.A. Berg (Eds.), *Intellectual development* (pp. 197–228). New York: Cambridge University Press.

Lave, J., Murtaugh, M., & de la Roche, O. (1984). The dialectic of arithmetic in grocery shopping. In B. Rogoff & J. Lave (Eds.), *Everyday cognition: Its development in social context* (pp. 67–94). Cambridge, MA: Harvard University Press.

Laipple, J.S. (1992). Problem-solving in young and old adulthood: The role of task interpretation. *Dissertation Abstracts International, 53*(1-B), 582.

Lazarus, R.S., & Folkman, S. (1984). *Stress, appraisal, and coping.* New York: Springer.

Loewen, E.R., Shaw, J.R., & Craik, F.I.M. (1990). Age differences in components of metamemory. *Experimental Aging Research, 16*, 43–48.

Meacham, J.A., & Emont, N.C. (1989). The interpersonal basis of everyday problem solving. In J.D. Sinnott (Ed.), *Everyday problem solving* (pp. 7–23). New York: Praeger.

Miller, K.A., & Kohn, M.L. (1983). The reciprocal effects on job conditions and the intellectuality of leisure time activities. In M.L. Kohn & C. Schooler (Eds.), *Work and personality* (pp. 217–241). Norwood, NJ: Ablex.

Mischel, W. (1984). Convergences and challenges in the search for consistency. *American Psychologist, 39*, 351–364.

Murtaugh, M. (1985). The practice of arithmetic by American grocery shoppers. *Anthropology and Education Quarterly, 16*, 186–192.

Naus, M.J., & Ornstein, P.A. (1983). Development of memory strategies: Analysis, questions and issues. In M.T.M. Chi (Ed.), *Trends in memory development research: Contributions to human development* (Vol. 9, pp. 1–30). Basel, Switzerland: Karger.

Neisser, U. (1976). General, academic, and artificial intelligence. In L. Resnick (Ed.), *Human intelligence: Perspectives on its theory and measurement* (pp. 179–189). Norwood, NJ: Ablex.

Neugarten, B.L., Moore, J.W., & Lowe, J.C. (1968). Age norms, age constraints, and adult socialization. In B.L. Neugarten (Ed.), *Middle age and aging* (pp. 22–28). Chicago: University of Chicago Press.

Piaget, J. (1972). *The psychology of intelligence.* Totowa, NJ: Littlefield Adams.

Pressley, M., Forrest-Pressley, D.L., Elliot-Faust, D., & Miller, G. (1985). Children's use of cognitive strategies: How to teach strategies, and what to do if they can't be taught. In M. Pressley & C.J. Brainers (Eds.), *Cognitive learning and memory in children: Progress in cognitive development research* (pp. 1–47). New York: Springer.

Ree, M.J., & Earles, J.A. (1993). *g* is to psychology what carbon is to chemistry: A reply to Sternberg and Wagner, McClelland, and Calfee. *Current Directions in Psychological Science, 1*, 11–12.

Rogoff, B. (1982). Integrating context and cognitive development. In M.E. Lamb & A.L. Brown (Eds.), *Advances in development psychology* (Vol. 2, pp. 125–169). Hillsdale, NJ: Erlbaum.

Rogoff, B., Gauvain, M., & Gardner, W. (1987). Children's adjustment of plans to circumstances. In S.L. Friedman, E.K. Scholnick, & R.R. Cocking (Eds.), *Blueprints for thinking* (pp. 303–320). New York: Cambridge University Press.

Rogoff, B., & Lave, J. (Eds.). (1984). *Everyday cognition: Its development in social context.* Cambridge, MA: Harvard University Press.

Salthouse, T.A. (1984). Effects of age and skill in typing. *Journal of Experimental Psychology: General, 113,* 345–371.

Salthouse, T.A. (1991). *Theoretical perspectives on cognitive aging.* Hillsdale, NJ: Erlbaum.

Salthouse, T.A. (1998). Relation of successive percentiles of reaction time distributions to cognitive variables and adult age. *Intelligence, 26,* 153–166.

Salthouse, T.A., & Somberg, B.L. (1982). Skilled performance: The effects of adult age and experience on elementary processes. *Journal of Experimental Psychology: General, 111,* 176–207.

Sansone, C., & Berg, C.A. (1993). Adapting to the environment across the life span: Different process or different inputs? *International Journal of Behavioral Development, 16,* 215–241.

Schaie, K.W. (1977/1978). Toward a stage theory of adult cognitive development. *International Journal of Aging and Human Development, 8,* 129–138.

Schaie, K.W. (1988). Variability in cognitive functioning in the elderly: Implications for societal participation. In A.D. Woodhead, M.A. Bender, & R.C. Leonard (Eds.), *Phenotypic variation in populations: Relevance to risk assessment* (pp. 191–212). New York: Plenum Press.

Schaie, K.W. (1996). *Intellectual development in adulthood: The Seattle Longitudinal Study.* New York: Cambridge University Press.

Schmidt, F.L., & Hunter, J.E. (1993). Tacit knowledge, practical intelligence, general mental ability, and job knowledge. *Current Directions in Psychological Science, 1,* 8–9.

Schmidt, F.L., & Hunter, J.E. (1998). The validity and utility of selection methods in personnel psychology: Practical and theoretical implications of 85 years of research findings. *Psychological Bulletin, 124,* 262–274.

Schooler, C. (1984). Psychological effects of complex environments during the life span: A review and theory. *Intelligence, 8,* 259–281.

Schooler, C. (in press). The intellectual effects of the demands of the work environment. In R.S. Sternberg & E.L. Grigorenko (Eds.), *Environmental effects on intellectual functioning.* Hillsdale, NJ: Erlbaum.

Scribner, S. (1984). Studying working intelligence. In B. Rogoff & J. Lave (Eds.), *Everyday cognition: Its development in social context* (pp. 9–40). Cambridge, MA: Harvard University Press.

Scribner, S. (1986). Thinking in action: Some characteristics of practical thought. In R.J. Sternberg & R.K. Wagner (Eds.), *Practical intelligence: Nature and origins of competence in the everyday world* (pp. 13–30). New York: Cambridge University Press.

Scribner, S., & Cole, M. (1981). *The psychology of literacy.* Cambridge, MA: Harvard University Press.

Sinnott, J.D. (1989). A model for solution of ill-structured problems: Implications for everyday and abstract problem solving. In J.D. Sinnott (Ed.), *Everyday problem solving: Theory and applications.* New York: Praeger.

Smith, J., & Baltes, P.B. (1990). Wisdom-related knowledge: Age/cohort differences in response to life-planning problems. *Developmental Psychology, 26*(3), 494–505.

Smith, J., Staudinger, U.M., & Baltes, P.B. (1994). Occupational settings facilitating wisdom-related knowledge: The sample case of clinical psychologists. *Journal of Consulting and Clinical Psychology, 62,* 989–999.

Sternberg, R.J. (1999). Intelligence as developing expertise. *Contemporary Educational Psychology, 24,* 359–375.

Sternberg, R.J., & Berg, C.A. (1992). *Intellectual development.* New York: Cambridge University Press.

Sternberg, R.J., Forsythe, G.B., Hedlund, J., Horvath, J., Snook, S., Williams, W.M., Wagner, R.K., & Grigorenko, E.L. (2000). *Practical intelligence.* New York: Cambridge University Press.

Sternberg, R.J., Grigorenko, E.L., & Gil, G. (1999). *Measuring everyday situational judgment skills.* Unpublished manuscript.

Sternberg, R.J., Nokes, K., Geissler, P.W., Prince, R., Okatcha, F., Bundy, D., & Grigorenko, E.L. (in press). The relationship between academic and practical intelligence: A case study in Kenya. *Intelligence.*

Sternberg, R.J., & Powell, J.S. (1983). The development of intelligence. In P.H. Mussen (Series Ed.), J. Flavell & E. Markman (Volume Eds.), *Handbook of child psychology* (3rd ed., Vol. 3, pp. 341–419). New York: Wiley.

Sternberg, R.J., & Wagner, R.K. (Eds.). (1986). *Practical intelligence: Nature and origins of competence in the everyday world.* New York: Cambridge University Press.

Sternberg, R.J., & Wagner, R.K. (1993). The geocentric view of intelligence and job performance is wrong. *Current Directions in Psychological Science, 2,* 1–5.

Sternberg, R.J., & Wagner, R.K. (Eds.). (1994). *Mind in context: Interactionist perspectives on human intelligence.* New York: Cambridge University Press.

Sternberg, R.J., & Wagner, R.K., & Okagaki, L. (1993). Practical intelligence: The nature and role of tacit knowledge in work and at school. In H. Reese & J. Puckett (Eds.), *Advances in lifespan development* (pp. 205–227). Hillsdale, NJ: Erlbaum.

Sternberg, R.J., Wagner, R.K., Williams, W.M., & Horvath, J.A. (1995). Testing common sense. *American Psychologist, 50,* 912–927.

Strough, J., Berg, C., & Sansone, C. (1996). Goals for solving everyday problems across the life span: Age and gender differences in the salience of interpersonal concerns. *Developmental Psychology, 32,* 1106–1115.

Vallacher, R.R., & Wegner, D.M. (1987). What do people think they're doing? Action identification and human behavior. *Psychological Review, 94,* 3–15.

Voss, J.F., Perkins, D.N., & Segal, J.W. (Eds.). (1991). *Informal reasoning and education.* Hillsdale, NJ: Erlbaum.

Wagner, R.K. (1987). Tacit knowledge in everyday intelligent behavior. *Journal of Personality and Social Psychology, 52,* 1236–1247.

Wagner, R.K. (2000). Practical intelligence. In R.J. Sternberg (Ed.), *Handbook of human intelligence* (pp. 380–395). New York: Cambridge University Press.

Wagner, R.K., Rashotte, C.A., & Sternberg, R.J. (1994). *Tacit knowledge in sales: Rules of thumb for selling anything to anyone.* Paper presented at the annual meeting of the American Educational Research Association, Washington, DC.

Wagner, R.K., & Sternberg, R.J. (1985). Practical intelligence in real-world pursuits: The role of tacit knowledge. *Journal of Personality and Social Psychology, 49,* 436–458.

Wagner, R.K., & Sternberg, R.J. (1990). Street smarts. In K.E. Clark & M.B. Clark (Eds.), *Measures of leadership* (pp. 493–504). West Orange, NJ: Leadership Library of America.

Wertsch, J.V. (1985). *Vygotsky and the social formation of mind.* Cambridge, MA: Harvard University Press.

Wertsch, J.V., & Kanner, B.G. (1994). A sociocultural approach to intellectual development. In R.J. Sternberg & C.A. Berg (Eds.), *Intellectual development* (pp. 328–349). New York: Cambridge University Press.

Wigdor, A.K., & Garner, W.R. (Eds.). (1982). *Ability testing: Uses, consequences, and controversies.* Washington, DC: National Academy Press.

Williams, S.A., Denney, N.W., & Schadler, M. (1983). Elderly adults' perception of their own cognitive development during the adult years. *International Journal of Aging and Human Development, 16,* 147–158.

Willis, S.L. (1989). Improvement with cognitive training: Which dogs learn what tricks? In L.W. Poon, D.C. Rubin, & B.A. Wilson (Eds.), *Everyday cognition in adulthood and late life* (pp. 300–329). New York: Cambridge University Press.

Willis, S.L., & Schaie, K.W. (1986). Practical intelligence in later adulthood. In R.J. Sternberg & R.K. Wagner (Eds.), *Practical intelligence: Nature and origins of competence in the everyday world* (pp. 236–270). New York: Cambridge University Press.

Worden, P.E., & Sherman-Brown, S. (1983). A word-frequency cohort effect in young versus elderly adults-memory for words. *Developmental Psychology, 19,* 521–530.

CHAPTER 8

Memory in Midlife

ROGER A. DIXON, CINDY M. DE FRIAS, and SCOTT B. MAITLAND

WHAT DO WE KNOW about how memory functions and changes during the middle years of adulthood? It is to this most general question that this chapter was initially addressed. In the course of examining research on midlife memory, five more specific forms of this general question were eventually developed. These questions became the guiding issues of this chapter. The first set of three questions concerned the scholarly literature on memory in midlife.

1. *How much systematic developmental research on midlife memory has been conducted?* With no comprehensive compendium available, it is not clear how research projects on memory performance or changes have been conducted (or published) with midlife participants. Moreover, the extent to which the multiple dimensions or systems of memory have been explored with midlife participants is also not immediately evident. Would a systematic review of the literature reveal sufficient evidence to offer reasonable conclusions about midlife and memory? Alternatively, would such a review reveal insufficient evidence regarding memory phenomena during this phase of life?

2. *Are midlife memory performances located intermediate to the performances of younger and older adults?* Given the extant research—and limitations accruing because of its possible lack of systematicity and restricted range of phenomena—are the observed memory performances generally closer to one age group than the other or typically located between those of younger and older adults? This

We gratefully acknowledge grant support from the National Institute on Aging (AG08235) to Roger Dixon.

question about level of memory performance in midlife leads to the next guiding issue.

3. *Is there something unique or even notable about memory phenomena in the middle years of adulthood?* Is there something unpredictable about midlife and memory, given the well-documented knowledge accumulated regarding memory in earlier and later adulthood?

The premise of these three basic questions is that this topic has previously received scant specific attention. Prospective reviewers might well be concerned that the answers to the preceding three questions could reveal that, as yet, there is relatively little unique or unexpected about midlife and memory. Thus, our final two guiding questions were formulated as follows.

4. *Should reviewers fear or embrace a possible unremarkable observation?* The potential observation would be that midlife memory performance, as presently evaluated, lies intermediate to that associated with early and late adulthood. What are the implications if the following scenario holds: Given memory task X, by knowing the performance of younger and older adults, respectively, the expected performance of middle-aged adults may be reliably derived.

5. *Could reviewers recommend more systematic research on midlife and memory?* The extent to which future resources should be devoted to studying midlife memory may depend in part on the answers to the previous four guiding questions. We defer an answer to this question until the end of this chapter.

As there are precious few empirical, theoretical, or review articles focusing on midlife and memory, we sought initial solutions for the guiding questions in two literatures. These were the prodigious cognitive literature pertaining to memory development throughout adulthood (e.g., Blanchard-Fields & Hess, 1996; Craik & Salthouse, 2000) and the growing general literature concerning midlife development (e.g., Lachman & James, 1997; Willis & Reid, 1999). Accordingly, we begin this chapter by reporting briefly on our background search for previous treatments of midlife memory, as they appear in scholarly reviews of cognitive aging phenomena and in recent reviews of the psychology of midlife. Next, we provide brief reviews of general memory systems and memory in the context of adult development. It is useful to begin the documentation of phenomena by addressing the larger theoretical and empirical context. In the subsequent section, we provide descriptive characteristics of recent empirical studies containing some attention to midlife memory. Finally, we close with some comments concerning where midlife memory research may lead.

SEARCHING FOR NEWS
ABOUT MIDLIFE MEMORY

In the larger literature of adult development and aging, researchers have produced vast arrays of theories and results regarding both cognitive and social processes. Reviewers have noted theoretically fascinating, empirically challenging, and practically useful aspects of life-span psychological development (e.g., Baltes, Lindenberger, & Staudinger, 1998; Hess & Blanchard-Fields, 1999). Regarding cognitive development in adulthood, we have previously argued that cognitive phenomena are both commonplace and essential throughout the life span (Dixon & Hertzog, 1996, p. 25):

> Throughout life we seek, process, and produce new information, acquiring and disseminating new knowledge. We solve novel problems, plan daily and future activities, resolve everyday hassles, and perform challenging tasks. We follow directions or find our way, participate in conversations, give or listen to advice, and remember past events. During our lifetimes we acquire new cognitive skills that require a prodigious investment of time and effort (e.g., a profession or a hobby such as chess) and perform complex skills with an automaticity verging on disinterest if not aplomb (e.g., driving an automobile). Rarely does a day, hour, or even minute pass without some form of cognitive activity. This is true as much for children and adolescents as it is for younger, middle-aged, and older adults.

Human cognitive activity is ubiquitous throughout all phases of the normal life span. Among the more basic cognitive processes—and among the more frequently used ones—is memory. Not surprisingly, research on memory development in adulthood is a vast and prominent field in the study of human aging. Numerous book chapters reviewing selected aspects of memory and aging have been published (e.g., Bäckman, Small, & Larsson, in press; Craik & Jennings, 1992; Howard, 1996; Hultsch & Dixon, 1990; Light, 1991; A.D. Smith & Earles, 1996), and the topic has been the focus of several books (e.g., Hultsch, Hertzog, Dixon, & Small, 1998; Kausler, 1994; Weinert & Perlmutter, 1988). The prominent theoretical issues in cognitive development have been explored in studies of memory development in adulthood. These include (1) the extent to which aging-related changes in memory performance are universal (happen to everyone in about the same way) or differential (show different directions and causes of aging-related change across individuals); (2) the extent to which memory is multidimensional or multisystemic and the implications for charting the direction(s) of change with aging; (3) the extent to which memory phenomena in adulthood are susceptible to interventions (e.g., practice or training); (4) the extent to which normal memory change with aging is incremental, decremental, or mixed; and (5) the extent to which memory change in adulthood may be predicted from more basic or more global indicators. Results of these reviews may be found in several compendiums (e.g., Blanchard-Fields & Hess, 1996; Craik & Salthouse, 1992, 2000; Kausler, 1994).

Overall, both unique and overlapping aspects and issues pertaining to memory development in adulthood have been addressed; we ignore these for the present discussion (see reviews cited previously). Instead, our current focus is on the extent to which these reviews address specifically issues of midlife and memory. In brief, midlife does not play a featured role in these reviews, and when it is addressed, it is typically only by implication. For example, a cursory examination of the subject indexes of several compendiums on cognition, memory, and aging reveals virtually no entries for terms such as midlife or middle-aged memory, and very few related to underlying biological changes that could be associated with memory in midlife (e.g., hormonal changes). Nevertheless, on closer examination it is possible to infer that midlife is represented in some reviews, at least by implication. Two illustrations of this from reviews will suffice. First, A.D. Smith and Earles (1996) presented numerous summary data and interpretations pertaining to memory changes in aging, with all but one figure comparing younger with older adults. The implication may be that middle-aged adults would perform intermediate to the younger and older adults, or if they perform more closely to one or the other extreme age group, it is not of substantial theoretical importance. Indeed, one adapted figure summarizes some historical memory results that included sampling of 30-, 40-, and 50-year-old adults. The performances represented seem to confirm the implication we have drawn from the absence of middle-aged data in this and other reviews. A second illustration contains somewhat more direct information. Although little specifically is made of results from middle-aged participants, several tables in the comprehensive Craik and Jennings (1992) chapter offer results or hypotheses emanating from middle-aged participants. In every case, middle-aged adults are represented as performing at a level precisely between younger and older adults. In one figure (Figure 2.2 in their chapter), theoretical functions are ordered from best to worst, in stepwise fashion, as follows: Normal Younger, Normal Middle-aged, Normal Older, and Alzheimer's Disease patients. A similar concentration on younger and older adult comparisons, with occasional representation of intermediate performance by middle-aged adults, may be found in even more extensive reviews (e.g., Kausler, 1994, Chapters 6 and 7).

Does the absence of specific attention to midlife and memory represent an implicit understanding by these cognitive scholars that midlife memory phenomena fall in terms of level robustly and precisely between younger and older adults? If so, it is arguably unnecessary to reflect that fact explicitly in reviews of memory performance in adulthood. Alternatively, the lack of specific attention to midlife and memory may reflect that there are relatively little systematic data pertaining to midlife memory. If this is true, it may have been wise for reviewers to omit explicit attention to an unknown phenomenon; the data on midlife memory may not have merited inclusion in these reviews. Naturally, these two alternatives are not mutually exclusive. In addition, certain conventions may be operating, including the expectation that reviews of memory aging are focused on contrasts between older adults and those much younger. We conducted literature searches for reviews of midlife memory. Thus far, we have found only one such review (i.e., Lavigne & Finley, 1990).

Memory is a major topic of cognitive aging researchers, certainly one of the most prominent. Researchers have also focused on metacognitive aspects, including beliefs, knowledge, and awareness of memory and memory changes. Coinciding with the prominence accorded memory in aging research, it has been documented that among the most frequent complaints of aging adults are those associated with memory failures, impairments, and complaints. Memory occupies a privileged position in the pantheon of scholarly research in human aging reflecting the considerable concern for memory phenomena displayed by aging adults. Does memory occupy a similarly privileged position in the scholarship devoted to midlife? We sought to explore this question by consulting selected volumes of scholarly and popular literature regarding midlife development.

Apart from the present volume, relatively few scholarly books are devoted to a broad swath of issues in midlife. In one of the early collections, edited by Hunter and Sundel (1989), two chapters focused on cognitive issues. Whereas Willis (1989) addressed issues pertaining to intellectual development, Labouvie-Vief and Hakim-Larson (1989) attended to structural and progressive aspects of adult cognitive development, devoting one section to selected aspects of memory development in adulthood. She noted that although most studies in the field feature only extreme age-group comparisons, one included a middle-aged group. The reported performance characteristics of this group were intermediate to those of the younger and older comparison groups, with similarity to the younger group in one aspect and similarity to the older group in another. The corresponding chapter by Willis on intelligence included rather systematic representation of midlife performance. Focusing on results from the Seattle Longitudinal Study (see also Schaie, 1996), some differential patterns for midlife participants were observed. Whereas for some abilities, longitudinal changes reached their peak in the middle years of adulthood, for other abilities midlife performance was intermediate to that of the adults in their earlier and later years (see also Chapter 7, this volume). Perhaps similar differential change phenomena could be identified for dimensions of memory performance.

We examined other collections, including the more recent edited volume by Lachman and James (1997). The focus of this volume is on more social aspects of midlife development, including attention to the self, interpersonal relationships, health and stress issues, and career patterns and influences. No chapter is overtly devoted to cognitive or memory issues, or with aspects of the underlying biological, sensory, or neurological substrate. Although there is no chapter on intelligence, a subject index item was found for the "intellective-cognitive domain, and career commitment." The chapter by Vandewater and Stewart (1997) presents self-report personality data including a dimension of intellectual efficiency. Finally, in the Willis and Reid (1999) compendium, Willis and Schaie (1999) present select longitudinal memory data in the context of their chapter on intellectual functioning at midlife. Two intriguing observations on verbal memory in midlife should be noted. First, verbal memory is among those cognitive functions that appears to peak longitudinally in the 50s. Second, the authors summarize that this pattern may be linked in part to midlife adults using compensatory strategies. In summary, some compendia of midlife development contain some attention to memory performance during this part of the life span (e.g., Hunter & Sundel, 1989; Willis & Reid, 1999), but there is little focused attention on this topic.

Recalling that memory complaints are among the most prominent issues noted by aging adults, we wondered whether more popular press books on midlife would reflect this everyday concern. One illustration will suffice. In her recent best-selling book, Sheehy (1995) devoted several pages to issues pertaining to memory in midlife. Two general topics are covered briefly in this book. The first is the relevance of menopause and hormone changes to cognitive performance in middle-aged women. In particular, the role of estrogen in brain activity and memory is noted (see also Warga, 1999). The second is the more general issue of normative change patterns across adulthood. Citing several research pieces, Sheehy presents an optimistic picture of middle- and late-life changes in the brain and in memory. She writes (Sheehy, 1995, p. 353):

> Most researchers agree that no functional mental decline occurs before 60 or 65. Short-term memory can become somewhat less reliable. But the vast memory banks in which we have been making deposits over a lifetime continue to grow more sophisticated over the years.

Two aspects of this quotation should be highlighted. First, Sheehy posits that there may be declines in memory performance over adulthood, but these changes are not of substantial functional significance. Second, and related to the first, she suggests that the declines that do occur may be localized to some specific aspects of memory (i.e., short-term memory) whereas other aspects (memory or knowledge) are spared—and indeed improve across adulthood. This point presents a natural transition to the next section, in which we summarize a prominent theoretical perspective on memory, in general, and memory development in adulthood, in particular. This perspective allows us to make theoretical inferences regarding Sheehy's second observation about memory in midlife.

OVERVIEW OF MEMORY
SYSTEMS AND AGING

Although there is a tendency in everyday discourse to treat memory phenomena as relatively unitary, many memory scholars view it as heterogeneous. That is, memory, like many psychological constructs of interest to researchers, is multidimensional. Observers vary in their interpretation of the definitions, number, characteristics, and interrelationships of these dimensions. These matters are not of interest in the present chapter. Rather, we adopt perhaps the most widely used perspective on the multiple systems of memory, applying it to a brief overview of issues in memory and aging. The principal purpose is not to review memory and aging research, but to provide a structure for organizing the empirical literature in midlife memory.

As attested in numerous reviews (e.g., Bäckman et al., in press; Craik & Jennings, 1992; Kausler, 1994; Light, 1992), a constancy-with-diversity pattern emerges when one examines a broad range of memory tasks performed by multiple adult age groups (Dixon, 2000). The "constancy" part of the pattern refers to the fact that a great deal of evidence for age-related decrements is observed. Younger adults typically perform better than older adults, and most long-term longitudinal profiles evince some degree of decline. The "diversity" part of the pattern refers to the notion that (1) there may be more maintenance (less longitudinal decline) in performance until late life than would have been expected, and (2) change profiles may vary across task and individual. How might this complex pattern be explained?

The *memory systems perspective* is useful for organizing the diversity of memory phenomena and can be profitably applied to memory development in adulthood (Bäckman et al., in press; Dixon, 2000). As described by Tulving and colleagues (e.g., Schacter & Tulving, 1994), five systems of memory may be identified. A memory system is defined as a set of related processes, linked by common brain mechanisms, information processes, and operational principles (Schacter & Tulving, 1994). A principal purpose of the perspective is to explicate the organization of the systems.

The bulk of research in memory—and in memory and aging—pertains to a system known as *episodic memory*. Episodic memory refers to memory for experienced events or information. Examples include such classic laboratory tasks as remembering lists of words, stories, pictures, and faces.

Age-comparative results robustly show that younger adults perform better than older adults. Much pertinent research has recently been conducted targeting moderating factors such as education, health, environmental support, biological processes, and ecological relevance. In addition, several longitudinal studies have reported aging-related profiles (e.g., Dixon, Wahlin, Maitland, Hertzog, & Bäckman, in press; B.J. Small, Dixon, Hultsch, & Hertzog, 1999; Zelinski & Burnight, 1997). Regarding midlife, an operative question would be: Is episodic memory similarly the most frequently studied system of memory and where are the performances of midlife participants located vis-à-vis those of younger and older adults?

A system of memory frequently documented in cross-sectional studies of cognition and aging is known as *semantic memory*. It is commonplace for cognitive experiments to report mean vocabulary performance by age group, although such performance is less frequently the target of theory-guided research. Vocabulary tests tap one important aspect of semantic memory, which is expressed through the acquisition and retention of generic facts, knowledge, and beliefs. Sensibly, as one progresses through life one is exposed to more generic facts pertaining to one's culture, and thus semantic memory may tend to increase throughout life. This is one form of memory for which older adults typically perform as well as younger adults on tests of general world knowledge, words, concepts, and facts. In addition, older adults typically display similar knowledge structures, although accessing these structures rapidly may become impaired with aging. Recent cross-sectional (Bäckman & Nilsson, 1996) and longitudinal (Hazlitt, 2000) studies have confirmed these patterns. Indeed, the former suggests that midlife participants perform intermediate to younger and older adults. This may be the system of memory to which Sheehy (1995) was referring when she noted that the vast "memory banks" remain intact if not continue to grow with aging.

A third system of memory is known variously as *short-term, primary, or working memory*. The basic issue is that some expressions of memory are brief, temporary, and not committed to a long-term store. Whereas some aspects of short-term memory are well-preserved in late adulthood, other aspects are not (see Bäckman et al., in press). A differentiating characteristic has to do with the extent to which the information is held passively (fewer age differences) or must be manipulated (magnified age differences). To what extent has this system of memory been investigated with midlife participants? At what age does the manipulation-of-information effect begin to affect the working memory performance of (middle-) aging adults?

The term, *procedural memory,* refers to the type of learning that occurs during skill acquisition, with skill defined broadly enough to include cognitive and behavioral skills. Although relatively few age-comparative studies have been conducted, a preliminary expectation would be that this system of memory is relatively unaffected by aging. Naturally, the research to date reveals a more complex pattern, with procedural memory performance being moderated by task demands and the extent to which the neurological and sensory systems are intact. Nevertheless, a straight-forward expectation regarding midlife procedural memory is that it would be relatively unaffected for most adults, with some exceptions for skills requiring exaggerated speeded components. A question for the present review concerns the extent to which tasks tapping procedural memory have been investigated with midlife adults.

The *perceptual representation system* is involved in identifying words and objects, and is often evaluated in implicit memory or priming tasks. In the growing body of priming and aging research, relatively small apparent effects of aging are often observed, but several qualifications have been detected (e.g., Howard, 1996). These qualifications pertain to extreme group comparisons—the circumstances under which older adults may perform worse than younger adults—and thus are not intrinsically relevant to the present review. In brief, it would not be expected that normal middle-aged adults would be seriously compromised in the memory abilities represented by these tasks. For those tasks in which aging effects are expected, however, midlife adults may perform at a level between that of younger and older adults.

The system that has been sketched provides us with a scheme for understanding the diversity of profiles observed in the vast literature of memory and aging. In addition, this system helps us to begin organizing the much smaller literature in which middle-aged adults have participated. Furthermore, knowing the five systems and the previous results pertaining to them is an aid in evaluating the level of performance typical of midlife adults. We turn now to our effort to organize the literature in midlife memory, using this scheme.

DESCRIPTIVE CHARACTERISTICS OF STUDIES OF MIDLIFE MEMORY

As noted, few reviews of memory development in adulthood have focused sustained attention on midlife performance or characteristics. No specific literature on midlife memory appears to be widely available or thoroughly documented. Midlife is rarely an organizing theme or keyword in the memory and aging literature, much less the larger cognitive aging or cognitive science literatures. For these reasons, we conducted a literature search with the following keywords: memory and middle age, memory and middle adult, memory and midlife. The search was constrained by date; specifically we searched the 22-year period from 1977 to the initial writing of this chapter (mid-1999). We used PsycInfo, allowing for journal articles, books, and book chapters to emerge. Under these conditions we initially obtained 269 citations for the keyword "memory and middle age," 21 citations for the keyword "memory and middle adult," and 7 for the keyword "memory and midlife." Some overlap was observed, and approximately 30% were ruled irrelevant or not usable for a variety of reasons (e.g., animal studies, unpublished dissertations, articles in languages other than English). Of the remaining 70%, about 14% were initially excluded because they appeared in journals unavailable in the available time frame. Thus, we identified 124 papers published between 1977 and 1999 in this literature search.

We reviewed these publications with several criteria in mind. Most importantly, we sought to sort these studies into the categories associated with the memory systems. In so doing, we could address several of our guiding questions. Our initial sort resulted in 118 articles being successfully sorted into our system (a 95% success rate). On further examination, we found that the remaining articles focused less on memory and more on metamemory, including beliefs, knowledge, and training. Thus, these articles addressed issues not covered in memory systems theory; their exclusion was reasonable. In Figure 8.1, we present the count of these articles by the year in which they appeared. A gradual increase in number of articles published per year is apparent.

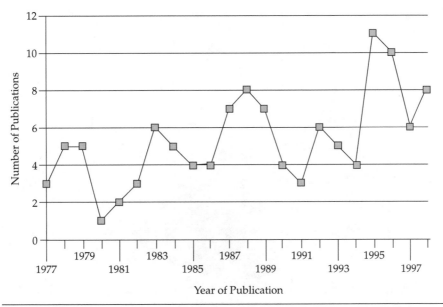

Figure 8.1   Tally of publications relevant to memory in midlife.

To what extent does research in midlife and memory represent the five comprehensive systems of memory? In Figure 8.2, we present the results of classifying the 118 articles in terms of a pie chart. The figure shows that episodic tasks are most frequently employed in midlife memory research, with 51% of the total articles published between 1977 and 1999. Although a similar meta-analysis is not available for the larger literature of memory and aging, this preponderance of episodic tasks is consistent with our expectations. Similarly, as expected, semantic memory tasks are also among the most frequently used ones in midlife research, with 17% of the total. Tasks reflecting short-term memory and the perceptual representation system were used at similar levels (17% and 12%, respectively). Only 2% of the published studies employed tasks that were classified as procedural memory.

The next step in our descriptive analysis was to table the studies according to memory system. These tables present information pertaining to citation, basic design (predominantly cross-sectional), age range of the midlife group used in the study, the midlife group size (*n*), a brief summary of the main age-related finding and whether a correlate or covariate was used. We present this information in the following tables: Table 8.1 (Episodic) and Table 8.2 (Semantic). The data pertaining to the less frequent memory systems are not tabled.

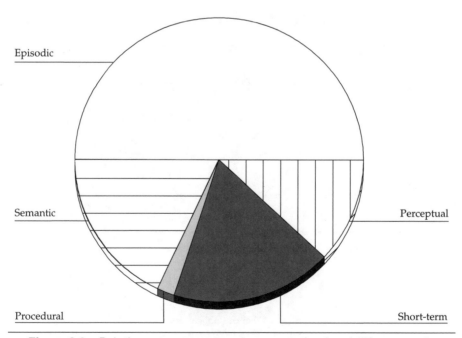

Figure 8.2   Relative memory system representation in midlife research.

Table 8.1

Selected Characteristics of Episodic Memory Studies Including Midlife Participants

Citation	Basic Design	Midlife Group Age Range	n	Age Finding	Correlates
Woodruff-Pak, Jaeger, Gorman, and Wesnes (1999)	C	45–55	47	Mid > O, Y > Mid and O	Classical conditioning
Commissaris, Ponds, and Jolles (1998)	C			Increase in prevalence of forgetfulness with age; 34% of middle aged reported forgetting	
Finkel and McGue (1998)	C	27–59	147	The magnitude of correlation between memory and cognitive factors varied across age groups (Y vs O) but the nature of the relationship did not.	
Maylor (1998)	C	53.5–63.5		O < Y and Mid	
Payton, Riggs, Spiro, Weiss, and Hu (1998)	C	M = 66.8 (Full sample)	141	Level of lead: low > high	Lead
Compton, Bachman, and Logan (1997)	C				Age, education
Levine and Bluck (1997)	C	46–70		Decrease with age	
Nilsson et al. (1997)	C			Age-related decline	Education
Erngrund, Mäntylä, and Nilsson (1996)	C			Age-related deterioration for item and source recall (SR)	Background variables, age, gender, and word comprehension were related to SR of well-known items; age and education were related to SR of unknown items

(continued)

259

Table 8.1 Continued

Citation	Basic Design	Midlife Group Age Range	n	Age Finding	Correlates
Maylor (1996)	C			Variation depending on memory type; individual differences	
McGinnis and Roberts (1996)	C	41–56		Y and Mid > O	
Park et al. (1996)	C			Speed and working memory explained age-related changes in cognitive aging; contributions of constructs vary as a function of type of memory task	Working memory and perceptual speed affect long-term memory
Finkel, Pedersen, and McGue (1995)		50–65	MTSADA sample: n = 80; Swedish sample n = 64	No age differences in the structure of the memory factor	Genetic influences
Finkel, Fox, and McGue (1995)	L	40–59	63	Y = Mid = O for mean absolute words gained; O > Y mean absolute words lost; % loss of words for O > Mid and Y; although O = Mid = Y for clustering of high-strength associates (relational encoding), clustering wasn't as effective for them in preventing loss of words (hypermnesic task)	

260

Study		Age	N		
Hess (1995)	C	Experiment 2: 36–58	32	O benefit more from being prompted to produce or actually produced a link between 2 sentences (sentence 1 is cue for recall of 2nd)	
Lipman, Caplan, Schooler, and Lee (1995)	C	Experiment 1: 47–69 Experiment 2: 47–67		Year of occurrence versus life event organization of calendars; effects for O	
Small, La Rue, Komo, Kaplan, and Mandelkern (1995)	C		91		Parietal asymmetry, sex, and baseline verbal memory scores predicted change in verbal memory
Coleman, Dwyer, and Casey (1994)	C	40–55	26		
de Wall, Wilson, and Baddeley (1994)	C				
Goldstein et al. (1994)	C	50+			
Webster (1994)	C	32–58	22	Memory remoteness was predicted by age; O retrieved older memories	High Openness and women; reminisce > frequently
Friedman, Berman, and Hamberger (1993)	C	M = 48.9	15		ERPs recognition tasks
Yarmey (1993)	C	30–44		Y and Mid > O	Confidence, accuracy
Chodzko-Zajko, Schuler, Solomon, Heinl, and Ellis (1992)	C	60–65	22	Age differences on a free-recall task	Fitness
Denney, Dew, and Kihlstrom (1992)	C	40–55	54		

(continued)

Table 8.1 Continued

Citation	Basic Design	Midlife Group Age Range	n	Age Finding	Correlates
Howes and Katz (1992)	C	40–55	24		Autobiographical
West and Crook (1992)	C		62		
Denney, Miller, Dew, and Levav (1991)	C	40–55	54		Contextual memory
Lipman (1991)	C			Landmark salience relates to route learning for older adults.	
Arbuckle, Vanderleck, Harsany, and Lapidus (1990)	C				
Crook and West (1990)	C	40–60		Y > Mid	
Friedman, Putnam, and Hamberger (1990–1991)	C	M = 48.9	15		ERPs, heart rate
Larrabee and Crook (1989)	C				
Pratt, Boyes, Robins, and Manchester (1989)	C	26–55	20	O lowest on memory span; no age differences in complexity of conjunction usage	
Yarmey (1989)	C	30–45		Y and Mid > O	
Hyland and Ackerman (1988)		45–55	24	Y and O report frequent reminiscence; time to respond to prompt words increases with age	
Kausler, Salthouse, and Saults (1988)	C	40–59			
Read (1988)	L	50–59	209	Mid > O	
Telakivi et al. (1988)	C	41–52	106		Snoring, hypoxia

Study		Age	N	Results	
Miller, Berrios, and Politynska (1987)	C				Impairment and benzhexol
Nixon, Kujawski, Parsons, and Yohman (1987)	C		136		Alcoholics
Perlmuter, Tun, Sizer, McGlinchey, and Nathan (1987)	C	55–64	111		Diabetes
Rodin (1987)	C				Attractiveness and age relevance of photos
J.L. Thomas (1987)	C	39–50	30	Y and Mid > O	
Waddell and Rogoff (1987)	C				Spatial memory
Yoder and Elias (1987)	C	35–45	16		
Cohen and Faulkner (1986)	C	40–59	32	Y and Mid > O	Memory for names poorer than places, occupations, or hobbies
Lehman and Mellinger (1986)	C	38–50	16	O < Mid and Y	
R.J. Smith, Roberts, Rodgers, and Bennett (1986)					Postoperative memory deficits were related to duration of anesthesia
Bäckman and Nilsson (1985)	C				
Emery (1985)	C	30–42	20	Mid > O	Language and aging
Loriaux, Deijen, Orlebeke, and de Swart (1985)	C	55–65	30		Drugs improve sensory register and short-term, differentially by age group
J.L. Thomas (1985)	C	M = 43.2			Map learning
Mergler, Faust, and Goldstein (1984–1985)	C				Story telling
Rankin, Karol, and Tuten (1984)	C	M = 46.67	18		Clustering, imagery

(continued)

263

Table 8.1 Continued

Citation	Basic Design	Midlife Group Age Range	n	Age Finding	Correlates
Shelton, Parsons, and Leber (1984)	C	M = 42.4 alcohol M = 42.5 controls	72	Mid > O	Alcoholism and learning
Stanton, Jenkins, Savageau, Zyzanski, and Aucoin (1984)	C	40–69	322		Age, level of education
Zivian and Darjes (1983)	C	35–44; 36–49		In-school vs. out-of-school categories—like groups were similar to each other than the Mid groups of each category	Years of schooling
Till, Bartlett, and Doyle (1982)	C	57–70	32		
Waddell and Rogoff (1981)	C	31–59	20	O = Mid contextual task, O < Mid noncontextual task	
Kausler and Puckett (1981)	C	42.49.2	Decrease in processing capacity. Onset by middle age.		
Charman (1979)	C	58	20		
Rankin and Kausler (1979)	C	M = 45		Y > Mid and O	
Simon (1979)	C	M = 42.7			
Weingartner, Caine, and Ebert (1979)	case study	41–53	8		Huntington's disease

264

Study	Design	Age range		Finding
Dye and Klisz (1978)	C	44–87 (Full sample)	30	Memory has a negative correlation with age
Rawling and Lyle (1978)	C	50–64		
A.D. Smith and Winograd (1978)	C			Y > O
Zelinski, Walsh, and Thompson (1978)	C	55–70	49	
Pershad and Wig (1977)	C	45–70		

Note: C = cross-sectional design; Y = young adults; Mid = middle-aged adults; O = older adults; *M* = mean; ERP = event-related potential; MTSADA = Minnesota Twin Study of Adult Development and Aging.

Table 8.2

Selected Characteristics of Semantic Memory Studies Including Midlife Participants

Citation	Basic Design	Midlife Group Age Range	n	Age Finding	Correlates
Payton, Riggs, Spiro, Weiss, and Hu (1998)	C	$M = 66.8$ (Full sample)	141	Level of lead: low > high	Lead
Marshall, Morelli, Calise, and Phillips (1997)	C	46–55	20	O > Mid	
Nilsson et al. (1997)	C			No differences	Education
Bäckman and Nilsson (1996)	L	35–50	300	No differences	Education
Maylor (1996)	C			Variation depending on memory type; individual differences	
Chan et al. (1995)	C				
Dubow (1995)		> 35		Y > O	
Karayandis, Andrews, Ward, and McConaghy (1993)	C	40–59	15		ERPs, age
Perfect and Rabbitt (1993)	C	50–59	29		Age, Gf, Gc
Cohen, Stanhope, and Conway (1992)	C	41–60			
Calev, Nigal, and Chazan (1989)	C	39–69	8		Depressed, bipolar, manic versus controls
Fisk, McGee, and Giambra (1988)	C	37–50		Y and Mid > O	

Study	Design	Age	N	Results
Fullerton (1988)	C	40–59	34	
Howes and Katz (1988)	C	$M = 48.11$	24	Mid > O
Perlmuter, Tun, Sizer, McGlinchey, and Nathan (1987)	C	55–64	111	Diabetes
Dixon and Hultsch (1983)	C	39–58	86	Relationship of MIA and text recall
Petros, Zehr, and Chabot (1983)	C			
West and Boatwright (1983)	C	40–59		
Light, Zelinski, and Moore (1982)	C			Y > O for facts
Bartlett and Snelus (1980)	C	$M = 45.6$	32	Mid few recognition responses to songs pre-dating their birth
Rankin and Kausler (1979)	C			Mid and O > Y on false recognition
Stones (1978)	C	$M = 49$	16	
J.C. Thomas, Fozard, and Waugh (1977)	C			

Note: C = cross-sectional design; L = longitudinal design; Y = young adults; Mid = middle-aged adults; O = older adults; *M* = mean; ERP = event-related potential; Gf = Fluid intelligence, Gc = Crystallized intelligence; MIA = Metamemory in Adulthood instrument.

Table 8.1 is the largest table. Midlife participants range in age from the 40s through about 60. Results indicate that midlife performance is typically intermediate to younger and older adults (when present), although some midlife groups perform more like younger adults for some tasks and others perform more like older adults for other tasks. Although this is the most frequently used task, little programmatic work has been conducted with midlife participants. Thus, overall conclusions are not available for episodic memory performance in midlife.

Some 23 studies were classified as containing a semantic memory task in Table 8.2. As noted, the largest of these uniformly cross-sectional studies was the Bäckman and Nilsson (1996) report, which featured $n = 300$ adults ranging from 35 to 50 years of age. No age differences were observed in this life-span study. This result is consistent with much research in memory and aging.

Overall, a diverse array of tasks, even within a system, have been employed in extant midlife memory research. The samples are typically small, and the designs are predominantly cross-sectional. Midlife is defined broadly, although reasonably, across these studies. Several studies have considered covariates, although these are not consistently incorporated into the analyses. Although gender differences in life-span memory research are of considerable interest (e.g., Herlitz, Nilsson, & Bäckman, 1997), only a small proportion of the midlife memory studies have examined this factor.

REPRISE OF THE GUIDING QUESTIONS

We began this chapter aware that research on midlife memory would represent a relatively small proportion of research in the larger field of memory in adulthood. Accordingly, we developed five general questions to guide our search for memory phenomena during the middle years of adulthood. The first question concerned how much published research would be available. Given our search criteria, we found an average of about 5 articles containing midlife participants that were published annually during the past 20 or so years. However, virtually none of these studies was focused on midlife. Rather, they were identified because they included a midlife age group. Nevertheless, the proportions of studies sorted into the five memory systems were roughly similar to what we would expect for the larger field of memory aging. Little evidence of programmatic research is available, however, with multiple authors employing multiple tasks and diverse definitions of middle-aged groups. Thus, the number of studies published on midlife memory is not insignificant, but the literature is in need of further systematic treatment.

The second and third guiding questions concerned the performances of midlife participants, and whether there was evidence of some special or unpredictable characteristic of memory phenomena in this age group. General conclusions are risky for this small and selective literature, but the overall impression we have gained is that midlife memory performance is neither startlingly superior (e.g., to that of older adults) or startlingly inferior (e.g., to that of younger adults), nor is it qualitatively differentiated from memory performance in other phases of adulthood. To be sure, the reviewed research was not directed at uncovering an answer to these guiding questions, but no research report appears to suggest anything contrary to this conclusion. Nevertheless, the data sets from which this conclusion is drawn are not nearly as complete as they could be, and further studies directed more specifically at midlife memory may reveal a different pattern. Accordingly, three potentially interesting avenues for future research can be noted. First, researchers focusing attention on midlife phenomena may be able to generate specific theory-guided predictions about midlife cognitive performance that cognitive developmental psychologists may not have previously considered. Now that we have some overview of what we know about midlife memory, midlife researchers may be able to inform memory and aging researchers of useful avenues for future studies.

A second avenue for future midlife memory research would be to pursue topics that are linked to biological processes associated with midlife. Hormonal changes occur during this period, and emerging research has linked several pertinent hormones to some facets of cognitive performance. For example, a growing area of research links the effects of estrogen on memory performance in postmenopausal women. While selective effects of estrogen on memory tasks have been documented (e.g., Kampen & Sherwin, 1994; Kimura, 1995; Phillips & Sherwin, 1992; Resnick, Metter, & Zonderman, 1997; Robinson, Friedman, Marcus, Tinklenberg, & Yesavage, 1994), other studies have found no benefit (e.g., Hogervorst, Boshuisen, Riedel, Willeken, & Jolles, 1999; Polo-Kantola, Portin, Polo, Helenius, Irjala, & Erkkola, 1998). Reasons for the inconsistent findings among studies may include the use of different estrogen preparations and dosages, whether circulating levels of estrogen were measured, inclusion of naturally or surgically menopausal women, sample size, and memory measures (with greater support for an association between estrogen and verbal memory than visual-spatial memory) (Sherwin, 1997, 1998). Clearly, the association between estrogen and memory warrants further investigation.

A third new avenue for midlife research could be that of awareness or metamemory in midlife. Of the articles originally identified in our literature search, 12% presented data on various aspects of metamemory, including memory knowledge and memory-related affect (e.g., L.M. Miller &

Lachman, 2000). Given that midlife scholars have identified images and awareness of middle-aging as a phenomenon of interest (e.g., Lachman, Lewkowicz, Marcus, & Peng, 1994) then quite possibly awareness of cognitive middle-aging would be a topic of considerable import. Although future work in this area may be profitable, there is no obvious promise that midlife metamemory phenomena will be more differentiated than midlife memory phenomena.

Our fourth and fifth guiding questions concerned issues that we have already begun to discuss. Most pertinent, perhaps, is the question of the extent to which we would recommend further research in midlife memory. Indeed, further research is necessary, as we have yet to develop a broad sense of the phenomenon, given the diversity of its representations. However, we do not recommend a strategy in which researchers fill in the gaps by employing *this* or *that* previously unexamined (in midlife) memory task. Rather, further contributions to building a *systematic* description of the phenomenon are required. In addition, explanatory work, such as linking memory performance with other well-understood biological or social processes would be welcome. There is much more to know about midlife memory, and specialists in neighboring facets of adult development should be consulted.

CONCLUSION

Midlife is an increasingly studied phase of life. As is illustrated in Figure 8.1, there appears to be a gradual shift to including midlife participants in cognitive aging studies. Although encouraging, this is not tantamount to systematic research on midlife memory. For this to occur, we should encourage theory-guided research, linking midlife social or biological processes to midlife cognitive phenomena. Such promising areas of research provide opportunities for fruitful collaborative and interdisciplinary efforts.

REFERENCES

Arbuckle, T.Y., Vanderleck, V.F., Harsany, M., & Lapidus, S. (1990). Adult age differences in memory in relation to availability and accessibility of knowledge-based schemas. *Journal of Experimental Psychology: Learning, Memory, and Cognition, 16,* 305–315.

Bäckman, L., & Nilsson, L.G. (1985). The avoidance of age differences in single-trial free recall. *Annals of the New York Academy of Sciences, 444,* 523–524.

Bäckman, L., & Nilsson, L.G. (1996). Semantic memory functioning across the adult life span. *European Psychologist, 1,* 27–33.

Bäckman, L., Small, B.J., & Larsson, M. (in press). Memory. In J.G. Evans, T.F. Williams, B.L. Beattie, J-P. Michel, & G.K. Wilcock (Eds.), *Oxford textbook of geriatric medicine.* Oxford, England: Oxford University Press.

Baltes, P.B., Lindenberger, U., & Staudinger, U.M. (1998). Life-span theory in developmental psychology. In R.M. Lerner (Ed.), *Handbook of child psychology: Vol. 1, Theoretical models of human development* (5th ed., pp. 1029–1143). New York: Wiley.

Bartlett, J.C., & Snelus, P. (1980). Lifespan memory for popular songs. *American Journal of Psychology, 93,* 551–560.

Blanchard-Fields, F., & Hess, T.M. (Eds.). (1996). *Perspectives on cognitive change in adulthood and aging.* New York: McGraw-Hill.

Calev, A., Nigal, D., & Chazan, S. (1989). Retrieval from semantic memory using meaningful and meaningless constructs by depressed, stable bipolar and manic patients. *British Journal of Clinical Psychology, 28,* 67–73.

Chan, A.S., Butters, N., Salmon, D.P., Johnson, S.A., Paulsen, J.S., & Swenson, M.R. (1995). Comparison of the semantic networks in patients with dementia and amnesia. *Neuropsychology, 9,* 177–186.

Charman, D.K. (1979). The aging of iconic memory and attention. *British Journal of Social and Clinical Psychology, 18,* 257–258.

Chodzko-Zajko, W.J., Schuler, P., Solomon, J., Heinl, B., & Ellis, N.R. (1992). The influence of physical fitness on automatic and effortful memory changes in aging. *International Journal of Aging and Human Development, 35,* 265–285.

Cohen, G., & Faulkner, D. (1986). Memory for proper names: Age differences in retrieval. *British Journal of Developmental Psychology, 4,* 187–197.

Cohen, G., Stanhope, N., & Conway, M.A. (1992). Age differences in the retention of knowledge by young and elderly students. *British Journal of Developmental Psychology, 10,* 153–164.

Coleman, K.A., Dwyer, J.T., & Casey, V.A. (1994). Accuracy of memories from childhood and adolescence related to growth and size. *Current Psychology: Developmental, Learning, Personality, Social, 13,* 233–240.

Commissaris, C.J.A.M., Ponds, R.W.H.M., & Jolles, J. (1998). Subjective forgetfulness in a normal Dutch population: Possibilities for health education and other interventions. *Patient Education and Counseling, 34,* 25–32.

Compton, D.M., Bachman, L.D., & Logan, J.A. (1997). Aging and intellectual ability in young, middle-aged, and older educated adults: Preliminary results from a sample of college faculty. *Psychological Reports, 81,* 70–90.

Craik, F.I.M., & Jennings, J.M. (1992). Human memory. In F.I.M. Craik & T.A. Salthouse (Eds.), *The handbook of aging and cognition* (pp. 51–110). Hillsdale, NJ: Erlbaum.

Craik, F.I.M., & Salthouse, T.A. (Eds.). (1992). *The handbook of aging and cognition.* Hillsdale, NJ: Erlbaum.

Craik, F.I.M., & Salthouse, T.A. (Eds.). (2000). *The handbook of aging and cognition* (2nd ed.). Mahwah, NJ: Erlbaum.

Crook, T.H., & West, R.L. (1990). Name recall performance across the adult life span. *British Journal of Psychology, 81,* 335–349.

Denney, N.W., Dew, J.R., & Kihlstrom, J.F. (1992). An adult developmental study of the encoding of spatial location. *Experimental Aging Research, 18,* 25–32.

Denney, N.W., Miller, B.V., Dew, J.R., & Levav, A.L. (1991). An adult developmental study of contextual memory. *Journal of Gerontology, 46,* P44–P50.

de Wall, C., Wilson, B.A., & Baddeley, A.D. (1994). The Extended Rivermead Behavioural Memory Test: A measure of everyday memory performance. *Memory, 2,* 149–166.

Dixon, R.A. (2000). Concepts and mechanisms of gains in cognitive aging. In D. Park & N. Schwarz (Eds.), *Cognitive aging: A primer* (pp. 23–41). Philadelphia: Psychology Press.

Dixon, R.A., & Hertzog, C. (1996). Theoretical issues in cognition and aging. In F. Blanchard-Fields & T.M. Hess (Eds.), *Perspectives on cognitive change in adulthood and aging* (pp. 25–65). New York: McGraw-Hill.

Dixon, R.A., & Hultsch, D.F. (1983). Metamemory and memory for text relationships in adulthood: A cross-validation study. *Journal of Gerontology, 38,* 689–694.

Dixon, R.A., Wahlin, Å., Maitland, S.B., Hertzog, C., & Bäckman, L. (in press). Episodic memory change in late adulthood: Generalizability across samples and performance indices. *Memory and Cognition.*

Dubow, J.S. (1995). Advertising recognition and recall by age—including teens. *Journal of Advertising Research, 35,* 55–60.

Dye, C.J., & Klisz, D.K. (1978). The interrelationship of memory functions in a nursing home population. *Experimental Aging Research, 4,* 493–503.

Elias, J.W., Wright, L.L., & Winn, F.J. (1977). Age and sex differences in cerebral asymmetry as a function of competition for "time" and "space" in a successive auditory matching task. *Experimental Aging Research, 3,* 33–48.

Emery, O.B. (1985). Language and aging. *Experimental Aging Research, 11,* 3–60.

Erngrund, K., Mäntylä, T., & Nilsson, L.G. (1996). Adult age differences in source recall: A population-based study. *Journals of Gerontology, 51B,* P335–P345.

Finkel, D., Fox, P.W., & McGue, M. (1995). Age differences in hypermnesia: Word gain versus word loss. *Experimental Aging Research, 21,* 33–46.

Finkel, D., & McGue, M. (1998). Age differences in the nature and origin of individual differences in memory: A behavior genetic analysis. *International Journal of Aging and Human Development, 47,* 217–239.

Finkel, D., Pedersen, N.L., & McGue, M. (1995). Genetic influences on memory performance in adulthood: Comparison of Minnesota and Swedish twin data. *Psychology and Aging, 10,* 437–446.

Fisk, A.D., McGee, N.D., & Giambra, L.M. (1988). The influence of age on consistent and varied semantic-category search performance. *Psychology and Aging, 3,* 323–333.

Friedman, D., Berman, S., & Hamberger, M. (1993). Recognition memory and ERPs: Age-related changes in young, middle-aged, and elderly adults. *Journal of Psychophysiology, 7,* 181–201.

Friedman, D., Putnam, L., & Hamberger, M. (1990–1991). Cardiac deceleration and E-wave brain potential components in young, middle-aged and elderly adults. *International Journal of Psychophysiology, 10,* 185–190.

Fullerton, A.M. (1988). Adult age differences in solving series problems requiring integration of new and old information. *International Journal of Aging and Human Development, 26,* 147–154.

Goldstein, F.C., Levin, H.S., Presley, R.M., Searcy, J., Colohan, A.R.T., Eisenberg, H.M., Jann, B., & Bertolino-Kusnerik, L. (1994). Neurobehavioral consequences of closed head injury in older adults. *Journal of Neurology, Neurosurgery and Psychiatry, 57,* 961–966.

Hazlitt, J.E. (2000). *Longitudinal changes in semantic memory performance of older adults.* Unpublished master's thesis, University of Victoria, Victoria, British Columbia, Canada.

Herlitz, A., Nilsson, L.G., & Bäckman, L. (1997). Gender differences in episodic memory. *Memory and Cognition, 25,* 801–811.

Hess, T.M. (1995). Aging and the impact of causal connections on text comprehension and memory. *Aging and Cognition, 2,* 216–230.

Hess, T.M., & Blanchard-Fields, F. (Eds.). (1999). *Social cognition and aging.* San Diego, CA: Academic Press.

Hogervorst, E., Boshuisen, M., Riedel, W., Willeken, C., & Jolles, J. (1999). The effect of hormone replacement therapy on cognitive function in elderly women. *Psychoneuroendocrinology, 24,* 43–68.

Howard, D.V. (1996). The aging of implicit and explicit memory. In F. Blanchard-Fields & T.M. Hess (Eds.), *Perspectives on cognitive change in adulthood and aging* (pp. 221–254). New York: McGraw-Hill.

Howes, J.L., & Katz, A.N. (1988). Assessing remote memory with an improved public events questionnaire. *Psychology and Aging, 3,* 142–150.

Howes, J.L., & Katz, A.N. (1992). Remote memory: Recalling autobiographical and public events from across the lifespan. *Canadian Journal of Psychology, 46,* 92–116.

Hultsch, D.F., & Dixon, R.A. (1990). Learning and memory in aging. In J.E. Birren & K.W. Schaie (Eds.), *Handbook of the psychology of aging* (3rd ed., pp. 258–274). San Diego, CA: Academic Press.

Hultsch, D.F., Hertzog, C., Dixon, R.A., & Small, B.J. (1998). *Memory change in the aged.* New York: Cambridge University Press.

Hunter, S., & Sundel, M. (Eds.). (1989). *Midlife myths: Issues, findings, and practice applications.* Newbury Park, CA: Sage.

Hyland, D.T., & Ackerman, A.M. (1988). Reminiscence and autobiographical memory in the study of the personal past. *Journal of Gerontology, 43,* P35–P39.

Kampen, D.L., & Sherwin, B.B. (1994). Estrogen use and verbal memory in healthy postmenopausal women. *Obstetrics and Gynecology, 83,* 979–983.

Karayanidis, F., Andrews, S., Ward, P.B., & McConaghy, N. (1993). Event-related potentials and repetition priming in young, middle-aged and elderly normal subjects. *Cognitive Brain Research, 1,* 123–134.

Kausler, D.H. (1994). *Learning and memory in normal aging.* San Diego, CA: Academic Press.

Kausler, D.H., & Puckett, J.M. (1981). Adult age differences in memory for sex of voice. *Journal of Gerontology, 36,* 44–50.

Kausler, D.H., Salthouse, T.A., & Saults, J.S. (1988). Temporal memory over the adult lifespan. *American Journal of Psychology, 101,* 207–215.

Kimura, D. (1995). Estrogen replacement therapy may protect against intellectual decline in postmenopausal women. *Hormones and Behavior, 29,* 312–321.

Labouvie-Vief, G., & Hakim-Larson, J. (1989). Developmental shifts in adult thought. In S. Hunter & M. Sundel (Eds.), *Midlife myths* (pp. 69–96). Thousand Oaks, CA: Sage.

Lachman, M.E., & James, J.B. (Eds.). (1997). *Multiple paths of midlife development.* Chicago: University of Chicago Press.

Lachman, M.E., Lewkowicz, C., Marcus, A., & Peng, Y. (1994). Images of midlife development among young, middle-aged, and older adults. *Journal of Adult Development, 1,* 201–211.

Larrabee, G.J., & Crook, T.H. (1989). Performance subtypes of everyday memory function. *Developmental Neuropsychology, 5,* 267–283.

Lavigne, V.D., & Finley, G.E. (1990). Memory in middle-aged adults. *Educational Gerontology, 16,* 447–461.

Lehman, E.B., & Mellinger, J.C. (1986). Forgetting rates in modality memory for young, mid-life, and older women. *Psychology and Aging, 1,* 178–179.

Levine, L.J., & Bluck, S. (1997). Experienced and remembered emotional intensity in older adults. *Psychology and Aging, 12,* 514–523.

Light, L.L. (1991). Memory and aging: Four hypotheses in search of data. *Annual Review of Psychology, 42,* 333–376.

Light, L.L. (1992). The organization of memory in old age. In F.I.M. Craik & T.A. Salthouse (Eds.), *The handbook of aging and cognition* (pp. 111–165). Hillsdale, NJ: Erlbaum.

Light, L.L., Zelinski, E.M., & Moore, M. (1982). Adult age differences in reasoning for new information. *Journal of Experimental Psychology: Learning, Memory, and Cognition, 8,* 435–447.

Lipman, P.D. (1991). Age and exposure differences in acquisition of route information. *Psychology and Aging, 6,* 128–133.

Lipman, P.D., Caplan, L.J., Schooler, C., & Lee., J.S. (1995). Inside and outside the mind: The effects of age, organization, and access to external sources on retrieval of life events. *Applied Cognitive Psychology, 9,* 289–306.

Loriaux, S.M., Deijen, J.B., Orlebeke, J.F., & de Swart, J.H. (1985). The effects of nicotinic acid and xanthinol nicotinate on human memory in different categories of age: A double blind study. *Psychopharmacology, 87,* 390–395.

Marshall, R.C., Morelli, C.A., Calise, G.A., & Phillips, D.S. (1997). Retrieval of famous names on a Rebus Riddle task by middle-aged and older subjects. *Perceptual and Motor Skills, 85,* 1492–1494.

Maylor, E.A. (1996). Older people's memory for the past and the future. *Psychologist, 9,* 456–459.

Maylor, E.A. (1998). Changes in event-based prospective memory across adulthood. *Aging, Neuropsychology, and Cognition, 5,* 107–128.

McGinnis, D., & Roberts, P. (1996). Qualitative characteristics of vivid memories attributed to real and imagined experiences. *American Journal of Psychology, 109,* 59–77.

Mergler, N.L., Faust, M., & Goldstein, M.D. (1984–1985). *International Journal of Aging and Human Development, 20,* 205–228.

Miller, E., Berrios, G.E., & Politynska, B. (1987). The adverse effect of benzhexol on memory in Parkinson's disease. *Acta Neurologica Scandinavica, 76,* 278–282.

Miller, L.M.S., & Lachman, M.E. (2000). Cognitive performance and the role of control beliefs in midlife. *Aging, Neuropsychology, and Cognition, 7,* 69–85.

Nilsson, L.G., Bäckman, L., Erngrund, K., Nyberg, L., Adolfsson, R., Bucht, G., Karlsson, S., Widing, M., & Winblad, B. (1997). The Betula prospective cohort study: Memory, health, and aging. *Aging, Neuropsychology, and Cognition, 4*, 1–32.

Nixon, S.J., Kujawski, A., Parsons, O.A., & Yohman, J.R. (1987). Semantic (verbal) and figural memory impairment in alcoholics. *Journal of Clinical and Experimental Neuropsychology, 9*, 311–322.

Park, D.C., Smith, A.D., Lautenschlager, G., Earles, J.L., Frieske, D., Zwahr, M., & Gaines, C.L. (1996). Mediators of long-term memory performance across the life span. *Psychology and Aging, 11*, 621–637.

Payton, M., Riggs, K.M., Spiro, A. Weiss, S.T., & Hu, H. (1998). Relations of bone and blood lead to cognitive function: The VA normative aging study. *Neurotoxicology and Teratology, 20*, 19–27.

Perfect, T.J., & Rabbitt, P.M. (1993). Age and the divided attention costs of category exemplar generation. *British Journal of Developmental Psychology, 11*, 131–142.

Perlmuter, L.C., Tun, P.A., Sizer, N., McGlinchey, R.E., & Nathan, D.M. (1987). Age and diabetes related changes in verbal fluency. *Experimental Aging Research, 13*, 9–14.

Pershad, D., & Wig, N.N. (1977). P.G.I. Memory Scale: A normative study on elderly subjects. *Indian Journal of Clinical Psychology, 4*, 6–8.

Petros, T.V., Zehr, H.D., & Chabot, R.J. (1983). Adult age differences in accessing and retrieving information from long-term memory. *Journal of Gerontology, 38*, 589–592.

Phillips, S.M., & Sherwin, B.B. (1992). Effects of estrogen on memory function in surgically menopausal women. *Psychoneuroendocrinology, 17*, 485–495.

Polo-Kantolo, P., Portin, R., Polo, O., Helenius, H., Irjala, K., & Erkkola, R. (1998). The effect of short-term estrogen replacement therapy on cognition: A randomized, double-blind, cross-over trial in postmenopausal women. *Obstetrics and Gynecology, 91*, 459–466.

Pratt, M.W., Boyes, C., Robins, S., & Manchester, J. (1989). Telling tales: Aging, working memory, and the narrative cohesion of story retellings. *Developmental Psychology, 25*, 628–635.

Rankin, J.L., Karol, R., & Tuten, C. (1984). Strategy use, recall, and recall organization in young, middle-aged, and elderly adults. *Experimental Aging Research, 10*, 193–196.

Rankin, J.L., & Kausler, D.H. (1979). Adult age differences in false recognitions. *Journal of Gerontology, 34*, 58–65.

Rawling, P., & Lyle, J.G. (1978). Cued recall and discrimination of memory deficit. *Journal of Consulting and Clinical Psychology, 46*, 1227–1229.

Read, D.E. (1988). Age-related changes in performance on a visual-closure task. *Journal of Clinical and Experimental Neuropsychology, 10*, 451–466.

Resnick, S.M., Metter, E.J., & Zonderman, A.B. (1997). Estrogen replacement therapy and longitudinal decline in visual memory: A possible protective effect? *Neurology, 49*, 1491–1497.

Robinson, D., Friedman, L., Marcus, R., Tinklenberg, J., & Yesavage, J. (1994). Estrogen replacement therapy and memory in older women. *Journal of the American Geriatrics Society, 42,* 919–922.

Rodin, M.J. (1987). Who is memorable to whom: A study of cognitive disregard. *Social Cognition, 5,* 144–165.

Schacter, D.L., & Tulving, E. (1994). What are the memory systems of 1994? In D.L. Schacter & E. Tulving (Eds.), *Memory systems 1994* (pp. 1–38). Cambridge, MA: MIT Press.

Schaie, K.W. (1996). *Intellectual development in adulthood: The Seattle Longitudinal Study.* New York: Cambridge University Press.

Sheehy, G. (1995). *New passages: Mapping your life across time.* Toronto, Canada: Random House

Shelton, M.D., Parsons, O.A., & Leber, W.R. (1984). Verbal and visuospatial performance in male alcoholics: A test of the premature-aging hypothesis. *Journal of Consulting and Clinical Psychology, 52,* 200–206.

Sherwin, B.B. (1997). Estrogen effects on cognition in menopausal women. *Neurology, 48,* S21–S26.

Sherwin, B.B. (1998). Estrogen and cognitive functioning in women. *Proceedings of the Society for Experimental Biology and Medicine, 217,* 17–22.

Simon, E. (1979). Depth and elaboration of processing in relation to age. *Journal of Experimental Psychology: Human Learning and Memory, 5,* 115–124.

Small, B.J., Dixon, R.A., Hultsch, D.F., & Hertzog, C. (1999). Longitudinal changes in quantitative and qualitative indicators of word and story recall in young-old and old-old adults. *Journal of Gerontology, 54,* P107–P115.

Small, G.W., La Rue, A., Komo, S., Kaplan, A., & Mandelkern, M.A. (1995). Predictors of cognitive change in middle-aged and older adults with memory loss. *American Journal of Psychiatry, 152,* 1757–1764.

Smith, A.D., & Earles, J.L.K. (1996). Memory changes in normal aging. In F. Blanchard-Fields & T.M. Hess (Eds.), *Perspectives on cognitive change in adulthood and aging* (pp. 192–220). New York: McGraw-Hill.

Smith, A.D., & Winograd, E. (1978). Adult age differences in remembering faces. *Developmental Psychology, 14,* 443–444.

Smith, R.J., Roberts, N.M., Rodgers, R.J., & Bennett, S. (1986). Adverse cognitive effects of general anaesthesia in young and elderly patients. *International Clinical Psychopharmacology, 1,* 253–259.

Stanton, B.A., Jenkins, C.D., Savageau, J.A., Zyzanski, S.J., & Aucoin, R. (1984). Age and educational differences on the Trail Making Test and Wechsler Memory Scales. *Perceptual and Motor Skills, 58,* 311–318.

Stones, M.J. (1978). Aging and semantic memory: Structural age differences. *Experimental Aging Research, 4,* 125–132.

Telakivi, T., Kajaste, S., Partinen, M., Koskenvuo, M., Salmi, T., & Kaprio, J. (1988). Cognitive function in middle-aged snorers and controls: Role of excessive daytime somnolence and sleep-related hypoxic events. *Sleep, 11,* 454–462.

Thomas, J.C., Fozard, J.L., & Waugh, N.C. (1977). Age-related differences in naming latency. *American Journal of Psychology, 90,* 499–509.

Thomas, J.L. (1985). Visual memory: Adult age differences in map recall and learning strategies. *Experimental Aging Research, 11,* 93–95.

Thomas, J.L. (1987). Localization versus featural information in adult visual memory. *Journal of Human Behavior and Learning, 4,* 16–22.

Till, R.E., Bartlett, J.C., & Doyle, A.H. (1982). Age differences in picture memory with resemblance and discrimination tasks. *Experimental Aging Research, 8,* 179–184.

Vandewater, E.A., & Stewart, A.J. (1997). Women's career commitment patterns and personality development. In M.E. Lachman & J.B. James (Eds.), *Multiple paths of midlife development* (pp. 375–410). Chicago: University of Chicago Press.

Waddell, K.J., & Rogoff, B. (1981). Effect of contextual organization on spatial memory of middle-aged and older women. *Developmental Psychology, 17,* 878–885.

Waddell, K.J., & Rogoff, B. (1987). Contextual organization and intentionality in adults' spatial memory. *Developmental Psychology, 23,* 514–520.

Warga, C. (1999). *Menopause and the mind.* New York: Touchstone.

Webster, J.D. (1994). Predictors of reminiscence: A lifespan perspective. *Canadian Journal on Aging, 13,* 66–78.

Weinert, F.E., & Perlmutter, M. (Eds.). (1988). *Memory development: Universal changes and individual differences.* Hillsdale, NJ: Erlbaum.

Weingartner, H., Caine, E.D., & Ebert, M.H. (1979). Imagery, encoding, and retrieval of information from memory: Some specific encoding-retrieval changes in Huntington's disease. *Journal of Abnormal Psychology, 88,* 52–58.

West, R.L., & Boatwright, L.K. (1983). Age differences in cued recall and recognition under varying encoding and retrieval conditions. *Experimental Aging Research, 9,* 185–189.

West, R.L., & Crook, T.H. (1992). Video training of imagery for mature adults. *Applied Cognitive Psychology, 6,* 307–320.

Willis, S.L. (1989). Adult intelligence. In S. Hunter & M. Sundel (Eds.), *Midlife myths: Issues, findings, and practice applications* (pp. 97–111). Newbury Park, CA: Sage.

Willis, S.L., & Reid, J.D. (Eds.). (1999). *Life in the middle: Psychological and social development in middle age.* San Diego, CA: Academic Press.

Willis, S.L., & Schaie, K.W. (1999). Intellectual functioning in midlife. In S.L. Willis & J.D. Reid (Eds.), *Life in the middle: Psychological and social development in middle age* (pp. 233–247). Boston: Academic Press.

Woodruff-Pak, D.S., Jaeger, M.E., Gorman, C., & Wesnes, K.A. (1999). Relationships among age, conditioned stimulus-unconditioned stimulus interval, and neuropsychological test performance. *Neuropsychology, 13,* 90–102.

Yarmey, A.D. (1989). Recognition memory and expressive behavioral correlates of self as an imaginal prototype in younger and older men and women. *Journal of Mental Imagery, 13,* 161–170.

Yarmey, A.D. (1993). Adult age and gender differences in eyewitness recall in field settings. *Journal of Applied Social Psychology, 23,* 1921–1932.

Yoder, C.Y., & Elias, J.W. (1987). Age, affect, and memory for pictorial story sequences. *British Journal of Psychology, 78,* 545–549.

Zelinski, E.M., & Burnight, K.P. (1997). Sixteen-year longitudinal and time-lag changes in memory and cognition in older adults. *Psychology and Aging, 12,* 503–513.

Zelinski, E.M., Walsh, D.A., & Thompson, L.A. (1978). Orienting task effects on EDR and free recall in three age groups. *Journal of Gerontology, 33,* 239–245.

Zivian, M.T., & Darjes, R.W. (1983). Free recall by in-school and out-of-school adults: Performance and metamemory. *Developmental Psychology, 19,* 513–520.

CHAPTER 9

Personality and the Self in Midlife

MARGIE E. LACHMAN and ROSANNA M. BERTRAND

MUCH HAS BEEN WRITTEN about personality and the self in adulthood and old age (Bengtson, Reedy, & Gordon, 1985; Neugarten, 1977). However, there has been little focus on the nature of personality and the self during the middle years of adulthood. Among those who have written about personality and the self in midlife, there are a wide variety of perspectives. Some have said that midlife is the peak time for adaptive functioning (e.g., Neugarten, 1968). Others have said that midlife is a time of turmoil and crisis (e.g., Levinson, 1977). Another perspective presents midlife as a time of quietude and stability in terms of personality (Costa & McCrae, 1994). Regardless of whether and in what ways personality and the self change during midlife, there is increasing evidence that the nature and experiences of midlife and later adulthood are determined in large part by individual differences in personality and the self.

In this chapter, we examine the nature of personality and the self in midlife from multiple perspectives, first providing a historical overview of theoretical approaches and then presenting more recent empirical findings. We offer an overview of key concepts and issues in personality and the self that are most relevant for midlife. We cover the key theoretical perspectives especially those which take a life-span approach to personality (e.g., Erikson, 1963; Jung, 1933; Levinson, Darrow, Klein,

We would like to acknowledge the generous support of the John D. and Catherine T. MacArthur Foundation Research Network on Successful Midlife Development and the National Institute on Aging #AG17920 (ML) and T32 AG 00204 (RB).

Levinson, & McKee, 1978; Vaillant, 1977). We also examine trait approaches (Costa & McCrae, 1994) to personality, less in terms of whether there is stability or change, but more in terms of how individual differences in personality shape the midlife experience. Contextual models of personality, which represent the complexities of person-environment interactions, are illustrated in the work of Caspi (1987), Helson (1984), and Neugarten and Gutmann (1968), The phenomenological approach to personality is also of great interest during midlife and some of the key findings about subjective personality change are discussed. For the self, we examine specific constructs such as identity, self-concept and multiple selves, sense of control, and well-being. Finally, we provide an assessment of the field and suggest directions for future research.

WHEN IS MIDLIFE?

There is much controversy about the timing of the middle years. The most common conception is that midlife begins at 40 and ends at 60 or 65 when old age is believed to begin (Lachman et al., 1994; Lachman & James, 1997). Although 40 to 60 are the modal entry and exit years reported in most surveys, there is tremendous variability in the timing of midlife (Lachman et al., 1994). The timing of midlife is also positively correlated with age. The older the person the later one expects midlife to begin. This is tied to the notion of subjective age in which most people think of themselves as 10 to 15 years younger than their chronological age (Montepare & Lachman, 1989). In fact, feeling younger than one's age is associated with greater well-being and health. In a recent study conducted by the National Council on the Aging (2000), almost half of the respondents ages 65 to 69 considered themselves middle-aged. This pattern is similar to the findings in a study of Boston-area adults, in which half of the men and women between the ages of 60 and 75 considered themselves to be in middle age (Lachman, Maier, & Budner, 2000).

The use of chronological age as a determinant of midlife may not be ideal as age norms are less stringent in midlife. Many people of the same chronological age are in different life phases with regard to social, family, or work-related events and responsibilities. For example, at age 40 some adults may have become a parent for the first time while another 40-year-old may have just become a grandparent. Social/family events place people of the same age in very different contexts for midlife. Being off-time, either early or late, for an event or life transition may have a major impact on one's self-conception (Neugarten, 1968). When considering personality and the self during midlife, it is useful to keep in mind that it is a complex and diffuse period in the life span.

HISTORICAL BACKGROUND

Development beyond young adulthood is a contemporary conceptualization. Propositions set forth by early theorists focused on development from birth to young adulthood proclaiming or at least intimating that development beyond this point in the life course was nonexistent. According to early developmentalists, personality in middle and older adulthood was impermeable to change. William James's classic statement, that by the age of 30, character is "set like plaster, and will never soften again" (James, 1890, p. 121), echoed the dominant perspective. For Freud and his early disciples, intrapsychic development occurred within an even narrower age boundary. That is, according to the psychoanalytic theory, personality is determined some time during middle childhood..Psychological change beyond this point in life is seen as the consequence of early experiences and not as the result of continued development. The tradition of embracing a childcentric view of development dates from Rousseau (1762/1948) and has been reinforced not only by the writings of Freud (1905), but by the contributions of many other preeminent theorists such as Piaget (1936/1974) and Bowlby (1982).

The view of development as a life-span process has its roots in early philosophers and can be traced to work by Quetelet, Carus, and Tetens in the eighteenth and nineteenth centuries (Baltes, 1983). More modern views of life span emerged in the early twentieth century with work by C. Jung, C. Buhler, G. Stanley Hall, and E. Erikson. Jung's (1933) psychoanalytic theory dealt primarily with issues of adulthood and aging, while Erikson (1963) introduced the notion of lifelong development by expanding Freud's theory to include later life stages. Jung's theory emphasized that each aspect of an individual's personality contains opposing poles (e.g., masculinity versus femininity). Psychological immaturity, inherent in childhood and early adulthood, results in an imbalance between opposing poles. During adulthood, when psychological maturity can be achieved, the individual is able to seek a balance between the rival forces through the process of individuation. Some of the recent work that has supported and expanded on Jung's and Erikson's theoretical propositions will be presented later in the chapter.

Fueled primarily by the advances made by Erikson toward a view of development as a lifelong process, research and theory over the past three decades has moved beyond a childcentric approach (Lachman & James, 1997) and culminated in a substantial body of literature from a life-span perspective (e.g., Baltes, 1987; Baltes, Lindenberger, & Staudinger, 1997; Featherman & Lerner, 1985; Lachman & Baltes, 1994; Lerner, 1976). Furthermore, aided by the development of sophisticated methodological techniques, considerable research initiatives have focused on personality and the self in the later years of the life cycle within the context of the life-span perspective (e.g., Schaie, 1996). In particular, longitudinal research designs have provided the data to model intraindividual change over time. As a result, our perspective of the aging process has been broadened beyond the narrow view of aging as an inevitable, pervasive decline to include the possibility of stability and even growth in some areas of development.

Although the increase of interest in the life-span perspective has served to advance efforts at understanding psychological development in older adulthood, until very recently, it has done little to foster research and theory of middle adulthood. Compared with other age periods, midlife has received much less emphasis, as is apparent by the dearth of volumes and journals devoted to midlife (Lachman & James, 1997).

Lachman and James (1997) have identified four possible reasons for the scientific oversight of midlife development. First, and probably most important is the assumption that little happens in midlife. Although many associate the entry into midlife as a time of crisis, it is often thought that the rest of the long period of midlife is relatively quiet and uneventful.

The second problem that has deterred scientific interest in the middle years is that midlife is not a clearly demarcated life stage. Sociological age-graded markers such as entry and graduation from school and participation in the employment cycle that help to delineate other periods of the life span are not available to define midlife. As Lachman and James (1997) argue, it is easier to place an individual in midlife according to the attainment of a specific event such as menopause or the empty nest than by a particular chronological or sociological age marker. Further, the definition of midlife varies as a function of cohort, culture, and context (Lerner, 1983).

Another factor that may help to explain the lack of research on the psychology of midlife is that middle-age individuals are underrepresented in studies on adulthood. A hallmark feature of midlife is engagement in multiple roles. Responsibilities toward jobs, children, aging parents, and civic and social commitments make it difficult for middle aged adults to participate in studies, especially if they require time away from home or work. It is quite common for studies of adult psychological behavior to use samples that are convenient to obtain, such as college-age and older adults rather than middle-aged individuals.

Finally, the study of midlife has been seen as an enormous undertaking due to the diversity and variation in form that it takes as a function of experience, choices, and genetic makeup (Lachman & James, 1997). Until recently, models of development to study such varied patterns were nonexistent. Rather, theory and research were dominated by stage models in which development is viewed as unfolding in a sequential, lockstep fashion. Stage models do not easily incorporate the variability and complexity necessary to capture the diverse adult experience.

Quite recently, however, midlife as a relevant life stage has been experiencing a growth phase. The explanation for this phenomenon is twofold. The first reason lies in the current demographic trend in our society (Moen & Wethington, 1999). The increase in longevity and the decline in fertility have created an extended post-childbearing period that may last decades before the onset of old age. This is a recent cultural phenomena given that at the beginning of the twentieth century, the survival rate for women in the United States after the birth of the last child was only a few years. Today's women can look forward to many decades after the birth of their last child that are free of age-related disease and disability.

The second explanation for the recent increase of theory and research on the middle years is based on methodological innovations and can be viewed as an extension of the work on older adulthood. With the introduction of longitudinal designs and the conceptualization of the life-span developmental perspective, the complexity of the midlife experience can be captured (e.g., Baltes, 1987; Featherman & Lerner, 1985). Longitudinal methods allow modeling of intraindividual development so that change patterns throughout the life span can be explored. The life-span approach, incorporating a comprehensive family of theories, recognizes the rich historical, cultural, and genetic sources of variation in personality and the self (Baltes, 1987). By employing the life-span framework to build on the work of early theorists (e.g., Erikson, 1963; Jung, 1933), and utilizing longitudinal methodologies to examine change over time, the diversity and complexity of midlife personality and self-development can be studied.

PERSONALITY

PERSPECTIVES

Over the past few decades, the literature on midlife personality has grown. For example, Caspi (1987) and Neugarten (1968) emphasize the importance of sociocultural influences in shaping personality throughout adulthood. In addition to contextual models that embrace a life-span approach, some more traditional models have been employed to examine the midlife experience. Trait theorists (e.g., Costa & McCrae, 1988; Roberts & DelVecchio, 2000) support the notion that personality structures have a genetic basis and are consistent across adulthood, while stage theorists believe that personality continues to evolve throughout adulthood in a predetermined, sequential way (e.g., Erikson, 1963; Levinson, 1977). To get a good representation of the complexities inherent in midlife development, it is useful to explore personality from multiple perspectives.

Trait Models

Traits, by definition, are enduring characteristics, which are expected to remain stable over time and consistent across situations. Although there was much debate about the utility or even the existence of traits in the field of personality (Mischel, 1968), most personality psychologists now acknowledge that there are broad propensities for behavior that have their origin in early temperament, develop at a relatively young age, and remain constant throughout adulthood. Although there are many approaches to assessing traits, most empirical studies reveal five broad traits: Extraversion, Neuroticism, Openness to Experience, Agreeableness, and Conscientiousness (Costa & McCrae, 1994). Much of the empirical work shows long-term stability in terms of maintaining rank orders. For example, those who are high in extraversion maintain their high level relative to others. Nevertheless, there is converging evidence both longitudinally and cross-sectionally that there are age-related mean changes in some of the traits (Costa & McCrae, 1994). Extraversion tends to decline with age, especially the components associated with activity and thrill-seeking. Neuroticism also tends to decline with age, so that with age adults become less anxious and less self-conscious. Openness to experience also has shown decreases with age, suggesting that with aging people become less likely to explore new horizons.

Costa and McCrae (1994) have found that personality forms the backbone of adult development. The key question for studying adulthood is to determine how aging will vary as a function of different personality styles (Lachman, 1989). One interesting finding is that those adults who are more neurotic are more likely to experience a midlife crisis (Costa & McCrae, 1980). This suggests a long-term pattern of difficulty dealing with transitions. Thus, the adult who experiences a midlife crisis is likely to have had a difficult time during adolescence and early adulthood as well (Jung, 1933).

According to Costa and McCrae (e.g., 1988), trait consistency should be reached by the age of 30. However, the findings reported from several empirical studies cast doubt on this position (e.g., Field & Millsap, 1991; Helson & Wink, 1992; Roberts, 1997). As noted by Roberts and DelVecchio (2000), many longitudinal studies reveal changes in trait dimensions during middle and later adulthood (e.g., Field & Millsap, 1991; Helson & Wink, 1992; Roberts, 1997).

Although many studies debunk the notion that personality traits reach maximum consistency as early as suggested by Costa and McCrae (1988), there have been few investigations that explore the alternatives. To fill this gap in the literature, Roberts and DelVecchio (2000) conducted a meta-analysis of 124 longitudinal studies and examined rank order consistency on personality trait dimensions over time. In addition, these investigators attempted to pinpoint the age or period of life when trait consistency peaks, and to determine whether personality traits reach a level high enough to justify the assertion that they are impermeable to change.

Findings from these analyses indicate high levels of rank-order stability across the life course. However, the consistency estimates between age groups were not high enough to support the notion that personality traits are resistant to change in adulthood. The study demonstrated that trait consistency increased in a linear, stepwise manner until it peaked during the fifth decade (i.e., 50–59). The dramatic increase in consistency that was detected during middle age (i.e., between 40–49 and 50–59) stabilized between later middle age (i.e., 50–59) and old age (i.e., 60–73). Roberts and DelVecchio (2000) summarized their findings by stating that although there is high consistency in personality traits during adulthood, throughout adulthood, a "dynamic quality" is also maintained. Based on this research, it can be concluded that the personalities of midlife adults are not impervious to change. Indeed, they are "open systems that remain susceptible to the pressures of life and the potential socialization effects of life experiences" (Roberts, 1997, p. 208).

The Midlife in the United States (MIDUS) survey was conducted by the John D. and Catherine T. MacArthur Foundation Research Network on Successful Midlife Development (MIDMAC) (Ryff & Kessler, in press). A national probability sample of households with at least one telephone was selected using random digit dialing. The sample of 3,485 noninstitutionalized adults was administered the Midlife Development Inventory (MIDI). This entailed an interview for 20 to 30 minutes by telephone (70% response rate) and a two-booklet self-administered questionnaire sent in the mail. This questionnaire was returned by 3,032 respondents (87% response rate). The age ranged from 25 to 75 years old ($M = 47.06$, SD = 13.11). Men comprised 49% of the sample. The majority of the sample were Caucasian (89%) and over half were married (64%). Of the total sample, 10% had less than a high school diploma, 29% had completed high school or a G.E.D., 31% had completed some college, and 30% had attained a baccalaureate or advanced degree.

The MIDUS survey included a list of 30 personality attributes that were selected from existing attribute rating lists developed by Goldberg (1992), John (1990), and Trapnell and Wiggins (1990). Respondents rated the attributes according to whether they were "a lot like me" to "not at all like me." The attributes can be used to index the Big Five personality factors. Agreeableness was measured with the following 5 items: helpful, warm, caring, softhearted, and sympathetic. Conscientiousness was measured with the following 4 items: organized, responsible, hardworking, and careless. Extraversion was measured with the following 5 items: outgoing, friendly, lively, talkative, and active. Neuroticism was measured with the following 4 items: Moody, worrying, nervous, and calm. Openness to experience was measured with the following 7 items: creative, imaginative, intelligent, adventurous, curious, broad-minded, and sophisticated.

Young, middle-aged and older adults were compared on the Big Five traits. These cross-sectional results revealed significant age differences on agreeableness, openness, neuroticism, and conscientiousness (Markus & Lachman, 1996). Agreeableness showed increases with age, conscientiousness showed a peak in midlife, and openness and neuroticism showed decreases with age. Gender differences were more pronounced than age differences. Women had higher levels of agreeableness, extraversion, conscientiousness as well as neuroticism than men. Men, on the other hand, showed higher levels of openness to experience.

An interesting portrait of Americans in midlife emerges based on endorsement of the "a lot like me" category in the attribute ratings (Markus & Lachman, 1996). The attributes most frequently rated as "a lot like me" in the representative sample were: responsible (72%), hardworking (72%), caring (67%), friendly (63%), helpful (57%), sympathetic (55%), warm (52%), softhearted (52%). There were some interesting patterns of gender differences. Women were more likely than men to describe themselves as responsible, caring, hardworking, friendly, sympathetic, helpful, warm, softhearted, organized, outgoing, talkative, lively, worrying, sophisticated, and nervous. Men were more likely than women to describe themselves as active, self-confident, imaginative, calm, adventurous, and forceful. Education also played an important role in shaping personality descriptors for men and women. Those with a college education were more likely to endorse attributes associated with agency (self-confident, forceful, assertive, outspoken, and dominant) and openness to experience. In general, these characteristics were more likely to be endorsed by men than women. However, education seems to be an equalizer in that women who had college education were as likely as men to endorse these characteristics. Thus, the midlife experience for women may be tied to their educational attainment. More research is needed to determine how education changes beliefs about the self as well as how personality affects educational choices.

Stage Models

Stage models provide another framework for examining the midlife experience. Studies that are based on trait models generally demonstrate relative personality consistency across adulthood (Costa & McCrae, 1988; Roberts & DelVecchio, 2000), whereas those that are framed by a stage approach demonstrate change throughout the life course (e.g., Erikson, 1963; Levinson, 1977).

In general, stage models attempt to describe normative, sequential patterns of personality change. Each period is associated with a particular developmental task that, when successfully resolved, provides a firm foundation for the next stage in the sequence (Havighurst, Neugarten, & Tobin, 1968). If a task is not successfully accomplished, healthy development in the following, consecutive period may be compromised.

The stage model of development is represented by many theories used to study midlife personality. Influenced primarily by Erikson's classic eight-stage model of psychosocial development (1963), several other researchers (e.g., Gould, 1978; Levinson, 1977; Levinson et al., 1978; Vaillant, 1977) have created theories that focus primarily on development in adulthood. Similar to Erikson, these researchers hypothesize that midlife personality change is linked to external demands that coincide with a particular transitional phase of life. A glimpse at the work of Erikson, Levinson, and Vaillant provides a basis for understanding change patterns in midlife personality structures as they are described in early stage model research.

According to Erikson's psychosocial theory, each of eight stages are marked by a tension or crisis between two opposing forces. The crises are resolved through a dynamic interaction between inner ego strength and outer societal demands. The result of each crisis is a strengthened or weakened ego that then becomes the basis for resolving the crisis in the succeeding stage. The stages proceed in a predetermined, sequential pattern that is based on the epigenetic principle. That is, the ego evolves out of a biologically programmed plan and different facets of the ego have the opportunity to develop at specified times. Later stages are built on the foundation of previous ones and it is not until older adulthood, if all eight stages have been resolved, that the possibility of complete psychosocial strength can be acquired. A close examination of the writings of Erikson (see Whitbourne, Zuschlag, Elliot, & Waterman, 1992) reveals that although during optimal development the stage sequence is followed precisely, environmental circumstances can derail an individual on his or her course and change the timing and pattern of development. An altered trajectory will result in a weakened ego and negatively impact present and future development. The emphasis of societal and cultural influences on ego development is another important contribution that Erikson's work has made to the field of developmental psychology. Prior to the writings of Erikson (1963), Freudian thought prevailed and it was believed that inner forces alone determined ego development.

Erikson (1963) posited that during midlife, the adult must grapple with the tension between generativity and stagnation (see Chapter 12, this volume). That is, the adult is torn between a sense of responsibility for establishing and guiding the next generation and self-absorption. Generativity, as defined by Erikson, is not limited to parenting; it can also be carried out through roles such as teaching and mentoring, and by activities that lead to productivity and creativity (Erikson, 1963). The healthy resolution of the crisis between generativity and stagnation results in ego strength and a sense of trust in the next generation. Failure to find a venue for generative efforts results in self-focus and an underdeveloped ego in this domain. Furthermore, an ego weak in generativity will be ill equipped to straddle the final hurdle of life, ego integrity versus despair. Similarly, if the crisis in young adulthood, intimacy versus isolation, is not successfully resolved, the resultant imbalance toward isolation will weaken the ego and inhibit the establishment of generativity in midlife. The virtue that develops out of the fulfillment of the need to nurture the next generation is caring, "a widening commitment to take care of the persons, the products, and the ideas one has learned to care for" (Erikson, 1982, p. 67).

Erikson's life-span model of psychosocial development has spawned numerous theoretical conceptualizations on the development of personality in adulthood (e.g., Levinson, 1977; McAdams, this volume; Vaillant, 1977). However, it has been difficult to quantify and study empirically. As a result, only a few studies (e.g., Whitbourne et al., 1992) have tested the model. In addition, Erikson's framework has been criticized for assuming male development and Western culture as the norm (e.g., Gilligan, 1982; Kahn, Zimmerman, Csikszentmihalyi, & Getzels, 1985). It is argued that women and non-Western cultures demonstrate very different developmental trajectories.

Although limitations can be identified, the significant contributions of Erikson's work including the expansion of personality development into midlife and later adulthood, the recognition that societal and cultural influences impact the developmental trajectory of the individual, and the inspiration that his work has had on other theorists, cannot be ignored.

A researcher whose work was influenced substantially by the work of Erikson is Levinson (1977; Levinson et al., 1978). Levinson conceptualized a theory of adult developmental processes that is also identified by distinct, sequential stages; however, rather than confronting a crisis at each stage as framed in Erikson's theory, Levinson's model fluctuates between a phase of relative stability (life structure) and a phase of transition (Levinson, 1986). The primary task of the transitional phase is to reappraise the existing life structure and to explore the possibility of change. The end product of the transitional phase is a committed choice around which a new life structure is built and a phase of stability is begun. Each phase is marked by its own developmental task and when accomplished, it becomes the foundation for the next life structure.

Framed in a Jungian context, the transition phase of middle adulthood is associated with four sets of opposing sources of conflict: young versus old, destruction versus creation, masculine versus feminine, and attachment versus separation. It is the task of midlife adults to reconcile these polarities by accepting the coexistence of both sides within themselves, "the neglected parts of the self urgently seek expression and stimulate a man to reappraise his life" (Levinson, 1977, p. 108). The crisis during middle adulthood, according to Levinson, hinges on the tension and stress caused by the process of resolving these conflicts. For example, qualitative findings based on retrospective biographical sketches of 40 men between the ages of 35 and 45 revealed that the majority of subjects underwent a crisis at about the age of 40 or 45 (Levinson et al., 1978). Levinson writes that during this time the men heard "internal voices that have been silent or muted for years and now clamor to be heard" (1977, p. 108). According to Levinson et al. (1978), the middle-aged men in his study reported intense internal struggles that were similar to depressive symptoms.

Levinson's theory is important because it was one of the first to focus primarily on development in middle adulthood. In addition, it is worth noting because of the attention that it has received from the media as a result of the publication, *The Seasons of a Man's Life* (Levinson et al., 1978) and a related popular book, *Passages,* by Gail Sheehy (1976). Indeed, the media fascination with the phenomenon of the "midlife crisis" is responsible for popularizing the term and for inextricably associating Levinson's and Sheehy's names with it. However, Levinson's research has several important limitations that raise questions about the validity of his findings. First, his initial conceptualizations of adult development were based on a small number of exclusively white, middle-class males. He subsequently applied his theory to women's lives and found similar results (Levinson, 1996). However, there is some question about the generalizability or universality of the findings. Second, this research was based on interview data and was not subjected to rigorous statistical analyses. Qualitative, retrospective reports are by nature subjective and susceptible to reporter and interpreter bias. Finally, the descriptive study was conducted as a snapshot design (i.e., one point in time) and examined only one cohort of individuals. As a result, it is difficult to make statements regarding change in behavior across stages or to generalize from one cohort to another. Given the weak methodological strategies of the study on which Levinson based his developmental conceptualizations, the model should be interpreted with skepticism. Nonetheless, he can be credited with drawing public and scientific attention to the intrapsychic and environmental influences on development in the middle adulthood years.

Another important body of work that was influenced by Erikson's fundamental ideas is Vaillant's research, summarized in the publication *Adaptation to Life* (1977). This book reports on the findings of a subsample of 95 men from the Grant Study of Harvard Graduates, a longitudinal interview study that began in 1937. Vaillant, whose framework is grounded in psychoanalytic theory, examined the maturation, adaptive styles, and external adjustment of the participants. Based on the compilation of interviews, he concluded that over time, mature defenses are used with more frequency. For example, he found that denial and projection were utilized less often and that intellectualization, sublimation, and humor were used more often. According to Vaillant (1977), throughout middle adulthood, ego defenses continue to evolve and mature.

Extending Erikson's idea of generativity in midlife, Vaillant noted that the men in the Grant Study (1977) demonstrated a tendency toward career commitment and responsibility for others during middle adulthood and that their lives were shaped by important sustained relationships. Interestingly, although many of these midlife men claimed to be in crisis, tangible evidence to support the existence of a midlife crisis such as a major career change, divorce, or depression was rare (Vaillant, 1977). Vaillant also identified a stage referred to as "Keepers of the Meaning," among men in their fifties. This phase is characterized by a philosophical approach to life involving a concern for carrying on and teaching others the cultural views.

A major asset of the Grant Study (Vaillant, 1977) is its longitudinal design. With multiple measurements taken over time, the investigators were able to examine change in the phenomena of interest. Vaillant was able to demonstrate change in ego defense mechanisms across adulthood. In addition, with longitudinal data, it was revealed that men in middle adulthood were no more likely than men at other ages to experience the major life transitions that have been associated with the "midlife crisis." However, the Grant Study also has limitations. First, it is based on a group of well educated, white, middle-class males; therefore, generalizations to other groups must be made with caution. Second, the data were examined as descriptive narratives and were not analyzed with statistical procedures. The qualitative analysis places some limits on the interpretability of the findings. Nevertheless, Vaillant and Milofsky (1980) examined and tested their theory with a group of poor inner city adults. They found similar stages of change and comparable use of defense mechanisms to those found in the Grant study, lending support for the applicability of their theory to different socioeconomic groups.

Overall, research based on stage models has supported the assumption that development occurs during adulthood. Although according to Erikson (1963), Levinson et al. (1978), and Vaillant (1977), change and growth are possible throughout the adult years, the available data about the developmental trajectories of women, non-Western cultures, diverse ethnicities, or SES groups other than middle class are limited. Further, with the exception of the Grant Study (1977), most of the work that has been conducted to test the models have utilized cross-sectional data. As a result, statements regarding direct change in personality development over time can not be made. Although theoretically strong, the models are based on interviews and clinical data and were not tested with statistical techniques. Finally, the three models described focus on ego development and view inner forces as the primary motivator of developmental change, even though external contributors are acknowledged.

In contrast to models that emphasize inner motivating forces as the main determinants of personality development, the following section presents a model that emphasizes an interaction between external circumstances and personality characteristics. Contextual models consider historical and sociological circumstances as influential determinants of personality development and place special significance on the role of cultural age norms in this process. For example, Caspi (1987) examines the influence of person-environment interactions through age-graded roles, whereas Helson (1984) and Neugarten (1968) utilize the analogy of the social clock to explore adult personality development.

Contextual Models

According to the contextual framework, developmental trajectories are viewed over an extended period through a multidisciplinary lens. For example, social transitions have different meanings for different individuals due to the influence of factors such as historic context, culturally prescribed age norms, socioeconomic resources, and personal life histories (Elder & Caspi, 1990). Moreover, the dynamic interaction among these parameters is considered to hold important developmental implications for the individual. The synchronization between individual development and social history causes "ripple effects" that trigger continuous or discontinuous effects throughout the life course (Elder & Hareven, 1994).

The study of personality change and stability is most commonly approached by employing longitudinal methods to examine behavior over time without reference to historical or sociocultural implications (Caspi, 1987). The nomothetic emphasis, indicative of trait models, provides information about the trajectory of a particular personality dimension (i.e., trait) across the life span and compares individuals' standings on the characteristic.

Contextual models have an idiographic orientation in which the diverse trajectories of subtypes of individuals are followed over time. An idiographic emphasis suggests the mapping of multiple pathways resulting not only from response to changing environmental conditions and life events, but also from the individual's selection of environmental context given particular personality characteristics (Kogan, 1990). The trajectories of two individuals of similar personality characteristics are likely to diverge if they experience significantly disparate life events in different historical contexts.

The work of Avshalom Caspi is an outstanding example of the contextual model as applied to the study of personality (e.g., Caspi, 1987; Caspi & Moffitt, 1993; Caspi & Roberts, 1999). Among the assumptions embedded in his framework is the use of personality dimensions as an antecedent of later life outcomes. The assumption is that personality characteristics bring about three distinct effects: (1) They help to explain the choices made at age-related transitional phases, (2) they help to assure continuity in lifestyles across contexts, and (3) they serve to regulate the degree of adaptation to new settings (Caspi, 1987). Inherent in this description is Caspi's belief in the coherence of personality traits across the life course, leading to a congruent, consistent way of responding to experiences across time and across situations. Framed within a dynamic, interactional model, Caspi maintains that it is the interaction of psychological and environmental factors that explain the coherence of personality traits over time and context.

Furthermore, Caspi argues that personality traits play an increasingly important role in the selection and maintenance of lifestyles as one ages. Personality influences the selection of environments as well as the impact the environments will have on the person (Caspi, 1987). Although Caspi leans toward a deterministic view, he emphasizes the importance of the dynamic interaction between personality traits and environmental contexts.

Of particular importance in Caspi's contextual framework is the relevance of culturally prescribed, age-graded norms; that is, the culturally acceptable age at which an individual is expected to cross a particular social marker (e.g., marriage, college graduation). Caspi argues that the way individuals confront, adapt, and adjust to these age-graded roles and transitions throughout the life course is the core developmental task and the essence of one's personality (Caspi, 1987).

To explore the effects of role transitions on individual personalities across time and across circumstance, Caspi (1987) used a sample of children drawn from the Berkeley Guidance Study. This 40-year longitudinal research endeavor contains data collected during late childhood, young adulthood, and middle adulthood, across multiple situations, and makes it possible to examine the behavior of specific types of individuals in specific situations at specific points in their development (Caspi, 1987).

Findings from this work support Caspi's hypothesis that personality characteristics are consistent over time and across situations, and have consequences for outcomes in multiple domains. Results revealed that undercontrolled individuals, who suffered explosive temper tantrums in late childhood, had difficulty in various roles in adulthood such as educational attainment and job status. Furthermore, this work demonstrated that the trajectories of subtypes of individuals of similar personality traits given different social contexts were not parallel. Middle-class boys showed a greater downward spiral in socioeconomic status than working-class boys. Ill-tempered boys from middle-class backgrounds demonstrated a progressive deterioration of social status over time lending them indistinguishable from their working-class peers by midlife. For women, childhood temperament played an increasingly important role in their lives by midlife. Women who had been ill-tempered at childhood were significantly more likely to marry men with low-status jobs in young adulthood and more likely to be divorced by midlife than their even-tempered counterparts. They also were more likely to be rated as poor mothers.

Caspi, Bem, & Elder (1989) also examined the life course continuity of behaviors among withdrawn or inhibited as well as dependent children. They found evidence that shy children delayed events in adulthood such as higher education or marriage and attained less occupational achievement and stability. For women, being shy was associated with a conventional pattern of marriage, child-bearing, and homemaking. Dependent children, especially women, tended to marry earlier and to have more children. Dependent boys fared relatively well in their adult roles.

The findings reported here suggest that behavior across the life span demonstrates stability rather than change. Indeed, Caspi argues that it is during times of social discontinuity or transition that consistent personality characteristics emerge (Caspi & Moffitt, 1993). The authors note the paradox of this statement in light of prior ideas that regard life events and transitional phases as the primary catalyst for change. Caspi and Moffitt hypothesize that novel and stressfully demanding situations cause an individual to fall back on emotional responses of the past. Change is produced only when old options for responses are blocked and scripts for new responses are readily available.

Framed by Caspi's theoretical perspective, psychological development at midlife is viewed as relatively stable. Behavior is consistent across the life course due to cumulative and interactional continuity (Caspi et al., 1989). An individual's personality leads to the selection of similar environments across time that reinforce one's personal style (cumulative continuity). One's personality style also tends to elicit similar responses from others across situations, thereby recreating similar reactions and interactions over time (interactional continuity). However, not all theorists who use a contextual framework support the notion of stability across the life span. Helson and Neugarten, for example, remain open to the possibility of discontinuity and view major life events as markers of developmental change.

Helson and Neugarten use a model of development that is based on the timing of events. As ascribed by this framework, people develop in response to when key events or transitions occur in their lives. Neugarten (1977) noted that development over the life course may occur on-time or off-time (early or late) with regard to cultural norms. Helson (1984) popularized the term "social clock" and noted that a major source of personality change in adulthood is related to how in tune individuals are to its rhythm (Helson, Mitchell, & Moane, 1984, p. 1081). When individuals confront events at culturally prescribed, age-appropriate times, they are considered "on time" and the integrity of the pattern of personality development is maintained. When individuals are "off time," however, life events become demanding and stressful because they are not ingrained into their understanding of the social system (Helson et al., 1984). As a result, the pattern of normal development may be interrupted and open the opportunity for change.

Helson and colleagues illustrate the usefulness of the social clock framework to study life-span personality development with findings from a longitudinal study of female college graduates (Helson et al., 1984). These researchers explored three social clock patterns: (1) the Feminine Social Clock (FSC), starting a family by early to middle 20s; (2) the Masculine Occupational Clock (MOC), choosing a career with status potential by age 28, and; (3) Neither Social Clock (NSC), adhering to neither social clock by age 28.

An individual differences approach revealed two major findings that lend support to the primary concepts of the contextual model. First, results confirm that personality characteristics are related to life outcomes across adulthood. For example, it was revealed that personality characteristics identified in young adulthood could distinguish those who would later depart from the FSC pattern from those who would not. Second, findings from this study support the importance of the timing of events. On the one hand, women who by age 28 had either started a family or obtained a potentially high-status career demonstrated a normative positive pattern of personality development. These on-time women scored high on scales of well-being and effective functioning in midlife. On the other hand, by their early 40s, women who failed to adhere to a social clock (i.e., NSC) reported feeling depressed, alienated, and embittered.

Helson and colleagues note that this work illustrates that the social clock serves as a barometer by which individuals evaluate their success in the world. When one remains on time with age-graded, culturally expected transitions and events, the individual receives social approval and a positive feeling of being that comes from playing in tune with society. Those off-time individuals who sway to their own rhythm, experience a lack of social acceptance that results in a painful, unsettling feeling of disengagement from social norms (Helson et al., 1984).

In more recent work, Helson and colleagues (Mitchell & Helson, 1990; Helson & Wink, 1992) reexamined the aforementioned group of female graduates from a small West Coast college to further explore women's midlife experiences. Hierarchical regression analysis demonstrated that a sense of well-being in early midlife (i.e., age 43) significantly predicted self-reported quality of life among women in their early 50s (Mitchell & Helson, 1990). This finding builds on previous evidence that shows that personality characteristics continue to influence later life outcomes.

Helson and Wink (1992) utilized the longitudinal data to examine personality change over time. Results support the hypothesis that change in personality across the life span is possible. Evidence for instability was found in the early 40s followed by a period of stability in the early 50s. Interestingly, the scales measuring masculinity/femininity were among those that revealed the greatest magnitude of change between the ages of 43 and 52. Older midlife women scored significantly lower on femininity than younger midlife women, indicating a trend toward characteristics normally identified with masculinity. Women in this sample showed an increase in variables that are associated with masculine traits such as decisiveness and action orientation, and a decrease in those associated with feminine characteristics such as vulnerability.

Similar findings were revealed in an earlier study of the same sample of women. Mitchell and Helson (1990) hypothesized that as midlife women gained freedom from child rearing, they would experience a reversal of sex roles including the feelings of power and status that are normally associated with the masculine identity. However, the data did not entirely support this notion. Instead of a reversal, a balance between masculine and feminine traits was associated with quality of life among middle-aged women. These findings add credibility to the writings of Jung (1933) in which he posits that achieving a balance between opposing intrapsychic forces is the hallmark of psychological maturity.

The prolific writings of Neugarten and her colleagues at the University of Chicago have also lent support to Jung's theoretical propositions. Using data from the Kansas City Studies of personality and aging, Neugarten and Gutmann (1968) report that during midlife, men become more receptive to their own affiliative and nurturant side, whereas women become more responsive toward their assertive and agentic impulses. According to Neugarten and colleagues (Havighurst, Neugarten, & Tobin, 1968), these shifts occur before external situations demand them. It is believed that at midlife, adults seek to evaluate their psychosocial position and to put energy into the neglected and unrealized aspects of their personality.

Neugarten's research, followed by Levinson's and Helson's, illustrates some of the personality shifts that were outlined decades earlier by Jung (1933). Inherent in the theoretical doctrine regarding the gender-role shift that occurs during middle adulthood is the assumption that there is the possibility of change in personality characteristics. Older midlife participants (i.e., age 55) from the Kansas City Study were significantly more likely than younger midlife participants (i.e., age 43) to create a story that described a passive man and an assertive woman when presented with an ambiguous picture (Neugarten & Gutmann, 1968). These projective data were interpreted as support for the hypothesis that personality has a dynamic quality and is susceptible to change throughout the middle years of life.

Most would agree that contextual models of development provide a richer, more complex view of personality development than either stage or trait models. Contextual models take a life-span approach by viewing development over time in an interdisciplinary, dynamic interactive framework. From this perspective, it is believed that personality is formed by a continuous reciprocity between what the person brings to a situation, socially constructed and objective external conditions, and situations, all of which are couched in a particular historic time period. The innovative theoretical conceptualizations of Caspi, Helson, and Neugarten have advanced the field of personality psychology by adopting a life-span view and by bringing to the forefront the importance of the context in which personality evolves. Their pioneering work has shed light directly on the middle-adult years and has made an enormous contribution to our understanding of the complexity of the midlife experience.

Paradoxically, while the advantage of the contextual framework is its multilevel, multidimensional model, it is also a disadvantage. The sophisticated methodological and statistical techniques needed to analyze change over time and complex relationships among antecedents and consequences has become available relatively recently. As a result, conclusions drawn from some of the research framed by the contextual model were incomplete due to the necessary exclusion of some valuable data, or based, in part, on qualitative reports that were not subjected to multivariate statistical analysis (e.g., Mitchell & Helson, 1990). However, with the availability of newer statistical techniques such as hierarchical linear modeling and structural equation modeling, studies to test the complexities of this model may be conducted.

SUBJECTIVE CONCEPTIONS OF PERSONALITY CHANGE

Most analyses of personality development in adulthood have made cross-sectional or longitudinal comparisons on a variety of dimensions. Cross-sectional studies compare people of different ages to examine whether there are differences in personality as a function of age or cohort. The longitudinal approach analyzes data on the same people over time at different ages. These developmental approaches enable examination of actual changes in personality. As previously summarized, much of this developmental work on personality traits has shown that stability of personality is common, and change is less often found. Another approach to examining personality is to examine phenomenological changes. The classic example of this approach was conducted by Birren and Woodruff (1972). They examined a cohort of college students upon graduation at age 21 and again 20 years later during midlife, using the California Personality Inventory (CPI). Two instructional sets were used in the midlife assessment. Respondents were asked to fill out the CPI based on their current personality in the standard fashion. In addition, they were asked to complete the test as they used to be at age 21. The pattern of results from the longitudinal comparison of scores from 21 to 41 showed a high degree of stability. In contrast, when the retrospective data were compared with the concurrent data, differences were found. Respondents answered the questions as if they had shown changes over the 20 years. The findings showed that the subjects remembered their psychological adjustment to be lower than it actually was. This suggests that there is a tendency for adults to expect change, especially growth, in personality during adulthood.

Other researchers (Fleeson & Heckhausen, 1997; Lachman, Walen, & Staudinger, 2000; Ryff, 1995) have also found perceived changes in personality. The design for these studies has been to ask subjects to rate their personalities in the present (the typical personality assessment mode) as well as in the past and in the future. Thus, retrospective and prospective comparisons can be made relative to the concurrent assessments. The time frame varies across studies from 5-year to 10-year intervals, or to specific age anchors (e.g., 25 or 65). The findings typically show that adults have experienced changes from the past to the present and that they expect additional changes in the future. The nature of the perceived changes includes both gains and losses (Heckhausen, Dixon, & Baltes, 1989; Lachman, Lewkowicz, Marcus, & Peng, 1994). On some dimensions, the expectation is for continued growth throughout adulthood. In contrast, some aspects of personality are expected to decline. A gain may be characterized by either increases on a desirable characteristic or a decrease in a negative characteristic. A loss may be represented by a decline in a desirable trait or an increase in an undesirable trait. In general, middled-aged adults are seen to be at the peak of their competence, ability to handle stress, sense of control, purpose in life, productivity, social responsibility, self-reliance, assertiveness, and authority (Lachman et al., 1994).

Another approach to examining subjective change is to compare the predictive value of perceived changes relative to objective measures. Using representative samples from the United States and Germany, Fleeson and

Baltes (1998) found that perceived changes in personality traits contributed significantly over and above the effects of concurrent ratings of personality when predicting health and well-being. Personality ratings become more meaningful when placed within the context of the life course. Two people may have a similar score on a measure of extraversion or agreeableness, yet have very different life-course experiences. For example, a person who has reached a given level of agreeableness after experiencing declines is likely to function differently than someone who has maintained the same levels of agreeableness over time. Moreover, different expectations of stability or change in the future may affect functioning.

PERSONALITY AS A PREDICTOR OF MIDLIFE OUTCOMES

Although much research on personality focuses on examining which dimensions change and which remain stable, another important consideration for understanding midlife is the role of individual differences in personality (Lachman, 1989). Personality characteristics can have a major impact on the nature and course of development in adulthood. As mentioned, those who are more neurotic are more likely to experience a midlife crisis (Lachman, Maier, & Budner, 2000). Although Jacques (1965) thought that the midlife crisis was driven by a fear of impending death, other theorists have identified personality as a key factor predisposing some to experience crises at transition points throughout the life course (Costa & McCrae, 1980). According to Jung, "as formerly the neurotic could not escape from childhood, so now he cannot part with his youth" (1933, p. 106). It is likely that the personality is the driving force behind the experience and the resolution of the midlife crisis, as it is with crises at other age periods. According to findings from a representative sample of 300 adults from the Boston area, about one-third of the time, the so-called midlife crisis is precipitated by external events such as job loss, financial problems, or illness, which can occur at other times in the life course, not just in midlife (Lachman et al., 2000). The way a person negotiates the losses and challenges of midlife is the key to whether a crisis will occur.

Caspi et al. (1989) found that personality had a long-term effect on educational and occupational attainment as well as marital stability. Personality also predicts well-being and health (see Chapter 5, this volume). There is evidence that childhood and early adult personality traits such as conscientiousness predict longevity (Friedman et al., 1995). Using longitudinal data from the Terman Life Cycle study, Friedman and colleagues found that personality has long-term consequences for adaptation to adulthood. Conscientious children were likely to be healthier and live longer as adults perhaps because they were more likely to engage in adaptive health behaviors.

THE SELF AT MIDLIFE

Scholars who embrace the self-concept model of personality development take a slightly different slant than those discussed thus far. According to these researchers, self-concept is the essence of personality and involves a cognitive dimension. The self-concept focuses on the way individuals view themselves. Proponents of this model view personality development as an evolving phenomenon that is guided by the integration of new environmental information into existing knowledge structures.

The self-concept is conceived as a web of mental constructions called schemas that guide and regulate an individual's behavior. Schemas are subjective interpretations of past reality that either adjust to new experience or remain the same by filtering out new information that is interpreted as threatening to the self-concept (Markus, 1977). Throughout the day, every individual faces experiences that require existing schemas, through subjective interpretation, to adjust, conform, or reject environmental information. As a result, the self-concept is in a continual state of flux between stability and change.

Some of the commonly studied aspects of the self are identity, sense of control, self-efficacy, self-concept, and well-being. All these aspects of the self may show changes in response to environmental or personal stresses. However, the self has been found to be relatively resilient in adulthood. Thus, although the self is vulnerable to change, it also can serve as a resource to the adult in the face of changes associated with midlife.

IDENTITY

Adapted from Piaget's theory of childhood cognitive development, Whitbourne (1987; Whitbourne & Connolly, 1999) formulated a self-concept model that focuses on identity development. Identity, as defined by Whitbourne and Connolly, is the sense of self-definition within personality over time and in different domains, "the individual's self-appraisal of a variety of attributes along the dimensions of physical and cognitive abilities, personal traits and motives, and the multiplicity of social roles including worker, family member, and community citizen" (p. 28). Whitbourne's cognitive perspective on personality development views the identity as flexible and susceptible to change across the life span.

The identity process model (Whitbourne, 1987), moves beyond Piaget's view, however, in that it is used to explain the life-span construct. This construct is an organizing schema that represents the individual's conceptualizations of past and future scenarios; it is a view of the self as existing over time (Whitbourne, 1985). For example, if a midlife individual defines himself in terms of his high school football career, football-related events would form his life-span construct.

According to the identity process model (Whitbourne, 1987), identity styles are created when the individual's experiences are interpreted through the processes of assimilation and accommodation. Assimilation is the process through which individuals incorporate life events and new experiences into their identity. In contrast, accommodation is the process through which individuals change their identity to conform to the new experiences.

Whitbourne and Connolly (1999) suggest that although a balance or equilibrium between the two opposing process styles is desirable, it is the imbalance of one over another that leads to the formation of different identity styles. When in balance, the processes produce a healthy approach to new experiences. When out of balance, however, leaning more toward assimilation or accommodation, the approach is likely to be neurotic or otherwise mentally unstable. For example, individuals with a strong assimilative identity style are seen as rigid and inflexible. As middle-aged adults, these individuals might deny age-related changes such as physical limitations. They may react either by placing blame elsewhere (e.g., the exercise routine has become more difficult) or by avoiding situations in which their physical prowess is challenged. These individuals see themselves as unchanging across middle adulthood (Whitbourne & Connolly, 1999). On the other hand, those with a proclivity toward a strong accommodative identity style have a weak, incoherent identity and overreact to changes. For example, the first sign of gray hair on a middle-aged adult may be the catalyst that causes this adult to take on the identity of an old person. In addition, accommodative adults fail to set goals or make commitments. It may be extremely difficult for this individual to parent teenage or young adult children as they are likely to overreact to criticism and challenges. The parent will be inconsistent and indecisive and it is quite possible that the dyad may experience role-reversal (Whitbourne & Connolly, 1999).

Whitbourne's model of identity processing is useful for understanding the complexity and dynamic qualities of personality. It allows one to grasp the notion of an evolving identity and how change can occur across the life span. However, similar to models previously discussed (e.g., Erikson's stage model), it is difficult to test. Cross-sectional data do not provide the basis to answer questions regarding age-related changes in identity across time or across situation. Longitudinal data among community-dwelling adults are necessary to adequately test the theoretical propositions proposed in Whitbourne's model.

Markus and Nurius have also developed a theoretical model of the self-concept that describes the formation of identity across the life span. The possible selves theory (Markus & Nurius, 1986) suggests that individuals' subjective evaluation of their progress in relation to their social surroundings is integrated into their self-concept. These evaluations represent what individuals could become, what they would like to become, and what they are afraid of becoming. Feelings of hope over whom they may become and dread over whom they are afraid of becoming are internalized into the structure of the self and utilized as motivators or defense strategies throughout adulthood. Individuals' behavior is based on their efforts to either realize their hoped for selves or avoid their dreaded selves and in the process, protect the current view of the self (Markus & Nurius, 1986). Ultimately, positive psychological outcomes result when hoped for selves are realized and feared selves are successfully avoided. However, when the individual perceives that he or she has become the feared or dreaded self at the expense of the hoped for self, the self-concept becomes threatened and negative outcomes result.

Cross and Markus (1991) tested the possible selves model among a sample of volunteers between the ages of 18 and 86. Findings demonstrate that midlife adults (i.e., ages 40–59) reported less hope for expansive changes (e.g., new beginnings or drastic changes), but more hope for enjoyment and achievement in current roles and responsibilities (e.g., work, family). The hoped for selves of middle-aged adults seemed to be more grounded and connected to their current self than the hoped for selves of the younger cohorts. For the younger cohorts, their hoped for selves seemed removed from their current selves and lives. However, the focus in middle age on hoped for possible selves that involve an increased richness in current roles, shift in old age to a focus on preventing possible selves involving illness and dependency (Cross & Markus, 1991). These data clearly emphasize the modifications and adjustments that are made in the identity across the life span. According to these findings, personality is not cast in stone, but rather it is flexible over time.

The possible selves model provides a framework from which to view personality development across the life span. As demonstrated by the work of Cross and Markus (1991), the concept of possible selves facilitates individuals' adaptation to new roles and transitions across the life span and provides evidence of the motivation to change and seek new directions or goals. Furthermore, similar to the contextual model, the possible selves framework suggests a reciprocal element where an individual may change or adjust his or her possible selves in response to external influences and personal growth.

THE SENSE OF CONTROL

One of the most frequently studied aspects of the self is the sense of control. There are many different components under the rubric of control including self-efficacy, locus of control, attributions, and primary and secondary control (Bandura, 1997; Rodin, 1986). The focus of the control construct is on the degree to which individuals believe they influence outcomes in their lives. The outcomes occur in many different domains of life (e.g., work, family, health), and beliefs about control may vary across these areas (Clarke-Plaskie & Lachman, 1999; Lachman & Weaver, 1998). There is evidence that beliefs about control change in adulthood. In the MacArthur Foundation study of midlife (Lachman & Weaver, 1998), adults were found to develop an increased sense of control over their work, finances, and marriage. In contrast, there was evidence for reduced control over sex life and children. Declines in perceived control have also been found for health and memory (Lachman, 1991).

The sense of control is related to health and well-being in midlife. Those who believe they are responsible for outcomes in their lives are more likely to engage in effortful and persistent behavior working toward goals in the academic, professional, as well as the physical realm. Thus, those who believe that what they do matters will be more likely to act in accordance with their desired outcomes. Those who believe that health is under their own control are more likely to engage in health-promoting be-haviors such as exercise, eating a healthy diet, and going to the doctor (Lachman & Prenda, in press). As a consequence those with a greater sense of control are healthier. Maintaining a sense of control during midlife may serve as an important psychosocial resource by fostering both preventive and remedial behaviors.

A sense of control is also associated with a greater sense of well-being. Feeling that one can have an impact on what happens contributes to a sense of satisfaction (Lachman et al., 2000). Those who believe they are in control of their lives are also more likely to expect positive changes in the future.

Other aspects of control have been investigated in midlife such as pri-mary and secondary control (see Chapter 11, this volume). There is evi-dence that with aging, there is a shift from the use of primary to secondary control strategies when faced with uncontrollable situations or difficult challenges (Heckhausen & Schulz, 1995). Primary control strategies involve working toward reaching a goal by changing the situation or the environ-ment. Secondary control strategies focus on changing the self to accommo-date to the situation or environmental constraints. Wrosch, Heckhausen, and Lachman (2000) found that among older adults use of secondary con-trol strategies was more adaptive whereas use of primary control strategies was more adaptive for younger and middle-aged adults.

WELL-BEING

What constitutes living well in midlife? Brim has defined the good life for those in midlife as comprised of psychological well-being, good physical health, and a sense of social responsibility (Brim, 1992). It is not necessary to be successful in all three areas, however, to have a sense of well-being. For example, there are cases of people who are happy despite having a grave illness.

Is a crisis a necessary part of midlife? Empirical studies (Lachman et al., 1994; Lachman et al., 2000) suggest that the midlife crisis is not highly prevalent, and that when it does occur it is manifested in many different ways. A large percentage (about 70%) of those surveyed in a small highly educated convenience sample believed there is such a thing as a midlife crisis (Lachman et al., 1994). In a larger more representative sample in the Boston area, about 46% reported knowing someone who had a midlife crisis, whereas only about 25% said they personally had experienced one (Lachman et al., 2000). The most common experiences associated with the midlife crisis are: concerns about getting older, self-questioning, a period of maladjustment, and a reappraisal of life. For many adults, this reappraisal and questioning of the self had positive consequences for personal growth and psychological well-being.

Ryff (1995) has defined well-being along six dimensions: positive relations with others, environmental mastery, self-acceptance, having a purpose in life, personal growth, and autonomy. Adults are more likely to maintain or increase well-being in terms of self-acceptance, positive relations with others, autonomy, and environmental mastery as they reach midlife and beyond. However, purpose in life and personal growth are more likely to show declines in later adulthood. Mroczek and Kolarz (1998) found evidence that midlife is a time for increased well-being. Using the MIDUS sample, they found that positive emotions increased and negative emotions decreased as adults reached midlife and beyond. Thus, midlife is a period in which there is a positive balance of emotions and well-being.

CONCLUSIONS AND FUTURE DIRECTIONS

The study of personality and the self in adulthood has focused mainly on young adulthood and old age, leaving somewhat of a gap in our understanding of the middle years. This chapter provides a summary of what we do know about personality and the self as it applies to midlife. We have a good sense of which aspects of personality change and which are stable in midlife. We also know which dimensions of personality and the self are antecedents of successful outcomes such as health and well-being. However, little is known about the processes whereby personality and aspects of the self influence health and well-being. More research is needed to discover the mediators of personality and adaptive outcomes such as health in midlife. It is likely that there are multiple factors that contribute to the links between personality variables and health. One class of variables includes behavioral factors such as health-promoting behaviors. Physiological mechanisms such as stress hormones and immune functioning also are beginning to surface as important ingredients. Further work is needed to develop and test models of how personality influences the course of development in midlife and into old age. It will be challenging to determine how middle-aged adults are able to maintain high levels of well-being in the face of the significant stresses and strains associated with the multiple roles and demands of this period of life. Research is needed to better understand how the self can serve as a buffer against stress and to what extent the self is related to resilience in midlife. It is important to determine how the self appraises and deals with changes in the body and appearance. Further research is needed to identify which aspects of the personality and self can serve as the focus for interventions for enhancing functioning during midlife. It remains to be seen whether personality and the self in midlife can provide a window to the nature and quality of life in the later years. If so, the opportunities for developing preventive strategies for optimizing later life functioning will be enormous.

REFERENCES

Baltes, P.B. (1983). Life-span developmental psychology: Observations on history and theory revisited. In R.M. Lerner (Ed.), *Developmental psychology: Historical and philosophical perspectives* (pp. 79–111). Hillsdale, NJ: Erlbaum.

Baltes, P.B. (1987). Theoretical propositions of life-span developmental psychology: On the dynamics between growth and decline. *Developmental Psychology, 23*, 611–626.

Baltes, P.B., Lindenberger, U., & Staudinger, U.M. (1997). Life-span theory in developmental psychology. In R.M. Lerner (Ed.), *Handbook of child psychology: Theoretical models of human development* (5th ed., Vol. 1, pp. 1029–1143). New York: Wiley.

Bandura, A. (1997). *Self-efficacy: The exercise of control.* New York: Freeman.

Bengtson, V.L., Reedy, M.N., & Gordon, C. (1985). Aging and self-conceptions: Personality processes and social contexts. In J.E. Birren & K.W. Schaie (Eds.), *Handbook of the psychology of aging* (2nd ed., pp. 544–593). New York: Van Nostrand-Reinhold.

Birren, J.E., & Woodruff, D.S. (1972). Age changes and cohort differences in personality. *Developmental Psychology, 6*, 252–259.

Bowlby, J. (1982). *Attachment and loss* (Vol. 1). New York: Basic Books.

Brim, G. (1992). *Ambition: How we manage success and failure throughout our lives.* New York: Basic Books.

Caspi, A. (1987). Personality in the life course. *Journal of Personality and Social Psychology, 53*(6), 1203–1213.

Caspi, A., Bem, D.J., & Elder, G.H., Jr. (1989). Continuities and consequences of interactional styles across the life course. *Journal of Personality, 57,* 375–406.

Caspi, A., & Moffitt, T.E. (1993). When do individual differences matter? A paradoxical theory of personality coherence. *Psychological Inquiry, 4*(4), 247–271.

Caspi, A., & Roberts, B.W. (1999). Personality continuity and change across the life course (pp. 300–326). In L.A. Pervin & O.P. John (Eds.), *Handbook of personality: Theory and research* (2nd ed.). New York: Guilford Press.

Clarke-Plaskie, M., & Lachman, M.E. (1999). The sense of control in midlife. In S.L. Willis & J.D. Reid (Eds.), *Life in the middle.* New York: Academic Press.

Costa, P.T., & McCrae, R.R. (1980). Still stable after all these years: Personality as a key to some issues in adulthood and old age. In P.B. Baltes & O.G. Brim, Jr. (Eds.), *Life-span development and behavior* (Vol. 3, pp. 65–102). New York: Academic Press.

Costa, P.T., & McCrae, R.R. (1988). Personality in adulthood: A six-year longitudinal study of self-reports and spouse ratings on the NEO Personality Inventory. *Journal of Personality and Social Psychology, 54,* 853–863.

Costa, P.T., & McCrae, R.R. (1994). Set like plaster? Evidence for stability of adult personality. In T.F. Heatherton & S.L. Weinberger (Eds.), *Can personality change?* (pp. 21–40). Washington, DC: American Psychological Association.

Cross, S., & Markus, H. (1991). Possible selves across the life span. *Human Development, 34,* 230–255.

Elder, G.H., Jr., & Caspi, A. (1990). Studying lives in a changing society: Sociological and personological explorations. In A. Rabin, R. Zucker, R. Emmons, & S. Frank (Eds.), *Studying persons and lives* (pp. 201–247). New York: Springer.

Elder, G.H., Jr., & Hareven, T.K. (1994). Rising above life's disadvantage: From the Great Depression to war. In G.H. Elder, J. Modell, & R.D. Parke (Eds.), *Children in time and place: Developmental and historical insights* (pp. 47–72). New York: Cambridge University Press.

Erikson, E. (1963). *Childhood and society* (2nd ed.). New York: Norton.

Erikson, E.H. (1982). *The life cycle completed: A review.* New York: Norton

Featherman, D.L., & Lerner, R.M. (1985). Ontogenesis and sociogenesis: Problematics for theory and research about development and socialization across the lifespan. *American Sociological Review, 50,* 659–676.

Field, D., & Millsap, R.E. (1991). Personality in advanced old age: Continuity or change? *Journal of Gerontology: Psychological Sciences, 46,* 299–308.

Fleeson, W., & Baltes, P.B. (1998). Beyond present-day personality assessment: An encouraging exploration of the measurement properties and predictive power of subjective lifetime personality. *Journal of Research in Personality, 12,* 125–136.

Fleeson, W., & Heckhausen, J. (1997). More or less "me" in past, present, and future: Perceived lifetime personality. *Psychology and Aging, 12,* 125–136.

Freud, S. (1905). Three contributions to the theory of sex. *The basic writings of Sigmund Freud* (A.A. Brill, Trans.). New York: Modern Library.

Friedman, H.S., Tucker, J.S., Schwartz, J.E., Martin, L.R., Tomlinson-Keasy, C., Wingard, D.L., & Criqui, M.H. (1995). Childhood conscientiousness and longevity: Health behaviors and cause of death. *Journal of Personality and Social Psychology, 68,* 696–703.

Gilligan, C. (1982). *In a different voice: Psychological theory and women's development.* Cambridge, MA: Harvard University Press.

Goldberg, L.R. (1992). The development of markers for the Big-Five factor structure. *Psychological Assessment, 4,* 26–42.

Gould, R.L. (1978). *Transformations: Growth and change in adult life.* New York: Simon & Schuster.

Havighurst, R.J., Neugarten, B.L., & Tobin, S.S. (1968). Personality and patterns of aging. In B.L. Neugarten (Ed.), *Middle age and aging* (pp. 173–177). Chicago: University of Chicago Press.

Heckhausen, J., Dixon, R.A., & Baltes, P.B. (1989). Gains and losses in development throughout adulthood as perceived by different adult age groups. *Developmental Psychology, 25,* 109–121.

Heckhausen, J., & Schulz, R. (1995). A life-span theory of control. *Psychological Review, 102,* 284–304.

Helson, R. (1984). E. Nesbit's 41st year: Her life, times, and symbols of personality growth. *Imagination, Cognition, and Personality, 4*(1), 53–68.

Helson, R., Mitchell, V., & Moane, G. (1984). Personality and patterns of adherence and nonadherence to the social clock. *Journal of Personality and Social Psychology, 46*(5), 1079–1096.

Helson, R., & Wink, P. (1992). Personality change in women from the early 40s to the early 50s. *Psychology and Aging, 7,* 46–55.

Jacques, E. (1965). Death and the midlife crisis. *International Journal of Psychoanalysis, 46,* 502–514.

James, W. (1890). *The principles of psychology.* New York: Dover.

John, O.P. (1990). The Big-Five factor taxonomy: Dimensions of personality in the natural language and in questionnaires. In L.A. Pervin (Ed.), *Handbook of personality theory and research* (pp. 66–100). New York: Guilford Press.

Jung, C. (1933). *Modern man in search of a soul.* New York: Harcourt Press & World.

Kahn, S., Zimmerman, G., Csikszentmihalyi, M., & Getzels, J.W. (1985). Relations between identity in young adulthood and intimacy at midlife. *Journal of Personality and Social Psychology, 49,* 1316–1322.

Kogan, N. (1990). Personality and aging. In J.E. Birren & K.W. Schaie (Eds.), *Handbook of the psychology of aging* (pp. 330–346). San Diego, CA: Academic Press.

Lachman, M.E. (1989). Personality and aging at the crossroads: Beyond stability versus change. In K.W. Schaie & C. Schooler (Eds.), *Social structure and aging: Psychological processes* (pp. 167–190.). Hillsdale, NJ: Erlbaum.

Lachman, M.E. (1991). Perceived control over memory aging: Developmental and intervention perspectives. *Journal of Social Issues, 47*(4), 159–175.

Lachman, M.E., & Baltes, P.B. (1994). Psychological aging in lifespan perspective. In M. Rutter & D.F. Hay (Eds.), *Development through life: A handbook for clinicians* (pp. 583–606). London: Blackwell Scientific.

Lachman, M.E., & James, J.B. (1997). Charting the course of midlife development: An overview. In M.E. Lachman & J.B. James (Eds.), *Multiple paths of midlife development* (pp. 1–17). Chicago: University of Chicago Press.

Lachman, M.E., Lewkowicz, C., Marcus, A., & Peng, Y. (1994). Images of midlife development among young, middle-aged, and elderly adults. *Journal of Adult Development, 1,* 201–211.

Lachman, M.E., Maier, H., & Budner, R. (2000). *A portrait of midlife.* Unpublished manuscript, Brandeis University, Waltham, MA.

Lachman, M., & Prenda, K. (in press). The adaptive value of feeling in control in midlife. In C. Ryff & R. Kessler (Eds.), *A portrait of midlife in the United States.* Chicago: University of Chicago Press.

Lachman, M.E., Walen, H., & Staudinger, U. (2000). *Perceived trajectories of subjective well-being: Patterns and predictors in German and American adults.* Unpublished manuscript, Brandeis University, Waltham, MA.

Lachman, M.E., & Weaver, S.L. (1998). Sociodemographic variations in the sense of control by domain: Findings from the MacArthur Studies of Midlife. *Psychology and Aging, 13,* 553–562.

Lerner, R.M. (1976). *Concepts and theories of human development.* Reading, MA: Addison-Wesley.

Lerner, R.M. (1983). A "goodness of fit" model of person-context interaction. In D. Magnusson & V.L. Allen (Eds.), *Human development: An interactional perspective* (pp. 279–294). New York: Academic Press.

Levinson, D.J. (1977). The mid-life transition. *Psychiatry, 40,* 99–112.

Levinson, D.J. (1986). A conception of adult development. *American Psychologist, 41*(1), 3–13.

Levinson, D.J., & Levinson, J.D. (1996). *The seasons of a woman's life.* New York: Ballantine Books.

Levinson, D.J., Darrow, C.N., Klein, E.B., Levinson, M.H., & McKee, B. (1978). *The seasons of a man's life.* New York: Knopf.

Markus, H. (1977). Self-schemata and processing information about the self. *Journal of Personality and Social Psychology, 35*(2), 63–78.

Markus, H., & Nurius, P. (1986). Possible selves. *American Psychologist, 41*(9), 954–969.

Markus, H.R., & Lachman, M.E. (1996, September). *Attributes and traits: Collective and individual approaches.* Paper presented at the MIDMAC meeting, Cambridge, MA.

Mischel, W. (1968). *Personality and assessment.* New York: Wiley.

Mitchell, V., & Helson, R. (1990). Women's prime of life: Is it the 50s? *Psychology of Women Quarterly, 14,* 451–470.

Moen, P., & Wethington, E. (1999). Midlife development in a life course context. In S.L. Willis & J.D. Reid (Eds.), *Life in the middle: Psychological and social development in middle age* (pp. 3–23). San Diego, CA: Academic Press.

Montepare, J.M., & Lachman, M.E. (1989). You're only as old as you feel: Self-perceptions of age, fears of aging, and life satisfaction from adolescence to old age. *Psychology and Aging, 4,* 73–78.

Mroczek, D.K., & Kolarz, C.M. (1998). The effect of age on positive and negative affect: A developmental perspective on happiness. *Journal of Personality and Social Psychology, 75,* 1333–1349.

National Council on the Aging. (2000, March). *Myths and realities 2000 survey results.* Washington, DC.

Neugarten, B.L. (1968). The awareness of middle age. In B.L. Neugarten (Ed.), *Middle age and aging* (pp. 93–98). Chicago: University of Chicago Press.

Neugarten, B.L. (1977). Personality and aging. In J.E. Birren & K.W. Schaie (Eds.), *Handbook of the psychology of aging* (pp. 626–649). New York: Van Nostrand-Reinhold.

Neugarten, B.L., & Gutmann, D.L. (1968). Age-sex roles and personality in middle age: A thematic apperception study. In B.L. Neugarten (Ed.), *Middle age and aging* (pp. 58–71). Chicago: University of Chicago Press.

Piaget, J. (1974). *The origins of intelligence in children* (M. Cook, Trans.). New York: International Universities Press. (Original work published 1936)

Roberts, B.W. (1997). Plaster or plasticity: Are work experiences associated with personality change in women? *Journal of Personality, 65,* 205–232.

Roberts, B.W., & DelVecchio, W.F. (2000). The rank-order consistency of personality traits from childhood to old age: A quantitative review of longitudinal studies. *Psychological Bulletin,126*(1), 3–25.

Rodin, J. (1986). Aging and health: Effects of sense of control. *Science, 233,* 1271–1276.

Rousseau, J.J. (1948). *Emile or education* (B. Foxley, Trans.). London: J.M. Dent and Sons Limited. (Original work published 1762)

Ryff, C.D. (1995). Psychological well-being in adult life. *Current Directions in Psychological Science, 4,* 99–104.

Ryff, C.D., & Kessler, R. (in press). *Portraits of midlife in the United States.* Chicago: University of Chicago Press.

Schaie, K.W. (1996). *Intellectual development in adulthood: The Seattle Longitudinal Study.* New York: Cambridge University Press.

Sheehy, G. (1976). *Passages.* New York: Dutton.

Trapnell, P.D., & Wiggins, J.S. (1990). Extension of the Interpersonal Adjective Scales to include the Big Five dimensions of personality. *Journal of Personality and Social Psychology, 59,* 781–790.

Vaillant, G.E. (1977). *Adaptation to life.* Boston: Little, Brown.

Vaillant, G., & Milofsky, E. (1980). Natural history of male psychological health: IX. Empirical evidence for Erikson's model of the life cycle. *American Journal of Psychiatry, 137,* 1348–1359.

Whitbourne, S.K. (1985). The psychological construction of the life span. In J.E. Birren & K.W. Schaie (Eds.), *The handbook of the psychology of aging* (pp. 594–618). New York: Van Vostrand-Reinhold.

Whitbourne, S.K. (1987). Personality development in adulthood and old age: Relationships among identity style, health, and well-being. In K.W. Schaie & C. Eisdorfer (Eds.), *Annual review of gerontology and geriatrics* (Vol. 7, pp. 189–216). New York: Springer.

Whitbourne, S.K., & Connolly, L.A. (1999). The developing self in midlife. In S.L. Willis & J.D. Reid (Eds.), *Life in the middle: Psychological and social development in middle age* (pp. 25–45). San Diego, CA: Academic Press.

Whitbourne, S.K., Zuschlag, M.K., Elliot, L.B., & Waterman, A.S. (1992). Psychosocial development in adulthood: A 22-year sequential study. *Journal of Personality and Social Psychology, 63*(2), 260–271.

Wrosch, C., Heckhausen, J., & Lachman, M.E. (2000). Primary and secondary control strategies for managing health and financial stress across adulthood. *Psychology and Aging, 15,* 387–399.

CHAPTER 10

Emotional Development during the Middle Years

CAROL MAGAI and BETH HALPERN

A BOTTLE OF NOVELTY CANDY packaged to look like prescription medicine depicts a red sports car on the label and suggests that the "pills" be used for the treatment of the following symptoms: emotional crises, bad haircuts, and the purchasing of a new wardrobe. These candy pills are humorously labeled "Middle-Aged Pills." A The packaging draws on the stereotype of the middle-aged adult in crisis who buys a sporty new car and behaves in uncharacteristic ways. The notion of midlife as a time of crisis, precipitous change, and instability is alive and well in popular culture. Within the field of psychology, the picture is changing. In the past, the idea of midlife as a time of crisis and upheaval accompanied by painful emotional states was supported by research that focused on in-depth interviews with small groups of individuals (Gould, 1978; Levinson, 1986; Levinson, Darrow, Klein, Levinson, & McKee, 1978). More recently, a study of nearly 10,000 men and women ranging in age from 30 to 60 indicated no association between middle age and feelings of turmoil, confusion, family dissatisfaction, or meaninglessness (McCrae & Costa, 1990). Most relevant to the present chapter's focus on emotions and midlife, the study included a scale of emotional instability, which

Work on this chapter was supported by a grant to the first author from the Minority Biomedical Research Support Program and the National Institute of Aging (1 SO6 GM54650–01).

showed no tendency toward increasing instability during midlife. Nevertheless, questions concerning the existence and/or parameters of a midlife juncture filled with tension and turmoil continue to be debated in the literature (Bumpass & Aquilino, 1995; Helson, 1997; Hunter & Sundel, 1989; Klohen, Vandewater, & Young, 1996).

A somewhat easier topic to address is the range of years encompassed by the construct of midlife, though even here there is not consistent agreement. For the purposes of the present discussion, midlife as a developmental period will be used to describe the years between 40 and 60. Such a definition, obviously, only applies to populations in which the life expectancy of adults approaches or surpasses 80 years, but this will suffice for the present task since the vast bulk of literature on midlife is based on studies conducted in Western, industrialized countries and this is the literature we review.

The study of emotional development in midlife has generally been approached in one of two ways. The first body of theory and research treats midlife as a point along a trajectory of development. Thus, emotional development in midlife is understood within the context of emotional development across the life span. A second body of theory and research has examined the midlife adult's emotional functioning by focusing on events that are considered to be singularly characteristic of midlife and particularly infused with emotional salience. These include adjusting to the "empty nest" in the postparental years, entering or reentering the workforce, becoming the caretaker for an elderly parent, and experiencing the death of one's parents. From this second point of view, emotional development in midlife is embedded within specific events or changes that are typical of this stage of life. Although the two approaches are not incompatible, generally they have not been integrated. What follows is an overview of these approaches, beginning with theories that describe a trajectory of emotional development across the life span.

TRAJECTORY MODELS— THEORETICAL FORMULATIONS

We present the theoretical formulations of each model first followed by a review of the literature that addresses evidence supporting the models. Of the six "trajectory" theories reviewed here, some address the midlife period directly, while others leave implicit the particulars of midlife emotional development. The theories also vary in terms of whether they address the subjective, expressive, or regulatory aspects of the emotion system. Finally, the last three theories are explicit about the assumption that much of emotional development is linked to interpersonal process, whereas the first three do not address the issue explicitly.

DIFFERENTIAL EMOTIONS THEORY

This theory, which originated with Carroll Izard (1971, 1977, 1991), derives its name from emphasis on the qualitatively different nature of the primary or basic emotions. Each basic emotion, such as fear, anger, and joy, is said to have different neurophysiological, phenomenological, physiognomic, and motivational properties. According to the theory, the emotion system constitutes a separate subsystem of personality although it interacts with the other subsystems and constitutes the primary organizer of human thought and behavior. In a review of research informed by the theory, Dougherty, Abe, and Izard (1996) note that although most of differential emotions theory research has focused on early development, the theory can be applied to an understanding of life-span emotional development as well. The theory assumes that there are aspects of the emotion system that contribute to constancy as well as change across development.

A tenet of differential emotions theory is that the feeling states accompanying the discrete emotions do not change with time or development. That is, what it feels like to be sad or angry does not change with age. This constancy in emotional experience is attributed in part to each discrete emotion being associated with a distinct feeling that drives thought and action in a particular direction and toward a particular goal. These pairings of emotion and motivation and emotion and mental state are thought to be "hardwired" in the nervous system and to remain stable from infancy to old age. Thus, whether one is a toddler, teenager, or middle-aged adult, interest will always be experienced as a heightened awareness and will always motivate a focusing of attention; fear will always be experienced as dread and will motivate protective behaviors; and anger will always provoke feelings of frustration and irritation and will motivate efforts toward overcoming obstacles toward desired goals, and so forth.

According to differential emotions theory, the stability of the emotion system across the life span serves several adaptive functions (Dougherty, Abe, & Izard, 1996; Izard & Ackerman, 1998). First, it provides for a stable sense of self. The individual can thus move through broad developmental changes in cognition and behavior which might be destabilizing were they not embedded in an emotion system that provided for an underlying constancy of experience. Second, the complexity of interpersonal functioning might not be navigable if it were not for the temporal stability of emotion states and their associated motivational properties. In support of this view, Dougherty and her colleagues cite findings from the field of clinical neurology that social skills and social functioning become impaired when they are no longer organized and informed by the emotion system, as in cases in which the neural underpinnings of the emotion system are damaged. Finally, the stability of the subjective experience of an emotion ensures that the individual will be motivated to perform the adaptive behavior associated with that emotion. Otherwise, developmental changes in what it feels like to be afraid or to be angry might result in the individual not performing the behaviors that would be most adaptive in a situation of danger or impeded access to a goal.

Despite the elements of stability thus far described, differential emotions theory also admits that certain elements of emotional behavior and experience are modifiable over the course of development. According to Izard and colleagues (Dougherty et al., 1996; Izard & Ackerman, 1998), the capacity for significant developmental change is not located within the emotion system itself, but rather in the connections among the emotion, cognition, and action systems. One example of an emotion-cognition connection that changes over time is the ability to anticipate the emotional response of another person based on knowledge of that person. While the connection is initially dependent on the development of essential cognitive capacities in the child, a lifetime of accumulated interpersonal experience fosters an increasingly complex and multifaceted ability to anticipate emotion in others. A second example of an emotion-cognition connection that changes over time is improved facility at modulating expressive behavior to meet the more nuanced understanding of interpersonal processes. Such changes in turn create feedback and feedforward loops that influence one's social network, ideally facilitating the development and maintenance of social support systems. Other elements of change include the association of a discrete emotion with images and thoughts that greatly increase in number with experience.

Expressive behavior is another aspect of the emotion system that changes with maturation. Whereas the emotion expressions of young infants appear to be instinctlike responses to preemptive stimuli, there being little or no ability to postpone or alter the timing or shape of the response, in older children and adults expressive behavior is considerably modulated. There are changes in the formal aspects of emotion expression, such as the frequency and configuration of expressive signals. Changes are thought to occur throughout the life span (Izard & Malatesta, 1987; Malatesta & Izard, 1984).

Differential emotions theory does not specifically address emotional development during the midlife period. For example, the theory does not identify particular tasks or challenges to be managed by the emotion system during midlife. Rather, the theory assumes that crises and challenges will be present throughout the life span, not necessarily to a greater degree during midlife. Furthermore, differential emotions theory asserts that the emotion system provides a stable sense of self and personality across the life span; this stability would be maintained regardless of whether midlife is a time of emotional ease or emotional difficulty.

However, differential emotions theory also asserts that the links among the emotion, cognition, and action subsystems of personality grow in density and complexity over time. While this aspect of the emotion system is described as adaptive, increasing complexity may be experienced differentially by different individuals. Some persons in midlife may view increasing emotional complexity (mixed or blended feelings, ambivalence, appreciation of the multiple emotional ramifications of events) as an enriching aspect of the aging process while others may experience the increasing complexity of experience as perplexing and confusing and seek tension reduction through defensive coping patterns (Carstensen, 1998; Labouvie-Vief, 1996; Labouvie-Vief & DeVoe, 1991; Malatesta, Izard, Culver, & Nicholich, 1987).

Differential emotions theory proposes that certain aspects of emotional life are stable, whereas others may undergo change. Fundamental feeling states associated with discrete emotions are stable over the life course, but increasing maturity of the cognitive and behavioral subsystems of personality permits greater modulation in expressive behavior, greater complexity of emotional experience, and more nuanced understanding of interpersonal process.

Cognitive-Affective Developmental Theory

Labouvie-Vief offers a life-span theory of emotion that specifically addresses the midlife period, and that embeds emotional development within cognitive processes (Labouvie-Vief, 1996, Labouvie-Vief & DeVoe, 1991). Labouvie-Vief proposes that the trajectory of emotional development runs parallel to changes in both cognition and ego functioning. The theory assumes that the experience of emotion becomes qualitatively restructured as the maturing individual acquires more complex forms of cognition with which to reflect on the world and a more differentiated and integrated self. Using neo-Piagetian and postformal cognitive models, she asserts that the cognitive sophistication accompanying maturation processes across the life span provides an ever more complex scaffolding to support differentiated experiences of emotion and emotion regulation. However, since she also believes that cognitions must satisfy certain emotional conditions, there is also the possibility that the cognitive system misrepresents emotions, which accounts for the direction her most recent work has taken.

Although Labouvie-Vief does not delineate fixed stages of emotional development, the theory proposes a trajectory of adult emotional development linked to levels of cognitive/ego development. Generally, that trajectory is as follows. In late adolescence, as adulthood approaches, formal operations allows the individual to regulate emotions according to abstract ideals and societal standards. At this stage, the individual has internalized the rules and norms by which culture defines competent emotional behavior, accepts a conventional stance in which the inner emotional life is devalued as being immature, and adopts the customs and standards that are ascribed to adult emotional functioning; as such, the cognitive-affective system remains grounded in conventional language, symbols, and norms that stress conformity rather than change and transformation. Emotion regulation at this stage, while linked to a generalized abstraction reaching beyond the egocentrism of the young child, also includes a fairly rigid internalization of social rules and norms about emotional experience and behavior. Labouvie-Vief maintains that there is a need for the individual to reintegrate self-reference into the cognitive-emotional system to achieve emotional maturity.

In the beginning of early adulthood, and continuing on through the middle years, there is a shift away from the conventional orientation toward one that becomes increasingly contextualistic. Rules and norms for behavior are no longer viewed as absolute, but rather relativistic and context-dependent; thus cognitions and behavior become more individualized and customized to particular times and circumstances. This is accompanied by a growing subjectivity, autonomy, and self-exploration. These advances in cognitive and ego complexity usher in an important reorganization of self and emotional development. The more mature adult relies not only on objective, abstract ideals for emotion regulation, but incorporates a subjective perspective into a process of emotional regulation that previously relied on "objective" reality only. Labouvie-Vief refers to the process leading to this integration as a "de-repression of emotions" that becomes more prominent during the middle years. This greater conceptual and emotional complexity of the individual in the middle years permits increased flexibility of self-regulation and more mature emotion regulation. However, at the emotional level, the greater awareness of inner states, in which conflicting feelings may war with one another, makes for a certain degree of tension. Some individuals may not be capable of sustaining and resolving this tension, which may prompt a retreat into more defensive modes of operating. Alternatively, an individual may intensify his or her efforts at reconciliation and integration, and advance in ego level as well as emotional maturity. Further growth may accrue into old age, as well, though there may be limits. Although Labouvie-Vief's growth-oriented model suggests improvements in self-regulation over the life course, at least for some individuals, it also acknowledges that extreme old age nevertheless brings a number of reversals in cognitive and emotional adaptations.

In the context of this theory, Labouvie-Vief describes affective organization and change in terms of "cognitive/affective complexity," differentiating between two aspects of affect regulation related to the self. One involves maintenance of a positively valenced view of the self, with a corresponding tendency to regulate the self's behavior and values in line with social norms so as to avoid conflict. The other aspect of emotional development involves intrapsychic differentiation, greater blending of positive and negative affect, greater cognitive complexity, tolerance of ambiguity, and flexible affect regulation. The theory entertains the thesis that there may be both general, developmental trends reflecting improvement with age (although experience, ego level, and other cognitive phenomena, rather than age per se are implicated), as well as individual differences in the extent to which an individual has a preference for positivity or complexity.

Labouvie-Vief's theory maintains that the course of emotional development over the adult years involves qualitative changes in the subjective aspects of emotional life linked to increasing cognitive/affective complexity. There are changes as well in emotional regulation, as culturally defined proscriptions for affective behavior are loosened and a more self-authored system of management emerges.

CONTROL THEORY OF EMOTION

Richard Schulz's life-span theory of control asserts that emotions are not ends in themselves (Schulz & Heckhausen, 1997). Thus, affect regulation is not a goal of development. Rather, his theory relies on the construct of "control" to characterize all aspects of human development, including emotional development. According to this life-span theory of control, humans strive to control their environment and to experience events as contingent on their own behavior. Emotions provide feedback that enables individuals to regulate their control strivings. This regulatory aspect of emotion is the primary focus of the aspect of the theory that deals with emotion, although other functions of emotion are acknowledged. In Schulz's view, positive affect often serves to maintain control strivings while negative affect can motivate the individual to reroute control efforts in another direction more likely to result in control over the environment. This theory construes emotions as a kind of energy or fuel that enhances efforts toward control over the environment thus maximizing the chances for survival. If emotions were ends in themselves, the evolutionary goal of survival might be impeded were the organism to solely strive after engaging in pleasurable activities.

Schulz's life-span theory specifically addresses the midlife period. He suggests that the need to exert primary control over one's immediate external environment follows an inverted U pattern over the life span. He hypothesizes that primary control strivings peak around age 45–50 and then continue to decline into old age. However, secondary control strivings, which target the self and the self's internal processes, steadily increase over the life span, even into old age. Thus midlife is seen as a period during which an unprecedented shift occurs. After a lifetime of ever-increasing effort to control the external environment, primary control strivings reach their zenith in later middle age, followed by a steady decline. In contrast, attempts to regulate the self's internal processes continue unabated. Therefore, the theory implies that there is a significant shift from an external focus to an internal focus during later middle age. Schulz suggests that this shift allows for greater self-regulation of affect as individuals move toward old age.

This theory stresses the instrumental nature of emotions, its feedback functions, and emotion regulation. A trajectory is outlined in which outer-directed control shifts to inner-directed control during midlife with increasingly effective self-regulatory management of emotion.

Selectivity and Optimization Theories of Emotion

Like Schulz, Powell Lawton and Laura Carstensen have also focused on changes in affect regulation over the life course, but for them, emotions are central psychological processes rather than the means toward another end. Both authors propose that adults become more sophisticated at emotion regulation over the adult years. Of the two, only Carstensen's work explicitly addresses emotional life during the middle years.

Lawton (1989) has suggested that older individuals actively create environments that optimize the mix of emotionally stimulating versus insulating features toward the goal of "affective optimization." That is, older adults choose contexts and relationships that permit sufficient intellectual and emotional stimulation and they also tend to avoid situations that might provoke negative affect and conflict.

In a similar vein, but in the context of a more elaborated theoretical framework addressing midlife development Carstensen's (1992, 1995) socioemotional selectivity theory indicates that older individuals exercise a selectivity about interpersonal relationships linked to emotional goals, including efforts to regulate emotions and conserve energy. Indeed, the theory embeds emotional development across the life span within relationships (Carstensen, 1995, in press; Carstensen, Graff, Levenson, & Gottman, 1996; Carstensen, Gottman, & Levenson, 1995).

According to Carstensen, age-related changes in the interpersonal realm form the basis of changes that occur in emotion experience and emotion regulation over the course of the adult life span. As originally formulated, her theory was an attempt to account for the well-established observation that social networks narrow in later life, and to offer an alternative to disengagement and activity theories. According to socioemotional selectivity theory, the control of the opportunity to engage or not engage in social interaction is an adaptive strategy people use to regulate emotion, a strategy that is particularly important for the maintenance of well-being in later life because of aging effects that include heightened physiological arousability, reduced physical energy, and increased physical frailty. Social contacts decline in frequency and become limited to relationships that maximize positive outcomes (a sense of support, companionship, assistance) and minimize sources of negative affect such as interpersonal conflict. The observed changes in social relationships in old age, when viewed within a life-span developmental framework, then, is more appropriately viewed as highly adaptive and as contributing to successful aging, rather than a harbinger of decline.

Carstensen's theory assigns an agentic role to the individual, who in later life actively chooses social interactions with the goal of regulating affect; it also assumes that people are attuned to how much time they have left in their lives and that concomitant with the process of maturation and aging is a more keenly emerging awareness that time is limited. Socioemotional selectivity theory proposes that social interaction is motivated by basic human goals that change with age. There is a move away from the goal of experiencing novelty and acquiring new information toward the goal of achieving emotional satisfaction and maintaining a positively valenced emotional life; optimal emotion regulation characterizes development from young adulthood through old age. With the amount of time left to live inexorably receding over the adult years, there is a shift from the individual's focus on future-oriented goals to a focus on present-centered goals, which makes emotional experiences and associated socioemotional relationships more salient and important.

Carstensen's theory explicitly construes midlife as a time during which the goal of pursuing knowledge about the self and the social world, highly salient since adolescence and young adulthood, may still be paramount, given the continued demands of establishing a career and family (Fung, Carstensen, & Lang, in press). Knowledge seeking may be pursued during midlife even at the expense of emotional satisfaction. However, the shift toward pursuit of emotion regulation, with the goal of maintaining positive affect—a paramount goal in later life—seems to begin during the middle years (Carstensen, 1992; Fung et al., in press). From middle adulthood until later adulthood, frequency of contact with acquaintances should decrease, contact with intimate social partners increase, and emotion regulation improve.

The theoretical formulations of Lawton and Carstensen have primarily focused on emotion regulatory characteristics, processes, and functions over the adult years. Both construe aging as involving the process of acquiring more efficacious emotion regulation skills that help reduce the experience of negative affect.

ATTACHMENT THEORY AS A LIFE-SPAN THEORY OF EMOTION

Although not expressly formulated as a life-span theory of emotional development, Bowlby (1979) described attachments as central to human well-being "from the cradle to the grave" (p. 129). Unlike Izard in the previous section and Magai in the following section, who argue that emotion is the primary organizing force in development over the life span, attachment theory accords this role to attachment-related strivings. However, feelings and emotions are viewed as the basic "material" out of which attachments develop, and differential materials that accrue during development are at the heart of differential attachment styles and patterns of relating.

Research in this field, initially focused on infancy and early childhood, has subsequently grown to include the study of attachments in adulthood. This work has been led by Mary Main and colleagues (Main, Kaplan, & Cassidy, 1985) within the field of developmental psychology, and Cindy Hazan and Phil Shaver (Hazan & Shaver, 1987) within the social personality field. Attachment styles forged in infancy are thought to be carried forward from infancy through the development of "internal working models" of the primary attachment relationship that then generalize to other social partners. In general, researchers distinguish among three distinct attachment patterns—secure, avoidant, and ambivalent—which are associated with different emotional profiles.

The three attachment styles are associated with different styles of attentional strategy, affective communication patterns, and strategies of emotion regulation. Secure attachment is associated with a balanced affective repertoire and ability to contend with negative events without ignoring them or becoming unduly dysregulated. The avoidant or dismissive style is associated with dampened expressivity, a tendency to shunt negative affect from consciousness, and a tendency to engage in avoidance coping. The ambivalent or preoccupied pattern is associated with heightened affect expression, hypervigilence for distress, and emotionally demanding behavior (Magai, 1999; Magai & McFadden, 1995).

Attachment theory suggests that attachment styles, whether they be secure, avoidant, or ambivalent, should remain relatively stable once formed although changes in these patterns are possible through the adjustment of internal working models based on subsequent life experiences. Since attachment relationships are emotionally salient and significant conditions of life, a possible prediction from the theory is that changes in attachment patterns, if they occur more frequently during the middle years—as the midlife crisis formulations would have it—might substantiate the existence of midlife turbulence.

Different attachment styles are associated with different emotional configurations, emotion communication styles, and patterns of regulating affect. Attachment styles have been hypothesized to remain relatively stable once established. Study of changes in attachment styles over the life course might provide another means of gauging the quality of emotional experience over the life course and fluctuations therein. The attachment framework also permits us to hypothesize that changes in interpersonal relationships may precipitate some of the more turbulent emotional experiences of life and be a catalyst to changes in the structure of emotional organization.

A DISCRETE EMOTIONS FUNCTIONALIST THEORY OF EMOTION

This theory, as articulated by Carol Magai (Malatesta-Magai) had its beginnings in the early 1980s when she first proposed a life-span perspective on emotional development (Malatesta, 1981, 1982). This was followed by two later papers (Izard & Malatesta, 1987; Malatesta & Wilson, 1988), which began to sketch some of the theory's basic tenets. Earlier versions of the theory were primarily focused on describing the role that structuralized emotion played in personality functioning, whereas more recent formulations have attempted to address the role of emotions in precipitating change in personality structure.

As a discrete emotions model, this theory is in the tradition of Izard (1971, 1977) and Tomkins (1962, 1963), although a number of aspects of the theory are unique or offer more detailed exposition of certain facets, including life-span issues, formulations concerning the role of trait emotion in personality development, attention to expressive changes in adult development, and the addition of dynamic systems theory to account for personality change over the life course (e.g., Magai & Haviland-Jones, in press; Magai & Nusbaum, 1996; Malatesta, 1982, 1990; Malatesta & Izard, 1984). Its functionalist element calls attention to the functional properties of the different emotions as adaptations to life circumstances. As such, the theory addresses why emotions become structuralized in the personality over time as emotion traits, as well as why this structure may change over time.

In early development, certain emotional states are experienced more frequently than others. Those that are experienced repetitively over time come to characterize the self and become prominent features of personality. By the same token, feeling states that are experienced less frequently or that are disavowed or dissociated, also come to characterize the self, in this case, by their absence. By late childhood, these biases in emotional experience and disposition become ever more centered in personality. They become "crystallized" or structuralized in the personality. That is, they become central organizing aspects of personality that affect a wide array of information processing functions, behavior, and interpersonal process (Magai & McFadden, 1995). As implied by the term "structural-ized," these emotional biases or dispositions are thought to be relatively stable aspects of personality, meaning that individuals will be predisposed to experience certain prevailing emotion states and to respond to the world in certain characteristic ways.

Despite the evidence that emotions become crystallized in development leading to distinctive emotional traits that affect a wide array of psychosocial processes in personality, this model proposes and has documented some of the conditions of change (Magai, 2000; Magai & Haviland-Jones, in press; Magai & Nusbaum, 1996). Although there is substantial evidence for the stability of personality traits, especially those that are linked to temperament (Costa, McCrae, & Zonderman, 1987), there is also sufficient evidence for change to suggest that personality is not immutable to change over the span of the adult years.

One of the more challenging questions facing developments today is that of determining the processes underlying personality change. It is Magai's thesis that not only are emotional events and experiences formative features of personality and lend them a traitlike aspect, but emotions also are largely responsible for personality change. Emotional turmoil attendant on major life events constitutes one such occasion for deflection of the life course, but it is not typically sufficient. While experience with strong emotion—of either a positive or negative nature—may set structural changes into motion, for personality change to consolidate, the emotional experiences that are galvanized during meaningful junctures in life must be followed by sustained cognitive and emotional work. Magai has also suggested that certain emotional constellations are particularly vulnerable to the perturbation of life events, whereas others are more resistant (Magai & Haviland-Jones, in press; Magai & McFadden, 1995).

The theory further assumes that events that involve interpersonal processes are likely to generate the greatest degree of turbulence during disruptions to attachment bonds or during the emergence of new attachment attractions. Moreover, just as interpersonal process is assumed to play a key role in the development of emotional biases in children, interpersonal process is assumed to constitute a crucial factor in the destabilization of emotion traits in adult development. This aspect of the theory borrows liberally from dynamic systems theory to model changes in the personality structure of individuals with respect to emotional organizations.

In terms of expressive behavior, the theory assumes that emotional expressions undergo modification with neurological, intellectual, and social maturation, as individuals orient increasingly to the display rules of the family and the larger culture and learn to modulate expressive behavior in accordance with these conventions. Aspects of expressive behavior that are hypothesized to undergo change include the frequency, range, discreteness, and complexity of expressive behavior (Izard & Malatesta, 1987; Malatesta & Izard, 1984).

The theory has suggested that over the course of the life span, expressive behaviors undergo change to address functional needs for social integration, that individuals develop emotional dispositions or biases that affect a wide array of social, intellectual, and behavioral processes, and that life events involving interpersonal perturbations can precipitate change in emotional structures. This theory makes no assumptions about what distinguishes emotions in midlife development. However, major life events may precipitate the kind of emotional turbulence that has been hypothesized to be one of the crucial ingredients in personality change. Because these events may occur at a greater frequency during midlife due to changes in work and family roles and alterations in interpersonal relationships common during the middle years (see later section on event-related aspects of emotion in midlife), the theory does not discount the possibility that midlife may provoke greater opportunity for structural changes in the personality. Although there may be a greater sheer density of life changes involving social networks—loss of spouse and friends—in the elderly versus the middle-aged individual, the greater regulatory capacities that seem to characterize old age may act as a stabilizing factor, mitigating such change.

TRAJECTORY MODELS—EMPIRICAL WORK ON EMOTIONAL DEVELOPMENT OVER THE ADULT YEARS

In this section, we consider the supporting evidence for the several theoretical models previously reviewed. Since the theories are primarily focused on stability or change in the subjective, regulatory, and expressive aspects of the emotion system, and in the structure of personality, we have organized our treatment of the empirical literature so as to address issues of change in each of these four areas. As indicated, the data suggest that for the most part, as adults age, emotional functioning improves, certainly through middle age and perhaps well beyond, although some authors urge caution with respect to this interpretation (Labouvie-Vief & DeVoe, 1991, 1996; Magai, 1998).

SUBJECTIVE EXPERIENCE

In contrast to studies conducted 20 to 40 years ago using largely institutionalized samples of older adults, which suggested that aging is accompanied by an increase in negative affect (Malatesta, 1981), more recent studies based on community-dwelling show a different pattern.

Changes in Positive and Negative Affect

In terms of positive affect, several studies indicate that positive affect either remains the same or increases over the adult years until very late life, when there is a decline. A cross-national study of 169,776 people in 16 countries found that reported level of happiness was constant from ages 15 to 65+ (Inglehart, 1990). The National Opinion Research Center's General Social Survey (GSS; Davis & Smith, 1995), which has measured well-being over the past 25 years, found that the percentage of people state that they are "very happy" rises incrementally across age cohorts until reaching the oldest, when it then declines. A similar finding was obtained in the Berlin Aging Study (Staudinger, Freund, Linden & Maas, 1999). In two longitudinal studies that compared levels of positive affect in the young-old and old-old, researchers found that positive affect declines only in the oldest individuals.

In terms of negative affect, Almeida (1998) examined daily, weekly, and monthly recall of distress (anxiety, sadness, anger) in 1,031 adults ranging in age from 25 to 74 years, as part of the National Survey of Midlife in the United States. Negative affect, as reported on both a monthly and a weekly basis, significantly decreased with age. However, no age-related pattern was found for measures of negative emotion experienced on a daily basis. These data might be construed as suggesting that negative affect lingers longer in young adults.

In a study that examined both positive and negative affect in a large sample of adults ranging in age from the mid 20s to mid 70s, Mroczek and Kolarz (1998) found that an array of complex factors underlie the relation between age and affect. While significant age effects were found for both positive and negative affect, the age effects were small, accounting for less than 1% of the variance. On the surface, the findings are easily summarized with regard to age: negative affect was highest among young adults and lowest among older adults. However, a more complex picture emerged when multiple factors were taken into account. For example, age and negative affect were unrelated for women and unmarried men. The inverse relation between age and negative affect held for married men. With regard to positive affect, the findings are equally complex. A nonlinear relation between age and positive affect, in the form of an accelerating curve, was found for the entire sample. Analyzed by gender, a simple linear effect of increasing positive affect with age was found for men, but a curvilinear relationship held for women. Interestingly, an interaction effect was found whereby introverted men experienced the most marked increase in positive affect with age. In other words, the linear relationship between age and positive affect was amplified by the personality variable of introversion. In contrast, extroversion moderated the age-related increase in positive affect such that extroverted men reported high levels of positive affect at all ages, with some increase in older age. The authors' findings suggest that future research should ask not just whether affect rises or falls with age, but "for whom does affect rise or fall with age" (p. 1345).

Finally, in the first experience-sampling study of emotion using a cross-sectional sample that included nearly the entire age range of adulthood, Carstensen, Pasupathi, Mayr and Nesselroade (2000) investigated emotions in everyday life. Rather than use global judgments of emotional experience that might have elicited participants' implicit theories about their own emotional functioning, Carstensen and her colleagues gathered data on emotional experiences as they occurred in everyday life, repeatedly sampling the same subjects many times a day over the period of one week. The findings are in keeping with much of the empirical work discussed so far. Early adulthood was associated with the most frequent experiences of negative affect. With age, negative emotions declined until approximately age 60, the upper bound of midlife, after which there was a nonsignificant increase. There was no association between positive emotion and age, although a very small, nonsignificant correlation existed that was similar to the significant but small correlation in Mroczek and Kolarz's (1998) study. No age variation in subjective intensity of positive or negative emotion was found. Finally, experiences of highly positive affect were more stable among older men and women. Periods of highly negative emotion were less stable among older men.

Changes in Affective Complexity

Several studies suggest that affective experience becomes more complex with age. Carstensen and colleagues' (2000) experience-sampling study of emotion found that age was linearly associated with more complex emotional experiences. Older respondents reported more experiences involving several emotions, suggesting that emotional experiences come to be infused with a certain mixed, bittersweet, or "poignant" quality, to use their term, even as affect regulation improves. Emotions become more complex and experienced more keenly as the limits of time and mortality become more salient. Carstensen and her colleagues explicitly link the quality of poignancy to a keener appreciation for what one has in life. Thus the emotional complexity that comes with aging, although bittersweet, is seen as an ultimately rewarding and deepening experience.

Labouvie-Vief and colleagues have been engaged in research on affective complexity for over a decade. One of their first studies (Labouvie-Vief, DeVoe, & Bulka, 1989) involved a content analysis of emotion narratives collected from younger and middle-aged adults, and the data indicated a developmental trend with respect to changes in subjective experience. They found that younger individuals rarely spoke of inner subjective feelings, were likely to describe their experiences in terms of normative proscriptions, and controlled their emotions through such metacognitive strategies as forgetting, ignoring, or distracting the self. In contrast, the middle-aged individuals in their sample were able to acknowledge complex feelings, sustain feelings of conflict and tension without resolving them prematurely, and were less influenced by conventional norms and rules.

Further work on changes in the affective quality of subjective experience is found in Labouvie-Vief's subsequent work on changes in self attributes over the life span. In a recent study, Labouvie-Vief and colleagues (Labouvie-Vief, 1998; Labouvie-Vief & Medler, 1998) examined how the self-concepts of people of different ages were organized and assessed the affective quality of self-attributes. There were 280 participants, roughly balanced for gender, comprising 5 age groups spanning the years 15 to 70+. Participants were asked to make self-attribute ratings of traits related to the big five personality factors. They also indicated how central or peripheral each attribute was to their self-concept by representing the self as a series of concentric circles, and indicated how affectively positive or negative they viewed these traits. Participants described both the real self and the dreaded self. Labouvie-Vief and colleagues found that younger individuals tend to maintain a positively valenced self-concept by allocating positively rated attributes to the core and negatively rated attributes to the periphery; however, for the elderly, this polarization was much less pronounced. In addition, the degree to which core positivity—the tendency to concentrate positive affect at the core of the self—predicted adaptive outcomes that varied with age. When core positivity was low, it was associated with higher depression in younger adults but with lower depression in older adults. In contrast, when core positivity was high, it predicted lower depression in both age groups. Thus, polarizing positive and negative self-aspects appeared to be important in early adulthood, but less so in later adulthood, suggesting that there is greater integration of affect with age. It also appears that there are two groups of older adults: One includes those who maintain high core positivity and thus avoid depression; and the other, those for whom maintaining less polarization is more adaptive.

In terms of scores on the personality traits, there were few age differences, with the following exceptions. Older adults (60–69) had significantly lower neuroticism scores than adolescents and middle-aged adults (46–59), with the scores for the other age groups falling in between. In addition, older adults described their self-attributes as less emotionally labile than those of adolescents and middle-aged adults.

In several other studies, however, Labouvie-Vief and colleagues found that there were age-linked changes in emotional development when other measures of affective organization were used. In one study (Labouvie-Vief;

1998, Labouvie-Vief & Medler, 1998; Labouvie-Vief, Romano, Diehl, Monos-Nigro, & Bourbeau, 1999), 149 participants were distributed over 7 age groups, ranging from 11 to 86 years. Measures of the study included an index of depression, well-being, verbal ability, and a measure of conceptual complexity of self-representations. For the latter, participants were asked to write a brief paragraph about the self, including likes and dislikes, and thoughts about the self. These statements were subsequently coded for conceptual self-complexity (i.e., complexity levels in the organization of emotion-relevant and self-relevant statements); thus, it may be best described as a measure of cognitive/affective complexity. At the heart of the coding scheme was an assessment of the degree of differentiation and integration of affective experiences, the use of reflection; differentiation of the self from parents, peers, norms, and institutions; the awareness of reciprocity in affective transactions; and an examination of the affective self in terms of complex psychological process and transformation.

The material was also independently coded for affective valence, that is, the degree to which individuals' descriptions expressed positive or negative affect about the self, or whether it indicated a blend of the two. In a series of regression analyses, the researchers determined that affective valence and conceptual complexity are separate aspects of emotional development. Moreover, trend analysis indicated a quadratic effect of conceptual (cognitive/affective) complexity, with elderly adults (71–86) scoring significantly lower than the adult (30–45) and middle-aged adult (47–60) groups. The latter findings are in accord with previously reported age differences in conceptual complexity with young and old individuals scoring lower than middle-aged adults (Labouvie-Vief, Chiodo, Goguen, Diehl, & Orwoll, 1995; Labouvie-Vief, Diehl, Chiodo, & Coyle, 1995).

The findings were more differentiated when subgroups were formed based on whether they were high or low on the valence or affective complexity dimensions. These groups represented quite different emotion regulation styles:

- The high positive affect/high complexity group appeared to be the most well-adjusted overall. They combined high conceptual complexity, openness, objectivity, and tolerance of ambiguity with high positive affect, low negative affect, low levels of depression, and high levels of well-being. This group was the group most likely to report secure attachment.
- The high positive affect/low complexity group, in contrast, showed the lowest level of objectivity, tolerance, intellectual ability, and openness. Yet this group had the highest level of positive affect overall, as well as the highest self-ratings on subjective well-being, denial, and repression. However, objective indicators showed that this group may

misreport important adaptive outcomes such as medications taken. This group was most likely to report avoidant attachment.

- The low positive/high complexity group was the highest in objectivity and tolerance. However, they were lower in positive affect and well-being and higher in depression, negative affect, and affect blends. Persons in this group were the most likely to report fearful attachment.
- The low positive affect/low complexity group represented the poorest picture, with low intellectual functioning and complexity but high levels of negative affect, depression, and low well-being. This group was the most likely to report preoccupied attachment.

Age differences in the distribution of these styles were not found, though this may be due to the small sample size.

From the preceding studies, it would appear that emotional complexity—the interaction and integration of emotion and cognition—is enhanced with age, supporting the theories of Labouvie-Vief and Izard. Further, the greatest enhancement is seen during the middle years. However, the general trend toward increasing affective complexity up to and throughout the middle years does not hold for all individuals (Diehl, Coyle, & Labouvie-Vief, 1996; Labouvie-Vief, 1996). Moreover, the research of Labouvie-Vief and colleagues suggests that adults who do not have a well-developed capacity for cognitive/affective complexity may be limited in their use of the more mature coping strategies that are necessary for adaptive emotion regulation. Thus increasing age may be associated with greater limitation in emotion functioning rather than a deepening of experience.

Our review of the literature on subjective emotional experience indicates that positivity (positive affect) and cognitive/emotional complexity appear to be two different aspects of emotional development. Recent studies indicate that positive affect is preserved over the course of the adult years, and that there may even be gains, although for the oldest old there appears to be a decline. The data also suggest that there is a curvilinear function with respect to cognitive/affective complexity from young adulthood to old age, with the highest level attained during the middle years.

CHANGES IN EMOTION REGULATION

Emerging data seem to indicate that emotion regulation strategies change with age. In the Labouvie-Vief (1998; Labouvie-Vief & Medlar, 1998) study mentioned previously, there appeared to be two aspects of emotional development—a positively valenced self-core that remains positive over the adult years and a more complex, reflective aspect that is related to cognitive complexity and shows a curvilinear relation to age. Both styles may be different core emotion regulation strategies or facets of affect regulation. Labouvie-Vief (1998) refers to the style that is responsible for maintaining an affectively positive core as involving an equilibrium-regulating strategy; negative affect is dampened and deviation from positive affect forestalled. The other strategy permits movement into a zone that is "far from equilibrium"; it tolerates deviation and even seeks it out; this style is referred to as one of "deviation amplification through exploration." The first style relies on creating a self-structure that optimizes positive affect by keeping positive and negative aspects of the self at maximal distance from one another. The other style is more drawn to exploration, and places a premium on objectivity, flexibility, tolerance for ambiguity, and the ability to explore and understand complex emotional experiences; deviation amplification eventually integrates positive and negative affect into a new structure. There are likely substantial individual differences in preference for these two strategies of emotion regulation as well as age-related changes in use of these two styles. In old age, given greater physical frailty and reduced energy reserves, there may well be a shift to preference for maintaining a positive equilibrium for the self. If so, this would explain why older persons seem oriented toward optimizing positive affect by avoiding conflict and seem better at this kind of emotion regulation than younger individuals. It would also help explain Carstensen's socioemotional selectivity effects—the preference for familiarity when it comes to social relationships and the reduction in novelty seeking, with both apparently involving equilibrium-maintaining strategies.

Another study by Diehl et al. (1996) has also reported changes in emotion regulation with age in a sample of individuals ranging in age from early adolescence to old age. Several age-related differences in emotion regulation were found. Older adults were more likely than younger adults to suppress their feelings in response to situations of conflict. They preferred to delay the expression of their feelings until an appropriate time. Older adults were also more likely to offer positive and cheerful interpretations of conflict situations. The authors interpret these differences as indicating that the older adult uses more mature defenses and exhibits better impulse control, although it seems equally appropriate to interpret the data as indicating that the older adults were better able to regulate their affect in response to stress. All age trends were linear with no special effects noted for the period of middle age.

The foregoing studies support the theoretical formulations of both Labouvie-Vief and Carstensen, to the effect that emotion regulation capacities of people improve with age. Schulz's control theory is supported as well by the finding that older adults seemed more willing to accept that some factors of life are beyond personal external control (primary control) and it is best to accept these factors (secondary control) rather than try to alter them.

Collectively, the data on subjective experience of emotion and emotion regulation suggests improvement in mood and a deepening of affective experience with age, at least until very old age. With aging, whether through social selectivity, increasing integration of affect and cognition, or a shift in focus to regulating the self rather than the environment, adults learn to regulate their negative emotions more effectively.

EXPRESSIVE BEHAVIOR: CHANGES IN THE EXPRESSION OF EMOTION

The vast bulk of research on the nonverbal communication of emotion has been conducted on facial expressions. Research has shown that there is increasing conventionalization of facial expressions across the childhood years, which in large measure involves adopting familial and cultural display rules and includes a general dampening of expressive behavior. Changes however, accrue during adulthood.

Malatesta-Magai and colleagues (Malatesta-Magai, Jonas, Shepard, & Culver, 1992) studied the facial expressions of younger (< 50 years) and older (> 50 years) individuals using an emotion induction procedure in which participants relived and recounted emotionally charged experiences involving anger, fear, sadness, and interest. Older individuals were found to be more emotionally expressive than younger subjects in terms of the frequency of expressive behavior under all four emotion induction conditions. The older people expressed a higher rate of anger expressions in the anger-induction condition, a higher rate of sadness during the sadness induction, greater fear under the fear induction condition, and greater interest during the interest induction.

The facial expressive behavior of older adults also appears to be more expressive in another sense. Malatesta and Izard (1984) videotaped and subsequently coded the facial expressions of a group of young, middle-aged, and older women as they recounted emotional experiences. They found that although the middle-aged and older women used fewer component muscle movements in facial displays than younger women, their expressions were more complex and consisted of more instances in which different emotions combined in one expression.

The preceding studies indicated that emotional expressivity is preserved, and perhaps even heightened, in later life when objective facial affect coding criteria are applied by skilled coders. However, there is some question about the communicative significance of facial expressions in older adults in interpersonal contexts involving ordinary untrained individuals. The musculature of the human face tends to lose some of its elasticity over the adult years, and with advanced age develops deep lines and furrows. Such changes may interfere with the clarity of the affective signal. Malatesta, Fiore, and Messina (1987) had a group of untrained adult judges rate, from videotapes, the emotional intensity and quality of emotion expressions of young, middle-aged, and older individuals who were describing emotional events in their lives. These naive decoders found the older faces somewhat more difficult to judge; moreover, the accuracy with which they judged the class of emotional event subjects described varied with age congruence between judges and emotion expressors, suggesting a decoding advantage accruing though social contact with like-aged peers. Thus, older individuals may have greater facility in discounting the "noise" of facial wrinkling so that they can discern the essential emotional messages of older social partners.

Though the data from the studies are cross-sectional and need to be replicated in longitudinal research, there appear to be developmental trends indicating increased complexity of facial expressions in terms of greater interindividual variability and the presence of more blended affects; this would appear to parallel the studies indicating increased affective complexity as judged by verbal behavior. Changes in facial musculature appear to obscure the meaning of affective signals in older people, but not appreciably so. These observed changes in facial expressions of adults over the life span are in accord with the theoretical formulations of both Izard and Magai.

STABILITY AND CHANGE IN EMOTIONAL PATTERNS AND PERSONALITY ORGANIZATION

Attachment Patterns

Despite the large and growing literature on adult attachment relationships, estimated at over 800 articles and chapters since 1987 (Crowell, Fraley, & Shaver, 1999), the vast majority of studies are based on a restricted age range. Stability studies conducted with infants and children and with young adults over two or three points in time all indicate that about 70% of individuals retain their original attachment classifications (Baldwin & Fehr, 1995; Campos, Barrett, Lamb, Goldsmith, & Stenberg, 1983). There are at present no stability studies explicitly looking at the middle adult years or late life. This means that Bowlby's formulation regarding attachment stability over the life-course is as yet unsupported. For our present purposes, such data would also be of importance to emotions researchers since changes in attachment patterns in the middle and later adult years might provide another means of gauging the quality of emotional experience over the life course and fluctuations therein.

Stability and Change in Affective Organizations

The stability of affective organizations has been measured using frequency measures of emotion such as the differential emotions scale (Izard, 1972), mood scales, and by clinical and/or personality measures of depression, anxiety, shame, and anger. Evidence across these various measures indicates that emotional dispositions are quite stable during adulthood. For example, Epstein and colleagues (1980) have demonstrated highly stable patterns of anxiety as measured under authentic arousal conditions. A study by Berry and Webb (1985) demonstrated that there is substantial intraindividual stability for other classes of affect-specific moods as measured by the Lorr Mood Test; day-to-day correlations for the mood scales for cheerful, energetic, angry, anxious, depressed, inert-fatigued, thoughtful, and composed over three days ranged from .20 to .87, with a median of .66. The data were interpreted as indicating relatively stable underlying traits. Other studies report comparable stabilities over longer stretches of time. Izard, Libero, Putnam, and Haynes (1993) assessed the stability of 12 emotions in a group of postpartum women. The 3-year test-retest stabilities ranged from a low of .33 for fear to a high .71 for contempt with an average of .56. Williams (1984) reported that the 4-year test-retest correlation for trait hostility was .84. Finally, Magai (2000) obtained 8-year stability coefficients for anxiety, depression, interest, anger-in, anger-out, and total anger, that ranged from .47 to .75. Only anger-out showed significant change over the 8 years.

A handful of studies have looked at the factors that may be involved in changes in personality/affective organization; interpersonal factors were prominent. McCrae (1993) assessed the role of private self-consciousness, personal agency, self-monitoring, and openness to experience as potential moderators of the stability of personality. These personal characteristics were not found to moderate stability. On the other hand, Noberini and Neugarten (1975) found that losing a spouse was associated with a drop in coping ability. Miller and C'deBaca (1994) studied individuals who underwent radical change and found that interpersonal processes were prominent; one fifth of the respondents had been in therapy, and a number of narratives were striking for their depiction of the respondent's involvement in a group, workshop, or retreat, where intense affiliative relationships were experienced. Ullman (1989) examined factors involved in religious conversion experiences and found that such changes were precipitated by a sudden infatuation with a real or imagined figure of intense emotional salience. Finally, Magai (2000) examined the factors that may mediate changes in personality in a sample of 63 adults who provided self-report data on the degree to which they felt their perspectives, goals, personality, feelings, and ways of relating had changed over 8 years. Respondents reported moderate changes in all five areas and their reports of change were significantly correlated with reports by outside informants for all areas but goals. Overall personality change (an aggregate measure of all indices) was associated with positive and negative interpersonal life events of an intimate nature such as marriage, divorce, and death of loved ones that took place over the past 8 years, and was unassociated with other high and low points in people's lives involving careers, changes in residence, and more distant social relationships.

These studies lend support to Magai's thesis that emotion-related changes in personality in the face of emotional events are more likely to obtain in cases that involve interpersonal process—events that involve the initiation or termination of intimate relationships or other intense affiliative experiences, although additional longitudinal work is necessary.

The studies reviewed here, based on a wide range of methodologies, generally support the trajectory theories of emotional development previously outlined and indicate that emotional functioning is preserved and even somewhat improved over the course of the adult years. However, some caveats apply. First, in some cases large samples contributed to significant results in which the age effects for emotion were actually relatively small. Second, all the studies used a cross-sectional design and were potentially confounded by cohort effects. Longitudinal research by Carstensen and Labouvie-Vief, presently underway, should eventually help to disambiguate these results. Finally, as Mroczek and Kolarz (1998) and Malatesta-Magai et al. (1992) have pointed out, the improvement in emotional well-being and emotion functioning with age found in the various cross-sectional studies may be linked to a selective survivorship effect. It may be that happier and more expressive people live longer or that chronic unhappiness and emotion inhibition is associated with dying younger. Thus, survivorship, would account for the higher levels of positive affect, lower levels of negative affect, and greater facial expressivity in older versus younger adults.

Finally, attempts to fully understand the links between emotion and aging are necessarily limited when using a linear systems perspective (Fogel & Thelen, 1987; Haviland & Walker-Andrews, 1992). Affective organization across the life span sometimes changes in a saltatory, discontinuous way that may be best understood using dynamic systems theory (Magai & Haviland-Jones, in press; Magai & Nusbaum, 1996) and ideographic methods. Magai's discrete emotions, functionalist theory suggests that major life events may generate powerful emotional experiences that may be instrumental in precipitating life change and even personality change.

Though the issue of the normativness of life crises has not yet been resolved, we can examine midlife as a time of particular vulnerability to certain events that will occur with greater frequency at midlife and it is to this literature that we now turn.

EVENT-FOCUSED RESEARCH ON EMOTION DURING THE MIDDLE YEARS

In this section, we treat the literature dealing with midlife events that are not necessarily universal, but are certainly more common at midlife than in early development or old age. They are events that tend to generate emotional distress of varying degrees of intensity. The majority of studies on midlife stressors deal with issues of changes in family or work roles, the empty nest, assumption of caretaking responsibilities for aging parents, and the death of parents. While we cannot do a comprehensive treatment of these areas within the limitations of this review chapter, we have selected some studies as being particularly relevant or representative.

CHANGES IN FAMILY AND WORK ROLES

Stewart and Vandewater (1999) investigated potential consequences of the midlife review—the tally of goals so far achieved and those still in progress—an event widely assumed to be part and parcel of midlife. Their study focuses on the emotion of regret and asked, what is the value of acknowledging regret when reviewing one's life? Stewart and Vandewater theorized that the experience of regret in midlife accompanied by a wish to make major changes would be more common in those women who as young adults chose a traditionally feminine path: being a wife, mother, and homemaker; in contrast, women who were able to integrate work outside the home into their marriage and mothering would be less regretful and less desirous of major change in midlife.

Two longitudinal samples of college-educated women were assessed at multiple points during the midlife period. These cohorts were seen as coming of age when education and career opportunities for women were expanding. Furthermore, they entered adulthood under one set of social pressures, those of the late 1960s, yet they were experiencing midlife under another set of social pressures.

Consistent with the researchers' predictions, most regrets early in midlife were about having chosen a traditionally feminine role with a focus on marriage, mothering, and the home. Most of the regretors wished to make changes in the future that involved developing a career or pursuing educational goals. Very few regrets concerned not having pursued motherhood or other aspects of a traditionally feminine role. When the women were assessed later in midlife, those regretors who had not made the desired changes were significantly more depressed, significantly more anxious, and reported feeling significantly less physically healthy. When regret did not trigger positive change, there was a deleterious effect on well-being, mostly seen in the realm of emotional functioning. In a similar study, Carr (1997) analyzed the data for over 3,000 women at midlife who were participants in a longitudinal study. She found that the women who had not fulfilled their earlier career aspirations were significantly more depressed and felt less of a sense of purpose in life at midlife, even when controlling for the effects of social background, resources, and physical health.

In the Stewart and Vandewater (1999) study, an attempt was made to determine some of the factors predicting failure to achieve change. Examining Time 1 personality traits, they found that low personal efficacy and high tendency to ruminate or focus on negative life events predicted those women for whom early midlife regret was followed by failing to attain the desired positive changes in later midlife. The women who were able to change did not face any fewer contextual barriers, such as caregiving responsibilities for young children or an unemployed or ill spouse, than the women who did not.

The authors conclude that the experience of regret alone is not sufficient to motivate midlife change in women who made a decision early in life to pursue a traditional female role and in later life wished to achieve educational and career goals. The regret must be accompanied by personality variables favorable to effecting desired change. However, when regret is successfully transformed into change in the realm of career and educational goals, a greater sense of well-being occurs.

THE EMPTY NEST AND OTHER PARENTING ISSUES

For individuals who were occupied with parenting small children in early adulthood, midlife may be a time of separation from children who have grown up and left home. Thus, the empty nest is another typical midlife marker with significant emotional consequences. While the phrase "empty nest" conjures up images of bereft middle-aged parents facing a loss of purpose, the emotional impact of children leaving home may actually be more positive than negative (Adelman, Antonucci, Crohan, & Coleman, 1989; Carstensen et al., 1996; Glenn, 1975). Marriages improve and happiness increases. In particular, couples who maintain a positive relationship with their grown children seem to experience a second honeymoon after the children leave (White & Edwards, 1990). Carstensen and her colleagues (1996) studied the developmental course of marriage and found that positive emotions within the marriage follow a curvilinear pattern: initially high, declining during the first 20 years and becoming high again late in marriage. Some of this pattern was attributable to the finding that marital satisfaction decreased during the early years of raising young children and improved considerably when the children left home. All in all, the empty nest seems to increase positive emotion in midlife adults.

Certainly not all midlife adults are parents of grown children. It is no longer uncommon for women to delay childbearing until their later 30s or early 40s. Alternatively, some adults in midlife who have large families will still have young children at home during the middle years. Others will not have had children at all. Little research has been conducted on the emotional impact of becoming a parent for the first time in midlife or on the emotional impact of deviating from societal expectations by not having children at all. For adults who decided in early adulthood not to have children or who delayed having children, midlife may be a time when the decision of whether to become a parent becomes especially salient because of the decline in fertility associated with aging. In a study of midlife women without children, Ireland (1993) distinguished between the "traditional" woman who tried earlier in adulthood to become a mother but could not because of medical reasons, the "transitional" woman who became childless because of delay, and the "transformative" woman who consciously chose not to have children. The grief associated with being childless during middle age was most profound for the first group, traditional women.

BECOMING A CAREGIVER FOR AN AGING PARENT

Becoming the primary caregiver for an elderly or ill family member, usually a parent, is another midlife event that has become increasingly common, given the longer life spans of individuals in industrialized nations. Adults who take on such a role are subject to feelings of distress as well as pleasure. Williamson and Schulz (1990) examined what causes some caregivers of family members diagnosed with Alzheimer's disease to experience more negative affect than positive affect. They found that female caregivers reported more depression than males, regardless of the quality of the relationship with the family member for whom they were caring. Female caregivers also felt more burdened than their male counterparts, even when the amount of caregiving being provided was equivalent.

In an attempt to look beyond the gender differences in depression that are typically seen in the general population, the authors generated several alternative explanations for the greater incidence of depression in female caregivers. They suggest that the social constraints of the female role may make women feel more torn than men between their caregiving role and their wish for self-development and self-fulfillment in other arenas. They also hypothesize that female caregivers may have other nurturing responsibilities, again in line with the traditional social role of women, and are thus more likely to have sacrificed social and recreational activities to assume caregiving for the ill relative. The authors also suggest that women may be more disturbed than men by assuming yet another caregiving role relatively late in life, as they may have begun to pursue career goals when their own children grew up, only to be thrust back into the role of caregiver. By contrast, men who assume the role of caregiver after a lifetime of working or developing a career may welcome the shift of focus from that work to the domestic sphere.

DEATH OF A PARENT

As adults age, not only may caregiving roles shift, but encounters with loss and grief increase. The death of a parent is one of the most common events of midlife (Umberson, 1996). However, relatively few studies have focused on filial grief and the course it runs in midlife. (Douglas, 1991; Scharlach, 1991; Scharlach & Fredriksen, 1993). Umberson considered the death of a parent to be one of the most stressful events of midlife, one that has considerable impact on individuals' relationships with their own adult children. In an investigation of the impact of parental death during the middle years, Scharlach found an association between the extent of both initial and unresolved grief and the expectedness of the parent's death. In a subsequent study, Scharlach and Fredriksen interviewed adults in midlife who had lost a parent within the previous 1 to 5 years. They found that over half continued to experience emotional reactions to the death. The death of a parent in midlife has a long-lasting effect on emotional functioning. Finally, Douglas (1991) found some gender differences among midlife adults who experienced the loss of a parent. In response to the death of a father, women reported greater affect than men; in response to the death of a mother, both men and women reported strong affect. These results seem to reflect the gender differences in affectivity typically found in the population and underscore the role of the mother as primary caregiver. However, more research is necessary to understand the vicissitudes of filial grief in ways particularly relevant to midlife emotional development.

MENOPAUSE

No discussion of midlife change would be complete without a discussion of how this hormonal event affects a woman's emotional life. No matter whether a woman in midlife has already become a mother, is starting a family, or has chosen not to parent, her reproductive capacity undergoes a dramatic shift during midlife. Menopause is certain to occur sometime during the middle years. Much like the midlife crisis, this biological marker of midlife has long been associated with depression and emotionality and has been assumed to be a central event in the emotional lives of women (Barnett & Baruch, 1978). However, evidence suggests this is not the case. The biological changes that occur during menopause do not seem to be associated with depression (Matthews, 1992; McKinlay, McKinlay, & Brambilla, 1987). Yet some assert that the cultural narrative of the menopausal woman is negative and may have a deleterious effect on women's emotional functioning in midlife unless alternative models of well-being in the menopausal years are made available (McQuaide, 1998). Others suggest that the majority of women, regardless of ethnicity or socioeconomic status, have neutral feelings toward menopause (Wilbur, Miller, & Montgomery, 1995).

There is evidence that for some women menopause is associated with distressing symptoms that are exacerbated by coexisting negative affective experiences such as depression, anxiety, and embarrassment (Slade & Amalee, 1995; Wilbur et al., 1995). Without prospective studies, however, it is not possible to know whether the negative emotions experienced by these women predated their menopausal years. Further investigations are needed to elucidate the relations among cultural stereotypes of affective instability during menopause, emotional dispositions prior to menopause, and women's subjective experiences of menopause.

Research on event-related factors, much of it atheoretical in nature, has typically been propelled by the notion that midlife is a significant milestone accompanied by profound life changes. That is, the middle years of adulthood are frequently visited by life events of particular emotional salience and intensity. The areas we covered in this chapter touched on varied phenomena of midlife, including the assumption of new roles and burdens, changing reproductive capacities, conflicts between the drive toward self-fulfillment or self-development and social responsibilities, and profound losses. The fact that middle-aged adults often sustain such new pressures, conflicts, burdens, and losses with grace and—based on what the literature on age trends in positive and negative affect indicate, without retreating into deep and lasting depression—speaks to the resilience of the human spirit. However, this might be said about other epochs of life as well. Certainly, individuals during early adulthood face comparable challenges and often disappointments in the context of finding and keeping a mate, establishing a career, adjusting to the restricting of freedom that comes with having children, and so forth. In old age as well, deaths of spouse and friends, the emergence of major health challenges, and the like are occasions that typically generate considerable emotional distress.

Contemporary emotions theory helps us understand resilience during such events. Unlike earlier perspectives on emotion that regarded emotions as disruptive and dysadaptive forces in mental life, contemporary theories view human emotions as part of an evolutionarily grounded and fundamentally adaptive system. Emotional experiences and feelings motivate the pursuit of goals and provide for functional adjustments in behavior, and emotional expressions signal needs and intentions to others, thereby facilitating interpersonal support in times of difficulty. Life is filled with challenges and the emotion system helps us adapt; it also permits us to experience and savor the joys and pleasures that accrue from life's experiences. Midlife seems to be no exception.

CONCLUSION

Theory with respect to the course of emotional development over the life span has had a relatively short history, dating back only to the early 1980s, with the single exception of an early attempt by Banham (1951) that provoked little attention and failed to stimulate research (Malatesta, 1981). In this chapter, we reviewed six models of emotional development and noted that only half of them dealt explicitly with the middle years. The six theories address issues revolving around stability and change in the subjective experience of emotion, emotion regulation, expressive behavior, and continuity and change in affective organization over the adult years. The empirical literature was reviewed to assess support for these theories and for the most part sustained the theoretical formulations. The subjective experience of emotion with respect to overall positive or negative affect does not appear to change much over the adult life course, excepting for the very end when it is likely that severe and chronic illnesses alter the trajectory in an adverse fashion. Emotional experience appears to become more complexly textured, as judged by narrative material as well as facial expressions, with the greatest affective complexity in terms of verbal material being observed during the middle years, which is apparently linked to a derepression of affect. Emotion regulation appears to improve over the course of the adult years if our yardstick is the ability to maintain positive affect; the maintenance of positivity in later life appears to result from socioemotional selectivity and a shift in control tactics. It also includes defensive strategies that may involve avoidance of negative environments and repression of negative affect, although it is still not possible to rule out selective survivorship effects and cohort factors.

Research on stability and change in affective organizations indicates that emotion-based aspects of personality are relatively stable during the adult years and at least one study indicates that there may be no greater emotional instability during the middle years. Nevertheless, some emerging work also indicates that personality change is possible during the adult years and most likely involves affective elements and interpersonal processes.

There is need for further work in all of these areas to replicate and clarify the pattern of findings from this important body of theory and research. Longitudinal studies and those that include analysis of the middle years are especially needed.

REFERENCES

Adelman, P.K., Antonucci, T.C., Crohan, S.F., & Coleman, L.M. (1989). Empty nest, cohort and employment in the well-being of midlife women. *Sex Roles, 20,* 173–189.

Almeida, D. (1998). *Age differences in daily, weekly, and monthly negative affect.* Paper presented at the meeting of the American Psychological Association, San Francisco.

Baldwin, M.W., & Fehr, B. (1995). On the instability of attachment style ratings. *Personal Relationships, 2,* 247–261.

Banham, K.M. (1951). Senescence and the emotions: A genetic theory. *Journal of Genetic Psychology, 78,* 175–183.

Barnett, R.C., & Baruch, G.K. (1978). Women in the middle years: A critique of research and theory. *Psychology of Women Quarterly, 3,* 187–197.

Berry, D.T.R., & Webb, W.B. (1985). Mood and sleep in aging women. *Journal of Personality and Social Psychology, 49,* 1724–1727.

Bowlby, J. (1979). *The making and breaking of affectional bonds.* London: Tavistock.

Bumpass, L.L., & Aquilino, W.S. (1995). *A social map of midlife: Family and work over the middle life course.* Madison, WI: Center for Demography and Ecology.

Campos, J.J., Barrett, K.C., Lamb, M.E., Goldsmith, H.H., & Stenberg, C. (1983). Socioemotional development. In P.H. Mussen (Ed.), *Handbook of child psychology* (4th ed., pp. 783–915). New York: Wiley.

Carr, D. (1997). The fulfillment of career dreams at midlife: Does it matter for women's mental health? *Journal of Health and Social Behavior, 38,* 331–344.

Carstensen, L.L. (1992). Social and emotional patterns in adulthood: Support for socioemotional selectivity theory. *Psychology and Aging, 7,* 331–338.

Carstensen, L.L. (1995). Evidence for a life-span theory of socioemotional selectivity. *Current Directions in Psychological Science, 4,* 151–156.

Carstensen, L.L. (1998). A life-span approach to social motivation. In J. Heckhausen & C. Dweck (Eds.), *Motivation and self-regulation across the life span* (pp. 341–364). New York: Cambridge University Press.

Carstensen, L.L., Gottman, J.M., & Levenson, R.W. (1995). Emotional behavior in long-term marriage. *Psychology and Aging, 10,* 140–149.

Carstensen, L.L., Graff, J., Levenson, R.W., & Gottman, J.M. (1996). Affect in intimate relationships. In C. Magai & S.H. McFadden (Eds.), *Handbook of emotion, adult development, and aging* (pp. 227–242). San Diego, CA: Academic Press.

Carstensen, L.L., Gross, J.J., & Fung, H.H. (1997). The social context of emotional experience. In M.P. Lawton (Series Ed.) & K.W. Schaie (Vol. Ed.), *Annual review of gerontology and geriatrics: Focus on emotion and adult development* (Vol. 17, pp. 325–352). New York: Springer.

Carstensen, L.L., Pasupathi, M., Mayr, U., & Nesselroade, J. (2000). Emotional experience in everyday life across the adult life span. *Journal of Personality and Social Psychology, 79,* 644–655.

Costa, P.T., Jr., McCrae, R.R., & Zonderman, A.B. (1987). Environmental and dispositional influences on well-being: Longitudinal follow-up of an American national sample. *British Journal of Psychology, 78,* 299–306.

Crowell, J.A., Fraley, R.C., & Shaver, P.R. (1999). Measurement of individual differences in adolescent and adult attachment. In J. Cassidy & P.R. Shaver (Eds.), *Handbook of attachment: Theory, research, and clinical applications* (pp. 434–465). New York: Guilford Press.

Davis, J.A., & Smith, T.W. (Producer and Distributor). (1995). *General social surveys: 1972–1994.* Cumulative file (ICPSP 6217) [Electronic database]. Ann Arbor, MI: International Consortium of Political and Social Research.

Diehl, M., Coyle, N., & Labouvie-Vief, G. (1996). Age and sex differences in strategies of coping and defense across the life span. *Psychology and Aging, 11,* 127–139.

Dougherty, L.M., Abe, A., & Izard, C.E. (1996). Differential emotions theory and emotional development in adulthood and later life. In C. Magai & S.H. McFadden (Eds.), *Handbook of emotion, adult development, and aging* (pp. 27–38). San Diego, CA: Academic Press.

Douglas, J.D. (1991). Patterns of change following parent death in midlife adults. *Omega: Journal of Death and Dying, 22,* 123–137.

Epstein, S. (1980). The stability of behavior: II. Implications of psychological research. *American Psychologist, 35,* 790–806.

Fogel, A., & Thelen, E. (1987). Development of early expressive and communicative action: Reinterpreting the evidence from a dynamic systems perspective. *Developmental Psychology, 23,* 747–761.

Fung, H.H., Carstensen, L.L., & Lang, F.R. (in press). Age-related patterns in social networks among European-Americans and African-Americans: Implications for socioemotional selectivity across the life span. *International Journal of Aging and Human Development.*

Glenn, N.D. (1975). Psychological well-being in the post-parental stage: Some evidence from national surveys. *Journal of Marriage and the Family, 53,* 261–270.

Gould, R.L. (1978). *Transformations: Growth and change in adult life.* New York: Simon & Schuster.

Haviland, J.M., & Walker-Andrews, A.S. (1992). Emotion socialization: A view from development and ethnology. In V.B. Van Hasselt & M. Hersen (Eds.), *Handbook of social development* (pp. 29–50). New York: Plenum Press.

Hazan, C., & Shaver, P. (1987). Romantic love conceptualized as an attachment process. *Journal of Personality and Social Psychology, 52,* 511–524.

Helson, R. (1997). The self in middle age. In M.E. Lachman & J.B. James (Eds.), *Multiple paths of midlife development* (pp. 21–43). Chicago: University of Chicago Press.

Herbert, T.B., & Cohen, S. (1993). Depression and immunity: A meta-analytic review. *Psychological Bulletin, 113,* 472–486.

Hunter, S., & Sundel, M. (1989). *Midlife myths: Issues, findings and practice implications.* Newbury Park, CA: Sage.

Inglehart, R. (1990). *Culture shift in advanced industrial society.* Princeton, NJ: Princeton University Press.

Ireland, M.S. (1993). *Reconceiving women: Separating motherhood from female identity.* New York: Guilford Press.

Izard, C.E. (1971). *The face of emotion.* New York: Appleton-Century-Crofts.

Izard, C.E. (1972). *Patterns of emotions: A new analysis of anxiety and depression.* New York: Academic Press.

Izard, C.E. (1977). *Human emotions.* New York: Plenum Press.

Izard, C.E. (1991). *The psychology of emotions.* New York: Plenum Press.

Izard, C.E., & Ackerman, B.P. (1998). Emotions and self-concepts across the life span. M.P. Lawton (Series Ed.) & K.W. Schaie (Vol. Ed.), *Annual review of gerontology and geriatrics: Focus on emotion and adult development* (Vol. 17, pp. 1–26). New York: Singer.

Izard, C.E., Libero, D.Z., Putnam, P., & Haynes, O.M. (1993). Stability of emotion experiences and their relations to traits of personality. *Journal of Personality and Social Psychology, 64,* 847–860.

Izard, C.E., & Malatesta, C.Z. (1987). Emotional development in infancy. In J. Osofsky (Ed.), *Handbook of infant development* (2nd ed., pp. 494–554). New York: Wiley.

Klohen, E., Vandewater, E., & Young, A. (1996). Negotiating the middle years: Ego-resiliency and successful midlife adjustment in women. *Psychology and Aging, 11,* 431–442.

Labouvie-Vief, G. (1996). Emotion, thought and gender. In C. Magai & S.H. McFadden (Eds.), *Handbook of emotion, adult development, and aging* (pp. 101–115). San Diego, CA: Academic Press.

Labouvie-Vief, G. (1998, August). *Processing of negative affect in later life.* Paper presented at the annual meeting of the American Psychological Association, San Francisco.

Labouvie-Vief, G., Chiodo, L.M., Goguen, L.A., Diehl, M., & Orwoll, L. (1995). Representations of self across the life span. *Psychology and Aging, 10,* 404–415.

Labouvie-Vief, G., & DeVoe, M.R. (1991). Emotion regulation in adulthood and later life: A developmental view. In M.P. Lawton (Series Ed.) & K.W. Schaie (Vol. Ed.), *Annual review of gerontology and geriatrics: Focus on emotion and adult development* (Vol. 17, pp. 172–194). New York: Springer.

Labouvie-Vief, G., DeVoe, M., & Bulka, D. (1989). Speaking about feelings: Conceptions of emotion across the life span. *Psychology and Aging, 4,* 425–437.

Labouvie-Vief, G., Diehl, M., Chiodo, L.M., & Coyle, N. (1995). Representations of self and parents across the life span. *Journal of Adult Development, 2,* 207–222.

Labouvie-Vief, G., & Medler, S.M. (1998, November). *Positive, negative, and complex affect: Their roles in life span development.* Paper presented at the annual meeting of the Gerontological Society of America.

Labouvie-Vief, G., Romano, E.H., Diehl, M., Nonos-Nigro, E., & Bourbeau, L. (1999). *Differentiation and affective valence of self-facets: A life-span developmental study.* Manuscript in preparation.

Lawton, M.P. (1989). Environmental proactivity and affect in older people. In S. Spacapan & S. Oskamp (Eds.), *The social psychology of aging* (pp. 135–163). Newbury Park, CA: Sage.

Levenson, R.W., Carstensen, L.L., Friesen, W.V., & Ekman, P. (1991). Emotion, physiology, and expression in old age. *Psychology and Aging, 6,* 28–35.

Levinson, D.J. (1986). A conception of adult development. *American Psychologist, 41,* 3–13.

Levinson, D.J., Darrow, C.N., Klein, E.B., Levinson, M.H., & McKee, B. (1978). *The seasons of a man's life.* New York: Knopf.

Magai, C. (1999). Affect, imagery, attachment: Working models of interpersonal affect and the socialization of emotion. In J. Cassidy & P. Shaver (Eds.), *Handbook of attachment theory and research* (pp. 787–802). New York: Guilford Press.

Magai, C. (2000). Personality change in adulthood: Loci of change and the role of interpersonal process. *International Journal of Aging and Human Development, 49,* 339–352.

Magai, C., & Haviland-Jones, J. (in press). *The genius of emotion: Dynamic trajectories of lives.* New York: Cambridge University Press.

Magai, C., & McFadden, S.H. (1995). *The role of emotions in social and personality development: History, theory, and research* (Series on emotion and personality). New York: Plenum Press.

Magai, C., & Nusbaum, B. (1996). Personality change in adulthood: Dynamic systems, emotions, and the transformed self. In C. Magai & S. McFadden (Eds.), *Handbook of emotion, adult development and aging* (pp. 403–420). San Diego, CA: Academic Press.

Main, M., Kaplan, N., & Cassidy, J. (1985). Security in infancy, childhood, and adulthood: A move to the level of representation. *Monographs of the Society for Research in Child Development, 50*(1–2, Serial No. 209).

Malatesta, C. (1981). Affective development over the lifespan: Involution or growth? *Merrill-Palmer Quarterly, 27,* 145–173.

Malatesta, C. (1982). The expression and regulation of emotion: A lifespan perspective. In T.M. Field & A. Fogel (Eds.), *Emotion and early interaction* (pp. 1–24). Hillsdale, NJ: Erlbaum.

Malatesta, C. (1990). The role of emotion in the development and organization of personality. In R. Dienstbier & R. Thompson (Eds.), *Nebraska symposium on motivation* (Vol. 36, pp. 1–56). Lincoln: University of Nebraska Press.

Malatesta, C., Fiore, M.J., & Messina, J. (1987). Affect, personality, and facial expressive characteristics of older individuals. *Psychology and Aging, 1,* 64–69.

Malatesta, C., & Izard, C.E. (1984). The ontogenesis of human social signals: From biological imperative to symbol utilization. In N. Fox & R. Davidson (Eds.), *The psychobiology of affective development* (pp. 161–206). Hillsdale, NJ: Erlbaum.

Malatesta, C., Izard, C.E., Culver, C., & Nicholich, M. (1987). Emotion communication skills in young, middle-aged, and older women. *Psychology and Aging, 2,* 193–203.

Malatesta, C., & Wilson, A. (1988). Emotion/cognition interaction in personality development: A discrete emotions, functionalist analysis [Special issue]. *British Journal of Social Psychology, 27,* 91–112.

Malatesta-Magai, C., Jonas, R., Shepard, B., & Culver, C. (1992). Type A personality and emotional expressivity in younger and older adults. *Psychology and Aging, 7,* 551–561.

Matthews, K.A. (1992). Myths and realities of the menopause. *Psychosomatic Medicine, 54,* 1–9.

McCrae, R.R. (1993). Moderated analyses of longitudinal personality stability. *Journal of Personality and Social Psychology, 65,* 577–585.

McCrae, R.R., & Costa., P.T., Jr. (1990). *Personality in adulthood.* New York: Guilford Press.

McKinlay, J.B., McKinlay, S.M., & Brambilla, D. (1987). The relative contributions of endocrine changes and social circumstances to depression in mid-aged women. *Journal of Health and Social Behavior, 28,* 345–363.

McQuaide, S. (1998). Women at midlife. *Social Work, 43,* 21–31.

Miller, W.R., & C'deBaca, R. (1994). Quantum change: Toward a psychology of transformation. In T.F. Heatherton & J.L. Weinberger (Eds.), *Can personality change?* (pp. 253–280). Washington, DC: American Psychological Association.

Mroczek, D.K., & Kolarz, C.M. (1998). The effect of age on positive and negative affect: A developmental perspective on happiness. *Journal of Personality and Social Psychology, 75,* 1333–1349.

Noberini, M., & Neugarten, B.L. (1975, October). *A followup study of adaptation in middle-aged women.* A paper presented at the annual meeting of the Gerontological Society, Louisville, KY.

Scharlach, A.E. (1991). Factors associated with filial grief following the death of an elderly parent. *American Journal of Orthopsychiatry, 61,* 307–313.

Scharlach, A.E., & Fredriksen, K.I. (1993). Reactions to the death of a parent during midlife. *Omega: Journal of Death and Dying, 27,* 307–319.

Schulz, R., & Heckhausen, J. (1997). Emotion and Control: A Life-Span Perspective. In M.P. Lawton (Series Ed.) & K.W. Schaie (Vol. Ed.), *Annual review of gerontology and geriatrics: Focus on emotion and adult development* (Vol. 17, pp. 185–205). New York: Springer.

Slade, P., & Amalee, S. (1995). The role of anxiety and temperature in the experience of menopausal hot flushes. *Journal of Reproductive and Infant Psychology, 13,* 127–134.

Staudinger, U.M. Freund, A.M., Linden, M., & Maas, I. (1999). In P.B. Baltes & K.U. Mayer (Eds.), *The Berlin Aging Study: Aging from 70 to 100.* Cambridge, MA: Cambridge University Press.

Stewart, A.J., & Vandewater, E.A. (1999). "If I had it to do over again . . .": Midlife review, midcourse corrections, and women's well-being in midlife. *Journal of Personality and Social Psychology, 76,* 270–283.

Tomkins, S.S. (1962). *Affect, imagery, consciousness, Vol. 1: The positive affects.* New York: Springer.

Tomkins, S.S. (1963). *Affect, imagery, consciousness, Vol. 2: The negative affects.* New York: Springer.

Ullman, C. (1989). *The transformed self: The psychology of religious conversion.* New York: Plenum Press.

Umberson, D. (1996). Demographic position and stressful midlife events: Effects on the quality of parent-child relationships. In C.D. Ryff & M.M. Seltzer (Eds.), *The parental experience in midlife* (pp. 493–531). Chicago: University of Chicago Press.

White, L., & Edwards, J. (1990). Emptying the nest and parental well-being: An analysis of national panel data. *American Sociological Review, 55,* 235–242.

Wilbur, J., Miller, A., & Montgomery, A. (1995). The influence of demographic characteristics, menopausal status, and symptoms on women's attitudes toward menopause. *Women and Health, 23,* 19–39.

Williams, R.B. (1984, March). *Psychological concomitants of cardiovascular disease in the elderly.* Paper presented at the NIMH conference on mental health aspects of physical disease in late life, Bethesda, MD.

Williamson, G.M.S., & Schulz, R. (1990). Relationship orientation, quality of prior relationship, and distress among caregivers of Alzheimer's patients. *Psychology and Aging, 5,* 502–509.

CHAPTER 11

Adaptation and Resilience in Midlife

JUTTA HECKHAUSEN

THIS CHAPTER DISCUSSES developmental regulation in midlife, particularly the way adults in midlife adapt to the challenges of developmental growth and are resilient to developmental losses. Adaptation to growth potential and resilience in managing losses are two major components of developmental regulation (J. Heckhausen, 1999). Midlife more than any other period of the life span requires the conjoint mastery of both these components of regulating one's own development.

One of the most intriguing puzzles of life-span developmental psychology is the myth of a midlife crisis (Chiriboga, 1989; Hunter & Sundel, 1989; Whitbourne, 1986). In 1965, Elliot Jacques (1965) proposed the midlife crisis as a normative crisis in early middle adulthood on the basis of a psychoanalytic approach to the awareness of death surfacing first in early midlife (mid-30s). Although the notion of a midlife crisis has received much acclaim, both in the scientific and public debate, it has failed to receive empirical support ever since then. Empirical investigations have resulted in midlife developmental patterns of continuous development, maintained well-being, adaptivity, and resilience throughout midlife (Farrell & Rosenberg, 1981; see reviews in Hunter & Sundel, 1989; Whitbourne, 1986), and did not uncover a midlife crisis in mental health as a universal or very common developmental experience. Despite this negative empirical evidence, the notion of a midlife crisis has survived as a public myth about development in the 4th and 5th decade of life. This survival of the midlife myth in itself is an intriguing pheonomenon, which calls for scientific explanation (Rosenberg, Rosenberg, & Farrell, 1999). It seems likely that this myth fulfills an adaptive function that lends it credibility and resilience. I will get back to this question in the section on midlife resources for adaptation and resilience.

Interesting theories and a lot of empirical research are available about coping and developmental regulation in adults at various age levels, including age-group comparative studies. However, many of them focus on comparing young and old or young-old and old-old adults, either ignoring the middle-aged adult group or addressing midlife without differentiating age levels within a broad category of middle-agedness. As a consequence, we still know much less about the specific characteristics of adaptation and resilience during middle adulthood compared with our knowledge about old age. However, there was a pioneer generation of studies about midlife development in the 1970s, which have been reviewed extensively elsewhere (e.g., Helson, 1997; Rosenberg et al., 1999; Whitbourne & Connolly, 1999). Many early studies on midlife development suffer from a restriction to specific subgroups in terms of gender (see review in Brim, 1976; Levinson, Darrow, Klein, Levinson, & McKee, 1978; Vaillant, 1977), socioeconomic status or profession (e.g., Gould, 1972; Sheehy, 1976; Vaillant, 1977), and to qualitative data collection and analyses (e.g., Lowenthal, Fiske, & Chiriboga, 1972; Lowenthal, Fiske, Thurnher, & Chiriboga, 1975; Neugarten, 1968; Sheehy, 1976), thus not providing the kind of empirical material and evidence that is comparable to research about the beginning or the end of the life span, childhood and old age.

A major contribution to our in-depth understanding of the processes involved in continuity and change of midlife personality as well as cohort-differential contexts are five longitudinal studies of college-educated women, that have been "harvested" in terms of publishing findings (see overview in Stewart & Ostrove, 1998): Ravenna Helson's longitudinal study of Mills College graduates of 1958 and 1960 (Helson, 1993), the Radcliffe Longitudinal Study of the class of 1964 (Stewart & Vandewater, 1993), a sample of 1964 graduates from Smith College (Stewart & Ostrove, 1998), graduates of the Class of 1967 of the University of Michigan (Tangri & Jenkins, 1993), and African American graduates of the University of Michigan from around 1967 (Cole & Stewart, 1996). These studies provided a rich set of findings and resulted in valuable insights about personality development throughout midlife. However, these studies also are restricted in social strata, and, only included women. Thus, it was time for increased efforts to promoting empirical research about midlife development in a sample that is heterogeneous and more differentiated in terms of gender, age, socioeconomic status, and ethnic background. This was the major objective for the MIDUS study conducted by the MacArthur Foundation Research Network on Successful Midlife Development (MIDMAC, director: Orville G. Brim). These efforts are just now in the process of bringing in the harvest (e.g., Ryff & Kessler, 2000).

This chapter starts by identifying on conceptual and, as available, on empirical grounds the specific developmental challenges of midlife adults. Subsequently, the major external and internal resources available to adults in midlife are discussed in terms of their effectiveness to attain adaptive developmental outcomes, and to be resilient with regard to the impact of major losses on psychological functioning. In this context, I pinpoint a set of key phenomena that are selectively characteristic of midlife and then investigate the available empirical evidence about midlife adaptation and resilience with regard to these phenomena.

DEVELOPMENTAL CHALLENGES DURING MIDLIFE

What developmental challenges characterize midlife and distinguish it from young adulthood and old age? First, we should take a broad life-span view of development and identify the overall age trajectories of key developmental dimensions. Second, we can then zoom in to the particular developmental tasks and transitions in midlife, which represent midlife-specific challenges for adaptation and resilience.

THE POSITION OF MIDLIFE IN DEVELOPMENTAL CHANGE THROUGHOUT THE LIFE SPAN

Two characteristics of midlife developmental challenge that result from their age-temporal position in the life course are discussed in this section. First, the composition of gains and losses is considered as unique between the first half of the life span with predominant growth and the last part of the life span with predominant losses. Second, the issue of lifetime finitude and its implications for developmental regulation is addressed particularly with regard to social motivation. This latter issue is recurrent throughout this chapter and also leads to a specific model of developmental regulation to be proposed in the last section of this chapter.

Midlife as a Life-Span Period of Continued Growth and Emerging Decline

When we take a wide-angle view of midlife as a period of development within the life span, its most characteristic feature is its position between a part of life with predominant growth, addition, perfection, and gains and a part of life associated with decline, restriction, and losses. Based on life-span research as well as on laypersons' conceptions about development, there is a gradual shift across adulthood from a very large dominance of chances for developmental gains to increasing risks for developmental losses (J. Heckhausen, Dixon, & Baltes, 1989). In a study on conceptions about adult development, we asked young, middle-aged, and old adults to rate a large set of psychological attributes with regard to their change during adulthood (increase, decrease, stability), the expected onset and closing ages of this change, and their desirability (J. Heckhausen et al., 1989). Figure 11.1 gives the percentages and absolute numbers of developmental changes going on at consecutive decades of adult life, separately for expected developmental gains (i.e., desirable changes in terms of desirable attributes increasing or undesirable attributes decreasing) and losses (i.e., undesirable changes in terms of undesirable attributes increasing or desirable attributes decreasing). As shown in Figure 11.1, the midlife decades of the 40's, 50's and 60's are marked by a radical increase in loss-related changes relative to the early adulthood decades, when undesirable changes

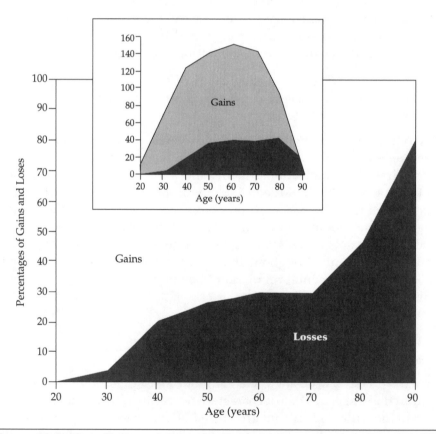

Figure 11.1 Quantitative relation of gains and losses across the adult life span. Percentages and absolute numbers. Adapted from Heckhausen, Dixon, and Baltes, 1989.

are perceived to be almost absent. Moreover, the absolute numbers of expected changes, displayed in the insert to Figure 11.1, illustrate that both gains and losses peak in number during midlife and early old age, (i.e., between the 40's and the 70's), with a total of about 120 to 140 developmental changes going on during the 40's, 50's, and 60's.

Many developmental growth processes that start in early adulthood (e.g., expertise development, improved emotional balance) continue well into old age. However, changes related to restricted time perspective and declining physical functioning, which continue into old age, will have started in midlife. What does this mean for midlife? In their middle years, adults have to manage the joint occurrence of growth and decline. Some areas, such as professional expertise or getting along with adolescent children are marked by finally realized perfection or continued learning. In some other areas, mostly those associated with high-level functioning in the physical domain (e.g., team sports, fertility), irreversible losses start to occur for the first time. This situation of simultaneous growth and decline involving various increases in stressors and challenges is reflected in the specific images about midlife held by adults at various age levels. Lachman, Lewkowicz, Marcus, and Peng (1994) found perceived trajectories of change from young adulthood across midlife to old age to involve notions of continued growth throughout midlife, continued decline, stability, and maximum or minimum growth, thus comprising a picture of more pronounced multidirectionality and multidimensionality (Baltes, 1987) in changes than any other period of the life span.

This situation of conjoint growth and decline requires a differentiated approach on the part of the midlife person. It is not any more a question of proactive "go-for-it," nor is it one of focusing on the maintenance of functioning. Instead, regulatory resources have to be carefully invested in select areas of individual growth and select maintenance of certain levels of functioning. Future research should address the ways in which midlife adults master the challenges of conjoint growth and decline, and investigate which socio-structural, biographical, and personality characteristics are associated with adaptive versus maladaptive development.

Growing Salience of the Finitude of Lifetime during Midlife

Another key characteristic and one closely related to the myth of midlife crisis is the notion that during midlife people realize with heightened awareness the finitude of life. Empirical evidence for this awareness of time running out is reported by Gould (1972). Endorsement of the item "There is still plenty of time to do most of the things I want to do" dropped between ages 35 and 40 and remained stable throughout the 50s (Gould, 1972). This increased awareness brings about a shift in perspective from one focusing on life lived from birth to life left till death (Neugarten, 1968). Erikson's (1963) psychosocial model conceptualizes the acceptance of life's finitude and an achievement of ego integrity as the major challenge of old age, marking the end of midlife. However, stage-theories of adult personality development such as the ones by Erikson, Levinson (Levinson et al., 1978), Gould (1978) and Vaillant (1977) all emphasize that it is during midlife when the fundamental challenges of a satisfying family and work life either are met or fail. Thus, midlife is the final "testing ground" for success or failure in life. It is what you achieve in midlife that allows or prevents a satisfactory life review and thus ego integrity.

Recently, the developmental challenge of constrained time perspective has received renewed attention from research on social behavior in young, middle-aged, and old adults (Carstensen, Isaacowitz, & Charles, 1999). Carstensen and her colleagues argue that constraints in future time perspective, or as they call it "social endings," lead to a reorientation of social behavior and perception from an instrumental and information-gathering mode directed at optimizing future behavior to a focus on optimizing socioemotional experiences. An expansive future perspective leads to a focus on knowledge-related goals and directs social behavior (Fredrickson & Carstensen, 1990; Lang & Carstensen, 1994) and information processing (Carstensen, 1998; Carstensen & Fredrickson, 1998; Carstensen & Turk-Charles, 1994) accordingly toward new and potentially informative social partners. Younger adults are more interested in getting to know new people, from which they can learn new information that might prove helpful for future action. In contrast, a limited or constrained time perspective renders information less valuable and leads to a greater appreciation of emotional benefits involved in social interactions. Therefore, older adults are expected to prefer, and selectively maintain contacts with social partners (see also Lang, 2000), they have known for a longer time and who promise emotionally meaningful experiences.

Figure 11.2 illustrates the hypothetical trajectories of information and knowledge-related goals versus emotion-related goals in social behavior across the life span. Interestingly, the figure places midlife at the crossover of the emotion and the knowledge-related trajectory. During midlife, the motivation for social behavior is expected to shift from information gathering to maximizing emotionally meaningful experiences. This hypothetical model of trajectories is supported by empirical evidence on age differences in the recall of emotional and nonemotional information after reading a story (Carstensen & Turk-Charles, 1994).

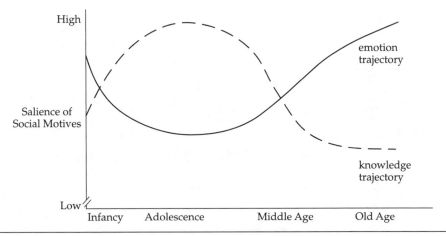

Figure 11.2 Idealized model of socioemotional selectivity theory's conception of the salience of two classes of social motives across the life span (adapted from Carstensen, Gross, & Fung, 1997).

Figure 11.3 displays the mean proportions of emotional material recalled by young adults, early-midlife adults, late-midlife adults, and older adults. It is between the early and late midlife group that the major increase in recalling emotional material occurs. So indeed, midlife seems to be the critical period when the shift from a predominant knowledge-orientation to an emotion-orientation occurs.

The conceptual and empirical contribution of the socioemotional selectivity theory is considerable and most intriguing, particularly because of its emphasis on lifetime as a determinant of developmental challenge to the individual. Time perspective is surely a fundamental factor in directing individuals' behavior and emotions. However, is time the ultimate latent variable in this context? In my view, time perspective may be a proxy for the amount of control the individual can muster at a given point in time. Based on a control-theory perspective, time is a major control resource in the following sense. The more time is left in the future, the more opportunities the individual can expect to bring to bear his/her control resources. Severely constrained future time perspectives render current states of affairs irreversible. Thus, from a control-theory perspective, it is the amount of control expected for the future and determined by future time extension that renders information versus emotion more or less useful. A critical test for this assumption would be to investigate the behavioral implications of domain-differential control expectations at a common age level and thus a common general future time extension. Under such circumstances, a control-based mechanism would bring about domain-differential behavior,

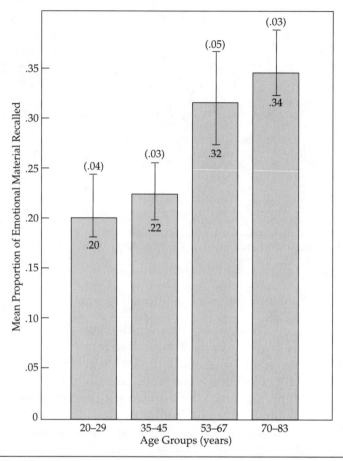

Figure 11.3 Mean proportions of emotional propositions recalled by age group. Means are: *M* = .20 (*SD* = .19) for young subjects, *M* = .22 (*SD* = .16) for mid-aged subjects, *M* = .32 (*SD* = .23) for older subjects, and *M* = .34 (*SD* = .15) for elderly subjects. Adapted from Carstensen, Isaacowitz, and Charles, 1999.

whereas a time-perspective based mechanism would have domain-universal effects. This issue is taken up again later is this chapter (see section on developmental deadlines).

SPECIFIC CHALLENGES OF MIDLIFE DEVELOPMENT

This section addresses specific challenges of midlife, some of which result from the implications of the temporal position of midlife in the life course for goal striving and dealing with failure. The first issue is the one of multiple challenges overlapping in time. The second addresses the challenges to developmental regulation that result from time running out for achieving long-term ambitious goals and associated emotional and motivational phenomena such as regret and feelings of urgency. The third issue involves the different challenges posed by age-normative and nonnormative events.

Multiple Simultaneous Challenges, Overburdening, and Vulnerability

Midlife holds a sandwiched position between early adulthood and old age and also between the generation of parents and of children. This sandwiched position brings with it a multitude of responsibilities and developmental tasks, and along with these multiple roles. When viewing these multiple roles from a perspective of limited resources and coping capacity, they may well give rise to excess burdening during midlife. Thus, one may refer to this pheonomenon of overburdering in midlife as the "midlife squeeze," "generational squeeze," or "sandwich generation" (Bengtson, Cutler, Mangen, & Marshal, 1985; Bengtson, Rosenthal, & Burton, 1990; Chiriboga, 1989; Hagestad, 1986). However, the resources of midlife are as outstanding as its challenges, and thus the key to successful development is the proper balance between stressors and coping resources (see also Chiriboga, 1989). Moreover, the burdening with multiple responsibilities at a given period of time does not affect a majority of middle-aged adults. Only about a fifth of midlife adults appear to be involved in assisting both a child and an elderly parent (e.g., Ward & Spitze, 1998).

The multiple challenge hypothesis about midlife is prototypically represented by women in midlife, who have to care for their elderly parents in addition to their other responsibilities as partners, mothers, and workers (Brody, 1990; Chiriboga, Weiler, & Nielsen, 1989; Moen, Robison, & Fields, 1994; Robinson & Thurner, 1979; Sommers & Shields, 1987). Brody investigates the burdening that results from adding the task of caregiving for elderly parents to the other responsibilities of midlife women (Brody, 1990). Women in midlife appear more vulnerable to stress because of the various social roles and their respective demands that compete for their personal resources. Parris Stephens, Franks, and Townsend (1994) found that role-related stress in midlife women accumulated in its effect on well-being across the three roles of wife, mother, and caregiver for elderly parent. Women with stress experiences in more than two roles reported worse physical health and role overload, and less positive and more negative affect. However, there was an upside to multiple roles. Multiple roles also hold the potential for rewarding experiences. Having rewarding experiences in more than one role proved to be beneficial with regard to enhancing positive affect and reducing role overload. Yet, it has to be said that the negative cumulative effect of stressors was more generalized across the indicators of well-being compared with the positive cumulative effect of role rewards. Further evidence about the benefits of multiple roles and identities is discussed in the section about internal resources for adaptivity and resilience in midlife.

DEVELOPMENTAL DEADLINES FOR ATTAINING AMBITIOUS GOALS

Another challenge related to the management of multiple goals and roles concerns long-term goals that hold the status of what Levinson et al. (1978) calls "The Dream." During midlife, the individual either fulfills or ultimately fails and has to give up many long-standing ambitions with regard to career, family life, property, or lifestyle. Thus, although younger adults may have fewer resources for attaining such long-term goals, they still can entertain the (potential) illusion to ultimately achieve their dream. However, midlife is the period of proof whether ambitious expectations can be met or finally prove to be unrealistic. Although these two constellations (young adult and midlife adult) in self-efficacy or control beliefs may look alike in terms of overall scale means, they represent very different outlooks on personal mastery (Heise, 1990). This illusion-reality shift in midlife is closely related to two particularly characteristic and taxing challenges of midlife, the experience of regret, and the management of developmental deadlines.

Because of the perspective of restricted lifetime resources, midlife is also when regret of earlier decisions about developmental paths can occur and lead either to activity that revises the wrong decision or to inactivity and thus potential dispair. Stewart and Vandewater (1993, 1998, 1999; see also Stewart & Ostrove, 1998) report findings about midlife regret from two longitudinal studies with women college graduates (Radcliffe and Michigan). A large percentage (34% in the Radcliffe and 61% in the Michigan sample) of the women interviewed at age 37 expressed regret about their past life-course pattern. However, when the regrets had motivated these women to redirect their life and achieve life changes by their mid-40s, well-being and mental health of the women with earlier regrets was similar to the nonregret group. Only those who had early-midlife regret and did not change their lifes in the regret-relevant domain experienced impaired well-being, more depression and rumination, and less effective instrumentality. This pattern of findings illustrates how perceived stressors can be compensated for by active attempts to regulate one's own development, a phenomenon to be discussed in greater detail when addressing the resources for adaptivity and resilience in midlife development.

The other time-related phenomenon of midlife is final time constraints for the attainment of developmental goals, referred to as "developmental deadlines" (J. Heckhausen, 1999; Wrosch & Heckhausen, 1999). The human life span is not homogeneous with regard to the opportunities to attain developmental goals. Having your first child in young adulthood is biologically facilitated and favored by society, although it would also be possible at somewhat younger or older ages. In many cases, these restrictions and norms about the age-timing of certain events and transitions not only regard the ideal timing, but also the latest possible or final timing representing an age-graded deadline for attaining a certain developmental goal. Because of its position in the middle between early and late adulthood, midlife involves a lot of such developmental deadlines. Before midlife, it is too early to have attained final achievements in long-term goals, and after midlife the individual moves out of a state of optimal resources in most domains of life and of functioning. Therefore, midlife is the heyday of developmental deadlines for long-term developmental or life goals.

AGE-NORMATIVE AND NONNORMATIVE CHALLENGES

Given that adults in a given society know about the biological and social constraints that accompany certain age transitions, they can also anticipate when a deadline for a given goal runs out. Such expectancies about upcoming deadlines can bring about anxieties to fail attaining the goal ultimately. Upcoming deadlines should spark urgent efforts by individuals, who cherish the goal threatened by the deadline. Moreover, the individual who passes the perceived deadline without attaining the goal needs to disengage from the futile goal and emotionally balance the loss of control, a difficult challenge that holds much potential for individually differential courses of resilience.

Thus, developmental deadlines represent prototypical and uniquely characteristic challenges of midlife development. Again, the burdening impact of upcoming or passed deadlines depends on the kind and age-appropriateness of the individual's attempts to regulate their challenge. A model of adaptive developmental regulation around deadlines for developmental goals along with findings from a set of studies is presented in the section on resources of midlife adaptivity and resilience.

Finally, as in any age segment of the life span, the issue of normativity of life events and transitions moderates the degree of challenge or threat an event has for an individual's system, of behavior regulation. Life-span developmental psychology has always emphasized the importance of distinguishing between different kinds of influences on life-span development, with age-normative influences being one of the three key categories (Baltes, 1987). Age-normative influences hold a close statistical relation to chronological age, either by way of biological (e.g., menopause) or societal (e.g., retirement) influences. This age-normativity makes these events predictable and therefore accessible by anticipatory primary (preparation) and secondary control (advanced disengagement). Moreover, age-normative events are familiar in the social community, and thus may involve more social support in terms of companionship in fate, as well as more salient and accessible social models of coping with them. In contrast to all these favorable aspects of age-normative events, events that are nonnormative can neither be anticipated, nor do they typically involve access to others with similar burdens, which would help as models or supportive companions (Schulz & Rau, 1985). Therefore, it has been argued that the lower the correlation with age, the lower the probability of occurrence, and the lower the commonness of a life event in a given population the greater the demands of a life event on the individual's resilience (Brim & Ryff, 1980; Schulz & Rau, 1985). However, there is little systematic research on the issue of differential burdening by more or less age-normative events, and therefore, future work should address this topic more directly.

Midlife development holds exceptional and highly taxing challenges for the individual's developmental regulation. The midlife challenges focus around a growing awareness about the limitations of personal control over one's life course. However, whether these challenges overload the individual and lead to detrimental outcomes of functioning and well-being depends on the resources available for developmental regulation. Among these resources, strategies and modes of developmental regulation and control in general hold a central role.

RESOURCES, PROCESSES, AND STRATEGIES FOR ADAPTATION AND RESILIENCE IN MIDLIFE

All the general, age-period specific and domain-specific burdens and challenges discussed in the previous section may lead one to the conclusion that individuals at midlife are overburdened by challenges. However, one needs to take into account that adults in midlife also have acquired substantial resources for mastering developmental demands and stress. Middle-aged adults may be at a significant advantage compared with less experienced and less resourceful young adults and also compared with older adults, who have decreased physical, psychological, and social resources to cope with stressors, negative life events, and developmental challenges in general. In this section, I consider conceptual models and empirical findings about three types of regulatory resources available to varying degree to midlife adults and moderating their ability to master the general life-course related and domain-specific challenges that confront them. These are resources associated with the immediate or broader social context including social support, general psychological resources, and specific techniques and strategies for regulating stress and challenge at midlife. Before considering in some detail these different types of resources and their influence on adaptation and resilience in midlife, I briefly address general conceptual models of resilience.

MODELS OF RESILIENCE AND PROTECTIVE FACTORS

The classic conceptions of resilience come from longitudinal research about children and adolescents who grew up under unfavorable developmental conditions (e.g., parents mentally ill, poverty, disrupted family) and yet attained comparatively adaptive developmental outcomes. These earlier conceptions and research programs, which laid the groundwork for empirical research on resilience and protective factors (Masten & Garmezy, 1985; Rutter, 1985), defined resilience as the adaptive role of an individual's response to adversity or stress (Rutter, 1990), the capacity to recover and/or maintain adaptive functioning after threats or weakenings of functional capacity (Garmezy, 1991; Masten, 1989), or sustained competence under stress (Werner, 1995; Werner & Smith, 1992).

Building on this work, Ryff, Singer, Love, and Essex (1998) propose a definition of resilience as the maintenance, recovery, or improvement in mental and physical functioning following challenge. This definition of resilience goes beyond the earlier conceptions in that it includes the possibility of improvement and developmental growth after a challenge that initially compromised developmental potential. Resilience and growth potential go hand in hand in that the mechanism allowing for resilience in overall functioning is also the key to a refocused investment into further developmental growth. It is through adaptation of goals and of goal-related control strategies that the individual confronted with taxing challenges not only can achieve psychological and physical equilibrium, but also can turn attention and resources to promising goal pursuits for the future. I present a theory and model for such adaptations of goals in midlife, which addresses the functional relations, phase-sequential activation, and adaptive capacity of control processes involved in developmental regulation.

Protective factors can be identified at multiple levels. Werner (1995) identified three levels of protective factors: within the individual (e.g., personality and temperament in infancy, childhood, and adolescence), in the family (e.g., close parent-child bonds), or in the community (e.g., support by peers and others in the community). Regarding the stressors that tax these resources and protective factors, Chiriboga (1997) proposed a similar multilevel differentiation between "microstressors" of everyday life (i.e., daily hassles), "mezzostressors" such as life transitions and life events, which may be anticipated to unexpected, and "macrostressors," which are given at the societal level and include historical events and transitions (e.g., war, technologicalization).

RESOURCES OF SOCIOSTRUCTURAL CONTEXT AND SOCIAL RELATIONS

Socioeconomic Status

A major resource for adaptation and resilience is socioeconomic status with all its facets, such as financial, educational, and environmental benefits. Socioeconomic status has direct material effects on physical and mental health (Adler et al., 1994; Dohrenwend, Levav, & Shrout, 1992; Kessler & Cleary, 1980; Marmot, Ryff, Bumpass, Shipley, & Marks, 1997). A detailed review of these effects is given in Carol Ryff's chapter (see Chapter 2, this volume) on social structural influences. Moreover, socioeconomic status may have indirect effects on the individual's capacity to control challenges and stresses. Kivett, Watson, and Busch (1977) found that middle-aged adults working in administrative and operative jobs had more internal control beliefs compared with adults in clerk or laborer types of jobs. Similarly, Lachman and Weaver (1998) found that middle-aged adults who perceived their work as involving high constraints, also reported less confidence in personal control than adults who perceived their jobs as involving less constraints.

Potential for Social Mobility in a Given Society

Another even more macrolevel resource of the larger social system is the potential for social mobility in a given society. The permeability of a social system in terms of upward or downward social mobility can be seen as a challenge or risk, as a resource or chance. The important implication for midlife development is that it is typically during midlife when the individual can achieve his or her final social position. Thus, an individual's ultimate success or failure with regard to intergenerational and life-course social mobility is decided during midlife. One can expect that associated feelings of triumph or defeat will be stronger in societies and birth cohorts with much social mobility than in those with little. An empirical illustration of the effects of life-course mobility present for middle-aged American men is the study by Farrell and Rosenberg (1981). They report about their sample of 200 early adulthood and 300 middle adulthood men, that professionals and middle-class executives attain comfortable, asymptotic modes of development during midlife with no indication of midlife emotional upheaval or even midlife crisis. In contrast, men who have remained unskilled laborers during midlife begin to show severe signs of personal disorganization and psychopathology during middle age. In between these two extremes of winners and losers, the lower-middle class men (skilled or clerical workers, small business-men) in Farrell and Rosenberg's study appear in their majority to manage life and keep feelings of disappointment, depression, or lethargy at bay by means of denial and avoidance. Despite temporary afflictions with doubt and regret, these men seem to be able to avoid major emotional upheaval, although a minority of 12% did in fact experience overt midlife crises.

Sociohistorical Differences in Normative Conceptions about Women's Life

A related phenomenon of societal or cohort differences in institutional constraints for developmental regulation regards the role of women, their family and work involvement. This is reflected in differences of images of midlife reported by different birth cohorts of women. Woods and Mitchell (1997) compared perceptions of midlife in different cohorts of women born between 1935 and 1955. Younger women in this study describe midlife more in terms of work and personal achievements than women from the older cohorts. Thus, it may well be that politicohistorical change during the 1960s radically reduced the gender-based constraint on women's roles and identities.

A most revealing study about cohort differences in life-course constraints for women was done by Helson, Stewart, and Ostrove (1995). They found that women who came of age during the 1960s had more integrated identities than women coming of age in the 1950s. In the younger more "liberated" women, moreover, well-defined identity was associated with better psychological well-being, whereas the older more constrained women were unaffected in their well-being by the quality of their identities. It is as if the women in the younger cohort had gained the capacity to make their own life, identity, and well-being, whereas for the older women, roles and constraints were set in such a narrow way as to not allow for psychological resources to even make a difference.

Another example of politicohistorical change in norms about the women's roles and the proper path through midlife is the role of marriage. Ever larger proportions of younger birth cohorts are likely to reach midlife or old age being single, either never married, divorced, or widowed. Half of the women currently in early midlife will reach old age unmarried (Uhlenberg, Cooney, & Boyd, 1990). Marks (1996) reviews the available evidence on relationship between marriage status and psychological well-being, concluding that there is an ever narrowing gap in well-being between the married and never-married across birth cohorts (see also Glenn & Weaver, 1988). Thus, "flying solo at midlife" (Marks, 1996, p. 917) may become an increasingly accepted lifestyle rather than a stigmatized life-course pattern. Marks also provides most revealing evidence about protective factors on psychological well-being to be discussed in the next section.

Social Support

Marital status may also have important implications for the availability of social support. Marital status has been identified as a major protective factor against negative developmental outcomes in adulthood. Married women and men exhibit greater longevity, better health, and greater psychological well-being than unmarried persons (Tower & Kasl, 1996; Waite, 1995). While marital status has many implications, what is the specific effect of social support provided by a spouse? In her study about the effects of marital status on well-being in middle-aged adults, Marks (1996) identifies three major protective factors for psychological well-being. Financial income was found to positively influence well-being. More importantly, though, the social support provided by a kin confidant was found to be a strong positive predictor of all components of well-being for both men and women (the only exception was autonomy in men). Thus, the midlife adults greatly profited from having "a person in the family with whom you can really share your private feelings and concerns" (Marks, 1996, p. 923). For a subset of well-being components, having a nonkin confidant was found to be beneficial, too. Given that married and unmarried adults differ in their access to financial resources and to a kin confidant, part of the negative effect of single status (never married or divorced) may be compensated when having sufficient financial resources and a kin or nonkin confidant. Moreover, this finding suggests that maybe the major benefit of married status may reside in the social support provided by the spouse confidant in a successful marriage.

Overall, research on social support in adulthood has found that protective effects of social relationships are especially salient when the individual has to deal with nonnormative events or chronic stress (Cohen & Wills, 1985; Schulz & Rau, 1985; Staudinger, Marsiske, & Baltes, 1995). Interestingly, it is not so much the number of persons included in the social network, but certain structural characteristics of social networks that determine whether social support can really serve as a buffer to stress. Hirsch (1980) studied the effect of the density of social networks on the health and subjective well-being of young and middle-aged widows. He found that women with less dense networks reported significantly better support and better mental health. Similar findings in terms of negative effects of high-density networks were obtained in a study on women whose spouses had suffered a heart attack (Finlayson, 1976). Maybe the reason for this is that within closely knit social networks such as families or vocational teams, the negative effect and shock associated with a major stressful event in the life of one of its members is enhanced by a kind of repercussion or multiple-feedback effect. It would seem more beneficial for the person affected by a negative event to have social contacts that allow her to take a break from venting the problem. Moreover, Hirsch (1980; see also Staudinger et al., 1995) has speculated that a less dense and more varied social network can provide multidimensional role models and expectations.

Finally, one may ask how differences in social support at midlife come about, and how adults may accumulate social support resources. Von Dras and Siegler (1997) investigated characteristics of social support behavior in a very large sample of participants of the North Carolina Alumni Heart Foundation during their 40s. Midlife adults who had high scores on Extraversion at the time of their college entry, during midlife exerted more social activity, perceived receiving greater social support, and also were more likely to seek support when faced with a stressful problem in midlife. Emotional closeness to parents in college-age young adults was associated with social closeness at midlife in terms of number of close contacts providing emotional and instrumental support (Graves, Wang, Mead, Johnson, & Klag, 1998). Moreover, a 32-year longitudinal study found that satisfactory peer social adjustment, no angry behavior, and a mentor relationship in young adulthood predicted a large percentage of the variance (26%) of overall mental health in midlife, including quality of social integration (Westermeyer, 1998). Thus, the development of sociability, outgoingness, and emotional closeness during adolescence and early adulthood appears to have long-term cumulative effects on the structure, functioning, and adaptiveness of social support at midlife.

PERSONALITY CHARACTERISTICS AS PSYCHOLOGICAL RESOURCES

Similar to the long-term cumulative effects of early sociability on midlife social support patterns, psychological resources of midlife individuals reflect the accumulated benefits of long-term maturation. Summarizing their findings about laypersons' conceptions about midlife, Lachman, Lewkowicz, et al. (1994) conclude, "Midlife was seen as a period with many responsibilities, increased stress in several domains, and little time for leisure, but also as a peak in competence, ability to handle stress, sense of control, productivity, and social responsibility" (p. 201). It may well be that one of the reasons most adults achieve an untroubled midlife transition is that by midlife they have developed their personality and effective strategies, so that the midlife challenges can be more or less smoothly met by psychological resources.

The prototypical personality resource to promote adaptiveness and resilience would probably have to be what is captured in Jack Block's concept of ego resiliency (Block & Block, 1980). Ego resilience is defined as the generalized capacity for flexible and resourceful adaptation to external and internal stressors. It "is a personality resource that allows individuals to flexibly modify their characteristic level and mode of impulse expression so as to most effectively encounter, function in, and shape their immediate and long-term environmental contexts" (Klohnen, Vandewater, & Young, 1996, p. 432). Klohnen et al. investigated the adaptive potential of ego resiliency in a sample of the Mills College and the Radcliffe college study. Self-reported and observer-based indicators of ego resiliency at age 43 were found to be significantly correlated with various measures of psychological well-being, quality of partnership, engagement in the work domain, physical health, and body image at age 52. Moreover, ego resilience at age 43 also predicted the change in various outcome measures between 43 and 52 years of age. These relationships seem impressive. However, one is left with the question of how to disentangle a concept that basically comprises the prototypical syndrome of adaptive functioning as an undifferentiated positive manifold. In addition, with a very broad concept of adaptive personality as is ego resiliency, semantic overlap with indicators of well-being and effective psychological functioning is likely to be substantial. Thus, in the end predicting adaptive psychological functioning in later midlife from ego resiliency in earlier midlife may amount to assessing the 10-year stability of adaptive functioning. Such information is interesting and far from trivial. However, it also does not reveal much about the psychological processes involved in mastering the midlife years.

The following studies focus on more specific, albeit still fairly broad personality characteristics and their relation to adaptive functioning in midlife adults. Particularly with regard to women, emotional and motivational functioning at midlife appears to be superior compared with adolescence and young adulthood or old age. For a subsample of the Mills Study of College Graduates and their spouses, Helson and Klohnen (1998) found increases in positive emotionality and decreases in negative emotionality between 27 and 43 years of age with a stability thereafter. These positive changes in emotional resources were related to concurrent increases in interests and social potency in terms of being motivated and powerful beyond one's inner family cycle. Moreover, they were also associated with decreases in emotional and self-image vulnerability, and increases in confidence and pragmatism between young adulthood and early midlife.

Similarly, Helson and Wink (1992) found for the women of the Mills Study that changes in personality during their 40s were not associated with salient events, such as menopause or a child leaving home. Instead, personality changes, in the context of much stability, appeared to be age-normative in this sample of early midlife women. During their 40s, these women seem to have become less feminine (high CPI-scores can be interpreted as being more decisive, action oriented, and objective; Gough, 1957/1987), less vulnerable, more responsible, responsive, and cooperative to others, self-disciplined and conscientious. Wink and Helson (1993), who studied a subsample of women from the Mills Study along with their spouses during the parental (around age 27) and postparental (around age 43) period, also report decreasing personality differences between the genders. Women in their early 40s attained higher scores on the factors competence and self-confidence, and lower scores on the factor succorance when compared with the scores obtained in their late 20s.

Moreover, for age 52 compared with age 43, Helson and Wink (1992) report superior coping styles in these Mills College graduates in terms of intellectuality, logical analysis, tolerance of ambiguity and substitution (goal flexibility). These characteristics may well have allowed these women to more adaptively respond to adverse or otherwise challenging events in their midlife.

Convergent findings in terms of femininity and with regard to specific protective processes come from a study by Bromberger and Matthews (1996). They report on a sample of postmenopausal 42- to 50-year-old women that personality characteristics associated with femininity (Spence & Helmreich, 1979), private self-awareness, and anger suppression put these women at risk for depressive symptoms. In a short longitudinal study covering 3 years, vulnerability for depressive symptoms (measured by Beck's Depression Inventory) was enhanced for women with low instrumentality and high self-consciousness at study entry (with initial depression level controlled for). And even more interestingly from a process-oriented perspective, women with high self-consciousness and the tendency to not express anger were selectively more vulnerable to the negative effects of ongoing problems and menopausal symptoms serious enough to be treated with hormone replacement therapy. Women with these personality characteristics at early midlife experienced more depressive symptoms when encountering ongoing problems with hormonal changes and in other life domains. Future research should address the ways in which specific personality characteristics render a person resilient or vulnerable during particularly challenging phases of life.

PROCESS-TYPE INFLUENCES ON ADAPTIVE AND RESILIENT MIDLIFE DEVELOPMENT

In this section, some key processes are considered, that are likely to or have been shown to influence adaptation and resilience in midlife.

The first process potentially influential for midlife developmental outcomes is beliefs about personal control and self-efficacy. The second kind of processes probably mediating between midlife opportunities and developmental engagement is experience and knowledge about adult development. The third issue relates to the benefits and risks of multiple identities and the degree to which identities are interdependent. The fourth issue is conceptually related to the second in its focus on the benefits of selection and density, but is addressing the domain of social relations and social support.

Perceived Personal Control and Self-Efficacy

One of the major mediating variables between the actual change of resources and challenges and an individual's behavior is the perception of controllability, personal control, and self-efficacy. It is only when the individual is aware of changes for better or worse in opportunities and constraints for pursuing certain goals, that he or she will alter behavior to match these changes of circumstance. The important mediating role of beliefs about self-efficacy or control has been demonstrated in numerous studies (Bandura, 1989). One exemplar study experimentally induced massed failure experiences and investigated the responses of middle-aged-adult subjects in terms of appraisals of positive challenge, threat, and loss of self-efficacy (Jerusalem & Schwarzer, 1992). Subjects with high self-efficacy perceived more challenge, and less threat or loss than subjects with low self-efficacy. Moreover, high self-efficacious subjects maintained their optimistic appraisals longer and kept perceptions of threat or loss at bay for longer. The abundant evidence for the mediating role of control beliefs indicates that this should also be a major resource for managing the challenges and threats of midlife development. The findings about changes in control perception across adulthood are quite inconsistent (see reviews in Clark-Plaskie & Lachman, 1999; Lachman, 1986). Some areas such as intellectual functioning and health involve decline in perceived internal control across adulthood. For other domains such as the political and interpersonal control domain, beliefs reflected stable control perceptions across adulthood (Lachman, 1991; Lachman, Ziff, & Spiro, 1994).

From a domain comparative perspective, the evidence suggests that the work domain plays a central role during midlife, both in terms of goal investment and in terms of perceived control. Clark and Lachman (1994) found that the work domain attracted more personal goals (36% of all goals) than any other domain. Moreover, work-related goals were perceived to be more under the individual's control than goals in any other domain. And finally, work-related and overall control beliefs mutually influenced each other during midlife. The degree of internal control beliefs was found to influence work success, which in turn enhanced general expectancies of personal control (Andrisani & Nestel, 1976). These findings suggest that during midlife control beliefs and general self-efficacy may be more closely tied to goal investments and actual attempts to realize control. This may restrict the potential to hold illusory control beliefs. Thus, in contrast to ages involving less objective control resources, such as adolescence, midlife affords to take control beliefs to the test of active goal pursuit and thus the potential experience of failure (see also Clark-Plaskie & Lachman, 1999; Heise, 1990).

On the other hand, there is certainly enough interindividual variability left to make control beliefs an important moderator of developmental outcomes, even over and above objective determinants of control. This is demonstrated in a study by Lachman and Weaver (1998), who examined social class differences in a large national probability sample of 25- to 75-year-old adults (study conducted by the MacArthur Foundation Research Network of Successful Midlife Development) with regard to two aspects of control, mastery and perceived constraints. On the one hand, it was found that lower income was associated with lower perceptions of mastery and higher perceptions of constraints to control. Thus, the subjects expressed beliefs about control that were in line with the objective conditions they were experiencing in their everyday life. On the other hand, though, mastery-focused control beliefs enabled these adults, irrespective of their level of income, to achieve better developmental outcomes in terms of physical health and psychological well-being. This way, enhanced mastery beliefs served as a buffer against the negative effects of lower income on health and well-being. Research in this area should refocus on the delicate calibration of control perceptions to realistically reflect developmental potential on the one hand and encourage the individual to take charge of her own development on the other hand.

Experience and Knowledge about Adult Development

Laypersons' knowledge about psychological changes and life transitions in midlife should influence the attempts of midlifers to influence their own development. They set the stage for possible goals, anticipated losses, and efforts for preventing such losses. Research on age-normative conceptions about adult development has revealed that middle-aged adults have substantially more elaborated conceptions than young adults about psychological development and aging, both in terms of the multidimensionality of expected change and with regard to the differentiation of expectations about the timing of change (onset and closing ages of change). Figure 11.4 shows results from a study by Heckhausen et al. (1989), who requested young, middle-aged, and old adults to rate the

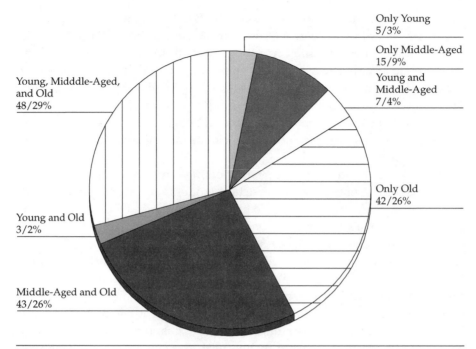

Only Young
5/3%

Only Middle-Aged
15/9%

Young and
Middle-Aged
7/4%

Young, Midddle-Aged,
and Old
48/29%

Only Old
42/26%

Young and Old
3/2%

Middle-Aged and Old
43/26%

Figure 11.4   Attributes perceived as undergoing strong development increases in young, middle-aged, and old adults. Adapted from Heckhausen, Dixon, and Baltes, 1989).

changeability of psychological attributes throughout adulthood and old age. Figure 11.4 indicates that the three age groups had increasingly rich conceptions about development with higher age levels. The midlife group showed, however, much overlap between their own pool of attributes rated as change-sensitive and the one nominated by the older adults. In fact, this overlap was significantly larger than the overlap shared between young and middle-aged adults. This pattern of findings suggests that midlife adults have acquired a substantial knowledge system which may enable them to anticipate and prevent, ameliorate, and/or emotionally cope with these age-normative changes. To date, we know little about the extent to which such knowledge systems about development, transitions, and/or mastering such transitions vary interindividually and may be influential for developmental regulation.

Multiple Identities and Roles

Another psychological resource that may set up a middle-aged adult for adaptive regulation and resilience is the availability of multiple identities and roles. Thoits (1983) studied the effect of social identities (spouse, parent, child, employee, student, neighbor, etc.) on distress in middle-aged adults. He showed that with an increasing number of social identities women and men at midlife reported less psychological distress. This finding converges with research on identity structure in late midlife adults by Ogilvie (1987). In his detailed analysis of idiosyncratic identity hierarchies in 50- to 70-year-olds, Ogilvie found that those adults who reported spending more time in higher-order identities that integrated multiple roles of the self, also expressed greater life satisfaction.

Vandewater and colleagues (Vandewater, Ostrove, & Stewart, 1997) provide another slant to the multiple identity puzzle with their two studies on midlife women who had graduated in the middle to late 1960s (Radcliffe College, 1964, and University of Michigan, 1967). These studies show that it is not the number of roles a women holds during midlife (age 48 and age 47 for the two samples respectively) that predicts life satisfaction, effective psychological functioning and psychological well-being. Instead, the number of roles in early adulthood (28 years in both studies) influences the structure of identity and the quality of roles related to family, work, and generativity. These in turn have a promotive influence on the various facets of adaptive psychological functioning. Thus, we have a life-course sequential pattern of multiple roles, high-quality identities and roles for the key domains of life, and psychological outcomes, that allows for a narrowing of roles during midlife, while keeping the benefits of diversified roles in young adulthood. This pattern appears particularly adaptive in the light of findings from the Thoits study to be reported next, which point to the perils of multiple and densely interrelated identity or role structures.

In Thoits's study (1983) of middle-aged adults, gains and losses in social identities were more consequential for those who started out (during midlife) with more and interrelated identities than for those who started with few and segregated identities. Gaining an identity was very beneficial for those who had more and integrated identities tying together closely interrelated social networks. On the other hand, losing an identity out of a large and well-integrated system of identities had particularly adverse effects on psychological distress. This latter finding converges nicely with the recurrent finding in social support research that dense social support networks are less beneficial for dealing with negative events. While during times of serenity and growth, highly interrelated social contacts and identities may provide a rich and satisfactory meaning system, they might turn into risk factors at times of trauma and loss. The very strength of mutually supportive and interdependent identities and social contacts, turn into perils when loss in some part of the identity and social network system endangers and drags down all the related other parts.

The pattern of findings reported about the benefits of multiple identities and perils of dense, closely interrelated self-conceptions, roles, and social networks raises questions about theoretical conceptions of adaptive selectivity both in terms of optimizing internal, psychological resources and in terms of social networks. The model of selective optimization with compensation (Baltes & Baltes, 1990; Freund & Baltes, 2000; Marsiske, Lang, Baltes, & Baltes, 1995) proposes that selecting domains of functioning for investment of behavioral resources is a major adaptive mechanism of successful development. While most researchers in life-span development would agree that selection is required for developmental progression, the question needs to be answered: What are the critical limits of adaptive selection at various age levels and developmental ecologies? Overselection certainly bears major risks of rendering the individual vulnerable for loss in either of the selected areas. An analogous weakness is implied by too closely interrelated domains of functioning, which may drag each other down in case of severe losses in either subdomain.

Size and Density of Social Networks

The issue of overselection and adverse interdependence or density is also a critical issue for the domain of social relations and social support. Thus, a similar argument as developed in the previous section on multiple identities may also be relevant for Carstensen's socioemotional selectivity theory (Carstensen, 1993, 1998; Carstensen et al., 1999). Socioemotional selectivity theory proposes that with the gradual shift from informational to socioemotional needs that occurs during adulthood, individuals cumulatively narrow down their social networks to exclude less close to the benefit of very close social partners (see also Lang, 2000; Lang & Carstensen, 1994). Such a process of ever narrowing social networks might well leave the individual with precariously small sets of close social partners insufficient to fulfill even the most select needs for close emotional relations. Thus, adaptive management of social networks should probably not be a unidirectional process of accumulated selection. Instead, an overall selection process across adulthood should be counterbalanced to some extent by periods of diversification of one's social network, especially during and after developmental transitions (J. Heckhausen & Schulz, 1999). It seems likely that cycles of diversification and contraction of social networks occur during developmental segments of the life course, such as during college time, work life, and retirement. At the beginning of a new period in life (e.g., parent with child at home to empty nest transition), individuals will expand their social networks. Then the individual will structure these social networks in terms of closeness (i.e., differentiating into closer and less close social partners) and start the winnowing-out process. Finally, toward the end of the developmental period when "social ending" (Carstensen, 1993) such as retirement draws near, the individual should narrow down social networks to the close and dear with regard to the developmental tasks of the recent past, and at the same time open up the social network for new social contacts related to developmental tasks in the near future. Such a model of diversification and contraction of social contacts might be particularly appropriate during midlife, when major transitions from parenthood to empty nest, or from career striving to preparing retirement have to be managed. Such transitions may be facilitated by new social partners who are models and companions on the path to a changed lifestyle and new developmental period. Future research should investigate such transition-related expansion and contraction cycles of social networks.

STRATEGIES OF CONTROL FOR ADAPTIVE AND RESILIENT MIDLIFE DEVELOPMENT

In this section, a set of specific strategies for mastering midlife developmental challenges is examined. These strategies are discussed in the context of the life-span theory of control (J. Heckhausen & Schulz, 1995; Schulz & Heckhausen, 1996). This discussion also provides one explanation for the resilience of the myth of the midlife crisis despite mounting counterevidence. The main part of this section addresses age sequentially organized strategies of control, which are adapted to the expected time course of developmental opportunities and constraints during midlife. In this context, an action-phase model of developmental regulation and the concept of developmental deadlines is presented along with some first empirical studies about its applicability to midlife development.

A Model of Developmental Regulation Based on the Life-Span Theory of Control

The concept of control is central for any consideration of adaptation and resilience. From the beginning of their lives, humans strive to control their immediate environment (White, 1959; see also review in J. Heckhausen & Schulz, 1995). The effort to control the environment and produce effects that are contingent on one's own behavior is likely to be an outcome of evolutionary selection, not only characteristic for the human species but for broader strata, including mammals and probably all vertebrates (J. Heckhausen, 2000). This type of control directed at the environment is referred to as "primary control" (J. Heckhausen & Schulz, 1995; Rothbaum, Weisz, & Snyder, 1982).

However, even though primary control is a universal striving, it needs to be organized to effectively invest behavioral and motivational resources.

Thus, the individual needs to select goals that are accessible to personal control, and avoid or deactivate those that are beyond the reach of available control resources or would drain resources without producing reasonable gains. In short, primary control striving needs to be selective.

In addition, the great variability and plasticity of human behavior also implies that advanced performance in each domain has to be acquired, rather than being preadapted by instinctual patterns. Processes of learning and acquisition typically involve many failure experiences. In fact, acquisition is most promoted at intermediate levels of difficulty when failures occur in about 50% of the trials. Thus, individuals also have to deal with frequent failure experiences.

These requirements of human control striving, the need to be selective, and the need to compensate for potential negative consequences of loss or failure experiences call for means to regulate the internal motivational and emotional responses of the individual. During the course of action, when deciding for a goal of primary control, striving for it, and succeeding or failing at it, the individual needs to activate different motivational states that are functionally adapted to the respective action phase. These requirements of internal regulation can be met by what Rothbaum et al. (1982) have called "secondary control."

Secondary control attempts are directed at the internal world of the individual and serve to optimize his or her motivational and emotional resources. The life-span theory of control, developed by Heckhausen and Schulz (1995; Schulz & Heckhausen, 1996) proposes that primary control striving holds functional primacy. Secondary control striving serves primary control striving by optimizing the motivational resources for ongoing actions and for long-term primary control. This function of secondary control can be realized in two ways (see right side of Table 11.1). First, motivational resources have to be focused for an ongoing primary control striving. Alternative and potentially competing goals need to be ignored, even devalued, while the chosen goal for primary control striving should be perceived as particularly valuable, as well as controllable. This type of control is referred to as "selective secondary control." Second, compensatory secondary control strategies serve to compensate for the negative effects of failure or loss experiences on an individual's motivational and emotional resources. After a failure, individuals may feel threatened in their self-esteem, perceived personal competence, or even more generally in their personal control perceptions. These negative effects of failure can undermine the long-term motivational resources for control. Compensatory secondary control counteracts this by disengaging from the goal and protecting positive perceptions about the self. Self-protection can be achieved, for example, by comparing oneself favorably with others who are worse off than oneself, or by finding causal attributions for the failure

Table 11.1

OPS-Model: Optimization in Primary and Secondary Control

Optimization

Adaptive goal selection: long-term and age-appropriate goals

Management of positive and negative trade-offs for other life domains and future life course

Maintenance of diversity, avoidance of dead ends

Selective Primary Control	*Selective Secondary Control*
Invest effort, abilities	Enhance goal value
Invest time	Devalue competing goals
Learn new skills	Enhance perception of control
Fight difficulties	Anticipate positive consequences of goal attainment
Compensatory Primary Control	*Compensatory Secondary Control*
Recruit others' help	Goal disengagement (sour grapes)
Get others' advice	Self-protective attributions
Use technical aids	Self-protective social comparisons
Employ unusual means	Self-protective intraindividual comparisons

---

Source: Adapted from Heckhausen and Schulz, 1995.

that take the blame off oneself. In the paragraphs to follow, I discuss a few prototypical secondary control strategies that are particularly adaptive in midlife.

Before getting to that, the overarching regulatory mechanisms of optimization need to be addressed. Selective goal striving, disengagement from goals, and self-protection are not adaptive in and of themselves, but only in regard to the developmental ecology of opportunities and constraints for primary control in which they occur. Therefore, the control system cannot function adaptively without a higher-order process, which addresses the selection of a particular goal and then activates the respective control strategies accordingly. This higher-order regulatory process is referred to as "optimization" (see top section of Table 11.1). Optimization functions on the basis of three principles:

1. For adaptive goal selection, the individual has to take into account the appropriateness of the age timing (opportunities are most favorable, less than optimal, or unfavorable) and the long-term consequences.
2. When choosing a certain track of action or development, implications both in terms of positive transfer or negative trade-off need to be considered.
3. The individual needs to maintain a certain degree of diversity to avoid excessive vulnerability that results from too narrow selections

(see also earlier discussion on multiple identities, network size, and density).

Secondary Control by Adaptively Selecting Reference Frames

Some secondary control strategies are particularly suited to developmental regulation at midlife. Before getting to these specific control processes, however I will briefly summarize the findings with regard to age differences in general primary control striving and secondary control striving, irrespective of the specific processes involved. Research on age differences in primary and secondary control striving has overall supported a pattern of stability for primary control striving across adulthood and increase for secondary control striving (J. Heckhausen, 1997, 1999; J. Heckhausen & Schulz, 1995; Peng & Lachman, 1993). This conclusion is based on various studies conducted by Heckhausen and colleagues (J. Heckhausen, 1997; J. Heckhausen, Diewald, & Huinink, 1994) and Peng and Lachman (1993; Peng, 1993) comparing young, middle-aged, and old adults. Brandtstädter and colleagues (Brandtstädter & Renner, 1990) report partially converging evidence for the age trends in their assimilative and accommodative tendency, which overlap with the distinction between primary and secondary control. They find increasing goal flexibility (accommodation) with higher ages in middle adulthood. However, they also report decreases in tenaciousness (assimilation). J. Heckhausen (1999; see also J. Heckhausen et al., 1994) reports data indicating that the decrease in tenaciousness may be due to differential age trends of two subsets of items in the tenaciousness scale (positively phrased items increased, negatively phrased items decreased).

I now turn to the adaptive selection of reference frames as a means of secondary control. As discussed in the first section on the position of midlife and its challenges in the life course, the major challenges of midlife are the concurrence of developmental gains and losses, and the growing awareness about the finitude of life. Midlife confronts the individual with unprecedented challenges because time and opportunities to completely change one's life path and reverse earlier decisions are not available any more. In this context, secondary control strategies that are unbiased in terms of avoiding premature disengagement, while serving self-protective needs are most needed and adaptive.

A most important and effective general strategy of mastering challenges related to developmental change is to reconsider the change in the context of a strategically selected reference frame. The various ways this can be done will be explained for the case of loss. When experiencing a negative event or loss, such as the failure to be promoted or the disappointment about the school career of a child, the individual can respond in various ways. Some of these responses imply that the individual keeps trying to reverse the loss; others imply that the loss is accepted and that striving to undo the loss is given up. Both types of strategies have their specific risks. Giving up active control too early is problematic because one loses out on the potential benefits of one's own actions. However, not giving up a futile cause is maladaptive, too, because it may drain one's resources without producing any benefits. When the individual has insufficient information to decide which of the two routes to take, there is still a possible avenue for improving one's appraisal of the loss. This is to reframe the event in the sense of comparing it in a different context that makes the loss appear less severe, or that diminishes the loss's diagnostic value for the self. Such reframings are particularly adaptive because they do not require a distorted representation of reality such as positive illusions. Instead, they leave the representation of the loss itself untouched, while recontextualizing and improving its interpretation and thus its impact for motivational resources. This way, the individual can protect his or her motivational and emotional resources from the impact of negative events, while maintaining a realistic account of control potential. Two major reference frames can be used for such reframing purposes. One is temporal comparison within the individual (intraindividual comparison); the other one is social comparison across individuals (interindividual intraindividual comparison).

Ryff (1991) has studied temporal intraindividual comparisons in young (mean age = 19.3), middle-aged (mean age = 46.0), and older adults (mean age = 73.4) with regard to the six dimensions of her psychological well-being scale. Subjects were requested to rate themselves as they are at present, were in the past (for young: as adolescents; for middle-aged: 20–25 years; for old: 40 to 50 years), will be in the future (for young: 40 to 50 years; for middle-aged: 65 to 70 years; for old: 10 to 15 years later). Moreover, subjects were asked to provide ratings for their ideal self. The pattern of ratings across instructional conditions and age groups reflects disengagement from unrealistic goals and a balancing of ratings across temporal perspectives such that across age groups equivalent mean appreciations of one's own standing resulted. Across age groups ideal ratings declined steadily, with the older adults holding the lowest ideal images of their own well-being, which actually closely resembled their present ratings. Present ratings were stable across the age groups for most of the six dimensions. These findings imply that these older adults are well satisfied with major aspects of their lives and of their personal characteristics. However, future ratings by the older adults were decreasing on all six dimensions. At the same time, ratings of past well-being increased across age groups with the older adults perceiving their past self as more favorable than the middle-aged and young adults. Thus, these older adults may construct an overall life-course balance of positive well-being, evening out expected losses in the future by enhancing perceptions of the past. This can be conceived as a compensatory secondary control strategy of reevaluating expected decline by putting it in the context of the overall life-course attainment of well-being. Such reinterpretation is much more adaptive than illusory expectations about future growth or maintenance would be, since such illusions would lead to dysfunctional attempts to achieve unrealistic goals.

What was the pattern of temporal perceptions in the middle-aged group studied by Ryff (1991)? Compared with young adults, middle-aged adults perceived similar future prospects for all dimensions, similar present status for all dimensions, except for higher (!) ratings for environmental mastery and autonomy, and similar past status, except for higher ratings in autonomy. They also expected future improvement with regard to self-acceptance, autonomy, positive relations with others, and environmental mastery (only women), and future stability with regard to purpose in life, personal growth, and mastery (only men). Thus, the early midlife position (mean age, 46 years) of this sample makes them in many ways similar to the young adults, in that they still hold substantial potential for growth. However, these young middle-aged adults already anticipate that some domains of well-being will not yield further improvements. One may speculate that an older middle-aged group would have expressed less ambitious ideals, a tendency already apparent in the data but failing to reach significance. Moreover, such an older midlife group might have reported less optimistic expectations for the future and greater satisfaction with past status, thus balancing these two temporal perspectives. It would be fascinating to see when, under which conditions, and with regard to which dimensions of well-being (e.g., environmental mastery, autonomy, purpose in life) the shift to future expectations involving decline occurs.

Another reference system that can be used for secondary control is the comparison with others. Festinger (1954) has proposed a "unidirectional drive upward" for self-improvement, which is served by upward comparisons with others who are superior or more advanced than oneself in a certain domain of functioning. However, the main purpose of social comparison for Festinger was self-assessment by comparing oneself with similar others. That way, the individual can validate and differentiate knowledge about the self and calibrate aspirations. Finally, going beyond Festinger's conceptions about social comparisons, it has been proposed that a third function of social comparison is self-enhancement (Wills, 1981; Wood, 1989). This function is served best by comparison with someone inferior to oneself, so that the self appears enhanced. Such downward social comparisons are particularly adaptive when the individual experiences failure or threat, especially when this failure is uncontrollable (e.g., Diener, 1984; Taylor & Lobel, 1989; Taylor, Wood, & Lichtman, 1984;

Wills, 1981). Numerous studies have shown that individuals under threat or after loss choose others with lower status or less fortunate fate for comparison. Downward social comparisons can be seen as a compensatory secondary control strategy in response to perceived threat to the self, expected loss or stress, and a perceived uncertainty about the self in general. This has been shown in research about coping with progressive disability (Schulz & Decker, 1985), severe illness (Taylor & Lobel, 1989; Taylor et al., 1984), and victimization by crime (A. Burgess & Holmstrom, 1979; J. Burgess & Holmstrom, 1979).

In a study on laypersons' conceptions about development in adulthood, J. Heckhausen and Krueger (1993) asked young (20 to 35 years), middle-aged (40 to 55 years), and old adults (over 60 to 80 years) to rate adjectives representing psychological characteristics associated with the positive versus negative end of the Big Five personality factors (extraversion, agreeableness, neuroticism, conscientiousness, intellectual functioning) with regard to the extent and direction of change expected throughout adulthood between 20 and 80 years. Ratings were requested with regard to two instructional targets, for the self and for most other people. Figure 11.5 depicts the perceived trajectories of increase and decrease of desirable and undesirable attributes across adulthood, as pertaining to the self and as attributed to most other people, and separately for young (top panel), middle-aged (middle panel), and old adults (bottom panel). The trajectories reflect substantial congruence between self and other in that at higher ages beyond the 30s positive attributes were perceived to show less increase and after the 60s even decrease. All age groups expected some increase in undesirable attributes beginning in the 60s at the latest. Notable differences between the age groups were revealed with regard to the differentiation between self and other. Younger adults anticipated close to identical trajectories for self and others throughout adulthood. In contrast, middle-aged and old adults expressed divergent expectations for the self and for most other people. For the self compared with the other-related conceptions, decrease of desirable attributes in old age was less pronounced and delayed. Similarly, increase in undesirable attributes was less severe and delayed for the self when compared with expectations about most other people. This self-enhancing divergence between self and other-related conceptions about developmental gains and losses was most pronounced in the older adults. Thus, the age group most imminently affected by aging-related loss also showed the strongest tendency to view the developmental prospects of age-peers less favorably than for oneself. It is interesting though that the middle-aged adults exhibited a similar, albeit somewhat less pronounced tendency to view their own developmental prospects less negatively than the prospects ascribed to most other people. Apparently for the middle-aged group, aging-related

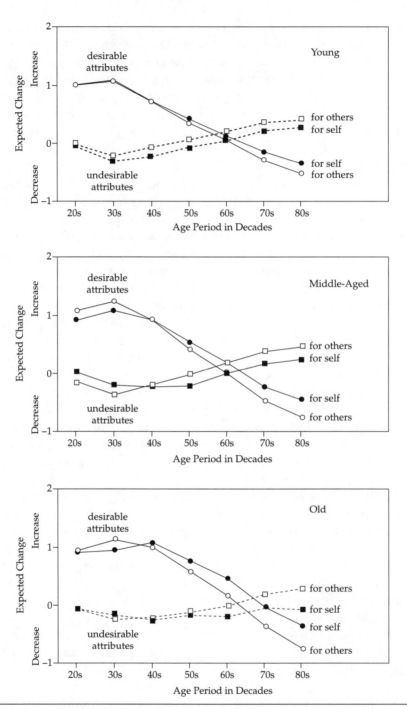

Figure 11.5 Change in desirable and undesirable attributes expected for the self and most other people; separate for young, middle-aged, and old adults. Adapted from Heckhausen and Krueger, 1993.

loss is close enough in the future to motivate a more salient and self-protective self-other contrast.

The findings of the Heckhausen and Krueger (1993) study addressed a type of social comparison that makes use of conceptions about a generalized other (here "most other people"), rather than comparing the self with a specific individual. This type of social comparison has been found in other contexts such as in studies about stereotypes of aging. Harris and Associates (1975, 1981) found that older people when asked to rate the extent to which they perceive problems in a given domain of life (health, finances, loneliness, etc.) attribute severe problems to other old adults but much less or no problems to themselves. O'Gorman (1980) provided a secondary analysis of the Harris Survey and revealed that perceived discrepancy between problem severity in self and other was associated with perceived personal burdening. Those older adults who reported substantial problem burdening themselves in a given domain were more likely to attribute particularly severe problems to most other old adults. Thus, personal burdening and threat seems to motivate older adults to see the respective problem as a normative burden of old age. This would allow them to not blame themselves for having the problem, and to have companions in the loss.

In a survey study covering a broad adult age range from 18 years to old age, Heckhausen and Brim (1997) investigated perceived problem severity for the self and for "most people your age" with regard to the domains of money, health, friends, marriage, stress, meaning of life, sex, attractiveness, job, children, leisure time, and fitness. For each domain and all age groups, self-related problem ratings were less severe than other-related problem ratings. This supported our prediction that social downgrading is not unique to old age, but pertains to other adult ages too. Moreover, the severity of problems attributed to "most people my age" was clearly influenced by one's own problem-burdening. Those who experienced problems in a given domain, also expressed that other people their age have similar problems. Finally, this tendency to attribute problems suffered personally to others similar in age, was most pronounced among the elderly. However, it was present in the young and middle-aged adults, too. This finding of pervasive usage of social downgrading and its selectively enhanced usage when being personally burdened or threatened indicates the important role of strategic social comparison and the construction of suitable social stereotypes to compare oneself with.

Implications for the Resilience of the Midlife Crisis Myth

Heckhausen and Brim (1997) argued that these kinds of phenomena involving comparisons with groups of generalized others can be conceptualized as "social downgrading." We propose that social downgrading based on negative age stereotypes is a compensatory secondary control strategy used by adults who experience loss or threat. Moreover, such age-related stereotypes are not only present with regard to old age, but also exist for midlife. The myth of the midlife crisis may serve just this function. The midlife crisis may be a useful conception to organize a social stereotype about midlife, that allows social downgrading and thereby self-enhancement. In this way, the myth of the midlife crisis is an adaptive stereotype much like the negative stereotypes about aging. Another adaptive implication of the midlife crisis myth is that it renders predictable certain problems, such as the increased tendency for feelings of regret, disappointment, and lack of purpose and meaning, which are probably more likely to be experienced at midlife because of the growing salience of finite lifetime. Thus, based on expectations implied in the notion of a midlife crisis, individuals might move into midlife anticipating and prepared to disengage from certain goals, that have become obsolete.

These two advantages of the midlife crisis myth, providing a socially downgraded reference frame and preparing a normative expectation of negative changes, probably go a long way to keep the myth of the midlife crisis alive. Despite tremendous efforts of gerontologists to eradicate negative views about old age and aging, negative conceptions about aging reflect common sense and the backdrop of everybody's experience of his/her own aging. It seems very difficult to create a more differentiated or positive view among the public. Similarly, scholars have been puzzled by the resilience of the myth about the midlife crisis despite numerous studies showing no common pattern indicative of a crisis in the middle years (e.g., Chiriboga, 1989; Hunter & Sundel, 1989; Whitbourne, 1986). It may be that part of this resilience of the midlife crisis myth lies in its benefit to anticipate the worst at midlife and be pleasantly surprised by one's own comparatively smooth sail.

Developmental Regulation as Goal Engagement and Disengagement around Developmental Deadlines

Developmental regulation can be conceptualized as control behavior involved in engagement and disengagement around developmental goals. Opportunities and constraints for attaining developmental goals are not equally distributed across the life span. Instead, they follow an age-graded and sequentially organized pattern along the age axis. This holds for midlife just as well as for other periods of the life span. The specific feature of midlife is that it does hold a lot of growth potential, but at the same time for many important and common developmental goals lifetime is running out. This means that individuals during midlife encounter various developmental deadlines that imply a "now or never" situation. They have to urgently strive to attain these deadline-dependent goals, so as to not have to give them up forever. However, if the individual fails at attaining the goal before the deadline runs out, he or she needs to switch from urgent goal pursuit to goal disengagement.

Based on the life-span theory of control and action-theoretical conceptions of sequential phases of goal selection, pursuit, and disengagement, an action-phase model of developmental regulation was developed that is organized around developmental deadlines (J. Heckhausen, 1999; Wrosch & Heckhausen, 1999). Figure 11.6 displays the action-phase model of developmental regulation. It is organized in three levels. The top level informs about two critical transitions, one is the decisional Rubicon (H. Heckhausen, 1991; J. Heckhausen, Wrosch, & Fleeson, in press), which Heinz Heckhausen and his colleagues have identified as a shifting point from a deliberative predecisional motivation to implementation-oriented postdecisional volition (Gollwitzer, 1990; Gollwitzer, Heckhausen, & Steller, 1990; H. Heckhausen, 1991; H. Heckhausen & Gollwitzer, 1987). The other critical transition, which is characteristic for our model is the transition of the developmental deadline, after which opportunities for goal attainment are radically reduced. The second level addresses the functions of the different action phases. Our model differentiates between a nonurgent and an urgent action phase before the deadline has passed. On the third level (see bottom of Figure 11.6), the specific control processes required for adaptive developmental regulation in the respective action phase are identified. The urgency phase just before passing the deadline calls for increased behavioral and motivational investment in goal striving. After passing the deadline, goal intentions have either been realized or failed. Those who failed the deadline (see postdeadline "failure" condition, Figure 11.6) need to shift radically from intense goal engagement to compensatory goal disengagement and self-protective interpretations. In contrast, those who were successful (see postdeadline "success" condition, Figure 11.1) can invest in further primary control striving and capitalize on the action resources strengthened by their success.

What are the implications of the deadline model for developmental regulation in midlife? First, we should examine what are the most important and common developmental goals. Clark and Lachman (1994) found that work-related goals was the category with the greatest frequency (36% of all goals) of all goals nominated by middle-aged adults. Heckhausen (1997) asked young, middle-aged, and older adults about the five most important goals for the next 5 to 10 years. As in Clark and Lachman's study, Heckhausen found that work-related goals were the most frequently nominated, followed by family-related goals, then health goals, followed by financial, leisure, and community-related goals.

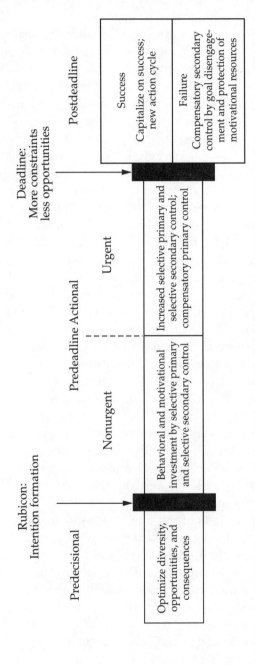

Figure 11.6 Action-phase model of developmental regulation (adapted from Heckhausen, 1999).

When examining the literature on regret, psychological turning points (Wethington, Cooper, & Holmes, 1997), and reorientations during midlife, it becomes clear that they are often connected to experiences of limited control and relinquished hopes to realize a long-standing dream or goal, all being experiences that are most likely based on reaching a deadline. A number of studies employed qualitative methodology of in-depth interviews to examine such processes of simultaneously looking forward and looking back during midlife. Shifting from goal-engagement to disengagement and reorientations have been studied on the basis of such a phenomenological approach in the domain of childbearing (Jarrett & Lethbridge, 1994), finding (again) an intimate partner (Lewis & Moon, 1997), and mastering new challenges at work (Karp, 1987). With regard to career goals, Carr (1997) has also conducted a large survey study on fulfillment of women's career dreams. According to Carr's findings from the Wisconsin Longitudinal Study, women who have fallen short of their earlier career goals suffer from lower purpose of life and a greater number of depressive symptoms.

The Project "Motivational Psychology of Ontogenesis," based at the Berlin Max Planck Institute for Human Development, has conducted a research program on developmental regulation around developmental deadlines (J. Heckhausen, 1999; Wrosch & Heckhausen, 1999). The deadlines studied in his research program are located in the core of midlife. The two developmental deadlines studied were the "biological clock" deadline for childbearing (J. Heckhausen et al., in press), and the deadline associated with rapidly waning chances of finding a new intimate partner during midlife (Wrosch, 1999; Wrosch & Heckhausen, 1999).

Heckhausen et al. (in press) investigated developmental regulation in groups of women, whose age put them before versus after a presumed developmental deadline for childbearing at age 40. In two studies, we examined control processes associated with being engaged with the goal of having a child and being disengaged from this goal.

In the first study, we compared women without children at age 27 to 33 (urgency group) at age 40 to 46 ("passed-deadline" group) and women who had a young child and varied in age between 19 and 44 years. These women were requested to nominate the five most important goals for the next 5 to 10 years. Moreover, we conducted an incidental memory task to see whether these women showed selective recall of sentences that reflect goal engagement versus goal disengagement in accordance with their position in the life course and their parental status. It was found that women in the predeadline urgency group expressed the most goals about childbearing. In general, predeadline women and those with a child nominated more child and family-related goals than women in the passed-deadline group. In contrast, childless women after the deadline were more focused on self-development, promoting one's health, and improving their social network and relations to friends. With regard to the selective recall task, our results indicate that women in the urgency group showed superior recall of various types of sentences about children, irrespective of positive (good things about having children) or negative (bad things about having children) valuations implied. Childless women in the passed-deadline group had particularly good recall of sentences about causal attributions that avoid self-blame (e.g., "Having children is largely a matter of luck"). Finally, on findings revealed differential relations of action-phase congruent versus incongruent selective recall and psychological well-being. Childless women in the passed deadline group who also showed selective recall for child-related sentences, also expressed higher negative affect. In contrast, those passed-deadline women who selectively recalled substitute goals for childbearing (e.g., being a good aunt) and recalled fewer sentences about the benefits of having children expressed higher positive affect.

In the second study (J. Heckhausen et al., in press), we added two further groups to our design by including pregnant women and women who have long passed the deadline, thus having a five-group design: group with child (18 to 41 years), pregnant group (21 to 39 years in third trimester of pregnancy), urgency group (29 to 35 years, "just passed" deadline group (39 to 46 years), and long passed deadline group (49 to 56 years). Again we investigated the goals nominated. In addition, we employed a new measurement instrument for assessing control strategies (*Optimization in Primary and Secondary Control-Scales*, OPS-Scales; J. Heckhausen, Schulz, & Wrosch, 1998), which was specifically adapted to the childbearing domain. Similarly to Study 1, we found that predeadline women and women with a child nominated goals related to childbearing, child rearing, and family. In contrast, women in the two passed-deadline groups expressed other nonfamily goals regarding leisure, friends, and self more frequently. The control strategies showed a pattern across the groups that reflected goal engagement in the predeadline groups and the group with a child and disengagement in the postdeadline groups. Goal engagement in the pregnant and urgent group as well as the group with a child was reflected in selective primary control, selective secondary control, and compensatory primary control. Goal disengagement and self-protection was shown in higher ratings for compensatory secondary control in the two passed-deadline groups. Finally, we investigated the predictive relations between congruency of reported control strategies and pre-and post-deadline action phases and depressive symptoms (CES-D; Radloff, 1977). In the urgency group, women profited from using selective primary control strategies by reducing their risk for depressive symptoms.

Conversely, women in the passed-deadline groups who reported more selective primary control striving suffered more depressive symptoms. This pattern of findings supports our model of adaptive control strategies in different action phases before and after passing a developmental deadline.

The other domain of midlife development we studied using the research paradigm of developmental deadline is the partnership domain. National German statistics show that opportunities to remarry decline sharply from 80% for 30-year-olds to 20% at age 60 (Braun & Proebsting, 1986), thus creating a shift in opportunities to realize goals for an intimate partnership. Wrosch (1999; Wrosch & Heckhausen, 1999) investigated the reported control striving in four groups of adults: young (20 to 34 years) and recently committed to a new partner, young and recently separated, late midlife (49 to 59) and recently committed, late midlife and recently separated. The partnership-related goals nominated by these groups reflected their pre- and postdeadline status. Figure 11.7 gives the number of goals oriented toward achieving gains (e.g., finding a new partner, improving the partnership) and toward avoiding losses (e.g., separating, not getting on). As can be seen in Figure 11.7, younger adults irrespective of whether they were committed or separated focused on

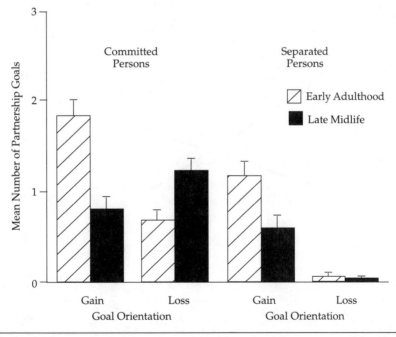

Figure 11.7 Number of gain-oriented and loss-avoiding partnership goals in recently committed and separated adults in early adulthood and late midlife. The error bars reflect the respective standard error. Adapted from Wrosch and Heckhausen, 1999.

gains. Late midlife adults, in contrast, were less gain-oriented, and particularly focused on avoiding loss of the partner when they had recently found a new partnership. It is as if these late midlife adults wanted to protect this uncommon and thus precious luck of a late love.

In the partnership study, we also investigated domain-specific control strategies. The findings reflect predeadline goal engagement in terms of enhanced selective primary and selective secondary control in the young adults irrespective of their partnership status. For the older midlifers, goal engagement control strategies were high only in the group that was recently committed. Those middle-aged adults who had recently separated, expressed higher compensatory secondary control and lower selective primary and selective secondary control. With regard to indicators of selective information processing, an incidental recall task was given using adjectives describing partnerships in positive (e.g., happy, important) or negative (e.g., deceptive, constraining) ways. It was found that younger separated persons recalled relatively more positive compared with negative words about partnerships, whereas older adults recalled relatively more negative words. Wrosch also conducted a longitudinal follow-up 15 months after the initial data collection. As illustrated in Figure 11.8, high ratings in compensatory

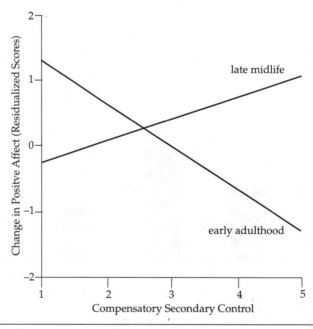

Figure 11.8 Compensatory secondary control as a predictor of change in positive affect in separated individuals in early adulthood and late midlife. Adapted from Worsch and Heckhausen, 1999.

secondary control, that is, disengagement from partnership goals and self-protection about a failing partnership, proved to be a differential predictor for young and older separated adults' change in affect during the 15-month period. For older midlifers, compensatory secondary control striving was beneficial in that it predicted enhanced positive affect in the longitudinal follow-up. In contrast, young adults who had expressed disengagement with partnership goals deteriorated in positive affect over the 15-month period.

The studies about midlife developmental regulation around deadlines for important life goals show the adaptive value of anticipated age changes in opportunities for goal attainment. These age-structured opportunities and constraints allow the middle-aged adult to use life time effectively. With the time-schedule in mind, midlife adults can for a while put off, and then intensely pursue important goals and developmental tasks for which time runs out. The age-normative shifts in opportunities also provide prompts when to disengage and focus on self-protection, thus avoiding negative affect and depressive symptoms. This allows the individual to cherish his or her motivational resources for future primary control pursuits of still attainable goals. Further research should address other deadlines relevant in midlife (e.g., children's career, health status) and investigate the longitudinal sequencing and shifts from one goal engagement cycle to the next.

CONCLUSION

Midlife is a period of life with extraordinary challenges including the co-occurrence of and shift from processes of growth to processes of decline; the multiplicity of roles, identities, and burdens; and not least the growing salience of the finitude of life. With the latter comes the awareness that certain life goals and dreams may not be attained after all. However, these great challenges are typically matched by impressive resources on the part of the midlife adult, who has accumulated and optimized material resources, social networks, personality characteristics, and specific strategies of control. There are interindividual variations in the availability of these resources, but the overall message is that most people in midlife sucessfully adapt to the transition and show resilience to burdening events and circumstances. As Bert Brim (1992) stated, the key to understanding developmental mastery during midlife is to investigate how ordinary people change their life so as to cope with "just manageable" goals, stresses, and challenges in general. It means adapting one's goals to a more realistic view of the controllable, and being resilient with regard to the loss of objective control and particularly with regard to disillusionment of adolescent and young adulthood dreams about prime-of-life achievements and ways of life that have proven unobtainable and obsolete. Normative expectations about ideal timing and final deadlines for attaining important goals are most helpful scaffolds in this process of adaptation. Maybe the myth of the midlife crisis itself is an adaptive tool for anticipating the worst and being prideful and pleasantly surprised by one's comparatively smooth sail through the middle years.

REFERENCES

Adler, N.E., Boyce, T., Chesney, M.A., Cohen, S., Folkman, S., Kahn, R.L., & Syme, S.L. (1994). Socioeconomic status and health: The challenge of the gradient. *American Psychologist, 49*, 15–24.

Andrisani, P.J., & Nestel, G. (1976). Internal-external control as contributor to and outcome of work experience. *Journal of Applied Psychology, 61*, 156–165.

Baltes, P.B. (1987). Theoretical propositions of life-span developmental psychology: On the dynamics between growth and decline. *Developmental Psychology, 23*, 611–626.

Baltes, P.B., & Baltes, M.M. (1990). Psychological perspectives on successful aging: The model of selective optimization with compensation. In P.B. Baltes & M.M. Baltes (Eds.), *Successful aging: Perspectives from the behavioral sciences* (pp. 1–34). New York: Cambridge University Press.

Bandura, A. (1989). Human agency in social cognitive theory. *American Psychologist, 44*, 1175–1184.

Bengtson, V.L., Cutler, N.E., Mangen, D.J., & Marshall, V.W. (1985). Generations and intergenerational relations. In R. Binstock & E. Shanas (Eds.), *Handbook of aging and the social sciences* (2nd ed.). New York: Van Nostrand-Reinhold.

Bengtson, V.L., Rosenthal, C., & Burton, L. (1990). Families and aging: Diversity and heterogeneity. In R. Binstock & L. George (Eds.), *Handbook of aging and the social sciences* (pp. 263–287). New York: Academic Press.

Block, J.H., & Block, J. (1980). The role of ego-control and ego-resiliency in the organization of behavior. In W.A. Collins (Ed.), *Development of cognition, affect, and social relations* (pp. 39–101). Hillsdale, NJ: Erlbaum.

Brandtstädter, J., & Renner, G. (1990). Tenacious goal pursuit and flexible goal adjustment: Explication and age-related analysis of assimilative and accommodative strategies of coping. *Psychology and Aging, 5*, 58–67.

Braun, W., & Proebsting, H. (1986). Heiratstafeln verwitweter Deutscher 1979/82 und geschiedener Deutscher 1980/83 [Marriage tables of widowed, 1979/82, and divorced, 1980/83, Germans]. *Wirtschaft und Statistik*, 107–112.

Brim, O.G. (1976). Theories of the male mid-life crisis. *Counseling Psychologist, 6*, 2–9.

Brim, O.G. (1992). *Ambition: How we manage success and failure throughout our lives.* New York: Basic Books.

Brim, O.G., & Ryff, C.D. (1980). On the properties of life events. In P.B. Baltes & O.G. Brim (Eds.), *Life-span development and behavior* (Vol. 3, pp. 367–388). New York: Academic Press.

Brody, E.M. (1990). *Women in the middle: Their parent-care years.* New York: Springer.

Bromberger, J.T., & Matthews, K.A. (1996). A "feminine" model of vulnerability to depressive symptoms: A longitudinal investigation of middle-aged women. *Journal of Personality and Social Psychology, 70,* 591–598.

Burgess, A.W., & Holmstrom, L.L. (1979). *Rape: Crisis and recovery.* Bowie, MD: Brady.

Burgess, J.M., & Holmstrom, L.L. (1979). Adaptive strategies and recovery from rape. *American Journal of Psychiatry, 136,* 1278–1282.

Carr, D. (1997). The fulfillment of career dreams at midlife: Does it matter for women's mental health? *Journal of Health and Social Behavior, 38,* 331–344.

Carstensen, L.L. (1993). Motivation for social contact across the life-span: A theory of socioemotional selectivity. In J. Jacobs (Ed.), *Nebraska symposium on motivation* (Vol. 40, pp. 205–254). Lincoln: University of Nebraska Press.

Carstensen, L.L. (1998). A life-span approach to social motivation. In J. Heckhausen & C. Dweck (Eds.), *Motivation and self-regulation across the life span* (pp. 341–364). New York: Cambridge University Press.

Carstensen, L.L., & Fredrickson, B.F. (1998). Socioemotional selectivity in healthy older people and younger people living with the human immunodeficiency virus: The centrality of emotion when the future is constrained. *Health Psychology, 17,* 1–10.

Carstensen, L.L., Gross, J., & Fung, H. (1997). The social context of emotion. *Annual Review of Geriatrics and Gerontology, 17,* 325–352.

Carstensen, L.L., Isaacowitz, D.M., & Charles, S.T. (1999). Taking time seriously: A theory of socioemotional selectivity. *American Psychologist, 54,* 165–181.

Carstensen, L.L., & Turk-Charles, S. (1994). The salience of emotion across the adult life span. *Psychology and Aging, 9,* 259–264.

Chiriboga, D.A. (1989). Stress and loss in middle age. In R.A. Kalish (Ed.), *Midlife loss: Coping strategies* (pp. 42–88). Newbury Park, CA: Sage.

Chiriboga, D.A. (1997). Crisis, challenge, and stability in the middle years. In M.E. Lachman & J. Boone James (Eds.), *Multiple paths of midlife development. Studies on successful midlife development: The John D. and Catherine T. MacArthur Foundation series on mental health and development* (pp. 293–322). Chicago: University of Chicago Press.

Chiriboga, D.A., Weiler, P.G., & Nielsen, K. (1989). The stress of caregivers. *Journal of Applied Social Sciences, 13,* 118–141.

Clark, M.D., & Lachman, M.E. (1994, August). *Goals and perceived control: Age differences and domain effects.* Poster presented at the meeting of the American Psychological Association, Los Angeles.

Clark-Plaskie, M.D., & Lachman, M.E. (1999). The sense of control in midlife. In S.L. Willis & J.D. Reid (Eds.), *Life in the middle: Psychological and social development in middle age* (pp. 182–208). San Diego, CA: Academic Press.

Cohen, S., & Wills, T.A. (1985). Stress, social support, and the buffering hypothesis. *Psychological Bulletin, 98,* 310–357.

Cole, E.R., & Stewart, A.J. (1996). Meanings of political participation among Black and White women: Political identity and social responsibility. *Journal of Personality and Social Psychology, 71,* 130–140.

Diener, E. (1984). Subjective well-being. *Psychological Bulletin, 95,* 542–575.

Dohrenwend, B.P., Levav, I., & Shrout, P.E. (1992). Socioeconomic status and psychiatric disorders: The causation-selection issue. *Science, 255,* 946–951.

Erikson, E.H. (1963). *Childhood and society* (2nd ed.). New York: Norton.

Farrell, M.P., & Rosenberg, S.D. (1981). *Men at midlife.* Boston: Auburn House.

Festinger, L. (1954). A theory of social comparison processes. *Human Relations, 7,* 117–140.

Finlayson, A. (1976). Social networks as coping resources. *Social Science and Medicine, 10,* 97–103.

Fredrickson, B.C., & Carstensen, L.L. (1990). Choosing social partners: How old age and anticipated endings make people more selective. *Psychology and Aging, 5,* 335–347.

Freund, A.M., & Baltes, P.B. (2000). The orchestration of selection, optimization, and compensation: An action-theoretical conceptualization of a theory of developmental regulation. In W.J. Perrig & A. Grob (Eds.), *Control of human behaviour: Mental processes and consciousness* (pp. 17–33). Mahwah, NJ: Erlbaum.

Garmezy, N. (1991). Resilience in children's adaptation to negative life events and stressed environments. *Pediatric Annals, 20,* 459–466.

Glenn, N.D., & Weaver, C.N. (1988). The changing relationship of marital status to reported happiness. *Journal of Marriage and the Family, 50,* 317–324.

Gollwitzer, P.M. (1990). Action phases and mind-sets. In E.T. Higgins & R.M. Sorrentino (Eds.), *Handbook of motivation and cognition: Foundations of social behavior* (Vol. 2, pp. 53–92). New York: Guilford Press.

Gollwitzer, P.M., Heckhausen, H., & Steller, B. (1990). Deliberative and implemental mind-sets: Cognitive tuning toward congruous thoughts and information. *Journal of Personality and Social Psychology, 59,* 1119–1127.

Gough, H.G. (1987). *Manual for the California Personality Inventory.* Palo Alto, CA: Consulting Psychologists Press. (Original work published 1957)

Gould, R. (1972). The phases of adult life: A study in developmental psychology. *American Journal of Psychiatry, 129,* 521–531.

Gould, R. (1978). *Transformations.* New York: Simon & Schuster.

Graves, P.L., Wang, N-Y., Mead, L.A., Johnson, J.V., & Klag, M.J. (1998). Youthful precursors of midlife social support. *Journal of Personality and Social Psychology, 74,* 1329–1336.

Hagestad, G.O. (1986, Winter). The aging society as a context for family life. *Daedalus,* 31–49.

Harris, L., & Associates. (1975). *The myth and reality of aging in America.* Washington, DC: National Council on the Aging.

Harris, L., & Associates. (1981). *Aging in the eighties: America in transition.* Washington, DC: National Council on the Aging.

Heckhausen, H. (1991). *Motivation and action.* New York: Springer.

Heckhausen, H., & Gollwitzer, P.M. (1987). Thought contents and cognitive functioning in motivational and volitional states of mind. *Motivation and Emotion, 11,* 101–120.

Heckhausen, J. (1997). Developmental regulation across adulthood: Primary and secondary control of age-related challenges. *Developmental Psychology, 33,* 176–187.

Heckhausen, J. (1999). *Developmental regulation in adulthood: Age-normative and sociostructural constraints as adaptive challenges.* New York: Cambridge University Press.

Heckhausen, J. (2000). Evolutionary perspectives on human motivation [Special issue]. *American Behavioral Scientist, 43,* 1015–1029.

Heckhausen, J., & Brim, O.G. (1997). Perceived problems for self and others: Self-protection by social downgrading throughout adulthood. *Psychology and Aging, 12,* 610–619.

Heckhausen, J., Diewald, M., & Huinink, J. (1994). *Control agency means-ends in adulthood questionnaire—short version.* Unpublished questionnaire, Max Planck Institute for Human Development, Berlin, Germany.

Heckhausen, J., Dixon, R.A., & Baltes, P.B. (1989). Gains and losses in development throughout adulthood as perceived by different adult age groups. *Developmental Psychology, 25,* 109–121.

Heckhausen, J., & Krueger, J. (1993). Developmental expectations for the self and most other people: Age grading in three functions of social comparison. *Developmental Psychology, 29,* 539–548.

Heckhausen, J., & Schulz, R. (1995). A life-span theory of control. *Psychological Review, 102,* 284–304.

Heckhausen, J., & Schulz, R. (1999). Biological and societal canalizations as adaptive constraints in individuals' developmental regulation: Optimization of developmental selectivity by sequential pursuit of age-graded developmental goals. In J. Brandtstädter & R. Lerner (Eds.), *Development and action: Origins and functions of intentional self-development* (pp. 67–103). London: Sage.

Heckhausen, J., Schulz, R., & Wrosch, C. (1998). *Developmental regulation in adulthood: Optimization in primary and secondary control.* Unpublished manuscript, Max Planck Institute for Human Development, Berlin, Germany.

Heckhausen, J., Wrosch, C., & Fleeson, W. (in press). Developmental regulation before and after a developmental deadline: The sample case of biological clock for childbearing. *Psychology and Aging.*

Heidegger, M. (1979). *Sein und Zeit* [Being and time]. Tübingen, Germany: Niemeyer. (Original work published 1927)

Heise, D.R. (1990). Careers, career trajectories, and the self. In J. Rodin, C. Schooler, & K.W. Schaie (Eds.), *Self-directedness: Cause and effects throughout the life course* (pp. 59–84). Hillsdale, NJ: Erlbaum.

Helson, R. (1993). Comparing longitudinal samples: Towards a paradigm of tension between stability and change. In D.C. Funder, R.D. Parke, C. Tomlinson-Keasey, & K. Widaman (Eds.), *Studying lives through time* (pp. 93–119). Washington, DC: American Psychological Association.

Helson, R. (1997). The self in middle age. In M.E. Lachman & J.B. James (Eds.), *Multiple paths of midlife development* (pp. 21–43). Chicago: University of Chicago Press.

Helson, R., & Klohnen, E.C. (1998). Affective coloring of personality from young adulthood to midlife. *Personality and Social Psychology Bulletin, 24,* 241–252.

Helson, R., Stewart, A.J., & Ostrove, J. (1995). Identity in three cohorts of midlife women. *Journal of Personality and Social Psychology, 69,* 544–557.

Helson, R., & Wink, P. (1992). Personality change in women from the early 40s to the early 50s. *Psychology and Aging, 7,* 46–55.

Hirsch, B.J. (1980). Natural support systems and coping with major life changes. *American Journal of Community Psychology, 8,* 159–172.

Hunter, S., & Sundel, M. (1989). Introduction: An examination of key issues concerning midlife. In S. Hunter & M. Sundel (Eds.), *Midlife myths: Issues, findings, and practice implications* (pp. 8–28). Newbury Park, CA: Sage.

Jacques, E. (1965). Death and the midlife crisis. *International Journal of Psychoanalysis, 46,* 502–514.

Jarrett, M.E., & Lethbridge, D.J. (1994). Looking forward, looking back: Women's experience with waning fertility during midlife. *Qualitative Health Research, 4,* 370–384.

Jerusalem, M., & Schwarzer, R. (1992). Self-efficacy as a resource factor in stress appraisal processes. In R. Schwarzer (Ed.), *Self-efficacy: Thought control of action* (pp. 195–213). Washington, DC: Hemisphere.

Karp, D.A. (1987). Professionals beyond midlife: Some observations on work satisfaction in the fifty- to sixty-year decade. *Journal of Aging Studies, 1,* 209–223.

Kessler, R.C., & Cleary, P. (1980). Social class and psychological distress. *American Sociological Review, 45,* 463–478.

Kivett, V.R., Watson, J.A., & Busch, J.C. (1977). The relative importance of physical, psychological, and social variables to locus of control orientation in middle age. *Journal of Gerontology, 32,* 203–210.

Klohnen, E.C., Vandewater, E.A., & Young, A. (1996). Negotiating the middle years: Ego-resiliency and successful midlife adjustment in women. *Psychology and Aging, 11,* 431–442.

Lachman, M.E. (1986). Personal control in later life: Stability, change and cognitive correlates. In M.M. Baltes & P.B. Baltes (Eds.), *The psychology of control and aging* (pp. 207–236). Hillsdale, NJ: Erlbaum.

Lachman, M.E. (1991). Perceived control over memory aging: Developmental and intervention perspectives. *Journal of Social Issues, 47,* 159–175.

Lachman, M.E., Lewkowicz, C., Marcus, A., & Peng, Y. (1994). Images of midlife development among young, middle-aged, and elderly adults. *Journal of Adult Development, 1,* 201–211.

Lachman, M.E., & Weaver, S.L. (1998). The sense of control as a moderator of social class differences in health and well-being. *Journal of Personality and Social Psychology, 74,* 763–773.

Lachman, M.E., Ziff, M., & Spiro, A. (1994). Maintaining a sense of control in later life. In R. Abeles, H. Gift, & M. Ory (Eds.)., *Aging and quality of life* (pp. 116–132). New York: Sage.

Lang, F.R. (2000). Endings and continuity of social relationships: Maximizing intrinsic benefits within personal networks when feeling near to death? *Journal of Social and Personal Relationships.*

Lang, F.R., & Carstensen, L.L. (1994). Close emotional relationships in late life: Further support for proactive aging in the social domain. *Psychology and Aging, 9,* 001–0010.

Levinson, D.J., Darow, C.N., Klein, E.B., Levinson, M.H., & McKee, B. (1978). *The seasons of a man's life.* New York: Knopf.

Lewis, K.G., & Moon, S. (1997). Always single and single again women: A qualitative study. *Journal of Marital and Family Therapy, 23,* 115–134.

Lowenthal, M.F., Fiske, M., & Chiriboga, D. (1972). Transition to the empty nest. *Archives of General Psychiatry, 26,* 8–14.

Lowenthal, M.F., Fiske, M., Thurnher, M., & Chiriboga, D. (1975). *Four stages of life.* San Francisco: Jossey-Bass.

Marks, N.F. (1996). Flying solo at midlife: Gender, marital status, and psychological well-being. *Journal of Marriage and the Family, 58,* 917–932.

Marmot, M., Ryff, C.D., Bumpass, L.L., Shipley, M., & Marks, N.F. (1997). *Social inequalities in health—a major public health problem.* Unpublished manuscript.

Marsiske, M., Lang, F.R., Baltes, P.B., & Baltes, M.M. (1995). Selective optimization with compensation: Life-span perspectives on successful human development. In R.A. Dixon & L. Bäckman (Eds.), *Compensating for psychological deficits and declines: Managing losses and promoting gains* (pp. 35–79). Mahwah, NJ: Erlbaum.

Masten, A.S. (1989). Resilience in development: Implications of the study of successful adaptation for developmental psychopathology. In D. Cicchetti (Ed.), *The emergence of a discipline: Rochester symposium on developmental psychopathology* (Vol. 1, pp. 261–294). Hillsdale, NJ: Erlbaum.

Masten, A.S., & Garmezy, N. (1985). Risk, vulnerability, and protective factors in developmental psychopathology. In B.B. Lahey & A.E. Kazdin (Eds.), *Advances in clinical child psychology* (Vol. 8, pp. 1–52). New York: Plenum Press.

Moen, P., Robison, J., & Fields, V. (1994). Women's work and caregiving roles: A life-course approach. *Journal of Gerontology: Social Sciences, 49,* S176–S186.

Neugarten, B.L. (1968). *Middle age and aging.* Chicago: University of Chicago Press.

Ogilvie, D.M. (1987). Life satisfaction and identity structure in late middle-aged men and women. *Psychology and Aging, 2,* 217–224.

O'Gorman, H.J. (1980). False consciousness of kind: Pluralistic ignorance among the aged. *Research on Aging, 2,* 105–128.

Parris Stephens, M.A., Franks, M.M., & Townsend, A.L. (1994). Stress and rewards in women's multiple roles: The case of women in the middle. *Psychology and Aging, 9,* 45–52.

Peng, Y. (1993). *Primary and secondary control in American and Chinese-American adults: Cross-cultural and life-span developmental perspectives.* Unpublished doctoral dissertation, Brandeis University, Waltham, MA.

Peng, Y., & Lachman, M.E. (1993). *Primary and secondary control: Age and cultural differences.* Paper presented at the 101st annual convention of the American Psychological Association, Toronto, Canada.

Radloff, L. (1977). The CES-D Scale: A self-report depression scale for research in the general population. *Applied Psychological Measurement, 1,* 385–401.

Robinson, B., & Thurner, M. (1979). Taking care of aged parents: A family cycle transition. *Gerontologist, 19,* 586–593.

Rosenberg, S.D., Rosenberg, H.J., & Farrell, M.P. (1999). The midlife crisis revisited. In S.L. Willis & J.D. Reid (Eds.), *Life in the middle: Psychological and social development in middle age* (pp. 47–73). San Diego, CA: Academic Press.

Rothbaum, F., Weisz, J.R., & Snyder, S.S. (1982). Changing the world and changing the self: A two-process model of perceived control. *Journal of Personality and Social Psychology, 42,* 5–37.

Rutter, M. (1985). Resilience in the face of adversity: Protective factors and resistance to psychiatric disorder. *British Journal of Psychiatry, 157,* 598–611.

Rutter, M. (1990). Psychosocial resilience and protective mechanisms. In J. Rolf, A.S. Masten, D. Cicchetti, K.H. Neuchterlein, & S. Weintraub (Eds.), *Risk and protective factors in the development of psychopathology* (pp. 181–214). New York: Cambridge University Press.

Ryff, C.D. (1991). Possible selves in adulthood and old age: A tale of shifting horizons. *Psychology and Aging, 6,* 286–295.

Ryff, C.D., & Kessler, R.C. (Eds.). (2000). *A portrait of midlife in the U.S.* Manuscript in preparation.

Ryff, C.D., Singer, B., Love, G.D., & Essex, M.J. (1998). Resilience in adulthood and later life. In J. Lomranz (Ed.), *Handbook of aging and mental health: An integrative approach* (pp. 69–96). New York: Plenum Press.

Schulz, R., & Decker, S. (1985). Long-term adjustment to physical disability: The role of social support, perceived control, and self-blame. *Journal of Personality and Social Psychology, 48,* 1162–1172.

Schulz, R., & Heckhausen, J. (1996). A life-span model of successful aging. *American Psychologist, 51,* 702–714.

Schulz, R., & Rau, M.T. (1985). Social support through the life course. In S. Cohen & L. Syme (Eds.), *Social support and health* (pp. 129–149). New York: Academic Press.

Sheehy, G. (1976). *Passages: Predictable crises of adult life.* New York: Dutton & Co.

Sommers, T., & Shields, L. (1987). *Women take care: The consequences of caregiving in today's society.* Gainesville, FL: Triad.

Spence, J.T., & Helmreich, R. (1979). *Masculinity and femininity: Their psychological dimensions, correlates and antecedents.* Austin: University of Texas Press.

Staudinger, U.M., Marsiske, M., & Baltes, P.B. (1995). Resilience and reserve capacity in later adulthood: Potentials and limits of development across the life span. In D. Cicchetti & D. Cohen (Eds.), *Developmental psychopathology* (Vol. 2, pp. 801–847). New York: Wiley.

Stewart, A.J., & Ostrove, J.M. (1998). Women's personality in middle age: Gender, history, and midcourse corrections. *American Psychologist, 53,* 1185–1194.

Stewart, A.J., & Vandewater, E.A. (1993). The Radcliffe class of 1964: Career and family social clock projects in a transitional cohort. In K.D. Hulbert & D.T. Schuster (Eds.), *Women's lives through time* (pp. 235–258). San Francisco: Jossey-Bay.

Stewart, A.J., & Vandewater, E.A. (1998). Women's personality in middle age: Gender, history, and midcourse corrections. *American Psychologists, 53,* 1185–1194.

Stewart, A.J., & Vandewater, E.A. (1999). "If I had it to do over again . . .": Midlife review, midcourse corrections, and women's well-being in midlife. *Journal of Personality and Social Psychology, 76,* 270–283.

Tangri, S., & Jenkins, S. (1993). The University of Michigan class of 1967: The women's life paths study. In K.D. Hulbert & D.T. Schuster (Eds.), *Women's lives through time* (pp. 259–281). San Francisco: Jossey-Bass.

Taylor, S.E., & Lobel, M. (1989). Social comparison activity under threat: Downward evaluation and upward contacts. *Psychological Review, 96,* 569–575.

Taylor, S.E., Wood, J.V., & Lichtman, R.R. (1984). Attributions, beliefs about control, and adjustment to breast cancer. *Journal of Personality and Social Psychology, 46,* 489–502.

Thoits, P.A. (1983). Multiple identities and psychological well-being: A reformulation and test of the social isolation hypothesis. *American Sociological Review, 48,* 174–187.

Tower, R., & Kasl, S. (1996). Gender, marital closeness, and depressive symptoms in elderly couples. *Journal of Gerontology: Psychological Sciences, 51B,* P115–P129.

Uhlenberg, P., Cooney, T., & Boyd, R. (1990). Divorce for women after midlife. *Journal of Family Issues, 13,* 390–409.

Vaillant, G.E. (1977). *Adaptation to life.* Boston: Little, Brown.

Vandewater, E.A., Ostrove, J.M., & Stewart, A.J. (1997). Predicting women's well-being in midlife: The importance of personality development and social role involvements. *Journal of Personality and Social Personality, 72,* 1147–1160.

Von Dras, D.D., & Siegler, I.C. (1997). Stability in extroversion and aspects of social support at midlife. *Journal of Personality and Social Psychology, 72,* 233–241.

Waite, L. (1995). Does marriage matter? *Demography, 32,* 483–507.

Ward, R.S., & Spitze, G. (1998). Sandwiched marriages: The implications of child and parent relations for marital quality in midlife. *Social Forces, 77,* 647–666.

Werner, E.E. (1995). Resilience in development. *Current Directions in Psychological Science, 4,* 81–85.

Werner, E.E., & Smith, R.S. (1992). *Overcoming the odds: High risk children from birth to adulthood.* Ithaca, NY: Cornell University Press.

Westermeyer, J.F. (1998). Predictors and characteristics of mental health among men at midlife: A 32-year longitudinal study. *American Journal of Orthopsychiatry, 68,* 265–273.

Wethington, E., Cooper, H., & Holmes, C.S. (1997). Turning points in midlife. In I.H. Gotlib & E. Wethington (Eds.), *Stress and adversity over the life course: Trajectories and turning points* (pp. 215–231). Cambridge, England: Cambridge University Press.

Whitbourne, S.K. (1986). *The me I know: A study of adult identity.* New York: Springer.

Whitbourne, S.K., & Connolly L.A. (1999). The developing self in midlife. In S.L. Willis & J.D. Reid (Eds.), *Life in the middle: Psychological and social development in middle age* (pp. 25–45). San Diego, CA: Academic Press.

White, R.W. (1959). Motivation reconsidered: The concept of competence. *Psychological Review, 66,* 297–333.

Wills, T.A. (1981). Downward comparison principles in social psychology. *Psychological Bulletin, 90,* 245–271.

Wink, P., & Helson, R. (1993). Personality change in women and their partners. *Journal of Personality and Social Psychology, 65,* 597–605.

Wood, J.V. (1989). Theory and research concerning social comparison of personal attributes. *Psychological Bulletin, 106,* 231–248.

Woods, N.F., & Mitchell, E.S. (1997). Women's images of midlife: Observations from the Seattle midlife women's health study. *Health Care for Women International, 18,* 439–453.

Wrosch, C. (1999). *Entwicklungsfristen im Partnerschaftsbereich: Bezugsrahmen für Prozesse der Aktivierung und Deaktivierung von Entwicklungszielen [Developmental deadlines in the partnership domain: Reference frame for activating and deactivating developmental goals].* Münster, Germany: Waxmann.

Wrosch, C., & Heckhausen, J. (1999). Control processes before and after passing a developmental deadline: Activation and deactivation of intimate relationship goals. *Journal of Personality and Social Psychology, 77,* 415–427.

CHAPTER 12

Generativity in Midlife

DAN P. MCADAMS

IN HIS LANDMARK VOLUME, *Childhood and Society,* Erik Erikson (1950) identified *generativity* as the defining psychosocial feature of midlife. It is in the middle-adult years, Erikson maintained, that men and women are most likely to be concerned about the well-being of future generations and involved in various life projects, from parenting to political action, aimed at generating a positive legacy that will ultimately outlive the self. Younger adults are more likely to be involved in the complicated business of establishing an *identity* and building up long-term bonds of *intimacy,* Erikson argued. By contrast, old age brings a concern with what Erikson called ego *integrity,* as the elderly man or woman takes stock of life and, ideally, reaches a point of acceptance. It is in the middle—in that long and vaguely demarcated epoch in the life course, when people are no longer "young" but not yet "old"—that men and women take on the challenges and experience the joys and failures of generativity. It is in that long middle of life that adults should and often do provide care, guidance, inspiration, instruction, and leadership for children, youth, students, protegees, subordinates, followers, and those many others who, individually or collectively, represent those who will come of age, who will reach full maturity in the future. It is in the long middle when men and women make their most significant contributions to future generations and to society.

Preparation of this manuscript was facilitated by grants to the author from the Spencer Foundation and the Foley Family Foundation. The author thanks Ed de St. Aubin and the many contributors to the edited volume, *Generativity and Adult Development,* and Tae-Chang Kim and the contributors to the 1998 and 1999 Kyoto conferences on generativity and future generations for shaping and enriching his understanding of generativity in midlife.

Generativity is the concern for and commitment to promoting future generations through parenting, teaching, mentoring, and generating products and outcomes that aim to benefit youth and foster the well-being and development of individuals and social systems that will outlive the self (McAdams & de St. Aubin, 1998). In their roles as parents, teachers, coaches, mentors, leaders, helpers, and volunteers, generative adults serve as norm bearers and destiny shapers in families, schools, churches, neighborhoods, and the workplace. From a psychological standpoint, generativity may be experienced both as an inner desire or proclivity on the one hand and an age-appropriate expectation or demand on the other. As Erikson wrote, the midlife man or woman "needs to be needed, and maturity needs guidance as well as encouragement from what has been produced and must be taken care of" (1963, pp. 266–267). In simple terms, mature adults need and want to care for others, and indeed society expects them to need and want this, and to act accordingly. From the standpoint of society and culture, furthermore, generativity is a critical resource that may undergird social institutions, encourage citizens' contributions and commitments to the public good, motivate efforts to sustain continuity from one generation to the next, and initiate social change. Consequently, generativity is a psychosocial concept in two related senses. First, adults can be generative only in social arenas that sustain their generative efforts. Second, social contexts and institutions themselves may be more or less generative. There are generative people, generative groups, generative situations, even generative societies. Likewise, there are people, groups, situations, and even societies that are more or less lacking or deficient in generativity (Kotre, 1999; Moran, 1998).

Despite its theoretical richness and intuitive appeal for understanding human lives, generativity remained a dormant concept in the social sciences for at least 30 years following the publication of *Childhood and Society*. Beginning in the 1980s, however, theorists and researchers began to examine the concept in some detail. Recent years have witnessed an upsurge of creative theorizing and systematic research on the concept of generativity, much of it holding implications for how social and behavioral scientists understand midlife. The goal of this chapter is to synthesize much of the best theoretical and empirical work on generativity within a life-course perspective, with special emphasis on how this work informs the study of midlife. The chapter begins with a history of the concept of generativity, going back 2,000 years. Next, it considers the ways in which generativity is a developmental construct, contrasting life-cycle and life-course perspectives on the relation between generativity and midlife. Finally, the chapter considers empirical research on generative lives in the middle-adult years, examining relations between generativity on the one hand and psychological, social, and cultural phenomena on the other. The chapter ends with proposals for new directions in future research and theorizing.

HISTORY OF THE CONCEPT

Although Erikson is credited for bringing the word generativity into the modern psychological lexicon, the concept has been around, at least in Western traditions, for over two thousand years. Indeed, the history of the concept of generativity may be neatly divided into three phases: (1) the long period preceding Erikson's seminal writings; (2) Erikson's theory itself; and (3) developments that have followed Erikson, in some cases taking issue with Erikson's emphases and themes.

BEFORE ERIKSON

Wakefield (1998) argues that the first full-blown theory of generativity appears in Plato's *Symposium.* In this ancient Greek dialogue concerning the nature of love, Plato spells out a conception of generativity, without ever using the Greek equivalent of the word, that underscores its connections to love and the desire for immortality. Plato proposes that love is the desire to possess that which is good and beautiful in the other. The possession of good things makes men (and women) happy, he maintains. But it is not enough to possess the good. The lover wishes to possess the good indefinitely, to continue to have that which is beautiful in the beloved over a prolonged period of time, indeed forever. In that all forms of human love aim at the everlasting possession of the good, love presupposes the human desire for immortality. Heterosexual love, furthermore, reveals an even closer connection to immortality:

> Then if this be the nature of love, can you tell me further what is the manner of the pursuit? What are they doing who show all this eagerness and heat which is called love, and what is the object which they have in view? . . . Well, I will teach you—the object which they have in view is birth in beauty, whether of body or of soul. . . . There is a certain age at which human nature is desirous of procreation—procreation which must be in beauty and not in deformity; and this procreation is a union of man and woman, and is a divine thing; for conception and generation are an immortal principle in the mortal creature. . . . Beauty, then, is the destiny or goddess of parturition who presides at birth, and therefore, when approaching beauty, the conceiving power is propitious, and diffusive, and benign, and begets and bears fruit; at the sight of ugliness she frowns and contracts and has a sense of pain, and turns away, and shrivels up, and not without a pang refrains from conception. And this is the reason why, when the hour of conception arrives, and the teeming nature is full, there is such a flutter and

ecstasy about beauty, whose approach is the alleviation of the pain of travail. For love, Socrates, is not, as you imagine, the love of the beautiful only. . . . It is the love of generation and of birth in beauty. . . . Because to the mortal creature generation is a sort of eternity and immortality, and if, as has been already admitted, love is of the everlasting possession of the good, all men will necessarily desire immortality together with good—wherefore love is of immortality. (Jowett, 1956, *Plato's Symposium*, pp. 47–48)

The prototype of generativity is what Plato depicted as "birth in beauty." To be generative is to give birth to a beautiful (e.g., healthy, well-formed, useful, elegant, good) product. The adult gets to generativity through love. The aim of love is to possess the beauty of the beloved, in the hope and expectation that it will inspire one to bring forth something good out of oneself. In the case of erotic love between male and female, generativity may be expressed through procreation, as the product of sexual union is literally (and ideally) born in beauty. More generally, furthermore, love may inspire the birth of many other kinds of beautiful products, including works of art and ideas. In Plato's view, all people are pregnant with physical or mental generative products, awaiting the inspiration for their birthings that can only come through a loving relationship with another person. As Wakefield puts it, "Generativity is essentially a triadic relationship among the generative individual, a generative love object that serves as a catalyst for the creation and nurturance of the generated product, and a generative product that is brought forth because of the relationship to the love object" (1998, p. 149). It would seem that one cannot be generative on one's own.

The products of generativity help to assuage the human desire for immortality, Plato argued. It is expected that one's children will live on after one's death, and it is hoped that they, too, will generate offspring that are good and beautiful and (eventually) generative themselves. Of course, generativity does not end with conception. Parents must work hard and sacrifice a great deal to assure that their children survive and flourish—this was recognized in Plato's time as clearly as it is today. But children are only one road to immortality. Most adults cultivate a good reputation, Plato maintained, and they strongly hope that that reputation will endure after they are gone. Indeed, children are valued not only for the good and beautiful persons they may be, Plato suggested, but also for their role in keeping the parents' good memory alive after they have died. Beyond this, however, the adult may attain an enduring positive reputation through a wide range of heroic exploits (e.g., victory in war, sacrifice for others), industrious activities (making crafts, manufacturing implements), and contributions of the mind (e.g., art, philosophy, teaching). An especially important form of generativity, Plato suggested, is active involvement in social institutions and social reform. When the adult comes to understand that families, social institutions, and laws order society and shape the young of future generations, the lover of wisdom and virtue wants to impart these qualities to others and thus plays an active role in ordering society's institutions and laws consistent with the ideal of justice, and thus encouraging virtue in the citizenry. Laws and institutions provide the structures that nurture all of the procreation, productivity, creativity, and other virtues in a culture. Therefore, social reform is an especially high form of generativity. From Solon to Martin Luther King, Jr., social reformers may earn an exceptionally long-lasting and positive reputation.

Plato's ideas anticipated themes that have gathered around the concept of generativity in the discourse of twentieth-century psychology, especially in writings coming out of the psychoanalytic tradition. As a general desire to possess the beautiful in another, Plato's eros is a direct intellectual ancestor of Freud's (1905/1953) libido, or sexual instinct. The prudent and socially useful investment of libido into objects and people that are worthy of such an investment is the cardinal feature of adaptive ego functioning, Freud argued. Put more simply, psychological adaptation and maturity in the adult years involve the ability to love well and to work usefully—*Lieben und Arbeiten,* as Freud is thought to have put it. Blending ideas from Freud and Marx, Erich Fromm (1941, 1947) sought to understand how modern adults might love and work well within modern societal arrangements that are not always conducive to generativity. How do modern adults find expression for their basic needs within the rules of culture, those rules ranging from the strictures of totalitarian states to the norms of winner-take-all capitalist economies? The interactions of personal needs and societal contexts give rise to a wide range of nongenerative character types in adulthood, such as the receptive (passive and conforming), the hoarding, the exploitative, and the marketing (opportunistic, market-driven) types. By contrast, the *productive type* fulfills his or her inner potential to become a creative worker and lover within a well-defined social identity. The productive adult is autonomous, spontaneous, loving, creative, and committed to the social good.

Otto Rank (1936, 1968) and Ernest Becker (1973) picked up on the Platonic desire for immortality as it plays itself out in adult lives. For these psychoanalytic theorists, the fear of death proves the great motivator for human behavior, inspiring both humankind's greatest achievements and most shameful follies. Adults work hard and love earnestly in their efforts to deny death and to build up some kind of legacy on earth that will endure. To denote these death-denying projects in work and love, Becker employed the term *heroism,* whose meaning approximates aspects of generativity (McAdams, 1985). According to Becker (1973), "the most that any one of us can seem to do is to fashion something—an object or ourselves—and drop it into the confusion, make an offering of it, so to speak, to the life force" (p. 285). Yet people differ with respect to the "gifts" they may offer. The *neurotic* man or woman is unable to make an offering and instead erects an impenetrable character shield that keeps him or her from engaging the world in a productive manner. The *average* man or woman offers "the gift that society specifies in advance" (p. 173). Conforming and dependable, the average person finds a conventional niche in the social world and performs the heroic behaviors—builds a home, raises children, contributes to society—that society deems appropriate. The adult who offers the most heroic, authentic, and influential gift, however, is the *artist*. Becker employs this label to denote the person who most successfully transforms the fear of death into creative activity that helps to transform society or culture in a positive manner. The gift that the artist offers has a lasting value, transcending the here-and-now to speak to the "highest powers." "The artist's gift is always to creation itself, to the ultimate meaning of life, to God" (p. 173).

Outside the psychoanalytic tradition, references to psychological phenomena and processes akin to generativity appear in the writings of such early-twentieth-century life-span theorists as Buhler (1933) and Frenkel (1936). Examining life histories written by almost 400 European men and women in the 1930s, Buhler and Frenkel identified "rather sharply demarcated phases through which every person passed in the course of" life (Frenkel, 1936, p. 2). They argued that while young adults tend to be strongly oriented toward their own personal goals and bodily needs, the midlife man or woman tends to be more preoccupied with internalized duties that one "has set himself [or herself], or which have been set for him [or her] by society, or which have come from some code of values such as religion or science" (Frenkel, 1936, p. 15). The cultivation of those values and their transmission to the next generation becomes an especially salient developmental task in midlife and beyond.

ERIKSON'S THEORY

Beginning in *Childhood and Society* and running through a series of books published over a 32-year span, Erikson (1950, 1964, 1969, 1982) conceived the human life course as a sequence of eight stages. The individual moves through each stage in a cultural context that holds expectations and provides socializing influences that pertain to the stage. Each stage, then, spells out how biological, cognitive, and emotional changes on the one hand interact with corresponding societal and cultural forces and factors on the other. Each stage is defined by a central, constellating contrast or dialectic. For example, Erikson viewed the first stage of life (infancy) through the contrast of *trust versus mistrust*. In this first stage, important aspects of the infant's behavior and experience concern the eventual establishment of a trusting attachment bond with caregivers and the concomitant first experiences of mistrust or anxiety in the face of separation, novelty, and other sources of potential danger. The infant's social world, furthermore, is geared to expect and provide for this first developmental task. Caregivers implicitly know that babies require comfort and attention, and caregivers invest considerable energy, according to the cultural norms of the day, to promoting the development of a secure (i.e., trusting) attachment bond. The more-or-less successful movement through this first stage paves the way for healthy development in subsequent stages, as the toddler now moves into a second stage of *autonomy versus shame and doubt,* within which the toddler and the toddler's world face a new set of developmental challenges.

Fast-forwarding to adolescence and adulthood, Erikson's theory introduces the stages of identity, intimacy, and generativity. After moving through the fifth (late-adolescent) stage of *identity versus role confusion* and the sixth (young-adult) stage of *intimacy versus isolation,* the adult confronts *generativity versus stagnation*—the key issue of Erikson's seventh stage, associated with the long period of the middle-adult years. In the ideal Eriksonian scenario, the individual first consolidates a sense of who he or she is and how he or she fits into society (identity) and then commits him- or herself to others through marriage and long-term friendship (intimacy) before he or she is psychosocially ready to devote considerable time and effort to the well-being of generations to come. Parenting is perhaps the prototypical expression of generativity, but adults can be generative in many other ways as well, especially through creative and productive activities and through leadership and teaching. Failures and frustrations in generativity may be experienced as stagnation, wherein the adult feels that he or she is unable to create or produce a satisfying legacy of the self, or as self-preoccupation, wherein the adult focuses attention mainly on the care and maintenance of the self rather than others. The latter instance is a curious example of infantilization. The adult comes to see him- or herself to be like a child, needing constant attention and care lest it come to feel neglected.

Erikson identified *care* as the signal virtue associated with the generativity stage. A primary arena for expression of care is the family, and the primary objects of generativity for many adults are their own children and/or the young people in their immediate community. But generativity can also be expressed on a larger public stage, even to the point of caring for society as a whole. In *Gandhi's Truth,* Erikson (1969) showed how one man's generativity mission came to encompass the well-being of an entire nation. As a spiritual leader and a fatherly caregiver for his own people, Gandhi played out his generativity in a dramatic public fashion, even as he failed to be a good father to his biological children at home.

The trade-off of public and private expressions of generativity is an especially salient theme in the life histories of prominent women and men, who have sought, like Becker's artist, to exert a transformative effect on society at large (e.g., Colby & Damon, 1992).

Erikson described generativity as stemming from both inner needs or drives and external forces in society. He speculated that generativity may ultimately be traced from some kind of biological urgings, related perhaps to sexuality and procreation, but he also underscored how society's expectations for generative behavior shape the expression of generativity and care in adulthood. Furthermore, while Erikson's stage model suggests that generativity versus stagnation is a normative developmental issue, adults still differ significantly from one another with respect to the strength and scope of their generative feelings, attitudes, and expressions. Individual differences in generativity may stem from many causes, Erikson argued. Among the more intriguing may be what Erikson (1963, p. 267) called a "belief in the species"—a faith in the ultimate goodness and worthwhileness of the human enterprise. Generativity always involves hard work, and people who lack a belief in the species may find it difficult to summon forth the energy and commitment that are needed to support that work and sustain the hope that it will all pay off in the long run. It is difficult to be generative, Erikson maintained, if one is not at least moderately optimistic about the future and about the fate of one's family, community, or people.

Generativity motivates behavior aimed at promoting the greater good. But Erikson also emphasized how generativity can be good for the generative person. Not only is generativity a sign of psychosocial maturity in Erikson's developmental scheme, but it should also be associated with mental health and well-being. Psychoanalytically informed theorists and clinicians have argued that generativity represents the full expression of love and work. Vaillant (1977) placed generativity at the center of healthy adaptation in the adult years. Elaborating on Erikson's ideas, Vaillant suggested that in early-to-middle adulthood generativity is often expressed through parenting and through one's activities in the workplace but that as adults move through midlife their generative expressions expand to encompass the maintenance of important societal institutions. In midlife, Vaillant wrote, especially generative adults may come to function as society's "keepers of the meaning." Following Erikson, other life-span theorists have identified generativity as a key component to psychosocial adaptation in midlife: Gould (1980), Gutmann (1987), Havighurst (1972), Helson and Wink (1992), Levinson (1978, 1996), Neugarten (1968), and Roberts and Newton (1987).

There are intriguing parallels between Plato's ancient and Erikson's modern conceptualizations of generativity. Both views, for example, suggest a tight relationship between adult love and generativity. For Plato, love catalyzes or inspires the generation of self-extending offspring, whether those offspring be children or artistic masterpieces. For Erikson, mature adult love, or what he calls intimacy, is developmentally prior to generativity in the stage scheme. Generativity's fullest expression awaits the successful resolution of the intimacy versus isolation contrast of young adulthood. For both views, furthermore, procreation exists as something of a prototype for generativity, but generativity also comes to encompass a wide variety of creative and productive activities. Both Plato and Erikson viewed generativity through a moral lens, and in both views generativity is deemed to be good or virtuous. It is right and good that adults should focus their attentions on promoting the next generation; artistic, intellectual, and political expressions of generativity, furthermore, are held in very high esteem. By way of difference, Erikson deemphasized the extent to which generativity stems from desires for immortality, though the idea is not absent in his writings (e.g, his analysis of Gandhi; Erikson, 1969). More than Plato, Erikson emphasized the softer and more nurturing aspects of generativity. Generativity is first and foremost about *caring for* the next generation, Erikson maintained. While Plato's philosopher-king and Becker's heroic artist may make contributions that profoundly impact the worlds around them, thereby assuring a noteworthy reputation for generations to come, Erikson left more room for everyday acts of kindness and care, even when those acts are displayed in the most local of scenes by the most anonymous of actors, and even when those actions are soon to be forgotten. There is a democratic, egalitarian spirit in Erikson's writings (Friedman, 1999). He seemed to believe that all adults could, in principle, be generative.

After Erikson

Although Erikson's overall stage model of psychosocial development proved to be an extraordinarily influential framework for the social and behavioral sciences, and even in some branches of the humanities, the concept of generativity attracted little notice in the years following the publication of his first work. With only a few exceptions (e.g., Browning, 1975), little scholarly or scientific attention was paid to generativity through the 1970s. Virtually no empirical research was conducted on the topic, although generativity was sometimes included in more large-scale studies of Erikson's overall stage scheme (e.g., Constantinople, 1969; Ochse & Plug, 1986; Vaillant, 1977). Generativity featured prominently in some psychoanalytically inspired case studies and psychobiographies (Anderson, 1981), but little effort was made to flesh out the construct or to test hypotheses that might be derived from it.

The situation began to change in the early 1980s. The first theorist to expand significantly on Erikson's ideas about generativity was John Kotre (1984). Kotre distinguished among four different forms of generativity. In *biological* generativity, adults beget, bear, and nurse their offspring; the generative object is the infant. In *parental* generativity, adults nurture and discipline offspring, initiate them into family traditions, and continue to support, guide, protect, teach, and advise them through their adolescent years; the generative object, thus, is the child. In *technical* generativity, the adult teaches skills and offers instrumental training to those who require these competencies for successful adaptation to the world; the generative objects are both the skill itself and the apprentice for the skill. Finally, in *cultural* generativity, the adult creates, renovates, or conserves a symbol system—the "mind" of a culture—and explicitly passes that system on to the next generation; here the generative objects are the culture itself—its institutions and ideas—as well as those disciples or students to whom culture is transmitted. Cutting across the four forms of generativity, furthermore, are two different styles or modes. Following Bakan (1966), Kotre identified especially *communal* modes of generativity as involving nurturance and care for others while especially *agentic* modes encompass creative and/or powerful extensions of the self, as in some forms of leadership, entrepreneurial activity, scientific achievement, and so forth.

Kotre defines generativity as "the desire to invest one's substance in forms of life and work that will outlive the self" (1984, p. 10). Like Plato, Becker, and Rank, then, Kotre suggests that generativity involves extending the self beyond the end of one's own life, generating an enduring personal legacy. Unlike these theorists, however, and in contrast to Erikson as well, Kotre contends that generativity is not necessarily a virtue in life. As such, generativity may be used for good or ill. One person's efforts to produce legacies that will outlive the self may be seen by others as misguided, destructive, or even evil. Kotre exposes the dark side of generativity—how generativity can sometimes lead to fanaticism, for example, and how the outcomes of one's best generative efforts can sometimes turn out to be bad. At the same time, a person's generativity can also take the form of transforming a bad legacy into a good one, or of assuring that something bad from the past (e.g., a family history of abuse, a destructive cultural practice) is actively blocked so that it will not be repeated in future generations. In this latter example, the generative person functions as an intergenerational buffer, filtering out the negative legacies and seeking to pass on only those meanings and practices from the past that are deemed to be positive (Kotre, 1999; Kotre & Kotre, 1998).

Drawing on Erikson, Kotre, and Becker, Dan McAdams and his colleagues (McAdams, 1985; McAdams & de St. Aubin, 1992; McAdams, Hart, & Maruna, 1998) have developed an integrative model of generativity that emphasizes the multiple levels on and modes through which generativity may be expressed. McAdams agrees with Kotre that generativity may take agentic or communal forms, but he goes on to suggest that the fullest expressions of generativity are fundamentally *both* agentic and communal. The very concept of generativity brings together two seemingly incompatible sets of desires. On the one hand, generativity challenges adults to produce, create, or generate some product or outcome that may potentially, in Kotre's terms, "outlive the self." This sense of generativity suggests a trace of narcissism, of creating something in one's own image, a powerful act of self-expansion. On the other hand, that which is generated must be cared for, nurtured, and eventually granted its own autonomy, to live on as, in Becker's words, a "gift" for/to/of the next generation. Therefore, while the first sense of generativity bespeaks agency, the second sense suggests communion, even to the point of sacrificing the self for the good of that which and those who will follow. Generativity can prove to be a curious blend of narcissism and altruism aimed toward future generations. Bringing together power and love, agency and communion, self-expansion and self-surrender, generativity may embody a motivational paradox, making for a wide range of complex and even contradictory expressions in any given adult life.

McAdams argues that generativity is a configuration of seven psychosocial features—desire, demand, concern, belief, commitment, action, and narration—all of which center on the individual and societal goal of providing for future generations. As shown in Figure 12.1, generativity begins with (1) agentic and communal *desires* that motivate a person to seek out opportunities for both symbolic immortality and caring nurturance for others and (2) age-graded cultural *demands* that provide standards and expectations concerning how people may and should begin to take responsibility for the next generation as they move into and through middle adulthood. As Erikson suggested, therefore, generativity comes from within and without. Agentic and communal desires combine with and are structured by cultural norms, expectations, and influences that specify when and how adults are to engage in generative behaviors in a given social milieu. Motivated by inner desires and outer demands, adults develop (3) a conscious *concern* for the next generation. They begin to expand their purview of concern to encompass the well-being of others who will survive them. They become more interested in those institutions and cultural practices designed to promote positive functioning and social life into the future—schools, churches, charities, community organizations, professional societies, and so on. They become more concerned with intergenerational relations. They begin to see that they may have something to offer others, that the time may be right to "give something back" to society, to move from being the recipient to being the agent of care and concern.

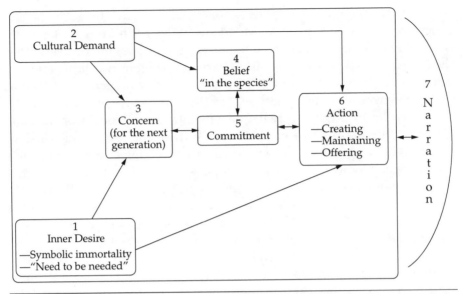

Figure 12.1   Seven features of generativity (from McAdams, Hart, & Maruna, 1998, p. 9).

Interacting with desire, demand, and concern are (4) *beliefs* pertaining to how advisable it may be to invest in others and in the future and how worthy others may be of one's care. Erikson saw a "belief in the species" as a key attitudinal support for generative behavior. These kinds of beliefs may take many forms—faith in the goodness of humankind, hope for redemption in the future, optimism about the prospects of future prosperity for one's family, belief in a just world, and so on. By contrast, deep pessimism, cynicism, despair, and hopelessness undermine generativity, for they suggest that investments in the future are not likely to bring positive returns (Van De Water & McAdams, 1989). A positive belief in the species, then, may help to buttress the adult's efforts to translate concerns into behavior through plans, goals, and other generative (5) *commitments*. Not all manifestations of generativity are planned in advance, of course. Unexpected pregnancy is the most obvious example, and in many other lives adults find that generative opportunities or challenges are as much thrust on them as they are developed out of their own life agendas. Sooner or later, however, generativity virtually always results in some kind of long-term commitment, entailing goals and plans. Ideally, the commitments lead to generative (6) *actions*. Many different kinds of actions may be construed as generative. Most common, however, are behaviors that involve creating or generating new things and people (developing an innovation, giving birth to a child), maintaining and caring for those things (and people) deemed to be good (preserving religious traditions, raising children), and passing on that which has been created or maintained as a "gift" (Becker, 1973) to the next generation (teaching a skill, "launching" a son or daughter into the adult world).

The last of McAdams's seven features is generative (7) *narration*. As they translate their concerns and beliefs into commitment and action designed to promote the well-being of the next generation, adults construct personal narrations or tellings of their generative efforts, which eventually become incorporated into the larger, autobiographical tellings that comprise their life stories. These tellings are designed both for public and private consumption; people tell each other stories about their own lives, and they tell themselves their own stories—consciously and unconsciously—to make narrative sense of their own lives as they are living them. McAdams integrates the concept of generativity within his overall life-story theory of adult identity. The basic premise of the theory is that modern adults provide their lives with a sense of unity and purpose by constructing and internalizing self-defining life stories, complete with settings, scenes, characters, plots, and themes (McAdams, 1985, 1993, 1996b). Within this evolving life story, narrations of generativity become increasingly central and salient as the adult moves into and through midlife (McAdams, 1996a). These narrations specify how the adult has worked and/or will continue to work to fashion a positive legacy for the future. As such, a narration of generativity functions to provide an adult with a potentially satisfying sense of an "ending" for his or her life story (Kermode, 1967), in that the generativity narration anticipates how one's life may ultimately result in the generation of offspring, products, and outcomes that will outlive the self. Following Becker, adults craft self-defining life stories whose endings defy death, in a narrative sense; for (the author hopes) even though one's own life will end, it may give birth to new beginnings.

In recent years, a number of other psychologists have begun to articulate further the concept of generativity. For example, Abigail Stewart and Bill Peterson have argued that generative *motivation* should be distinguished from generative *realization* (Peterson, 1998; Peterson & Stewart, 1996; Stewart & Vandewater, 1998) Young adults may have strong motivations to be generative, but they may not be able to actualize or realize these desires until they have achieved the necessary resources that may attend midlife. By then, their generative motivations may have flagged somewhat, but their behavioral realizations of generativity are likely to reach their peak. A counterpoint to generative motivation is what John Snarey (1993) has described as *generativity chill*. Increasingly salient as one moves through midlife, generativity chill is the anxiety and dread caused by a threatened loss of one's generative products. Other theorists have underscored the variability of generativity across different life domains (MacDermid,

Franz, & De Reus, 1998). While one adult may express generativity in work or volunteer roles, another may be especially generative in the family. Like Gandhi (Erikson, 1969), many people may be specialists in generativity, expressing high levels of care and commitment in some social roles but not in others. Beyond the strength and scope of generativity, therefore, individual differences in generative expression can be understood with respect to a person's idiosyncratic patterning of social roles. Still other theorists have underscored the ethical dimensions of generativity (Browning, 1999; Dollahite, Slife, & Hawkins, 1998; Snarey & Clark, 1998). Snarey and Clark define *generative ethics* as a moral stance predicated on the principle of caring for future generations. Linking generativity to religiously based ethical codes, Dollahite et al. have developed an elaborate regimen for family counseling, designed to help "families keep faith with the next generation" (p. 449).

GENERATIVITY AS A DEVELOPMENTAL CONSTRUCT

Because it defines the seventh stage in Erikson's highly influential model of psychosocial development, the concept of generativity most readily summons forth the discourse of developmental psychology. This is to say that although Erikson described generativity as a biologically determined drive, a need to be needed, a criterion of mental health, and a dimension of individual differences, among other things, generativity is nonetheless most often construed by psychologists (and laypersons familiar with Erikson's writings) as a *stage*. And even though more recent theoretical expansions of the concept (e.g., Kotre, McAdams, Stewart & Peterson) have endeavored to articulate a wider range of discourses about generativity (e.g., generativity as a desire for symbolic immortality, generativity as cultural demand, generativity as a way of telling a life, individual differences in generativity, generativity motivation vs. realization), it is still the developmental, purportedly stage-like features of generativity that many people think of as central to the construct. What, then, is the status of generativity as a developmental construct? To what extent may generativity be viewed as a discrete stage of (mid)life? What is generativity's place in the human life course?

IS GENERATIVITY A MIDLIFE STAGE?

Erikson's stage model is often read as a theory of the human life cycle. The metaphor of a life "cycle" suggests that development is more or less regular and predictable, that each developmental stage has its own particular place and time in the cycle (epigenesis), and that human lives themselves have something of a repetitive, cyclical quality. With respect to the last idea, Erikson's model implies that human beings come full circle by the time they reach the last stage of life; ego integrity (Stage 8) brings forth qualities and experiences that are reminiscent of basic trust (Stage 1). In addition, the cyclical nature of life derives from the relations that individuals have to the lives and developmental trajectories of preceding and subsequent generations. Wakefield describes this idea:

> Each individual is nurtured by the previous generation in a way that allows the individual ultimately to nurture the next generation in a way that allows that generation to go on and nurture the following generation. The generative strivings of one generation match the needs for nurturance of the next and result from the generative nurturance of which they themselves were the recipients earlier in their lives. The repetition of the generations, the dovetailing of developmental histories of the generations, and in particular, the movement from passive recipient to active provider of generative nurturance constitute the cycle. (1998, p. 137)

In Erikson's life-cycle model, the stage of midlife is defined by the psychosocial dialectic of generativity versus stagnation. The psychosocial way for generativity is paved by the resolution of developmentally prior issues (most immediately intimacy versus isolation in young adulthood) and by the welling up of inner desire and cultural demand that attend this period in the life cycle. During midlife, then, psychosocial development should be centered on generativity, in the same way, Erikson suggested, that psychosocial development in the first year of life centers around trust versus mistrust. It might be expected, then, that in midlife a person's generative concerns, commitments, and behaviors should increase, relative to their respective levels in young adulthood. Furthermore, it would be expected that generative concerns, commitments, and behaviors should decrease as the individual moves into the last of Erikson's stages—"old age" (never clearly defined by Erikson), with its issue of ego integrity versus despair. It might also be predicted that generativity would become a greater source of both fulfillment and frustration as the adult moves into midlife, and that its salience in this regard should diminish somewhat in the later years. To date, data speaking to these hypotheses come from case studies, cross-sectional studies, and longitudinal investigations.

Stewart and her colleagues have carried out a series of quantitative case studies examining Eriksonian stages. Their method is to code open-ended autobiographical data—such as published diaries and autobiographies—for stage-related themes of identity, intimacy, and generativity. Their carefully drawn coding systems provide reliable quantitative indexes for each of these three stages. Stewart, Franz, and Layton (1988) focused on the writings of Vera Brittain, an early-twentieth century feminist and peace activist who published a celebrated autobiographical chronicle of her adolescent and early-adult years, entitled *Testament of Youth* (Brittain, 1933/1970). Coding her diaries and her retrospective account in *Testament of Youth,* the researchers found that concerns about identity vastly outweighed concerns about intimacy and generativity during Brittain's early years. Peterson and Stewart (1990) coded fiction and diaries written by Brittain during early adulthood (age 21–23, during World War I), early middle age (39–43, just before World War II), and later middle age (46–50, during World War II) for the same themes. They found a clear decrease in identity and intimacy concerns and a clear increase in generativity concerns over this time period. Still, identity themes tended to predominate throughout. Brittain's case suggests, then, that generativity may increase as a concern into midlife, but that developmentally prior identity themes remain relatively prominent. A case analysis of the written correspondence of an adolescent girl who eventually emigrated from her nation of origin showed that generativity themes can nonetheless appear at high levels in the adolescent years. Espin, Stewart, and Gomez (1990) found that generativity themes increased significantly between the age of 13 and 22 in these letters. At age 22, the young woman became a mother.

Cross-sectional studies have examined generativity scores, assessed in a variety of ways, among different age cohorts. While these studies cannot disentangle age and cohort effects, they do offer some of the most direct assessments of generativity in the empirical literature. An early study by Gruen (1964) used judges' ratings of the degree to which individuals achieved a positive resolution of each of Erikson's eight stages, based on two-hour interviews of adults ranging in age from 40 to 65 years. The study revealed no age differences (and no gender or class effects) for generativity. By contrast, Ryff and Heincke (1983) employed a variety of self-ratings made by young (mean age = 21), middle-aged (mean age = 48), and older (mean age = 69) adults. Middle-aged adults rated themselves as higher on a rationally derived scale of generativity in the present than they recalled being in the past and more generative than they anticipated being in the future. Younger adults anticipated scoring higher on generativity in middle age than they were at present. Older adults recalled their being higher in generativity in midlife than they rated themselves in the present. The results suggest that in evaluating their own lives, adults expect to be most generative in their middle-adult years. However, this is not the same as saying that middle-aged persons actually score higher on generativity than do older and younger persons. In fact, Ryff and Heincke reported that the youngest of the three cohorts tended to show the highest generativity scores overall.

A more direct cross-sectional study of generativity was conducted by McAdams, de St. Aubin, and Logan (1993). The researchers employed a well-validated self-report measure of generativity, the 20-item Loyola Generativity Scale (McAdams & de St. Aubin, 1992), which is designed to assess individual differences in adults' conscious generative concerns. They also employed measures of generative commitments (open-ended reports of daily goals or strivings), generative actions (a checklist of generative behaviors displayed in the prior two months), and generativity themes in autobiographical narratives. These four measures were administered to three age cohorts: young adults (ages 22–27, born in late 1960s), midlife adults (ages 37–42, baby boomers), and older adults (ages 67–72, born before World War II). The overall quadratic trend in the data showed that the midlife cohort scored significantly higher in generativity than the young and older adults, in keeping with Eriksonian predictions. This trend was strongest for the measures of generative acts and generative themes in accounts of consequential autobiographical scenes. On the Loyola Generativity Scale, however, young adults scored just as high as midlife adults, and both groups scored significantly higher than older adults. By contrast, the measures of generative commitments (assessed via daily goals) showed extremely low scores for young adults and significantly higher scores for both midlife and older adults. The accounts of daily goals provided by older adults were just as strong in generativity content as those provided by the midlife adults. Therefore, while midlife adults did tend to score higher on generativity than younger and older adults in this study, different measures of the construct showed somewhat different age-related patterns.

More recently, Keyes and Ryff (1998) examined the relation between age and generativity in a large national probability sample for the MacArthur Foundation's Successful Midlife National Study. The sample, drawn with random-digit dialing procedures, consisted of noninstitutionalized, English-speaking adults, age 25 to 74, in the 48 contiguous states of the United States. For ease of description, the researchers divided the age range into young (age 25–39), middle-aged (40–59), and older (60–74) adults. The researchers employed three types of measures of generativity: (1) behavioral measures of the extent to which the respondent regularly provides emotional support and unpaid assistance to others (including children and grandchildren); (2) measures of generative commitment as indicated in obligations to help family and friends and in civic obligations (e.g., serving on a jury); and (3) three measures of self-construal (how generative a respondent sees him- or herself overall), one of which included items from the aforementioned Loyola Generativity Scale (McAdams & de St. Aubin, 1992).

The results from Keyes and Ryff (1998) showed that age impacts all three dimensions of generativity, though the impact sometimes interacted with effects by education levels and/or gender. Middle-aged and older adults reported that they provided more emotional support and unpaid assistance to others (behavioral measures of generativity) than did younger adults.

With respect to generative commitment, midlife and older adults also showed higher levels of civic responsibility, but younger adults scored higher than the two older cohorts on obligations to help children and other people directly. With respect to self-construals, midlife adults scored higher on the Loyola Generativity Scale than did young and older adults, while age was linearly related to the endorsement of trait-descriptors indicative of generativity. With respect to the last finding, adults viewed themselves as increasingly caring, wise, and knowledgeable with age.

Few longitudinal studies have been explicitly designed to assess the course of generativity over the human life cycle. Instead, researchers have tried to adapt measures employed for other purposes to the generativity construct, with varying degrees of success. For example, Jones and Meredith (1996) found increases in cognitive commitment around age 30 and in self-confidence around age 40 in the Oakland Growth and Berkeley Guidance Studies. To the extent that cognitive commitment and self-confidence might be related to generativity, the results are consistent with Eriksonian prediction. Similarly, Helson and her colleagues have documented increases in overall scores for self-confidence, responsibility, self-control, responsiveness, and tolerance for ambiguity among women graduates of Mills College, as they moved from early adulthood into their early 50s (Helson & Moane, 1987; Helson & Stewart, 1994; Helson & Wink, 1992). These results suggest developmental increases in autonomy and maturity from young to middle-adult years, which is certainly consistent with Eriksonian theory but not directly informative for generativity. By contrast, one longitudinal study that directly assessed individual differences in generativity found no support for an increase from young adulthood to early midlife. Whitbourne, Zuschlag, Elliot, and Waterman (1992) employed a sequential design covering ages 20 through 42 years and administered a self-report inventory of Erikson's stages developed by Constantinople (1969) and modified by Waterman and Whitbourne (1981). Longitudinal analysis did not show significant change over time in generativity from ages 31 to 42 for Cohort 1 or ages 20 to 31 years for Cohort 2.

Finally, Stewart and Vandewater (1998) traced longitudinal changes in generativity motivation (the desire to be generative) in two cohorts of college-educated women: the Radcliffe Longitudinal Study of the class of 1964 (Stewart & Vandewater, 1993) and a stratified random sample of women graduating from the University of Michigan in 1967 (Tangri & Jenkins, 1993). For the Radcliffe study, data were collected when the women were ages 31, 36, and 43 years. For the Michigan study, data were collected when the women were ages 21, 24, 31, and 47. The researchers measured generativity motivation through content analysis of the respondents' imaginative stories told in response to ambiguous picture cues (the Thematic Apperception Test) and open-ended accounts of future goals. The results showed that generativity motivation decreased over time. By the time the women had reached their 40s, their scores on the desire for generativity were significantly lower than they had been when the women were in their early 20s. Stewart and Vandewater argue that generativity motivation is conceptually distinct from most other measures of generativity, which tend to assess what Stewart and Vandewater call generativity realization, or accomplishment. They propose that while generativity motivation may decrease from young adulthood to midlife, generativity accomplishment tends to increase. Young adults may have strong nascent desires to be generative, but it is not until midlife that many of them have the material and social resources to accomplish generative goals. Interestingly, Stewart and Vandewater suggest that it may be at the same time—in midlife—that desires for generativity may, in fact, be declining.

The empirical literature provides something of a mixed picture concerning the relation between generativity and age. Longitudinal studies are arguably the most persuasive for documenting developmental changes over time. Yet, extant longitudinal investigations tend not to be well designed for the direct charting of generativity over time. One longitudinal study with direct evidence to report (Whitbourne et al., 1992) shows no age effect, though the study follows respondents only into their early 40s. And Stewart and Vandewater's (1998) longitudinal study shows an unexpected decrease in generativity motivation in women graduates of two elite universities from early adulthood to the mid-40s. By contrast, cross-sectional data tend to show marked age differences in generativity. While these differences may be due more to cohort than developmental effects, the results are consistent with the life-cycle prediction of an increase in various aspects of generativity from young adulthood into middle age. While some young adults may show relatively strong desires to be generative and strong generative concerns for one's family and friends, measures of generative behaviors and generative commitments (especially those involved with community and civic responsibilities) tend to be higher among midlife adults than younger adults, at least in the American samples employed. Whether older adults show significantly lower generativity scores than midlife adults, however, remains an open question. The cross-sectional studies have not examined adults beyond their early 70s. Within this age range, some measures of generativity do show lower levels among older adults compared with midlife adults (e.g., generative concern as assessed on the Loyola Generativity Scale), but other measures suggest that healthy older adults, at least into their early 70s, tend to express levels of generativity comparable to those expressed by adults in their 40s and 50s. As documented later in this chapter, furthermore, large individual differences in generativity can be seen at all points heretofore studied across the adult life span (McAdams et al.,

1998). Mean differences between age/cohort groups should not disguise that many young adults score quite high on various measures of generativity, and many middle-aged and older adults score quite low.

In light of the findings reviewed, it may be claiming too much to claim that generativity is a "midlife stage" in adult development. While some data do support the life-cycle prediction that generative concerns, behaviors, and commitments tend to increase from young- to middle-adulthood, the empirical picture is too ambiguous to delineate a clearly demarcated stage of generativity in the middle of the adult life course. It is not clear when such a stage would begin, and it is particularly difficult to determine when (and if) it would end. Given the long life expectancy for citizens of most modern Western societies, furthermore, one wonders how useful it is to posit a life stage specifically centered on generativity that could encompass more than 50 to 60 years of an individual's life. Much more is happening, psychosocially speaking, between the ages of, say, 30 and 80, than the expression of generativity. Erikson's placement of generativity within the large middle of the human life span seems sensible enough. But the strong epigenetic message of life-*cycle* theory may be too strong when it comes to considering the complexities and vicissitudes of generativity in adulthood. A full developmental understanding of the construct, therefore, requires a more contextualized life-*course* perspective.

Generativity in the Life Course

In their argument against strict stage models and in favor of a life-course approach to the study of generativity, Cohler, Hostetler, and Boxer (1998) write this:

> Efforts to portray the course of lives in terms of predefined, sequential, and age-ordered stages, phases, or tasks have provided little lasting understanding of the manner in which people maintain the experience of personal integrity or continuity over time. The course of development is much less clearly ordered than such stage theories would predict and cannot be understood apart from either larger social and historical trends or unique events within particular lives. Certain sequentially negotiated tasks across the adult life course, related to work, intimate partnership, providing for the next generation, and dealing with the finitude of life, appear to be ubiquitous within contemporary society, yet no simple checklist can capture the full range of variation in developmental pathways or the ways in which certain tasks and prescribed social roles are experienced. (p. 266)

In contrast to life-cycle stage models such as Erikson's original epigenetic framework, a life-course perspective offers a more nuanced and situated approach to adult development. Individual lives are viewed in their full social, cultural, and historical contexts, allowing for the tremendous variability in developmental pathways that is observed across many different lives, across cultures, and across historical epochs (Bronfenbrenner, 1994; Dannefer, 1984; Elder, 1995). Generativity is contoured by economic conditions, cultural norms, social change, historical events, and even chance happenings. At the same time, individuals exert their own, agentic influence on the course of development, actively co-constructing their lives in a complex and evolving social context (Bandura, 1989). A life-course perspective on generativity, therefore, brings to the fore (1) social time and timing, (2) social roles and relationships, (3) social structure, and (4) the role of human agency and individual variability in psychosocial development in the adult years.

Social timing "refers to the incidence, duration, and sequence of roles and to related age expectations and beliefs" concerning the course of human life as understood in a given society or social context (Elder, 1995, p. 114). Thus, the extent to which a given social event or role assumption is "on time" or "off time" is of prime importance for social life and individual well-being. Cohler and Boxer (1984) have argued that the experience of positive morale, or life satisfaction, is significantly determined by the sense of being on time for expectable role transitions or life changes. Different societies and different groupings within a society offer markedly different timetables for assuming generative roles. Becoming a parent at age 16 is generally considered off time in middle-class American society even though teenage pregnancy may be biologically routine (and may be viewed as especially on time in a different kind of society). The healthy 45-year-old man who feels he is "not ready yet" to invest time and energy into any kind of nurturing relationship with others may be viewed as especially immature or perhaps narcissistic. If he were 25 years old, society might be more forgiving; but 20 years later, the timing seems off. An important manifestation of what McAdams and de St. Aubin (1992) categorize as cultural demand with respect to generativity, then, is general developmental expectations or assumptions about the timing of generative roles in the life course. These culturally constructed developmental guidelines may be fairly elastic in some societies, but there are always limits—biological and cultural—beyond which the guidelines cannot readily be stretched. Therefore, within U.S. society, social timing expectations urge adults to assume generative roles as they move into their 30s and 40s; those who do not do so are typically considered to be off time.

As Elder and Caspi (1990) and others have shown, the timing of historical events can have a significant impact on individual development. Wars, economic downturns, political revolutions, and the like affect human lives in myriad ways that are partly determined by where in the life course a given individual is positioned (Stewart & Healy, 1989).

Across historical time, different cohorts or generations (Mannheim, 1928) may develop their own characteristic patterns of attitudes and expectations about the life course, about what is possible to achieve in life and what is not, about what is good and what is bad, whom to trust and what to fear. While Ryff and Heincke (1983) found that three different cohorts all believed that generativity should peak as a personal characteristic in midlife (reflecting a shared sense of social timing), the young adult cohort in their study showed the highest self-ratings of generativity overall. Historical cohorts may also show different understandings of what generativity is and should be. In an intensive qualitative analysis of the life stories of Jewish survivors of the Holocaust, Kay (1998) discovered that their generative strivings in late midlife and into old age were strongly, almost obsessively, driven by their desire to provide for the material well-being of their biological offspring, while shunning close emotional connections with the next generation.

In a fundamental sense, generativity is tied up with a society's overall conception of time (McAdams et al., 1998). In that generativity refers to the creation (generation) of new forms that will outlive the self, generativity points to the future. In that generativity also refers to the maintenance, preservation, and passing on of that which has been valued in a given social context, it points to the past. In its linking of generations, generativity links past and future time. The linkage is not without tension, however, for the demands of the future may be seen as undercutting the verities and virtues of the past. Such a tension may be especially salient in modern societies, in which the struggle between tradition (past) and progress (future) can undermine community and even tear families apart. Amidst the dizzying cultural change experienced in many modern societies, youth may no longer value the wisdom of their elders, for that wisdom may be seen as specific to a bygone time. An older generation may seek to be generative through passing on traditional values and ways of life, but the targets of those efforts—the younger generation—may want and need guidance and resources that better address new challenges in the future. Parents are not always able to give children what they need, and children do not always value what parents have to offer. Although generativity mismatches are surely as old as civilization itself, they take on added salience under conditions of rapid social change, as is often witnessed in modern societies.

Overall, modernity affirms a progressive and developmental understanding of time as it demythologizes the authority of the past (Giddens, 1991; Habermas, 1987). From the modern point of view, economic growth promotes the advance of society; medical research lengthens the expected life span and improves the quality of life; science and technology lead to progress in society; and political systems promise a better world in the future. Notions such as growth, advancement, improvement, and progress strike the modern ear as especially generative ideas. However, such potentially generative notions become highly problematic when modern worldviews (1) threaten to destroy those things most cherished in the past or (2) fail to deliver on their promises for a better world in the future. What some scholars describe as the contemporary turn toward cultural postmodernism represents, in part, a rejection of the modern faith in progressive time (Gergen, 1992; Sloan, 1996). If it is true that modern men and women have typically imported the discourse of progressive time into their attempts to make sense of their generative efforts, one wonders what mental forms generativity will take when people lose faith in the idea that the future can be better than the past. In its deepest sense, probably experienced unconsciously, an adult's orientation toward time is bound to the religious and spiritual dimensions of life, touching on apprehensions of life-in-time, immortality, death, and ultimate meaning.

Social timing often concerns the sequencing and patterning of *social roles*. MacDermid et al. (1998) have underscored the importance of work, marital, parental, civic, and religious roles in the expression of generativity. Generative involvements are spread unevenly across different roles, their research suggests, and the strength or quality of generativity in one role is no predictor of the strength or quality of generativity in another. Within any given life, furthermore, generativity may move around from one role to another, according to dictates of the social clock, on-time and off-time events, and a host of other factors. Over the adult life course, generativity ebbs and flows and spreads itself across different roles and life domains, sometimes in an unpredictable manner. Further contouring the development and expression of generativity are close and long-term personal relationships. Life-course theorists speak of *linked lives* (Elder, 1995) and *social convoys* (Kahn & Antonucci, 1981) to underscore the many senses in which individual development is thoroughly interdependent. The complex patterning of roles and relationships making up the social ecology of any given person's life influence the timing, quality, strength, and meaning of that person's generativity.

Gender, race, and variables of *social structure* strongly shape generativity, as well. Keyes and Ryff (1998) examined how education and gender, in addition to age, influence levels of generativity in the aforementioned MacArthur Foundation's Successful Midlife National Study. The results of their study show that education is positively associated with some, though not all, of their generativity measures. (Modest associations between education and generativity have also been observed by McAdams et al., 1998, though they have not found associations between generativity and family income.) In particular, more educated adults in Keyes and Ryff's study showed higher levels of civic obligation, compared with less educated adults. In addition, education interacted with age and gender in the contouring of generativity. For example, education predicted higher levels of providing emotional support among midlife and older adults, but not in the cohort of young adults. Women with more education defined themselves as more characteristically generative than did less-educated women, but higher educational attainment did not coincide with enhanced generative self-construals for men. In addition, women scored significantly higher than men on generativity via providing others with emotional support and via obligations to family and friends By contrast, other studies of generativity have typically not found significant gender effects in mean levels (McAdams et al., 1998); different measures of generativity provide different results in this regard. However, McAdams and de St. Aubin (1992) reported that the interaction of gender and parenting role predicted scores on the Loyola Generativity Scale. Men who had never been fathers scored especially low in generativity, whereas men who had at one time or another been fathers scored relatively high. For women, the parenting role was not significantly associated with generativity scores.

Beyond mean differences, the characteristic ways in which people understand and express generativity and the different roles and social timing schedules they employ are likely to be a function of gender, class, ethnicity, and other macro variables. Gender stereotypes would predict, for example, that men may express more agentic aspects of generativity while women may show more communal manifestations (Kotre, 1984). To date, however, little research has directly examined this claim. Nor has research directly examined the hypothesis, derived from Gutmann (1987) and other proponents of midlife gender crossover, that men's generativity expressions might move toward the communal in and after midlife, whereas women might channel generativity into more agentic pursuits at this time. Peterson and Stewart (1996) found that highly generative woman with careers found gratification through work, whereas generative women not working in careers experienced gratification through parenting. In recent years, many theorists and researchers have moved gender to the center of life-course inquiries, and these developments surely hold implications for understanding generativity in midlife.

Stewart and Ostrove (1998) examined several key features of adult development, including generativity, in the cohort of American women born during the baby boom. By focusing on women in this group and comparing their experience with that of older cohorts and research on men, the authors demonstrate the need for models of aging that take account of the intersections of history, gender, and individual development. Stewart and Ostrove assert that "middle age is gendered differently for different generations" (p. 1186). Graduating from college just before the women's movement gathered steam in the United States, many baby-boom women began young adulthood with rather traditional views of gender roles. By the time they reached age 40, longitudinal studies suggest, a large number of them were experiencing what Stewart and Ostrove call a "mid-course correction" (p. 1188). This process was most consequential among women with traditional role regrets, and for some of them it set off a process involving pursuit of educational or career opportunities that had been abandoned much earlier. For many, the correction brought with it a concerted, and sometimes painful, life review. By their late 40s, most of the baby-boom women studied by Stewart and Ostrove reported high levels of identity certainty and enhanced power as a generative agent in the world. For these women, nascent desires to be generative may have been squelched or channeled into traditional family roles in young adulthood, Stewart and Ostrove argue, but profound social changes—most importantly, the rise of the women's movement—ultimately instigated mid-life-course corrections, which in turn functioned to broaden generative scope and to strengthen women's confidence in their generative abilities.

The role of race/ethnicity in generativity has been highlighted recently by Cole and Stewart (1996) and by Hart, McAdams, Hirsch and Bauer (in press). Cole and Stewart found that among both African American and White women, student activism in college predicted generativity at midlife. In addition, midlife generativity was positively associated with midlife political participation. In this study, Black women in midlife showed significantly higher scores on generativity and politicization compared with their White counterparts. Hart et al. found that individual differences in generativity among both Black and White men and women, ranging in age from 35 to 65 years, predicted a wide range of social involvements, from social support to political and religious participation. Controlling for social class differences, Blacks, scored slightly higher on some measures of generativity compared to Whites. In addition, Hart et al. found that Black adults showed much higher levels of religious participation and social support compared with Whites, and their accounts of especially generative experiences were more likely to contain references to religious activities and intergenerational family events. The study by Hart et al. suggests that self-report measures of generativity and objective correlates of the measures may be similar for African American and Anglo-American adults, but the culturally informed meanings of living a generative life may nonetheless differ somewhat as a function of race/ethnicity. In a study to be described later in this chapter, McAdams, Bowman, Lewis, Hart, and Cole (1999) focused on possible differences in meanings in a qualitative examination of generativity and life stories among 35 middle-aged African American adults.

The research just described highlights the role of human *agency* and *individual differences* in generativity in midlife. Rather than passive adherents to social norms and cultural constraints, adults actively construct their lives within social contexts. As Cohler et al. (1998) show in their persono-logical portraits of generativity among three gay men, adults often defy social clocks and fly in the face of conventional social norms to create personal meaning and exert positive impacts on the next generation. Within a given age cohort, furthermore, people differ markedly with respect to the strength, scope, and meanings of their generativity. Researchers have developed and attempted to validate measures of individual differences in generativity. Peterson and Klohnen (1995) developed a Q-sort profile for generativity realization or accomplishment in which descriptors such as "behaves in a giving way toward others" and "is turned to for advice and assistance" code for high generativity. The measure is independent of the aforementioned TAT-measure of generativity motivation, but Peterson (1998) has shown that applying the two measures in concert can provide extremely useful profiles of generativity.

McAdams and de St. Aubin (1992) developed the Loyola Generativity Scale (LGS), a 20-item self-report measure that includes such items as "I try to pass along knowledge I have gained through my experience" and "I feel as though my contributions will exist after I die." The scale shows high levels of internal consistency and good test-retest reliability over short periods of time. Himsel, Hart, Diamond, and McAdams (1997) have shown that self-reports on the LGS are strongly positively associated with Peterson and Klohnen's (1995) Q-sort measure. McAdams et al. (1998) also regularly employ behavior checklists to assess individual differences in generative actions and a variation on Emmons's (1986) method for collecting personal strivings (daily goals), that are coded for generativity content and viewed as a rough index of current generative commitments. Measures of generative concern (LGS), generative actions (behavior checklist), and generative commitments (daily goals) tend to be significantly positively correlated with each other, but the correlations are not so high as to suggest that the three measures are assessing exactly the same thing (McAdams et al., 1998). Rather, each of the three appears to be getting at a different feature of the general construct of generativity. Other self-report measures of generativity include the survey scales employed by Keyes and Ryff (1998) in the MacArthur nationwide study and omnibus self-report inventories for Eriksonian stages (e.g., Ochse & Plug, 1986; Waterman & Whitbourne, 1981). Various rating scales, informed by Eriksonian theory and/or clinical practice, have also been used in studies by McAdams, Ruetzel, and Foley (1986), Snarey (1993), and Vaillant and Milofsky (1980), among others.

Measures of generativity, then, typically assess the relative strength and/or scope of a person's concerns, commitments, or actions associated with generativity. The higher the score, the stronger the generativity. This form of measurement, however, is blind to individual differences in the meanings of people's generative efforts. Instead, meanings are complexly embedded in the stories that people construct to make sense of their lives in time (Cohler, 1982; McAdams, 1993; Polkinghorne, 1988). Cohler et al. (1998) argue that social timing, social roles, and the impact of social structures come together in personal narratives of lived experience. The life course perspective on generativity "provides a unique opportunity for the study of the manner in which shared cultural meanings become the foundation for the construction of particular lives. These shared meanings are appropriated by individuals and portrayed in a story, or narrative," that serves to reconstruct the past and anticipate the future in such a way as to confer on a human life a sense of unity and coherence (p. 268). A life-course perspective on generativity, therefore, should consider the shared stories about providing for the next generation that prevail within a given culture and the individual life narratives, constructed as idiosyncratic variations on cultural themes, that convey how adults make personal and psychosocial sense of their projects, programs, hopes, fears, accomplishments, and frustrations in generativity.

GENERATIVE LIVES IN CONTEXT: RECENT RESEARCH

Individual variation in generativity is a central theme in contemporary generativity research. The development of measures to assess individual differences in generativity has spurred research into the correlates of the construct, especially in the realms of parenting, political activity, and community involvements. Researchers have also tested hypotheses concerning the relation between generativity on the one hand and mental health and adaptation on the other. In addition, researchers have begun to examine especially generative lives in detail through the use of narrative frames of analysis and qualitative methodologies. Supplementing quantitative studies of generativity's antecedents and consequences, therefore, are more qualitative examinations of the meanings of generativity in individual lives.

PARENTING

The prototype of generativity is probably the bearing and raising of children. One's own biological child is literally an extension of the self, biologically generated in one's own image, flesh of one's flesh, nurtured, cared for, mentored, educated, disciplined, and eventually granted some degree of autonomy to carry forward life for generations to come. It is in the bearing and raising of children that many adults confront their biggest challenges, fulfillments, and frustrations in generativity. Parenting, therefore, can be seen as a primary instantiation of generativity itself.

However, simply being a parent, Erikson argued, does not make an adult a generative person. Generative parenting involves adequate care for one's children and an enduring commitment to the well-being of the next generation (Erikson, 1963; Snarey, 1993). Consequently, individual differences in generativity may be reflective of or associated with individual differences in the quality of parenting.

The relation between parental status itself (that is, whether an adult becomes a parent) and generativity remains unclear. The one study reporting results on this relation showed a mixed picture, with generativity being positively associated with fatherhood but unrelated to motherhood (McAdams & de St. Aubin, 1992). One interpretation of this correlational result is that becoming a father may have a significant impact on a man's overall concern for the next generation. Controlling for age and other demographic effects, men who were not fathers in this study showed especially low scores in generativity. It is possible that women may show slightly stronger concern for the next generation to begin with, compared with men, but that once parenthood is achieved men and women show relatively comparable scores overall. Another possibility, though probably too simplistic, is that it is generative men to begin with who, for the most part, become parents. But given that becoming a parent is a highly overdetermined accomplishment and subject to a wide range of internal and external factors, and given that so little research has examined this problem, it is unwise to draw any firm conclusions about parental status and generativity at this point.

Are parents who score high on measures of generativity more caring and committed parents than those who score low in generativity? This is a difficult question to answer because of disagreements among scholars and laypersons alike concerning what constitutes good parenting and because of cross-cultural differences in parenting approaches and values. Nonetheless, a handful of studies have examined relations between self-report measures of generativity and certain well-defined aspects of parenting. Peterson and Klohnen (1995) found that highly generative women who were also mothers invested considerably more energy and commitment in parenting and showed an "expanded radius of care" (p. 20) compared with less generative mothers. In two other investigations, researchers found that generativity was associated with an *authoritative* approach to parenting. Peterson, Smirles, and Wentworth (1997) found that middle-aged parents of college students expressed more authoritative attitudes about parenting if they were high in generativity. Pratt, Norris, Arnold, and Filyer (1999) found that generativity among mothers of teenage children predicted authoritative styles, but generativity among fathers was unrelated to parenting style. Authoritative parenting combines an emphasis on high standards and discipline with a child-centered and caring approach to raising children. Authoritative parents provide their children with a good deal of structure and guidance, but they also give their children a strong voice in making family decisions. In studies done primarily in the United States, authoritative patterns of parenting have been consistently associated with a number of positive outcomes in children, including higher levels of moral development and greater levels of self-esteem (Maccoby & Martin, 1983). In Peterson et al. (1997), authoritative parenting predicted attitudinal similarity between parents and college-age children, and it was negatively associated with parent/child conflict.

A large-scale study of parents of children enrolled in Chicago elementary schools showed that for both mothers and fathers high scores on generativity concern (assessed via an abbreviated version of the LGS) were strongly predictive of the extent to which parents were involved in their children's schooling. Mothers and fathers scoring high in generativity tended to help their children with their homework more, showed higher levels of attendance at school functions, and evidenced greater knowledge about what their children were learning and doing in school, compared with parents scoring low in generativity (Nakagawa, 1991). In a sample of both African American and White parents, Hart et al. (in press) found that high levels of generativity were associated with valuing trust and communication with one's parents and viewing parenting as an opportunity to pass on values and wisdom to the next generation. While Black and White parents showed some differences in their descriptions of their own approaches to parenting, generativity predicted the same parenting qualities for both groups.

Given the small body of research supporting a link between generativity on the one hand and caring and committed parenting on the other and given the intuitive appeal of generativity as a construct, family therapists and child advocates have begun to speak of generativity as a key factor in improving family life in the United States. Snarey and Clark (1998) argue that a fuller appreciation of the concept of generativity can enhance the role of fathers in American society. They report research showing that involved fathers have positive impacts on their children, especially sons, and that involvement in fatherhood is associated with other indexes of psychosocial adaptation, such as marital harmony and occupational success. In addition, they illustrate how a father's generative involvements change over time in a moving case study of one particular father-son relationship, charted across four decades. Dollahite et al. (1998) outline principles of *generative counseling* for work with families. They spell out procedures whereby the family counselor can help families sustain "generative connections," maintain "generative convictions," make "generative choices," keep "generative commitments," develop "generative capabilities," and initiate "generative changes" (p. 455).

SOCIETAL INVOLVEMENTS

While parenting is closely associated with generativity, it is intriguing to note that Erikson chose as his exemplary personification of generativity a man whose generative accomplishments were played out in the bright light of public action rather than in the private realm of the family. Although Mahatma Gandhi generated biological children of his own, Erikson viewed him as a paragon for generativity because of his mission to deliver and care for an entire nation. Indeed, Gandhi knew many failings as a father of his own children. But his commitment to the well-being of his people, the nation of India, defined a life whose generativity was as impressive and exemplary as any witnessed in the twentieth century. In *Gandhi's Truth,* Erikson (1969) showed how generativity may be expressed in public political actions as well as in the crucible of family and local life.

If parenting within the family, then, is seen as the most private and local realm of generative expression, social involvements among one's peers, in churches, in the community, and through political action offer opportunities for a more public expression of generativity. It would be expected, therefore, that some highly generative adults would show especially strong involvements in civic and/or religious affairs. In their study of African American and Anglo-American adults between the ages of 35 and 65 years, Hart et al. (in press) found that high levels of generativity were associated with more extensive networks of friends and social support in the community and greater levels of satisfaction with social relationships. In addition, generativity was positively associated with church attendance and with involvement in church activities. Adults scoring high in generativity, furthermore, were more likely than those scoring lower to have voted in the last U.S. presidential election, to have worked for a political party or campaigned for a candidate, and to have called or written to a public official about a social concern or problem. Cole and Stewart (1996) found that generative concern among both Black and White women in midlife correlated highly with measures of sense of community and political efficacy, suggesting that adults with strong generative concerns also tend to express strong feelings of attachment and belongingness in their communities and tend to view themselves as effective agents in the political process. Peterson et al. (1997) showed that generativity is positively associated with interest in political issues. And Peterson and Klohnen (1995) found that highly generative women showed more prosocial personality characteristics.

Themes of generativity are very apparent in the social-scientific literature on altruism, volunteerism, and political activism (Andrews, 1991; Colby & Damon, 1992). A prime motivation undergirding the commitments that many adults show toward social causes, political parties, religious traditions, and a wide range of other social and cultural institutions is the concern for the well-being of the next generation. In a critique of American social life entitled, *The Good Society,* Robert Bellah and his colleagues (Bellah, Madsen, Sullivan, Swidler, & Tipton, 1991) argue that the most pressing problems facing large-scale American institutions—such as schools, churches, and governing bodies—reflect failures in generative care. Bellah calls on American citizens and their leaders to embrace a "politics of generativity," through which American adults may be able to "anchor our economic and political institutions firmly in the moral discourse of citizens concerned about the common good and the long run" (Bellah et al., 1991, p. 279). Outside the United States, Japanese social scientists and policy makers have turned their attention to the concept of generativity and its implications for developing a public philosophy to promote the survival and well-being of future generations (Kim & Tough, 1994).

PSYCHOLOGICAL WELL-BEING

Erikson believed that generativity was good for society and for the individual, too. The benefits of generativity should be seen in the strengthening of social institutions and the linking of individuals to both benevolent cultural traditions and progressive social change. At the same time, generativity should benefit the generative adult him- or herself. Erikson viewed generativity to be a sign of both psychological maturity and psychological health in the adult years. But what do the data show?

The data show that Erikson was probably right. Longitudinal investigations by Vaillant (1977) and Snarey (1993) have shown that ratings of generativity are positively associated with the use of mature coping strategies during times of stress and with clinically derived ratings of overall psychosocial adaptation. McAdams and his colleagues have consistently found that measures of generativity are positively correlated with self-reports of life satisfaction, happiness, self-esteem, and sense of coherence in life and negatively associated with depression among midlife men and women, Black and White (de St. Aubin & McAdams, 1995; McAdams et al., 1998). Similarly, Ackerman, Zuroff, and Moscowitz (in press) showed that generativity was positively associated with positive affectivity, satisfaction with life, and work satisfaction among midlife adults. Among young adults, generativity predicted positive affect at home. Among midlife adults, self-report generative concern, assessed on the LGS, is negatively correlated with trait measures of neuroticism (de St. Aubin & McAdams, 1995; Peterson et al., 1997). In the Radcliffe and Michigan longitudinal studies, Stewart and Ostrove (1998) reported that, among a host of variables, quality of midlife roles and generativity were the only significant direct predictors of later midlife well-being.

In their nationwide survey, Keyes and Ryff (1998) have provided the most extensive documentation of generativity's relation to psychological well-being. The researchers found that nearly all of their measures of generativity significantly predicted a composite measure of psychological and social well-being. Supporting more people emotionally, feeling more obligated to society, having more generative concern, seeing oneself as a generative resource, and possessing more generative personal qualities were all associated with higher levels of psychological and social well-being. As the authors conclude, "Generative behavior, generative social obligations, and generative self-definitions are key ingredients in the recipe for psychological wellness" (Keyes & Ryff, 1998, p. 249). However, one of the authors' indexes of generativity turned out to be negatively associated with well-being. Feeling strong obligations to family and friends was inversely related to measures of social well-being. Keyes and Ryff suggest that some generative commitments may exact personal costs. Strong obligations to care for family members and ailing friends may sometimes prove burdensome, undercutting the quality of social life.

The main goal of the analysis provided by Keyes and Ryff (1998) was to link social structural variables, generativity, and psychological and social well-being. Their argument was that while structural variables contour generativity, generativity may in turn contour well-being. Survey studies have consistently shown that education levels are significant predictors of well-being. More educated people are generally happier, all other things being equal, than less educated people. Keyes and Ryff suggest that education may impact well-being by way of generativity. Education enhances opportunities and personal accomplishments, which may "motivate generativity by instilling social concern and engendering the desire for reciprocity" (p. 231). In other words, more educated and (assumedly) successful adults may be more motivated to "give something back" to society. Higher levels of education, therefore, should predict higher levels of generativity, which in turn should predict well-being. Keyes and Ryff provide strong empirical evidence for these linkages, and their statistical analyses, furthermore, show that a significant portion of the variance in well-being associated with education can be accounted for by generativity. Generativity components explained between 30% and 40% of the relationship between education and well-being in the nationwide data collected by Keyes and Ryff.

While a positive association between generativity and psychological well-being in midlife seems well established, some caveats are in order. First, the correlations obtained in these studies, while significant, are typically relatively modest, ranging between +.25 and +.40 in the studies reported by McAdams and his colleagues. Second, many of the significant associations reported are between self-report indexes. People who report high levels of generativity tend to report high levels of well-being. Future research, however, needs to employ other forms of measurement, so that researchers can be assured that these associations reflect more than a method bias. Third and related, the assessments of psychological and social well-being that have typically been employed have been designed, for the most part, to assess individual differences in nonclinical samples. Measures of clinical symptomatology and other more direct measures of mental illness per se have generally not been employed. Erikson's theory would certainly predict that adults suffering from serious mental illness would be significantly less generative than well-functioning adults, but this hypothesis has not been directly tested. Fourth, with the exception of Stewart and Ostrove (1998), studies have not been able to tease out cause-and-effect relationships over time. Does being highly generative lead to higher levels of well-being? Or are happier people to begin with more likely to become generative in adulthood? Perhaps both possibilities are true, but research to date cannot reach any conclusion on this issue.

In conclusion, the positive associations between well-being and generativity should not overshadow that (1) generativity is only one factor among many that predict well-being in adulthood, (2) being highly generative is not a surefire guarantee of health and happiness, (3) some highly generative men and women are sure to be unhappy, even miserable, and (4) some especially nongenerative, narcissistic, and self-indulgent adults may indeed feel perfectly fine about their lives. With the exception of one finding from Keyes and Ryff, furthermore, researchers have not seriously considered the possible costs and dangers of high generativity, both psychological and social. Kotre (1984, 1999) has written eloquently of the dark side of generativity. But little research to date has followed this lead.

NARRATING THE GENERATIVE LIFE

Beginning with Erikson's (1969) psychobiography of Gandhi, social scientists have explored themes of generativity in life narrative. Kotre (1984) portrayed different ways in which adults make sense of generativity challenges in eight life-story accounts. For each case, Kotre created a dramatic narrative encapsulating what he believed to be the heart of the story obtained from his extensive interviews of the adult, and then he analyzed the story in terms of two or three key themes of generativity. A major idea in some of the stories concerned the ways in which efforts to create legacies of the self and then offer them to others may encounter insurmountable and even tragic obstacles. Some adults who desperately want to have children cannot. Some adults who seek to be generative in artistic, political, scientific, literary, or social ways find their efforts stymied and their generated products rejected. Some adults, by design or unwittingly,

damage (and even kill) their own creations. The dynamic between generating and destroying legacies is a major theme in de St. Aubin's (1998)
psychobiography of the American architect, Frank Lloyd Wright. A similar dynamic is portrayed in Lee's (1998) study of generativity in the life
and career of Martha Graham, the American dancer.

A life course perspective on generativity should be sensitive to the myriad ways in which adults appropriate shared cultural meanings and make
sense of social roles and social timing through the production of life narratives (Cohler et al., 1998). A growing number of philosophers, psychologists, social scientists, and social critics have argued in recent years that
adults living in modern societies tend to provide their lives with a sense of
identity by constructing, internalizing, sharing, and revising life stories
(Bruner, 1990; Giddens, 1991; Hermans & Kempen, 1993; Kenyon, 1996;
MacIntyre, 1981; McAdams, 1985, 1997, 1999; Singer & Salovey, 1993; Taylor, 1989). According to this view, the dilemma of modern identity is fundamentally a problem in storytelling. Beginning in late adolescence and
young adulthood, many people living in modern societies face the daunting challenge of constructing a life and fashioning a niche in society that
provides them with a sense that they are unified and purposeful beings
and that their lives display some intrinsic meaning or value (Bluck &
Habermas, 1999; McAdams, 1985). In that modern societies typically offer
no consensus as to how to achieve this psychosocial task, people draw on a
wide range of cultural resources to fashion a conception of the self that integrates them into the adult world but also distinguishes them in some
meaningful way from others. This is accomplished, more or less, through
fashioning and internalizing a story that reconstructs the past and anticipates the future in order to provide a followable and vivifying narrative of
the self. As modern men and women continue to fashion self-stories
through midlife and beyond, they draw on the established literary traditions in their culture, rending life stories that contain origin myths set in
early family experience, turning points in which the protagonist gains new
insights, heroes and heroines who support the protagonist's strivings and
villains who stand in the way, and endings that resolve conflict and bring
events to a satisfying conclusion (Denzin, 1989; Rosenwald, 1992). Within
the modern world, therefore, "a person's identity is not to be found in behavior, nor—important though this is—in the reactions of others, but in
the capacity *to keep a particular narrative going*" (Giddens, 1991, p. 54).

Generativity is an important story line in the narratives that midlife
adults construct to provide their lives with unity and purpose. Many
adults include within their self-defining life stories detailed accounts of
their efforts to promote the well-being of the next generation. A common
theme in many life stories told in midlife is the realization that because
others have provided me with care in the past it is now my turn to give

something back to my family, my people, or my society. Accounts like these may be called *generativity scripts* (McAdams, 1985, 1993). For some adults, generativity scripts may dominate the plot lines in their life stories. For others, generativity may be played out in but a small number of life-story scenes.

Employing quantitative measures of generativity and lengthy life-story interviews, McAdams and his colleagues have analyzed life stories constructed by highly generative adults and compared them with the life stories told by adults scoring very low on measures of generativity (Mansfield & McAdams, 1996; McAdams, Diamond, de St. Aubin, & Mansfield, 1997; McAdams, Reynolds, Lewis, Patten, & Bowman, in press). The vast majority of the subjects in these studies are in their 30s, 40s, and 50s. In describing how they reconstruct their own past and anticipate their own future, highly generative midlife adults are significantly more likely than their less generative counterparts to highlight scenes in their life stories in which extremely bad events (e.g., death, loss, failure, frustration) are followed by good outcomes (e.g., revitalization, improvement, growth, enlightenment). This way of telling a story about oneself may be called a *redemption sequence.* A bad scene is redeemed, salvaged, made better by that which follows. The opposite narrative movement is a *contamination sequence,* whereby an extremely good scene is ruined, spoiled, or sullied by a bad scene that follows it. Highly generative adults rarely construct contamination sequences in accounting for their lives, while less generative adults are more likely to speak of good scenes turning bad.

What is the connection between redemptive imagery in life stories and generativity? First, some adults see their own generative efforts as explicit attempts to redeem their own lives. A striking example of this phenomenon is documented in Maruna's (1997) study of published autobiographies of ex-convicts. Maruna found that men who eventually desist from crime after spending many years in criminal activity tend to tell the same kind of story of their reform. In the standard account, the criminal experiences a dramatic turning point in life, sometimes a life-threatening scene or a spiritual epiphany, that signals a move away from crime and toward a mature life of love and work. However, the move toward a socially acceptable lifestyle may suffer many setbacks and frustrations and the person may fall back into crime, until he or she is able to experience the self as an effective agent who is integrated into a supportive interpersonal community. Once the protagonist of the story finds agency and communion (Bakan, 1966) in life, he is now ready to "give something back" as a kind of payment or penitence for a life of crime. Generativity becomes an effort to achieve redemption in life. It becomes very important that the ex-convict be able to tell his story to other young people who may be headed toward antisocial behavior. The life story becomes dominated by a generativity script that affirms the author's redemption and provides a cautionary tale aimed to protect the next generation.

Second, generativity itself may entail an implicit understanding of human redemption. The hard work that the highly generative adult displays in his or her efforts to promote the well-being of future generations may entail a good deal of pain, suffering, and sacrifice. But the hardships of today may pay off in good dividends in the future. Scenes of sacrifice and hard work, therefore, may lead to scenes of blessing and reward—a redemption sequence of sorts. It is rare, furthermore, to find a man or woman in middle age who still believes that his or her life is perfect or unsullied. Adult life is full of mistakes, frustrations, and missed opportunities for most people; yet the promise of a new generation is that those same mistakes will not be made again, that frustrations will pass, and new opportunities will be grasped and fulfilled in the generation to come (Kotre & Kotre, 1998). Again, the hope is that the imperfections of today will be followed by a better tomorrow. Generativity is often couched, then, in terms of progress, improvement, transforming the bad into good. At the same time, however, generativity challenges people and societies to preserve that which is good from the past in order to benefit the future. In this case, the effort to preserve the good is often itself viewed to be difficult or onerous. It is not easy to pass on the good from one generation to the next. There is always a battle to be fought with the forces that oppose such a transmission. The discourse on generativity, therefore, is filled with stories about people suffering and making sacrifices in order that the future will be good (Kotre, 1999; McAdams, 1985). The stories are variations on a more general theme of transforming bad into good—the essence of redemption. Redemption is an idea that appears in one form or another in all of the major world religions and in many cultural myths (James, 1902/1958).

The theme of redemption is often part of a larger and more complex life-story form that McAdams and his colleagues describe as a *commitment story*. McAdams et al. (1997) identified the commitment story as an especially prevalent life-story format in interviews of highly generative adults. The commitment story comprises five narrative themes: (1) early blessing, (2) suffering of others, (3) moral steadfastness, (4) redemption sequences, and (5) prosocial goals for the future. In their intensive study of 70 life stories, McAdams et al. showed that highly generative adults tend to construct life narratives that more closely approximate the commitment story form than do less generative adults. Although every adult's life story is unique, the study suggests that highly generative adults appropriate some of the same kinds of themes and images in making sense of their lives in time, and that their stories as a group differ significantly from those constructed by less generative adults.

In the prototypical commitment story, the protagonist comes to believe early on (in childhood) that he or she has a special advantage (e.g., a family blessing, a special talent, a lucky break) that separates him or her out from others. The highly generative adult, therefore, tends to reconstruct the past in such a way as to identify a blessing or advantage that he or she enjoyed at a very early age. The blessing stands in sharp contrast, however, to the realization, again early in childhood, that other people suffer, that while I am blessed, others are not so fortunate. Thus, compared with less generative adults, highly generative adults are significantly more likely to recall and describe scenes from childhood in which they became aware of the suffering of other people. The clash between early blessing and the suffering of others sets up a tension in the story and motivates the protagonist to see him- or herself as "called" or "destined" to be of good use to other people. As a result, the protagonist comes to articulate a clear and convincing system of personal beliefs, sometimes rooted in religion but sometimes not, that continues to guide his or her behavior throughout the (reconstructed) life span (moral steadfastness). Compared with less generative adults, highly generative adults tell a story of continuity and certainty in moral beliefs—they have known what is "right" since very early in their lives; they have organized their beliefs into a coherent system that centers their life strivings; and they have continued to hold to this belief system ever since, recalling few periods of strong doubt or significant change in their beliefs. Moving ahead with the confidence of early blessing and steadfast belief, the protagonist of the commitment story encounters an expectable share of personal misfortune, disappointment, and even tragedy in life, but these bad events often become transformed or redeemed into good outcomes (redemption sequences), sometimes because of the protagonist's efforts and sometimes by chance or external design. Thus, bad things happen, but they often turn into good things, whereas when good things happen they rarely turn bad. Looking to the future with an expanded radius of care, the protagonist sets goals that aim to benefit others, especially those of the next generation, and to contribute to the progressive development of society as a whole and to its more worthy institutions.

The commitment story appears to be a highly effective life-narrative form for supporting the adult's generative efforts, an efficacious matchup of narrative identity and generative behavior. The adult who works hard to guide and foster the next generation may make sense of his or her strong commitment in terms of a story that suggests that he or she has been called or summoned to do good things for others and that the calling is deeply rooted in childhood, reinforced by a precocious sensitivity to the suffering of others, and bolstered by a clear and convincing ideology that remains steadfast over time. Perceiving one's own life in terms of redemption sequences, furthermore, provides the hope that may sustain generative efforts as private as raising one's own child and as public as committing oneself to the advancement of one's society or even one's own people (Erikson, 1969). A commitment story provides a language or discourse for the self that supports a caring, compassionate, and responsible approach to social life. In *Acts of Compassion*, Robert Wuthnow (1991, p. 45) wrote: "The possibility of compassion depends as much on having an appropriate discourse to interpret it as it does on having a free afternoon to do it. To ask whether compassion is possible, therefore, is to ask about the language in which its very conceivability depends." A commitment story, therefore, would appear to provide a powerful language or discourse for generativity.

Variations on the commitment story have been identified in the life stories constructed by highly generative African American adults, in a qualitative study conducted by McAdams, Bowman, et al. (1999). Employing a grounded-theory, qualitative approach (Glaser & Strauss, 1967) to the analysis of 35 life-story interviews, the authors discovered that highly generative Black adults crafted life stories in which the protagonist enjoyed an early advantage, bad scenes were redeemed by good outcomes, and the future was anticipated with hope and prosocial goals. These differences between highly generative and less generative Black adults were consistent with those found in the McAdams et al. (1997) mainly White sample. However, the stories of midlife African American adults who were high in generativity also depicted plots that were developed in a progressive, stage-like and goal-directed manner, whereas the life stories of Black adults scoring low in generativity contained fixated and chaotic plot structures in which main characters repeated frustrated and troubling goal sequences again and again. For both highly generative and nongenerative African American adults, furthermore, the life-narrative accounts were noteworthy for the early emergence of danger and threat in the story, the clear identification of a (bad) antagonist against whom the (good) protagonist struggled, and the powerful and beneficent role of religion and extended kin networks in coping with the dangers and the antagonists that life presents.

The study by McAdams et al. (1999) on the life stories of midlife African American adults differing in generativity illustrates three points concerning the narration of generative lives. First, in constructing self-defining life narratives, highly generative Black adults appropriate some of the same shared cultural meanings that have been observed in the life stories of highly generative American Whites. In particular, three of the five central themes of what McAdams et al. (1997) identified as the commitment story figure prominently in the life stories of generative Blacks in this small sample. Like their White counterparts, highly generative Blacks make sense of their own lives in terms of an early advantage they enjoyed, the transformation of bad events into good outcomes, and the anticipation of prosocial goals for the future. Second, comparing the life stories of highly generative and less generative African American adults revealed themes that have not been highlighted in past research with Whites. In particular, generativity among Blacks was associated with a tight, stage-like, and goal-driven plot structure in which the protagonist steadily progressed over time; whereas the stories of less generative adults showed fixated plots and the repetition of chaotic or frustrating scenes. Third, the study showed how the life stories of Black adults at midlife, regardless of their generativity level, draw on shared cultural meanings that depart dramatically from those observed in stories of mainly middle-class White Americans. The emic quality of this analysis was most evident in the characteristic ways in which the African American adults developed plot lines against a backdrop of perceived danger and threat and vis-à-vis strong antagonists in the environment. As adaptive coping resources for the struggles they perceive, furthermore, midlife African American adults draw on religious faith and the support provided by extended family networks, which is consistent with the main thrusts of empirical literature on psychosocial adaptation among African Americans across the adult life course (e.g., Bowman, 1990).

CONCLUSION

From Plato's writings on love and immortality through Erikson's life-cycle theory and to the current flowering of research and theorizing on the concept, generativity has become established as a central psychosocial issue for the middle adult years. Sharing Plato's belief that generativity follows directly from the successful establishment of long-term intimate relationships in young adulthood, Erikson situated generativity as a discrete midlife stage in his epigenetic life-cycle scheme. Empirical research generally supports the idea that generativity is important to midlife adults, but it also argues against a rigid stage scheme and in favor of variability in the developmental pathways that people follow in the adult years. A life-course perspective on generativity underscores the determinative influences of social timing, social roles, social structure, and human agency in the contouring of generativity over time. Research examining individual differences in generativity shows that highly generative adults tend to be highly invested in their children's growth and education, to be constructively involved in civic and religious activities, and to experience high levels of psychological and social well-being, compared with adults scoring low on measures of generativity. Life-narrative studies have begun to document the different ways in which highly generative adults make sense of their lives and the life course, underscoring the themes of redemption, progress, and personal destiny in the culturally anchored meanings that generative adults appropriate and articulate in their self-defining life stories.

Empirical research on generativity is still in a very early stage. Future studies are likely to go in a multitude of directions. For example, many important developmental hypotheses coming out of Erikson's writings on generativity have not been adequately tested. Chief among them may be the proposed developmental linkages between intimacy and generativity. Are adults who have successfully resolved Erikson's intimacy versus isolation dynamic more likely to be generative in the next phase of life? Does generativity feed back to enhance, or undermine, intimacy? To what extent do important developments in generativity fundamentally alter intimacy and identity? Does successful generativity presage the establishment of ego integrity at the end of life?

Considering generativity from a life-course perspective, researchers will need to explore in much more detail the commonalities and variations in social timing, social roles, and social structural influences across different social contexts and cultures. Researchers need to address the complex ways in which generativity is gendered in different generations (Stewart & Ostrove, 1998) and how generativity is contoured by class, ethnicity, race, and historical events. More creative methods of assessing generativity may also be required, and the many measurement methods already employed will need to be refined further and linked more meaningfully to each other. Especially useful would be the development and validation of more ecologically valid measures that tap directly into the everyday experience of generativity.

Several intriguing questions about generativity have received virtually no research attention at all (McAdams & de St. Aubin, 1998). First among these is the question of the *developmental antecedents* of generativity. How is it that some people become more generative than others? Can the roots of strong generativity be traced back to the childhood and adolescent years? While life narrative studies provide some hints in this regard, long-term longitudinal studies are needed to do justice to these developmental questions. Cross-national studies have examined the development of civic responsibility and the role of community service in adolescence (Yates & Youniss, 1999), and a growing literature on social responsibility in adulthood has also begun to take shape (Colby & Damon, 1992; Parks-Daloz, Keen, Keen, & Daloz-Parks, 1996). Generativity research may benefit from connections to and indeed may even shed light upon these other lines of research.

A second question that has not been adequately addressed concerns the precise relation between *generativity and creativity*. Erikson suggested that generativity shares space with the concept of creativity. Many expressions of generativity appear to involve some form of creativity, as in procreation and the making of products and outcomes designed to outlive the self. One might ask whether highly creative people are especially generative. In some ways they may be, and in some ways not. Part of the indeterminacy here comes from the difficulty in defining creativity. Gardner (1993) suggested that creativity exists not so much within a single individual as in the nexus of the individual, the domain, and the field. Creative individuals work within a particular domain of expression that exists as part of a rule-governed field. The field's rules are determined by various experts such as literary critics and book reviewers (for the field of literature) and granting agencies and peer review panels (for sciences). To a large extent, the experts decide who and what is creative in a given field. In a loose sense, the same might be said for generativity. It is perhaps worthwhile to ponder what and who the experts are and how the rule-governed fields may operate for the different domains of generative expression.

A third question: What are the *limits, costs, and excesses* of generativity? Kotre (1984) was the first to suggest that generativity may have a dark side. Because generativity involves the creation and passing on of products and outcomes from one generation to the next, the extent to which a community views particular generative expressions as "good" depends on the shifting social constructions of the potential worth embodied in those products and outcomes. Madmen and tyrants may view their own efforts as especially generative, in that they aim to craft enduring legacies for what they may consider to be "the good." But even the most well-meaning generative expressions can go wrong, for one cannot control what one's products will lead to in the future, even if one cares for and nurtures those products in a wise and compassionate way. Kotre and Kotre (1998) make another significant contribution to theorizing about generativity by identifying the phenomenon of intergenerational buffering, which is generativity in the service of not transmitting something from one generation to another. The buffer insists that "the damage stops here." Nonetheless, damage is sometimes the main result of one's best generative efforts. Beyond the writings of Kotre, this troubling conundrum has not generally been addressed.

Finally, what is the *role of suffering* in generativity? Snarey (1993) defines generativity chill as the anxiety experienced when one encounters the possibility of losing either the fruits of one's generative efforts or one's very power to be generative. From the realm of parental generativity come such obvious examples as infertility and facing the possibility of losing one's child. Snarey found that the most generative fathers were those who had, at one time or another, encountered an episode of generativity chill. In a similar vein, Kay (1998) intimates that the Holocaust experience seemed to intensify the generative strivings of survivors, who showed much stronger generative inclinations than a matched sample of adults who were refugees (rather than concentration camp inmates) during World War II. Peterson (1998) suggests that midlife women who showed high levels of both generativity motivation and generativity realization seemed to be compelled to continue their substantial efforts to achieve generative goals because of tension or frustration in an area of strong generative concern. McAdams et al. (1997) report that highly generative midlife adults tend to construct life stories that emphasize early recollections of the suffering of others and numerous examples in their own lives in which suffering paved the way for growth, insight, and fulfillment.

Is it necessary to experience deep suffering to be especially generative? Is generativity enhanced or undermined by suffering? One can imagine examples of both: ways in which personal anxiety, frustration, or deprivation might help to make a person more generative or might contribute to stagnation, self-preoccupation, and despair. What is the relation between experiencing personal misery or witnessing the misery of others on the one hand and what Erikson identified as the "belief in the species" that sustains the necessary faith for generativity on the other?

When one thinks hard about generativity, one is challenged to ask some of the most important questions about the psychological, social, ethical, and existential dimensions of midlife. These questions beckon the systematic inquiries that social and behavioral scientists can offer. The concept of generativity should continue to generate creative theorizing and informative scientific research on midlife adult development through the twenty-first century and for generations to come.

REFERENCES

Ackerman, S., Zuroff, D., & Moscowitz, D.S. (in press). Generativity in midlife and young adults: Links to agency, communion, and well-being. *International Journal of Aging and Human Development.*

Anderson, J.W. (1981). Psychobiographical methodology: The case of William James. In L. Wheeler (Ed.), *Review of personality and social psychology* (Vol. 2, pp. 245–272). Beverly Hills, CA: Sage.

Andrews, M. (1991). *Lifetimes of commitment: Aging, politics, psychology.* Cambridge, England: Cambridge University Press.

Bakan, D. (1966). *The duality of human existence: Isolation and communion in Western man.* Boston: Beacon Press.

Bandura, A. (1989). Human agency in social cognitive theory. *American Psychologist, 44,* 1175–1184.

Becker, E. (1973). *The denial of death.* New York: Free Press.

Bellah, R.N., Madsen, R., Sullivan, W.M., Swidler, A., & Tipton, S.M. (1991). *The good society.* New York: Knopf.

Bluck, S., & Habermas, T. (1999). *The life story schema: Adolescent development and lifespan function.* Paper presented at the annual convention of the American Psychological Association, Boston.

Bowman, P.J. (1990). Coping with provider role strain: Adaptive cultural resources among Black husband-fathers. *Journal of Black Psychology, 16,* 1–21.

Brittain, V. (1970). *Testament of youth.* New York: Wideview Books. (Original work published 1933)

Bronfenbrenner, U. (1994). Ecological models of human development. In T. Husten & T.N. Postlethwaite (Eds.), *International encyclopedia of education* (2nd ed.). New York: Elsevier.

Browning, D. (1975). *Generative man.* New York: Dell.

Browning, D. (1999). *An ethical analysis of Erikson's concept of generativity.* Paper presented at the international conference on Generativity and Future Generations, Kyoto, Japan.

Bruner, J. (1990). *Acts of meaning.* Cambridge, MA: Harvard University Press.

Buhler, C. (1933). *Der menschliche lebenslauf als psychologisches problem.* Leipzig, Germany: S. Hirzel Verlag.

Cohler, B.J. (1982). Personal narrative and the life course. In P. Baltes & O.G. Brim (Eds.), *Life span development and behavior* (Vol. 4, pp. 205–241). New York: Academic Press.

Cohler, B.J., & Boxer, A. (1984). Personal adjustment, well-being, and life events. In C.Z. Malatesta & C.E. Izard (Eds.), *Emotion in adult development* (pp. 85–100). Beverly Hills, CA: Sage.

Cohler, B.J., Hostetler, A.J., & Boxer, A.M. (1998). Generativity, social context, and lived experience: Narratives of gay men in middle adulthood. In D.P. McAdams & E. de St. Aubin (Eds.), *Generativity and adult development* (pp. 265–309). Washington, DC: American Psychological Association.

Colby, A., & Damon, W. (1992). *Some do care: Contemporary lives of moral commitment.* New York: Free Press.

Cole, E.R., & Stewart, A.J. (1996). Meanings of political participation among Black and White women: Political identity and social responsibility. *Journal of Personality and Social Psychology, 71,* 130–140.

Constantinople, A. (1969). An Eriksonian measure of personality development in college students. *Developmental Psychology, 1,* 357–372.

Dannefer, D. (1984). Adult development and social theory: A paradigmatic reappraisal. *American Sociological Review, 49,* 100–116.

Denzin, N.K. (1989). *Interpretive biography.* Newbury Park, CA: Sage.

de St. Aubin, E. (1998). Truth against the world: A psychobiographical exploration of generativity in the life of Frank Lloyd Wright. In D.P. McAdams & E. de St. Aubin (Eds.), *Generativity and adult development* (pp. 391–427). Washington, DC: American Psychological Association.

de St. Aubin, E., & McAdams, D.P. (1995). The relations of generative concern and generative action to personality traits, satisfaction/happiness with life, and ego development. *Journal of Adult Development, 2,* 99–112.

Dollahite, D.C., Slife, B.D., & Hawkins, A.J. (1998). Family generativity and generative counseling: Helping families keep faith with the next generation. In D.P. McAdams & E. de St. Aubin (Eds.), *Generativity and adult development* (pp. 449–481). Washington, DC: American Psychological Association.

Elder, G.H., Jr. (1995). The life course paradigm: Social change and individual development. In P. Moen, G.H. Elder, Jr., & K. Luscher (Eds.), *Examining lives in context: Perspectives on the ecology of human development* (pp. 101–139). Washington, DC: American Psychological Association.

Elder, G.H, Jr., & Caspi, A. (1990). Studying lives in a changing society: Sociological and personological explorations. In A.I. Rabin, R.A. Zucker, R.A. Emmons, & S. Frank (Eds.), *Studying persons and lives* (pp. 201–247). New York: Springer.

Emmons, R.A. (1986). Personal strivings: An approach to personality and subjective well-being. *Journal of Personality and Social Psychology, 51,* 1058–1068.

Erikson, E.H. (1950). *Childhood and society.* New York: Norton.

Erikson, E.H. (1963). *Childhood and society* (2nd ed.). New York: Norton.

Erikson, E.H. (1964). *Insight and responsibility.* New York: Norton.

Erikson, E.H. (1969). *Gandhi's truth: On the origins of militant nonviolence.* New York: Norton.

Erikson, E.H. (1982). *The life cycle completed.* New York: Norton.

Espin, O., Stewart, A.J., & Gomez, C.A. (1990). Letters from V: Adolescent personality development in sociohistorical context. *Journal of Personality, 58,* 347–364.

Frenkel, E. (1936). Studies in biographical psychology. *Character and Personality, 5,* 1–35.

Freud, S. (1953). Three essays on the theory of sexuality. In J. Strachey (Ed. and Trans.), *The standard edition of the complete psychological works of Sigmund Freud* (Vol. 7). London: Hogarth Press. (Original work published 1905)

Friedman, L. (1999). *Identity's architect: The life and work of Erik H. Erikson.* New York: Pantheon Books.

Fromm, E. (1941). *Escape from freedom.* New York: Farrar & Rinehart.

Fromm, E. (1947). *Man for himself.* Greenwich, CT: Fawcett.

Gardner, H. (1993). *Creating minds.* New York: Basic Books.

Gergen, K.J. (1992). *The saturated self: Dilemmas of identity in contemporary life.* New York: Basic Books.

Giddens, A. (1991). *Modernity and self-identity: Self and society in the late modern age.* Stanford, CA: Stanford University Press.

Glaser, B.G., & Strauss, A.L. (1967). *The discovery of grounded theory.* Chicago: Aldine.

Gould, R.L. (1980). Transformations during early and middle adult years. In N.J. Smelser & E.H. Erikson (Eds.), *Themes of love and work in adulthood* (pp. 213–237). Cambridge, MA: Harvard University Press.

Gruen, W. (1964). Adult personality: An empirical study of Erikson's theory of ego development. In B.L. Neugarten (Ed.), *Personality in middle and late life: Empirical studies* (pp. 1–14). New York: Atherton.

Gutmann, D. (1987). *Reclaimed powers: Toward a new psychology of men and women in later life.* New York: Basic Books.

Habermas, J. (1987). *The philosophical discourse of modernity.* Cambridge, MA: MIT Press.

Hart, H.M., McAdams, D.P., Hirsch, B.J., & Bauer, J., (in press). Generativity and social involvements among African-American and among Euro-American adults. *Journal of Research in Personality.*

Havighurst, R. (1972). *Developmental tasks and education* (3rd ed.). New York: David McKay.

Helson, R., & Moane, G. (1987). Personality change in women from the early forties to the early fifties. *Journal of Personality and Social Psychology, 53,* 176–186.

Helson, R., & Stewart, A.J. (1994). Personality change in adulthood. In T.F. Heatherton & J. Weinberger (Eds.), *Can personality change?* (pp. 201–225). Washington, DC: American Psychological Association.

Helson, R., & Wink, P. (1992). Personality change in women from early 40s to early 50s. *Psychology and Aging, 7,* 46–55.

Hermans, H.J.M., & Kempen, H.J.G. (1993). *The dialogical self: Meaning as movement.* New York: Academic Press.

Himsel, A.J., Hart, H., Diamond, A., & McAdams, D.P. (1997). Personality characteristics of highly generative adults as assessed in Q-sort ratings of life stories. *Journal of Adult Development, 4,* 149–161.

James, W. (1958). *The varieties of religious experience.* New York: New American Library. (Original work published 1902)

Jones, C.J., & Meredith, W. (1996). Patterns of personality change across the life span. *Psychology and Aging, 11,* 57–65.

Jowett, B. (1956). *Plato's symposium* (Trans.). Indianapolis, IN: Bobbs-Merrill.

Kahn, R., & Antonucci, T. (1981). Convoys of social support: A life-course approach. In S. Kiesler, J. Morgan, & V. Oppenheimer (Eds.), *Aging: Social change* (pp. 383–405). New York: Academic Press.

Kay, A. (1998). Generativity in the shadow of genocide: The Holocaust experience and generativity. In D.P. McAdams & E. de St. Aubin (Eds.), *Generativity and adult development* (pp. 335–359). Washington, DC: American Psychological Association.

Kenyon, G.M. (1996). The meaning/value of personal storytelling. In J. Birren, G.M. Kenyon, J.E. Ruth, J.J.F. Schrot, & J. Svendson (Eds.), *Aging and biography: Explorations in adult development* (pp. 21–38). New York: Springer.

Kermode, F. (1967). *The sense of an ending.* New York: Oxford University Press.

Keyes, C.L.M., & Ryff, C.D. (1998). Generativity in adult lives: Social structural contours and quality of life consequences. In D.P. McAdams & E. de St. Aubin (Eds.), *Generativity and adult development* (pp. 227–263). Washington, DC: American Psychological Association.

Kim, T-C., & Tough, A. (1994). Thinking about the well-being of future generations: A one-year learning effort. In T-C. Kim (Ed.), *Creating a new history for future generations.* Kyoto, Japan: Institute for the Integrated Study of Future Generations.

Kotre, J. (1984). *Outliving the self: Generativity and the interpretation of lives.* Baltimore: Johns Hopkins University Press.

Kotre, J. (1999). *Making it count: How to generate a legacy that gives meaning to your life.* New York: Free Press.

Kotre, J., & Kotre, K.B. (1998). Intergenerational buffers: The damage stops here. In D.P. McAdams & E. de St. Aubin (Eds.), *Generativity and adult development* (pp. 367–389). Washington, DC: American Psychological Association.

Lee, S.A. (1998). Generativity and the life course of Martha Graham. In D.P. McAdams & E. de St. Aubin (Eds.), *Generativity and adult development* (pp. 429–448). Washington, DC: American Psychological Association.

Levinson, D.J., Darrow, C.N., Klein, E.B., Levinson, M.H., & McKee, B. (1978). *The seasons of a man's life.* New York: Knopf.

Levinson, D.J., & Levinson, J.D. (1996). *The seasons of a woman's life.* New York: Ballantine Books.

Maccoby, E.E., & Martin, J.A. (1983). Socialization in the context of the family: Parent-child interaction. In P. Mussen (Ed.), *Handbook of child psychology* (4th ed., Vol. 4, pp. 1–102). New York: Wiley.

MacDermid, S.M., Franz, C.E., & De Reus, L.A. (1998). Generativity: At the crossroads of social roles and personality. In D.P. McAdams & E. de St. Aubin (Eds.), *Generativity and adult development* (pp. 181–226). Washington, DC: American Psychological Association.

MacIntyre, A. (1981). *After virtue.* Notre Dame, IN: University of Notre Dame Press.

Mannheim, K. (1928). The problem of generations. In K. Mannheim (Ed.), *Essays on the sociology of knowledge* (pp. 276–322). London: Routledge & Kegan Paul.

Mansfield, E.D., & McAdams, D.P. (1996). Generativity and themes of agency and communion in adult autobiography. *Personality and Social Psychology Bulletin, 22,* 721–731.

Maruna, S. (1997). Going straight: Desistance from crime and life narratives of reform. In R. Josselson & A. Lieblich (Eds.), *The narrative study of lives* (Vol. 5, pp. 59–93). Newbury Park, CA: Sage.

McAdams, D.P. (1985). *Power, intimacy, and the life story: Personological inquiries into identity.* New York: Guilford Press.

McAdams, D.P. (1993). *The stories we live by: Personal myths and the making of the self.* New York: Morrow.

McAdams, D.P. (1996a). Narrating the self in adulthood. In J.E. Birren, G.M. Kenyon, J-E. Ruth, J.F. Schrot, & T. Svensson (Eds.), *Aging and biography: Explorations in adult development* (pp. 131–148). New York: Springer.

McAdams, D.P. (1996b). Personality, modernity, and the storied self: A contemporary framework for studying persons. *Psychological Inquiry, 7,* 295–321.

McAdams, D.P. (1997). The case for unity in the (post)modern self: A modest proposal. In R. Ashmore & L. Jussim (Eds.), *Self and identity: Fundamental issues* (pp. 46–78). New York: Oxford University Press.

McAdams, D.P. (1999). Personal narratives and the life story. In L. Pervin & O. John (Eds.), *Handbook of personality: Theory and research* (2nd ed., pp. 478–500). New York: Guilford Press.

McAdams, D.P., Bowman, P.J., Lewis, M., Hart, H.M., & Cole, E. (1999). *Generativity and the construction of life stories among African-American adults: A qualitative study.* Unpublished manuscript, Northwestern University, Evanston, IL.

McAdams, D.P., & de St. Aubin, E. (1992). A theory of generativity and its assessment through self-report, behavioral acts, and narrative themes in autobiography. *Journal of Personality and Social Psychology, 62,* 1003–1015.

McAdams, D.P., & de St. Aubin, E. (Eds.). (1998). *Generativity and adult development: How and why we care for the next generation.* Washington, DC: American Psychological Association.

McAdams, D.P., de St. Aubin, E., & Logan, R.L. (1993). Generativity among young, midlife, and older adults. *Psychology and Aging, 8,* 221–230.

McAdams, D.P., Diamond, A., de St. Aubin, E., & Mansfield, E.D. (1997). Stories of commitment: The psychosocial construction of generative lives. *Journal of Personality and Social Psychology, 72,* 678–694.

McAdams, D.P., Hart, H.M., & Maruna, S. (1998). The anatomy of generativity. In D.P. McAdams & E. de St. Aubin (Eds.), *Generativity and adult development* (pp. 7–43). Washington, DC: American Psychological Association.

McAdams, D.P., Reynolds, J., Lewis, M., Patten, A.H., & Bowman, P.J. (in press). When bad things turn good and good things turn bad: Sequences of redemption and contamination in life narrative and their relation to psychosocial adaptation in midlife adults and in students. *Personality and Social Psychology Bulletin.*

McAdams, D.P., Ruetzel, K., & Foley, J.M. (1986). Complexity and generativity at midlife: Relations among social motives, ego development, and adults' plans for the future. *Journal of Personality and Social Psychology, 50,* 800–807.

Moran, G. (1998). Cares for the rising generation: Generativity in American history, 1607–1900. In D.P. McAdams & E. de St. Aubin (Eds.), *Generativity and adult development* (pp. 311–333). Washington, DC: American Psychological Association.

Nakagawa, K. (1991). *Explorations into the correlates of public school reform and parental involvement.* Unpublished doctoral dissertation, Human Development and Social Policy, Northwestern University, Evanston, IL.

Neugarten, B.J. (Ed.). (1968). *Middle age and aging.* Chicago: University of Chicago Press.

Ochse, R., & Plug, C. (1986). Cross-cultural investigation of the validity of Erikson's theory of personality development. *Journal of Personality and Social Psychology, 50,* 1240–1252.

Parks-Daloz, L.A., Keen, C.H., Keen, J.P., & Daloz-Parks, S. (1996). *Common fire: Lives of commitment in a complex world.* Boston: Beacon Press.

Peterson, B.E. (1998). Case studies of midlife generativity: Analyzing motivation and realization. In D.P. McAdams & E. de St. Aubin (Eds.), *Generativity and adult development* (pp. 101–131). Washington, DC: American Psychological Association.

Peterson, B.E., & Klohnen, E.C. (1995). Realization of generativity in two samples of women at midlife. *Psychology and Aging, 10,* 20–29.

Peterson, B.E., Smirles, K.A., & Wentworth, P.A. (1997). Generativity and authoritarianism: Implications for personality, political involvement, and parenting. *Journal of Personality and Social Psychology, 72,* 1202–1216.

Peterson, B.E., & Stewart, A.J. (1990). Using personal and fictional documents to assess psychosocial development: A case study of Vera Brittain's generativity. *Psychology and Aging, 5,* 400–411.

Peterson, B.E., & Stewart, A.J. (1993). Generativity and social motives in young adults. *Journal of Personality and Social Psychology, 65,* 186–198.

Peterson, B.E., & Stewart, A.J. (1996). Antecedents and contexts of generativity motivation at midlife. *Psychology and Aging, 11,* 21–33.

Polkinghorne, D. (1988). *Narrative knowing and the human sciences.* Albany, NY: State University of New York Press.

Pratt, M., Norris, J., Arnold, M.L., & Filyer, R.J. (1999). Generativity and moral development as predictors of value-socialization narratives of young persons across the adult life span: From lessons learned to stories shared. *Psychology and Aging, 14,* 414–426.

Rank, O. (1936). *Truth and reality.* New York: Norton.

Rank, O. (1968). *Art and artist: Creative urge and personality development.* New York: Agathon Press.

Roberts, P., & Newton, P.M. (1987). Levinsonian studies of women's adult development. *Psychology and Aging, 2,* 154–163.

Rosenwald, G.C. (1992). Conclusion: Reflections on narrative self-understanding. In G.C. Rosenwald & R.L. Ochberg (Eds.), *Storied lives: The cultural politics of self-understanding* (pp. 265–289). New Haven, CT: Yale University Press.

Ryff, C.D., & Heincke, S.G. (1983). Subjective organization of personality in adulthood and aging. *Journal of Personality and Social Psychology, 44,* 807–816.

Singer, J., & Salovey, P. (1993). *The remembered self.* New York: Free Press.

Sloan, T. (1996). *Damaged life: The crisis of the modern psyche.* London: Routledge.

Snarey, J. (1993). *How fathers care for the next generation: A four-decade study.* Cambridge, MA: Harvard University Press.

Snarey, J., & Clark, P.Y. (1998). A generative drama: Scenes from a father-son relationship. In D.P. McAdams & E. de St. Aubin (Eds.), *Generativity and adult development* (pp. 45–74). Washington, DC: American Psychological Association.

Stewart, A.J., Franz, E., & Layton, L. (1988). The changing self: Using personal documents to study lives. *Journal of Personality, 56,* 41–74.

Stewart, A.J., & Healy, J.M., Jr. (1989). Linking individual development and social changes. *American Psychologist, 44,* 30–42.

Stewart, A.J., & Ostrove, J.M. (1998). Women's personality in middle age: Gender, history, and midcourse corrections. *American Psychologist, 53,* 1185–1194.

Stewart, A.J., & Vandewater, E.A. (1993). The Radcliffe class of 1964: Career and family social clock projects in a transitional cohort. In K.D. Hulbert & D.T. Schuster (Eds.), *Women's lives through time* (pp. 235–258). San Francisco: Jossey-Bass.

Stewart, A.J., & Vandewater, E.A. (1998). The course of generativity. In D.P. McAdams & E. de St. Aubin (Eds.), *Generativity and adult development* (pp. 75–100). Washington, DC: American Psychological Association.

Tangri, S., & Jenkins, S. (1993). The University of Michigan class of 1967: The women's life paths study. In K.D. Hulbert & D.T. Schuster (Eds.), *Women's lives through time* (pp. 259–281). San Francisco: Jossey-Bass.

Taylor, C. (1989). *Sources of the self: The making of the modern identity.* Cambridge, MA: Harvard University Press.

Vaillant, G.E. (1977). *Adaptation to life.* Boston: Little, Brown.

Vaillant, G.E., & Milofsky, E. (1980). The natural history of male psychological health: IX. Empirical evidence for Erikson's model of the life cycle. *American Journal of Psychiatry, 137,* 1348–1359.

Van de Water, D., & McAdams, D.P. (1989). Generativity and Erikson's belief in the species. *Journal of Research in Personality, 23,* 435–449.

Wakefield, J.C. (1998). Immortality and the externalization of the self: Plato's unrecognized theory of generativity. In D.P. McAdams & E. de St. Aubin (Eds.), *Generativity and adult development* (pp. 133–174). Washington, DC: American Psychological Association.

Waterman, A.S., & Whitbourne, S.K. (1981). The inventory of psychosocial development. *JSAS Catalog of Selected Documents in Psychology, 11*(5). (Ms. No. 2179).

Whitbourne, S.K., Zuschlag, M.K., Elliot, L.B., & Waterman, A.S. (1992). Psychosocial development in adulthood: A 22-year sequential study. *Journal of Personality and Social Psychology, 63,* 260–271.

Wuthnow, R. (1991). *Acts of compassion: Caring for others and helping ourselves.* Princeton, NJ: Princeton University Press.

Yates, M., & Youniss, J. (Eds.). (1999). *Roots of civic identity: International perspectives on community service and activism in youth.* Cambridge, England: Cambridge University Press.

SECTION IV

SOCIAL FACTORS

CHAPTER 13

The Role of Work in Midlife

HARVEY L. STERNS and MARGARET HELLIE HUYCK

ONE OF THE MOST intriguing issues in adult development and aging is the importance of work in people's lives. Havighurst (1982, p. 771) pointed out that "every society has its ways of earning its living, of getting its food and clothing and shelter." The selection of an occupation is a complex interaction of values, attitudes, interests, personality, experiences, and chance. Recent discussion has emphasized the role that all these factors may play in selecting a job or career as well as the changing organizational structure where the work opportunity takes place (Avolio & Sosik, 1999; Farr, Tesluk, & Klein, 1998). A person's work life may be a series of jobs, or it may be appropriate to talk about a person's career or careers. Life-span models have been utilized in industrial/organizational psychology in specific areas such as aging and workplace issues (H. Sterns & Doverspike, 1989; H. Sterns, Matheson, & Park, 1997; H. Sterns & Miklos, 1995; H. Sterns & Gray, 1999).

Atchley (1988) has emphasized in his discussions of work and retirement that jobs end but work never ends. There are always things to be done, cooking, cleaning, lawn care, taking out the garbage. Jobs start and finish. We thus have the issue of job, jobs, and when appropriate careers.

The meaning of work in individuals' lives, its importance, and priority are central themes. Work opportunity was a critical theme of earlier generations. In the past, many individuals died during their working years. Today, many issues have emerged in how we think about work through the life span. A critical issue is whether an individual will be able to continue to do the kind of work that he or she wants to do now and in the future. How one negotiates through his or her work role in the middle years and beyond is a major focus of this chapter.

Another theme to be considered is the role that generational difference may play in a person's work life. Workers coming from different generations/cohorts have different social cultural experiences that may affect attitudes regarding work and co-workers, career, leisure, and family life (Zemke, Raines, & Filipczak, 2000).

Age is not a good predictor of who can perform a job successfully. Whether changes in physical abilities are relevant to job performance depends on the characteristics of the job and level of performance needed to be successful. People stay mentally competent with normal aging. People maintain intelligence and learning abilities into late life. While declines in information processing and attention have been found in lab studies, these may not directly translate to actual work settings. A careful task analysis of a job will reveal the requisite skills and the minimum levels of performance required. Most jobs do not require maximal mental or physical performance and can be performed by healthy, moderately educated adults regardless of age (H. Sterns & Sterns, 1995a).

In terms of mental and physical capability, there are few obstacles for a large number of middle-aged adults and older adults. In the future, more older adults will be active and healthy, and we can expect them to have the capacity to work and continue to do so for as long as they have skills, knowledge, and abilities that are useful to an employer. The drive to be productive, receive income, have social interactions, and contribute to the success of an organization are all reasons people want to work. Additionally, some people keep working because they need additional income in later life (H. Sterns & Sterns, 1995a).

One of the most important determinants of remaining in the workforce is one's attitude toward work and the motivation to be current and competitive. Feeling valued, appreciated, and respected within the company context has been an important part of the desire to continue to work. A change has been found from extrinsic (financial priorities) factors at age 50 to more intrinsic values with regard to work after the age of 60. Employees' attitudes apparently become increasingly important in determining whether an individual will work into late life. However, new work environments and fast-changing workplaces now make apparent that "the objective in a job is not self expression but to put bread on the table. Knowing this will save you painful disillusionment later" (Mirvis & Hall, 1996, p. 72).

Employers are becoming more positive about capable older workers, but at the current time are decidedly mixed. Cost containment issues are prominent today, and this impacts negatively on older workers. However, future policies on retirement and healthcare and a better understanding of the cost/benefit ratio associated with employing older workers should improve opportunities for middle-aged and older workers.

Physical and mental changes with age can be sensitively accommodated through the use of human factors approaches. These approaches can support the older worker through careful job design and restructuring the work environment. ADA requires an employer to make reasonable accommodations so that a disabled worker, young or old, can perform the job. Training can also facilitate older workers to perform in unfamiliar job situations. With normal aging and continued maintenance of skills, older workers can continue to work and be competitive (A. Sterns, Sterns, & Hollis, 1996).

Future work opportunities will be more intellectual and less physical. Most jobs will be well within the range of older adults' skills and abilities. Capable, able, older adult workers can perform most jobs with great success. Evidence indicates that experience and knowledge make older workers competitive with workers of all ages. Nevertheless, workers need to be proactive about maintaining their skills and updating them to remain competitive. They need to be responsible for their own careers and perhaps their pension and health benefits. Most older workers can look forward to continuing involvement in work for as long they have the ability to carry out needed activities.

Workers of today get a mixed set of messages regarding continued work or retirement from their workplace, and society at large. There is much to be said in support of an anticipatory period of the retirement decision (Ekerdt, 1998). People are trying to make meaningful decisions about their futures.

The decision to continue to work, modify work, or retire is influenced by many factors. Time left (at work or in the labor force) is part of a decision process influenced by eligibility for Social Security, employer pension, and norms (Sheppard, 1991). This extended stream of decision making for retirement can be observed in the changing plans and intention toward retirement that workers entertain over time.

WHO'S AT WORK

The majority of people age 40 to 59 work. Twenty percent of people in this age range do not work. Of people 51 to 59, 24% do not work. Among the nonworkers: (1) 54% are retired and, have worked some time in the past 5 years, but are no longer in the workforce; (2) 46% are dependents who have never worked more than a few months or have not worked in the past 20 years; (3) 85% of nonworking men are retired and 44% of nonworking women are retired.

Sixty-one percent of older workers aged 60 to 69 are working full time and 36% are working part time; 28% of workers 70 and older are working full time and 72% are working part time.

Fifty-five percent of retirees aged 51 to 59 say a health condition or impairment limits the amount and type of work they can do. Retirees in this age group are three times more likely to be in fair or poor health than those who are working. Of people 60 and older who are working, 48% are in very good to excellent health, 36% are in good health, and 16% are in fair to poor health. For people 60 and older who are nonworkers, 26% are in good to excellent health, 35% are in good health, and 34% are in fair to poor health (National Academy on an Aging Society, 2000).

ATTITUDINAL CHANGES AND DESIRE TO WORK

Psychosocial definitions of older workers (H. Sterns & Doverspike, 1989) are based on social perceptions including age typing of occupations, perceptions of the older worker, and the aging of knowledge, skill, and ability sets. The individual's self-perception is also considered. How individuals perceive themselves and their careers at a given age may be congruent or incongruent with societal image. Relatively little research has addressed the basic question of how we know when workers will perceive themselves, or be perceived by others as old. Timing norms are discussed as prescriptive about when and how one retires, influenced by level of commitment to the work organization, modes and styles of exiting, and pension incentives. Timing norms become the "bearer of societal, firm level or reference group preferences for retirement" in the Ekerdt (1998) analysis. His analysis of the Health and Retirement Study 1992 baseline wave (aged 51–61) reveals support for the concept of a usual age for retirement that may vary in different work settings and occupational categories. Plan incentives influence timing of retirement behavior and 85% of workers reported that they planned to leave at or prior to the local, usual age for retirement. In addition, over 80% of respondents did not plan to work beyond the usual age.

Lawrence (1987) broadly defines age effects as outcomes within an organization attributed to the age of employees. In her discussion, chronological age and age distributions impact age norms. Age distributions are the actual age distributions in the organization, while the age norms are shared perceptions of the normal ages within an organization or role. Individual age expectations are also important, as they reflect the degree to which the individual applies the social norm to him- or herself. Age norms are likely to occur when the range of perceived ages is narrow and agreement on typical ages is high. Organizational tenure is expected to increase recognition of age group distinctions as individuals of roughly the same age and organizational tenure will have shared history and experience. These age norms may provide a context that influences judgments about individuals.

One can look to parents and peers for models, but each person's circumstances, feelings, and situations may be very different. Recent discussions of the future of retirement (H. Sterns & Gray, 1999) tell us that nothing less than a paradigm shift is under way that will affect how people will have to save and invest, how they will fantasize about and plan for the future. Uncertainty regarding what present and future employment will offer is true for individuals who presently have job security, stable working conditions, and choices about their retirement. This can change quickly with corporate buyouts, new public policies, and changing attitudes on the part of workers themselves. The possibility of losing one's job, being faced with an early buyout, or uncertainty regarding future prospects are all part of the current scene. At the same time, capable people are continuing in fairly traditional careers. Others may lose jobs but reenter the job search to discover it is a major challenge to find a new position at the same or better salary. Often the person has to settle for reduced salary and benefits, if any. It appears that somewhere between 10% and 20% of older adults want to work beyond traditional retirement age. In any case, it is important to focus on individuals who will continue to work.

Over the past two decades, employees' attitudes toward working have become increasingly more important in efforts by organizations to predict worker behavior (Warr, 1994). The attitudes people hold about work contribute to their desire to continue to work and to maintain the skills required to excel. The work environment itself also influences employees' attitudes about continuing to work and job performance. The desire to continue working in an organization has been researched under the topic of organizational commitment.

Meyer and Allen (1984) distinguish between two dimensions of organizational commitment that affect work attitudes in different ways. The first, *continuance commitment,* is the employee's perceived cost of leaving or a perceived lack of alternatives to replace or make up investments in the benefits of the current job. Benefits include one's position, salary, seniority, and pension. Individuals remain at work because they are not willing to risk salary loss, health benefits, or pension investment. This is especially relevant to our discussion of older adults. As workers increase their tenure with an organization, they may feel increasing continuance commitment because they have established a home and friendships in the area, they have become specialized in a skill that they feel cannot be transferred, or feel they could not get the same salary, benefits, or pension if they moved to a new organization.

Affective commitment is the second dimension of organizational commitment and refers to the employee's affective or emotional orientation to the organization. Affective commitment is concerned with the individual's interest in the work and loyalty to the organization and its goals. Affective commitment gives employees an emotional tie to the organization that motivates them to remain, not because they cannot afford to leave, but because they feel a sense of contribution and growth from and with the organization.

An organization that encourages employees to maintain and improve job skills while it also provides challenging work and the opportunity to inject new ideas will not only be more likely to stay ahead of competitors, but also will have reduced turnover and retain more productive employees.

An organization can measure the success of its efforts to improve the work environment by examining organizational-based self-esteem (Pierce, Gardner, Cummings, & Dunham, 1989). Organizational-based self-esteem (OBSE) is assessed by measuring the degree to which organizational members believe they are valuable, worthwhile, and effectual employees (Pierce et al., 1989).

Matheson (1991) carried out a research study on the influence of organizational-based self-esteem on job satisfaction and commitment. She divided the employees in a northeastern instrument company into three age groups (20–35, 36–50, and 51 years and up) and collected attitudinal information using a questionnaire and objective measures of absenteeism and turnover. She found that organizational satisfaction, continuance commitment, and global self-esteem (a measure of a person's overall perceived self-worth) increased as age increased. But, after controlling for job and organizational tenure, two variables that have been found to be related to age, only global self-esteem was significantly associated with age. In Matheson's study, employees over age 50 had significantly higher global self-esteem than did younger age groups. Employees who perceived that they were valuable as organizational members were more satisfied with their jobs and organizations, were committed to the organization both effectively and in terms of perceived sacrifice, and were less likely to leave. This finding shows the importance of understanding an employee's perceptions and interpretations of organizational policies, procedures, and culture.

Older adults bring experience and extensive skills to any job. They have had a lifetime of communicating, overcoming hardships, solving problems, and acquiring lessons learned. Older employees have had years to integrate their knowledge with practical experience to develop efficient methods of accomplishing their work. When new techniques arise, open-minded older workers are often the best source to determine how successful new ideas will be and how best to implement them.

Evidence is mounting that intrinsic rewards of work, satisfaction, relationships with co-workers, and a sense of participating in meaningful work become more important as an individual ages. Most jobs allow older adults to continue to participate in these benefits until they feel that they have the financial resources and personal network outside the workplace to retire (Brady, Fortinsky, Norland, & Eichar, 1989).

MODELS OF CAREER DEVELOPMENT

One of the best ways to understand the evolution of how development has been treated in career development is to review various theories over the past 60 years. There has been a gradual recognition that middle-aged and older workers have continuing growth potential. The following discussion builds on H. Sterns and Sterns (1995b).

1940s

Much of the aging and work literature of the past has focused on general statements regarding older workers. Industrial gerontologists in Great Britain began to focus on the issue of career development at the end of World War II. Belbin and Belbin (1972) initiated training specifically designed to address the needs of older adults. This may be the earliest example of a career development activity designed for older adult workers.

1950s

In 1957, Super proposed a fixed sequence of career stages. He theorized that children from birth to age 14 develop certain interests and abilities by role-playing activities. This he termed the growth stage. Between ages 15 and 24, people are in a stage of exploration making tentative career choices and entering the labor market. From ages 25 to 44 comes the establishment stage in which occupational changes sometimes occur and an effort is made to stabilize a career. By ages 45 to 65, people are expected to hold on to what they have in the so-called maintenance stage. Finally, from age 65 on, the person enters into a stage of decline, where the pace is slowed and retirement occurs.

1960s

The early 1960s continued to focus on a linear career path. Wilensky (1961) defined an orderly career as an endeavor in which a person can grow in responsibility and competence as well as income, can plan for the future, and can invest his or her time and energy with the certainty of future gain (Havighurst, 1982).

The 1960s also led to the development of the person-environment fit model. Holland (1959, 1962) defined work using for characteristics change, simplicity, instrumentation, and data. Holland proposed that a finite number of work environments exists within the American society. These environments are realistic, investigative, social, conventional, enterprising, and artistic.

1970s

The 1970s saw age and life stage as an important determinant of behavior. Numerous models suggested that the mobility rates of younger persons (up to around age 30) are much higher than those of older persons (Hall & Nougaim, 1968; Super, 1957; Veiga, 1973) as the younger generations move about seeking their niche in life and the older ones maintain theirs as they plan for retirement.

Schein (1971) describes three stages in a career: socialization, performance, and obsolescence versus the development of new skills. In the third stage, the obsolete person may be retained as "deadwood," with no options for mobility, or may be retrained, transferred into a lateral position, or forced into early retirement. Although career development could be helpful to the employee in all three stages, it seems likely that the person who would most strongly desire such help would be in the third stage of Schein's model. In terms of actual research, "mobility in the earliest stage of one's career bears an unequivocal relationship with one's later career" (Rosenbaum, 1979; Veiga, 1981, 1983). Thus, the person who is mobile early on is most likely to be mobile in the latter career stages.

Hall's model of career growth (1971) conceptualizes career planning from a goal-setting perspective. Once a person makes a career-goal decision, such as the decision to engage in training or retraining, then goal attainment should lead to identity growth and enhanced self-esteem. Such enhanced self-esteem may then lead to greater commitment to future career-developmental goals. Goal attainment enhances self-esteem, which may increase perceptions of self-efficacy and future commitment to career-development activities.

Research on actual mobility rates seem to bear out these hypotheses (Byrne, 1975; Saben, 1967; Sommers & Eck, 1977; Veiga, 1983). Veiga also found that age correlated significantly and negatively with propensity to move. With regard to career development, S. Gould (1979) predicted that career planning would be highest during Super's stabilization period (aged 31–44), when there is stable growth as the person attempts to secure a place within the occupation. Research support has not been found for this hypothesis.

In the late 1970s, theories of career progression began to be criticized for following a linear life plan, the pattern in which education is a task for the young, work is for the middle-aged, and leisure is for the elderly. The criticism of using the linear life plan as a basis for theory is that it perpetuates the notion that these are the appropriate tasks for each life stage, discouraging intermixing all three tasks across the life span.

The work of Levinson (Levinson, Darrow, Klein, Levinson, & Mckee, 1978) added new dimensions to stage theories by incorporating biological, psychological, and social development constructs. Levinson et al. (1978) and Sheehy (1976) contributed by popularizing the idea of mid-life transition issues and raising the possibility of different career development patterns for males and females.

1980s

The life-span orientation combines the previous approaches with a recognition that behavioral change can occur over the entire life cycle. This approach emphasizes substantial individual differences in aging (P. Baltes, Reese, & Lipsitt, 1980). Individuals are influenced by normative, age-graded biological and environmental influences (physical and cognitive changes as one ages), normative, history-graded factors (generational events), and nonnormative influences unique to every individual. The influences interact to determine an individual's career path. Over the course of a career, a person will be presented with increasingly complex work roles, which play a crucial role in stimulating the development of cognitive structures. Individuals begin with different potentials and will improve at differing rates.

Katz (1980) moved the focus of career development into the organizational setting. In a model of job longevity, Katz describes three successive stages: socialization, innovation, and adaptation. Stage I, socialization, occurs during the first few months on the job. During this stage, one tries to establish a situational identity, decipher situational norms, learn role expectations, build social relationships, and prove oneself as an important contributing member of the organization. Stage II, innovation, is characterized by a transition in employee job concerns. Occurring approximately between the sixth month and the third year of job longevity, the major concern is on achievement and accomplishment. Attempts are made to improve special skills, enlarge the scope of one's contributions, enhance visibility and promotional potential, and influence the organizational surroundings. Gradually, however, if promotion or movement does not occur, tasks become less challenging and more routine, and the person enters into Stage III, adaptation. In this stage, the individual must adapt to the job or leave the organization. If the individual adapts to the job, extrinsic motivators of the job efforts are made to protect one's autonomy and minimize vulnerability. If the organization is left, then the socialization phase of job longevity is reentered. Katz views socialization as a process that can occur throughout the span of the career.

In the early 1980s, Veiga (1983) discussed "individual barriers to moving" and the issues of seniority and age. Veiga suggested that perceptions of one's own marketability may strongly influence one's efforts to explore alternative career opportunities, both within one's own organization or in an outside firm. Holding a particular position within the same organization for an extended period may only reinforce one's feeling of specialization and/or obsolescence rather than one's feelings of marketability potential. Similarly, the longer a person remains with a company and the older that person gets, the more likely he or she will be to think twice about risking any benefits accrued through the years by moving to a new organization. The same may be true for the person who strongly values job security, regardless of age. Mobility implies a certain degree of risk to one's job security; in which case career-development programs may be seen as a waste of time if there is little motivation to move.

Veiga also identified five motives for moving which significantly influenced propensity to leave: fear of stagnation; career impatience; and dissatisfactions with one's salary, recognition, and/or advancement. Again, we assume that people expressing a desire to move will react positively to the initiation of a career-development program that could conceivably help them on their way.

Since the 1980s, life-cycle and stage theories have been criticized for using male workers as the basis for the development. It is becoming increasingly evident that career progressions of women may be quite different from those of men, as the former juggle the roles of student, housewife, paid worker, mother, and so forth. Life-cycle and stage approaches have also been criticized for failure to test propositions adequately. Particularly lacking is longitudinal research using subjects over age 50. A criticism of stage and with-job theories is that they tend to ignore the interaction of work and nonwork aspects of life (Sonnenfeld & Kotter, 1982).

In his 1980 theory update, Super (1980) retains these age-stage categories as a general description of lifelong career progression. However, he also notes that career growth, exploration, maintenance, and decline may occur at any or at many points in the life span.

H. Sterns and Patchett (1984) and H. Sterns (1986) have attempted to develop a model of adult and older adult career development that is non-age-specific. The model assumes that transition in work life may occur many times throughout a career (see Figure 13.1).

1990s

Although the work of Hall and associates covers a 30-year period, two of the most important publications appeared in the 1990s (Hall & Mirvis, 1995a, 1995b; Hall & Associates, 1996). *The Career Is Dead—Long Live the Career* (Hall & Associates, 1996) presents the strongest statements regarding the protean career, which are referred to throughout the chapter. The emphasis is on self-management of career in a dramatically changing work environment.

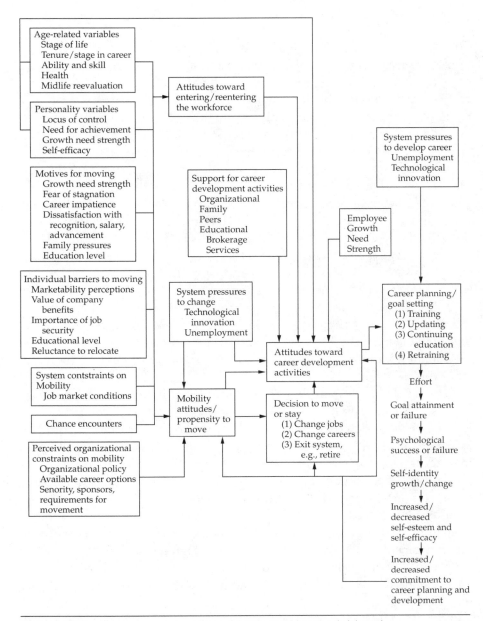

Figure 13.1 Career progression in middle and later adulthood.

MODELS OF WORK AT MIDLIFE

The most widely accepted model for examining changes over time in human functioning, generally, is a developmental-contextual one. This model assumes that biogenetic, maturational, psychological, and socio-cultural aspects must all be considered when positing reasons for patterns of behavior. However, while most theorists and researchers give homage to this perspective, often they prefer, in fact, to focus on one or two aspects rather than strive for the enormous complexity posed. If we wish to assemble a more holistic view of development, we must still rely on a patchwork of interesting data sets and models that take serious account of some, but not all, of the possible variables.

All life-span models include some attention to the middle years—but not all give much detailed attention to the role of work. Virtually all of the models of male adult development put work at the center, with the assumption that how a man negotiates entry, progress, and exit from the domain of whatever the culture recognizes as work is a centrally organizing force in his development. Models that describe women's development are more varied. Most emphasize relational aspects, many include mothering and home management as a work equivalent, and some more contemporary models examine the varying patterns of involvement in the paid labor force.

Some of the models are described as universally or widely applicable. This is seldom justified. Some of the best-known models have utilized select samples, restricted in age, gender, culture, social class, and cohort. For example, Jaques (1965) drew on biographies and autobiographies of great men to develop his model of the centrality of the awareness of death in prompting the inevitable midlife crisis. Levinson drew on intensive study of 40 men (most were White) born in the 1920s and early 1930s and living around New Haven when interviewed (Levinson et al., 1978) and 45 women born two decades later (Levinson & Levinson, 1996); Helson assessed women born in the late 1930s who graduated from an elite women's college in California (Helson & Moane, 1987). The model with the most diverse database is that offered by Gutmann (1994), who examined American men in Kansas City, Navajo Native Americans in the Southwest, Highland and Lowland Mayan Indians in South America, Druze in Israel, and psychiatric patients in Chicago; he also reviewed anthropological reports, literature, and artistic creations. Each sample was small, but he was searching for common themes across time and culture.

The shortcomings identified do not mean that the studies or the models are not valuable, but it means that we must look for themes and patterns across samples. And we must remember that none of the data sets include representative samples of racial/ethnic minorities, persons with disabilities, or persons with a homosexual orientation.

THEMES IN MIDLIFE DEVELOPMENT MODELS

MIDLIFE IS DYNAMIC

Not surprisingly, theorists and researchers who focus on the middle adult portion of the life course believe there are significant and interesting changes emerging during these years. Erikson (1963) proposed a model describing developmental challenges for ego processes that arise from biological, psychological, or sociocultural shifts. The relative importance of each of these factors may vary, but he described them as interacting to produce the emergent challenges to rework earlier resolutions in ways adequate for the current realities. Colarusso and Nemiroff (1981, p. 6) wrote, "The adult is always becoming." They also postulated that the nature of the developmental process is basically the same in children and adults, and that the fundamental developmental issues of childhood continue as central aspects of adult life, but in altered form. Development during adulthood is influenced by the adult past, as well as the childhood past, and there are central, phase-specific themes of adult development (Nemiroff & Colarusso, 1988).

Gender Shapes Midlife Experience

Because biological sex and social-psychological gender are so important, virtually all models recognize that midlife experiences will be different for men and women. Erikson (1963, 1974) couched the differences primarily in terms of reproductive potentials. Young men must form a secure occupational identity to function as adequate men and fathers. Young women should form a preliminary identity only in order to make their final identity fit with the man who would be her husband and father to their children. His model has been roundly criticized for this emphasis on the centrality of motherhood for women, but he remained certain that his perspective was accurate for most women in most cultures across time. In Erikson's model, paid work is central for men, and incidental for women. Similarly, Gutmann (1994) has proposed a model of ego mastery styles predicated on the importance of gender-differentiated parenting demands (providing physical security for fathers and emotional security for mothers).

Levinson et al. (1978) initially built his model on men, and suggested that it would be applicable to women. The subsequent exploration with women, in collaboration with his wife, made it clear that women's lives were more complex. Levinson and Levinson (1996) ended up emphasizing the importance of "gender splitting . . . that permeates every aspect of human life" (p. 6). They compared homemakers and two kinds of career women. The emphasis on exploring varying experiences of women based on involvement in paid work is also evident in models proposed by Baruch, Barnett, and Rivers (1983) and Gerson (1985).

Midlife Should Probably Be Separated into Early and Later Phases

This theme is not explicit in most models, but emerges from examining the ages of persons considered in developing the model, and the issues identified. Some of the models cited so far deal with the transition into midlife, how one becomes aware that one has become middle-aged (Neugarten, 1968) and the issues (or crises) that this engenders (Baruch et al., 1983; Jaques, 1965; Levinson & Levinson, 1996; Levinson et al., 1978). The issues in the first portion often revolve around recognizing the limits of career progress and deciding whether to shift gears or remain in place, and rebalancing work and family needs as children become more independent (but may need even more costly investment in higher education). During the second phase, the career issues revolve increasingly around the decisions about how much energy and ambition to invest in work, and decisions about withdrawal from paid employment.

Normal Biological Changes Are Important as Signifiers

The physical changes that emerge in midlife are less dramatic than those of childhood, adolescence, and advanced old age. The wrinkles, grey hair, reduced sensory capacities, altered fat distribution, and even menopause are significant primarily because they signal to the self and to others that one is moving along the life course. What they signify is variable. Minimally, they provide cues to others about one's age, and to the extent that others respond differently to a person who is thought to be middle-aged the individual may be forced to acknowledge changes (Neugarten, 1968). Some theories emphasize the awareness of personal death as a crucial marker of midlife, an awareness that is not based on the actual nearness of death so much as the recognition that underlying biological changes are occurring, unbidden, to them (Colarusso & Nemiroff, 1981; Jaques, 1965; Levinson et al., 1978). Biological changes become central when they are diseases, many of which emerge in midlife and have the potential to dramatically redirect the course of life.

The impact of biological changes on work depends substantially on the individual and the context. In times and settings where stereotypes persist that midlife and older persons are less desirable workers, individuals strive to mask external signs of age (through hair coloring, plastic surgery, systematic exercise, fashion, avoiding references to earlier experiences that would date them, etc.). Men and women who work in physically demanding jobs often seek relief in early retirement; men and women who have a chronic disease or disability may be forced to withdraw from employment, or they may find settings that accommodate their altered capacities.

COGNITIVE AND EMOTIONAL CHANGES ARE IMPORTANT

The evidence is substantial that overall intelligence remains quite stable through the middle years (Schaie, 1996), but several models posit ways in which qualitative thinking and problem solving change during this period. Jaques (1965) described shifts from a "natural," driven style of creativity to a more thoughtful, considered mode in midlife. Labouvie-Vief and Hakim-Larson (1989) document early midlife shifts in the way complex problems are viewed, from the young adult search for certainty and a single correct answer to the appreciation that many problems have no single solution and that any solution may be good and bad at the same time. It was found that while young adults were focused on controlling their emotions, middle-aged persons described their feelings more vividly and differentiated an inner realm of emotional experience from an outer realm of convention; they tried to acknowledge their inner experience while recognizing that the two realms often conflict. Vaillant (1977) reported that the men in the longitudinal Grant Study (all Harvard graduates of 1942–1944) showed a maturing of defense mechanisms. By 35, these men were four times as likely to use dissociation, suppression, sublimation, and altruism than as young adults, and they were far less likely to use projection, masochism, or hypochondriasis. The net effect is to make cognitive and emotional perceptions less marked by defensive distortions.

Another shift often described in models of midlife is of self-in-the-world, with an overall shift from outer-world orientation to an inner-world one. Buehler (1935) described this shift on the basis of her studies of biographies. Levinson et al. (1978) and Levinson and Levinson (1996) emphasize the BOOM/BOOW—Becoming One's Own Man/Woman—as a critical thrust signaling a preparation for middle age. Gutmann (1994) assumes that young adults repress aspects of the self in the service of the social-psychological demands of parenting, and that midlife offers the opportunity to reclaim these aspects to become more individualized and whole. The concept is clearly heralded as an opportunity and even a mandate in many of the popular books on midlife (e.g., Sheehy's model of a second adulthood where one can "choose your own path") (Sheehy, 1981, 1995; Sher, 1998).

The impact on work of these changes is discussed in several of the models. Generally, middle-aged persons are perceived as potentially better workers because they have a more complex, holistic view of issues, and are more attuned to their own contributions to both problems and solutions. On the other hand, the increased focus on self-determination may lead individuals to withdraw investment in career building in favor of greater attention to family, friends, or self-development. This conflicts with current expectations that all workers remain engaged, ambitious, eager to update, and flexible in meeting the changing demands of their workplace.

SOCIAL ROLE CHANGES MARK MIDLIFE

Taking a social role perspective shifts the emphasis to the rights and responsibilities associated with moving along the life course. Such conceptions are ancient, as seen in the Indian phrasing of the male life course, which differentiates the householder phase of active engagement in socially productive roles and the elder phase of withdrawal to spiritual contemplation. Havighurst's (1972) model was explicitly framed in this perspective. Among the midlife challenges he listed are to "exercise the powers of midlife wisely" and "be ready to mentor younger persons and turn over power to them." His description of adult developmental tasks have been criticized for reflecting expectations for White, middle-class Western adults—and they increasingly seem less applicable in an era when family structures are fluid and varied and when management positions may be held by young adults supervising their elders.

Probably the most notable example of the social perspective was offered by Neugarten and her colleagues in the description of the power of age norms to shape behaviors in all domains (Neugarten & Hagestad, 1976; Neugarten, Moore, & Lowe, 1965). One consequence is the development of a social clock by which progress is charted according to one's personal timetable and according to the one held by others in the social system. In this perspective, jobs and career progress are both governed by age norms (as well as gender norms). There are "young men's jobs" and "midlife jobs." Neugarten (1968) described the shift in relations between generations, particularly evident in workplaces; the shift from apprentice to becoming part of the command generation and mentor to the younger workers was an important marker of feeling middle-aged among high achieving adults. Neugarten later deemphasized age norms and argued that America had become a largely "age irrelevant" society (Neugarten, 1996b).

The social role model has clear applications to the work realm, since role defines one's place in social structures. A review of career development literature and first person accounts makes it clear that many persons who are now middle-aged and older came of age when career ladders were anticipated, and expectations of progress were tied to age. By age 35 to 40, men knew whether they were likely to be promoted in their line of work or sidelined, and this awareness had significant repercussions (e.g., Howard & Bray, 1988; Huyck, 1970; Levinson et al., 1978). Personal identity was heavily invested in the work role and in the degree of competence, author-ity, and power implied in titles such as journeyman, master craftsman, as-sistant vice-president, lieutenant colonel, and CEO. In addition, social relationships, within the workplace and even in the wider community were governed by work role status. In the current era, when adults are likely to change careers several times, organizational structures are less hierarchi-cal, and promotion is based more on expertise than tenure, the previous notions of "appropriate work roles for middle age" have been challenged. The models developed on earlier realities may not fit in the future.

The other way in which roles influence work behavior concerns parent-ing. Most of the earlier models assumed that most adults become parents; fatherhood mobilizes men toward greater seriousness in work productiv-ity (see, especially, Gutmann, 1994); motherhood brings a primary de-mand for involvement in unpaid family work; and the middle years are marked by a freedom, especially for women, to reconsider involvement in paid work. Some of the current models of young adulthood try to identify factors that lead men and women into parenthood or not, and to different combinations of work and family involvement for both parents. The con-sequences of such decisions for the middle years are not yet clear.

EXPERIENCES DURING THE MIDDLE YEARS VARY BY SOCIAL CLASS, COHORT, RACE/CULTURE, HISTORICAL TIME, AND INDIVIDUAL DIFFERENCES

Such variability is not news, but, there are no studies that meet the gold standard of sequential designs, across cultures, which could tease out the contributions of these different influences. There is, thus, no basis for a comprehensive model of adult development during midlife in all domains.

The challenges of the middle years are influenced by cohort, a concept that assesses how the historical-cultural times shape the opportunities and assumptions of individuals who came of age during that time. Sheehy sug-gested that five different generations (or cohorts) now occupy contempo-rary adulthood (Sheehy, 1995). She drew on a unique database created from Census Bureau data to compare what is happening at any stage to a partic-ular cohort group over its lifetime, in terms of educational and occupa-tional achievement, labor force status, income level, marriage, childbearing, and divorce patterns. The five generational cohorts are designated as World War II (aged 16–19 from 1937 to 1944), Silent (aged 16–19 from 1952 to 1959), Vietnam (aged 16–19 from 1974 to 1984), and Endangered (aged 16–19 from 1982 to 1989). Her analysis, supported by other researchers, points out the ways in which the content of challenges perceived during the early 40s, for example, is strongly influenced by generation.

Some of the reports provide data about individuals who do not fit into the primary model identified. For example, Vaillant (1977) noted that some of the men, whom he labeled "perpetual boys," did not develop more mature defense mechanisms. Newman (1998) examined the lives of middle-aged African Americans living in the Harlem section of New York City. Although their neighborhood had been a safe haven when they were young, their middle years are beset with fears about physical safety, struggles to continue parenting damaged children and dependent grand-children, and a loss of opportunities. This image of vulnerable and constricted middle age is very different from the optimistic portraits of the command generation involved in expansion and release from parenting responsibilities.

Generally, the best reports on subgroup developmental themes during midlife will probably come from researchers who are focusing on those groups and approaching the study of their lives much as the early researchers did with the European Americans included in the current models. It is likely that work experiences—and perhaps other "normal" transformations—during the middle years will vary among those with substantial inherited wealth, the "underclass," men and women of color, persons with disabilities, persons with mild retardation, persons with mental illnesses, and so forth.

NEGOTIATING MIDLIFE AS A WORKER

H. Sterns and Gray (1999) emphasize the challenges faced by midlife workers in terms of self-management. As organizations transition from pyramid to flatter more streamlined configurations through downswing and restructuring, employees may experience job loss, job plateauing, and skills obsolescence (Farr et al., 1998; H. Sterns & Miklos, 1995). Older workers may be singled out in downsizing efforts on the basis of stereotypic traits such as being unsuitable for retraining or fast-paced work environments (Hall & Mirvis, 1995a, 1995b; Mirvis & Hall, 1996). Furthermore, depending on age of career entry, middle-aged and older workers may be more likely to occupy the midlevel managerial positions that are often the focus of downsizing and restructuring strategies. Additionally, slow company growth may lead to less opportunity for advancement (Farr et al., 1998). These changes suggest older workers may need to take increased involvement and responsibility in terms of career management.

Organizational changes are also altering the nature of the relationships between organizations and employees (Hall & Mirvis, 1996). Employers' commitment to employees may last only as long as there is a need for their skills and performance. Similarly, employees' commitment to the employer may last only as long as their expectations are being met. These changes place greater emphasis on employees' adaptability and abilities in learning to learn (Hall & Mirvis, 1996).

CAREER SELF-MANAGEMENT

The idea of career self-management is well captured in the discussions of Hall and Mirvis (1996) of the protean career. A protean career is directed by the individual rather than the employing organization. Greater responsibility for learning, skill mastery, and reskilling is also placed on the individual (Hall & Mirvis, 1995a). The individual is in charge, in control, and able to change the shape of his or her career at will—similar to a free agent in sports (Hall & Mirvis, 1996). This perspective and the goals of this type of career (e.g., psychological success, identity expansion, and learning) also recognize the artificiality of the distinction between work and nonwork life. Personal roles and career roles are highly interrelated and the boundaries between these roles tend to be fuzzy rather than clear-cut (Hall & Mirvis, 1995a). One disadvantage of protean careers is that an individual's identity is not likely to be tied to any one organization. Problems of self-definition may result in that one's personal identity is not connected to a formal organizational work role.

Mirvis and Hall (1996) also suggest that taking the responsibility of career self-management may hold special benefits for older workers. Greater tenure in a protean-type career may lead to increased value of older workers. It may be rather expensive to replace such knowledgeable, adaptable, and continuously learning employees with younger workers with less protean-type career experience. Protean careers may increase the organization's options for deploying older workers. Similarly, the options older workers may pursue in changing their careers are also increased (Mirvis & Hall, 1996). Potential alternatives include moving to a new field (i.e., second or third careers), building new skills in their present field, changing organizations, phasing into retirement, or joining the contingent workforce.

Older workers, however, may also be at a disadvantage in terms of moving toward greater career self-management. Transitioning from a typical, organizational-driven career to a protean career may be a daunting task, particularly if an individual initially entered the workforce with a one career-one employer ideal. Additionally, stereotypic beliefs about older workers may lead to the underutilization of this group within the new relationships between organizations and employees (Mirvis & Hall, 1996).

MAINTAINING COMPETENCE

A decade ago, Willis and Dubin (1990) raised this important issue of remaining current and up to date in one's work.

Professional competence involves the ability to function effectively in the tasks considered essential within a given profession or job. Professional competence involves two broad domains. First, there are proficiencies specific to the profession or discipline: (1) the discipline-specific knowledge base; (2) technical skills considered essential in the profession or job; and(3) ability to solve problems encountered within the profession or job. Second, the concept of professional competence represents general characteristics of the individual that facilitate the individual's development and maintenance of professional competence: intellectual ability, personality traits, motivation, attitudes, and values.

Professional competence is reflected in the performance of the individual. It is through performance in particular professional or job domains that persons demonstrate their level of competence. Management or supervisory personnel assess level of competence by observing the person's performance. Assessment procedures associated with licensure or recertification involve obtaining a sample of the professional's behavior (performance) via tests, simulation tasks, and the like. A behavior sample is considered to represent the person's level of competence.

SELF-AWARENESS: THE APPRAISAL PROCESS AT MIDLIFE

One of the common themes, at least in contemporary Western culture, is that midlife spurs the reassessment of one's whole life. This belief permeates the popular culture. Age-theme birthday cards designed for those turning 40, especially, play on fears associated with aging: loss of potency (especially sexual) among men, loss of attractiveness among women (Huyck, 1988). An ad for a charge card featuring a snazzy red convertible asks, "Was it the midlife crisis—or was it the miles?" (frequent flyer credit miles one could obtain by charging the car). Messages floating through the Internet point out "great truths that adults have learned" including "Middle age is when you choose your cereal for the fiber, not the toy." The general image is one of confronting loss of youthful energy, possibility, and promise.

There is also a large selection of popular psychology self-help books to help individuals cope with midlife. Some of them constitute another kind of literature of middle age. Certainly the most well-known are the propositions offered by Gail Sheehy, who has augmented academic studies with her own surveys, interviews, and lively prose to describe the adult life cycle. In *Passages* (Sheehy, 1976) charted the territory of the "Trying Twenties," the "Catch-30 Transition," the Thirties, and the "Deadline Decade"; this first work drew heavily on the research of Levinson et al. (1978) and R. Gould (1978). Following the phenomenal success of *Passages,* she outlined *Further Passages* (Sheehy, 1995), which extended the model through the middle years and speculated about the late years. Sheehy also published *Pathfinders* (1981), focusing on how adults overcome crises to find well-being; *The Silent Passage* (1992) about menopause; and *Understanding Men's*

Passages (1998). The phrases and images she provides about the contemporary life cycle, transmitted in her publications, lectures, and media coverage have permeated the American culture.

Sheehy interprets the data to signify a radical restructuring of the adult life course to include Provisional Adulthood (18–30), First Adulthood (30–45), and Second Adulthood (45–85+). In her more recent model, phases are described as the Tryout Twenties, Turbulent Thirties, Flourishing Forties, Flaming Fifties, Serene Sixties, Sage Seventies, Uninhibited Eighties, Nobility of the Nineties, and Celebratory Centenarians. In this paradigm, the mid-40s are marked by an early midlife crisis and a "Little Death" of First Adulthood, as individuals realize that they have been living too much governed by the desire to please significant powerful adults (especially parents and bosses), and that the anticipated rewards are not forthcoming or are not as meaningful as hoped. The Meaning Crisis dominates much of Second Adulthood, "the search for meaning in whatever we do . . . based on a spiritual imperative: the wish to integrate the disparate aspects of ourselves, the hunger for wholeness, the need to know the truth" (Sheehy, 1995, p. 148).

This theme of searching for an authentic self and finding ways of investing that self into meaningful activities appears in many other self-help publications. For example, Barbara Sher (1998) draws on her clinical experience (and includes no references) to show readers how to identify the illusions governing their earlier years and reclaim their "original self" to guide decisions in their "second life." A similar theme, presented as a popular version of a research project including interviews with 73 men and women, is illustrated in *In Our Fifties: Voices of Men and Women Reinventing Their Lives* (Bergquist, Greenberg, & Klaum, 1993).

This theme has been sounded before. Robert Havighurst first proposed his list of Developmental Tasks for each phase of the life course in 1953 (Havighurst, 1953). In adults aged 40 to 50, he saw the challenges revolving around "exerting and asserting oneself"; he noted that most men were at their peak during this phase, though they might have more power later on. "A person who has leadership potential commences to assert his leadership at this time—or he never does do so at all" (p. 31). During the decade from 50 to 60, the task is "creating a new life style." He noted that many strive to maintain the power achieved so easily in the prior decade, but begin to doubt their occupational power, social power, and intellectual power. Havighurst believed that the ego turns toward the self, thought begins to replace action as a mode of dealing with the world, and many shift investment from one set of roles to another that "pays" better in satisfaction. During the next decade, individuals decide whether to disengage and how; some become jealous of and hostile to younger colleagues. Havighurst also indicated that while most resist pressures to disengage, their only choice really becomes how, not whether. This last observation is probably the one that is most variant with contemporary portrayals of options in the 60s, with the current emphasis on renewal, new life, and options for extending healthy functioning—as well as altered legal requirements for retirement.

Sheehy and Havighurst both note that their models of midlife do not extend to individuals who are struggling to gain a secure footing in the social system (e.g., those with significant challenges posed by disability, poverty, or illness).

Erik Erikson (1963) proposed that the distinctive challenge of midlife is to resist the temptation of self-absorption and become generative, capable of fighting to preserve values, traditions, and structures that will be best for the coming generations. A substantial body of research is accumulating on how women and men experience generativity, and which adults are most likely to develop this capacity (Antonucci & Akiyama, 1997; MacDermid, Heilbrun, & DeHaan, 1997; McAdams, & de St. Aubin, 1998).

Some believe this reassessment is linked to the awareness of personal mortality (Jaques, 1965) and the concern about how much time is left to accomplish youthful dreams and ambitions; or the signs of biological aging in appearance, reduced energy, and lessened recuperative powers. Others anchor such reappraisals to changes in social roles and the contexts in which social roles are enacted. Changes may be age-graded, to the extent that strong age norms persist about the "right age" to be promoted, to finish bearing children, for adult children to be married.

There remains substantial disagreement whether reappraisals occur on a predictable timetable for all adults (Levinson & Levinson, 1996; Levinson et al., 1978), or occur only at times when individual circumstances prompt such reassessment. There is also great disagreement about whether reappraisal signifies crisis. The general stance now seems to be to recognize a continuum of minimal appraisal through serious crisis, dependent on complex interactions of individual needs and ambitions, current circumstances and options, and anticipated future outcomes. For example, Florine Livson (1981) used longitudinal data to explore psychological well-being during the middle years. She found that some men and women showed little evidence of crisis or reappraisal from age 40 to 50. The stable women were quite traditional, feminine and confident; they became even more poised and charming with age. Another group of women looked very troubled at 40; by age 50 they had rebounded to very positive mental health. These "changers" had been less traditionally feminine even in high school—more intellectual, more assertive, and impatient. They experienced substantial dislocation in early midlife, but—often following divorce, psychotherapy, and/or career changes—redirected themselves. Gutmann and Huyck (1994) compared men who handled the changes of midlife well with those who had troubles. Most men expanded their gender styles with minimal dislocation; some showed substantial distress when either they recognized their own desire to become more passive or their wife became what they perceived as dangerously assertive. Such studies highlight the importance of the fit between personality styles and the current setting.

Menon and Shweder (1998; see also Chapter 2 this volume) argue that midlife reappraisal—and the concept of midlife itself—is a cultural invention, a convenient myth of modern Western societies. They offer anthropological evidence that the experience of a specific phase of life called middle age, marked by chronological age (e.g., the 40th birthday), expectations of biological decline, and social perceptions of lessened desirability as an employee, is limited to the kinds of adults studied in the United States. For example, in many traditional cultures, changes for women are linked not to chronological age but role relations. An adolescent girl marries and relocates into her husband's family compound, where she becomes the hardworking servant; she moves into a somewhat higher status when a younger son marries and brings home a newer wife to become the lowest-ranking daughter-in-law. The major transition, however, comes when her first son marries and brings home a wife to serve her; she then takes over substantial control of the household—and her mother-in-law moves into the old-age role of observer in the household (Kakar, 1998; Menon & Shweder, 1998). Movement into what we might consider middle age is dictated by family role changes, and carries connotations of power and authority, rather than decline. There is no evidence of a personal reappraisal of life priorities, perhaps because the life course is highly structured culturally. Shweder's work reminds us of the importance of considering the cultural context in building models of adult development.

NEGOTIATING WORK, FAMILY, AND FRIEND INVOLVEMENTS

As indicated, whatever reappraisals occur during midlife resonate with the full set of roles and psychological investments during that phase. Most midlife workers lead complex lives; what happens at work often affects other aspects of their life, just as other commitments often affect employment attitudes and behaviors. One of the common refrains is the desire to balance work and other commitments more successfully. The most familiar version of this challenge occurs with parents of young children. However, the challenges do not cease when parents move into the middle years. In fact, family involvement often becomes more complex, with marital, parental, grandparental, and filial roles competing with work for energy.

Probably the most complex ties are the intergenerational ones. Some 90% of adults aged 35 to 64 are parents. According to a review of some of the research, "No single trajectory is characteristic of all or even most families during the middle years of parenthood" (Seltzer & Ryff, 1994). It is, thus, impossible to generalize neatly about the midlife family given the changes in timing of births, marriage, divorce and remarriage, and blended families. Instead, parenting experiences vary by social class, gender, life events and transitions, and psychological functioning in both generations. Generally, Whites, married couples, and unmarried fathers have more material resources than do minority group parents, unmarried parents, and single mothers. Divorced parents report more strain in and less support from parenting, and are generally less satisfied with parenting during these years. The majority of parents need to tend both to work and parenting: 81% of the fathers and 64% of mothers aged 35 to 44 have children at home and are employed (Seltzer & Ryff, 1994).

Launching children into adulthood is a long, complex process. One of the first studies of this process was undertaken in Parkville, with a deliberate sample of 150 geographically and maritally stable families (Huyck, 1989). One young adult child (aged 21–31) and his or her parents were interviewed, with the guiding assumption that both generations would be influencing each other. When asked about the ideal time to leave home, it became clear there was no community norm. Rather, each family—and perhaps each dyad—felt responsible for determining how to handle the transition process. In fact, children moved in and out of the family home, so that a family with several children was very likely to have a resident young adult child at any particular time—though each one might stay a relatively short time. The Parkville study included the first examination of how mothers and fathers define parenting during this phase—and some had a difficult time describing it. Most (80%) characterized it as giving advice and encouragement, having special personal interactions (67%), giving financial assistance (60%) or nonfinancial assistance (36%); the majority (58%) emphasized that parenting was limited compared with prior years. The shift was from responsibility to concern. Similar to other reports of parenting during this phase (Seltzer & Ryff, 1994), mothers were more emotionally involved with young adult children, were less likely to define parenting as providing financial assistance, and were more likely to describe their parenting in terms of providing nonfinancial assistance. It was clear that even in this privileged group of parents (middle and working class, in long-term marriages, White), the responsibilities and delights of parenting were very important realities of their middle years.

Grandparenting is a relationship with many meanings and varied enactments (Robertson, 1977). In contrast to the stereotyped images of sedentary, cookie-making, or fishing grandparents, many grandparents now are very involved in vigorous, complex lives of their own. With the rise in unwed maternity, divorce, and substance abuse, more grandparents—especially grandmothers—have found themselves playing an active parental role with grandchildren, and many grandparents have fought for legal recognition of grandparent's rights. While some grandparents have little contact with their grandchildren, others are thrust into responsibilities they thought they had left behind.

Many middle-aged children have living parents, and the wish and/or the need to be involved in their lives can pose another balancing challenge. For comparison, in 1800 a 60-year-old woman had only a 3% chance of having a living parent; by 1980 that had risen to 60% (Watkins, Menken, & Bongaarts, 1987). The increased longevity of elders means that four- and five-generation families are increasingly common. Many of the elders are still involved in nurturing younger generations. However, the increased longevity, the relatively low fertility of women who are now elderly, and the changes in the healthcare system mean that families are providing more care and more difficult care over longer periods of time than ever before in history (Brody, 1990). Family members even provide around 80% of the care given to bedridden elders.

Elaine Brody (1990) described the situation of "women in the middle," with the recognition that "women" included others who provide care. A 1992 Harris survey of adults over 55 found that 29% of men and 29% of women are caregivers for spouses, parents, other relatives, friends, and neighbors (The Commonwealth Fund, 1993). The heroic balancing efforts of family caregivers have been well documented. Many caregivers feel pulled between spouse, children, parents, and employment. Work may be, in such cases, a relief from otherwise-relentless pressures. Some women, however, find they must reduce work to part time, or withdraw altogether.

Many middle-aged people are in committed relationships; most are heterosexual marriages or nonmarried arrangements, and some are same-sex unions (Huyck, 1995). One aspect of such relationships is that partners generally try to coordinate their work and family so that each partner feels able to function as well as possible in all domains, while honoring the time and attention needed to nurture their relationship. This means juggling schedules for family work, paid employment, and shared and individual pleasures. The traditional mode was to have one partner (usually the wife in heterosexual unions) be primarily responsible for unpaid family work; this system has been disrupted by the widespread employment of women. Most middle-aged dual-career couples did not start out married life assuming they would be "social pioneers" (Gilbert & Davidson, 1989); changed expectations and greater opportunities for women, and the perceived need for two incomes, contributed to keeping more women in the labor force. At midlife, married women with children and satisfying work are the most satisfied (Barnett, 1997). However, there is also substantial complexity, as each partner goes through the appraisal process of whether their work has provided the anticipated benefits, and been worth the sacrifices of the past. Dual-career couples often have additional complexities in terms of parenting—deciding whether, and when to have children. Those who delayed parenting may find themselves still involved with dependent or adolescent children in middle age. The complexities about career reappraisal, parenting, and family obligations may be very similar in homosexual couples (Huyck, 1995).

There are likely to be different issues with women who have had interrupted career patterns. Women who have returned to school and launched a career in early (or even middle) middle age often have the enthusiasm, ambition, and energy of younger adults venturing forth into their adult responsibilities. Many men who have been employed long enough to become disenchanted are ready to shift their emphasis to family sharing. While they are often relieved to share the financial burdens with an employed wife, some men are ambivalent or hostile when they feel their wife is competing on their own turf, and is not as available for companionship now that they are (finally) ready. Issues of retirement timing also emerge as troubling for many couples; men often feel they have worked long enough and women feel they are just getting started (Sheehy, 1995). Women often feel very conflicted about their loyalties (Dinnerstein, 1992). Presumably the women and men who are entering middle age with the current assumptions about long-term commitments to paid work will have more balanced assessments of how much they wish to invest in employment, though there are certainly no guarantees that even long-term relationships guarantee comparable timing and intensity of investment in work.

Some divorce in midlife. Men generally remarry, and there are likely to be only short-term repercussions on their focus on work. On the other hand, women are likely to experience downward economic status after divorce; most find they need to enter employment, or to place more emphasis on earning money or obtaining benefits if they wish to have reasonable financial security for the rest of their adult lives (Huyck, 1999). Thus, divorce often prompts serious realignment in priorities assigned to family, work, and self-development.

Women who do not divorce in midlife typically face a period of caring for an ill husband and widowhood; men who survive midlife may end up caring for their ill wives in old age. In same-sex and heterosexual couples, partners may end up caring for each other, and putting increased time and energy into the enterprise as they grow older. Employment of women is often disrupted by spousal caregiving; men are more likely to hire help, while women are likely to provide direct care themselves. The death of a spouse may mean a widow must find employment to provide adequate financial resources; some widows are financially secure enough to pursue self-development or employment interests.

A minority of middle-aged women and men have never married; some are in partnerships, but some are not. Never-married men are more likely to be less-educated than average men, and have lower-status work; homosexual men are an exception to this generalization. Never-married women are likely to have more education and higher status careers than average women. They are somewhat more likely to be involved in parent care, since the current preference seems to be to call on the adult child with the fewest competing responsibilities (Suitor, Pillemer, Keeton, & Robison, 1995). And, unmarried adults may have networks of close friends whom they regard as important as blood kin.

Thus, many men and women are struggling to achieve a new balance among the domains of complex lives. However, we should not lose sight that some individuals are not seeking any kind of more even balance: They want, instead, to concentrate fully on work, or on family relations, a hobby, or volunteer work.

PERSONAL GROWTH: TAKING ACTION OUTSIDE WORK

If we accept the premise that some reappraisal is a common aspect of midlife in America, the challenge becomes to understand how individuals translate contemplation into actions to redirect their lives. The common theme in many models of psychological development is that with maturity comes an increased capacity to experience the self and life in more realistic, complex terms, and the desire to move beyond self-protection and into using potentials more fully. As mentioned, Erik Erikson described the midlife challenge as one of moving into generativity and overcoming stagnation or self-preoccupation (Erikson, 1950/1980). Generativity was initially described in terms of "the concern in establishing and guiding the next generation . . . including more popular synonyms as *productivity* and *creativity*" (Erikson, 1950, 1980, p. 267). Others have clarified the kinds of expectations and experiences that could qualify as generative (e.g., McAdams & de St. Aubin, 1998). The first large-scale ($n = 3,032$), national study of adults aged 25 to 74 used behavioral, commitment, and self-construal measures of generativity to explore relationships with age, gender, and education (Keyes & Ryff, 1998). They found that, as predicted, young adults scored lower in most measures of generativity than midlife and older adults—with one interesting exception. Young adults reported they felt more of a "primary obligation" to care for children and other people in their intimate circles; middle-aged and older adults are more likely to feel a sense of civic obligation; and midlife adults are the most likely to feel they have personal generative qualities—they are resources for teaching, guiding, and assisting others. These age patterns are consistent with those identified in longitudinal studies of two samples of adult women (Stewart & Vandewater, 1998). Young adult women were high in their *desire* to be generative, whereas actual generative *accomplishments* were higher in midlife. Thus, it seems that becoming more generative is a normal aspect of adult development.

Other social experiences, in addition to those associated with age, seem to shape generativity. Studies using special measures of generativity show that women are higher in generativity than are men (Keyes & Ryff, 1998). On the other hand, 27% of women and 25% of men over 55 are volunteers in addition to working and helping their family and friends; most (63%) volunteer less than 5 hours per week, but 13% volunteer more than 11 hours per week (The Commonwealth Fund, 1993). More educated adults (beyond high school) are higher in generativity (Keyes & Ryff, 1998). Some gay men show generativity in caring for members of their community (particularly those dealing with AIDS) and working for social change (Cohler, Hostetler, & Boxer, 1998).

Those who are more generative show higher well-being, both in psychological well-being and confidence in the social system (Keyes & Ryff, 1998; Stewart & Vandewater, 1998). Among adults over 55, 71% of those who volunteer are very satisfied with their lives, compared with 58% of those who do not volunteer (The Commonwealth Fund, 1993). Psychological well-being is associated with generativity when expressed in one's role as a spouse or a worker, though not with the parental role (MacDermid, Franz, & DeReus, 1998). (Perhaps this is because heavy involvement in the parental role at midlife is often an indication that children—or grandchildren—need more attention and concern than is considered desirable.)

Generativity may be connected with a renewed appreciation of spirituality or religious framework. The evidence for this is largely anecdotal. Half of the volunteering of adults over 55 is done through religious organizations (The Commonwealth Fund, 1993). Some individuals explain that their actions helping others, working to become more effective, or striving to alter the social-political system have meaning because they are embedded in a larger set of meanings. Such meanings may be phrased in terms of acceptable religious beliefs and organizations, or they may be described as "spiritual."

The psychologist Mihaley Csikszentmihalyi (1990) described an experience of "flow" reported by many adults. Flow occurs when an individual is intensely focused on the challenge at hand; generally people say they feel strong, alert, in effortless control, unselfconscious, and at the peak of their abilities. They have a sense of accomplishment and personal affirmation on completion. Flow experiences are not motivated by external approval or anticipated rewards. Once experienced, people are drawn back to the situations in which flow is possible. Researchers have found that many individuals report flow experiences in their paid work, though they are also frequent in leisure pursuits.

For some in midlife, leisure time may provide opportunities for personal growth. Although there is no clear definition of leisure, generally, it involves an activity done primarily for its own sake, with an element of enjoyment, pursued during unobligated time (McGuire, Boyd, & Tedrich 1996). Leisure may be used in meaningful activities (e.g., they provide a sense of acceptance, appreciation, affection, achievement, and amusement), and meaningful activities allow the participant to avoid senses of fear, frustration, inferiority, and guilt (Burdman, 1986, cited in McGuire, Boyd, & Tedrich 1996). There are several patterns of later life leisure: expanders, who add new activities throughout life, contractors, who shed activities, and maintainers (McGuire & Dottavio, 1986–1987, cited in McGuire, Boyd, & Tedrich 1996). During the early middle years, leisure activities are apt to be closely linked to career development, with skills and contacts nurtured during leisure pursuits contributing directly or subtly to greater success in current work or toward redirecting one's career. During later middle years, leisure may increasingly become the focus of activities that can be maintained through retirement into the later years of life.

One challenge seems to be getting the desired amount of leisure. Some middle-aged people have too much leisure, particularly those who have been laid off work or are employed part time when they would prefer full-time work. Probably more have too little leisure, and feel continuously torn by responsibilities to employment and family responsibilities.

One additional way in which reappraisal becomes action is in health. Neugarten identified "body monitoring" as one of the hallmarks of midlife (Neugarten, 1969/1996a). In the past several decades, middle-aged individuals have become even more aware of the health threats of later life, and of actions to defer, avoid, or manage health problems. A minority of adults seem to be following the prescriptions regarding diet, exercise, checkups, and stress management. Some adults seem more preoccupied with the appearance of aging, and focus on hair coloring, plastic surgery, and other cosmetic attempts to conceal evidence of advancing age.

HOW EMPLOYERS VIEW MIDLIFE WORKERS

In the past, many employers have had negative impressions about middle-aged and older workers believing them to be slow, undependable, unadaptive, accident-prone, costly, and unable to meet the physical and mental demands of work (Cahill & Salomone, 1987). But there is growing evidence that these attitudes are changing (Ferraro & Sterns, 1990).

Many human resource managers consider older individuals to be excellent workers (Dennis, 1988). However, older people bring with them the expectation of increased costs for salary and benefits. In the current economic climate, human resource managers are understandably concerned with cost containment and may look less favorably on middle-aged and older workers. And negative stereotypes remain. Older workers are often considered to be less flexible people, who are unwilling to learn or change their ways. Some human resource managers subscribe to the notion that older workers have a different work style that clashes with the work style of younger workers (H. Sterns & Gray, 1999).

The new global economy and a renewed emphasis on current economic issues have placed new pressures on organizations and the people who work for them. Many of these pressures, in the form of company emphasis, are advantageous to both older workers and older consumers.

Organizations increasingly emphasize consumer satisfaction and customer relations. Older workers are perceived to be more skilled than younger workers in interpersonal communication and in giving attention to customers. William McNaught and Michael Barth (1992) examined differences between older (over 50) and younger (under 50) employees at the Days Inns Reservation Center in Atlanta. Older workers spent more time talking on the telephone to callers seeking reservations but were more successful in booking reservations. Younger workers' booking rates increased substantially after their first six months, but high turnover rate meant that few younger workers remained on the job for that length of time. Increased attention to customers resulted in improved sales, and the experiences of older workers appeared to contribute to their sales success. Another study, examining a building supply store chain in Britain, found older employees to be friendlier and more cooperative than younger workers (Hogarth & Barth, 1991).

The kinds of customers perceived to make up the market also have changed. Compared with decades past, certain sectors of older people have more disposable income and command increasing attention from business. Older adults may prefer doing business with people their own age, providing expanded opportunities for older adults (H. Sterns & Sterns, 1995a).

Overall, employers have a contradictory view of the value of older people as workers. They are seen as being excellent, hard-working, reliable, and motivated workers by most employers today. At the same time, organizations are looking for ways to cut expenses and see older workers as potentially costly. Paying for retirement benefits, such as pensions and healthcare plans, are among the concerns of human resource managers.

Cutting older workers is viewed as a way of providing a short-term solution to reducing operating costs (Hochstein, 1992).

However, older workers may more readily meet the business demands of the modern corporation. Older people may be interested in the flexibility of part-time and contract work following their main career. Such work is called contingent employment, and such jobs for older people are referred to as bridge jobs because they bridge the period between a person's major long-term work commitment and retirement. The need for workers in the present economy is the greatest in 40 years. Middle-aged and older workers should fare well in this period.

THE NEW MIDLIFE WORKER

Aging affects individuals at the personal, organizational, and societal levels. Industrial gerontology focuses on the employment and the retirement of middle-age and older workers. The aging of the workforce creates several issues including career patterns and retirement, training and retraining, performance, health and physical capacity, and potential staffing shortages. Whether middle-aged and older workers continue to occupy their jobs or change jobs will be determined by opportunities, career choices, retraining experiences, health, and retirement preferences (H. Sterns & Miklos, 1995).

The life-span approach to work emphasizes the possibility of behavioral changes at any point in the life span. Opportunities, choices, and decisions are not tied to any specific age. Individual differences in aging and development are also central to this perspective. The unique status of each individual results from age-graded, history-graded, and nonnormative life influences (P. Baltes & Graf, 1996).

The metamodel of selective optimization with compensation (SOC) has been advanced to describe and explain successful adaptation to aging-related changes by proposing the interplay of three processes: selection, compensation, and optimization (M. Baltes & Carstensen, 1996). The SOC model is also being used in discussions within Industrial/Organizational Psychology (Abraham & Hanson, 1995; B. Baltes & Dickson, 2000). The three processes form a system of behavioral action that generate and regulate development and aging. Selection processes deal with the choice of goals, life domains, and life tasks. Compensation becomes relevant when specific behavioral capacities or skills are lost or reduced below the level for adequate functioning. Such efforts can be automatic or planned. Compensation may require the acquisition of new knowledge, skills, or abilities. Optimization involves the creation of opportunity for desired outcomes using present or new abilities or settings.

A person-centered approach using the SOC model as well as exploring the use of the model in various settings at work sets the stage for the future. Self-management of career, leisure, and retirement entails a lot of responsibility. Some individuals may accept this responsibility and respond proactively with success. Others, however, may respond ineffectively or be unable to respond at all. These individuals may not have the needed skills or psychological resources, or may be constrained by their circumstances.

The idea of career self-management is well captured in the discussions of Hall and Mirvis (1996) of the protean career mentioned earlier in this chapter. A protean career is directed by the individual rather than the employing organization. Greater responsibility for learning, skill mastery, and reskilling is also placed on the individual (Hall & Mirvis, 1995a). The new midlife worker is in charge, in control, and able to change the shape of his or her career at will. The focus is on selection. This perspective and the goals of this type of career (e.g., psychological success, identity expansion, and learning) also recognize the artificiality of the distinction between work and nonwork life. The use of compensation and optimization may be essential here.

Mirvis and Hall (1996) also suggest that taking on the responsibility of career self-management may hold special benefits for midlife and older workers. Greater tenure in a protean-type career may lead to increased value of older workers. It may be rather expensive to replace such knowledgeable, adaptable, and continuously learning employees with younger workers with less protean-type career experience. Protean careers may increase the organization's options for deploying older workers. Similarly, older workers may pursue more options in shaping their careers (Mirvis & Hall, 1996). Potential alternatives include moving to a new field (i.e., second or third careers), building new skills in their present field, changing organizations, phasing into retirement, or joining the contingent workforce. The application of the SOC model captures the dynamic quality of this process.

Middle-aged and older workers, however, may also be at a disadvantage in terms of moving toward greater career self-management. Transitioning from a typical, organizational-driven career to a protean career may be a daunting task, particularly if an individual initially entered the workforce with a one career-one employer ideal. Additionally, stereotypic beliefs about older workers may lead to the underutilization of their group within the new relationships between organizations and employees (Mirvis & Hall, 1996).

Finally, organizational or technological changes can lead to changes in the knowledge, skills, and abilities required for a job. H. Sterns and Patchett (1984) discussed these issues, proposing that employees in fast-paced industries will have greater interest in career development because of an ongoing need to update skills. Motivation may be an important factor in determining whether employees update skills. Compensation choices may be very important.

CONCLUSION AND FUTURE DIRECTIONS

Eighty percent of people aged 40 to 59 are employed. In the age group of 51 to 59, 24% do not work and over half of this group say a health condition or impairment limits the type of paid work they can do. One quarter of people aged 60 and older continue to work full or part time.

A critical issue of midlife is whether an individual will continue to be able to do the kind of work that he or she wants to do now and in the future. Mental and physical capability will not be an obstacle for a large number of middle-aged adults. One of the major predictors of remaining in the workforce is one's attitude toward work and the motivation to be current and competitive. Feelings and attitudes about the work context in midlife become increasingly important in determining whether an individual will work into late life. Organizational commitment (continuance and affectiveness) may influence the middle-aged and older worker. However, even in a period of full employment, downsizing, layoffs, and early buyouts still leave considerable ambiguity regarding future work opportunities or the need to seek new employment. Midlife may be a period of evaluation, reassessment, and reflection. Themes of midlife include: recognizing the limits of career progress, deciding to change jobs and/or careers, rebalancing work and family, further investing or withdrawing from work, and planning for retirement. Self-development and meaning may play an important role. Self-management of career and retirement place responsibilities with the person. Midlife workers lead complex lives; what happens at work often affects other aspects of their lives. Other commitments affect employment attitudes and behavior.

Self-reflection, appraisal, and reappraisal are recurring themes in midlife. Career self-management and the concept of protean career places the midlife worker in control and able to shape his or her career. Examples are deciding on full or part time work and planning for retirement, if desired.

Issues for future research include: When do workers perceive themselves to be in middle age and when do others see them as being in middle age? How does this self-perception or the perception by others affect the person's career and opportunities? Self-management of work and of career present great challenges. How well are people able to engage in self-management, self-appraisal, career planning, and taking action? At midlife do work and life experiences lead to insights and actions that are not possible earlier?

REFERENCES

Abraham, J.D., & Hanson, R.O. (1995). Successful aging at work: An applied study of selection, optimization, and compensation through impression management. *Journal of Gerontology: Psychological Sciences, 50B*(2), P94–P103.

Antonucci, T., & Akiyama, H. (1997). Concern with others at midlife: Care, comfort, or compromise? In M.L. Lachman & J.B. James (Eds.), *Multiple paths of midlife development* (pp. 145–170). Chicago: University of Chicago Press.

Atchley, R.C. (1988). *Social forces and aging: An introduction to social gerontology.* Belmont, CA: Wadsworth.

Avolio, B.J., & Sosik, J.J. (1999). Gender roles and gender identity in midlife. In S.L. Willis & J.D. Reid (Eds.), *Life in the middle: Psychological and social development in middle age* (pp. 249–274). New York: Academic Press.

Baltes, B.B., & Dickson, M.W. (2000, August 14). *Using life-span modules in industrial/organizational psychology: The theory of selective optimization with compensation (SOC).* Unpublished manuscript, Wayne State University, Detroit, MI, Psychology Department.

Baltes, M.M., & Carstensen, L.L. (1996). Social-psychological theories and their application to aging: From individual to collective. In V.L. Bengtson & K.W. Schaie (Eds.), *Handbook of theories of aging* (pp. 209–226). New York: Springer.

Baltes, P.B., & Graf, P. (1996). Psychology aspects of aging: Facts and frontiers. In D. Magnusson (Ed.), *The lifespan development of individuals: Behavioral, neurobiological and psychosocial perspectives* (pp. 427–460). Cambridge, England: Cambridge University Press.

Baltes, P.B., Reese, H.W., & Lipsitt, L.P. (1980). Life-span developmental psychology. *Annual Review of Psychology, 31,* 65–110.

Barnett, R.C. (1997). Gender, employment and psychological well-being: Historical and life course perspectives. In M.E. Lachman & J.B. James (Eds.), *Multiple paths of midlife development* (pp. 325–343). Chicago: University of Chicago Press.

Baruch, G., Barnett, R., & Rivers, C. (1983). *Lifeprints: New patterns of love and work for today's women.* New York: McGraw-Hill.

Belbin, E., & Belbin, R.M. (1972). *Problems in adult retraining.* London: Heinemann.

Bergquist, W.H., Greenberg, E.M., & Klaum, G.A. (1993). *In our fifties: Voices of men and women reinventing their lives.* San Francisco: Jossey-Bass.

Brady, E.M., Fortinsky, R.H., Norland, S., & Eichar, D. (1989). *Predictors of success among older workers in new jobs: Final report.* Gorham: University of Southern Maine, Human Services Development Institute.

Brody, E.M. (1990). *Women in the middle: Their parent-care years.* New York: Springer.

Buehler, C. (1935). The curve of life as studied in biographies. *Journal of Applied Psychology, 19,* 405–409.

Byrne, J.J. (1975). *Occupational mobility of workers* (Rep. No. 176). Washington, DC: U.S. Bureau of Labor Statistics, Special Labor Force.

Cahill, M., & Salomone, P.R. (1987). Career counseling for work life extension: Integrating the older worker into the labor force. *Career Development Quarterly, 35*(3), 188–196.

Cohler, B.J., Hostetler, A.J., & Boxer, A.M. (1998). Generativity, social context, and lived experience: Narratives of gay men in middle adulthood. In D.P. McAdams & E. de St. Aubin (Eds.), *Generativity and adult development: How and why we care for the next generation* (pp. 265–309). Washington, DC: American Psychological Association.

Colarusso, C.A., & Nemiroff, R.A. (1981). *Adult development.* New York: Plenum Press.

Commonwealth Fund, The. (1993, November). *The untapped resource: The final report of The Americans Over 55 at Work Program.* New York: Author.

Csikszentmihalyi, M. (1990). *Flow: The psychology of optimal experience.* New York: Harper Perennial.

Dennis, H. (1988). *Fourteen steps in maintaining an aging work force.* Lexington, MA: Lexington Books.

Dinnerstein, M. (1992). *Women between two worlds: Midlife reflections on work and family.* Philadelphia: Temple University Press.

Ekerdt, D.J. (1998). Workplace norms for the timing of retirement. In K.W. Schaie & C. Schooler (Eds.), *Impact of work on older adults* (pp. 101–123). New York: Springer.

Erikson, E.H. (1950). *Childhood and society.* New York: Norton.

Erikson, E.H. (1963). *Childhood and society* (2nd ed.). New York: Norton.

Erikson, E.H. (1974). Once more on the inner space: Letter for a former student. In J. Strouse (Ed.), *Women and analysis.* New York: Grossman/Viking Press.

Erikson, E.H. (1980). *Identity and the life cycle.* New York: Norton. (Original work published 1950)

Farr, J.L., Tesluk, P.E., & Klein, S.R. (1998). Organizational structure of the workplace and the older worker. In K.W. Schaie & C. Schooler (Eds.), Impact of work on older adults (pp. 143–185). New York: Springer.

Farrell, M., & Rosenberg, S. (1981). *Men at midlife.* Dover, MA: Auburn House.

Ferraro, K.F., & Sterns, H.L. (1990). 2020 vision and beyond. In K. Ferraro (Ed.), *Gerontology: Perspectives and issues* (pp. 357–360). New York: Springer.

Gerson, K. (1985). *Hard choices: How women decide about work, career and motherhood.* Berkeley: University of California Press.

Gilbert, L.A., & Davidson, S. (1989). Dual-career families at midlife. In S. Hunter & M. Sundel (Eds.), *Midlife myths: Issues, findings, and practice implications* (pp. 195–209). Newbury Park, CA: Sage.

Gould, R.L. (1978). *Transformation: Growth and change in adult life.* New York: Simon & Schuster.

Gould, S. (1979). Characteristics of career planners in upwardly mobile occupations. *Academy of Management Journal, 22,* 539–550.

Gutmann, D.L. (1994). *Reclaimed powers: Toward a new psychology of men and women in later life* (2nd ed.). Evanston, IL: Northwestern University Press.

Gutmann, D.L., & Huyck, M.H. (1994). Development and pathology in postparental men: A community study. In E.H. Thompson, Jr. (Ed.), *Older men's lives* (pp. 65–85). Thousand Oaks, CA: Sage.

Hall, D.T. (1971). Potential for career growth. *Personnel Administration, 34,* 18–30.

Hall, D.T., & Associates. (1996). *The career is dead: Long live the career.* San Francisco: Jossey-Bass.

Hall, D.T., & Mirvis, P.H. (1995a). Careers as lifelong learning. In A. Howard (Ed.), *The changing nature of work* (pp. 323–361). San Francisco: Jossey-Bass.

Hall, D.T., & Mirvis, P.H. (1995b). The new career contract: Developing the whole person at midlife and beyond. *Journal of Vocational Behavior, 47,* 269–289.

Hall, D.T., & Mirvis, P.H. (1996). The new protean career: Psychological success and the path with a heart. In D.T. Hall & Associates (Eds.), *The career is dead: Long live the career: A relational approach to careers.* San Francisco: Jossey-Bass.

Hall, D.T., & Nougaim, K. (1968). An examination of Maslow's need hierarchy in an organizational setting. *Organizational Behavior and Human Performance, 3,* 12–35.

Havighurst, R.J. (1953). *Human development and education.* New York: David McKay.

Havighurst, R.J. (1972). *Developmental tasks and education* (3rd ed.). New York: David McKay.

Havighurst, R.J. (1982). The world of work. In B.B. Wolman (Ed.), *Handbook of developmental psychology* (pp. 771–787). Englewood Cliffs, NJ: Prentice-Hall.

Helson, R., & Moane, G. (1987). Personality change in women from college to midlife. *Journal of Personality and Social Psychology, 53,* 176–186.

Hochstein, L.M. (1992). *Overview.* Paper presented at the Textbook Authors conference. Washington, DC: American Association of Retired Persons.

Hogarth, T., & Barth, M.C. (1991). Costs and benefits of hiring older workers: A case study of B & Q. *International Journal of Manpower, 12,* 5–17.

Holland, J.L. (1959). A theory of vocational choice. *Journal of Counseling Psychology, 6,* 35–45.

Holland, J.L. (1962). Some explorations of a theory of vocational choice: I. One- and two-year longitudinal studies. *Psychological Monographs, 76*(26, Whole No. 545).

Howard, A., & Bray, D.W. (1988). *Managerial lives in transition: Advancing age and changing times.* New York: Guilford Press.

Huyck, M.H. (1970). *Age norms and career lines in the military.* Unpublished doctoral dissertation, University of Chicago, Chicago.

Huyck, M.H. (1988, August). When you care enough: The gender scene in humorous birthday cards. In L. Troll & D. Rodehgeaver (Co-Chairs), *Creativity and humor in women.* Paper presented at the 96th annual convention of American Psychological Association, Atlanta, GA.

Huyck, M.H. (1989). Midlife parental imperatives. In R. Kalish (Ed.), *Midlife loss: Coping strategies* (pp. 10–34). Newbury Park, CA: Sage.

Huyck, M.H. (1995). Marriage and close relationships of the marital kind. In R. Blieszner & V.H. Bedford (Eds.), *Handbook of aging and the family* (pp. 181–200). Westport, CT: Greenwood Press.

Huyck, M.H. (1999). Gender roles and gender identity in midlife. In. S.L. Willis & J.D. Reid (Eds.), *Life in the middle: Psychological and social development in middle age* (pp. 209–232). New York: Academic Press.

Jaques, E. (1965). Death and the mid-life crisis. *International Journal of Psycho-analysis, 66,* 502–515.

Kakar, S. (1998). The search for middle age in India. In R.A. Shweder (Ed.), *Welcome to middle age!* (pp. 75–100). Chicago: University of Chicago Press.

Katz, R. (1980). The influence of job longevity on employee reactions to task characteristics. *Human Relation, 31,* 703–725.

Keyes, C.M., & Ryff, C.D. (1998). Generativity in adult lives: Social structural contours and quality of life consequences. In D.P. McAdams & E. de St. Aubin (Eds.), *Generativity and adult development: How and why we care for the next generation* (pp. 264–277). Washington, DC: American Psychological Association.

Labouvie-Vief, G., & Hakim-Larson, J. (1989). Developmental shifts in adult thought. In S. Hunter & M. Sundel (Eds.), *Midlife myths: Issues, findings, and practice implications* (pp. 69–96). Newbury Park, CA: Sage.

Lawrence, B.S. (1987). An organizational theory of age effects. *Research in the Sociology of Organizations, 5,* 37–71.

Levinson, D.J., Darrow, C.N., Klein, E.B., Levinson, M.H., & McKee, B. (1978). *The seasons of a man's life.* New York: Knopf.

Levinson, D.J., & Levinson, J.D. (1996). *The seasons of a woman's life.* New York: Ballantine Books.

Livson, F.B. (1981). Paths to psychological health in the middle years: Sex differences. In D.H. Eichorn, J.A. Clausen, N. Haan, M.P. Honzik, & P. Mussen (Eds.), *Present and past in middle life* (pp. 195–221). San Diego, CA: Academic Press.

MacDermid, S.M., Franz, C.E., & De Reus, L. (1998). Generativity: At the crossroads of social roles and personality. In D.P. McAdams & E. de St. Aubin (Eds.), *Generativity and adult development* (pp. 181–226). Washington, DC: American Psychological Association.

MacDermid, S.M., Heilbrun, G., & DeHaan, L.G. (1997). The generativity of employed mothers in multiple roles: 1979 and 1991. In M.E. Lachman & J.B. James (Eds.), *Multiple paths of midlife development* (pp. 207–240). Chicago: University of Chicago Press.

Matheson, N.S. (1991). *The influence of organizational-based self-esteem on satisfaction and commitment: An analysis of age differences.* Unpublished doctoral dissertation, University of Akron, OH.

McAdams, D.P., & de St. Aubin, E.D. (Eds.). (1998). *Generativity and adult development: How and why we care for the next generation.* Washington, DC: American Psychological Association.

McAdams, D.P., de St. Aubin, E.D., & Logan, R.L. (1993). Generativity among young, midlife, and older adults. *Psychology and Aging, 8*(2), 221–230.

McGuire, F., Boyd, R., & Tedrich, R. (1996). *Leisure and aging: Ulyssean living in later life.* Champaign, IL: Sagamon.

McNaught, W., & Barth, M.C. (1992). Are older workers "good buys"? A case study of Days Inns of America. *Sloan Management Review, 33,* 53–63.

Menon, U., & Shweder, R.A. (1998). The return of the "White Man's Burden": The moral discourse of anthropology and the domestic life of Hindu women. In

R.A. Shweder (Ed.), *Welcome to middle age!* (pp. 139–188). Chicago: University of Chicago Press.

Meyer, J.P., & Allen, N.J. (1984). Testing the side-bet theory of organizational commitment: Some methodological considerations. *Journal of Applied Psychology, 69,* 372–378.

Mirvis, P.H., & Hall, D.T. (1996). New organizational forms and the new career. In D.T. Hall & Associates (Eds.), *The career is dead: Long live the career: A relational approach to careers.* San Francisco: Jossey-Bass.

National Academy on an Aging Society. (2000). *Data profiles: Young retirees and older workers* (No. 1). Washington, DC: Author.

Nemiroff, R.A., & Colarusso, C.A. (1988). Frontiers of adult development in theory and practice. *Journal of Geriatric Psychiatry, 21*(1), 7–27.

Neugarten, B.L. (1968). The awareness of middle age. In B.L. Neugarten (Ed.), *Middle age and aging* (pp. 93–98). Chicago: University of Chicago Press.

Neugarten, B.L. (1996a). Continuities and discontinuities of psychological issues into adult life. In D.A. Neugarten (Ed.), *The meanings of age: Selected papers of Bernice L. Neugarten* (pp. 88–95). Chicago: University of Chicago Press.

Neugarten, B.L. (1996b). The young-old and the age-irrelevant society. In D.A. Neugarten (Ed.), *The meanings of age: Selected papers of Bernice L. Neugarten* (pp. 47–71). Chicago: University of Chicago Press.

Neugarten, B.L., & Hagestad, G.O. (1976). Age and the life course. In R.H. Binstock & E. Shanas (Eds.), *Handbook of aging and the social sciences* (pp. 35–55). New York: Van Nostrand-Reinhold.

Neugarten, B.L., Moore, J.W., & Lowe, J.C. (1965). Age norms, age constraints, and adult socialization. *American Journal of Sociology, 70,* 710–717.

Newman, K. (1998). Place and race: Midlife experience in Harlem. In R.A. Shweder (Ed.), *Welcome to middle age!* (pp. 259–293). Chicago: University of Chicago Press.

Pierce, J.L., Gardner, D.G., Cummings, L.L., & Dunham, R.B. (1989). Organization-based self-esteem: Construct definition measurement and validation. *Academy of Management Journal, 32,* 622–648.

Robertson, J.F. (1977). Grandmotherhood: A study of role concepts. *Journal of Marriage and the Family, 39,* 165–174.

Rosenbaum, J.E. (1979). Tournament mobility: Career patterns in a corporation. *Administrative Science Quarterly, 24,* 220–241.

Saben, S. (1967). *Occupational mobility of employed workers* (Rep. No. 84). Washington, DC: U.S. Bureau of Labor Statistics, Special Labor Force.

Schaie, K.W. (1996). *Intellectual development in adulthood: The Seattle Longitudinal Study.* New York: Cambridge University Press.

Schein, E.H. (1971). The individual, the organization, and the career: A conceptual scheme. *Journal of Applied Behavioral Science, 7,* 401–426.

Seltzer, M.M., & Ryff, C.D. (1994). Parenting across the life span: The normative and non-normative cases. In D.L. Featherman, R.M. Lerner, & M. Perlmutter (Eds.), *Life-span development and behavior* (Vol. 12, pp. 1–40). Hillsdale, NJ: Erlbaum.

Sheehy, G. (1976). *Passages.* New York: Dutton.

Sheehy, G. (1981). *Pathfinders.* New York: Morrow.

Sheehy, G. (1992). *The silent passage: Menopause.* New York: Random House.

Sheehy, G. (1995). *New passages: Mapping your life across time.* New York: Random House.

Sheehy, G. (1998). *Understanding men's passages: Discovering the new map of men's lives.* New York: Random House.

Sheppard, H.L. (1991). The United States: The privatization of exit. In J. Quadagno & D. Street (Eds.), *Aging for the twenty-first century: Readings in social gerontology* (pp. 351–377). New York: St. Martin's Press.

Sher, B. (1998). *It's only too late if you don't start now: How to create your second life after 40.* New York: Delacorte Press.

Shweder, R.A. (Ed.). (1998). *Welcome to middle age! (And other cultural fictions).* Chicago: University of Chicago Press.

Sommers, D., & Eck, A. (1977). Occupational mobility in the American labor force. *Monthly Labor Review, 100,* 3–19.

Sonnenfeld, J., & Kotter, J.P. (1982). The maturation of career theory. *Human Relations, 35,* 19–46.

Sterns, A.A., Sterns, H.L., & Hollis, L.A. (1996). The productivity and functional limitations of older adult workers. In W.H. Crown (Ed.), *Handbook on employment and the elderly* (pp. 276–303). Westport, CT: Greenwood Press.

Sterns, H., & Gray, H. (1999). Work, leisure and retirement. In J. Cavanaugh & S. Whitbourne (Eds.), *Gerontology* (pp. 355–390). New York: Oxford University Press.

Sterns, H.L. (1986). Training and retraining adult and older adult workers. In J.E. Birren, P.K. Robinson, & J.E. Livingston (Eds.), *Age, health, and employment* (pp. 93–113). Engelwood Cliffs, NJ: Prentice-Hall.

Sterns, H.L., & Doverspike, D. (1989). Aging and the training and learning process in organizations. In I. Goldstein & R. Katzell (Eds.), *Training and development in work organizations* (pp. 299–332). San Francisco: Jossey-Bass.

Sterns, H.L., Matheson, N.K., & Park, L.S. (1997). Work and retirement. In K. Ferraro (Ed.), *Gerontology: Perspectives and issues* (2nd ed., pp. 171–192). New York: Springer.

Sterns, H.L., & Miklos, S.M. (1995). The aging worker in a changing environment: Organizational and individual issues. *Journal of Vocational Behavior, 47,* 248–268.

Sterns, H.L., & Patchett, M. (1984). Technology and the aging adult: Career development and training. In P.R. Robinson & J.E. Birren (Eds.), *Aging and technology* (pp. 261–277). Englewood Cliffs, NJ: Prentice-Hall.

Sterns, H.L., & Sterns, A.A. (1995a). Age, health and employment capability of older Americans. In S. Bass (Ed.), *Older and active* (pp. 10–34). New Haven, CT: Yale University Press.

Sterns, H.L., & Sterns, A.A. (1995b, November 17). *Training and careers: Growth and development over fifty years.* Paper presented at the 48th annual scientific meeting of the Gerontological Society of America, Los Angeles.

Stewart, A.J., & Vandewater, E.A. (1998). The course of generativity. In D.P. McAdams & E. de St. Aubin (Eds.), *Generativity and adult development: How and why we care for the next generation* (pp. 10–75). Washington, DC: American Psychological Association.

Suitor, J.J., Pillemer, K., Keeton, S., & Robison, J. (1995). Aged parents and aging children: Determinants of relationship quality. In R. Blieszner & V.H. Bedford (Eds.), *Handbook of aging and the family* (pp. 223–242). Westport, CT: Greenwood Press.

Super, D.E. (1957). *The psychology of careers.* New York: Harper & Row.

Super, D.E. (1980). A life-span, life-space approach to career development. *Journal of Vocational Behavior, 18,* 282–298.

Vaillant, G. (1977). *Adaptation to life.* Boston: Little, Brown.

Veiga, J.F. (1973). The mobile manager at mid-career. *Harvard Business Review, 51,* 115–119.

Veiga, J.F. (1981). Plateaued versus non-plateaued managers: Career patterns, attitudes, and path potential. *Academy of Management Journal, 24,* 566–578.

Veiga, J.F. (1983). Mobility influences during managerial career stages. *Academy of Management Review, 8,* 23–32.

Warr, P. (1994). Age and employment. In H.C. Triandis, M.D. Dunnette, & L.M. Hough (Eds.), *Handbook of industrial and organizational psychology* (2nd ed., Vol. 4, pp. 485–550). Palo Alto, CA: Consulting Psychologists Press.

Watkins, S.C., Menken, J.A., & Bongaarts, J. (1987). Demographic foundations of family change. *American Sociological Review, 52,* 346–358.

Wilensky, H. (1961). Orderly careers and social participation: The impact of work history on social integration in the middle mass. *American Sociological Review, 26,* 521–530.

Willis, S.L., & Dubin, S.S. (1990). Maintaining professional competence: Directions and possibilities. In S.L. Willis & S.S. Dubin (Eds.), *Maintaining professional competence.* San Francisco: Jossey-Bass.

Zemke, R., Raines, C., & Filipczak, B. (2000). *Generations at work: Managing the clash of veterans, boomers, xers, and nexters in your workplace.* New York: American Management Association.

CHAPTER 14

Moving into Retirement:
Preparation and Transitions in
Late Midlife

JUNGMEEN E. KIM and PHYLLIS MOEN

IN THE 1950s, Friedmann and Havighurst (1954) developed the following five-point typology of the meanings of work: (1) a source of income, (2) a life routine structuring the use of time, (3) a source of personal status and identity, (4) a context for social interaction, and (5) a meaningful experience that can provide a sense of accomplishment. Throughout the twentieth century, employment came to be a central midlife role, for women as well as men, organizing days, weeks, and even the life course of workers and their families, and providing, in addition to income, meaningful activity as a context for personal growth, identity, and social relations.

Given the salience of paid work in midlife, retirement can be an abrupt transition marking the cessation of productive engagement. Exiting from one's career job is a key life change, transforming individuals' social and physical worlds in terms of their roles, relationships, and daily routines, along with concomitant shifts in income, health, and sometimes even residence. These transformations may well affect how individuals perceive themselves, their abilities, and their construction of the meanings of their retirement. Traditionally, retirement has marked not only the cessation of employment but also the movement from midlife to old age. However, as

Preparation of this chapter was supported in part by grants 96-6-9 and 99-6-23 from the Alfred P. Sloan Foundation (Phyllis Moen, Principal Investigator), grant IT50 AG11711 from the National Institute on Aging (Karl Pillemer and Phyllis Moen, Co-Principal Investigators), and support for the Pathways to Life Quality Study (John Krout and Phyllis Moen, Co-Principal Investigators).

we move into the twenty-first century, cultural and personal scripts regarding the nature and meaning of retirement are being rewritten (Moen, 1998a). Retirement is more than an objective life transition; it is also a developmental and social-psychological transformation related to physical and psychological well-being.

In this chapter, we draw on the research evidence to address three basic questions: (1) When and how do midlife workers plan and prepare for retirement? (2) Do retirement transitions influence the well-being of late midlife men and women, and if so, how? (3) What is the role of a sense of control and self-efficacy in retirement planning and retirement adjustment? We summarize the evidence regarding sociodemographic, social relational, and psychological factors that have been related to retirement planning and adjustment as well as the link between retirement planning and subsequent postretirement adjustment. We begin by locating the retirement transition in historical context.

CHANGING HISTORICAL CONTEXT

By the second half of the twentieth century, retirement, in terms of the final exit from employment, came to be a recognized phase of the life course, an almost universal event occurring in late midlife. However, several demographic and social trends are transforming both the timing and the nature of retirement, rendering it increasingly a transition *within,* rather than *from* midlife (Moen & Wethington, 1999).

LONGEVITY

First, there has been the lengthening of both the midlife years and late adulthood. The increase in human longevity and the decline in fertility, along with educational and medical advances, mean that individuals enter their 50s, 60s, and 70s healthier, better educated, and with the prospect of far more able years ahead of them than was the case for their parents or grandparents. This new demography is challenging the traditional, twentieth-century lockstep adult life course (Kohli & Rein, 1991; Moen, 1998a).

EARLY RETIREMENT TIMING

Second, economic transformations, along with changes in pensions and preferences, have produced a continued decline in the average age at retirement, at least for men. Growing numbers of workers are moving into retirement in their fifties, both by choice and as a consequence of early retirement incentives offered in tandem with corporate restructuring

(Atchley, 1991; Han & Moen, 1999). Historically, retirement is a relatively recent phenomenon, institutionalized in the United States with the Social Security Act of 1935. Since the 1950s, the change toward early retirement has been facilitated by legislation expanding coverage and the proliferation of public and private income programs (Fields & Mitchell, 1984; Graebner, 1980; Ruhm, 1989). This progressively earlier retirement age, coupled with the increases in longevity, means that retirement is no longer the upper boundary of midlife, as men and women face an extended postretirement phase of activity and vitality (Moen, 1994, 1996b; Moen, Fields, Quick, & Hofmeister, 2000).

The Changing Workforce

A third demographic trend is the changing nature of the labor force. The proportion of women in the workforce has increased dramatically in recent decades, whereas men's participation rates have declined, particularly for men aged 55 years and older (Moen, 1996a). While retirement in the second half of the twentieth century was principally a male transition, by the twenty-first century, it is a transition experienced by growing numbers of women as well. While the employment patterns across the life course of men and women now in their middle years are distinctive (Han & Moen, 1999), for future cohorts they will more closely resemble each other. Moreover, retirement is increasingly a *coupled* transition, with husbands and wives having to negotiate the timing and sequencing of both spouses' retirement, with implications for both marital quality and well-being (Kim & Moen, 2000; Moen, Kim, & Hofmeister, 2001).

THE MEANING OF RETIREMENT

Redefining Retirement

Retirement is typically defined as later life withdrawal from the workforce. It is usually thought of as a one-way, one-time individual status passage. Career employment and retirement are seen as antithetical, with individuals moving inevitably and irreversibly from one to the other as they age. In the middle of the twentieth century, "retirement" was defined by Social Security and private eligibility (Kohli, 1994). Men's modal age for exiting the workforce was age 65, the year they received maximum Social Security benefits. Most employers required their employees to retire by a certain age (typically 65). At the beginning of the twenty-first century, the very definition of retirement is in flux. Retirement is increasingly a phased phenomenon, involving multiple transitions out of and into paid and unpaid "work." The age-graded retirement norm has become blurred and the actual range of retirement age has expanded, making the transition longer and fuzzier (Kohli & Rein, 1991; Mutchler, Burr, Pienta, & Massagli, 1997). Social scientists traditionally conceptualized retirement as a final exit from the workforce. Some scholars operationalize retirement as receiving (or eligible to receive) either Social Security or a private pension (e.g., Han & Moen, 1999; Kim & Moen, 2000). Others operationalize it as being employed at a paid job less than full time (e.g., working less than 35 hours a week) along with a self-definition of being retired (e.g., Hayward, Grady, & McLaughlin, 1988; Mutran, Reitzes, & Fernandez, 1997).

RETIREMENT AS A "NORMLESS" TRANSITION

Societies, institutions, and groups develop expectations about behavior associated with particular positions (R.H. Turner, 1978). Although retirement has become an almost universal transition, there are no clear norms regarding the nature and goals of the role of retiree. Clearly defined functions or behaviors for retirees have not evolved in a society where work is the primary source of social status (Singleton, 1985). From one perspective, retired persons experience maximum autonomy in structuring their days, their social networks, and their identities. Alternatively, individuals may find themselves without the structure of goals and situational imperatives set forth by raising a family and seeking economic sufficiency or the organizational goals and imperatives imposed by their jobs. In the absence of socially constructed options and expectations, older persons may feel constrained by the lack of a position or status in society, a "roleless role" (Burgess, 1960). Also missing are the established and institutionalized patterns of socialization seen in the process of preparation for early adulthood and middle-aged roles (D. Jacobson, 1974).

TIMING RETIREMENT

Midlife workers' decisions to exit the workforce on a permanent basis are based on a wide range of personal and family circumstances. Prior to pensions and policy developments encouraging early retirement, most people worked as long as they could, and poor health was about the only cause of retirement, tied as it was with an inability to work. Along with poor health, expected retirement income seems to be of principal importance. Those who have greater confidence in their financial security generally retire and plan to retire at an earlier age. Not surprisingly, evidence from national surveys in the United States and the United Kingdom continue to show that pension eligibility is an important factor for retirement timing (e.g., Barfield & Morgan, 1969; Boskin, 1977; Fields & Mitchell, 1984; McGoldrick & Cooper, 1989; Parnes & Nestel, 1981; Quinn, 1981). In fact, the two most consistent predictors of retirement age are health (Barfield & Morgan, 1969; McPherson & Guppy, 1979; Parnes, 1981; Quinn, 1981; Talaga & Beehr, 1995) along with pension eligibility and financial circumstances (Atchley, 1979; Barfield, 1972; Barfield & Morgan, 1969, 1978; Evans, Ekerdt, & Bossé, 1985; Kilty & Behling, 1985; Morgan, 1992; Quinn, 1977; Quinn & Burkhauser, 1990).

Other midlife transitions also push or pull workers into retirement. For example, using data drawn from the National Longitudinal Surveys (NLS) Cohort of Mature Women 1967–1982 (ages 45–59), Morgan (1992) investigated whether termination of marriage had an influence on subsequent retirement plans. She found that both widowed and divorced women planned to retire at later ages than did their married counterparts, by 2 years or more. However, this study underscored the overwhelming importance of financial considerations in women's decision making about retirement age. Regardless of marital status, their planned ages for retirement were shaped by the age at which retirement pensions (if they had them) would be available. This study highlights that midlife women's decision making, like that of men's, is shaped by economic resources.

Other factors associated with a lower planned age of retirement include being male (Han & Moen, 1999; Singleton & Keddy, 1991), members of younger cohorts (Morgan, 1992; Singleton & Keddy, 1991), and married (Kilty & Behling, 1985). Additionally, a lower socioeconomic and occupational status (Dobson & Morrow, 1984; Palmore, George, & Fillenbaum, 1982; Singleton & Keddy, 1991) and an orderly career path (e.g., traditional, prototypical full-time careers; Han & Moen, 1999) predict earlier retirement.

Attitudes toward work also shape expected retirement age. Evidence from several cross-sectional studies show that dissatisfaction with job is related to a lower anticipated retirement age among both White and Black retirees regardless of gender (Gibson, 1993; Kilty & Behling, 1985; Kremer, 1984–1985; McPherson & Guppy, 1979; Richardson & Kilty, 1992). Analyzing data on 457 professional male and female workers (ages 25–64), Kilty and Behling (1985) found that alienation was one of the major predictors, with higher levels of work alienation (i.e., not seeing work as providing an active interest or as giving meaning to life) associated with younger projected ages for retirement. This finding was replicated among 234 Black male and female professionals (ages 25–64) by Richardson and Kilty; the more these professionals viewed work as a necessity (higher work alienation) the more likely they anticipated retiring at an earlier age.

PLANNING THE
RETIREMENT TRANSITION

In this section on retirement planning in midlife, we focus on three questions: First, what is the role of planning in the retirement process? Second, what factors are related to retirement planning behaviors? Finally, how does personal control affect retirement planning and subsequent retirement adjustment?

THE PREVALENCE OF RETIREMENT PLANNING

Most individuals, as they move through midlife, increase retirement preparation activities, especially informal retirement planning behaviors (so-called self-preparation), such as reading about retirement and discussing it with friends (e.g., Evans et al., 1985). In an early study (using 1960s data on a nationwide sample of 2,053 males who had retired before the mandatory age of 65 years), Pyron and Manion (1970) found that a high proportion had made retirement plans that in fact subsequently worked out satisfactorily. Although 60% of these early retirees reported that their companies had no programs to help prepare for retirement, only 18% had made no income plans, 31% no retirement activity plans, and 26% no healthcare plans prior to their retirement. By contrast, another study in the 1970s showed that, among 360 male workers (ages 55–64), only 20% reported that they had any definite plans for retirement, even though about 75% looked forward to retirement (McPherson & Guppy, 1979). Other studies in the 1970s and 1980s report that no more than 40% of late midlife workers do concrete planning prior to retirement (Fitzpatrick, 1978; McPherson & Guppy, 1979; Morse & Gray, 1980; Prentis, 1980; see also Ekerdt, 1989, for a review).

More recent work shows that, for most workers, preparation typically consists of financial, not lifestyle, planning. Using a large regional sample of 2,760 midlife workers (ages 40–65), M.J. Turner, Bailey, and Scott (1994) found that few respondents had been involved in any retirement planning behaviors beyond financial planning. Whereas up to 76% of the sample had done some kind of financial planning (e.g., set up retirement savings), only 2% to 20% of these midlife workers had been involved in other areas of planning (such as home equity, locational, and employment planning).

TYPES OF RETIREMENT PLANNING

Retirement planning occurs both formally, through participation in preretirement planning programs, and informally, as individuals develop strategies for dealing with life changes that accompany retirement. Whereas participating in preretirement planning programs seems to be most valuable regarding financial preparation, informal lifestyle planning assists individuals in their psychological preparation for retirement transitions. In a study of a preretirement education program, attendees were more likely to initiate financial planning activities and were more knowledgeable about healthcare and economics than nonattendees (Kamouri & Cavanaugh, 1986). Preretirement planning programs, however, are frequently faulted for being superficial (e.g., focusing exclusively on financial assistance), offered at too late an age to be helpful, and/or failing to reach the people who need help the most (e.g., Ekerdt, 1989; Glamser, 1981; Rowen & Wilks, 1987). Research on the effects of participation in formal planning programs continues to suggest that they are relatively limited and short-lived (Anderson & Weber, 1993; Dorfman, 1989; Taylor-Carter, Cook, & Weinberg, 1997).

By contrast, researchers have found that informal lifestyle planning has significant influences on favorable retirement expectations, retirement satisfaction, self-efficacy, and overall well-being after retirement (Dorfman, 1989; MacEwen, Barling, Kelloway, & Higginbottom, 1995; Taylor-Carter et al., 1997). In a sample of retirees in rural areas (ages 65–96), having attended preretirement classes or counseling sessions was not related to retirement satisfaction, whereas informal planning behaviors such as reading or being exposed to radio or TV programs about retirement were significant predictors of retirement satisfaction (Dorfman, 1989).

IMPLICATIONS OF RETIREMENT PLANNING

Atchley (1982) pointed out that successful adaptation to role transitions is contingent on a dual process: anticipatory socialization into the new role and psychological readiness to leave one's old role. These processes can be enhanced by both instrumental and emotional preparedness. As any major role transition calls for socialization into the differing expectations and demands of the new role, preretirement preparation should function as a kind of anticipatory socialization, permitting individuals to explore possibilities about when and how to confront social or physical environmental changes.

Planning and Retirement Timing

The more workers think about retirement and make definite plans the more likely they are to retire early (Kilty & Behling, 1985; McPherson & Guppy, 1979; Reitzes, Mutran, & Fernandez, 1998). Research findings suggest that individuals who have planned for their retirement are better prepared for it, are more likely to report earlier planned retirement ages and are more likely to actually retire (Dorfman, Kohout, & Heckert,

1985; Taylor & Shore, 1995). In a recent study using longitudinal data on married late midlife workers (ages 58–64), Reitzes and colleagues (1998) confirmed that retirement planning encourages early retirement. They concluded that planning seems to lead one to feel more confident about retiring at an earlier age.

Planning and Retirement Attitudes

Positive attitudes about retirement are also a function of planning (Kilty & Behling, 1985; Mutran et al., 1997). A study of 444 late midlife men and women (ages 58–64) demonstrated that workers more active in their retirement planning are more positive in their attitudes about retirement (Mutran et al., 1997). In this investigation planning was indeed the strongest predictor of attitudes toward retirement, over and above any social background factors. Planning may serve to demystify retirement by permitting retiring workers to invoke coping mechanisms required to effectively deal with the transition.

Planning and Retirement Adjustment

There is widespread support linking planning to better adjustment in retirement (Atchley, 1976; Blank, Ritchie, & Ryback, 1983; Feldman, 1994; McPherson & Guppy, 1979; Monk & Donovan, 1978; Palmore, 1982; Weiner, 1980). In the preretirement stage, unfavorable attitudes toward retirement are associated with absence of retirement planning and failure to seek information about retirement, which in turn are related to unsuccessful adaptation to retirement (Fuller & Redfering, 1976; Hendrick, Wells, & Faletti, 1982; McPherson & Guppy, 1979).

Studies have also found planning for retirement to be positively related to satisfaction during retirement (Dorfman, 1989; Glamser, 1981; Palmore, 1982; Quick & Moen, 1998; Szinovacz, 1982). Furthermore, there is evidence that retirement planning is positively related to life satisfaction (Anderson & Weber, 1993; Palmore, 1982) and lower anxiety and depression (Fretz, Kluge, Ossana, Jones, & Merikangas, 1989; MacEwen et al., 1995). In a small sample of retirees ($N = 33$), Palmore found that retirement planning course participants (compared with those who had not had a preretirement course) had more favorable changes in levels of well-being. Other studies involving preretirement planning programs, however, have found no such significant impact of participating in preretirement programs on satisfaction in retirement (e.g., Anderson & Weber, 1993; Glamser, 1981; Glamser & DeJong, 1975; Tiberi, Boyack, & Kerschner, 1978). Anderson and Weber (1993) investigated the impact of preretirement planning on satisfaction during retirement by analyzing data on three distinct groups of retirees:

those who had participated in structured preretirement planning programs (structured planners), those who planned their own retirement programs (self-planners), and those who did no planning (zero planners). The only significant difference in retirement satisfaction was found between self-planners and zero planners, with self-planners reporting significantly higher levels of retirement satisfaction. The results emphasize that retirees should take an active role in pursuing their retirement planning.

In a comparison of retirees who had attended a preretirement education program and those who had not, Kamouri and Cavanaugh (1986) found that mean levels of retirement satisfaction did not differ between attendees and nonattendees. The number of years retired correlated positively with retirement satisfaction for attendees, but negatively with retirement satisfaction for nonattendees. This finding suggests that nonattendees may become less satisfied with their retired life over time, whereas attendees may become more satisfied over the years of retirement. Recent related evidence of long-term effects of retirement planning was also reported by Mutran and colleagues (1997) who assessed the retirement planning of late midlife workers (ages 58–64). Using a composite measure of retirement planning (discussed retirement with others, read about retirement, attended a preretirement program, and actively planned for retirement through such things as trips, activities, and/or calculating retirement income), they found that retirement planning, measured at Time 1 (1992), predicted positive perceptions of retirement at Time 2 (1994), both for those who had retired by Time 2 and for those who continued to work.

Some studies report gender differences in factors associated with retirement planning. In a study of 451 older retirees (ages 65–96), Dorfman (1989) used three measures of planning for retirement including the amount of planning for retirement, having made financial plans, and having made plans for activities. She found all facets of planning to be significantly and positively correlated with higher retirement satisfaction of both men and women; but plans for work after retirement was positively related to the retirement satisfaction of men only. Szinovacz (1982) also reported that, among women retirees, financial plans did not significantly differentiate between satisfied and dissatisfied retirees; however, plans for activities did.

In general, research on retirement planning suggests that it may play an important role in the process of retirement adjustment. The act of planning for retirement appears to encourage preparation for financial well-being and involvement in leisure activities, thus facilitating the retirement transition. Retirement planning also seems to be an effective mechanism for handling the tensions and the psychological problems that may accompany approaching retirement (e.g., MacEwen et al., 1995). An important implication of the research on retirement planning is that the process of adjustment to retirement begins long before the actual retirement transition.

FACTORS RELATED TO RETIREMENT PLANNING

Given that both positive anticipation of retirement and concrete retirement planning are associated with subsequent adjustment in retirement, it is important to identify those who are most likely to engage in this long-range planning.

SOCIODEMOGRAPHIC VARIABLES

Research has shown that retirement planning is positively correlated with certain sociodemographic characteristics, including being closer to the normative retirement age, being both male and White, having higher levels of income and education, as well as being in better health. Older workers are more likely to participate in retirement preparation activities (Dobson & Morrow, 1984; Julia, Kilty, & Richardson, 1995; Singleton & Keddy, 1991). Men tend to be more likely to plan for retirement than women (Beck, 1984; Carp, 1997; Kroeger, 1982; Morse, Dutka, & Gray, 1983; Morse & Gray, 1980; Richardson, 1990) and to begin to do so significantly earlier than do women (Atchley, 1982; Han & Moen, 1999). A study using the National Survey of Black Americans (NSBA) data (1979–1980) provides similar findings, showing that, among African Americans, retired men were more likely than retired women to have planned their retirement even though men and women were equally likely to be willing to retire (Gibson, 1993).

In addition, men and women seem to engage in different kinds of planning behaviors. Kroeger (1982) interviewed 264 recent retirees in 1980–1981, finding that men were more likely to use informal sources (e.g., books, articles, or TV programs), whereas women tended to rely more on formal programs. Men typically substituted informal preparation for formal programs. Women, on the other hand, most often did nothing to prepare for retirement if formal programs were not available. They were much less likely than men to turn voluntarily to informal sources (such as widely available popular literature on retirement).

Women's planning may also be more susceptible to the impact of personal and situational exigencies. For example, one study found that married women were the least likely to seek information about retirement, tending to rely instead on their husbands' preparations (Slowik, 1991). This may reflect either women's traditional gender norms and values that emphasize dependence and passivity (Perkins, 1992) or their role as secondary wage earners. The finding of women's dependence on their husbands' retirement preparations may well not hold true for future cohorts.

Studies on retirement planning have found that persons with a higher socioeconomic status give more thought to and make more definite plans for retirement (Broderick & Glazer, 1983; Campione, 1988; Gibson, 1993; McPherson & Guppy, 1979; M.J. Turner et al., 1994). Those with higher incomes and more education typically have both greater flexibility concerning when they retire and more options concerning their postretirement lifestyle. Low-income workers with little education are the most likely to retire unexpectedly and unwillingly (Gibson, 1993). Several national surveys found that retirement preparatory behaviors are more frequently reported among White respondents (Ekerdt, 1989 for a review). Beck (1984), for example, in a national sample of older male workers (ages 60–74) found that Blacks not only prepared less for retirement than Whites but also were less likely to attend preretirement planning seminars.

Studies of retirement planning suggest that those who may need retirement planning the most are least likely to get it. Typically, women and persons with lower socioeconomic status are less inclined to take personal initiative in retirement planning. Moreover, they are also less likely to have access to retirement preparation programs. It is also unfortunate that most retirement research has concentrated heavily on a population that is White, better educated, and socially and economically advantaged (Torres-Gil, 1984). More investigations are needed to better understand how different ethnic and social class groups plan for the retirement transition.

SOCIAL AND PSYCHOLOGICAL VARIABLES

Individual differences in psychological resources and lifestyles also predict variations in retirement planning behaviors. In a study of 816 male workers (ages 45–75) who anticipated retiring in the next 15 years, involvement in retirement-oriented behaviors was higher among participants who placed greater importance on pastimes and hobbies (Evans et al., 1985). This is consistent with an earlier study by McPherson and Guppy (1979), showing that those who have the experience, means, and interest to utilize increased leisure time are more likely to plan for retirement. Broderick and Glazer (1983) also found a high degree of preretirement leisure participation to be correlated with a high degree of retirement planning. This evidence on the relationship between leisure orientations and retirement planning suggest that midlife experiences may play an important role in shaping later retirement experiences, for example, through continuity of lifestyle.

Little is known about the relationship between personality and retirement planning. Nevertheless, it is reasonable to expect that personality traits have significant impact on retirement planning behaviors. For example, individuals who volunteer to participate in preretirement planning programs (i.e., self-selected participants) and individuals who voluntarily turn to self-preparation for retirement may be those who are high in conscientiousness, characterized by being careful and serious about planning (Reis & Gold, 1993). More investigations with a personality focus are required for a fuller understanding of the determinants of successful retirement planning.

RETIREMENT TRANSITIONS AND WELL-BEING

Linking Retirement with Health and Psychological Well-Being

A number of theorists (e.g. Brandstaedter & Baltes-Goetz, 1990; Labouvie-Vief, 1982; Perun & Bielby, 1980; Riegel, 1975) have adopted a dynamic (or dialectical) view of the relationship between role transitions, life events, and psychological development. For example, the accumulation and the loss of social roles/identities have been linked to changes in psychological distress and well-being (Moen, 1997; Thoits, 1986).

Yet the empirical evidence is thus far inconsistent concerning the relationship between retirement and psychological well-being. Some researchers have identified a significant association between retirement and decreased life satisfaction or morale (Elwell & Maltbie-Crannell, 1981; Peretti & Wilson, 1975; Thompson, 1973; Walker, Kimmel, & Price, 1981) and greater psychological distress (Abramson, Ritter, Gofin, & Kark, 1992; Bossé, Aldwin, Levenson, & Ekerdt, 1987; Palmore, Fillenbaum, & George, 1984; Richardson & Kilty, 1991). Other researchers have found no deleterious psychological effects associated with retirement, report mixed findings, or else no relationship between retirement and morale or life satisfaction (Gall, Evans, & Howard, 1997; George & Maddox, 1977; Palmore et al., 1984; Stull, 1988), and no relationship between retirement and depression (Keith & Schafer, 1986; Ross & Drentea, 1998; Wright, 1990); or even a positive effect of retirement on health and reduced stress level (e.g., Ekerdt, Bossé, & LoCastro, 1983; McGoldrick & Cooper, 1989; Midanik, Soghikian, Ransom, & Tekawa, 1995; Palmore et al., 1984; Streib & Schneider, 1971).

Part of the reason for these diverse findings is that much of the extant research on retirement compared snapshots of retirees with nonretirees, rather than examining dynamic changes in the well-being of people from before to after they retire. The fact is that differences in well-being by retirement status at one point in time may or may not reflect *changes* in well-being as individuals move from employment to retirement over time. Given the cross-sectional nature of most prior studies, longitudinal analyses are essential to determine whether any differences between retirees and nonretirees capture the effects of the actual transition. Moreover, the culture and structure of both work and retirement are in flux: findings on late midlife men in the 1960s and 1970s may or may not be applicable to men and women in late midlife in the early twenty-first century.

FACTORS PREDICTING SUCCESSFUL RETIREMENT ADJUSTMENT

A number of studies have investigated the circumstances related to postretirement adjustment in terms of physical and psychological well-being (commonly indicated by good health, higher life satisfaction and morale, and lower depression). Research evidence points to three resources facilitating individuals' transitions into retirement.

Economic/Financial Resources

Income is a central factor in the process of adjusting to retirement, with inadequate incomes and financial problems associated with dissatisfaction and maladjustment in retirement (Atchley, 1975, 1976; Fields & Mitchell, 1984; Hendrick et al., 1982; Richardson & Kilty, 1991; Streib & Schneider, 1971). Retirees' perceptions of having an adequate income are also key in retirement adjustment (Dorfman, 1989; Kim & Moen, 2000).

Social Relationship Resources

Research has demonstrated that family and friendship networks, as well as group affiliations, also promote retirement adjustment (Cox & Bhak, 1978–1979; Dorfman & Moffett, 1987; George, 1990; Hendrick et al., 1982; Kilty & Behling, 1985). The retirement transition is easier if retirees have friends and family to support them in their new role. In a study of 753 late midlife retirees and workers (ages 58–64), marital status had a significant effect on positive attitudes toward retirement, indicating that being married may provide social support that buffers the uncertainty of retirement (Mutran et al., 1997). This is consistent with earlier findings by George and Maddox (1977), showing that being married was a significant factor accounting for retirement adjustment (morale). Kim and Moen (2000) further showed that marital quality, rather than simply marital status, is positively related to retirement adjustment. Their longitudinal study found that decreased marital satisfaction after retirement was related to declining morale among late midlife women (but there was no such relationship among late midlife men).

Personal Resources

Personal resources include not only socioeconomic status but also health and personality variables (such as self-concept or self-efficacy). Although it is difficult to assess the direction of causality, a substantial body of research has shown that better adjustment (e.g., higher morale and lower depression) to retirement is related to better health (Fillenbaum, George, & Palmore, 1985; Hendrick et al., 1982; Kim & Moen, 2000; McGoldrick, 1994; Richardson & Kilty, 1991). Having a higher education and higher occupational prestige level of preretirement job (Dorfman, 1989; George & Maddox, 1977) is also related to greater retirement satisfaction and higher morale.

Personality characteristics also appear to play a crucial role in retirement adaptation. Havighurst (1968) maintained that the adaptation process, in general, is ruled by the ego or personality. Evidence from a range of studies suggests that psychological resources such as self-efficacy and self-esteem are major factors that facilitate successful retirement adjustment (Abel & Hayslip, 1987; Cherry, Zarit, & Krauss, 1984; Fretz et al., 1989; Hendrick et al., 1982; Mutran et al., 1997; Taylor-Carter & Cook, 1995; Taylor & Shore, 1995).

For most people, pragmatic considerations, such as financial and health resources, appear to be paramount in both the retirement decision and subsequent adjustment. Evidence suggests that job-oriented variables account for less variance in retirement status than do health and financial concerns (e.g., Schmitt, Coyle, Rauschenberger, & White, 1979). While job dissatisfaction has been related to early retirement, work-related variables (such as prior organizational commitment and prior occupational characteristics) are not predictive of retirement adjustment (Adelmann, 1987; Bell, 1978–1979).

DIFFERENT PATHWAYS: THE SIGNIFICANCE OF GENDER AND OTHER CONTEXTS

WOMEN'S AND MEN'S EXPERIENCES

Most previous studies have focused exclusively on men's retirement, but evidence is accumulating that both employment and retirement are qualitatively different experiences for men and women (Han & Moen, 1999; Moen, 1996b; Quick & Moen, 1998). The whole process of retirement may be a different experience for women than for men, in part because of the historical difference in their attachment to the labor force. When men leave their jobs they are exiting from a role that has typically dominated their adult years (Weiss, 1997). Women, on the other hand, commonly experience greater discontinuity, moving in and out of the labor force, and in and out of part-time jobs in tandem with shifting family responsibilities (Clausen & Gilens, 1990; Moen, 1985; Rosenfield, 1980; Sorenson, 1983). Consequently, they are less likely to have the same duration of employment or accumulation of work experience as men (Han & Moen, 1999; Henretta & O'Rand, 1980; Quick & Moen, 1998). Given occupational segregation by gender and their less stable employment histories, women are also less likely to be covered by pensions than are men, and those with pensions have incomes far lower than men's. Differences in work histories between men and women may affect their decisions, planning, and adjustment in retirement.

Earlier findings from the 1960s and 1970s indicated that both the subjective experiences and the objective conditions of retirement differed for men and women. Women were shown to have more negative attitudes toward retirement than men, take longer to adapt to retirement, and see retirement as more disruptive. Retirement was also more likely to be linked with greater depression and loneliness for women than men (Atchley, 1976; C.J. Jacobson, 1974; Streib & Schneider, 1971). Research has continued to show that variables predicting retirement timing for men do not necessarily predict women's retirement timing. Investigation of both large-scale national and Duke longitudinal data on men and women (ages 46–70) showed that predictors of men's retirement included older age, lower education and occupational status, greater health limitations, and increased interactions with friends. By contrast, the only significant predictor of women's retirement was age (George, Fillenbaum, & Palmore, 1984). Using data on 820 men and women (ages over 50 and employed full time) from a small town community, Atchley (1982) found that men and women were quite similar in terms of the average age (64 years) at which they planned to retire. The dynamics of planned retirement age, however, seemed to be different for women compared with men. Among women, those who planned to retire late had lower social status, tended to be unmarried, and had a less positive view of retirement. Women's choice of late retirement appeared to be strongly influenced by negative economic factors. In contrast, men who planned to retire later were motivated by more positive attitudes toward their jobs and less positive attitudes toward retirement than by negative economic factors.

Szinovacz and Washo (1992) explored gender differences in the experience of life events surrounding the retirement transition and the effects of such life event experiences on men's and women's adaptation to retirement (using data from 441 female and 370 male Florida retirees, ages 50–85). Their findings revealed the greater vulnerability of women: Women in their study experienced more life events than men, and such exposure to postretirement events had a more negative effect on the retirement adaptation of recently retired women than was the case among recently retired men. Szinovacz and Washo noted that the observed gender differences in the effect of life event exposure on adaptation may be a function of women's greater involvement in social network crises as well as their dependence on social support (see also Kessler & McLeod, 1984). Other studies also have shown that, whereas men are more likely to retire for work-related reasons (Szinovacz, 1991), women are more apt to retire in response to such events as a spouse's or other family member's illness (Brody, Kleban, Johnson, Hoffman, & Schoonover, 1987; Gratton & Haug, 1983; Szinovacz, 1989, 1991; Talaga & Beehr, 1995).

Given their different work histories, employment status, and general life experiences, women may adjust to retirement differently than men (Calasanti, 1996; Quick & Moen, 1998; Romsa, Bondy, & Blenman, 1985). Research has suggested that women's retirement adjustment is more adversely affected by poor health and inadequate incomes than men's (Martin Matthews & Brown, 1987; Seccombe & Lee, 1986). In a recent longitudinal study using data from the Cornell Retirement and Well-Being study, Kim and Moen (1999) reported significant gender differences in the relationship between couples' work/retirement transitions and subsequent psychological well-being. Looking at married workers and retirees as well as those who became retired between Time 1 and Time 2 ($N = 534$, ages 50–74), Kim and Moen found that being (newly/continuously) retired is positively related to increased morale for men, especially when their wives remain employed. But becoming retired is related to increased depressive symptoms for women, especially when their husbands remain employed. This and other studies mentioned here underscore the complexity of the adaptation processes as late midlife men and women "negotiate" life transitions such as retirement.

The existing literature documents that retirement decisions and postretirement expectations and experiences differ by gender, as do occupational and familial experiences. Future studies need to acknowledge and explore gender variations in the circumstances of the retirement transition to obtain a better understanding how gender shapes the retirement experience.

COUPLED TRANSITIONS

Retirement increasingly involves couples' calculations, coordinations, and compromises (Moen, 1998b; Szinovacz, Ekerdt, & Vinick, 1992). The increased work attachment patterns of women in recent decades have made joint retirement among dual-earner couples an increasingly common retirement pattern and increased the importance of spouse factors, over and above work-related factors, as retirement contingencies. Spousal characteristics (such as their socioeconomic status, pension coverage, health, and retirement status) have been shown to be incorporated in individuals' retirement decision making (Gratton & Haug, 1983; Reitzes et al., 1998; Talaga & Beehr, 1995). For example, in a recent study of married, full-time workers (ages 58–64), the presence of working spouse encouraged both men and women to remain employed (Reitzes et al., 1998). Among 228 married, retired couples (ages 50–72), Smith and Moen (1998) found that retirement of one spouse is frequently collaboratively decided on within a marriage.

Although most past research of retirement and subsequent well-being has focused heavily on the retirement status of individuals, available research findings point to the importance of knowing couples' joint employment/retirement status for understanding retirement adjustment. Previous studies have found that the couple's joint retirement status matters for retirement satisfaction as well as postretirement marital quality and psychological well-being. Wan and Ferraro (1985) showed that dual-retired couples had more favorable attitudes toward retirement, compared with single-retired couples. There is some evidence that asynchronous retirement transitions are related to marital strain (Gilford, 1984; Lee & Shehan, 1989; Moen et al., 2001; Szinovacz, 1996). Based on data on 672 couples in the National Survey of Families and Households (ages 50–72), Szinovacz showed that the husband retired/wife employed pattern is associated with perceptions of lower marital quality, especially among couples with transitional gender role attitudes. A longitudinal study of 534 married workers and retirees from the Cornell Retirement and Well-Being study demonstrated that (1) recently retired husbands whose wives remained employed reported the greatest marital conflict, and (2) recently retired wives whose husbands also moved into retirement reported the lowest marital conflict (Moen et al., 2001).

ETHNIC DIFFERENCES

Few studies have considered potential race and ethnic differences in the retirement transition. Jackson, Antonucci, and Gibson (1995) documented, however, the nature of the aging experiences of workers from various ethnic groups. Other studies have shown that minority individuals tend to be in relatively precarious economic situations as they age, compared with White counterparts (Markides, 1983; Thompson, 1979), but little is known about racial/ethnic differences in actual retirement transitions.

Studies comparing Black and White workers and retirees showed that Blacks are more disadvantaged than Whites in almost all aspects of the retirement process (Fillenbaum et al., 1985; Palmore, Burchett, Fillenbaum, George, & Wallman, 1985). For example, Black retirees on the average have less personal postretirement income (Gibson, 1987; Jackson & Gibson, 1985). This may reflect the fact that African Americans typically have disadvantaged work experiences across the life course. Their restriction to unstable jobs with low earnings and few benefits relates directly to low levels of retirement pensions and Social Security benefits (Gibson, 1993).

Previous studies in fact found that Black men, if physically or functionally capable, are less likely to retire than are White men (Chirikos & Nestel, 1989; Choi, 1994; Gibson, 1993; Hayward, Grady, Hardy, & Sommers, 1989; Parnes & Nestel, 1974). Using data of 2,443 men (54–63 years on the initial wave) from two national longitudinal studies (the Social Security Administration's Retirement History Survey and the National Longitudinal Surveys), Fillenbaum and colleagues (1985) found differences between White and Black men in predictors of retirement. Factors important in determining retirement were greater for White men than for Black men. Specifically, only age predicted the retirement of Black men, whereas age, lower socioeconomic status, poor health, having a pension, and positive views of retirement predicted the retirement of White men. Bould (1980, 1986) further confirmed that the predictors of early retirement for Whites (such as pension eligibility, college education, family responsibilities, and health limitations) were not significant for Blacks. In a study on retirement experiences among Blacks, Gibson found significant race differences in the factors that determine the retirement decision. Data from the National Survey of Black Americans (1979–1980) demonstrated that Black Americans are least likely to retire "on time" (age 65 years) and most likely to retire at earlier ages (55–64). But about 15% of the sample retired at or after age 70. Poor health and disadvantaged labor force experiences were more influential on retirement timing for Blacks, whereas financial readiness is more influential for Whites.

Turning to research on Black women, in a sample of 258 White and Black women (ages 62–66) drawn from the membership of a health maintenance organization, Belgrave (1988) found that Black women were less likely to be retired (50%) than were White women (68%). Furthermore, the eligibility for pensions of Black women was not reflected in their retirement status. Regardless of race, poor health was the most important predictor of retirement; however, for Black women, average earnings over the past five years was also a significant predictor of retirement status, with those who had higher incomes less likely to be retired than those with lower earnings. According to Belgrave, Black women's greater tendency to remain in the labor force seems to reflect continuity over the life course, rather than result from poorer financial resources available for retirement. She maintained that as most have spent the majority of their lives as active participants in the labor force, Black women tend to remain in the labor force in their early 60s despite opportunities for retirement.

Retirement seems to have differential impacts on subjective well-being across different gender and ethnic groups. In a prospective investigation of the transition from full-time employment to retirement (over a 2-year period) of 749 workers, retirement (categorized as retired if working less than 35 hours a week) was related to increased depressive symptoms in African American men whereas it was related to decreased depressive symptoms in European American men and women, and African American women (Fernandez, Mutran, Reitzes, & Sudha, 1998). This study suggests that the loss of the work role may be particularly consequential for the psychological well-being of African American men.

Given the dearth of research evidence thus far, however, further investigations on ethnic differences in retirement adjustment are needed. What is required is the development of more comprehensive models of retirement transitions that can promote understanding of the ways in which ethnicity and culture contribute to the retirement process.

COHORT DIFFERENCES

Han and Moen (1999) examined the temporal patterning of retirement using life history data on three cohorts of recent United States retirees: (1) born 1922–1929, (2) born 1929–1934, and (3) born 1934–1944. At the time of 1994–1995 interview, these cohorts were ages (1) 66–72, (2) 60–65, and (3) less than 60, respectively. Significant cohort differences were found, indicating that respondents in the most recent cohort began to plan earlier, expected to retire earlier, and did in fact retire earlier. This is consistent with the secular trend in earlier retirement in the latter half of the twentieth century. Cohort, as a marker of historical context, was significant in explaining differences in the age respondents began planning, the age they expected to retire, and the age they actually retired.

Given that the current workers moving into retirement are younger, better educated, and healthier than ever in the past (Moen, 1996b), baby boomer cohorts now in midlife will have access to a wider range of social and personal resources with which to shape the retirement transition and life after retirement. But contemporary cohorts moving through midlife are also confronting a world in which the structure and culture of retirement are being recast, and will most likely participate in the constructing of new scripts, new pathways. Such social changes may render prior research findings on earlier cohorts suspect in terms of broad generalizability.

SOCIAL CLASS DIFFERENCES

Social class is a powerful external force affecting midlife career and retirement paths and passages. Social class is typically indexed by level of occupational prestige, educational attainment, and income level (Brown,

Fukunaga, Umemoto, & Wicker, 1996). We focus on these three dimensions of social class, summarizing research findings linking social class to both retirement timing and retirement adjustment.

High socioeconomic status has been linked to positive emotional outcomes throughout the life course, including in retirement. The literature suggests that the lower the socioeconomic status, the more negative the attitude toward retirement (Atchley & Robinson, 1982; Glamser, 1976; Goudy, Powers, Keith, & Reger, 1980). Persons lower on the socioeconomic hierarchy tend to retire earlier and for different reasons than those of higher classes (Dobson & Morrow, 1984; Fridlund, Hansson, & Ysander, 1992; McPherson & Guppy, 1979; Parnes & Nestel, 1974; Singleton & Keddy, 1991; Weis, Koch, Kruck, & Beck, 1994). Blue-collar or clerical workers tend to retire earlier than those in white-collar or professional occupations. In addition, men in clerical and service occupations are more likely than those in other jobs to leave the workforce as a result of disability (DeViney & O'Rand, 1988; Hayward et al., 1988; Hayward, Hardy, & Grady, 1989). Research on the retirement behavior among Black Americans found no significant social class differences in retirement age (Gibson, 1993). But, persons having lower income and less education were more likely than the higher groups to retire both unexpectedly and unwillingly. In one study of 298 White and 110 Black Americans who had similar work histories, Choi (1994) found that Black men's retirement timing was more strongly affected by their occupational status.

Preretirement occupational status and the amount of income reduction have been found to predict adjustment to retirement (Dorfman, 1989; Hendrick et al., 1982; Richardson & Kilty, 1991). For example, Richardson and Kilty, in a panel study of 250 men and women retirees (average age 60 years), found that retirees with low preretirement occupational status and retirees with the greatest drop in income were the most vulnerable to postretirement adjustment problems (measured as lower levels of life satisfaction, morale, and satisfaction with relationships).

RETIREMENT: PLANNING AND CONTROL

Retirement is a transition that involves role change, redefinition, and activity shifts. Individuals' ability to effectively use available sources to negotiate and manage the necessary shifts in role, identity, and activity accompanying retirement may depend on their psychological characteristics. Two psychological constructs—locus of control and self-efficacy (both related to personal control)—may serve as strong predictors of retirement planning and adjustment (Taylor-Carter & Cook, 1995).

THE ROLE OF CONTROL IN RETIREMENT

Rotter's (1966) internal-external locus of control concerns causal beliefs about action-outcome contingencies. Individuals with an internal locus of control believe that they can control many events in life, whereas individuals with an external locus of control believe that many of life's outcomes are the result of luck and chance and are not under their control. Those who evidence an internal locus of control are more likely to hold positive retirement expectations, based on the expectancy of controlling outcomes associated with retirement.

Self-efficacy is an individual's belief that he or she can deal with specific activities or problems appropriately, and with reasonable prospect of success (Bandura, 1977; Rowe & Kahn, 1998). Individuals with high self-efficacy would believe that they possess the knowledge and skill needed to effectively deal with retirement transition. Bandura (1982) pointed to the importance of self-efficacy in shaping an individual's behavior: How competent individuals feel affects what activities they take on and their persistence in them. From this perspective, individuals with high self-efficacy may be more active in planning for retirement, which should lead to better adjustment to retirement.

As people get older, they may well experience a decline in control, given that the environmental events accompanying old age limit the range of outcomes that are actually attainable (Rodin, 1990; Weisz, 1983). Moreover, biological changes that occur with aging may restrict control (Rodin, 1986). The relationship between retirement and control is not at all clear. Some scholars presume that retirement may mean the loss of one of the most meaningful sources of instrumental control in life, the work role (e.g., Schulz, 1976). Others suggest that retirement may offer more time and opportunities for realizing one's goals and carrying out plans thus increasing personal efficacy (e.g., Lachman, 1986b).

A large literature on personal control has documented that personal control (both perceived control and self-efficacy) is related to better health and greater psychological well-being in midlife and late adulthood (Abel & Hayslip, 1987; Hale, Hedgepeth, & Taylor, 1985–1986; Lachman, 1986a; Lachman & Weaver, 1998; Moen, 1996b, 1997; Rodin, Timko, & Harris, 1985; Rowe & Kahn, 1998; Ryff & Keyes, 1995). Likewise, research on psychological well-being has recognized a sense of control as one of the key aspects of well-being. Using confirmatory factor analyses on a national sample data of adults aged 25 or older, Ryff and Keyes showed that psychological well-being is a multidimensional construct that consists of six dimensions including "environmental mastery" (i.e., having a sense of mastery and competence in managing the environment) that is similar to a sense of control. Ryff (1989) further demonstrated that psychological well-being measures were correlated positively with self-esteem and internal locus of control and negatively with external locus of control such as powerful other control and chance control. When the profiles of well-being were compared among younger (18–29), middle-aged (30–64), and older (65 and older) adults, midlife and older adults were shown to report more environmental mastery than younger adults (Ryff, 1989). Particularly, there was a remarkable improvement of environmental mastery in midlife, compared with young adulthood, contributing to the highest overall well-being of midlife adults relative to those who were younger and older.

CONTROL, RETIREMENT PLANNING, AND RETIREMENT ADJUSTMENT

Research has shown that personal control has significant influences on retirement timing, planning, and adjustment. Individuals with higher retirement self-efficacy have been shown to plan to retire earlier than those who lack confidence in their ability to make the retirement transition, even after controlling for financial status (Taylor & Shore, 1995). Hendrick and colleagues (1982) studied predictors of retirement adjustment among 314 older retirees (mean age of 68 years) and found that retirement planning was the most powerful predictor of anomie (feeling of alienation). More specifically, individuals who were most vulnerable to feeling higher alienation during retirement were those who made no retirement plans and had less control over their retirement decisions (i.e., greater external pressures and less autonomy). In a study of the relationships among self-efficacy, planfulness, anxiety and depression about retirement, both a low sense of self-efficacy and low degree of planfulness were the best predictors of preretirement worry, in addition to concerns about money or health (Fretz et al., 1989). Similarly, a study of 213 Canadian employees (mean age of 44 years) showed that internality locus of control was positively related to both financial and activity planning. Retirement planning, in turn, had significant indirect influences on reduced retirement anxiety, through its impact on positive expectations of retirement (MacEwen et al., 1995).

Other studies have shown that involuntary retirement, which may well represent a serious diminishment of personal control, is negatively associated with retirement satisfaction and retirement adjustment (e.g., Kimmel, Price, & Walker, 1978; Palmore et al., 1984; Peretti & Wilson, 1975). In their 1986 survey of individuals ages 50 to 70, for example, Herzog, House, and Morgan (1991) found that those who stopped work and felt they had little or no choice reported lower levels of health and well-being, compared with those who voluntarily retired and those working the amount they would like. Burke (1991) also emphasized that disruptive events such as unanticipated retirement cause an interruption of the normal identity maintenance process, which in turn produces a loss of a sense of mastery and self-esteem.

The relationship between control and planning seems to be bidirectional. It appears not only that self-efficacy would lead a person to be engaged in more planning behaviors but also that planning would enhance confidence in making the retirement transition. In a study of a small sample of adults aged 26 to 61 ($N = 34$), informal leisure planning, but not financial planning, was significantly related to enhanced self-efficacy (Taylor-Carter et al., 1997).

LIFE AFTER RETIREMENT

Being retired in late midlife means, for many, the opportunities to pursue new life patterns. We discuss two types of postretirement lifestyle choices, postretirement employment and volunteering, as well as changes in self-identity following retirement. Both options afford opportunities for productive activity, social interaction, and identity defining status within society.

POSTRETIREMENT EMPLOYMENT

One increasingly common option after retiring from one's career job is to embark on a second or third career, whether undertaking an entirely different type of job or continuing one's previous work but at a reduced level. The lines between retirement and employment are blurring as a large proportion of retirees engages in some form of paid work after leaving their career jobs. Using data from the Cornell Retirement and Well-Being study, Kim and Moen (2000) found a significant positive impact of postretirement employment on psychological well-being. Retired and reemployed men reported higher levels of morale and lower levels of depressive symptoms, compared with not-yet-retired men and those who were retired but not employed. For women's psychological well-being, however, there were no significant differences across the three groups.

COMMUNITY SERVICE

A second possibility is unpaid work, whether as an informal volunteer or as an active participant in a community association. Volunteer participation in retirement may be either a continuation of activities begun earlier or a qualitative shift in relative emphasis from paid work to unpaid volunteer labor. Individuals who retire, however, do not necessarily "replace" their career jobs with community participation (i.e., in the form of volunteering and/or organizational membership) (Caro & Bass, 1995; Gilespie & King, 1985; Herzog & Morgan, 1993). Using data from both the 1974 Current Population Survey and a 1981 national survey, Chambré (1984, 1987) found that those in the labor force volunteered at higher rates than did retirees, but that retirees who were active volunteers tended to have a significantly higher level of commitment than volunteers who were still in the labor force. Similarly, in a study of 762 retirees and not-yet-retired workers (ages 50–74), Moen and Fields (2000) found little difference in community participation by retirement status. Although individuals did not increase their tendency to become volunteers in retirement, those who were already volunteers tended to increase their degree of involvement following retirement.

Participation as formal volunteers in community service is an important form of social integration as those in late midlife leave their paid jobs (Moen, 1997; Moen & Fields, 1999; Moen, Fields, et al., 1999). With respect to the consequences of involvement in unpaid volunteer activities, the preponderance of the literature (Chambré, 1984, 1987; Fischer & Schaffer, 1993; Moen, 1997; Moen, Dempster-McClain, & Williams, 1992; Moen & Fields, 2000; Moen et al., 2000; Okun, Stock, Haring, & Witter, 1984) concludes that involvement in unpaid work is positively related to well-being. The most positive attitudes about retirement were reported by the most socially active retirees, as evidenced by high postretirement participation in formal associations and volunteer involvement (Broderick & Glazer, 1983). In the study of late midlife retirees and not-yet-retired workers (ages 52–74, discussed earlier), Moen and Fields found formal volunteer activities (i.e., engaging in volunteering in community associations) predicted the well-being of retirees but not the well-being of those who were not yet retired. Moreover, the salutary effects of such community participation occurred only for those retirees who were not employed. This finding suggests that community participation in midlife may help to replace social capital lost when an individual exits the world of work. Volunteering in a formal context may more closely approximate the work situation of retirees who are not employed, and thereby serve a compensatory function. In addition, there was evidence that retired men benefit more from both paid work and volunteering than do retired women (Moen & Fields, 2000).

CHANGES IN SELF-CONCEPT

Scholars of psychological processes in midlife suggest that changes in identity, ways of thinking and reasoning, and self-concept may be brought on by normative life transitions and unexpected life events (e.g., George, 1993; Levinson, Darrow, Klein, Levinson, & McKee, 1978; McCrae & Costa, 1990; Moen & Wethington, 1999). Especially, in role transitions such as retirement, individuals actively strive to maintain a sense of well-being, and also a stable sense of identity, encompassing affective self-esteem and cognitive self-concept (George, 1980). In the cultural ideology that celebrates work as the source of identity and self-esteem, retirement may be regarded as a crisis for personal identity (Ekerdt, 1987), which results in negative psychological consequences including decline in self-esteem. No evidence, however, exists in the literature to show that retirement causes decline in self-esteem or negative changes in self-concept.

According to Atchley (1993), not only does middle age serve as a preparatory stage for retirement, but there is continuity between pre- and postretirement self-conceptions. Individuals continue to use ongoing family and friendship roles as sources of self-esteem and they may start a new career in paid or unpaid work or volunteering. Indeed, in a large-scale longitudinal study, preretirement self-esteem was found to be a powerful predictor of postretirement self-esteem (Reitzes et al., 1998). In a study of 753 late midlife retirees and workers (ages 58–64), Mutran and colleagues (1997) hypothesized that attitudes toward retirement are formed not just in response to the retirement event but also in response to self-concept. Consistent with their hypothesis, individuals who perceived themselves as being more competent workers (i.e., positive worker identity) and those who had higher self-esteem were more likely to show positive attitudes toward retirement.

FUTURE RESEARCH DIRECTIONS

LIFE-COURSE, ROLE-CONTEXT MODEL

We propose that midlife transitions such as retirement can be better understood using a paradigm of a life-course, role-context perspective (Kim & Moen, in press). The life-course approach highlights the dynamic processes of development and change over the life span (Elder 1995; Giele & Elder, 1998; Moen et al., 1992; Moen, Elder, & Lüscher, 1995). The related role context, ecological approach places particular roles (such as worker or retiree), in the social contexts of other roles, relations, and developmental processes (e.g., Bronfenbrenner, 1995; Moen, 1996b; Moen et al., 1992; Musick, Herzog, & House, 1999). Several themes emerge when viewing retirement from a life-course, role-context vantage point: a focus on biographical timing, process, the interdependency of linked lives, and the importance of human agency, all occurring in ecological context.

Timing in Context

Key to a life course formulation is its emphasis on timing (Elder, 1995; Giele & Elder, 1998; Moen et al., 1992). Though increasingly obsolete, culturally grounded norms and frames continue to shape individual expectations and beliefs about the "right" time for retirement (Hagestad & Neugarten, 1984; Rook, Catalano, & Dooley, 1989; Setterson, 1997). Role entries or exits that are experienced as "off time" (i.e., earlier or later than is socially prescribed) may be perceived as more stressful or disruptive than role transitions that are normatively "on time" (George, 1993). As discussed earlier, research has shown that workers who are unexpectedly forced into early retirement tend to experience this off-time transition as disruptive and psychologically stressful.

Process in Ecological Context

Social researchers are coming to regard retirement not as an "either-or" proposition but as a *process,* possibly extending over several years, involving a number of transitions between paid and unpaid work (e.g., Lowenthal & Robinson, 1976; Moen, 1998a; Reimers & Honig, 1989). An important proposition of life course analysis is that an understanding of any transition (such as retirement) requires it to be placed in the larger context of both current exigencies and other life pathways (Elder, 1995). Bronfenbrenner (1995) also points out that the cognitive response of individuals is related to both characteristics of the person and features of the environment, as well as the process that shapes and binds the two over time. Indeed, research has shown that family, educational, vocational, and other experiences all help to shape the retirement transition. For example, in the case of employment history, both occupational position and career pathways shape individuals' position in the broader opportunity structure, which in turn affects the range of strategies and options regarding retirement (e.g., Han & Moen, 1999; Hoff & Hohner, 1986; O'Rand, Henretta, & Krecker, 1992; Quick & Moen, 1998). Individuals located in different social ecologies experience their middle years in greatly disparate ways. For example, individuals entering midlife at the beginning of the twenty-first century are vastly different in their resources, expectations, and experiences from those entering midlife in the 1950s or at the beginning of the twentieth century.

Linked Lives in Context

Another key tenet of the life-course perspective is that lives are interdependent (Elder, 1995). Developmental processes always take place in the context of ongoing social relations. This is increasingly true regarding developmental shifts that occur with retirement. Individuals frequently decide to retire based on the health and/or retirement plans of others, and the implications of these transitions are played out in a network of shifting social relations. For example, consider that the dual employment of midlife spouses became the modal family division of market work by the 1980s (Szinovacz, 1989). Contemporary cohorts of couples are making conscious choices about retirement timing and whether to retire together (e.g., Henretta & O'Rand, 1983; Henretta, O'Rand, & Chan, 1993; Smith & Moen, 1998).

Human Agency in Context

Individuals in midlife take an active role in designing and redesigning their life biographies in the context of structural options and constraints (such as the availability of pensions and eligibility for retirement). As mentioned earlier, the transformation in the retirement transition is poised to produce unprecedented normlessness and variability in late midlife. This brings to mind a final life-course theme: that individuals help to construct their own lives and their own environments (Elder, 1995). As a social process, retirement transitions are creating opportunities for individuals to shape their middle years in unique ways—by acquiring new roles (e.g., volunteer) as well as continuing in other roles (e.g., friend or parent) and by developing new self-identities. There are opportunities as well for society to create new structures that will serve to expand the life chances and choices for those in the middle life course.

As documented, both retirement planning and retirement adaptation are closely related to choice and control over the decision of whether, and when, to retire. Planned or expected changes in roles and resources are more easily adapted to than are unanticipated life events. Research on retirement has recognized that individuals are active agents in planning their retirement (e.g., Evans et al., 1985; Taylor-Carter et al., 1997). However, changes in social behavior and cognitive responses accompanying retirement are related not only to choices by individual actors but also to features of their institutional environment shaping those choices (e.g., Riley, 1987). For example, when an early retirement option suddenly becomes mandatory in the face of downsizing, then individuals are no longer in control of the timing of their own retirement.

An important theoretical and practical implication of life-course perspective is that occupying particular roles at any one point in time may matter less in terms of psychological adjustment than the number and predictability of role entries and exits over the middle years, and the duration and the timing of role occupation in an individual's life course. As Moen and Wethington (1999) remind us, role continuities and changes (as workers or retirees) are tied to developmental trajectories involving shifts in physical health, emotional well-being, and subjective orientations throughout midlife.

CONCLUSION

In reviewing the literature on midlife preparation for and the transition to retirement, we see concerns that are both methodological and theoretical. First, most prior studies on retirement are cross-sectional in nature. From both life-span developmental and life-course, role-context perspectives, it is crucial to study how individuals change in their retirement-related behaviors and perceptions as they age, as well as how such changes affect long-term development. Studies concerning age effects on retirement-related behaviors are almost exclusively cross-sectional, comparing individuals of different age groups at one point in time. Yet we know that different cohorts are experiencing distinctive economic conditions and social norms surrounding retirement. Cross-sectional studies on this topic exacerbate the difficulties in interpreting differences across age groups as cohort effects or age effects. Moreover, most extant research on retirement involves cross-sectional comparisons of retirees with employed workers, so that it is not clear whether the differences are the consequences of the retirement transition. Researchers have failed to examine dynamic changes in the well-being of midlife workers as they plan and then carry out their retirement. It is critical that dynamic, longitudinal analyses be undertaken for capturing the actual retirement process and its developmental consequences.

Second, there is no consensus regarding the conceptualization or measurement of retirement planning or preparation. Neither is it clear what constitutes "effective" planning for retirement. Various measures have been developed and used—ranging from "having a savings plan for retirement" to "having thought about what to do when retire." Moreover, many studies simply asked retirees whether and how they had planned, raising the issue of retrospective bias (e.g., recall problems, post-hoc rationalization).

Third, there is a clear need for two kinds of investigations: (1) those of broad-based national samples and (2) community samples locating midlife workers in particular organizational, familial, and community contexts. Past research on retirement has documented mostly men's retirement experiences in cohorts where retiring at age 65 was the norm. Even with studies involving women, many researchers rely on a male model of retirement, looking at women whose careers are most similar to men's (Moen, 1998a). Much is left to learn about women's unique experiences in their pathways to and through retirement. The same dearth of evidence holds true for the experiences of members of diverse ethnic and cultural groups. Findings from the few studies of Black Americans document the distinctive retirement experiences of Black men and women from their White counterparts (e.g., Gibson, 1993). How organizational and family settings facilitate or constrain retirement preparation, timing, and consequences have both theoretical and policy relevance.

Finally, investigators studying retirement have yet to develop and test models of the psychological aspects of this key transition. For example, we know something about what social structural variables are implicated in shaping retirement-related behaviors, but little about how the psychological qualities individuals bring to this life stage affect their retirement preparation and experiences. The retirement process itself, as well as adjustment to it, is a product of biological (e.g., aging and health), social structural (e.g., economic and social conditions), and psychological (e.g., self-efficacy) factors. Accordingly, studies of retirement planning, expectations, and actual transitions must take a holistic approach that incorporates the biological, social structural, and psychological aspects of this key status passage. Research indicates that retirement is a process that spans a long period of time, not simply a one-way, one-time, homogeneous bounded event.

From a life course, role context perspective, the retirement transition is meaningful only when it is socially and temporarily situated in individuals' lives and in ecological context (e.g., Moen et al., 1992; Musick et al., 1999; O'Rand et al., 1992). This implies that contemporary midlife workers must prepare, not only for the changes that occur in their personal lives, but also for the changes in the social and organizational structures of work, retirement, careers, and the life course.

REFERENCES

Abel, B.J., & Hayslip, B. (1987). Locus of control and retirement preparation. *Journal of Gerontology, 42,* 165–167.

Abramson, J.H., Ritter, M., Gofin, J., & Kark, J.D. (1992). Work-health relationships in middle-aged and elderly residents of a Jerusalem community. *Social Science and Medicine, 34,* 747–755.

Adelmann, P.K. (1987). Occupational complexity, control, and personal income: Their relation to psychological well-being in men and women. *Journal of Applied Psychology, 72,* 529–537.

Anderson, C.E., & Weber, J.A. (1993). Preretirement planning and perceptions of satisfaction among retirees. *Educational Gerontology, 19,* 397–406.

Atchley, R.C. (1975). Adjustment to loss of job at retirement. *International Journal of Aging and Human Development, 6,* 17–27.

Atchley, R.C. (1976). *The sociology of retirement.* Cambridge, MA: Halsted Press.

Atchley, R.C. (1979). Issues in retirement research. *Gerontologist, 19,* 44–54.

Atchley, R.C. (1982). The process of retirement: Comparing women and men. In M. Szinovacz (Ed.), *Women's retirement: Policy implications of recent research* (pp. 153–168). Beverly Hills, CA: Sage.

Atchley, R.C. (1991). *Social forces and aging* (6th ed.). Belmont, CA: Wadsworth.

Atchley, R.C. (1993). Continuity theory and the evolution of activity in later life. In J.R. Kelly (Ed.), *Activity and aging: Staying involved in later life.* Newbury Park, CA: Sage.

Atchley, R.C., & Robinson, J.L. (1982). Attitudes toward retirement and distance from the event. *Research on Aging, 4,* 299–313.

Bandura, A. (1977). Self-efficacy: Toward a unified theory of behavioral change. *Psychological Review, 84,* 191–215.

Bandura, A. (1982). Self-efficacy mechanism in human agency. *American Psychologist, 37,* 122–147.

Barfield, R.E. (1972). Some observations on early retirement. In G.M. Shatto (Ed.), *Employment of the middle-age* (pp. 45–59). Springfield, IL: Thomas.

Barfield, R.E., & Morgan, J.N. (1969). *Early retirement: The decision and the experience.* Ann Arbor: University of Michigan, Institute of Social Research.

Barfield, R.E., & Morgan, J.N. (1978). Trends in planned early retirement. *Gerontologist, 18,* 13–18.

Beck, S.H. (1984). Retirement preparation programs: Differentials in opportunity and use. *Journal of Gerontology, 39,* 596–602.

Bell, B.D. (1978–1979). Life satisfaction and occupational retirement beyond the impact year. *International Journal of Aging and Human Development, 9,* 31–50.

Blank, A.M., Ritchie, P.J., & Ryback, D. (1983). Lack of satisfaction in post-retirement years. *Psychological Reports, 53,* 1223–1226.

Boskin, M.J. (1977). Social security and retirement decisions. *Economic Inquiry, 15,* 1–25.

Bossé, R., Aldwin, C.M., Levenson, M.R., & Ekerdt, D.J. (1987). Mental health differences among retirees and workers: Findings from the normative aging study. *Psychology and Aging, 2,* 383–389.

Bould, S. (1980). Unemployment as a factor in early retirement decisions. *American Journal of Economics and Sociology, 39,* 123–136.

Bould, S. (1986). Factors influencing the choice of social security early retirement benefits. *Population Research and Policy Review, 5,* 217–236.

Brandstaedter, J., & Baltes-Goetz, B. (1990). Personal control over development and quality of life perspectives in adulthood. In P.B. Baltes & M.M. Baltes (Eds.), *Successful aging: Perspectives from the behavioral sciences* (pp. 197–224). New York: Cambridge University Press.

Broderick, T., & Glazer, B. (1983). Leisure participation and the retirement process. *American Journal of Occupational Therapy, 37,* 15–22.

Brody, E.M., Kleban, M.H., Johnson, P.T., Hoffman, C., & Schoonover, C.B. (1987). Work status and parent care: A comparison of four groups of women. *Gerontologist, 27,* 201–208.

Bronfenbrenner, U. (1995). The bioecological model from a life course perspective: Reflections of a participant observer. In P. Moen, G.H. Elder, Jr., & K. Lüscher (Eds.), *Examining lives in context: Perspectives on the ecology of human development.* Washington, DC: American Psychological Association.

Brown, M.T., Fukunaga, C., Umemoto, D., & Wicker, L. (1996). Annual review, 1990–1996: Social class, work, and retirement behavior. *Journal of Vocational Behavior, 49,* 159–189.

Burgess, E.W. (1960). Aging in Western culture. In E.W. Burgess (Ed.), *Aging in Western society: A comparative study.* Chicago: University of Chicago Press.

Burke, P.J. (1991). Identity processes and social stress. *American Sociological Review, 50,* 836–849.

Calasanti, T.M. (1996). Gender and life satisfaction in retirement: An assessment of the male model. *Journal of Gerontology: Social Sciences, 51B,* S18–S29.

Campione, W.A. (1988). Predicting participation in retirement preparation programs. *Journal of Gerontology, 43,* S91–S95.

Caro, F.G., & Bass, S.A. (1995). Increasing volunteering among older people. In S.A. Bass (Ed.), *Older and active: How Americans over 55 are contributing to society* (pp. 71–96). New Haven, CT: Yale University Press.

Carp, F.M. (1997). Retirement and women. In J.M. Coyle (Ed.), *Handbook on women and aging* (pp. 112–128). Westport, CT: Greenwood Press.

Chambré, S.M. (1984). Is volunteering a substitute for role loss in old age? An empirical test of activity theory. *Gerontologist, 24,* 294–295.

Chambré, S.M. (1987). *Good deeds in old age: Volunteering by the new leisure class.* Lexington, MA: Lexington Books.

Cherry, D.L., Zarit, S.H., & Krauss, I.K. (1984). The structure of post-retirement adaptation for recent and longer term women retirees. *Experimental Aging Research, 10,* 231–236.

Chirikos, T.N., & Nestel, G. (1989). Occupation, impaired health, and the functional capacity of men to continue working. *Research on Aging, 11,* 174–205.

Choi, N.G. (1994). Racial differences in timing and factors associated with retirement. *Journal of Sociology and Social Welfare, 21,* 31–52.

Clausen, J.A., & Gilens, M.I. (1990). Personality and labor force participation across the life course: A longitudinal study of women's careers. *Sociological Forum, 5,* 595–618.

Cox, H., & Bhak, A. (1978–1979). Symbolic interaction and retirement adjustment: An empirical assessment. *International Journal of Aging and Human Development, 9,* 279–286.

DeViney, S., & O'Rand, A.M. (1988). Age, gender, cohort succession and labor force participation of older workers, 1951–1984. *Sociologist Quarterly, 29,* 525–540.

Dobson, C., & Morrow, P.C. (1984). Effects of career orientation on retirement attitudes and retirement planning. *Journal of Vocational Behavior, 24,* 73–83.

Dorfman, L.T. (1989). Retirement preparation and retirement satisfaction in the rural elderly. *Journal of Applied Gerontology, 8,* 432–450.

Dorfman, L.T., Kohout, F.J., & Heckert, D.A. (1985). Retirement satisfaction in the rural elderly. *Research on Aging, 7,* 577–599.

Dorfman, L.T., & Moffett, M.M. (1987). Retirement satisfaction in married and widowed rural women. *Gerontologist, 27,* 215–221.

Ekerdt, D.J. (1987). Why the notion persists that retirement harms health. *Gerontologist, 27,* 454–457.

Ekerdt, D.J. (1989). Retirement preparation. In L.M. Powell (Ed.), *Annual review of gerontology and geriatrics* (Vol. 9, pp. 321–356). New York: Springer.

Ekerdt, D.J., Bossé, R., & LoCastro, J.S. (1983). Claims that retirement improves health. *Journal of Gerontology, 38,* 231–236.

Elder, G.H., Jr. (1995). The life course paradigm: Social change and individual development. In P. Moen, G.H. Elder, Jr., & K. Lüscher (Eds.), *Examining lives in context: Perspectives on the ecology of human development* (pp. 101–140). Washington, DC: American Psychological Association.

Elwell, F., & Maltbie-Crannell, A.D. (1981). The impact of role loss upon coping resources and life satisfaction of the elderly. *Journal of Gerontology, 36,* 223–232.

Evans, L., Ekerdt, D.J., & Bossé, R. (1985). Proximity to retirement and anticipatory involvement: Findings from the normative aging study. *Journal of Gerontology, 40,* 368–374.

Feldman, D.C. (1994). The decision to retire early: A review and conceptualization. *Academy of Management Review, 19,* 285–311.

Fernandez, M.E., Mutran, E.J., Reitzes, D.C., & Sudha, S. (1998). Ethnicity, gender, and depressive symptoms in older workers. *Gerontologist, 38,* 71–79.

Fields, G.S., & Mitchell, O.S. (1984). *Retirement, pensions, and social security.* Cambridge, MA: MIT Press.

Fillenbaum, G.G., George, L.K., & Palmore, E.B. (1985). Determinants and consequences of retirement among men of different races and economic levels. *Journal of Gerontology, 40,* 85–94.

Fischer, L.R., & Schaffer, K.B. (1993) *Older Volunteers: A guide to research and practice.* Newbury Park, CA: Sage.

Fitzpatrick, E.W. (1978). An industry consortium approach to retirement planning: A new program. *Aging and Work, 1,* 181–188.

Fox, J.H. (1977). Effects of retirement and former work life on women's adaptation in old age. *Journal of Gerontology, 32,* 196–202.

Fretz, B.R., Kluge, N.A., Ossana, S.M., Jones, S.M., & Merikangas, M.W. (1989). Intervention targets for reducing preretirement anxiety and depression. *Journal of Counseling Psychology, 36,* 301–307.

Fridlund, B., Hansson, H., & Ysander, L. (1992). Working conditions among men before and after their first myocardial infraction: Implications for a rehabilitative care strategy. *Clinical Rehabilitation, 6,* 299–304.

Friedmann, E., & Havighurst, R.J. (1954). *The meaning of work and retirement.* Chicago: University of Chicago Press.

Fuller, R.L., & Redfering, D.L. (1976). Effects of pre-retirement planning on the retirement adjustment of military personnel. *Sociology of Work and Occupations, 3,* 479–487.

Gall, T.L., Evans, D.R., & Howard, J. (1997). The retirement adjustment process: Changes in the well-being of male retirees across time. *Journal of Gerontology, 52,* P110–P117.

George, L.K. (1980). *Role transitions in later life.* Belmont, CA: Brooks/Cole.

George, L.K. (1990). Social structure, social processes, and social-psychological states. In R.H. Binstock & L.K. George (Eds.), *Handbook of aging and the social sciences* (3rd ed., pp. 205–226). San Diego, CA: Academic Press.

George, L.K. (1993). Sociological perspectives on life transitions. *Annual Review of Sociology, 19,* 353–373.

George, L.K., Fillenbaum, G.G., & Palmore, E.B. (1984). Sex differences in the antecedents and consequences of retirement. *Journal of Gerontology, 39,* 364–371.

George, L.K., & Maddox, G.L. (1977). Subjective adaptation to loss of the work role: A longitudinal study. *Journal of Gerontology, 32,* 456–462.

Gibson, R.C. (1987). Reconceptualizing retirement for Black Americans. *Gerontologist, 27,* 691–698.

Gibson, R.C. (1993). The Black American retirement experience. In J.S. Jackson, L.M., Chatters, & R.J. Taylor (Eds.), *Aging in Black America* (pp. 277–297). Newbury Park, CA: Sage.

Giele, J.Z., & Elder, G.H., Jr. (1998). *Methods of life course research: Qualitative and quantitative approaches.* Thousand Oaks, CA: Sage.

Gilespie, D.F., & King, A.E. (1985). Demographic understanding of volunteerism. *Journal of Sociology and Social Welfare, 12,* 798–816.

Gilford, R. (1984). Contrasts in marital satisfaction throughout old age: An exchange theory analysis. *Journal of Gerontology, 39,* 325–333.

Glamser, F.D. (1976). Determinants of a positive attitude toward retirement. *Journal of Gerontology, 31,* 104–107.

Glamser, F.D. (1981). The impact of preretirement programs on the retirement experience. *Journal of Gerontology, 36,* 244–250.

Glamser, F.D., & DeJong, G.F. (1975). The efficacy of preretirement preparation programs for industrial workers. *Journal of Gerontology, 30,* 595–600.

Goudy, W.J., Powers, E.A., Keith, P.M., & Reger, R.A. (1980). Changes in attitudes toward retirement: Evidence from a panel study of older males. *Journal of Gerontology, 35,* 942–948.

Graebner, W. (1980). *A history of retirement.* New Haven, CT: Yale University Press.

Gratton, B., & Haug, M.R. (1983). Decision and adaptation: Research on female retirement. *Research on Aging, 5,* 59–76.

Hagestad, G.O., & Neugarten, B.L. (1984). Age and the life course. In R. Binstok & E. Shanas (Eds.), *Handbook of aging and the social sciences* (pp. 35–61). New York: Van Nostrand-Reinhold.

Hale, W.D., Hedgepeth, B.E., & Taylor, E.B. (1985–1986). Locus of control and psychological distress among the aged. *International Journal of Aging and Human Development, 21,* 1–8.

Han, S.K., & Moen, P. (1999). Clocking out: Temporal patterning of retirement. *American Journal of Sociology, 105,* 191–236.

Havighurst, R.J. (1968). A social-psychological perspective on aging. *Gerontologist, 8,* 67–71.

Hayward, M.D., Grady, W.R., Hardy, M.A., & Sommers, D. (1989). Occupational influences on retirement, disability, and death. *Demography, 26,* 393–409.

Hayward, M.D., Grady, W.R., & McLaughlin, S.D. (1988). Changes in the retirement process among older men in the United States: 1972–1980. *Demography, 25,* 371–386.

Hayward, M.D., Hardy, M.A., & Grady, W.R. (1989). Labor force withdrawal patterns among older men in the United States. *Social Science Quarterly, 70,* 425–558.

Hendrick, C., Wells, K.S., & Faletti, M.V. (1982). Social and emotional effects of geographical relocation on elderly retirees. *Journal of Personality and Social Psychology, 42,* 951–962.

Henretta, J.C., & O'Rand, A.M. (1980). Labor force participation of older married women. *Social Security Bulletin, 43,* 29–39.

Henretta, J.C., & O'Rand, A.M. (1983). Joint retirement in the dual worker family. *Social Forces, 62,* 504–520.

Henretta, J.C., O'Rand, A.M., & Chan, C.G. (1993). Joint role investments and synchronization of retirement: A sequential approach to couples retirement timing. *Social Forces, 71,* 981–1000.

Herzog, A.R., House, J.S., & Morgan, J.N. (1991). Relation of work and retirement to health and well-being in older age. *Psychology and Aging, 6,* 201–211.

Herzog, A.R., & Morgan, J.N. (1993). Formal volunteer work among older Americans. In S.A. Bass, F.G. Caro, & Y.P. Chen (Eds.), *Achieving a productive aging society* (pp. 119–142). Westport, CT: Auburn House.

Hoff, E.H., & Hohner, H.U. (1986). Occupational careers, work, and control. In M.M. Baltes & P.B. Baltes (Eds.), *The psychology of control and aging* (pp. 345–371). Hillsdale, NJ: Erlbaum.

Jackson, J.S., Antonucci, T.C., & Gibson, R.C. (1995). Ethnic and cultural factors in research on aging and mental health: A life-course perspective. In D.K. Padgett (Ed.), *Handbook on ethnicity, aging, and mental health* (pp. 22–46). Westport, CT: Greenwood Press.

Jackson, J.S., & Gibson, R.C. (1985). Work and retirement among the Black elderly. In Z. Balu (Ed.), *Current perspectives on aging and the life cycle* (pp. 193–222). Greenwich, CT: JAI Press.

Jacobson, C.J. (1994). Rejection of the retiree role: A study of female industrial workers in their 50s. *Human Relations, 27,* 477–492.

Jacobson, D. (1974). Planning for retirement and anticipatory attitudes towards withdrawal from work. *British Journal of Guidance and Counselling, 2,* 72–83.

Julia, M., Kilty, K.M., & Richardson, V. (1995). Social worker preparedness for retirement: Gender and ethnic considerations. *Social Work, 40,* 610–620.

Kamouri, A.L., & Cavanaugh, J.C. (1986). The impact of preretirement education programmes on workers' preretirement socialization. *Journal of Occupational Behaviour, 7,* 245–256.

Keith, P.M., & Schafer, R.B. (1986). Housework, disagreement, and depression among younger and older couples. *American Behavioral Scientist, 29,* 405–422.

Kessler, R.C., & McLeod, J.D. (1984). Sex differences in vulnerability to undesirable life events. *American Sociological Review, 49,* 620–631.

Kilty, K.M., & Behling, J.H. (1985). Predicting the retirement intentions and attitudes of professional workers. *Journal of Gerontology, 40,* 219–227.

Kim, J.E., & Moen, P. (1999). *Work/retirement transitions and psychological well-being in late midlife* (Working Paper No. 99-10). Ithaca, NY: Cornell University, Bronfenbrenner Life Course Center.

Kim, J.E., & Moen, P. (2000). *Retirement transitions, gender, and psychological well-being in late midlife.* Manuscript submitted for publication.

Kim, J.E., & Moen, P. (in press). Is retirement good or bad for subjective well-being? *Current Directions in Psychological Science.*

Kimmel, D.C., Price, K.F., & Walker, J.W. (1978). Retirement choice and retirement satisfaction. *Journal of Gerontology, 33,* 575–585.

Kohli, M. (1994). Work and retirement: A comparative perspective. In M.W. Riley, R.L. Kahn, & A. Foner (Eds.), *Age and structural lag: Society's failure to provide meaningful opportunities in work, family, and leisure* (pp. 80–106). New York: Wiley.

Kohli, M., & Rein, M. (1991). The changing balance of work and retirement. In M. Kohli, M. Rein, A.M. Guillemard, & H. van Gunsteren (Eds.), *Time for retirement: Comparative studies of early exit from the labor force* (pp. 1–35). New York: Cambridge University Press.

Kremer, Y. (1984–1985). Predictors of retirement satisfaction: A path model. *International Journal of Aging and Human Development, 20,* 113–121.

Kroeger, N. (1982). Pre-retirement preparation: Sex differences in access, sources, and use. In M. Szinovacz (Ed.), *Women's retirement: Policy implications of recent research* (pp. 95–111). Beverly Hills, CA: Sage.

Labouvie-Vief, G. (1982). Dynamic development and mature autonomy. *Human Development, 25,* 161–191.

Lachman, M.E. (1986a). Locus of control and aging research: A case for multidimensional and domain-specific assessment. *Psychology and Aging, 1,* 34–40.

Lachman, M.E. (1986b). Personal control in later life: Stability, change, and cognitive correlates. In M.M. Baltes & P.B. Baltes (Eds.), *The psychology of control and aging* (pp. 207–236). Hillsdale, NJ: Erlbaum.

Lachman, M.E., & Weaver, S.L. (1998). The sense of control as a moderator of social class differences in health and well-being. *Journal of Personality and Social Psychology, 74,* 763–773.

Lee, G.R., & Shehan, C.L. (1989). Retirement and marital satisfaction. *Journal of Gerontology, 44,* S226–S230.

Levinson, D.J., Darrow, C.N., Klein, E.B., Levinson, M.H., & McKee, B. (1978). *The seasons of a man's life.* New York: Knopf.

Lowenthal, M.F., & Robinson, B. (1976). Social networks and isolation. In R.H. Binstock & E. Shanas (Eds.), *Handbook of aging and the social sciences* (pp. 432–456). New York: Van Nostrand-Reinhold.

MacEwen, K.E., Barling, J., Kelloway, E.K., & Higginbottom, S.F. (1995). Predicting retirement anxiety: The roles of parental socialization and personal planning. *Journal of Social Psychology, 135,* 203–213.

Markides, K.S. (1983). Minority aging. In M.W. Riley, B. Hess, & K. Bond (Eds.), *Aging in society: Selected reviews of recent research* (pp. 15–37). Hillsdale, NJ: Erlbaum.

Martin Matthews, A.M., & Brown, K.H. (1987). Retirement as a critical life event: The differential experiences of women and men. *Research on Aging, 9,* 548–571.

McCrae, R., & Costa, P. (1990). *Personality in adulthood.* New York: Guilford Press.

McGoldrick, A.E. (1994). Stress, early retirement, and health. In K.S. Markides & C.I. Cooper (Eds.), *Reviews in Clinical Gerontology, 4,* 151–160.

McGoldrick, A.E., & Cooper, C.L. (1989). *Early Retirement.* Chichester, England: Gower.

McPherson, B.D., & Guppy, N. (1979). Pre-retirement life-style and the degree of planning for retirement. *Journal of Gerontology, 34*, 254–263.

Midanik, L.T., Soghikian, K., Ransom, L.J., & Tekawa, I.S. (1995). The effect of retirement on mental health and health behaviors: The Kaiser Permanente Retirement Study. *Journal of Gerontology, 50B*, S59–S61.

Moen, P. (1985). Continuities and discontinuities in women's labor force activity. In G.H. Elder, Jr. (Ed.), *Life course dynamics: Trajectories and transitions, 1968–1980* (pp. 113–155). Ithaca, NY: Cornell University Press.

Moen, P. (1994). Women, work and family: A sociological perspective on changing roles. In M.W. Riley, R.L. Kahn, & A. Foner (Eds.), *Age and Structural Lag: The mismatch between people's lives and opportunities in work, family, and leisure* (pp. 151–170). New York: Wiley.

Moen, P. (1996a). Change age trends: The pyramid upside down? In U. Bronfenbrenner, P. McClelland, E. Wethington, P. Moen, & S.J. Ceci (Eds.), *The state of Americans: This generation and the next* (pp. 208–258). New York: Free Press.

Moen, P. (1996b). A life course perspective on retirement, gender, and well-being. *Journal of Occupational Health Psychology, 1*, 131–144.

Moen, P. (1997). Women's roles and resilience: Trajectories of advantage or turning points? In I.H. Gotlib & B. Wheaton (Eds.), *Stress and adversity over the life course: Trajectories and turning points* (pp. 133–156). New York: Cambridge University Press.

Moen, P. (1998a). Recasting careers: Changing reference groups, risks, and realities. *Generations, 22*, 40–45.

Moen, P. (1998b). Reconstructing retirement: Careers, couples, and social capital. *Contemporary Gerontology, 4*, 123–125.

Moen, P., Dempster-McClain, D., & Williams, R.M., Jr. (1992). Successful aging: A life course perspective on women's roles and health. *American Journal of Sociology, 97*, 1612–1638.

Moen, P., Elder, G.H., Jr., & Lüscher, K. (Eds.). (1995). *Examining lives in context: Perspectives on the ecology of human development.* Washington, DC: American Psychological Association.

Moen, P., & Fields, V. (2000). *Retirement, social capital, and well-being: Does community participation replace paid work?* Unpublished manuscript, Cornell University, Ithaca, NY.

Moen, P., Fields, V., Quick, H., & Hofmeister, H. (2000). A life-course approach to retirement and social integration. In K. Pillemer, P. Moen, E. Wethington, & N. Glasgow (Eds.), *Social integration in the second half of life* (pp. 75–107). Baltimore: Johns Hopkins University Press.

Moen, P., Kim, J.E., & Hofmeister, H. (2001). Couples' work/retirement transitions, gender, and marital quality. *Social Psychology Quarterly.*

Moen, P., & Wethington, E. (1999). Midlife development in a life course context. In S.L. Willis & J.D. Reid (Eds.), *Life in the middle* (pp. 3–23). San Diego, CA: Academic Press.

Monk, A., & Donovan, R. (1978). Pre-retirement preparation programs. *Aged Care and Services Review, 1*, 1–7.

Morgan, L.A. (1992). Marital status and retirement plans: Do widowhood and divorce make a difference? In M. Szinovacz, D.J. Ekerdt, & B.H. Vinick (Eds.), *Families and retirement* (pp. 114–126). Newbury Park, CA: Sage.

Morse, D.W., Dutka, A.B., & Gray, S.H. (1983). *Life after early retirement: The experience of lower-level workers.* Totowa, NJ: Rowman & Allanheld.

Morse, D.W., & Gray, S.H. (1980). *Early retirement—boon or bane: A study of three large corporations.* Montclair, NJ: Allanheld, Osmun.

Musick, M.A., Herzog, A.R., & House, J.S. (1999). Volunteering and mortality among older adults: Findings from a national sample. *Journal of Gerontology, 54B,* S173–S180.

Mutchler, J.E., Burr, J.A., Pienta, A.M., & Massagli, M.P. (1997). Pathways to labor force exit: Work transitions and work instability. *Journal of Gerontology, 52B,* S4–S12.

Mutran, E.J., Reitzes, D.C., & Fernandez, M.E. (1997). Factors that influence attitudes toward retirement. *Research on Aging, 19,* 251–273.

Okun, M.A., Stock, W.A., Haring, M.J., & Witter, R.A. (1984). The social activity/subjective well-being relation: A quantitative synthesis. *Research on Aging, 6,* 45–65.

O'Rand, A.M., Henretta, J.C., & Krecker, M.L. (1992). Family pathways to retirement. In M.D. Szinovacz, D.J. Ekerdt, & B.H. Vinick (Eds.), *Families and retirement* (pp. 81–98). Newbury Park, CA: Sage.

Palmore, E.B. (1982). Preparation for retirement: The impact of preretirement programs on retirement and leisure. In N.J. Osgood (Ed.), *Life after work* (pp. 330–341). New York: Praeger.

Palmore, E.B., Burchett, B.M., Fillenbaum, G.G., George, L.K., & Wallman, L.M. (1985). *Retirement: Causes and consequences.* New York: Springer.

Palmore, E.B., Fillenbaum, G.G., & George, L.K. (1984). Consequences of retirement. *Journal of Gerontology, 21,* 109–116.

Palmore, E.B., George, L.K., & Fillenbaum, G.G. (1982). Predictors of retirement. *Journal of Gerontology, 37,* 733–742.

Parnes, H.S. (1981). *Work and retirement.* Cambridge, MA: MIT Press.

Parnes, H.S., & Nestel, G. (1974). Early retirement. In H.S. Parnes, A. Adams, P. Andrisani, A. Kohen, & G. Nestel (Eds.), *The retirement years: Five years in the work lives of middle-aged men* (Vol. 4, pp. 153–196). Columbus: Ohio University, Center for Human Resources Research.

Parnes, H.S., & Nestel, G. (1981). The retirement experience. In H.S. Parnes (Ed.), *Work and retirement: A longitudinal study of men* (pp. 155–197). Cambridge, MA: MIT Press.

Peretti, P.O., & Wilson, C. (1975). Voluntary and involuntary retirement of aged males and their effect on emotional satisfaction, usefulness, self-image, emotional stability, and interpersonal relationships. *International Journal of Aging and Human Development, 6,* 131–138.

Perkins, K.E. (1992). Psychosocial implications of women and retirement. *Social Work, 37,* 526–532.

Perun, P.J., & Bielby, D.D. (1980). Structure and dynamics of the individual life course. In K.W. Back (Ed.) *Life course: Integrative theories and exemplary populations* (pp. 97–119). Boulder, CO: Westview.

Prentis, R.S. (1980). White-collar working women's perception of retirement. *Gerontologist, 20,* 90–95.

Pyron, H.C., & Manion, U.V. (1970). The company, the individual, and the decision to retire. *Industrial Gerontology, 4,* 1–11.

Quick, H.E., & Moen, P. (1998). Gender, employment, and retirement quality: A life course approach to the differential experiences of men and women. *Journal of Occupational Health Psychology, 3,* 44–64.

Quinn, J.F. (1981). The extent and correlates of partial retirement. *Gerontologist, 21,* 634–642.

Quinn, J.F., & Burkhauser, R.V. (1981). The extent and correlates of partial retirement. *Gerontologist, 21,* 634–642.

Quinn, J.F., & Burkhauser, R.V. (1990). Work and retirement. In R.H. Binstock & L.J. George (Eds.), *Handbook of aging and the social sciences* (3rd ed., pp. 307–327). San Diego, CA: Academic Press.

Reimers, C., & Honig, M. (1989). The retirement process in the United States: Mobility among full-time work, partial retirement, and full retirement. In W. Schmall (Ed.), *Redefining the process of retirement: An international perspective.* Berlin, Germany: Springer-Verlag.

Reis, M., & Gold, D.P. (1993). Retirement, personality, and life satisfaction: A review and two models. *Journal of Applied Gerontology, 12,* 261–282.

Reitzes, D.C., Mutran, E.J., & Fernandez, M.E. (1998). The decision to retire: A career perspective. *Social Science Quarterly, 79,* 607–619.

Richardson, V. (1990). Gender differences in retirement planning among educators: Implications for practice with older women. *Journal of Women and Aging, 2,* 27–40.

Richardson, V., & Kilty, K.M. (1991). Adjustment to retirement: Continuity vs. discontinuity. *International Journal of Aging and Human Development, 33,* 151–169.

Richardson, V., & Kilty, K.M. (1992). Retirement intentions among Black professionals: Implications for practice with older Black adults. *Gerontologist, 32,* 7–16.

Riegel, K. (1975). Adult life crises: Toward a dialectical theory of development. In N. Datan & L. Ginsberg (Eds.), *Life span development and psychology: Normative life crises* (pp. 99–123). New York: Academic Press.

Riley, M.W. (1987). On the significance of age in sociology. *American Sociological Review, 52,* 1–14.

Rodin, J. (1986). Health, control, and aging. In M.M. Baltes & P.B. Baltes (Eds.), *Aging and the psychology of control* (pp. 139–165). Hillsdale, NJ: Erlbaum.

Rodin, J. (1990). Control by any other name: Definitions, concepts, and processes. In J. Rodin, C. Schooler, & K.W. Schaie (Eds.), *Self-directedness: Cause and effects throughout the life course* (pp. 1–17). Hillsdale, NJ: Erlbaum.

Rodin, J., Timko, C., & Harris, S. (1985). The construct of control: Biological and psychosocial correlates. In C. Eisdorfer, M.P. Lawton, & G.L. Maddox (Eds.), *Annual review of gerontology and geriatrics* (pp. 3–55). New York: Springer.

Romsa, G., Bondy, P., & Blenman, M. (1985). Modeling retirees' life satisfaction levels: The role of recreational, life cycle and socio-environmental elements. *Journal of Leisure Research, 17,* 29–39.

Rook, K.S., Catalano, R., & Dooley, D. (1989). The timing of major life events: Effects of departing from the social clock. *American Journal of Community Psychology, 17*, 233–258.

Rosenfield, R.A. (1980). Race and sex differences in career dynamics. *American Sociological Review, 42*, 210–217.

Ross, C.E., & Drentea, P. (1998). Consequences of retirement activities for distress and the sense of personal control. *Journal of Health and Social Behavior, 39*, 317–334.

Rotter, J.B. (1966). Generalized expectancies for internal versus external control of reinforcement. *Psychological Monographs, 80*(1, Whole No. 609).

Rowe, J.W., & Kahn, R.L. (1998). *Successful aging.* New York: Pantheon Books.

Rowen, R.B., & Wilks, C.S. (1987). Pre-retirement planning, a quality of life issue for retirement. *Employee Assistance Quarterly, 2*, 45–56.

Ruhm, C.J. (1989). Why older Americans stop working. *Gerontologist, 29*, 294–298.

Ryff, C.D. (1989). Happiness is everything, or is it? Explorations on the meaning of psychological well-being. *Journal of Personality and Social Psychology, 57*, 1069–1081.

Ryff, C.D., & Keyes, C.L.M. (1995). The structure of psychological well-being revisited. *Journal of Personality and Social Psychology, 69*, 719–727.

Schmitt, N., Coyle, B.W., Rauschenberger, J., & White, J.K. (1979). Comparison of early retirees and non-retirees. *Personnel Psychology, 32*, 327–340.

Schulz, R. (1976). Effects of control and predictability on the physical and psychological well-being of the institutionalized aged. *Journal of Personality and Social Psychology, 33*, 563–573.

Seccombe, K., & Lee, G.R. (1986). Gender differences in retirement satisfaction and its antecedents. *Research on Aging, 8*, 426–440.

Setterson, R.A., Jr. (1997). The salience of age in the life course. *Human Development, 40*, 257–281.

Singleton, J.F. (1985). Retirement: Its effects on the individual. *Activities, Adaptation and Aging, 6*, 1–7.

Singleton, J.F., & Keddy, B.A. (1991). Planning for retirement. *Activities, Adaptation and Aging, 16*, 49–55.

Slowik, C.M. (1991). The relationship of preretirement education and well-being of women. *Gerontology and Geriatrics Education, 11*, 89–104.

Smith, D.B., & Moen, P. (1998). Spouse's influence on the retirement decision: His, her, and their perceptions. *Journal of Marriage and the Family, 60*, 734–744.

Sorenson, A. (1983). Women's employment patterns after marriage. *Journal of Marriage and the Family, 45*, 311–321.

Streib, G.F., & Schneider, C.J. (1971). *Retirement in American society.* Ithaca, NY: Cornell University Press.

Stull, D.E. (1988). A dyadic approach to predicting well-being in later life. *Research on Aging, 10*, 81–101.

Szinovacz, M.E. (1982). Beyond the hearth: Older women and retirement. In E.W. Markson (Ed.), *Older women in society.* Lexington, MA: Heath.

Szinovacz, M.E. (1989). Decision-making on retirement timing. In D. Brinberg & J. Jaccard (Eds.), *Dyadic decision making* (pp. 286–310). New York: Springer.

Szinovacz, M.E. (1991). Women and retirement. In B.B. Hess & E.W. Markson (Eds.), *Growing old in America* (pp. 293–303). New Brunswick, NJ: Transaction Books.

Szinovacz, M.E. (1996). Couples' employment/retirement patterns and perceptions of marital quality. *Research on Aging, 18,* 243–268.

Szinovacz, M.E., Ekerdt, D.J., & Vinick, B.H. (1992). Families and retirement: Conceptual and methodological issues. In M. Szinovacz, D.J. Ekerdt, & B. Vinick (Eds.), *Families and retirement* (pp. 1–19). Newbury Park, CA: Sage.

Szinovacz, M.E., & Washo, C. (1992). Gender differences in exposure to life events and adaptation to retirement. *Journal of Gerontology, 47,* S191–S196.

Talaga, J.A., & Beehr, T.A. (1995). Are there gender differences in predicting retirement decisions? *Journal of Applied Psychology, 80,* 16–28.

Taylor, M.A., & Shore, L.M. (1995). Predictors of planned retirement age: An application of Beehr's model. *Psychology and Aging, 10,* 76–83.

Taylor-Carter, M.A., & Cook, K. (1995). Adaptation to retirement: Role changes and psychological resources. *Career Development Quarterly, 44,* 67–82.

Taylor-Carter, M.A., Cook, K., & Weinberg, C. (1997). Planning and expectations of the retirement experience. *Educational Gerontology, 23,* 273–288.

Thoits, P.A. (1986). Multiple identities: Examining gender and marital status differences in distress. *American Psychological Review, 51,* 259–272.

Thompson, G.B. (1973). Work versus leisure roles: An investigation of morale among employed and retired men. *Journal of Gerontology, 28,* 339–344.

Thompson, G.B. (1979). Black-White differences in private pensions findings from the retirement history study. *Social Security Bulletin, 42,* 15–22.

Tiberi, D.M., Boyack, V.I., & Kerschner, P.A. (1978). A comparative analysis of four preretirement education models. *Educational Gerontology, 3,* 355–374.

Torres-Gil, F. (1984). Preretirement issues that affect minorities. In H. Dennis (Ed.), *Preretirement preparation: What retirement specialists need to know* (pp. 109–128). Lexington, MA: Lexington Books.

Turner, M.J., Bailey, W.C., & Scott, J.P. (1994). Factors influencing attitude toward retirement and retirement planning among midlife university employees. *Journal of Applied Gerontology, 13,* 143–156.

Turner, R.H. (1978). The role and the person. *American Journal of Sociology, 84,* 1–23.

Walker, J.W., Kimmel, D.C., & Price, K.F. (1981). Retirement style and retirement satisfaction: Retirees aren't all alike. *International Journal of Aging and Human Development, 12,* 267–281.

Wan, T.T.H., & Ferraro, K.F. (1985). Retirement attitudes of married couples in later life. In T.T.H. Wan (Ed.), *Well-being of the elderly* (pp. 75–88). Lexington, MA: Lexington Books.

Weiner, A. (1980). Pre-retirement education: Accent on leisure. *Therapeutic Recreation Journal, 14,* 18–31.

Weis, J., Koch, U., Kruck, P., & Beck, A. (1994). Problems of vocational interation after cancer. *Clinical Rehabilitation, 8,* 219–225.

Weiss, R. (1997). Adaptation to retirement. In I.H. Gotlib & B. Wheaton (Eds.), *Stress, and adversity over the life course* (pp. 232–248). New York: Cambridge University Press.

Weisz, J.R. (1983). Can I control it? The pursuit of veridical answers across the life span. *Life-Span Development and Behavior, 5,* 233–300.

Wright, L.K. (1990). Mental health in older spouses: The dynamic interplay of resources, depression, quality of the marital relationship, and social participation. *Issues in Mental Health Nursing, 11,* 49–70.

CHAPTER 15

Families, Intergenerational Relationships, and Kinkeeping in Midlife

NORELLA M. PUTNEY and VERN L. BENGTSON

FAMILIES HAVE CHANGED, or so it seems. Relations between parents, children, grandparents, and grandchildren seem different than they used to be, the feelings of attachment and obligation toward one another less certain. The function of families, indeed the meaning of family itself, seems more tentative. Individuals and their families have been affected by dramatic demographic, socioeconomic, and historical changes during the last half of the twentieth century. Longer lives and fewer children, economic and political restructuring, the movement of women out of the home and into the labor force, increased marital instability and changing family structures—all have profoundly affected the direction and experience of individual lives. Our focus here, however, is on relations in families—multigenerational families—and how individual lives within those families are given form and meaning through interactions with intimate others who are bound together across generations and time. Within multigenerational families, those in midlife play a pivotal role.

Scholarly research on families and intergenerational relations points to several issues, frequently posed in the form of dilemmas, that are especially salient for those in midlife. In this chapter, we address four such midlife dilemmas. The first pertains to family caregiving and the often conflicting role demands placed on those in midlife. A mythology has grown up around the notions of "the sandwich generation" and "caregiving as normative stress," reflecting the purportedly increasing difficulties faced by caregivers in balancing the claims of family and work. Is there some truth here? Are caregivers truly overwhelmed, their situation extreme? We examine what the research has to say about this midlife dilemma.

The second issue addresses a relatively new phenomenon faced by midlife parents throughout the Western world—the increasingly prolonged dependency of their young adult children who stay in the parental home much longer than expected or who leave only to return after a failed attempt at independence, or because of a failed marriage. Grandchildren may accompany the returning adult child to the parental home. Or grandchildren may come alone. Increasingly, midlife grandparents are taking on parenting responsibilities for grandchildren because their own offspring are unable to do so. On the one hand, this fundamentally demographic and socioeconomic issue may present an unwelcome challenge to midlife parents. On the other hand, there may be benefits deriving from extended coresidence that increase individual well-being and strengthen family bonds.

The third issue concerns the paradox of "intergenerational solidarity and conflict in families" and what this means for the quality of family relationships and the health and well-being of family members. What are the implications of family conflict for the middle generation in the family lineage whose unique role it is to provide for the dependency needs of the youngest and oldest members? An important, and vexing, dilemma concerns the possibility that the bonds of multigenerational families are weakening and that members may be less able or willing to enact their protective function and support each other in time of need.

The fourth concern is kinkeeping, an important midlife role in multigenerational families. Kinkeeping refers to the work of maintaining strong bonds among the nuclear families within the extended family, a task usually undertaken by women. And herein lies the dilemma. Changes in women's lives—work, divorce and single parenting, shifting gender role expectations and opportunities—lead us to wonder whether family kinkeepers will be available in the future to tend to the solidarity needs of families.

In this chapter, we examine what recent research has to say about these midlife issues. We explore their contradictions and implications, and in so doing, can see what these midlife issues reveal about the strengths and vulnerabilities of intergenerational family bonds at the beginning of the twenty-first century. Throughout this discussion, we emphasize the heterogeneity of intergenerational relationships and midlife issues and variations by ethnicity, class, and gender as well as age cohort.

THE SANDWICH GENERATION: TRUTH OR MYTH?

Two decades ago, Elaine Brody alerted us to an impending crisis, that "having a dependent elderly parent was becoming a normative experience for many individuals and families and *exceeding the capacities of some of them*" (Brody, 1985, p. 20, italics added). In a community-based study of caregivers, Brody (1981, 1985) found that women in their middle years provided more support to their elderly parents, to their own children, and had worked more than had their elderly parents when the latter were in midlife. To cope with these competing demands, these contemporary midlife women had sacrificed their other activities and enjoyments. Focusing on the strain endured by middle-aged caregivers, mostly women, Brody called attention to two converging demographic and socioeconomic trends and their likely effects on family caregiving: the accelerated rate of increase in the very old population—those most likely to need care; and the rapid entry of middle-aged women—the traditional providers of parent care—into the workforce, affecting their availability for parent care and constituting a major claim on their time and energy. She referred to this generation of women with multiple and potentially conflicting roles as the "women in the middle" (Brody, 1981).

CHANGING DEMANDS ON THE MIDDLE GENERATION

A continuing theme in caregiving research is that the current cohorts of middle-aged adults, especially women, are increasingly finding themselves "in the middle" between two generations with caregiving responsibilities for both, or "sandwiched in" by the demands of competing family and work roles. Longer lives have meant a dramatic increase in the numbers of midlife adults who have surviving parents. An increasing proportion of those parents will survive to very old ages, although not without serious impairments. At the same time, declines in fertility have meant that fewer potential caregivers are available for the growing numbers of elderly. At midlife, the need to care for an elderly parent may coincide with the launching of one's own children, or caring for children still in the nest, or continuing responsibility for adult children who have returned to the nest, an increasingly common occurrence (discussed in the next section). Further, the proportion of midlife women in the workforce increased dramatically over the past three decades. By 1997, almost 80% of women aged 35 to 44 and over 75% of women aged 45 to 54 were employed, up substantially in the past 30 years (U.S. Bureau of Labor Statistics, 1997). Certainly the sandwich-generation scenario of being subjected to increasing cross-pressures on available time and energy seems plausible (Uhlenberg, 1993).

These dependency demands are at their highest during midlife. But is this portrayal true? Could it be that "the sandwich generation" is another "hydra-headed myth," as Ethel Shanas (1979) termed the misconception that American elderly are isolated from and abandoned by their children?

In the years since Brody's influential publications, there has been considerable debate over the extent of caregiver burden experienced by the sandwich generation, and indeed over the validity of the phenomenon itself. What is clear is that when elder care is needed, it often falls to kin at midlife to provide the tangible and emotional support that is needed. But are they sandwiched in? Until recently, there has not been adequate data by which to accurately determine the demographic potential and actual needs and exchange patterns between the generations in the family lineage that would allow us to make a judgment (Soldo, 1996; Uhlenberg, 1993). Most empirical data have been derived from nonrepresentative or local probability samples, or simulation models.

Recent studies have challenged the truth of a sandwich generation by asking: (1) For those currently at midlife, what is the demographic likelihood of experiencing the overlapping dependencies of parents, children, grandchildren? What is the sandwiched-in potential for the next cohort of midlife individuals? (2) How frequently does a potential sandwich situation become reality? (Bengtson, Rosenthal, & Burton, 1995). That is, what is the incidence and prevalence of occupying three or more roles simultaneously. Beyond looking at single points in time, what is the lifetime exposure of providing care to parents, children, or grandparents and grandchildren? (3) Are multiple roles necessarily stressful? Just how much pressure is generated on midlife adult children by their aging parents, and by the demands of children or adult children whether or not in the same household? Or can multiple care commitments also be satisfying? Rather than casting parent care as only burdensome, as a "normative stress," can parent care also be gratifying? Does employment add to the stress, or perhaps under some conditions does having a job mitigate the stress of competing family roles?

WHAT DO WE MEAN BY "SANDWICHED IN?"

Research on the sandwich-generation dilemma has focused on the issues of multiple role occupancy in the active provision of care to parents and children, in combination with the employee role, and their effects on well-being (Rosenthal, Martin-Matthews, & Matthews, 1996). If the commonsense notion of the sandwich generation is to be empirically tested, several methodological issues must be addressed. How broadly should we define the role configurations? In addition to elderly parent and midlife adult child caregiver, what other family roles should be included—for example, spouse, grandchild, grandparent, daughter-in-law? How should role enactment be measured? Provision of help to parents can be measured by type, volume, intensity, duration, or any combination of these (Martin-Matthews & Rosenthal, 1993). The broader the definition of help, the higher the estimate of the extent of helping (Gerstel & Gallagher, 1993).

How Do We Define Role Conflict?

What constitutes sufficient pressures, or hours of caretaking, to be considered sandwiched in (Bengtson et al., 1995)? Few studies on caregiving have addressed the broader aspects of assistance and exchange between generations. Might fulfillment of role responsibilities mean more than direct care—for example, socioemotional support, time, financial assistance, living space—and the trade-offs, both short and long term? The need to provide family caregiving can have multiple and reverberating employment, financial, and relationship implications. Caregiving commitments may compromise careers, financial resources, deflect money from retirement savings to pay for college tuition (Soldo, 1996). Marriage and other family relations must be renegotiated to accommodate the needs of elderly parents, or claims of dependent children or grandchildren. Soldo suggests broadening the "woman(or man) in the middle" conceptualization by situating parent care among the various intergenerational exchanges within the extended family, including siblings. This can provide a better estimation of ". . . the sheer volume of competing demands on adults children and provide insights into the division of labor within a family or the distribution of burden across midlife adults linked by blood or marriage" (p. S272).

In sum, the sandwich-generation debate revolves around two issues: first, multiple role occupancies and their demographic potential; second, whether multiple roles have negative consequences for well-being (Goode, 1960), or have positive consequences by providing benefits, such as gratification or feelings of self-efficacy or as a buffer for the stress from other roles (Thoits, 1986).

The Potential for Being Sandwiched In

In considering the structural opportunities for being sandwiched in, demographers have examined the prevalence of three-, four- and five-generation families, and the extent to which the age structures of generations align to present the midlife generation with a potential for concurrent care obligations to children and elderly parents (Uhlenberg, 1993). Data from the 1992–1994 National Survey of Families and Households show that for those at midlife ages 50 to 54, nearly 74% have a family containing at least three generations, and about 40% have four-generation families (Soldo, 1996). While these data show there is little generational overlap at a point when both elderly parents and children of middle-aged adults are likely to need care, parent care could coincide with the launching of young adult children, and at older ages, parent care may coincide with care commitments to grandchildren (Soldo, 1996; Szinovacz, 1998).

Rosenthal et al. (1996) suggest that the experience of being sandwiched in between being the adult child of elderly parents, the parent to dependent children, and employed worker is not typical. While 22% of women and 12% of men provided at least one type of help to a parent monthly, no more than 8% of women or men provide parent care while also having a dependent child and working. The authors conclude that the incidence of these Canadian midlife adult children actually being sandwiched in by competing responsibilities is relatively small. It should be noted that their measurement of help provided does not include emotional support, which is what most elderly say they need (Brody, 1985). Further, although the research is based on a national sample, the data are cross-sectional. In another study, Marks (1998) found that about one in eight employed, midlife adults reported they had given personal care for one month or more to a disabled or frail relative or friend during the past year and that overall by age 54 one in three had provided this type of care at some point in the past. The majority of midlife adults were not found to be sandwiched in at any one point by competing dependency and employment claims. Nevertheless, the experience of competing demands is not minor and should not be underestimated (Marks, 1998). When multiple role demands do occur, their effect can be severe (Rosenthal et al., 1996).

While much attention has focused on middle aged individuals who are sandwiched between the dependency needs of elderly parents and offspring, having concurrent responsibilities for old parents and *grandchildren* is typically overlooked (Szinovacz, 1998). Generally, the onset of grandparenthood occurs in midlife when individuals are in their 40s or 50s (Uhlenberg, 1996). More importantly in terms of the issue of being sandwiched in, the interval between the birth of an individual's last child and the first grandchild is typically less than 18 years. Therefore, the majority of grandparents will experience some overlap of active parenting and grandparenting, increasing the potential for experiencing concurrent caregiving responsibilities (Szinovacz, 1998).

ARE MULTIPLE ROLES STRESSFUL?

Issues of role overload or role enhancement become especially salient for those in midlife who add parent caregiving to their other roles as spouse, parent, or grandparent, and paid worker (Penning, 1998). There are three perspectives. The *role strain* hypothesis proposes that there is a fixed

quantity of time, energy, and commitment available for role-related responsibilities (Goode, 1960) and that multiple roles compete for the limited time and resources of the caregiver and cause psychological distress
(Brody, 1981, 1985). The *role enhancement* hypothesis holds that occupying
multiple roles is beneficial for caregivers wherein other roles provide supportive resources and respite, or buffer against other stresses (Hong &
Seltzer, 1995; Thoits, 1986). Alternatively, Moen, Robison, and Demptster-
McClain (1995) draw on a life course, *role context* perspective. Rather than
assuming caregiving is invariably stressful, or in fact is beneficial, this
approach suggests there is no simple or straightforward relationship between being a caregiver and psychological well-being. Moen et al. found
that family roles have remained highly salient for most women, although
increasing numbers are entering or remaining in the labor force. Earlier
experiences in previous roles and resources affect whether the midlife individual with multiple family caregiving and employment roles will feel
stressed. Timing matters; occupying the caregiving role positively relates
to mastery for women in their 50s and 60s but not those in their late 60s
and 70s. Regarding employment, women who are currently working and
have been caregivers are better off in terms of their psychological well-
being than those who are not employed. On the other hand, extended
caregiving has negative effects on married women's emotional health.
Hence, for women caregivers particular role combinations may have positive effects, such as caregiving and employment, and other combinations
may negatively affect well-being, such as caregiving and marriage.

Other research findings are mixed but demonstrate the usefulness of a
contextual approach. Spitze, Logan, Joseph, and Lee (1994) examined the
effects of various combinations of middle generation roles (adult child,
parent of adult child, paid work, spouse, parent of younger children) on
measures of psychological well-being (distress and life satisfaction) as
well as perceived family burden. For women, they found no evidence that
combining roles had any consequences for well-being—positive or negative. The effect of multiple role occupancy on men appears to be mixed.
For men, more help to parents increased their distress, but this was lessened when combined with employment. On the other hand, help to adult
children in combination with help to parents decreased men's life satisfaction. Perhaps women did not suffer negative consequences from the
multiple roles of parent care and child care because of their greater experience of juggling various family and work roles in the past. This research
does not support the notion that middle-aged men and women are sandwiched in by the overwhelming cross-pressures of family and work roles.
Rather, helping adult children appears to be rewarding and helping parents at the low levels found in the general population causes little distress
(Spitze et al., 1994).

More recently, Penning (1998) examined the implications of concurrent roles of spouse, parent, and paid workers for the perceived stress and physical and emotional health of parental caregivers. Supporting other studies, findings indicate that being caught in the middle of roles as caregiver to an older parent, parent to children and paid work is not a normative experience for middle-aged adults. However, adult children who are actually involved in parent care usually have other role commitments as well. Penning's findings offer only limited support to either role strain hypothesis or the competing role enhancement hypothesis and direct our attention to the meanings of various roles and their context. Marks (1998) found the caregiving role for those at midlife is not harmful to psychological well-being overall. Caregiving for immediate family members is associated with more psychological distress for employed midlife women, and midlife employed men who care for a disabled spouse experience poorer psychological well-being. These effects are largely attenuated once an adjustment is made for work-family conflicts. In fact, beneficial suppressed effects of caregiving on well-being emerge once work-family conflicts are held constant across caregiving and noncaregiving employed adults. Overall, these studies indicate the psychological health effects of occupying concurrent roles are small, suggesting that multiple role occupancy per se may not consistently affect the perceived well-being of parental caregivers.

The conclusions to be drawn here are that a majority of midlife adults are not sandwiched between the competing demands of caregiving to children and older parents, and employment (although some are). Brody's (1985) claims of caregiving as normative stress cannot be empirically supported (Loomis & Booth, 1995; Marks, 1998; Moen et al., 1995; Penning, 1998; Rosenthal et al., 1996; Spitze et al., 1994; Uhlenberg, 1993). Greater attention should be focused on the attitudes and subjective meanings people bring to their roles as well as the context within which these roles are enacted. But as has often been pointed out, the findings of scholarly research can fall on deaf ears and have little influence on popularly held myths, such as the beleaguered sandwich generation (Loomis & Booth, 1995) and the unbearable burden of parent care. What is unclear is whether the myth of the sandwich generation will have more validity for the upcoming cohorts of adult children who will bring very different work and family life experiences and expectations to their midlife roles.

PROLONGED PARENTING

Prolonged parenthood—when children remain home longer than expected, or don't leave, or return to the "empty nest" not because of their parents' needs but because of their own economic needs—has become a significant challenge in intergenerational relations at midlife.

A normatively prescribed midlife transition for parents is the successful launching of children from the parental home into responsible adulthood. Changing expectations and behaviors during this period require that parents and children negotiate a new relationship. Their relationship often becomes more peerlike (A. Rossi & Rossi, 1990). There may be disagreements or conflict as young adults move through the process of becoming independent and autonomous (Dunham & Bengtson, 1991). Recently, the timing of this life course transition has moved out and become more fluid, the boundaries of active parenting less clear.

In addressing the issue of prolonged parenting, we employ a life-course perspective that emphasizes the importance of transitions and their timing, the interdependence of lives, and the structural and historical contexts within which individuals are constrained and make choices (Bengtson & Allen, 1993; Elder, 1995). Drawing on the coresidency and home-leaving literature, three trends are evident: the recent increase in age at first leaving home; the changed reasons for leaving home; and the increased incidence of returning home. Less obvious are the cases where a transition did not occur—adult children who never left their parents' home. We also discuss a special case of prolonged parenting, the growing phenomenon of grandparents raising grandchildren.

It is instructive to examine the historical and cultural background of the prolonged parenting phenomenon. The completion of child rearing is a key transition in the adult life course, but its timing shifted during the last century. As with other major transition in adulthood—marriage, becoming a parent, retirement—its timing became increasingly sequenced and uniform. Specific age norms rather than the less structured or idiosyncratic needs of families came to regulate transition timing and duration, hence defining a "life course" (Hareven, 1996; Kohli, 1986). During the twentieth century, the life course became more segmented, its phases more differentiated; its patterning became institutionalized (Kohli, 1986). One consequence was that by mid-century the empty nest phase emerged for parents at midlife because age norms now specified a narrower time frame for childbearing, schooling, and exit from home (Hareven, 1996). In the past decade, however, there have been signs that the strict timing patterns of life course transitions are becoming more flexible and disordered (Bengtson & Dannefer, 1987; Hareven, 1996; Kohli, 1986). One manifestation is that the period of parenting has been extended. This new phenomenon has been called "the cluttered nest"; The returning adult children have been referred to as the "boomerang generation."

What are some micro- and macro-level factors that might account for home leaving or home returning? Is prolonged parenting disruptive or disappointing for midlife parents—or beneficial and satisfying? Has the "launching phase" been transformed into a new phase in the family life cycle? Scabini and Cigoli (1997) think so, coining the term "ongoing young adult families" to denote a period of coresidence of two adult generations. What does this all mean for intergenerational relationships in the future?

TRENDS IN CORESIDENCY AND NEST LEAVING

Over the past century, intergenerational coresidence, in particular where older parents and/or young adult children coreside with the middle generation nuclear family, declined in the United States and other developed countries (Goldscheider, 1997; Ruggles, 1996). In considering this trend, it is important to distinguish between coresidency with aging parents when help flows from middle-aged adult children to parents in need, and coresidency with young adult children in the midlife parents' home when help flows down the generational lineage. Historically, coresidence was a strategy for meeting the disability needs of aging parents. However, trends have now shifted the attention to young adult children and their needs. For those at midlife, parenting responsibilities have been extended.

In the United States and much of Europe, living outside the family setting in early adulthood only became common in the late 1960s. At the same time, leaving home for marriage has declined significantly over the past few decades (Goldscheider, 1997). Beginning about 1980, demographers noted a shift: The age of nest leaving began to increase in the developed countries. While it is still normative for young adults to leave their parents' home and establish independent residences before marriage (Goldscheider, 1997; Ward & Spitze, 1996), recent cohorts have delayed leaving and are increasingly returning to the family home during periods of economic hardship or marital problems. It is estimated that about 40% of recent cohorts of young adults have returned home after some period away (Goldscheider & Goldscheider, 1994). Those who leave to marry continue to be less likely to return. Those who leave to seek independence, including those who leave for cohabiting relationships, are more likely to return than was the case for previous cohorts. The never married are the most likely to move back into the parental home (Goldscheider & Goldscheider, 1993). Approximately half of coresiding adult children have *never* left home (Crimmins & Ingegneri, 1990).

The 1987–1988 National Survey of Families and Households indicates that 30% to 40% of parents aged 40 to 60 and 15% of those 60 and over coreside with adult children (Aquilino, 1990; Ward & Spitze, 1992, 1996). Ward and Spitze (1992) believe these cross-sectional views understate the lifetime prevalence of grown children coresiding with parents. Coresidence is dominated by unmarried, especially never-married, children, and typically involves parental households (Aquilino, 1990; Crimmins & Ingegneri,

1990, Goldscheider & Goldscheider, 1994). Recent research has found that it is the characteristics and needs of adult children that account for coresidence with middle-aged and older parents (White & Rogers, 1997). As a result of trends in delayed and aborted nest leaving, young adults receive a significant amount of parental support from midlife parents, both tangible and emotional, over a longer period. It is a stream of assistance that does not shift in the other direction until quite late in parents' lives, when the parents finally become net recipients, rather than net donors, of intergenerational transfers (Bengtson & Harootyan, 1994; Eggebeen & Hogan, 1990; A. Rossi & Rossi, 1990).

Factors Contributing to Home Leaving

The life course perspective calls attention to the economic, social, and historical changes over the twentieth century that have differentially affected the timing of nest leaving for different cohorts of young adults. Periods of economic decline can infringe on the ability of young adults to establish independent lives. Wars have caused young adults to leave their parents' home and delay schooling and marriage . The relatively prosperous, profamilist 1950s promoted early nest leaving through marriage (Goldscheider & Goldscheider, 1998).

In the United States, increased parental divorce and remarriage is one of the most important factors affecting the timing of young adults' departure from the parental home (Goldscheider, 1997; Marks, 1995). Disruption of the parental home and changes in family structure affect the resources parents can invest in their children as well as patterns of relating, which in turn may promote early home leaving. White and Lacy (1997) found that age at leaving home and the pathway from home have long-term consequences for children's educational attainment. Adult children benefit, particularly in terms of educational attainment, from continued parental sponsorship or coresidence into their early or mid-20s. They suggest that today both parents and children have unreasonable expectations about the age when adult children can be independent. Another parental influence on adult-child coresidence is parents' income, which can either promote leaving at later ages or discourage early departure.

To understand the nature and extent of filial responsibility in multigenerational families and their potential for providing support to one another, researchers have proposed alternate hypotheses to account for the changing patterns of coresidence. The *affluence perspective* states that increased financial resources allowed previously dependent kin to live independently because they now have the means to do so (Goldscheider & Lawton, 1998). But living independently does not mean there is a lack of willingness to assist family members if needed. Reflecting the cultural values of independence and autonomy in the United States, this desire for privacy and living outside the nuclear family is seen as positive; in economic terms, a normal good (McGarry & Schoeni, 1999). From the affluence perspective, coresidence has declined because it is no longer economically necessary. In fact, among the widowed over 65, there was a dramatic increase in the number living alone in the twentieth century and a corresponding decrease in the number living with family members. McGarry and Schoeni found this can be largely accounted for by the creation and expansion of Social Security. This does not mean that close relatives have backed off from a commitment to offer housing should the need arise. The affluence perspective implies that felt obligations to help family members in need has not declined.

⚫The second perspective argues that *changes in preference* for independent living may be as important as affluence in accounting for the declines in intergenerational coresidence (Ruggles, 1996). This implies that felt obligations to provide housing to family members in need have in fact weakened, and more generally, norms of filial obligation have declined over time. For young adults, coresidency infers failure to achieve autonomy, a key marker of the individualistic life. Affluence and preference may interact as well in that choices for independent living made possible by financial resources then reinforce the preference for privacy over interdependence (Goldscheider & Lawton, 1998).

CORESIDENCE AND PARENT-ADULT CHILD RELATIONS: DISAPPOINTING? SATISFYING? OR BOTH?

As noted, there is considerable research on the demographic and life course aspects of adult child-parent coresidence in the parental home. Less is known about the quality of their relationship and how it is affected by the coresidence experience. Do the economic and instrumental benefits of coresidence come at the expense of feelings of closeness and affection between parents and adult children? What are the implications of prior relationship quality for experiencing a satisfying coresidential relationship? And, are the effects of coresidence different for adult children than for their parents?

The findings are varied, conditioned by context, age of the adult child, and whether the adult child left and returned home, or never left. In a study of parents of adult children who resided in the parental home, Aquilino and Supple (1991) found generally high parent satisfaction and positive parent-child interactions. There were also some strains. These are often associated with frustrated expectations about the timing of leaving home and independence, particularly among adult children. Coresidence may be stressful because it is nonnormative in terms of the expectations of both parents and children, and because it implies the grown child's failure to successfully transition to adult occupational and family roles. Coresidence is more likely to intensify parent-child relations and the potential for conflict over money, household tasks, values and lifestyles (Ward & Spitze, 1992). At the same time, there is some indication among younger cohorts that the norms prescribing an independent household as a sign of successfully transitioning to adulthood may be weakening (Alwin, 1996).

As suggested by the intergenerational stake hypothesis (Giarrusso, Stallings, & Bengtson, 1995), there are differences in how parents and adult-children perceive their coresidential situation, with parents generally more positive than their adult children. For example, Spitze et al. (1994) found that for men, helping adult children increased life satisfaction when there were also coresident adult children. On the other hand. White and Rogers (1997) found that coresident young adults report somewhat lower affection toward their parents even though they give, receive, and perceive more support from their parents than nonresident children. Adult children are less satisfied with coresidence arrangements than their parents and expect shorter stays than their parents, even though coresidence in the parental home primarily reflects the needs of the younger generation. This may reflect different expectations concerning the tasks of achieving autonomy in young adulthood, with adult children experiencing greater strain than parents over exchanges in shared households. Ward and Spitze (1992) suggest that as coresident adult children grow older and the early adult norms regulating home-leaving become less salient, parents may have more positive feelings concerning the coresident relationship. Also, with time and age, parents and adult children can negotiate more positive and mutually satisfying relationships

As children reach adulthood, selection may become increasingly important in determining the quality of their coresident relationship. Having a close, supportive parent-child relationship in the past may increase the likelihood of a positive coresidence relationship. In some research, coresident adult children's well-being is shown to be strongly related to parents' reports of past relationship quality (Amato, Loomis, & Booth, 1995). But in a longitudinal analysis, White and Rogers (1997) found that the quality of prior family relationships has little effect on either the likelihood of coresidence or on children's perceptions of the coresident relationship. The authors suggest the important factors in accounting for coresidence may be the young adult's need and the parents' feelings of obligation, not necessarily feelings of closeness.

Goldscheider and Lawton (1998) found significant ethnic differences in attitudes toward intergenerational coresidence, with every group more supportive than White, nonfundamentalist Protestants. Hispanics and non-Hispanic Catholics are most supportive of both kinds of coresidence (aging parent and grown children). Attitudes among Blacks toward coresidence are more ambiguous in that their family structure has become more rather than less extended over the past several decades (Ruggles, 1996). Preferences are confounded with other determinants of coresidence such as inadequate resources and need for assistance.

GRANDPARENTS RAISING GRANDCHILDREN

As a special case of prolonged parenting, grandparents raising grandchildren has become an important—and unexpected—midlife challenge for many. In a nationally representative sample, using the grandparent as the reference, as many as 30% of Black grandmothers, 19% of Hispanic grandmothers, and 12% of White grandmothers have been surrogate parents for a grandchild at some point in their lives (Szinovacz, 1998). The number of grandchildren in the care of grandparents has risen dramatically over the past 30 years. By 1997, almost 4 million grandchildren were coresiding with head-of-household grandparents, representing more than one in 20 children in the United States (U.S. Census, 1999). Often grandparents become surrogate parents when the middle generation is disabled or otherwise unable to fulfill parental obligations (often due to drug addiction, AIDS-related illness and death, incarceration, divorce, and impoverishment)—the so-called skipped generation. Grandparents' care of grandchildren puts increased pressure on some older Americans' physical and financial resources.

HOME-LEAVING AND PROLONGED PARENTING: CROSS-CULTURAL COMPARISONS

The recent increase in the average age at leaving home is not unique to the United States, but has been observed in most Western nations since the early 1980s. In Europe and the United States, labor market conditions and youth unemployment in the past 15 years are seen as the most important factors in prolonging adult children's coresidence with midlife parents (Cherlin, Scabini, & Rossi, 1997). A corollary is the belief by parents and their children that an extended period of education is now needed, delaying the transition to adult autonomy. The norms and behaviors concerning marriage, cohabitation, and childbearing/rearing outside marriage also affect coresidency patterns. Goldscheider (1997) shows how these patterns interact with the labor market, employment policies, and youth employment prospects to explain national differences in delayed home leaving—whether adult children move to nonfamily, independent living arrangements (more typical of France, Germany, The Netherlands, and the United States), or remain in the parental home until forming a new family (as in Italy and Spain). Age at marriage has been pushed back in all of Western Europe as it has in the United States, due in part to unfavorable economic conditions, but also to marriage's apparent loss of value (Cherlin, 1999; G. Rossi, 1997).

In the southern European countries of Greece, Spain, and Italy, 65% of men ages 25 to 29 and 44% of women ages 25 to 29 live with their parents (Cordon, 1997). Examining the Italian patterns of nest leaving, Scabini and Cigoli (1997) found that the parents' generation continues for years to sustain its children until they decide to leave home, thereby lengthening the life cycle of the family. Italy may be unique; youth unemployment is especially high, a consequence of employment policies favoring the jobs and wages of those currently employed, that is, midlife parents. A pattern of nonfamily living has not developed in Italy (or Spain) as it has in western and northern European countries. This conditions the parent-adult child relationship in Italy, engendering the family's protective function and prolonging the parental role. In fact, parents play an active role in *delaying* their children leaving home (Scabini & Cigoli, 1997). Italian parents are portrayed as quite happy to have their adult children live with them and would find separation difficult.

In the European countries studied, the authors found that adult children's relationships with parents are generally positive, making coresidence more likely and attractive (Galland, 1997; Scabini & Cigoli, 1997). Today's young adults, raised in more egalitarian homes, have more positive relations with their midlife parents than young adults did even 30 years ago and less reason to leave home. In France, Galland found changes in employment and schooling accounted for half the extended stay of young adult children in the family home. The other half is explained by more favorable attitudes toward staying in the family home. In Italy and France, the mother appears to play the central relational role; her role is more esteemed when adult children remain dependent, whether unemployed or coresiding (Galland, 1997; Scabini & Cigoli, 1997.)

Recent data in the United States show that since the 1980s there has been some increase in age at leaving home. Among those ages 25 to 29, 20% of men and 12% of women are living at home (the figures are comparable for Germany, France, The Netherlands, and Great Britain). The more noteworthy shift is the large increase in young adults leaving home to live independently and the concomitant decrease in home leaving to get married. But this new living arrangement is tenuous, and the likelihood of young adults returning home increased dramatically in the past decade (Goldscheider, 1997).

INTERGENERATIONAL CORESIDENCE PREFERENCES REVISITED

While the long-term trend in U.S. attitudes toward family obligations and intergenerational coresidence has become more individualistic, there is some evidence suggesting a return toward more familistic values, at least among the younger cohorts. Using national data, Alwin (1996) examined attitudes toward coresidence between 1973 to 1991 and found overall a gradual shift toward greater approval of coresidence. Further, it is the more recent cohorts (born after 1940) that are more favorable to the idea of intergenerational coresidence, while the earlier-born cohorts are significantly less favorable. Also, younger cohorts have higher levels of contact with kin than older cohorts, and contact with kin is positively associated with endorsement of subjective norms of coresidence. Alwin suggests young adults may be more favorable toward living with their parents because it is more likely the parents are helping to support the younger generation. The family provides an important safety net when things go wrong.

And for those in midlife, parenting continues. The interesting question is, does this portend a shift toward greater interdependence among generations? It may be that delayed departure from the parental home or returning after attempting to establish an independent residence, as is now occurring, may positively affect intergenerational relations in the future by increasing interpersonal contacts and investments in parent-child relationships now.

INTERGENERATIONAL SOLIDARITY AND CONFLICT IN MIDLIFE

Are the roles and norms of intergenerational relations in midlife changing? Has this resulted in more conflict—and have family bonds been weakened? These are a few of the multiple challenges to intergenerational solidarity for today's middle-aged baby boomer family members. In addressing these issues, we are faced with an apparent paradox. In the context of the multigenerational family, are solidarity and conflict polar opposites, with high solidarity by definition reflective of low conflict? Or, can family relations be both cohesive and conflictual at the same time, as suggested by Bengtson (2001). Here we examine midlife generational issues using the family solidarity model and consider the paradox of both solidarity and conflict in family relationships over time.

INTERGENERATIONAL RELATIONS: A RESEARCH AGENDA

One consequence of longevity increases for multigenerational families has been longer periods of cosurvivorship, thus providing more opportunity for parents, adult children, grandparents and grandchildren to positively relate and support each other than ever before (Bengtson, 2001). But will they? We have to look deeper. What accounts for the cohesiveness of a family, or its resilience when faced with troubles? Why do families hold together and persist across time? And in what ways do strong intergenerational bonds promote individual family members' well-being?

Increasingly, studies are examining the quality of intergenerational relationships—why some families get along better than others, what conditions contributed to greater satisfaction, more affection, and less tension in the relationship (Clarke, Preston, Raksin, & Bengtson, 1999; Levitt, Guacci, & Weber, 1992; Marks, 1995; Pyke & Bengtson, 1996; Richards, Bengtson, & Miller, 1989; Whitbeck, Hoyt, & Huck, 1994). As longer lives increase the duration of shared lives as well as role occupancy in multi-generational families, such as grandparenthood, such questions take on new importance.

Over the past quarter century, the Longitudinal Study of Generations (LSOG) has attempted to answer these questions through the development and application of a theory of intergenerational solidarity (Roberts, Richards, & Bengtson, 1991; Silverstein & Bengtson, 1997). The LSOG, which began in 1971, is a study of linked members from some 300 three- and four-generation families as they have grown up and grown old during a period of dramatic social and economic change. Now with six waves of data, the LSOG examines long-term relationships between parents and children, (and grandparents and grandchildren) as they change over time, and their consequences for the well-being of family members over several generations. A specific focus has been on the theoretical and methodological explication of the structure of intergenerational relations. The intergenerational solidarity paradigm represents one of the few long-term efforts to develop a theory-driven, empirically tested model of family relationships over time. For over 25 years, the intergenerational solidarity paradigm has guided research on the aging family (e.g., Silverstein & Bengtson, 1997; Silverstein, Giarrusso, & Bengtson, 1998). In a multitude of studies, the strength of bonds—over time—between adult children and parents, and more recently grandparents and grandchildren (and soon to include great-grandparents) has been assessed.

Intergenerational Solidarity as a Metaconstruct

In its classical formulation (Durkheim, 1893/1984), group solidarity, or group cohesiveness, refers to the structural means or "glue" by which individuals are integrated within groups. Recognizing that families, as special instances of groups, differ from one another on the basis of cohesiveness, researchers have applied this concept to contemporary intergenerational relationships to assess and explain the principal sentiments and behaviors that link family members across generations (Roberts & Bengtson, 1990; Roberts et al., 1991).

Intergenerational solidarity is conceptualized as a metaconstruct with six distinct but interrelated dimensions: (1) affectual solidarity (the degree of emotional closeness and sentiment between generations); (2) consensual solidarity (the amount of intergenerational similarity or agreement in beliefs and values, seen as a primary source of intergenerational and societal continuity); (3) associational solidarity (the frequency of intergenerational contact and shared activities and time); (4) functional solidarity (the help and support that is exchanged between the generations, both emotional and instrumental support); (5) normative solidarity (the perceptions of obligations and expectations about intergenerational connections and assistance); and (6) structural solidarity (the opportunity structure for interactions, including such factors as family size and composition, geographic proximity, marital status, gender, age, ethnicity, and health). While there may be alternate ways to characterize the cognitive-emotional and behavioral interactions between parents and children, or grandparents and grandchildren, the dimensions of intergenerational solidarity can be theoretically and empirically supported (see Mangen, Bengtson, & Landry, 1988). To adequately describe intergenerational relationships, it is necessary to consider these several dimensions simultaneously, to determine whether they are latent or active, and to assess their potential for enactment in times of need (Silverstein & Bengtson, 1997). For example, functional exchanges may be intermittent over the life course, depending on the needs of each generation. Such forms of solidarity are crucially important when triggered and usually have latent forms of solidarity as their antecedents—affectual and normative solidarity (Silverstein & Bengtson, 1997).

Understanding the structural relationship among the dimensions of intergenerational solidarity is predictive of the prospects of receiving family support in old age. Lawton, Silverstein, and Bengtson (1994) examined the predictors and causal relationships of the solidarity dimensions of affection, association, and proximity. They demonstrated that the dimensions are interrelated that for women, but not for men, affection and association are reciprocal, and that parent's marital status was one of the most consistent predictors across the dimensions. Findings suggest that father-adult child bonds are more conditional than mother-adult child bonds and may be especially vulnerable when there is a divorce, which can lower the divorced father's reserves of family support when he becomes elderly. This analysis corresponds to other research findings concerning the negative effects of divorce, parental as well as the child's, on the quality of the adult child-parent relationships (Kaufman & Uhlenberg, 1998; Marks, 1995; Uhlenberg, 1993).

A TYPOLOGY OF THE STRUCTURE OF MULTIGENERATIONAL FAMILIES

Guided by the intergenerational solidarity model, Silverstein and Bengtson (1997) developed an empirically based multidimensional classification system of adult intergenerational relations, using a nationally representative sample. Five types of extended families are identified: tight-knit (25.5%), sociable (25.5%), intimate-but-distant (16%), obligatory (16%), and detached (17%). No one type is dominant, demonstrating the diversity of American family forms and styles. This methodology allows for the simultaneous contrasting of several dimensions of solidarity—some congruent, others discordant—and represents a more sophisticated approach toward understanding the greater complexity and contradictions of today's family configurations and attachments. As this study shows, gender matters in family relationships. In the analysis, family types are differentiated based on whether the adult child's relationship is with the mother or the father. Silverstein and Bengtson found that mother-adult child solidarity is stronger than that of father and adult child, a result consistent with other research findings concerning the strength of the maternal axis in intergenerational relations (Hagestad, 1985; A. Rossi & Rossi, 1990). On the affection dimension alone, 73% of adult children feel close to mothers while 57% feel close to fathers. Further,.divorced fathers have weaker emotional attachment with their adult children compared with married fathers, or compared with divorced mothers. The effect of parental divorce on the odds of having detached relations is about five times greater with fathers than it is with mothers. For adult child-mother relationships, the most common type is tight-knit (31%), and the least common is the detached type (7%). In contrast, for adult child-father relations, the most common type is detached (27%) while the least common is intimate-but-distant (14%).

Strong ethnic variations emerged. Blacks and Hispanics are less likely than non-Hispanic Whites to have obligatory relationships with mothers, and Blacks are less likely than Whites to have detached relationships (Silverstein & Bengtson, 1997). This corresponds to other research, which has found stronger maternal attachments in Black and Hispanic families than in White families (Burton, 1995; Taylor & Chatters, 1991).

An important research objective (Bengtson, 2001) has been to test the "demise of the family" thesis of Popenoe (1993). Silverstein and Bengtson (1997) demonstrate that while there is significant diversity among American families across the dimensions of solidarity, most do possess the latent solidarity resources needed to evoke intergenerational support and assistance in times of need. This study found latent kin attachment is an important characteristic of intergenerational relations, a fact overlooked by the "family values" contingent in their pronouncements of family disintegration (Silverstein & Bengtson, 1997). In fact, intergenerational family relations are alive and well. Analyses of 26 years of LSOG data on multigenerational families has found that about two thirds of parent-child relations consistently reflect high levels of intergenerational solidarity over time.

GRANDPARENT-GRANDCHILDREN RELATIONSHIPS

Several studies of grandparent-grandchild relationships have demonstrated the relevance and usefulness of the intergenerational solidarity framework (Silverstein et al., 1998). For example, in a longitudinal analysis of grandparent-grandchild relationships, Silverstein and Long (1998) found that contact and proximity declined over time while affection increased, suggesting a tendency for emotional attachments of family relationships to be independent of structural dimensions of family solidarity. Further, when compared at the same age, later born cohorts of grandparents exhibit steeper declines in contact and proximity over time than earlier born grandparents, even though there has been little change in the median age of grandparents during the century. One implication is that the grandparent role has changed in recent history. This seems plausible given the greater wealth, earlier retirement, and better health among more contemporary grandparents (many in midlife), which provides opportunity for alternative social roles (Silverstein & Long, 1998). While this suggests a cohort effect, the intergenerational solidarity construct is sufficiently broad to adequately describe and explicate the underlying structures and processes of the grandparent-grandchild relationship.

As described by Silverstein et al. (1998), the solidarity framework can address several unique aspects of the grandparent role: (1) its normative ambiguity; (2) the fact that grandparent-grandchild relations are mediated by the middle generation, with crucial implications for the strength or weakness of the grandparent-grandchild relationship when parents divorce, depending on custody arrangements; (3) the wider array of competing roles enacted by grandparents than in years past; and (4) the normative contradictions faced by grandparents—the norm of noninterference, and the norm of familial obligation and support. This dilemma is particularly evident in the case of the surrogate parenting of grandchildren.

INTERGENERATIONAL RELATIONS AS CONFLICT

The application of conflict principles to intergenerational relations has been less frequent, in part due to conceptual and operational difficulties (Clarke et al., 1999). Conflict theorists see an inherent paradox in families in that they demonstrate tendencies toward conflict, competition, and disagreement as well as order, stability, and cooperation toward others (Bengtson et al., 1995; Lüescher & Pillemer, 1998).

How is conflict to be defined? According to Straus (1979), conflict may refer to: (1) the collision of individuals' agendas and interests; (2) individuals' tactics or responses to conflicts of interest; or (3) hostility toward others. Conflict is not just a component of behavior, but also a state of relational being (Clarke et al., 1999). In its early stages of theoretical development, intergenerational solidarity was conceptualized as a unidimensional construct (Roberts & Bengtson, 1990). Solidarity and conflict were seen as located on a continuum. Focus was on the positive aspects of interaction, cohesion, sentiment, and support between parents and children or grandparents and grandchildren; intergenerational conflict was seen as their negative, conflictual, or nonaffirming aspects (Bengtson, 1996; Roberts et al., 1991). Subsequent research has shown that intergenerational solidarity is multidimensional and that conflict can coexist with one or more dimensions of solidarity. For example, one can experience high levels of filial obligation and have frequent contact with parents, but also have negative sentiments toward parents or experience anger and frustration in the relationship. Elder abuse by a coresident adult child in the caregiving situation may be the most extreme instance of the contradictions of family solidarity and conflict (Pillemer & Suitor, 1992). That solidarity is multidimensional—its components distinct and nonadditive yet interrelated—precludes a simple specification of conflict as its mirror opposite. "Long-term lousy relationships" have been found to characterize about one in eight adult intergenerational relationships in the LSOG sample (Bengtson, 1996). Our thinking now is that conflict is a quite different and theoretically orthogonal dimension of intergenerational relations (Bengtson et al., 1995). Solidarity and conflict are both aspects of intimate relationships and inevitably part of the interactions between and within generations over time. If this is so, then the more intriguing question is—and remains—how and why do families cohere and persist?

Lüescher and Pillemer (1998) argue against a solidarity-versus-conflict view of intergenerational relations. In a review of the adequacy of the solidarity paradigm, they note this research tradition has emphasized social roles, shared values across generations, normative obligations to provide help, and enduring ties between parents and children. In their view, what has been ignored is the presence of both positive and negative forces that are always operating in intergenerational relationships. What is also needed are analyses of intergenerational relations as dynamic structures of norms and counternorms, or conflicting structural situations and demands. They posit that a theory of ambivalence may better account for the observed complexity and fluidity of today's family structures and relationship processes. However, research using the solidarity paradigm has *not* neglected conflict in intergenerational relations. Several studies have examined the apparent contradictions of solidarity and conflict in families, some of which are discussed here.

A special challenge to midlife parents is the renegotiation of dependency issues with adolescent children as they press for autonomy in preparation for leaving the parental nest. During this time, family ties may be strained, solidarity in doubt. Intense conflict is not inevitable, however. Rueter and Conger (1995) tested a theory stating that the level of parent-adolescent conflict is determined by the family context. They hypothesized that interaction styles learned in the family of origin and transmitted to the next generation are an important moderator of later intergenerational bonds. In a warm and supportive family environment, disagreements can be negotiated to keep conflict at low or moderate levels. There is some suggestion that the open airing of disagreement can be adaptive in that problem-solving skills and self development are promoted while family bonds are maintained. However, where the family environment is coercive or hostile—where everyday interactions are characterized by criticism or arguing—adolescent-parent disagreements are less likely to be resolved and instead escalate to intense conflict. Over time, in fact, warm families tend to experience a greater reduction in parent-adolescent conflict than less supportive families, which experience increased conflict over time. Such conflict may be long-standing and weaken family ties (Rueter & Conger, 1995). Key is to identify the conditions that lead to healthy disagreements and resolution, and the conditions that result in harmful conflict.

In a qualitative study of 10 multigenerational families (a subsample of the LSOG) that explored family diversity and the seeming contradiction of individual family member change within family system continuity, Troll (1996) described one family whose bonds seemed to be the members' resentment and jealousy of each other. At the same time, they all wanted to get closer to each other and be part of the family. While the families in this study differed widely in terms of their intergenerational solidarity, even the least integrated families seemed to provide members with a sense of belonging. Troll found continuity over time despite individual development and generational changes. In another in-depth study of one LSOG multigenerational family, Richlin-Klonsky and Bengtson (1996) found a family beset by interpersonal antagonisms between and within generations, which nevertheless enacted the dual and contradictory themes of "drifting apart" and then "pulling together" over several decades, usually triggered by a family member's medical crisis.

Using the intergenerational solidarity paradigm within a life course framework, Whitbeck et al. (1994) investigated the effects of early family experiences on affectional solidarity and relationship strain between adult children and their parents at midlife, and the provision of social support to older parents. The study's particular focus was on family history and negative interaction styles learned early in life which can emerge in adulthood in times of family crisis or need to negatively affect family processes. They found family relationship histories characterized by parental rejection were consistently negatively associated with the quality of contemporary adult child-parent relationships (affectional solidarity and relationship strain). This had little effect on support outcomes, however. Filial concern—concern about parents' well-being—was the more consistent predictor of the inclination to provide assistance and emotional support to parents than was affectional solidarity. The effects of filial concern on providing instrumental support were independent of relationship quality, demonstrating the unique and sometimes contradictory effects of different dimensions of intergenerational solidarity.

SIBLING CONFLICT

Research on sibling relationships in contrast to parent-child relationships has often explored conflict issues. Conflict between siblings appears to diminish with age. This may be a consequence of less contact than is true for lineage relationships, the fact that sibling relationships are generally regarded as less important than parent-child or spousal relationships, or that sibling interactions are seen as more voluntary; siblings may feel less reticent to express their disagreements, or to leave if the relationship becomes too uncomfortable (Bengtson et al., 1995). Schmeeckle, Giarrusso, and Bengtson (1994) found that the salience of sibling relationships is curvilinear across the life course with siblings less close at midlife than at younger or older ages. This may reflect the more extensive role involvement of those at midlife (as parents and grandparents, adult children, spouses, workers, etc.), which competes with the attention given to sibling relationships. Gold (1989) found that about 10% of adult sibling relationships can be classified as hostile, with another 10% as apathetic. Bedford (1992) examined whether the awareness of having been a less favored sibling during childhood negatively affected intergenerational solidarity in adulthood. She found that the more adult children felt they had been treated worse than their siblings, the less affectional solidarity they perceived with their parents and the more conflict they felt in the relationship.

RESEARCHING FAMILY CONFLICT

Several factors have impeded research on conflict in intergenerational relations. First, there are measuring difficulties resulting from selective reporting biases. Respondents are often reluctant to discuss conflict in family relationships, so may provide socially desirable answers; or in describing parent-adult child relationships, older parents' reports tend to be more positive than children's reports—the intergenerational stake phenomenon (Giarrusso et al., 1995). Second, there is a lack of conceptual clarity as to how conflict is be defined and operationalized such that the interpretation of findings is often obscured (Clarke et al., 1999). Third, there are reservations about the adequacy of conflict scales designed for individuals when applied to families. For example, while quantitative research on family solidarity suggests that low consensual solidarity might indicate higher levels of conflict, a more complex, nuanced analysis is needed. The preceding limitations suggest that combining quantitative and qualitative methods may be a more useful approach in unearthing and understanding conflict in families.

It seems clear that we must conceptualize families as relationships involving both solidarity and conflict between and within generations. It is also the case there has been less research on conflict in multigenerational families than on solidarity (Bengtson et al., 1995). We need to know more about the structure and types of conflict, the tenuous balance between solidarity and conflict, and their interplay as family members age. With this in mind, Clarke et al. (1999) analyzed LSOG survey qualitative data and identified six principal themes of conflict between aging parents and their adult children: conflicts over (1) communication and interaction; (2) habits and lifestyle choices; (3) child-rearing practices and values; (4) politics, religion, ideology; (5) work habits and orientations; and (6) household standards of maintenance. They found generational differences. These results affirm the usefulness of examining intergenerational conflict within the context of solidarity in families.

Are Norms of Family Obligation Weakening?

Coincident with the secular trends toward greater individualism and focus on self fulfillment in social relations, several family researchers have documented the general weakening of normative prescriptions and constraints in American society, especially evident in the 1960s and 1970s and manifest in marital and childbearing behavior (Alwin, 1996; Hareven, 1996; Ruggles, 1996; Scott, Alwin, & Braun, 1996; Thornton, 1989). The implication is that family attachments are increasingly based on individual sensitivities rather than norms of obligation (Hareven, 1996), rendering the bonds of kinship more fragile than in times past. But are they? Are bonds of family attachment necessarily weaker if they are based more on preferences and personal commitment than normative requirements? To the extent the shift to personal choice and self-fulfillment has contributed to the escalating divorce rate and the more tenuous connection of divorced fathers to their adult children and family support systems (as we have seen), then the answer is yes. Other research is less conclusive.

Some recent studies in the United States suggest that beliefs about obligations in families are conditional rather than absolute. For example, the obligation to provide care to elderly parents is more likely to be seen as contextual—the conditions most cited being availability of resources and the quality of the relationship (Ganoug, Coleman, McDaniel, & Killian, 1998). Other studies suggests norms of filial obligation are not that crucial in terms of actual helping behavior. Eggebeen and Daley (1998) found it is the parent's experience of crisislike events that prompts adult children to provide support, not norms of familial assistance or patterns of ongoing intergenerational exchanges. These results reflect a contingent exchange perspective on intergenerational relations, also found by Silverstein and Bengtson (1991, 1994), which states that adult children provide support to parents contingent on circumstances and need, such as recent widowhood or deteriorating health. On the other hand, in a longitudinal analysis, Silverstein, Parrott, and Bengtson (1995) found that feelings of filial responsibility, in part, predicted adult child support of elderly parents. These findings are consistent with Riley and Riley's (1993) concept of the "latent kin matrix," where contemporary families increasingly will be characterized by cross-generational support patterns that become activated in times of family crises (Bengtson, 2001).

The strength of norms of familial obligation are not uniform across ethnic groups. Using a national sample, Lee, Peek, and Coward (1998) found that aged Blacks value and expect support from children more than do Whites. They suggest this reflects a more "collectivist" family belief system among Blacks (Pyke & Bengtson, 1996). In that normative filial responsibility is an aspect of culture, results affirm there are differences between races that can be attributed to culture even after controlling sociodemographic, health, and support factors. However, stronger norms of filial obligations do not translate into the actual provision of assistance when needed, where little or no race differences are found.

How are we to understand these differing results? One issue may be conceptual interpretation. Some researchers differentiate between "filial responsibility" an often used attitudinal approach to parent obligations, and "felt obligation," a relational approach (Stein, Wemmerus, Ward, Gaines, Freeberg, & Jewell, 1998). Filial responsibility in multigenerational relations conveys the presence of obligation as a general attitude or societal norm, for example, as a societal attitude toward adult children's duty to meet the needs of aging parents. Relational approaches to obligations, as reflected in the construct felt obligation, emphasize the salience of particular family relationships. Relational approaches acknowledge that there are social norms but stress that norms of obligation must be applied by individuals in the context of their ongoing family relationships (Stein et al., 1998), as several of the preceding studies seem to suggest. There may be indications that norms of filial responsibility have weakened, but not necessarily felt obligation to particular family members.

Pyke and Bengtson's (1996) qualitative study of individualistic and collectivist multigenerational families (a subsample of the LSOG) looks at the importance of normative obligations from a different perspective. This study examined the ideological orientations that guide the ways families organize and maintain ties to their members. While few families were uniformly of one type or another, collectivist families emphasized kinship ties and familial responsibilities over other nonfamily roles. Individualistic families emphasized independence, personal achievement, and loose kinship ties, with family relations more voluntary and egalitarian. The caregiving needs of elders in both types of families were met, but the strategies varied as did the outcomes. Individualists were motivated to provide care by feelings of obligation rather than affection and were more likely to use formal care and experience burden. Collectivists described caregiving as motivated by emotional sentiment toward parents, not obligation, and used caregiving to nurture family ties. They often shared the caregiving with other collectivist family members, and experienced less burden. Further, in these collectivist families, men were much more involved in caregiving than in the individualist families. The quality of past relationships with parents seems to matter. Findings indicate that the degree to which family relations are rewarding and meaningful instead of strained and difficult plays a key role in how families organize themselves to meet the dependency needs of its members over time.

KINKEEPING AND MAINTAINING INTERGENERATIONAL CONNECTIONS

Kinkeeping is often an important activity for those in midlife. But what is meant by kinkeeping? Kinkeeping has been variously described in the literature. In her seminal paper, "Kinkeeping in the Familial Division of Labor," Rosenthal (1985) focuses on the emotional labor involved in maintaining the ties among the nuclear families making up the contemporary extended family. The extended family, or kinship network, includes lineage members: parents, grandparents, children, grandchildren; as well as collateral relation: siblings, nieces and nephews, aunts and uncles, cousins (Fry, 1995). The "kinkeeper" is defined as someone who works at keeping these family members in touch with one another. Hence, kinkeeping is considered an essential aspect of intergenerational solidarity and continuity. Other researchers broaden the responsibilities of kinkeeping to include not only the emotional but the financial and physical labor required to sustain extended family ties, including caregiving to elderly relatives (Gerstel & Gallagher, 1993).

Whether narrowly or broadly defined, kinkeeping is concerned with what family members "do" in behalf of one another in the context of promoting family ties and collective well-being. Undergirding its enactment are dimensions of family solidarity, especially familial norms of obligation and bonds of affection, in varying degrees. It is also the case that kin-keeping and concern with intergenerational relations take on particular saliency at middle age. Fry (1995) suggests that kinkeeping in the middle years is a phenomenon of family life that is experienced across cultures.

THE KINKEEPER ROLE

Following Rosenthal's (1985) definition, a kinkeeper is conceptualized as a task-specific position within the family division of labor. Rosenthal found that over one half of family members were able to identity some-one as fulfilling the kinkeeper role in their families. Other task-specific positions in families may include the head of the family, comforter, financial manager, ambassador, and job-placement officer (Bengtson, Rosenthal, & Burton, 1990). The kinkeeper role involves a number of functions primarily concerned with family communication and inter-action. Kinkeepers act as communication links between family mem-bers. Their activities include telephoning, writing family members, visiting, and organizing or holding family gatherings. Kinkeeping is also associated with the challenges of maintaining relationships with siblings and their children. The more siblings in the extended family, the greater the likelihood of having a family kinkeeper (Rosenthal, 1985). This does not mean that families without designated kinkeepers do not engage in considerable informal sharing. But having a designated kinkeeper results in more family get-togethers, greater awareness of special objects of sentimental value in the family, and more sharing of family stories and rituals—all of which promote stronger family bonds over time.

Gerstel and Gallagher (1993) adopt an expanded interpretation of the kinkeeper role. They call attention to the wide range of kinkeeping labor that sustains contemporary families; it can include caring for disabled rel-atives as well as sustaining relations with a range of extended family members, doing such things as sending a gift, preparing a meal, or keep-ing in touch. In Gerstel and Gallagher's view, because of the research focus on caregiving to impaired family members, investigators have tended to emphasize that contemporary families activate their support and caregiving obligations only in times of crisis. Obscured is that kin work is ongoing, a demanding but normal part of everyday life. Gerstel and Gallagher point out that the extended family doesn't just persist. Family members expend a great of energy and work to maintain it.

Kinkeeping also promotes intergenerational continuity. Hagestad (1985) observes that with longer lives making multigenerational families more common, families ". . . are increasingly faced with the challenge of finding and maintaining a core of 'sameness,' transcending time and change . . ."

(p. 36). This sense of family continuity across generations has to be developed through an ongoing process of family interaction, the work of kinkeeping.

Why do people assume the role of kinkeeper? The most important reason is ". . . to keep the family together" (Rosenthal, 1985, p. 970), often prompted by the death or ill health of the previous kinkeeper. As research makes abundantly clear, the bonds of intergenerational solidarity are strong, and families often rely on the work of kinkeepers to make sure they stay that way (Bengtson et al., 1990). The death of a parent, especially a mother, can threaten family linkages with siblings and prompt an adult child to step into the kinkeeper role. The kinkeeper role often passes from mother to daughter. It is at midlife when one most commonly assumes the role of kinkeeper. Kinkeepers are often in this role for many years. Rosenthal (1985) found the median length of time was 20 years.

WOMEN AS KINKEEPERS

Most kinkeepers are women (Aronson, 1992; Brody, 1981, 1985; Gerstel & Gallagher, 1993; Hagestad, 1985; Rosenthal, 1985; A. Rossi & Rossi, 1990). Contact and exchanges between generations are often the purview of women. Men seem to benefit from the coordination that a kinkeeper provides in terms of interaction with siblings and other relatives (Rosenthal, 1985; A. Rossi & Rossi, 1990). Gerstel and Gallagher found there are significant differences in the amount and kinds of kin work done by women and men. Compared with husbands, wives help larger numbers of kin and spend three times as many hours helping kin, including parents and adult children. Women provide almost three-quarters of the caregiving to disabled husbands and elders (Cherlin, 1999). Women are significantly more likely to provide almost every type of care, with the exception of repairs (Gerstel & Gallagher, 1993).

Why are women generally designated as kinkeepers? Cultural definitions of gender roles have identified nurturance and caregiving with women's roles more than men's (Chodorow, 1978; Gilligan, 1982; Parsons & Bales, 1955). Gendered expectations about the emotional and caring work in families has meant that women—at least among the current midlife cohorts—take on these responsibilities. And despite the trend toward greater acceptance of egalitarian gender roles, both husbands and wives believe it is women who should maintain family relationships and do the caretaking (Aronson, 1992). Some have suggested women's greater investment in caregiving and kinkeeping activities in their early and middle life is a strategy to create obligations in men and children that lead to assistance in later life (Spitze & Logan, 1989). Others have found little support for the idea that reciprocity is central to understanding intergenerational flows of resources (Eggebeen & Hogan, 1990; A. Rossi & Rossi, 1990). Rossi and Rossi found that ties among women are stronger, more reciprocal, and less contingent on circumstances than those of men. They also found gender differences in affection and closeness. In mid and later life, mother dyads are closer than father dyads and mother-daughter relationships are the closest of all. This implies that women invest more in family relationships. Also, family roles are more salient in women's lives, while men have less experience in family work.

Grandparenting itself is an important kinkeeper role, one usually assumed at midlife. This is especially true for grandmothers. Because of their kinkeeping role, grandmothers have more frequent contact with grandchildren than do grandfathers. Similarly, Silverstein and Long (1998) found grandmothers have greater affection for their grandchildren than do grandfathers as well as greater affection for granddaughters than for grandsons. Researchers suggest the unusually close relationships between grandmothers and granddaughters are often explained by the kinkeeper role that women typically play in the family (Hagestad, 1985). Having an adult daughter as the link to the grandchildren is a salient factor for grandmothers although this is not the case for grandfathers (Uhlenberg & Hammill, 1998). In sum, many studies conclude that it is mainly women who do the work of kinship and supply the emotional and instrumental sustenance that keeps lineages and families together (Eggebeen & Hogen, 1990; Hagestad, 1985; A. Rossi & Rossi, 1990).

THE FEMINIZATION OF KINSHIP?

Several researchers have commented on the "matrifocal tilt" of intergenerational relationships and suggested that kinship systems are becoming increasingly feminized (Bengtson et al., 1995; Cherlin, 1999; Hagestad, 1985; A. Rossi, 1995). There are several reasons for this: the instability of marriage; the fact that children usually remain in the custody of their mothers after divorce and many divorced fathers do not maintain regular contact with their children; and, the much greater effort that women make to create and maintain kinship ties. Because men often rely on women to do the work of kinkeeping, even when they remarry—and divorced men are more likely to remarry than divorced women—they will rely on their wives as well as mothers, sisters, and other women relatives. Divorced older men have far less contact with their adult children than married ones (Uhlenberg, 1993). Widowed grandfathers have less contact with their grandchildren than married ones, presumably because they lack a wife to facilitate the maintenance of close kinship ties (Uhlenberg & Hammill, 1998). Divorced, separated or remarried grandfathers are especially unlikely, compared with their married counterparts, to maintain frequent contact with grandchildren.

DIVERSITY IN THE STRUCTURE OF KINKEEPING

Because involvement with and expectations about kin are linked to specific social and economic conditions, the structure of kinkeeping varies with social class and ethnicity and the associated values and preferences that have developed around those conditions (Fry, 1995). Further, increases in divorce and remarriage are forcing reconsideration of how families and kinship relations are defined (Chatters & Jayakody, 1995). For poor and minority families in particular, matrifocality has emerged as an important variant in American kinship (Fry, 1995). In poverty areas with chronic unemployment, young women come to rely less on marriage and husbands and more on other kinship ties for support: mothers who help them in raising their children, grandparents, siblings, other relatives, and fictive kin. The result is women-centered kinship in which the strongest bonds of support and caregiving occur among a network of women, most of them related (Cherlin, 1999). This type of kinship has come to characterize poor Black families. Contributing to the creation of woman-centered kinships is a pattern of teenage childbearing resulting in a compression of generations with relatively young grandmothers raising both their daughters and grandchildren (Bengtson et al., 1990). Overall, Blacks are more likely than Whites to reside in extended family households, with other kin living near by. Two thirds of Blacks report that there was someone in their family who was regarded as a fictive kin. Fictive kin may have the same rights and responsibilities as actual kin. (Chatters & Jayakody, 1995). Latinos are also more likely to reside in multigenerational households than Whites (Himes, Hogan, & Eggebeen, 1996).

Cherlin (1999) notes poor people actively construct extended kin networks by exchanging goods and services and establishing mutual obligations. These "created kinships" offer greater possibilities for receiving assistance than the "assigned kinship" structure characteristic of middle-class families where kin are related by blood or first marriage and supported by stronger social norms. On the other hand, created kinships require continuous work because they lack the strong social norms and biological ties that would otherwise bind multigenerational families together. In this sense, alternative family structures such as reconstituted and same-sex families are like created kinships. To maintain these types of kinship structures, active kinkeeping is essential.

A DILEMMA: WILL WOMEN CONTINUE TO DO MOST OF THE KINKEEPING WORK? WILL KINKEEPING DECLINE?

What are the implications of changing family gender roles for relationships between generations and the kinkeeper role? Several factors suggest that midlife women may not be as available, or willing, to assume the kinkeeping role in the future. First, women's continued involvement in the workplace is not likely to abate; their pattern of employment will continue to more closely resemble that of men. Over 75% of middle-aged women are in the workforce, squeezing the time and energy they have available for kinkeeping activity.

A second reason pertains to cultural changes and preferences. Noting the marked increase in nonfamily living arrangements among young adults over the past three decades, Goldscheider and Lawton's (1998) findings imply that women who left their parents' home early in their young adulthood, not for marriage but nonfamily living, may later value work and privacy more highly than kin work and be less inclined to take responsibility for maintaining family bonds and obligations to kin. For young adult daughters, staying home until marriage tends to reinforce the sense of commitment to caring for others. This is not the case for adult sons, probably because they have been less involved in the domestic sphere than adult daughters during their growing-up years (Goldscheider & Lawton, 1998). Third, feminists argue that women's kinkeeping activities are not really a choice and often are not welcome (Aronson, 1992). With few external resources and because men are reluctant to help in the caretaking of dependent elders, women have asked, "Who else is going to do it?" (p. 25). For such women, this type of kinkeeping is accompanied by guilt and anxiety and is often at the price of their employment and psychological well-being. While this may be less an issue for current women kinkeepers socialized into the traditional roles of family care, younger women influenced by the women's movement and who have spent much of their adult life in the workplace may feel more conflicted about the work of kinship. Younger women may have stronger individualistic orientations that may lessen their willingness to fill the kinkeeper role, at least to the exclusion of men. Perhaps in the future as the boundaries of gender-specific roles become more blurred, the disparate kinkeeping activities of men and women may converge with men assuming more of the kinkeeping responsibility.

Finally, because of reduced fertility, the need for a designated family kinkeeper may be less necessary in the future to the extent that a major function of kinkeeping is to maintain lateral siblings relationships within the extended family (Rosenthal, 1985). On the other hand, because of longer lives and the increasing verticalization of intergenerational family structures (Bengtson et al., 1995), a kinkeeper who keeps the family in touch and sees to the needs of the oldest and youngest generations may be especially needed.

SUMMARY AND CONCLUSION

We have addressed four important intergenerational relations issues facing those in midlife. Each issue is framed by a series of questions—or more accurately, dilemmas—having direct implications for the well-being of midlife adults and their family members.

First we examined the "truth" of the sandwich generation—the situation of being caught in the cross pressures of simultaneous caregiving to elderly parents and dependent children while balancing the demands of work and other roles. The encroachment of two social forces—longer lives with many more very elderly parents needing care, and the rapid entry of women, the traditional caregivers, into the workforce—prompted Brody (1981) to declare that the strain of caregiving would soon overwhelm families. The debate over caregiving as a normative stress has been an important theme in the caregiving literature and is especially relevant for women in midlife. The ability to assess the validity of the sandwiched-in phenomenon awaited adequate data which only recently became available. The evidence shows that the structural potential for generational overlap is small and that being sandwiched in by competing role demands is not typical. Among midlife caregivers, less than one-fifth experienced such multiple role pressures at any particular time. In terms of whether being caught in the middle is stressful or burdensome, research findings are more complex. Neither the role strain nor role enhancement hypotheses adequately explain multiple caregiving and work role effects. Much depends on prior life and family experience and context. Generally, women are found to experience little stress in these multiple roles. Men caregivers seem less adept at handling multiple role demands. In many cases, men and women caregivers who work have less distress than those who do not work. In general, helping children seems to be rewarding and helping elderly parents causes little distress. This is not to diminish how difficult and intense parent care in the context of other roles can be for some, but for most this is not the case.

We conclude that being sandwiched in cannot be empirically substantiated and is more myth than truth, at least for now. There are a few caveats. If government policy shifts more caregiving responsibilities to the private sector—that is, to families—we may see more "normative caregiving stress which may exceed the capacity of many." A second unknown concerns the availability and willingness of younger cohorts of potential caregivers to fill these roles at midlife. With very different lifetime experiences and expectations, those who are younger may value family less than their parents did at midlife; or these children of marital instability may value family more highly. They may not adapt as well to the stress of competing roles; or they may develop new strategies for combining the roles of family, work, and self.

A second dilemma confronting those in midlife is the relatively new phenomenon of prolonged parenting, when adult children delay departure from the family nest, or return to it, or don't leave at all. This is a dilemma for their young adult children as well, who may feel inadequate by their failure to achieve an independent life—a paramount American virtue. Parents and adult children are quite aware of the timing norms governing home leaving which in turn may negatively affect the quality of the parent-child relationship. Research shows this is not necessarily an unpleasant experience. Parents appear to experience coresidence positively and report strong feelings of affection. This may be less the case for their young adult children who may experience more help and support but lower feelings of affection, an effect more related to current living arrangements rather than to poor family relations. One clear benefit is that adult children who delay independence from their parents have higher educational attainment. Generally parents and adult children in other Western countries experience coresidence in a very positive way, where it meets the needs of both generations. What the issue of prolonged parenthood highlights is the powerful effect that macrolevel forces such as labor markets and government policies can have on family processes and relations among its members. We also discussed another type of prolonged parenting, the growing phenomenon of grandparents raising grandchildren due to the inability of their adult children to fulfill their parental roles. In a unique way, this instance of prolonged parenting demonstrates how family norms of obligation are activated and made manifest—often for extended periods of time and at considerable emotional and physical cost.

Prolonged parenting represents a new twist in the contract between generations for meeting the dependency needs of family members. In the past, it was the needs of elderly parents that prompted a coresidential arrangement with midlife children. Most of today's older parents—healthier, more active, and more financially secure than their parents before them—choose to live independently. Instead, young adult children are the ones in need of support by midlife parents. More than ever, midlife parents are a safety net for their children, and their grandchildren. But in another, perhaps paradoxical twist, prolonged parenting also increases the duration and frequency of interaction and mutual exchange between parents and their young adult offspring with the likely effect of enhancing long-term family bonds.

Third, we addressed the dilemma inherent in intergenerational solidarity and conflict in midlife. Here we shifted to a more abstract level, to theory. We presented a paradigm of intergenerational solidarity as comprising six distinct but interrelated dimensions: feelings of affection; agreement on values or consensus; association or the amount of time spent together; the giving and receiving of emotional and functional support; norms of familial obligation; and opportunity structure such as proximity, family size, and composition. Over the past 25 years, the intergenerational solidarity paradigm has guided research on multigenerational families and been used to assess the strength of bonds between adult children, parents, grandparents, and grandchildren over time. Solidarity and conflict coexist in families and are conceptually distinct. We presented research demonstrating the usefulness of the solidarity model in illuminating these seemingly contradictory aspects of intergenerational relations. Under some conditions, conflict may be long-standing and weaken family ties. In families characterized by warm and supportive relations, conflict levels can be contained; in more hostile family environments, conflicts can escalate. But, even in very troubled families, there remains a sense of belonging and family continuity.

What accounts for the cohesiveness of a multigenerational family and why does it persist across time even in the face of conflict? These questions have taken on new importance as longer lives increase the duration of family relationships. The central concern is whether the norms of family obligation are weakening as a consequence of continuing trends toward individualism and self-fulfillment in social relations, and what that implies for the bonds of familial attachment. Some point to the increase in divorce with its long-term negative effects on father-child bonds as evidence of the instability of family ties, which are based on individual sensitivities rather than norms of obligation. However, research on intergenerational families shows overwhelmingly that the bonds of solidarity are strong, that family members frequently interact and support one another and respond in times of need. If the norms of filial responsibility appear to be weakening—reflecting attitudes toward parental obligations in general—the more particularistic notion of felt obligation toward specific family members remains an important aspect of family solidarity that, as the research shows, can be activated in supportive behavior when needed.

Fourth, we discussed the kinkeeping role as an essential aspect of family solidarity and continuity. The kinkeeper role is usually assumed at midlife when concerns for family and the well-being of family members become especially salient. The desire to keep the family together as well as to maintain ties between siblings and their families are primary reasons for assuming the kinkeeper role. Kinkeeping is what family members "do" on an ongoing basis to promote communication and interaction and maintain strong extended family ties. Not all extended families have designated kinkeepers, but those that do seem to get together more often, share more family stories and rituals, have a stronger sense of family, and have stronger feelings of obligations to support each other in times of need.

To more fully understand kinkeeping at midlife and the diversity of kinship systems, we must examine the intersecting influences of gender, race, and class. Research consistently finds that most kinkeepers are women, a consequence of gendered role expectations that assign nurturance and family care to women more so than to men. Grandparenting itself involves kinkeeping functions, and this is especially the case for grandmothers. This matrifocal tilt in intergenerational relations suggests the feminization of kinship systems in the United States more generally, particularly among poor and minority families. We pointed out how social and economic conditions have produced considerable diversity in the structure of kinkeeping, including the construction of created kinships, extended kin networks of relatives and fictive kin that provide for mutual exchange and assistance and foster ties of obligations. But created kinships are more precarious than those based on biological ties, which are supported by strong social norms. Reconstituted and same-sex families structures are similarly created; all require the continuous work of kinkeeping to maintain their family bonds. Will the kinkeeping role continue? Will family caregiving in the context of competing roles become more arduous? As we have seen, the work of family is primarily the work of women. We suggested several reasons why midlife women in the future may not be as available, or willing, to assume the kinkeeping role or do parent care. Midlife women's continued commitment to the workplace will not only squeeze the time and energy they have available for caregiving or the ongoing work of kinkeeping, but may over time change their priorities concerning matters of family. Similarly, cultural values and preferences that extol privacy over collectivist ideals may erode support for these family roles and discourage their enactment. Feminists suggest that women's caregiving and kinkeeping activities are not really chosen, and future relaxation of prescribed gender roles will reduce the number of midlife women willing to assume these roles. In view of these changes, perhaps men will play a greater role maintaining family cohesiveness and well-being. Longer lives and the prospect of more generations alive together than ever before means kinkeeping and elder care will be especially needed.

The theme running throughout our discussion of these midlife intergenerational issues concerns the strength and stability of family bonds, and whether in the next century the multigenerational family will be there to provide emotional, social, and instrumental support to its members. Several family researchers believe that the push toward greater individualism over the past several decades has irreparably weakened the norms of family obligation and reciprocity between generations, and jeopardized the bonds of intergenerational solidarity. We conclude otherwise. Findings from empirical research show that while families are more diverse in structure and process, intergenerational attachments remain strong. Our review here suggests that individuals need the solidarity of the multigenerational family and will go to great efforts to preserve it. Longer periods of parent-young adult child coresidence mean more intergenerational exchange and support, which will promote long-term family attachments. Changes in life expectancy over the twentieth century have increased both the opportunity—and need—for the interaction and support across family generations that span more years than ever before (Bengtson, 2001). The theory of intergenerational solidarity explains how competing caregiving and work claims, unexpectedly longer years of parenting, and the work of kinship can be linked in the expression of family solidarity—how they can be understood in the context of intergenerational structures and processes and changing sociohistorical conditions. A theory of intergenerational solidarity is also very useful; it can illuminate the nature and source of family relationship problems and guide us to solutions. Despite the current challenges facing nuclear families, the bonds across generations remain vibrant and necessary. And in this continuing family drama, midlife adults are center stage.

Future research should address several issues. First, in considering intergenerational relationships in midlife, it is important to examine the life course development of multigenerational families and their outcomes over decades of time, as parents and children, grandparents and grandchildren, grow up and grow older in an increasingly aging society. Longitudinal studies are essential.

Second, research should focus on the complex ways in which longer lives, changing family structures and socioeconomic conditions may affect family roles and obligations in midlife, and particularly how these effects differ between men and women. For example, because of their greater attachment to the labor force, today's young adult women may be less inclined than their mothers to assume family support and kinkeeping responsibilities when they reach midlife. On the other hand, their greater work force experience may better prepare them, economically and psychologically, for their midlife family roles. To explore these alternative hypotheses, we need to understand how the changes in family structures, particularly divorce, and in younger women's work place experiences may interact to affect the willingness or ability of younger cohorts of women to move into these midlife family roles. We also need to understand the conditions under which middle aged men may assume greater responsibility for family care and kinkeeping.

Third, we found that most midlife adults are not burdened by the competing demands of the workplace and family caregiving. But this assessment may not be accurate in the future. We need more research on how, and under what conditions, employment demands at midlife may conflict with caring for dependent elders and children, and their effects on midlife adults' well-being. There needs to be further research on the conditions under which multiple roles at midlife are stressful or beneficial.

Fourth, we need more cross-national research on changing intergenerational family relationships. In particular, we need to pay attention to the timing adult life transitions, such as home leaving, marriage and child-bearing, and how this may be changing. Research is needed to better understand how structural phenomena such as changing labor markets and historic shifts in values affect family roles and functions.

Fifth, grandparenting is a central role for those in midlife. But increasingly, grandparents are becoming surrogate parents to their grandchildren. Some research suggests that the experience of middle aged grandparents raising their grandchildren inevitably results in stress with negative consequences for grandparent well-being. Other research indicates grandparents find this experience rewarding. More research is needed to find out if surrogate parenting is always stressful, or only under certain conditions, or if there are also significant rewards to grandparents who assume the responsibility at midlife of surrogate parenting.

REFERENCES

Alwin, D.F. (1996). Coresidence beliefs in American society: 1973–1991. *Journal of Marriage and the Family, 58,* 393–403.

Amato, P.R., Loomis, L.S., & Booth, A. (1995). Parental divorce, marital conflict, and offspring well-being in early adulthood. *Social Forces, 73,* 895–916.

Aquilino, W.S. (1990). The likelihood of parent-adult child coresidence: Effects of family structure and parental characteristics. *Journal of Marriage and the Family, 52,* 405–419.

Aquilino, W.S., & Supple, K.R. (1991). Parent-child relations and parent's satisfaction with living arrangements when adult children live at home. *Journal of Marriage and the Family, 53,* 13–27.

Aronson, J. (1992). Women's sense of responsibility for the care of old people: But who else is going to do it? *Gender and Society, 6,* 8–29.

Bedford, V.H. (1992). Memories of parental favoritism and the quality of parent-child ties in adulthood. *Journal of Gerontology: Social Sciences, 47,* S149–S155.

Bengtson, V.L. (1996). Continuities and discontinuities in intergenerational relations over time. In V.L. Bengtson & K.W. Schaie (Eds.), *Adulthood and aging* (pp. 246–268). New York: Springer.

Bengtson, V.L. (2001). Beyond the nuclear family: The increasing importance of multigenerational relationships in American society. *Journal of Marriage and the Family, 63.*

Bengtson, V.L., & Allen, K. (1993). The life course perspective applied to families over time. In P. Boss, W. Doherty, R. LaRossa, W. Schumm, & S. Steinmetz (Eds.), *Sourcebook of family theories and methods: A contextual approach* (pp. 469–498). New York: Plenum Press.

Bengtson, V.L., & Dannefer, D. (1987). Families, work, and aging: Implications of disordered cohort flow for the twenty-first century. In A.R. Ward & S.S. Tobin (Eds.), *Health in aging: Sociological issues and policy directions* (pp. 256–289). New York: Springer.

Bengtson, V.L., & Harootyan, R.A. (1994). *Intergenerational linkages: Hidden connections in American society.* New York: Springer.

Bengtson, V.L., Rosenthal, C.J., & Burton, L.M. (1990). Families and aging: Diversity and heterogeneity. In R.H. Binstock & L.K. George (Eds.), *Handbook of aging and the social sciences,* (3rd ed.) (pp. 263–287). New York: Academic Press.

Bengtson, V.L., Rosenthal, C.J., & Burton, L.M. (1995). Paradoxes of families and aging. In R.H. Binstock & L.K. George (Eds.), *Handbook of aging and the social sciences* (4th ed., pp. 253–282). San Diego, CA: Academic Press.

Brody, E.M. (1981). Women in the middle and family help to old people. *Gerontologist, 21,* 471–480.

Brody, E.M. (1985). Parent care as normative family stress. *Gerontologist, 25,* 19–29.

Burton, L.M. (1995). Intergenerational patterns of providing care in African-American families with teenage childbearers: Emergent patterns in an ethnographic study. In V.L. Bengtson, K.W. Schaie, & L.M. Burton (Eds.), *Adult intergenerational relations: Effects of social change* (pp. 79–96). New York: Springer.

Chatters, L.M., & Jayakody, R. (1995). Commentary: Intergenerational support within African-American families: Concepts and methods. In V.L. Bengtson, K.W. Schaie, & L.M. Burton (Eds.), *Adult intergenerational relations: Effects of social change* (pp. 97–118). New York: Springer.

Cherlin, A.J. (1999). *Public and private families: An introduction* (2nd ed.). New York: McGraw-Hill.

Cherlin, A., Scabini, E., & Rossi, G. (Eds.). (1997). Still in the nest: Delayed home leaving in Europe and the United States [Special issue]. *Journal of Family Issues, 18*(6), 572–575.

Chodorow, N. (1978). *The reproduction of mothering: Psychoanalysis and the sociology of gender.* Berkeley: University of California Press.

Clarke, E.J., Preston, M., Raksin, J., & Bengtson, V.L. (1999). Types of conflicts and tensions between older parents and adult children. *Gerontologist, 39,* 261–270.

Cordon, J.A.F. (1997). Youth residential independence and autonomy: A comparative study. *Journal of Family Issues, 18,* 576–607.

Crimmins, E.M., & Ingegneri, D.G. (1990). Interaction and living arrangements of older parents and their children: Past trends, present determinants, future implications. *Research on Aging, 12,* 3–35.

Dunham, C.C., & Bengtson, V.L. (1991). Generational continuity and change. In R.M. Lerner, A.C. Petersen, J. Brooks-Gunn (Eds.), *Encyclopedia of adolescence* (pp. 398–402). New York: Garland.

Durkheim, E. (1984). *The division of labor in society* (W.D. Halls, Trans.). New York: Free Press. (Original work published 1893)

Eggebeen, D., & Daley, A. (1998). Do safety nets work? The role of anticipated help in times of need. *Journal of Marriage and the Family, 60,* 939–950.

Eggebeen, D.J., & Hogan, D.P. (1990). Giving between generations in American families. *Human Nature, 1,* 211–232.

Elder, G.H., Jr. (1995). Life trajectories in changing societies. In A. Bandura (Ed.), *Self-efficacy in changing societies* (pp. 46–68). New York: Cambridge University Press.

Fry, C.L. (1995). Kinship and individuation: Cross-cultural perspectives on inter-generational relations. In V.L. Bengtson, K.W. Schaie, & L.M. Burton (Eds.), *Adult intergenerational relations: Effects of social change* (pp. 126–156). New York: Springer.

Galland, O. (1997). Leaving home and family relations in France. *Journal of Family Issues, 18,* 645–670.

Ganoug, C., Coleman, M., McDaniel, A.K., & Killian, T. (1998). Attitudes regarding obligations to assist an older parent or stepparent following later-life re-marriage. *Journal of Marriage and the Family, 60,* 595–610.

Gerstel, N., & Gallagher, S.K. (1993). Kinkeeping and distress: Gender, recipients of care, and work-family conflict. *Journal of Marriage and the Family, 55,* 598–607.

Giarrusso, R., Stallings, M., & Bengtson, V.L. (1995). The intergenerational stake hypothesis revisited: Parent-child differences in perceptions of relationships 20 years later. In V.L. Bengtson, K.W. Schaie, & L.M. Burton (Eds.), *Adult intergenerational relations: Effects of social change* (pp. 227–263). New York: Springer.

Gilligan, C. (1982). *In a different voice.* Cambridge, MA: Harvard University Press.

Gold, D.T. (1989). Sibling relationships in old age: A typology. *International Journal of Aging and Human Development, 28,* 37–51.

Goldscheider, F.K. (1997). Recent changes in U.S. young adult living arrangements in comparative perspective. *Journal of Family Issues, 18,* 708–724.

Goldscheider, F.K., & Goldscheider, C. (1993). *Leaving home before marriage: Ethnicity, familism and generational relationships.* Madison, WI: University of Wisconsin Press.

Goldscheider, F.K., & Goldscheider, C. (1994). Leaving and returning home in 20th-century America. *Population Bulletin, 48,* 2–33.

Goldscheider, F.K., & Goldscheider, C. (1998). The effects of childhood family structure on leaving and returning home. *Journal of Marriage and the Family 60,* 745–756.

Goldscheider, F.K., & Lawton, L. (1998). Family experiences and the erosion of support for intergenerational coresidence. *Journal of Marriage and the Family, 60,* 623–632.

Goode, W.J. (1960). A theory of role strain. *American Sociological Review, 25,* 483–496.

Hagestad, G.O. (1985). Continuity and connectedness. In V.L. Bengtson & J.F. Robertson (Eds.), *Grandparenthood* (pp. 31–48). Beverly Hills, CA: Sage.

Hareven, T.K. (1996). Historical perspectives on the family and aging. In R. Blieszner & V.H. Bedford (Eds.), *Aging and the family: Theory and research* (pp. 13–31). Westport, CT: Praeger.

Himes, C.L., Hogan, D.P., & Eggebeen, D.J. (1996). Living arrangements of minority elders. *Journal of Gerontology: Social Sciences, 51B,* S42–S48.

Hong, J., & Seltzer, M.M. (1995). The psychological consequences of multiple roles: The nonnormative case. *Journal of Health and Social Behavior, 36,* 386–398.

Kaufman, G., & Uhlenberg, P. (1998). Effects of life course transitions on the quality of relationships between adult children and their parents. *Journal of Marriage and the Family, 60,* 924–938.

Kohli, M. (1986). The world we forgot: A historical review of the life course. In V.W. Marshall (Ed.), *Later life: The social psychology of aging* (pp. 271–303). Beverly Hills, CA: Sage.

Lawton, L., Silverstein, M., & Bengtson, V.L. (1994). Affection, social contact and geographic distance between adult children and their parents. *Journal of Marriage and the Family, 56,* 57–68.

Lee, G.R., Peek, C.W., & Coward, R.T. (1998). Race differences in filial responsibility expectations among older parents. *Journal of Marriage and the Family 60,* 404–412.

Levitt, M.J., Guacci, N., & Weber, R.A. (1992). Intergenerational support, relationship quality, and well-being: A bicultural analysis. *Journal of Family Issues, 13,* 465–481.

Loomis, L.S., & Booth, A. (1995). Multigenerational caregiving and well-being: The myth of the beleaguered sandwich generation. *Journal of Family Issues, 16,* 131–148.

Lüscher, K., & Pillemer, K. (1998). Intergenerational ambivalence: A new approach to the study of parent-child relations in later life. *Journal of Marriage and the Family 60,* 413–425.

Mangen, D.J., Bengtson V.L., & Landry, P.H. (Eds.). (1988). *Measurement of intergenerational relations.* Newbury Park, CA: Sage.

Marks, N. (1995). Midlife marital status differences in social support relationships with adult children and psychological well-being. *Journal of Family Issues, 16,* 5–28.

Marks, N. (1998). Does it hurt to care? Caregiving, work-family conflict, and midlife well-being. *Journal of Marriage and the Family, 60,* 951–966.

Martin-Matthews, A., & Rosenthal, C.J. (1993). Balancing work and family in an aging society: The Canadian experience. In G. Maddox & M.P. Lawton (Eds.), *Annual review of gerontology and geriatrics* (Vol. 13, pp. 96–122). New York: Springer.

McGarry, K., & Schoeni, R.F. (1999, January). *Social security, economic growth and the rise in independence of elderly widows in the 20th century.* Paper presented at the colloquium series on Health and Aging, University of Southern California, Los Angeles.

Moen, P., Robison, J., & Dempster-McClain, D. (1995). Caregiving and women's well-being: A life course approach. *Journal of Health and Social Behavior, 36,* 259–273.

Parsons, T., & Bales, R.F. (Eds.). (1955). *Family, socialization and the interaction process.* New York: Free Press.

Penning, M.J. (1998). In the middle: Parental caregiving in the context of other roles. *Journal of Gerontology: Social Sciences, 53B,* S188–S197.

Pillemer, K., & Suitor, J.J. (1992). Violence and violent feelings: What causes them among family caregivers? *Journal of Gerontology: Social Sciences, 47,* S165–S172.

Popenoe, D. (1993). American family decline, 1960–1990: A review and appraisal. *Journal of Marriage and the Family, 55,* 527–555.

Pyke, D.K., & Bengtson, V.L. (1996). Caring more or less: Individualistic and collectivist systems of family eldercare. *Journal of Marriage and the Family, 58,* 379–392.

Richards, L.N., Bengtson, V.L., & Miller, R.B. (1989). The generation in the middle: Perceptions of changes in adults' intergenerational relationships. In K. Kreppner & R.M. Lerner (Eds.), *Family systems and life-span development* (pp. 341–366). Hillsdale, NJ: Erlbaum.

Richlin-Klonsky, J., & Bengtson, V.L. (1996). Pulling together, drifting apart: A longitudinal case study of a four-generation family. *Journal of Aging Studies, 10,* 255–279.

Riley, M.W., & Riley, J.W. (1993). Connections: Kin and cohort. In V.L. Bengtson & W.A. Achenbaum (Eds.), *The changing contract across generations* (pp. 169–189). New York: Aldine de Gruyter.

Roberts, R.E.L., & Bengtson, V.L. (1990). Is intergenerational solidarity a unidimensional construct? A second test of a formal model. *Journal of Gerontology: Social Sciences, 45,* S12–S20.

Roberts, R.E.L., Richards, L.N., & Bengtson, V.L. (1991). Intergenerational solidarity in families: Untangling the ties that bind. In S.K. Pfeifer & M.B. Sussman (Eds.), *Families: Intergenerational and generational connections* (pp. 11–46). Binghamton, NY: Haworth Press.

Rosenthal, C.J. (1985). Kinkeeping in the familial division of labor. *Journal of Marriage and the Family, 47,* 965–974.

Rosenthal, C.J., Martin-Matthews, A., & Matthews, S.H. (1996). Caught in the middle? Occupancy in multiple roles and help to parents in a national probability sample of Canadian adults. *Journal of Gerontology: Social Sciences, 51B,* S274–S283.

Rossi, A.S. (1995). Commentary: Wanted: Alternative theory and analysis modes. In V.L. Bengtson, K.W. Schaie, & L.M. Burton (Eds.), *Adult intergenerational relations: Effects of social change* (pp. 264–276). New York: Springer.

Rossi, A.S., & Rossi, P.H. (1990). *Of human bonding: Parent-child relations across the life course.* New York: Aldine de Gruyter.

Rossi, G. (1997). The nestlings: Why young adults stay at home longer: The Italian case. *Journal of Family Issues, 18,* 627–644.

Rueter, M.A., & Conger, R.D. (1995). Antecedents of parent-adolescent disagreements. *Journal of Marriage and the Family, 57,* 435–448.

Ruggles, S. (1996). Living arrangements of the elderly in America: 1880–1980. In T.K. Hareven (Ed.), *Aging and generational relations over the life course: A historical and cross-cultural perspective* (pp. 254–271). New York: Walter de Gruyter.

Scabini, E., & Cigoli, V. (1997). Young adult families: An evolutionary slowdown or a breakdown in the generational transition? *Journal of Family Issues, 18,* 608–626.

Schmeeckle, M., Giarrusso, R., & Bengtson, V.L. (1994, November). *Siblings: The role of a lifetime.* Paper presented at the annual meetings of the Gerontological Society of America, Atlanta, GA.

Scott, J., Alwin, D.F., & Braun, M. (1996). Generational changes in gender-role attitudes: Britain in a cross-national perspective. *Sociology: The Journal of the British Sociological Association, 30,* 471–492.

Shanas, E. (1979). *Use of home and community services by persons ages 65 and older with functional difficulties* (National Medical Expenditure Survey, Research Findings 5). Rockville, MD: Public Health Service.

Silverstein, M., & Bengtson, V.L. (1991). Do close parent-child relationships reduce the mortality risk of older parents? *Journal of Health and Social Behavior, 32,* 382–395.

Silverstein, M., & Bengtson, V.L. (1994). Does intergenerational social support influence the psychological well-being of older parents? The contingencies of declining health and widowhood. *Social Science and Medicine, 38,* 943–957.

Silverstein, M., & Bengtson, V.L. (1997). Intergenerational solidarity and the structure of adult child-parent relationships in American families. *American Journal of Sociology, 103,* 429–460.

Silverstein, M., Giarrusso, R., & Bengtson, V.L. (1998). Intergenerational solidarity and the grandparent role. In M. Szinovacz (Ed.), *Handbook on grandparenthood* (pp. 144–158). Westport, CT: Greenwood Press.

Silverstein, M., & Long, J.D. (1998). Trajectories of grandparents' perceived solidarity with adult grandchildren: A growth curve analysis over 23 years. *Journal of Marriage and the Family, 60,* 912–923.

Silverstein, M., Parrott, T.M., & Bengtson, V.L. (1995). Factors that predispose middle-aged sons and daughters to provide social support to older parents. *Journal of Marriage and the Family, 57,* 465–475.

Soldo, B.J. (1996). Guest editorial: Cross pressures on middle-age adults: A broader view. *Journal of Gerontology: Social Sciences, 51B,* S271–S273.

Spitze, G., & Logan, J.R. (1989). Gender differences in family support: Is there a payoff? *Gerontologist, 29,* 108–113.

Spitze, G., Logan, J.R., Joseph, G., & Lee, E. (1994). Middle generation roles and the well-being of men and women. *Journal of Gerontology: Social Sciences, 49,* S107–S116.

Stein, C.H., Wemmerus, V.A., Ward, M., Gaines, M.E., Freeberg, A.L., & Jewell, T.C. (1998). Because they're my parents: An intergenerational study of felt obligation and parental caregiving. *Journal of Marriage and the Family, 60,* 611–622.

Straus, M.A. (1979). Measuring intrafamily conflicts and violence: The Conflict Tactics (CT) Scales. *Journal of Marriage and the Family, 41,* 75–88.

Szinovacz, M.E. (1998). Grandparents today: A demographic profile. *Gerontologist, 38,* 37–52.

Taylor, R.J., & Chatters, L.M. (1991). Extended family networks of older Black adults. *Journal of Gerontology: Social Sciences, 46,* S210–S217.

Thoits, P.A. (1986). Multiple identities: Examining gender and marital status differences in distress. *American Sociological Review, 51,* 259–272.

Thornton, A. (1989). Changing attitudes toward family issues in the United States. *Journal of Marriage and the Family, 51,* 873–893.

Troll, L. (1996). Modified-extended families over time: Discontinuity in parts, continuity in wholes. In V.L. Bengtson (Ed.), *Adulthood and aging* (pp. 246–268). New York: Springer.

Uhlenberg, P. (1993). Demographic change and kin relationships in later life. In G.L. Maddox & M.P. Lawton (Eds.), *Annual Review of Gerontology and Geriatrics* (Vol. 13, pp. 219–238). New York: Springer.

Uhlenberg, P. (1996). Mortality decline in the twentieth century and supply of kin over the life course. *Gerontologist, 36,* 681–685.

Uhlenberg, P., & Hammill, B. (1998). Frequency of grandparent contact with grandchild sets: Six factors that make a difference. *Gerontologist, 38,* 276–286.

U.S. Bureau of the Census. (1999). *Coresident grandparents and grandchildren* (Current Population Reports, Series P23–198). Washington DC: U.S. Government Printing Office.

U.S. Bureau of Labor Statistics. (1997). Developments in women's labor force participation. *Monthly Labor Review, September 1977* (pp. 41–46). Washington DC: U.S. Government Printing Office.

Ward, R.A., & Spitze, G. (1992). Consequences of parent-adult child coresidence: A review and research agenda. *Journal of Family Issues, 13,* 553–572.

Ward, R.A., & Spitze, G. (1996). Will the children ever leave? Parent-child coresidence history and plans. *Journal of Family Issues, 17,* 514–539.

Whitbeck, L., Hoyt, D.R., & Huck, S.M. (1994). Early family relationships, intergenerational solidarity, and support provided to parents by their adult children. *Journal of Gerontology: Social Sciences, 39,* S85–S94.

White, L., & Lacy, N. (1997). The effects of age at home leaving and pathways from home on educational attainment. *Journal of Marriage and the Family, 59,* 982–995.

White, L.K., & Rogers, S.J. (1997). Strong support but uneasy relationships: Coresidence and adult children's relationships with their parents. *Journal of Marriage and the Family, 59,* 62–76.

CHAPTER 16

Dynamics of Social Relationships in Midlife

TONI C. ANTONUCCI, HIROKO AKIYAMA, and ALICIA MERLINE

LIFE-SPAN DEVELOPMENTAL RESEARCHERS are firmly committed to the exploration of both continuity and change (Baltes, 1987; Brim & Kagan, 1980; Caspi, Bem, & Elder, 1989; Dannefer & Uhlenberg, 1999; Fiske & Chiriboga, 1990; Haan, Millsap, & Hartka, 1986; Hagestad, 1985). These concepts are important to the experience of social relationships in midlife, especially at this historical moment. Many changes have taken place in the arena of midlife (Riley & Riley, 1993). In fact, it is probably appropriate to describe these changes as revolutionary (Harevan, 1996). The basic experience of midlife has changed in fundamental and radical ways. This is nowhere better demonstrated than in the social relationships of midlife men and women. The trials and tribulations, joys and rewards, indeed the very basic life goals and challenges of midlife have changed dramatically. And yet, at the same time, many of the old issues of midlife remain at the very core of the modern midlife experience. Family relationships are still centrally important; intergenerational relations are a constant factor, now more than ever, in the lives of most midlife individuals and their families. At the same time, friendship, community, and work relationships remain critical independent sources of both comfort and stress. Social relations at midlife have probably never been more dynamic—or more complicated.

We are grateful for the following sources of support: Social Relations and Mental Health over the Life Course MH46549; Convoys of Support in Old Age: A Cross-National Study AG13490; Aging in America: A Study of 3 Cohorts AG134010; Gender and Health: Historical & Cross Cultural Analysis MH48936.

We organize this chapter around the convoy model of social relations because it provides a theoretical framework within which to examine social relations at this point in the life span. It emphasizes the embeddedness of the individual in social relationships, both within and across time periods. In this chapter, we consider the traditional roles of midlife and reflect on how things have changed as the baby boom generation has moved into midlife. We begin by presenting the basic theoretical perspective of the convoy. We then present the available empirical evidence relating to the convoy model and social relations more generally in midlife both from the literature as well as from our own research program. Finally, we emphasize the need to recognize the implications of demographic, cultural, and ethnic diversity as we seek to understand midlife as experienced by the current, future, and ever-changing cohorts of middle-aged men and women.

THE CONVOY MODEL OF SOCIAL RELATIONSHIPS

In 1980, Kahn and Antonucci outlined the convoy model of social relationships to help reshape our thinking about relationships and to provide a conceptual framework for understanding social relationships across the life span. The concept of convoy was adopted from the work of the anthropologist David Plath (1980), who used the term to describe the cohort of agemates who in some societies share all their significant life events and major rites of passage. In the Convoy Model, Kahn and Antonucci envision a convoy of social support that, under ideal conditions, provides a protective layer of social relations to guide, socialize, and encourage individuals as they move through life. They emphasize the role of social support from family and friends that enables the individual to meet life's challenges. Kahn and Antonucci recognize, however, that these same family and friends under some circumstances can be detrimental to the individual by encouraging or rewarding poor choices or inappropriate behaviors.

The convoy model incorporated a life-span perspective in distinct contrast to the voluminous research generated by attachment theory, which focused on infancy (Ainsworth, Blehar, Waters, & Wall, 1978; Bowlby, 1969, 1973). Nevertheless, early research utilizing the Convoy Model actually focused on older people (Antonucci, 1985; Antonucci & Akiyama, 1987; Kahn & Antonucci, 1980; Levitt, Antonucci, Clark, Rotton, & Finley, 1985–1986). Later work also found the convoy model useful for younger people, but this work never specifically focused on midlife adults. Rather, it focused on school-age children (Levitt, Guacci-Franco, & Levitt, 1993), teenage mothers (Caldwell, Antonucci, & Jackson, 1998), and intergenerational relationships (Akiyama, Antonucci, & Campbell, 1997; Antonucci

& Akiyama, 1991; Levitt, Guacci, & Weber, 1992). In this chapter, we begin to address this limitation by specifically considering social relations in midlife.

The Convoy Model proposes that the more enduring Properties or Characteristics of the Person such as gender, race, religion, age, education, and marital status combine with Properties of the Situation such as role expectations, life events, financial stress, daily hassles, demands, and resources to influence Support Networks, Social Support, and Support Satisfaction. These factors, both additively and multiplicatively, are hypothesized to influence the Health and Well-being of the Individual. A modified version of the Convoy Model is presented in Figure 16.1.

Since the Properties or characteristics of individuals and their situation fundamentally influence the development and characteristics of the convoy, it is critical that the unique and changing nature of these properties be examined at midlife. We turn to the examination of these properties next.

PROPERTIES OF THE PERSON AT MIDLIFE

It is widely recognized that the basic demographics of midlife have changed dramatically in the past several decades (Popenoe, 1993; Uhlenberg, 1993). At the turn of the century, the average life expectancy was 47 years (Butler, Lewis, & Sunderland, 1991). Today it is 75 and, in many parts of the world, rising steadily. While people lived to be 47 in 1900, now most would argue that midlife begins at 30, about the time most people would be entering the last third of their life in 1900! Hence, not only is the individual experience of age and midlife radically different, this experience is being shared by an entire cohort. Similarly, in the early 1900s it was not uncommon for women to die much earlier than men, often in childbirth. The result was that an equal or greater number of those "old" 47-year-olds were men. Today, as we all know, older women far outnumber

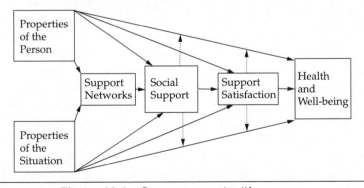

Figure 16.1   Convoys over the life course.

older men with the imbalance ratio increasing from 1.23 women for every man between age 65 and 69 to 2.59 for those aged 85 and older. Thus, in some ways midlife is a particularly new experience for women (Uhlenberg, 1993, 1996).

The experience of people, in terms of age, relationships, generation, and health of those around them, has changed no less dramatically. For many years, one could describe the population in this country and in most developed countries as pyramid shaped with many young people and few old people. This is now clearly changing. At least in most industrialized nations, it is more accurate to describe the population as having a beanpole shape evidencing an approximately equal number of people in the young, middle, and older generations with significant decreases in the population not evident until one reaches the oldest-old (Bengtson & Cutler, 1976). A dramatic reversal of the pyramid shape is feared in some countries, such as Italy, where so few children are being born that an inverted pyramid may best describe the population of the future.

The major roles of life (i.e., spouse, parent, child, and worker) have not changed, though their distribution throughout the population has. For example, trends in marriage have changed with people marrying later, having fewer children, and being more likely to divorce, remarry, and have additional children. The result is an increased diversity of marital statuses at midlife (Bumpass & Aquilino, 1995). It is now not uncommon to find men and women at midlife who may not yet have married, may never marry, may have been previously married, or may currently be in a second or third marriage. The influences of these changes on social relations are both fundamental and extensive. It is not difficult to see that the social relations of a single man or woman at midlife are likely to be significantly different from those of a married person with small children at midlife.

Parenthood has also changed. To look again at the turn of the twentieth century, it was not uncommon for a young child to be raised by a single parent, but the reasons for this situation were quite different from the current situation. At the beginning of the past century, single-parent families were most likely to be the result of the death of a parent: The mother may have died in childbirth or the child might be the youngest of many children, with the parents reaching the limits of their life expectancy before the child was full-grown. Now, however, the reason for single-parent families is most likely that the child was born to parents who have not married or to parents who were married but have since divorced. Parents who divorce often remarry, bringing children from previous marriages into the new marriage and sometimes having more children in the new marriage.

Once again, it is clear that the implications of societal change for social relations are enormous. People in midlife have different sets of social relationships depending on their marital status. People who have never married and have no children are much more likely to have social relationships with people in similar marital and parental situations. People who have small children but are not married are likely to seek social relations with other single-parent families. Another new twist on family and marital relationships is that people who have experienced one or more marriages also have been involved in a set of family relationships that are determined by marriage. With divorce these relationships often end. When children from one or two previous marriages are present, however, the family may maintain relationships with grandparents, aunts, uncles, and other relatives for the sake of the children—despite the end of the marriage. These convoys of social relationships can be complicated. While these changing marital patterns influence people of all ages, because of the high number of social roles that they occupy, the main participants in the experience of these changes are midlife men and women (Troll, 1996; Troll & Bengtson, 1982).

Employment status is another Property of the Person that changed radically in the past century. This change has been most dramatic for middle class women. During World War II, an enormous campaign was waged to persuade middle-class women to enter the workforce. Today, a large number of middle-class women work voluntarily. The changes that took place over the past 50 years have come in stages (Milkman, 1979). First, women worked while the men were at war, then just until they got married. Soon they worked until their first child was born and perhaps returned to work after their youngest child went to school. Now, the great majority of women work before and after their marriage, when their children are older and when they are young (Baruch, Barnett, & Rivers, 1983; Crosby, 1987). It is worth noting that while middle-class women are experiencing these changes, poor women always worked as a simple matter of necessity. In the early 1900s, middle-class women did not expect and were not expected to work outside the home. By contrast, middle-class women are now expected to contribute half the family income.

Many properties of the individual are changing, and it is impossible to consider them all here. It is critical, however, to recognize the importance of the changing racial, ethnic, and religious composition of this country (Bengtson, Rosenthal, & Burton, 1990; Fry, 1995; Wong, 1999). In the early years of the past century, this country was populated predominantly by individuals of European descent. Now, at a time when immigration is at an especially high level, the majority of immigrants come, not from Europe, but from Asia, South America, and the Middle East, and these immigrants are largely middle-aged. These regions of the world have customs, traditions, and religions that influence individual expectations and needs for social relations. Middle-aged immigrants struggle to nurture and maintain their traditions, transmitting the values, attitudes, and beliefs from their homeland to the younger generations. It is well recognized that due to the nature of assimilation and acculturation, these intergenerational links are not always without conflict. The midlife parent, who represents both the old and the new, must negotiate relationships across generations. Middle-aged parents who wish to nurture and maintain cultural traditions often experience conflict with their children.

In the preceding paragraphs, we have briefly summarized the unique Properties of the Person at midlife. The changing life-expectancy has redefined midlife from what it might arguably have been from 15 to 30 in 1900 (i.e., the middle third of a 47-year life span) to a 30-year-span from 30 to 60 in 2000, when many claim we are approaching a life expectancy of 100 years. Changing marital trends as well as later and multiple marriages influence the structure of family relationships. One acquires in-laws later when one marries later, and multiple marriages are likely to involve multiple sets of in-laws who may not be easy to divorce or leave behind when children are involved. But the changing and unique Properties of the Person at midlife are not the only influences on the development of one's convoy of social relations. Properties of the Situation are also fundamentally influential.

PROPERTIES OF THE SITUATION AT MIDLIFE

The Properties of the Situation refer to expectations, resources, and demands that characterize a situation. The situation for individuals at midlife has also changed radically with the biggest differences occurring quite recently, in the past 20 or 30 years.

Working might be considered a role or Property of the Person but role expectations are a Property of the Situation. Role expectations about work have changed considerably for women. Most economists tell us that whereas middle-class women might have worked for extra money for the family or for a feeling of accomplishment in the 1950s and 1960s, in the 1970s the downward turn in the economy made this second income a necessity for many families. The second income had become necessary if the average middle-income family was to maintain the high standard of living in the 1970s that they had achieved earlier. Once women became accustomed to working and the increased financial benefits to the family as well as the independence and equality they personally experienced, they were reluctant to give up employment. Now, more women work outside the home than at any other time in history. With the increase in women filling worker roles comes a parallel new issue of role demands and expectations experienced both differentially and similarly by men and women.

As is well documented, the roles of spouse and parent continue to have vastly different implications for men and women. Women are much more likely to be primarily responsible for child care, cooking, and cleaning regardless of whether they are working outside the home (Hochschild, 1989, 1997). These expectations have remained despite the increased number of women in the workforce. Women have been quite resourceful about finding ways to meet these expectations. They seek relatives, neighbors, family, and formal day-care providers to care for their children and use increasingly clever aids and conveniences offered by advancing technology (e.g., microwave ovens, food processors, and cleaning services). Since midlife is a time when both work and family expectations are at their highest, it is likely that the Properties of the Situation that accompany these multiple roles will have a critical influence on the network, support, and satisfaction with social relations at midlife.

Both men and women now occupy a high number of social roles at midlife. The roles of spouse, parent, child, and worker are examples of roles occupied by most people at midlife but never occupied so complexly or simultaneously as right now. These multiple roles are accompanied by opportunities and demands, advantages and disadvantages. For example, midlife women engaged in full-time employment outside the home were once thought to be severely stressed and burdened if the role of employee was added to the roles of wife and mother (Crosby, 1987). It has now been shown that while multiple roles do often mean multiple demands and multiple stressors, many women report that the ability to succeed at work may help offset some of the problems they face at home and that they are also advantaged by these multiple roles (Crosby, 1991; Hong & Seltzer, 1995; Martire, Stephens, & Townsend, 2000). On the other hand, men now seem to be playing a more active role in the rearing of their children in addition to their traditional full-time employment roles outside the home. These men often report that their family roles are among the most satisfying and gratifying activities in which they are engaged on a regular basis. Simple successes at home, such as playing a board game with one's 4-year-old or coaching the basketball team with one's 10-year-old as a member of the team, have been found to offset problems one may encounter on the job.

Two important lines of literature that have focused on the Properties of the Situation and received a great deal of attention is that of life events (Holmes & Rahe, 1967) and daily hassles (Lazarus, 1984). Life events, while not so frequent as to be termed normative, happen to enough people to be recognized as having a unique and often negative impact on the individual. Life events include such experiences as death of a loved one, losing a job, changing residence, marrying, divorcing, or having a child. While some of these events are positive, it is recognized that even positive events can cause stress for the individual (Dohrenwend & Dohrenwend, 1981). Within the context of the convoy model and understanding social relations, these life events are important because of the ways in which they impact an individual's convoy of social relations. For example, having lost a loved one means not only that an important source of one's social support is gone, but a significant void can be left in the structure of one's social network (Thoits, 1983). One's support network is also very likely to change when one moves or loses a job. Getting married or having a child is known to fundamentally impact the individual's social relations, with married people more likely to socialize with other couples and with parents more likely to socialize with people who have children. It is well documented that people experience more life events, both positive and negative, at midlife than at any other point in the life span (Aneshensel & Pearlin, 1987). Daily hassles are less dramatic but stressful events that occur in the individual's daily life. Traffic jams, job workload, minor health problems, being bothered by others, and being late for an appointment are examples. Hassles are often situational and fundamentally influence the experience of daily life (Coyne & DeLongis, 1986). There is some evidence that people at midlife are exposed to more daily hassles than people at other points in the life span.

Another characteristic of the situation that influences individuals is their membership in organizations. These include civic, religious, professional, political, and community organizations. Organizational membership is a source of social relationships influencing every facet of interpersonal interactions including the kind of social relationships that are considered necessary, the types of relationships that are likely to be formed, and the support exchanged within these relationships. Just as there are many family roles at midlife, it is also the time when people belong to the most organizations. Thus, the demands made by organizational membership as well as the benefits accrued from these memberships must be considered. Organizations differ considerably, as do their impact. Participation in a political party is likely to have a very circumscribed impact on the individual's situation. Similarly, membership in a labor union that is actively involved in influencing one's work environment will have a very different impact on the individual's situation than a religious affiliation.

Where one lives can also influence social relationships at midlife (Crimmins & Ingegneri, 1990; Forest, Murie, & Willams, 1990; Ruggles, 1996). A single home versus an apartment, urban versus rural environments, living with relatives or with relatives close by compared with living alone or at a great distance from other family members are all characteristics of the situation that will influence an individual's experience and the type of social relationships they will seek, require, and enjoy (Aquilino & Supple, 1991). An individual who lives alone may have trouble reaching out to form social relations with neighbors whereas a person who lives with and is surrounded by family members may feel no need to develop social relationships with nonfamily members. These situations represent another piece of the complicated set of factors that influence an individual's convoy of social relations.

Both the Properties of the Situation and the Properties of the Person influence social relationships. As individual circumstances have changed in recent times, so too have those of the Situation. Whereas at one time, multiple role occupancy by either men or women that was characterized by a true and complete involvement in these roles was seen as an anomaly, it is now both common and widely accepted. We recognize that these multiple roles are accompanied by multiple role expectancies that can offer gratification as well as distress (Crosby, 1991). Both the Properties of the Person and the Situation affect social relations that in turn influence both health and well-being. We turn now to a description of the special and unique characteristics of Support Network, Social Support, and Support Satisfaction and how these are affected by the Properties of the Person and Situation at midlife.

SOCIAL RELATIONS AT MIDLIFE

In this section we provide a broad overview of different aspects of social relations. We consider each of these separately because each has different properties that can potentially influence the health and well-being of the midlife individual.

Support Networks is the term often used to describe the structure of an individual's significant social relationships. Support Network refers to objective characteristics of the network such as the number of people in one's network, the number of family members, age, sex, proximity, or frequency of contact with network members. Support Network says nothing about the nature or quality of the relationships; it simply describes the people with whom the individual has social relationships. At midlife, the Properties of the Person and Situation significantly influence the structure of the individual's network. Since one occupies a large number of roles, such as child, spouse, and parent, it is natural that this is a time when there are numerous members of the support network, and that they differ widely in age and gender (Antonucci & Akiyama, 1997). Moreover, race/ethnic differences exist during midlife. When comparing African Americans with their White counterparts, Ajrouch, Antonucci, and Janevic (in press) examined a representative sample from a large midwestern city. They found that African Americans have a higher proportion of kin in their networks and are less likely to be married. On the other hand, Whites have larger networks and report on average more frequent contact with network members. More general findings indicate that most middle-aged Whites are married and hence have a close social connection to at least one member of the opposite sex. Both their mother and their father are likely to be alive and their children are likely to be young enough to still be dependent. While people have more family members as part of their support network at this time, it is worth noting that most people continue to mention at least a small number of significant friendships (Adams & Allan, 1998). It has also been noted that there are important unique characteristics of intergenerational support and extended family networks among African Americans (Chatters & Jayakody, 1995; Taylor & Chatters, 1991).

Social Support refers to the actual exchange of support, that is to the giving and receiving of aid, affect, or affirmation. There are several types of social support. Aid refers to instrumental or tangible support. Examples of this type of support include lending someone money, taking care of them when they are sick, and providing them with specific types of help that they might need. Affective support is considerably less tangible but no less important. It refers to the emotional support that one receives or provides by communicating that one is loved or cared for by close and significant others. Affirmation, while less specific than the two other types of support, is also seen as important. This type of support refers to an approval or agreement by others that your values and beliefs, goals, and aspirations are shared. One can see that all types of support are likely to be important throughout the life span but that there are special needs at midlife. People at midlife may need specific help providing instrumental support to their parents, spouse, or children. We know that people of all ages need to feel cared for and loved. This is no less true when one is surrounded by multiple generations of family members at midlife. And finally, when struggling with the tasks of midlife, it can be very helpful to know that others share your views, and understand and approve of your goals and aspirations. Midlife is a time of numerous and complex social relations (Scott, 1997). Many support demands are perceived and a great deal of support is exchanged during this period of life. There appears to be a decline in the perception of reciprocity in social relations at this time, with most people at midlife feeling that they are providing more support than they are receiving. Nevertheless, support exchanges continue to be significantly related to well-being. There are cultural differences, however, in views concerning intergenerational exchange and reciprocity across generations (Akiyama et al., 1997; Lee, Peck, & Coward, 1998).

Support Satisfaction refers to how people feel about their social relations. While support network refers to the actual composition of the individual's support networks and social support refers to the actual exchange of aid, affect, and affirmation, an evaluative dimension to these relationships is also important. Regardless of the objective characteristics of the support network and support exchanges, there are individual differences in how a person evaluates these experiences. By Support Satisfaction, we refer to this psychological and subjective dimension of social relations. People assess whether they are satisfied with their support relationships and if they are adequate to meet their needs (Kahn & Antonucci, 1980). They can feel that others make too many demands on them, or that others are available to provide exactly the amount of support they need or might request (Antonucci, Akiyama, & Lansford, 1998; Walen & Lachman, 2000). One can feel that one's relationships are completely positive, completely negative, or some combination of the two. What little data are available on this point show that while there is likely a relationship between the objective characteristics of the support network and the exchange of support, this relationship may not be linear. There is variation in what people need, what they think they need, how they react to specific events or supports and how they feel about specific people. Thus, the same amount of support to one person could seem to be just the right amount while another person might feel smothered by it. One kind of support behavior might be perceived as positive and therefore welcomed by one person, while another person might feel that the support provider is being too intrusive or excessively demanding. Regardless of the lack of objectivity to this evaluative dimension of social relations, there is no doubt that it is a powerful determinant of how effectively social relations influence the well-being of the individual.

HEALTH AND WELL-BEING AT MIDLIFE

The convoy model is designed to help us understand how the Properties of the Person and Situation uniquely combine to affect Social Relations, that is, support networks, social support, and support satisfaction. It is hypothesized that these characteristics interact to affect the health and well-being of the individual and there are data to support this claim (e.g., Cohen & Syme, 1985). There are effects of social relations on a variety of outcome variables, including physical and mental health, life satisfaction, happiness, and self-esteem (Silverstein & Bengtson, 1991). Our model is relatively broad in perspective, and we believe that these social and personal characteristics influence how the individual reacts to and feels about a variety of life situations. It has long been recognized that there is a negative relationship between socioeconomic status and health (Marmot et al., 1998). Certainly, organizational membership is a source of social relationships, influencing every facet of interpersonal interactions including the kind of social relationships that are considered necessary, the types of relationships that are likely to be formed and the support exchanged within these relationships. Recent work has identified the influence of social relations on the SES-Health link at midlife. We return to these findings later in this chapter.

The case of midlife is interesting. As with any life period, there are numerous dimensions on which individuals can evaluate themselves or be evaluated by others. At the same time, there are multiple life goals and outcomes converging on individuals at this particular point in their own life-span development (Lachman & James, 1997; McQuaide, 1998). In this chapter, we focus on several common outcomes represented in the literature. These include physical health such as subjectively evaluated health and number of health problems. We also consider psychological health as measured by depressive symptomatology. We turn now to a brief review of available evidence examining how various aspects of the Convoy Model affect the social relations of individuals at midlife.

EFFECTS OF PROPERTIES OF THE PERSON AND SITUATION ON SOCIAL RELATIONSHIPS

Many people speak of the changing nature of our culture, the increase in the stress and general pace of life. For example, Gleick's recent book entitled *Faster: The Acceleration of Just about Everything* (1999) documents the dramatic increase in the pace of our everyday lives. These changes are notable in the paragraphs outlining the current Properties of People and their Situation at midlife and are reflected in the changing characteristics of social relations. In the following paragraphs, we outline these characteristics at midlife as suggested by empirical evidence available both from our own studies and those in the literature. We report here from the Social Relations Study (Antonucci & Akiyama, 1994), which includes large, regionally representative, community-based samples in the United States and Japan. Earlier work (Antonucci & Akiyama, 1997) provided some preliminary evidence about social relations at midlife. There is very little difference between the composition of social networks at midlife and any other period in adulthood. Most people list family members as their closest relationships, including close family members (spouse, children, parents), with more distal family members, friends, and co-workers mentioned as people who are important but somewhat less close. The uniqueness of the midlife period, however, is that all these relationships are represented simultaneously. One can readily explain why this is the period when social networks are the most numerous. People are often married, in the workforce, still have living parents, and are likely to already have children.

Although there are not very many parallel data sets available in the literature, studies from New York (Peek & Lin, 1999) and Denmark (Due, Holstein, Lund, Modvig, & Avlund, 1999) yield very similar findings. Peek and Lin (1999) indicate that men and women in their sample have more people in their networks at midlife and a higher proportion of kin in their perceived network than older people. Due and colleagues examined social relations among people in the Danish Longitudinal Health Behaviour Study which included five cohorts of people born in 1975, 1965, 1940, 1930, and 1920 (see Due et al., 1999, for details). For our purposes, we are concentrating on the support information from 50-year-olds (the 1940 cohort). This is the group that is most likely to be married and have children. They are the most likely, compared with people older but not younger, to spend time weekly with relatives.

Data are available to compare Japanese and American men and women at midlife (Antonucci & Akiyama, 1994). As in the United States, Japanese people in midlife have a larger number of people in their network than those in the older groups. In Japan, the largest network size is reported by those in their 20s, while in the United States, the largest network size is reported by those in their 50s. In both countries, however, the two oldest groups are similar in that they each report fewer people in their social networks than younger people either at midlife or earlier. While the younger, 20-year-olds in Japan may still be in a formation stage of their life cycle among those apparently more established in an adult lifestyle, the middle aged in both countries appears to be most connected (i.e., have the largest social networks).

Data are now available that allow us to examine the influence of certain characteristics on social relationships. For example, we find that people who report experiencing financial strain are significantly more likely than those not reporting financial strain to indicate that their network is smaller in size and that they experience negative support from network members. These results reflect Krause, Jay, and Liang's (1991) findings with older people. Our data also indicate that both daily hassles and life events affect social relations. People at midlife who report a larger number of daily hassles in their lives are significantly more likely to have smaller networks, and to report negative affect from both their spouse and their child. Similarly, the larger the number of reported negative life events at midlife, the more likely the person is to report negative affect from spouse and child.

PERSONAL/SITUATIONAL PROPERTIES, SOCIAL RELATIONS, AND WELL-BEING

Personal and Situational Properties and all three types of Social Relations (i.e., Support Network, Social Support, and Support Satisfaction) can influence Health and Well-being. Among midlife men and women, the roles one occupies within the family, the quality of family relationships and one's satisfaction with these relationships are all known to influence well-being at midlife (Ryff, 1997). Vandewater, Ostrove, and Stewart (1997) have

shown that satisfaction with family roles and the quality of family relationships are related to well-being for midlife women. Our own data indicate that among the roles of spouse, parent and child, those who occupy
more roles express less depressive symptomatology.

SPOUSE

Of the possible family relationships in midlife, marriage has been examined most extensively. The quality of the marital relationship is consistently related to well-being at midlife. Traditionally, middle-aged
individuals are well-established in their marriages. Those who follow a
less traditional path may remain single, be divorced, or remarried at
midlife. Marital status is very likely to have an impact on well-being at
midlife. Being married at midlife seems to be generally beneficial and
positively related to well-being (Marks & Lambert, 1998). While the effects of marriage are generally positive, it does not necessarily follow that
the situation for those who are not married is completely negative. Unmarried individuals report higher levels of personal growth and autonomy than do married adults at midlife (Marks & Lambert, 1998). While
being single can place women at risk for lower well-being, friendships can
compensate for this resource deficit. Living with a female housemate and
having many casual friends are also related to high life satisfaction for
single women (Loewenstein, 1981).

For those who have followed the traditional course, marriages at
midlife are subject to a number of outside influences. Even stable marriages experience new pressures and challenges as changes take place at
work or within other relationships. When the youngest child leaves home,
the couple may find themselves alone together for the first time in many
years (Barber, 1989). Becoming grandparents for the first time may also
influence the relationship between husbands and wives at midlife. Taking on this new role may alter the identities of people at midlife and may
serve as a catalyst for change (Szinovacz, 1998).

Despite the continuing prevalence of the myth of the midlife crisis,
research on marriage at midlife shows that marital distress does not increase during this period of development (Blattberg & Hogan, 1994), except if one experiences widowhood and divorce. Widowhood is not a
common experience of midlife, although as one ages, the likelihood of a
spouse dying increases. While not a great deal of literature has focused
on this topic, widowed people are often more readily sympathized with
than divorced people. Even though widowhood at midlife is nonnormative, various rituals accompany widowhood. Certain customs and traditions are recognized and only very infrequently is anyone considered to
be at fault. The contrary seems to be true of divorce. Very few "rules"

seem to exist about how to behave, although everyone seems to choose sides and maintain a relationship with one but not both of the divorcing parties.

The valence of divorce's impact remains a topic of debate. It has been suggested that individuals who experience a divorce at midlife are more vulnerable to the effects of this transition than individuals who experience divorce during other phases of adulthood. However, there is also evidence that adults at midlife exhibit better coping with both divorcing and remaining single than do young adults (Marks & Lambert, 1998). Generally, there are negative correlates of a single marital status. An increase in the number of divorced individuals could mean that the overall well-being of individuals at this age is decreased. Other evidence, however, suggests that divorce may actually increase well-being for some individuals. Whatever the psychological consequences of midlife divorce, the financial consequences for women are overwhelmingly negative which, of course, has negative effects on individual well-being (Scott, 1997). Midlife remarriage is an option for both middle-aged widows and divorcees. However, it is an option not frequently chosen by or available to middle-aged women. Men are more likely than women to remarry (Julian, 1992).

PARENTS

Another significant relationship among adults at midlife is their relationship with their parents. Midlife can be the time during which the relationship between older parents and their middle-aged children shifts from one that is primarily egalitarian to one in which the middle-aged child has increasing power over and responsibility for his or her aging parent (Silverstein, Parrott, & Bengtson, 1995). For some, this can be a time of dependency, as the older adult parent can become financially dependent or physically frail (Spitze, Logan, Joseph, & Lee, 1994; Stein et al., 1998). These changes can alter the direction of power and influence between parent and child. This type of role reversal can be unsettling and uncomfortable for the older parent and middle-aged child. When an older parent needs assistance with the activities of daily life, it is frequently a daughter who bears this responsibility in the American culture (Scott, 1997; Soldo, 1996). While parent care can be experienced as a significant responsibility, many children report that this responsibility is accepted willingly as a natural progression of life. Adult children often indicate that they are pleased to be able to provide the support and care their parents need and feel it is only a minimal return on the bountiful gifts provided to them by their parents during their lifetime (Akiyama et al., 1997). There is also some evidence of race & cultural differences in expectations concerning filial responsibility (Fry, 1995; Lee et al., 1998).

Individuals at midlife often find that they must balance parent care with work responsibilities. The demands of these two roles can lead to stress. While many individuals find creative ways to meet the multiple demands of their lives, this doubling-up of roles often has negative consequences for the individual filling these roles (Gerstel & Gallagher, 1993; Gottlieb, 1994; Penning, 1998; Rosenthal, Martin-Matthews, & Matthews, 1996). Not every middle-aged child physically cares for his or her parent, and parent care can vary in scope and duration (Eckert & Schulman, 1996). However, the burden of care extends beyond physical care. Parent care can be defined more broadly to include responsibilities such as help with finances or healthcare planning. Therefore, even middle-aged persons who from one perspective may appear to have limited filial responsibilities may experience stress related to parent care that involves distal care and care management as well as anticipatory care planning (Marks, 1998; Moen, Robinson, & Dempster-McClain, 1995; Walen & Lachman, 2000).

Parent care can also shape the relationship between siblings at midlife. Siblings may be drawn together to provide support to their parents and to manage their financial situation. It has been suggested that if siblings do work together to care for their parents, this experience can strengthen their bond (Cicirelli, 1995; Gold, 1989). Struggles over parent care and finances can also increase conflict between siblings. Conflict can arise over who is seen as the person responsible for providing the care or the financial resources should a parent be needy. Another common source of conflict is the anticipated distribution of resources or inheritance should the parent have substantial resources.

CHILDREN

The third of the significant family relationships at midlife is with children. At midlife, it is normative to have children who are adolescents or young adults. Of course, even this can change in circumstances of late or remarriage accompanied by later childbearing. Having a young adult child means that one typically expects the child to live outside the parental home and to be relatively independent financially. The move of the youngest child away from the parental home may present a turning point in the midlife marriage. When parents experience what is called the "empty nest," they may experience a feeling of freedom and easing of responsibility (White & Edwards, 1990). Other couples may be confronted by a problem marriage that family responsibilities had obscured. The degree to which one's identity is dependent on the parental role may be a factor that determines the valence of the reaction to the empty nest. With few exceptions, most reports indicate that midlife women react quite positively to the empty nest, enjoying the time to reinvest in their marriage and to rediscover personal interests (Adelmann, Antonucci, Crohan, & Coleman, 1989).

The empty-nest period may not always occur uninterrupted. In fact, nearly half of the young people who leave home return again at some point (DeVanzo & Goldscheider, 1990). The reactions that middle-aged parents have to the return of their adult children may be dependent on the reasons for the return. Parents are generally supportive of children returning while they complete their education, but less supportive or at least less pleased when a failed marriage is the reason for return. In addition, when adult children bring their own children with them, parents at midlife may find that they are called on to provide child care at a time in their lives when they assumed that these responsibilities had concluded.

For some families, the empty nest does not come at the expected time. There are children who linger in the parental home past the normative time of transition to independent living. The effects of their presence in the home on middle-aged adults have been investigated (Aquilino, 1990). Adult children living in the parental home may cause tension, but the quality of the parent-child relationship determines the degree to which this living situation has an effect on the parent (Aquilino & Supple, 1991). The relationship between a middle-aged parent and a young adult child is still one in which it is normative for the parent to provide more support for the child than vice versa (Rossi & Rossi, 1990). However, this scenario is particularly middle class. Only children who have achieved some financial independence are likely to expect or be able to acquire independent living.

Often newly formed families of young people begin their early years as a family within the household of the older generation. Then, if the older generation loses financial ground, either through illness, job loss, or retirement without sufficient financial resources, the younger generation household members are available to pool their resources to meet the household obligations. Moreover, preliminary findings suggest that relationships with children have a differential impact on the physical well-being of middle aged men and women. Antonucci, Ajrouch, and Janevic (1999) found that in general social relations moderate the effect of education on health. Although social network size had no effect, instrumental and emotional support with spouse and children lessened the usual negative effect of low education on health. One exception is noteworthy. Among middle aged men and women with less education, those who confide in their spouse are less healthy, perhaps reflecting the greater vulnerability of middle aged, less educated people with significant health problems present.

If the next generation is also following the traditional trajectory, the individual at midlife may become a grandparent for the first time. However, there have been important changes in the timing of the family life cycle that have had an impact on the lives of middle-aged parents. For many segments of society, childbirth has been delayed, particularly for women with higher levels of education or higher economic status. In addition, the average age of first marriage has increased. These changes mean that many middle-aged parents can expect to have their own children living with them, often past what was once the normative time for children leaving the parental home.

Those who have been widowed young or who are not married may find that they have the task of single parenting at midlife. Demographic trends suggest that the proportions of middle-aged parents who are single or divorced will continue to increase.

Siblings

One additional close family relationship that is often neglected is the relationship among siblings (Bedford, 1992). The sibling relationship is usually the longest relationship in one's life. Even as parents, aunts, and uncles die, the remaining sibling can play a special role as a figure representing the idea of family. Most adults in middle age do have at least one sibling (Cicirelli, 1995). Young adulthood is typically a time when siblings drift apart. Additionally, a large number of roles and demands mean that middle-aged siblings are not in frequent contact. However, for those siblings who are in frequent contact, this relationship can be an important contributor to their well-being. Contact with siblings increases in late middle adulthood and into old age (Cicirelli, 1995). Some research has shown interaction between siblings to be lowest around age 30 with increases thereafter (Carstensen, 1992). Siblings act as confidants in midlife (Connidis & Davies, 1990) and sometimes as co-caregivers of their parents. Paul (1997) found that the quality of middle-aged men's relationships with their siblings related to their well-being. For example, if they reported positive feelings toward their siblings, this was related to low levels of loneliness and high morale. For women, sibling relationships also relate to well-being. Women who reported positive feelings toward their siblings scored higher on a measure of self-concept (Paul, 1997). Women who report few negative feelings toward their siblings also show less depressive symptomatology, and report less loneliness.

While most research on sibling relationships has focused on full, biological, sibling relationships, many siblings do not share the same two parents. Data from the National Survey of Families and Households (NSFH) indicate that this factor influences contact between siblings (White & Riedmann, 1992). The more time stepsiblings spend living together during childhood, the more likely they are to maintain contact as adults. While step- and half-siblings tend to keep in touch with each other, their contact is not as frequent as that between full siblings (White & Riedmann, 1992). Furthermore, half- and step-siblings have been found to provide less help to each other than do full siblings (White & Riedmann, 1992). These differences may diminish as blended families become more common. Alternatively, the well-being of midlife adults may decrease as a higher and higher proportion of them have no full siblings. Siblings have roles that bridge the qualities of family relationships and friendships. Like family members, they are not chosen, and many years of contact are normative. However, unlike other family members, siblings are typically around the same age and thus share many experiences typical of a given generation.

FRIENDS

Social relationships outside the family have been investigated less than family relationships, although it is well recognized that friendships have a significant impact on the well-being of the individual (Adams, 1997; Adams & Allan, 1998). Evidence is accumulating to suggest that friendships make an important contribution to the well-being of individuals at midlife. Socioemotional Selectivity Theory (Carstensen, 1992) would suggest that having a large number of friends is not as important to individuals at midlife as it is to young adults. Emphasis should be shifting to a smaller group of more intimate friends. There is some evidence to support this idea. Carney and Cohler (1993) argue that as adults move from middle age to late life, large social networks become less satisfying than they were earlier in adulthood. Because of the high number of social roles filled by individuals during midlife, middle age is typically the period that allows the least time for friendships. However, those who make time for friends benefit from these relationships.

Women with a confidant or a group of female friends report higher well-being than those women who lack these social resources (Loewenstein, 1981; McQuaide, 1998). In addition to having female friends, the quality of the relationships with these friends has an impact on well-being. Paul (1997) found that middle-aged women who express positive feelings toward their friends have lower levels of depressive symptomatology and higher morale. Friendships also have an impact on men's well-being. The impact of midlife friendships may extend into late life. Physical health at age 70 can be predicted by adequacy of social support, particularly from friends, at age 50 (Vaillant, 1998). Having many close friends has also been found to be important for men's well-being, but less important than feeling close to family members (Julian, 1992).

While there appear to be no differences in the quantity of friends among middle-aged male and female parents, childless women at midlife report having more friends than childless middle-aged men (Fischer & Oliker, 1983). Some have suggested that the multiple role occupancy of women at midlife, especially including the role of parent, precludes the availability of free time to maintain adult friendships. Certainly, many people at midlife can be heard lamenting the lack of time to engage in the type of leisure activities that would most likely include friends.

CO-WORKERS

Another social relationship outside the family is the work relationship. Co-workers can be an important source of support. For those who are feeling the need to contribute to future generations, mentoring at work may provide an outlet for feelings of generativity (MacDermid, Heilbrun, & Dehaan, 1997). Having friendly relationships with colleagues may buffer the effects of negative relationships elsewhere. This is an apparent contradiction to the stereotype in our culture: Working women have been found to report greater well-being. In the 1960s and 1970s, it was assumed that women who held jobs outside the home would have poorer health and relationships of a lower quality than would women without jobs (Barnett, 1997; Crosby, 1987). However, most research shows that the health and family relationships of working women are better than those of nonworking women. Perhaps the relationships they form at work account for some of this effect. As noted, research has documented that multiple role occupancy provides multiple stresses as well as multiple sources of reward and satisfaction. If one aspect of an individual's life is not going well, it may be possible to turn to another to garner some sense of accomplishment and success (Lachman & James, 1997).

OTHERS

Although much less information is available, it is now increasingly recognized that neighbors and volunteer organizations including religious groups may also be important sources of support and hence increase the health and well-being of individuals (Daniels, 1985; Herzog, Kahn, Morgan, Jackson, & Antonucci, 1989). This appears to be no less true, and perhaps more true, of men and women at midlife. Belonging to a religious community may expand one's social network. Many studies have shown higher levels of well-being among those who are actively religious. Perhaps the additional contact with a religious community contributes to the level of well-being. Volunteering may be an outlet for those who feel a drive for generativity, but have no children or opportunities for mentoring. Particularly for those who did not have, or did not help raise children, being a volunteer may lead to feelings of having contributed to the well-being of society and of having contributed to the future.

While we have explored these relationships individually, evidence suggests that diversity in relationships is important (Lepore, 1992). It may be possible for the positive aspects of some relationships to buffer the effects of other, more negative relationships. Therefore, persons with more social relationships may not suffer as much from the potentially detrimental effects of some negative relationship characteristics. However, some relationships are too significant to be easily substituted. Thus, a fight with one friend might be offset by a conversation with another friend but a conflictual relationship with one's spouse is not easily made up for by a nonconflictual one with a friend.

CONCLUSION AND FUTURE DIRECTIONS

This review of social relations at midlife as organized around the convoy model argues that social relations are developmental, continuous, and often lifelong. Changes in the Properties of the Person and the Situation especially the timing and experience of certain roles suggest that the experience of midlife has changed in ways that we would call revolutionary. At the same time, we caution that there remain many midlife activities that are traditional and unwavering. The lives of men and women at midlife are complex. It is a difficult task to weave traditional and emerging needs of family and friends with the old and new personal and situational characteristics of the individual. Responsive social relationships can help individuals achieve their goals and maintain their own health and well-being. As we seek to identify those aspects of the model that are most adaptive and most successful, it will be especially useful to remember that changing characteristics of the Person and the Situation also reflect societal changes such as the changing racial, ethnic, and religious makeup of our communities. While many of the fundamental goals of midlife are the same, many other aspects of the experience of midlife have changed. The challenges of midlife are complex and too often underestimated. People in midlife need multifaceted Support Networks and support exchanges to maintain satisfaction with their support relationships that will maximize the probability of positive outcomes in the achievement of the Health and Well-being of themselves and their loved ones.

As we look toward the future to determine how best to direct our research on social relations and midlife, several general areas seem to be in particular need of attention. It is widely recognized that the traditional nuclear family based on one marriage, consisting of one employed member, the father, one full-time homemaker, the mother, and two children who are full siblings (preferably a boy and a girl with a dog named Spot!) now represents less than 25% of the population at the same time we know very little about how the new "nontraditional" family styles

will affect the health, well-being, and life goals of men and women at
midlife. Nuclear and changing family membership; long and short-
term, obligatory and voluntary, family and nonfamily relationships; existing and changing ethnic, racial, and cultural traditions all combine to
influence social relations and midlife roles as they have traditionally
been known. Fortunately, as we come to recognize the uniqueness of intraindividual, intrafamilial life course development, parallel analytical
strategies are developing such as latent growth curve modeling that will
permit the examination and effects of their individual trajectories. We
are both theoretically and methodologically more sophisticated than we
ever have been before, which leaves us poised to learn and discover and
hence better understand midlife in the new millennium.

REFERENCES

Adams, R.G. (1997). Friendship patterns among older women. In J.M. Coyle
(Ed.), *Handbook on women and aging* (pp. 400–417). Westport, CT: Greenwood
Press.

Adams, R.G., & Allan, G. (1998). *Placing friendship in context.* Cambridge, MA:
Cambridge University Press.

Adelmann, P.K., Antonucci, T.C., Crohan, S.E., & Coleman, L.M. (1989). Empty
nest, cohort, and employment in the well-being of midlife women. *Sex Roles,
20,* 173–189.

Ainsworth, M., Blehar, M.C., Waters, E., & Wall, S. (1978). *Patterns of attachment:
A psychological study of the strange situation.* Hillsdale, NJ: Erlbaum.

Ajrouch, K.J., Antonucci, T.C., & Janevic, M.R. (in press). Social networks among
Blacks and Whites: The interaction between race and age. *Journal of Gerontology: Social Sciences.*

Akiyama, H., Antonucci, T.C., & Campbell, R. (1997). Exchange and reciprocity
among two generations of Japanese and American women. In J. Sokolovsky
(Ed.), *The cultural context of aging: Worldwide perspectives* (2nd ed. pp. 162–178).
Westport, CT: Greenwood Press.

Aneshensel, C., & Pearlin, L. (1987). Structural contests of sex differences in
stress. In R. Barnett, L. Biener, & G. Baruch (Eds.), *Gender and stress* (pp. 75–95).
New York: Free Press.

Antonucci, T.C. (1985). Personal characteristics, social support, and social behavior. In R.H. Binstock & F. Shamas (Eds.), *The handbook of aging and the social sciences* (2nd ed., pp. 94–120). New York: Van Nostrand-Reinhold.

Antonucci, T.C. Ajrouch, K., & Janevic, M. (1999). SES, social support, age, and
health. In N.E. Adler, M. Marmot, B.S. McEwen, & J. Stewart (Eds.), *Socioeconomic status and health industrial nations* (pp. 390–392). New York: New York
Academy of Sciences.

Antonucci, T.C., & Akiyama, H. (1987). Social networks in adult life and a preliminary examination of the convoy model. *Journal of Gerontology: Social Sciences, 42,* S519–S527.

Antonucci, T.C., & Akiyama, H. (1991). Convoys of social support: Generational issues. *Marriage and Family Review, 16*, 103–124.

Antonucci, T.C., & Akiyama, H. (1994). *Social relations and mental health over the life course.* Final report to the National Institute of Mental Health.

Antonucci, T.C., & Akiyama, H. (1997). Concern with others at midlife: Care, comfort, or compromise. In M. Lachman & J.B. James (Eds.), *Multiple paths of midlife development* (pp. 145–170). Chicago: University of Chicago Press.

Antonucci, T.C., Akiyama, H., & Lansford, J.E. (1998). The negative effects of close social relations among older adults. *Family Relations, 47*(4), 379–384.

Aquilino, W.S. (1990). The likelihood of parent-adult relations and parent's satisfaction with living arrangements when adult children live at home. *Journal of Marriage and the Family, 52*, 405–419.

Aquilino, W.S., & Supple, K.R. (1991). Parent-child relations and parent's satisfaction with living arrangements when adult children live at home. *Journal of Marriage and the Family, 53*, 13–27.

Baltes, P.B. (1987). Theoretical propositions of life-span developmental psychology: On the dynamics between growth and decline. *Developmental Psychology, 23*, 611–626.

Barber, C.E. (1989). Transition to the empty nest. In S.J. Bahr & E.T. Peterson (Eds.), *Aging and the family* (pp. 15–32). Lexington, MA: Lexington Books.

Barnett, R.C. (1997). Gender, employment, and psychological well-being: Historical and life course perspectives. In M.E. Lachman & J.B. James (Eds.), *Multiple paths of midlife development* (pp. 323–344). Chicago: University of Chicago Press.

Baruch, G., Barnett, R., & Rivers, C. (1983). *Life prints: New patterns of love and work for today's woman.* New York: McGraw-Hill.

Bedford, V.H. (1992). Memories of parental favoritism and the quality of parent-child ties in adulthood. *Journal of Gerontology: Social Sciences, 47*, S149–S155.

Bengtson, V.L., & Cutler, N.E. (1976). Generations and inter-generational relations: Perspectives on age groups and social change. In R. Binstock & E. Shanas (Eds.), *The handbook of aging and the social sciences* (pp. 130–159). New York: Van Nostrand-Reinhold.

Bengtson, V.L., Rosenthal, C., & Burton, L. (1990). Families and aging: Diversity and Hetrogeneity. In R.H. Binstock & L. K, George (Eds.), *Handbook of aging and the social sciences* (pp. 263–287). New York: Academic Press.

Blattberg, K.J., & Hogan, J.D. (1994). Marital distress across the mid-life transition among middle class Caucasian women. *Psychological Reports, 75*(1, Pt. 2, Special issue), 497–498.

Bowlby, J. (1969). *Attachment and loss: Vol. 1. Attachment.* New York: Basic Books.

Bowlby, J. (1973). *Attachment and loss: Vol. 2. Separation: Anxiety and anger.* New York: Basic Books.

Brim, O.J., Jr., & Kagan, J. (Eds.). (1980). *Constancy and change in human development.* Cambridge, MA: Harvard University Press.

Bumpass, L.L., & Aquilino, W.S. (1995). *A social map of midlife: Family and work over the middle life course.* Vero Beach, FL: MacArthur Foundation Research Network on Successful Midlife Development.

Butler, R.N., Lewis, M., & Sunderland, T. (1991). *Aging and mental health* (4th ed.). New York: Macmillan.

Caldwell, C.H., Antonucci, T.C., & Jackson, J.S. (1998). Supportive/conflictual family relations and depressive symptomatology: Teenage mother and grandmother perspectives. *Family Relations, 47*, 395–402.

Carney, J.K., & Cohler, B.J. (1993). Developmental continuities and adjustment in adulthood: Social relations, morale, and the transformation from middle to late life. *The course of life: Late adulthood* (Vol. 6, pp. 199–226). Madison, CT: International Universities Press.

Carstensen, L.L. (1992). Social and emotional patterns in adulthood: Support for socioemotional selectivity theory. *Psychology and Aging, 7*, 331–338.

Caspi, A., Bem, D.J., & Elder, G.H. (1989). Continuities and consequences of interactional styles across the life course. *Journal of Personality, 57*, 375–406.

Chatters, L.M., & Jayakody, R. (1995). Commentary: Intergenerational support within African-American families: Concepts and methods. In V.L. Bengtson, K.W. Schaie, & L.M. Burton (Eds.), *Adult intergenerational relations: Effects of social change* (pp. 97–118). New York: Springer.

Cicirelli, V.G. (1995). *Sibling relationships across the life span.* New York: Plenum Press.

Cohen, S., & Syme, L. (1985). *Social support and health.* New York: Academic Press.

Connidis, I.A., & Davies, L. (1990). Confidants and companions in later life: The place of family and friends. *Journals of Gerontology 45*, 141–149.

Coyne, J.C., & DeLongis, A.C. (1986). Going beyond social support: The role of social relationships in adaptation. *Journal of Consulting and Clinical Psychology, 54*, 454–460.

Crimmins, E.M., & Ingegneri, D.G. (1990). Interaction and living arrangements of older parents and their children: Past trends, present determinants, future implications. *Research on Aging, 12*, 3–35.

Crosby, F. (1987). *Spouse, parent, worker: On gender and multiple roles.* New Haven, CT: Yale University Press.

Crosby, F. (1991). *Juggling: The unexpected advantages of balancing career and home for women and their families.* New York: Free Press.

Daniels. A.K. (1985). Good times and good works: The place of sociability in the work of women volunteers. *Social Problems. 32*, 363–374.

Dannefer, D., & Uhlenberg, P. (1999). Paths of the life course: A typology. In V.L. Bengtson & K.W. Schaie (Eds.), *Handbook of theories of aging* (pp. 306–327). New York: Springer.

DeVanzo, J., & Goldscheider, F.K. (1990). Coming home again: Returns to the parental home of young adults. *Population Studies, 44*, 241–255.

Dohrenwend, B.P., & Dohrenwend, B.S. (Eds.). (1981). *Stressful life events and their contexts.* New York: Prodist.

Due, P., Holstein, B., Lund, R., Modvig, J., & Avlund, K. (1999). Social relations: Network, support and relational strain. *Social Science and Medicine, 48*, 661–673.

Eckert, J.W., & Schulman, S.C. (1996). Daughters caring for their aging mothers: A midlife developmental process. *Journal of Gerontological Social Work, 25*, 17–32.

Fischer, C.S., & Oliker, S.J. (1983). A research note on friendship, gender, and the life cycle. *Focial Forces, 62*, 124–133.

Fiske, M., & Chiriboga, D.A. (1990). *Change and continuity in adult life.* San Francisco: Jossey-Bass.

Forest, R., Murie, A., & Williams, P. (1990). *Home ownership: Differentiation and fragmentation.* London: Unwin Hyman.

Fry, C.L. (1995). Kinship and individuation: Cross-cultural perspectives on intergenerational relations. In V.L. Bengtson, K.W. Schaie, & L.M. Burton (Eds.), *Adult intergenerational relations: Effects of social change* (pp. 126–156). New York: Springer.

Gerstel, N., & Gallagher, S.K. (1993). Kinkeeping and distress: Gender, recipients of care, and work-family conflict. *Journal of Marriage and the Family, 55*, 598–607.

Gleick, J. (1999). *Faster: The acceleration of just about everything.* New York: Pantheon Books.

Gold, D.T. (1989). Sibling relationships in old age: A typology. *International Journal of Aging and Human Development, 28*, 37–51.

Gottlieb, B.H. (1994). Social support. In B.H. Gottlieb (Ed.), *Perspectives on close relationships* (pp. 307–324). Boston: Allyn & Bacon.

Haan, N., Millsap, R., & Hartka, E. (1986). As time goes by: Change and stability in personality over fifty years. *Psychology and Aging, 1*, 220–232.

Hagestad, G.O. (1985). Continuity and connectedness. In V.L. Bengtson & J.F. Robertson (Eds.), *Grandparenthood* (pp. 31–48). Beverly Hills, CA: Sage.

Harevan, T.K. (1996). Historical perspectives on the family and aging. In R. Blieszner & V.H. Bedford (Eds.), *Aging and the family: Theory and research* (pp. 13–31). Westport, CT: Praeger.

Herzog, A.R., Kahn, R.L., Morgan, J.N., Jackson, J.S., & Antonucci, T.C. (1989). Age differences in productive activities. *Journal of Gerontology: Social Sciences, 44*, S129–S138.

Hochschild, A. (1989). *The second shift.* New York: Avon.

Hochschild, A. (1997). *The time bind: When work becomes home and home becomes work.* New York: Metropolitan Books.

Holmes, T.H., & Rahe, R.H. (1967). The social readjustment rating scale. *Journal of Psychosomatic Research, 11*, 213–218.

Hong, J., & Seltzer, M.M. (1995). The psychological consequences of multiple roles: The nonnormative case. *Journal of Health and Social Behavior, 36*(4), 386–398.

Julian, T. (1992). Components of men's well-being at mid-life. *Issues in Mental Health Nursing, 13*, 285–299.

Kahn, R.L., & Antonucci, T.C. (1980). Convoys over the life course: Attachment, roles, and social support. In P.B. Baltes & O.J. Brim (Eds.), *Life-span development and behavior* (Vol. 3, pp. 253–286). New York: Academic Press.

Krause, N., Jay, G., & Liang, J. (1991). Financial strain and psychological well-being among the American and Japanese elderly. *Psychology and Aging, 6*, 170–181.

Lachman, M.E., & James, J.B. (1997). *Multiple paths of midlife development* Chicago: University of Chicago Press.

Lazarus, R.S. (1984). Puzzles in the study of daily hassles. *Journal of Behavioral Medicine, 7,* 375–389.

Lee, G.R., Peck, C.W., & Coward, R.T. (1998). Race differences in filial responsibility expectations among older parents. *Journal of Marriage and the Family, 60,* 404–412.

Lepore, S.J. (1992). Social conflict, social support, and psychological distress: Evidence of cross-domain buffering effects. *Journal of Personality and Social Psychology, 63,* 857–867.

Levitt, M.J., Antonucci, T.C., Clark, M.C., Rotton, J., & Finley, G.E. (1985–1986). Social support and well-being: Preliminary indicators based on two samples of the elderly. *International Journal of Aging and Human Development, 21,* 61–77.

Levitt, M.J., Guacci, N., & Weber, R.A. (1992). Intergenerational support, relationship quality, and well-being: A bicultural analysis [Special issue]. *Journal of Family Issues: Intergenerational Relationships, 13,* 465–481.

Levitt, M.J., Guacci-Franco, N., & Levitt, J.L. (1993). Convoys of social support in childhood and early adolescence: Structure and function. *Developmental Psychology, 29,* 811–818.

Loewenstein, S.F. (1981). A study of satisfactions and stresses of single women in midlife. *Sex Roles, 7,* 1127–1141.

MacDermid, S.M., Heilbrun, G., & Dehaan, L.G. (1997). The generativity of employed mothers in multiple roles: 1979 and 1991. In M.E. Lachman & J.B. James (Eds.), *Multiple paths of midlife development* (pp. 207–240). Chicago: University of Chicago Press.

Marks, N.F. (1998). Does it hurt to care? Caregiving, work-family conflict, and midlife well-being. *Journal of Marriage and the Family, 60,* 951–966.

Marks, N.F., & Lambert, J.D. (1998). Martial status continuity and change among young and midlife adults. *Journal of Family Issues, 19,* 652–686.

Marmot, M.G., Fuhrer, R., Ettner, S.L., Marks, N.F., Bumpass, L.L., & Ryff, C.D. (1998). Contribution of psychosocial factors to socioeconomic differences in health. *Milbank Quarterly, 76,* 403–445.

Martire, L.M., Stephens, M.A.P., & Townsend, A.L. (2000). Centrality of women's multiple roles: Beneficial and detrimental consequences for psychological well-being. *Psychology and Aging, 15,* 148–156.

McQuaide, S. (1998). Women at midlife. *Social Work, 43,* 21–31.

Milkman, R. (1979). Women's work and the economic crisis. In N.F. Cott & E.H. Pleck (Eds.), *A heritage of her own: Toward a new social history of american women.* New York: Simon & Schuster.

Moen, P., Robinson, J., & Dempster-McClain, D. (1995). Caregiving and women's well-being: A life course approach. *Journal of Health and Social Behavior, 36,* 259–273.

Paul, E.L. (1997). A longitudinal analysis of midlife interpersonal relationships and well-being. In M.E. Lachman & J.B. James (Eds.), *Multiple paths of midlife development* (pp. 171–206). Chicago: University of Chicago Press.

Peek, M.K., & Lin, N. (1999). Age differences in the effects of network composition on psychological distress. *Social Science and Medicine, 49*(5), 621–636.

Penning, M.J. (1998). In the middle: Parental caregiving in the context of other roles. *Journal of Gerontology: Social Sciences, 53B,* S188–S197.

Plath, D. (1980). *Long engagements: Maturity in modern Japan.* Stanford, CA: Stanford University Press.

Popenoe, D. (1993). American family decline, 1960–1990: A review and appraisal. *Journal of Marriage and the Family, 55,* 527–555.

Riley, M.A., & Riley, J.W. (1993). Connections: Kin and cohort. In V.L. Bengtson & W.A. Achenbaum (Eds.), *The changing contract across generations* (pp. 169–189). New York: Aldine de Gruyter.

Rosenthal, C.J., Martin-Matthews, A., & Matthews, S.H. (1996). Caught in the Middle? Occupancy in multiple roles and help to parents in a national probability sample of Canadian adults. *Journal of Gerontology: Social Sciences, 51B,* S274–S283.

Rossi, A.S., & Rossi, P.H. (1990). *Of human bonding: Parent-child relations across the life course.* New York: Aldine de Gruyter.

Ruggles, S. (1996). Living arrangements of the elderly in America: 1880–1980. In T.K. Hareven (Ed.), *Aging and generational relations over the life course: A historical and cross-cultural perspective* (pp. 254–271). New York: Walter de Gruyter.

Ryff, C.D. (1997). Experience and well-being: Explorations on domains of life and how they matter. *International Journal of Behavioral Development, 20,* 193–206.

Scott, J.P. (1997). Family relationships of midlife and older women. In J.M. Coyle (Ed.), *Handbook on women and aging.* Westport, CT: Greenwood Press.

Silverstein, M., & Bengtson, V.L. (1991). Do close parent-child relationships reduce the mortality risk of older parents? *Journal of Health and Social Behavior, 32,* 382–395.

Silverstein, M., Parrott, T.M., & Bengtson, V.L. (1995). Factors that predispose middle-aged sons and daughters to provide social support to older parents. *Journal of Marriage and the Family, 57,* 465–475.

Soldo, B.J. (1996). Guest editorial: Cross pressures on middle-age adults: A broader view. *Journal of Gerontology: Social Sciences, 51B,* S271–S273.

Spitze, G., Logan, J.R., Joseph, G., & Lee, E. (1994). Middle generations and the well-being of men and women. *Journal of Gerontology: Social Sciences, 49,* S107–S116.

Stein, C.H., Wemmerus, V.A., Ward, M., Gaines, M.E., Greenberg, A.L., & Jewell, T.C. (1998). Because they're my parents: An intergenerational study of felt obligation and parental caregiving. *Journal of Marriage and the Family, 41,* 75–88.

Szinovacz, M. (Ed.). (1998). *Handbook on grandparenthood.* Westport, CT: Greenwood Press.

Taylor, R.J., & Chatters, L.M. (1991). Extended family networks of older Black adults. *Journal of Gerontology: Social Sciences, 46,* S210–S217.

Thoits, P. (1983). Multiple identities and psychological well-being: A reformulation and test of the social isolation hypothesis. *American Sociological Review, 48,* 174–187.

Troll, L.E. (1996). Modified-extended families over time: Discontinuity in parts, continuity in wholes. In V.L. Bengtson (Ed.), *Adulthood and aging* (pp. 246–268). New York: Springer.

Troll, L.E., & Bengtson, V.L. (1982). Intergenerational relations throughout the life-span. In J. Wolman (Ed.), *Handbook of developmental psychology.* Englewood Cliffs, NJ: Prentice-Hall.

Uhlenberg, P. (1993). Demographic change and kin relationships in later life. In G.L. Maddox & M.P. Lawton (Eds.), *Annual review of gerontology and geriatrics* (Vol. 13, pp. 219–238). New York: Springer.

Uhlenberg, P. (1996). Mortality decline in the twentieth century and supply of kin over the life course. *Gerontologist, 38,* 681–685.

Vandewater, E.A., Ostrove, J.M., & Stewart, A.J. (1997). Predicting women's well-being in midlife: The importance of personality development and social role involvement. *Journal of Personality and Social Psychology, 72,* 1147–1160.

Vaillant, G.E. (1998). Are social supports in late midlife a cause or a result of successful physical aging? *Psychological Medicine, 28,* 1159–1168.

Walen, H.R., & Lachman, M.E. (2000). Social support and strain from partner, family, and friends: Costs and benefits for men and women in adulthood. *Journal of Social and Personal Relationships, 17,* 5–30.

White, K., & Riedmann, A. (1992). When the Brady Bunch grows up: Step/half- and full-sibling relationships in adulthood. *Journal of Marriage and the Family, 54,* 197–208.

White, L., & Edwards, J.N. (1990). Emptying the nest and parental well-being: An analysis of national panel data. *American Sociological Review, 55,* 235–242.

Wong, P. (1999). *Race, ethnicity, and nationality in the United States.* Boulder, CO: Westview Press.

Author Index

Abe, A., 312, 313
Abel, B.J., 500, 507
Ablondi, F., 129
Abraham, J.D., 477
Abramson, J.H., 498
Acker, J.D., 137
Ackerman, A.M., 262
Ackerman, B.P., 312, 313
Ackerman, S., 425
Acredolo, C., 205
Adams, M.E., 171
Adams, R.G., 580, 589
Adams, S.H., 144
Adelmann, P.K., 334, 500, 586
Adler, N., 142, 143, 157, 173, 174, 177, 358
Adolfsson, R., 259, 266
Aerssens, J., 126
Affleck, G., 177, 204
Ainsworth, M., 572
Ajrouch, K., 579, 587
Akimoto, S., 124
Akiyama, H., 468, 572, 573, 579, 580, 581, 582, 583, 585
Albert, M.S., 136
Aldwin, C., 169, 176, 178, 188, 191, 197, 198, 200, 201, 203, 204, 205, 206, 228, 231, 498
Allan, G., 580, 589
Allard, M., 82
Allen, K., 536
Allen, M.T., 203
Allen, N.J., 451
Almeida, D., 177, 323
Alperovitch, A., 140
Alvarez, H., 93, 94
Alves, S.E., 132

Alwin, D.F., 540, 543, 551
Amalee, S., 337
Amato, P.R., 540
Ames, D., 127
Ancoli-Israel, S., 137
Andersen, B.L., 172
Anderson, B.J., 172
Anderson, C.E., 493, 494
Anderson, C.V., 96
Anderson, J.W., 403
Anderson, K.M., 123
Anderson, N.B., 168, 171
Andrews, M., 424
Andrews, S., 266
Andrisani, P.J., 365
Aneshensel, C., 578
Antonovsky, A., 142
Antonucci, T., 334, 417, 468, 503, 572, 573, 579, 580, 581, 582, 583, 585, 586, 587, 590
Aquilino, W.S., 194, 311, 537, 539, 574, 578, 587
Araki, T., 141
Arbuckle, T.Y., 262
Arendt, T., 95
Arking, R., 77
Armeli, S., 177
Armstrong, E., 95
Armstrong, G.L., 160
Arnold, M.L., 422
Arnsten, A.F., 88, 89
Aromaa, A., 171
Aronson, J., 555, 558
Ashley-Montague, M.F., 80
Aspinwall, L., 201
Atchley, R.C., 7, 20, 195, 447, 489, 491, 493, 494, 496, 499, 501, 506, 511

Subject Index